# The Blue Guides

For Francesco
With all my gratitude for his help, encouragement and patience while I have been at work on many editions of this book.

# Sicily

## Alta Macadam

BLUE GUIDE

A&C Black • London
WW Norton • New York

Fifth edition 1999
Published by A & C Black (Publishers) Limited
35 Bedford Row, London WC1R 4JH

A CIP catalogue record of this book
is available from the British Library.

ISBN 0–7136–4908–9

Published in the United States of America by
WW Norton and Company, Inc
500 Fifth Avenue, New York, NY 10110

Published simultaneously in Canada by
Penguin Books Canada Limited
10 Alcorn Avenue, Toronto, Ontario M4V 3B2

ISBN 0–393–31935–0  USA

**Alta Macadam** has been a writer of Blue Guides since 1970. She lives in Florence with her
family (the painter Francesco Colacicchi and their children Giovanni and Lelia). Combined
with work on writing the guides she has also been associated with the Bargello Museum,
the Alinari photo archive and Harvard University at the Villa I Tatti in Florence. As author
of the Blue Guides to Northern Italy, Rome, Venice, Sicily, Florence, Tuscany and Umbria
she travels extensively in Italy every year in order to revise new editions of the books.

**Cover Picture**: interior of La Martorana, Palermo by Joe Cornish

Printed and bound in Great Britain by Butler and Tanner, Frome and London

# Contents

## The Guide

## Maps and plans

**Maps**
Sicily (*inside front and back covers*)

**Province maps**
Agrigento 184
Caltanissetta 208
Catania 291
Enna 216
Messina 322
Palermo 59
Ragusa 235
Siracusa 251
Trapani 140

**Town plans**
Agrigento 188–89
Catania 296–97
Enna 218
Erice 151
Lipari 355
Marsala 171
Messina 327
Noto 277
Palermo 68–9
Palermo environs 105
Ragusa 237
Siracusa 1: Ortygia 256
Siracusa 2: the mainland 263
Taormina 337
Trapani 143

**Ground plans**
Agrigento temples 191
Megara Hyblaea 289
Monreale cathedral 110
Morgantina (Serra Orlando) 233
Mozia (island of S. Pantaleo) 167
Palermo
    Cathedral 73
    La Martorana 71
    Museo Regionale Archeologico
        95/96
    Palazzo dei Normanni and the
        Cappella Palatina 77
Pantalica 286
Piazza Armerina, the Villa Romana
    229
Selinunte
    the ancient site 177
    the temples 178
Siracusa
    Cathedral 259
    Castello Eurialo 271

# Introduction

Sicily, the largest island in the Mediterranean, and the southernmost part of Italy, has had a remarkable history and many superb archaeological sites and beautiful buildings survive from the past. It also has lush sub-tropical vegetation around the coast, with wonderful mountain scenery in the interior. It is famous above all for its Greek remains, only rivalled by Greece itself, including the superb temples at Agrigento, Segesta and Selinunte, and the spectacular theatres at Taormina, Siracusa and Segesta. Palermo has fascinating Arab Norman buildings, especially famous for their wonderful mosaics (which also decorate the cathedrals of Monreale and Cefalù). Sicily has its own delightful Baroque architecture in the small towns in the south-east corner of the island which were all rebuilt after an earthquake in 1693 (the most famous of which are Noto and Ragusa).

The two main towns of the island, Palermo and Catania, after a period of decline in the 1960s and 1970s, have in the last few years become much more pleasant places to visit since the standard of living here has greatly improved. They are better kept and numerous restoration projects are in progress, more churches are open and there is more to do for the younger generation in the evenings. Palermo is a fascinating city with numerous large street markets in the streets of the old centre, and Catania is a Baroque city which, if it were wealthier, would rival some other European cities.

The natural beauty of the island is at last being preserved, with nature reserves at Vendicari and Zingaro on the coast, and the mountain ranges of the Nebrodi and Madonie now protected areas. The huge active volcano, Etna, is a national park. Sicily also has particularly beautiful offshore islands (especially the Aeolian islands, Ustica, Marettimo and Pantelleria).

The food of Sicily is extremely good and inexpensive, and local specialities ensure an interesting variety. The sweets and cakes, using pistachio, almond paste and ricotta as basic ingredients, are particularly delicious. Excellent fresh fish is served all over the island. Sicily is catching up with the rest of Italy in the provision of good small hotels, and some *agriturismo* accommodation is now available in farmhouses in the interior of the island.

Although the island has long been notorious as a centre of the Mafia, criminal professionals who have subjected the population to a 'protection' system, which has for years controlled almost every business transaction on the island, both private and state, it is necessary to emphasise that travellers to the island are in no way exposed to this problem. Sicilians are famous for their hospitality and are extremely kind and helpful to visitors. Sicily is as safe a place to visit as any other part of Italy. After the courageous stand taken by a number of Sicilians against the Mafia there are signs that it may lose two of its greatest strengths, its legitimacy and its invisibility.

## Acknowledgements

I am particularly grateful for the assistance provided by the provincial tourist boards in Sicily during my travels on the island. These include the APT of Caltanissetta; the APT of Catania (and in particular Daniela Locascio); the APT of Messina; the APT of Palermo (and in particular Lia Verdina); the APT of Siracusa (and in particular Giusi Di Lorenzo); the Azienda Autonoma Soggiorno e Turismo of Taormina (and in particular Franco Signorino); the APT of Trapani (and in particular Giuseppe Butera); and the Azienda Autonoma delle Isole Eolie.

I am also greatly indebted to Rosario Damiano of Capo d'Orlando, Maria Grammatico of Erice, Caterina Conti of Vulcano, Eva Greco of Siracusa, Maria and Giovanna Guccione of Favignana, Maria Amato of Noto and Roberto Sequi of the Riserva Marina of Ustica.

# How to use the Guide

The guide is divided into the nine provinces of Sicily: Palermo, Trapani, Agrigento, Caltanissetta, Enna, Ragusa, Siracusa, Catania, Messina. Within each province, sections are devoted to the provincial capitals and their immediate environs, and to other places of interest in the province, including towns, villages, areas known for their distinctive landscape and the offshore islands. The sections dedicated to the major towns are organised into a number of walking itineraries, with separate descriptions for the major monuments and museums.

An exhaustive section at the beginning of the book lists all the **practical information** a traveller is likely to need in preparation for a visit to Sicily and while on the journey. This information, which includes public transport, is integrated with specific details at the beginning of each chapter and at the beginning of the description of each town. Information has been given both for those who visit the area by car and those who travel by public transport.

A small selection of **hotels** is given at the beginning of each province section or sub-section within the province, with official star ratings to give an indication of price. For further information, see under **Accommodation** (see p.16) in the Practical information section.

**Restaurants** have also been indicated at the beginning of each province section or sub-section within the province, and these have been divided into three categories which reflect up-to-date price ranges: **A** indicates expensive luxury-class restaurants; **B** is for first-class but slightly cheaper restaurants, and **C** for simple, but excellent value *trattorie* and *pizzerie*. For further information, see under **Eating out** in the Practical information section (p.24).

The **most important monuments or works of art** in Sicily have been highlighted in bold letters throughout the text. The **Highlights** section on pages 11–12 singles out some of the major places of interest in the island which should not be missed.

All **churches** are taken as being orientated, with the entrance at the west end, and the altar at the east end, the south aisle on the right and the north aisle on the left.

In the larger towns all the main monuments have been keyed (i.e. map: 2) in the text against the double-page **town plans** which include a grid with numbered squares. On the ground plans of museums, figures or letters have been given to correspond with the description in the text.

The **local tourist boards** (APT or *Azienda di Promozione Turistica*), are usually extremely helpful and it is only through them that it is possible to secure up-to-date information on the spot about opening times and accommodation. The nine provincial offices have been listed with their telephone numbers on page 16, and the local information offices are listed at the beginning of each province section and in each town. On the town maps they are marked with the letter *i*, the symbol which is used on local signposts throughout Italy.

**Opening times** of museums and monuments have been given throughout the text, using the 24-hour clock (i.e. 09.00–14.00; Sun & PH 09.00–13.00), with the abbreviation PH indicating times for public holidays. However, opening times vary and often change without warning, so it is best to consult the local APT for up-to-date information on your arrival. Almost all churches close at 12.00 noon and do not re-open again until 16.00 or 17.00. For further information, see the section on Museums and churches in the Practical information section (p.31).

Although detailed town plans are provided, every traveller to Sicily, whether driving or using public transport, will also need a large-scale **map** of the island: the best is the one produced by the TCI (see p.20).

## *Abbreviations used in the guide:*

| | |
|---|---|
| APT | Azienda di Promozione Turistica (official local tourist office) |
| C | century |
| FS | Ferrovie dello Stato (Italian state railways) |
| PH | public holidays |
| S. and SS. | Saint and Saints (San, Santo, Santa, Santi etc.) |
| TCI | Touring Club Italiano |

The terms Quattrocento, Cinquecento, abbreviated in Italy '400, '500, etc., refer not to the 14C and 15C but to the 'fourteen hundreds' and 'fifteen-hundreds', i.e. the 15C and 16C.

For Glossary, see p. 367.

# Highlights

## *Ancient sites*

The most famous Greek buildings on the island are at Agrigento, Siracusa, Selinunte and Segesta. Other archaeological sites of great interest and in splendid positions include: Morgantina, Eraclea Minoa, Naxos, Mozia and Tindari. The Cave di Cusa provide a unique view of an ancient quarry. The Roman villa at Piazza Armerina has some of the most extensive and beautiful mosaics known, and the ancient theatre of Taormina has a spectacular view. Extremely important Greek fortifications are to be seen at Gela and the Castello Euralio, on the outskirts of Siracusa. Lesser known sites include Jetae, Solunto, Eloro, Akrai and Halaesa.

## *Archaeological museums*

Perhaps the most impressive archaeological museum on the island is now the one in Siracusa (re-opened in 1988). The regional archaeological museums at Palermo and Agrigento also have very fine collections with finds from all over Sicily. Particularly interesting local collections can be seen in Marsala, Gela and Lipari.

## Prehistoric Sicily

Some of the earliest traces of habitation on the island can be seen in the caves on Monte Pellegrino and the island of Levanzo. Excavations on Lípari have revealed the presence of man on the island from the Neolithic age onwards, and there are other prehistoric sites in the Aeolian Islands (Panarea, Salina and Filicudi). In the eastern part of the island is the most impressive of all the prehistoric sites in Sicily where the upland plateau of Pantalica has thousands of tombs cut in the rock face. The beautiful Cava Grande del Cassibile and Cava d'Ispica also have prehistoric tombs.

## Norman buildings

Palermo has the greatest concentration of Norman architecture, including the Cappella Palatina, the Zisa, Ponte dell'Ammiraglio, the Sala di Re Ruggero in the Palazzo dei Normanni and the wonderful churches of La Martorana, the Cappella di S. Cataldo, S. Giovanni degli Eremiti, La Magione and S. Giovanni dei Lebbrosi. The mosaic decoration of the Cappella Palatina and La Martorana is particularly splendid, and just outside the city at Monreale, the Norman cathedral has one of the greatest mosaic cycles ever produced. The presbytery of the cathedral of Cefalù also has very fine mosaics. Smaller, lesser known churches of this period can be seen on the east coast near Casalvecchio Siculo (SS. Pietro e Paolo d'Agro) and Itala (S. Pietro).

## Baroque towns

The most famous and best preserved Baroque town in Sicily is Noto, but other towns in the south-east corner of the island worth visiting, which were rebuilt after an earthquake in 1693, include Ragusa, Modica, Scicli and Comiso. Ortygia, the old part of Siracusa, also has some interesting Baroque buildings, as do Catania and Acireale.

## Small, well-preserved towns in picturesque positions

There are a number of well-preserved little towns in the centre of the island, including Polizzi Generosa, Petralia Soprana, Leonforte, Sperlinga, Sclafani Bagni, Castelbuono and Contessa Entellina. Erice on the west coast is a particularly enchanting place in a wonderful position. Other very small and little known places include Forza d'Agro in the Peloritani mountains and S. Marco d'Alunzio in the Nebrodi mountains.

## Offshore islands

The most beautiful group of islands are the Aeolian islands, and in particular Panarea, Salina, Alicudi and Lipari. Here the two volcanic islands, Stromboli and Vulcano, are also very interesting. Ustica has a particularly beautiful coastline and seabed, and Marettimo in the Egadi islands is well preserved. The distant Pantelleria, closer to Africa than to Sicily, has some fine scenery.

# Practical information

## When to go

The best months for travelling in Sicily are March, April, May, June, September, October and November. The island is famous for its cloudless skies and mild winters, and even in the rainiest months, November and December, there are usually many days of Indian summer. July and August are apt to be very hot, and the sirocco, which can blow for four or five days at a time, raises the temperature to 40°C. It is often very windy near the Strait of Messina and even in summer the sea here can be chilly. In March it is possible to combine swimming with skiing in the region of Etna.

**Passports** are necessary for all British and American travellers entering Italy. A lost or stolen passport can be replaced by the relevant embassy in Rome.

## Planning a visit

As many days as possible should be devoted to the city of Palermo and its environs (notably Monreale). Selinunte may then be reached via Segesta and the west coast (Trapani, Erice, the island of Mozia, and Marsala), or, if you have very little time, direct from Palermo (in this case Segesta can be visited on a detour or in a day from Palermo). Agrigento, reached from Selinunte along the south coast via Eraclea Minoa, deserves a visit of at least two days. The numerous medieval hill-towns and spectacular countryside in the interior of the island can be explored from Enna (reached via Caltanissetta from Agrigento). Piazza Armerina, with the famous mosaics in its Roman villa, and the ruins of Morgantina are near Caltagirone, another inland town. The coast road from Agrigento runs via Gela. In the south-east corner of the island are the fine Baroque towns of Ragusa, Modica and Comiso. The exploration of Siracusa and its environs (the Castello Eurialo, Noto, Palazzolo Acreide and the necropolis of Pantalica) requires at least three days. Catania, which can be visited in a day, is a good centre for the ascent of Etna and a circular tour of the foothills. The road between Catania and Messina passes Naxos and Taormina, where at least one night should be spent. On the road along the north coast, Tindari and Cefalù should not be missed.

### Italian tourist boards

General information can be obtained abroad from the Italian State Tourist Office (ENIT, *Ente Nazionale Italiano per il Turismo*), who provide detailed information on Sicily.

**Canada** 1 Place Ville Marie, Suite 1914, Montreal, ☎ (514) 886 7667, fax (514) 392 1429.
**Netherlands** Stadhoudestrade 2, 1054 ES Amsterdam, ☎ 6168246, fax 6188515.
**UK** 1 Princes Street, London WIR 8AY, ☎ 0171 408 1254, fax 0171 493 6695.
**USA** New York: 630 Fifth Avenue, Suite 1665, NY 10111, ☎ 245 4822, fax 586 9249. Chicago: 401 North Michigan Avenue, Suite 3030, ☎ 644 0996,

fax 644 3019. Los Angeles: 12400 Wiltshire Blvd, Suite 550, ☎ 820 1898, fax 820 6357.

### Tour operators

Among the numerous tour operators which offer package holidays to Sicily from the UK are: Prospect Music and Art Tours (☎ 0181 995 2163; fax 0181 742 1969); Specialtours (☎ 0171 732297; fax 0171 823 5035); Magic of Italy (☎ 0181 748 7575; fax 0181 748 3731); International Chapters (☎ 0171 722 9560); Italia nel Mondo (☎ 0171 828 9171; fax 0171 630 5184); Citalia (☎ 0181 686 5533; fax 0181 681 0712); Sunvil Holidays (☎ 0181 568 4499; fax 0181 568 8330); SAGA Holidays (☎ 0800 300 456; fax 01303 771 010).

# Getting there

### By air

Palermo and Catania are linked by air services with London by Alitalia (☎ 0171 602 7111 or 0181 745 8200). Flights to Palermo and Catania usually operate via Milan or Rome (direct flights in summer). There are also charter flights (often much cheaper) to Palermo and Catania. Details of these are available through travel agencies and listings sections in many of the national newspapers, especially the Sunday newspapers and the London *Evening Standard* and *Time Out*. Teletext and the internet also advertise flights and package holidays at competitive prices. Scheduled services offer special fares which are available according to season; there are reduced youth fares and fly-drive schemes can also be arranged.

Air services from the USA to Rome or Milan are operated by Alitalia (☎ 800 223 5730), which flies non-stop from New York, Boston, Chicago and Los Angeles. Flights from New York to Rome are also operated by Continental (☎ 800 231 0856), Delta (☎ 800 241 4141) and TWA (☎ 800 892 4141). United (☎ 800 538 2929) operate between Washington DC and Rome. British Airways, Air France, KLM and Sabena offer flights connecting through London, Paris, Amsterdam and Brussels and these are often more economical than direct flights.

Flights from the Italian mainland are operated by Alitalia. A frequent air service connects Reggio di Calabria and Catania. There are also daily services from Rome and Milan to Palermo and Catania. Flights also operate from Naples, Pisa, Florence and Cagliari to Palermo and Catania, and from Turin to Catania.

### By rail

Sicily is connected to the Italian mainland by numerous rail services. From Turin, Genoa and Milan mainline trains (via Rome and Naples) run to Villa San Giovanni and Reggio di Calabria, and through carriages for destinations in Sicily (Palermo, Catania, and Siracusa) continue via the ferry to Messina. Overnight trains (with sleeping accommodation) daily from Milan and Turin via Rome to Palermo. The Italian State Railways are represented in the UK by Citalia (☎ 0181 686 0677; fax 0181 686 0328).

Italy can be reached by through train from Paris Lyon overnight (by sleeper); there are now frequent trains from London Waterloo through the Eurotunnel via Calais to Paris Nord (in c 3hr). For more information, contact European Rail Ltd. (☎ 0171 387 0444; fax 0171 387 0888).

### By coach

A coach service operates in two days between London (Victoria Coach Station) and Rome (piazza della Repubblica) via Dover, Paris, Mont Blanc, Aosta, Turin, Genoa, Milan, Bologna and Florence, daily from June to September, and once or twice a week for the rest of the year. Reduction for students. Information from the National Express office at Victoria Coach Station (☎ 0171 730 0202), and from local National Express agents, or from Eurolines (☎ 01582 404511). In Italy, the offices of SITA will be able to advise on international coach travel.

From Rome daily coach services run by SAIS to Messina (going on to Catania and Siracusa) and to Palermo (in c 12–13hr). *Segesta* also run an overnight coach service from Rome to Palermo.

### By car

From northern Italy the motorway known as the *Autostrada del Sole* (A1) runs south to Rome, which is now bypassed well to the east, avoiding the congested ring-road around the capital. At Caserta, just north of Naples, the A30 motorway forks left to bypass Naples. At Salerno the A3 motorway (toll free) continues south via Cosenza to Reggio di Calabria, and the ferry for Messina. By this motorway Messina can comfortably be reached in a day from Naples.

Car sleeper train services operate from Paris and Boulogne, Hamburg, Vienna and Munich to Milan, Bologna, Rome, etc. Car transport by train in Italy is available from Turin, Milan, Bologna, Genoa and Rome to Villa S. Giovanni.

### By sea

The shortest sea approach is across the Strait of Messina from Villa S. Giovanni and Reggio di Calabria to Messina.

Car ferries on the Straits of Messina operate from Villa S. Giovanni (c every 20 min.) in 20 minutes to Messina. The ferries are run by the State Railways (FS) and private companies (*Caronte* and *Tourist Ferry Boat*). A frequent service is maintained, but there can be delays in the height of summer.

Frequent hydrofoil service operated by SNAV in 15 minutes between Reggio di Calabria and Messina. For further details, see p. 323.

To Palermo there are overnight car ferries from Naples, Cagliari, Tunis and Genoa (operated by *Tirrenia*, ☎ 091 6021111). Services by *Grandi Traghetti* (☎ 091 587801) from Livorno, Genoa, Tunis and Malta. Advance reservation is advised, particularly for a cabin or if with a car.

## On arrival

In Sicily the Regional State Tourist office is in Palermo: Assessorato Regionale del Turismo, 11 via Notarbartolo (☎ 091/6968033).

The nine provinces of Sicily each have their own tourist boards, called APT (*Aziende di Promozione Turistica*). These provide invaluable help to travellers on arrival: they supply a free list of accommodation (revised annually), including hotels, farm holidays, and campsites; up-to-date information on museum opening times and annual events; and information about local transport.

They also usually distribute, free of charge, illustrated pamphlets about the province, sometimes with good town plans, etc. The headquarters are normally open Monday–Saturday 08.00–14.00, but nearly all the provinces also have separate APT information offices which are often also open in the afternoon.

Subsidiary information offices are sometimes open in railway stations, airports, or ports (usually in summer only). In addition, some local tourist boards (*Aziende Autonome di Turismo*) still operate in the main tourist centres. All these offices are indicated, with their addresses in each section in the main text.

**The nine head offices of the APT of Sicily are as follows**:

| | |
|---|---|
| Palermo | 35 piazza Castelnuovo (☎ 091/583847; fax 091/331854). |
| Trapani | 27 via S. Francesco d'Assisi (☎ 0923/29000; fax 0923/29430). |
| Agrigento | 255 viale della Vittoria (☎ 0922/401352; fax 0922/25185). |
| Caltanissetta | 109 corso Vittorio Emanuele (☎ 0934/21089; fax 0934/21239). |
| Catania | 10 via Domenico Cimarosa (☎ 095/7306233; fax 095/316407). |
| Enna | 411 via Roma (☎ 0935/528228; fax 0935/528229). |
| Ragusa | 33 via Capitano Bocchieri, Ragusa Ibla (☎ 0932/621421; fax 0932/623467). |
| Siracusa | 45 via S. Sebastiano (☎ 0931/67710; fax 0931/67803). |
| Messina | via Calabria, isolato 301bis (corner of via Capra), (☎ 090/674236, fax 090/6411047). |

# Accommodation

Hotels in Italy are classified by stars as in the rest of Europe. Since 1985 the official category of *Pensione* has been abolished. There are five official categories of hotels, from the luxury 5-star hotels to the cheapest and simplest 1-star hotels.

An up-to-date selection of hotels in Sicily has been listed in the text. Their official star rating provides an indication of price. In making the selection for inclusion, smaller hotels have generally been favoured and those in the centre of towns, or in particularly picturesque rural situations.

Each provincial tourist board (APT, see above) issues a free annual list of hotels giving category, price and facilities. Local tourist offices help you to find accommodation on the spot. It is, however, advisable to book in advance, especially at Easter and in the summer. To confirm the booking you are usually asked to send a deposit (or give a credit card number and details); you have the right to claim this back if you cancel the booking at least 72 hours in advance. Hotels equipped to offer hospitality to the disabled are indicated in the APT hotel lists.

Up-to-date information about hotels and restaurants can be found in numerous annual specialised guides to Italy. These include *Alberghi d'Italia*, a selection of 3-star hotels published by Gambero Rosso, *Alberghi e Ristoranti d'Italia* published by the Touring Club Italiano, and the red guide *Italia: Hotel – Ristoranti* published by Michelin.

There is still a lack of good small hotels in Sicily. The nine provincial capitals all have adequate hotels (although Enna, Caltanissetta, Ragusa and Trapani have only a very small selection). The hotels in Erice and Taormina are particularly good. The grading is not standard, for example a 3-star hotel in Taormina may be better (and more expensive) than a 3-star hotel in a less fashionable town. The official categories are now established by the services offered (television in each room, private telephone, minibar, etc.) and do not necessarily reflect quality. The large hotels and tourist 'villages' built in the 1960s and 1970s on the coast of the island mainly cater for package holidaymakers.

**Breakfast** (which can be disappointing and costly) is by law an optional extra charge, although a lot of hotels try to include it in the price of the room. When booking a room, always specify if you want breakfast or not. If you are staying in a 2-star or 3-star hotel in a town, it is usually well worthwhile going round the corner to the nearest *pasticceria* or bar for breakfast. However, in the more expensive hotels some good buffet breakfasts are now provided. But even here the standard of the 'canteen' coffee can be poor: you can always ask for a *caffè* or *cappuccino* instead. There is a large supplement if you order breakfast in your room.

In all hotels the service charges are included in the rates. The total charge is exhibited on the back of the door of the hotel room. You should beware of **extra charges** added to the bill. The drinks in the *frigo bar* in your room are extremely expensive (it is always best to buy drinks outside the hotel). Telephone calls are also more expensive if made from your room; there is usually a pay telephone in the lobby which is the most economical way of telephoning (avoiding noisy public telephones in the streets). Hotels are now obliged by law (for tax purposes) to issue an official receipt to customers, you should not leave the premises without this.

**Accommodation services** from the UK are offered by Accommodation Line Ltd. (☎ 0171 409 1343; fax 0171 409 2606); Hotel Connect (☎ 0181 906 2686, fax 0181 906 262); and The Italian Connection (☎ 0171 486 6890, fax 0171 486 6891) who can arrange accommodation in hotels or self-catering apartments.

### Agriturismo and self-catering
Recently developed throughout Italy, this provides accommodation in farm-houses (*aziende agrituristiche*) in the countryside. Sicily now has some 80 autho-rised farms which offer this type of hospitality. Terms vary greatly from bed and breakfast, to full board or self-contained flats, and is highly recommended for travellers with their own transport, and for families, as an excellent (and usually cheap) way of visiting the country. Some farms require a stay of a minimum number of days. Cultural or recreational activities are sometimes also provided, such as horse-back riding. The local APT offices provide information, and *agrit-urismo* accommodation is now also usually listed in the annual lists of hotels published by the APT (and a selection has been given in the main text).

Terranostra publish an annual list of *agriturismo* accommodation under the title *Vacanze e Natura*. Agriturist also publish an annual guide.

### Camping
Camping is well organised throughout Italy. An international camping carnet is useful. In Sicily, campsites are included in the local APT hotel lists, giving their official category (from the most expensive 4-star sites to the simplest and cheapest 1-star sites) and details of all services provided, size of the site, etc. Their classification and rates charged must be displayed at the campsite office. Some sites have been indicated in the text, with their star ratings. In some sites caravans and campers are allowed.

Full details of the sites in Italy are published annually by the Touring Club Ital-iano in *Campeggi e Villaggi Turistici in Italia*. The Federazione Italiana del

Campeggio has an information office and booking service at 11 via Vittorio Emanuele, Calenzano, 50041 Florence (☎ 055 882391).

### Youth hostels

The Italian Youth Hostels Association (Associazione Italiana Alberghi per la Gioventù, 44 via Cavour, 00184 Rome, ☎ 06/4871152) has about 54 hostels in Italy. A membership card of the AIG or the International Youth Hostel Federation is required for access to Italian youth hostels. Details from the Youth Hostels Association, Trevelyan House, 8 St Stephen's Hill, St Albans, Herts AL1 2DY and the American Youth Hostel Inc, National Offices, PO Box 37613, Washington DC 20013 7613. In Sicily youth hostels are open at present only in Siracusa, Trapani, Castroreale (April–Oct), Lipari (March–October) and Erice (summer only).

# Getting around

### By car

The standard of roads on the island has improved in recent years. However, some of the main roads have rough stretches, while the condition of secondary roads can be unexpectedly good. The roads through the beautiful country in the mountainous centre of the island, with wonderful views, carry very little traffic but are often very windy and slow. In the larger towns the traffic tends to be chaotic (with excessive use of car horns), the roads congested and parking difficult. You are strongly recommended to park outside the centre and explore towns on foot. Signposting is erratic and can be virtually non-existent especially in large towns. However, hotels and restaurants are almost always clearly signposted (yellow signs). Information offices are marked with a yellow '*i*' symbol throughout Italy. Monuments of interest are also often signposted (yellow or brown signs).

The motorways (*autostrade*) are a convenient and fast way of travelling if you are restricted for time (and they often provide spectacular views of the countryside). They traverse the difficult terrain by means of viaducts and tunnels, usually built with little respect for the beauty of the landscape. Motorways link Messina to Catania, Catania to Palermo, Palermo to Trapani, and Palermo to Mazara del Vallo. The convenience of being able to reach Palermo from Catania in under three hours has transformed communications between the western and eastern half of the island. The motorway from Messina to Palermo has been awaiting completion for years (work on the gap in the middle between Furiano and Cefalù is still underway). The project to build a motorway from Catania to Siracusa and (via the coast) to Gela seems to have been shelved.

Tolls are charged according to the rating of the vehicle and the distance covered, although no tolls are charged on the last stretch of the motorway on the mainland from Salerno to Reggio di Calabria, and in Sicily the motorways from Palermo to Catania, and from Palermo to Mazara del Vallo, are also toll free. There are service areas on most motorways, open 24 hours a day. Some of the main motorways have SOS points every two kilometres. Unlike in France, motorways are indicated by green signs (and normal roads by blue signs). At the entrance to motorways, the two directions are indicated by the name of the most important town (and not by the nearest town) which can be momentarily confusing.

*Superstrade* are dual carriageway fast roads which do not charge tolls. They do not usually have service stations, SOS points, or emergency lanes. They are also usually indicated by green signs. A new *superstrada* (624) from Palermo to the south coast at Sciacca was finally completed (the work took 37 years!) in 1997 which provides a fast way of reaching Agrigento from Palermo.

**Petrol stations** are open 24 hours on motorways, but otherwise their opening times are: 07.00–12.00, 15.00–20.00; winter 07.30–12.30, 14.30–19.00. There are now quite a number of self-service petrol stations open 24hrs operated by bank notes (10,000 or 50,000 lire). Unleaded petrol is now available all over Sicily. Petrol in Italy costs more than in England, and a lot more than in America.

**Car parking**. Although most towns on the Italian mainland have at last taken the wise step of closing their historic centres to traffic, many town centres in Sicily (including Palermo) are still open to cars. This makes driving and parking extremely difficult. On approaching a town, the white signs for *centro* (with a bull's eye) should be followed towards the historic centre. Car-parks are also sometimes indicated by blue P signs; where parking is a particular problem, the best places to park near the centre have been mentioned in the main text. Some car-parks are free and some charge an hourly tariff. In the larger towns it is usually a good idea to look for a garage which provides parking space (these usually have a blue P sign and a blue-and-white striped entrance); tariffs are charged by the hour, by the day, or overnight. It is forbidden to park in front of a gate or doorway marked with a *passo carrabile* (blue and red) sign. Always lock your car when parked and never leave anything of value inside it.

**Car hire** is available in the main Sicilian towns and at Palermo and Catania airports. Firms include: Sicily by Car (Palermo, ☎ 091/328531; Rome, ☎ 06/8840235; Milan, ☎ 02/29403525), Maggiore, Avis and Hertz. Arrangements for car hire in Italy can also be made through Alitalia or British Airways (at specially advantageous rates in conjunction with their flights).

Temporary membership of the Automobile Club d'Italia (ACI) can be taken out on the frontier or in Italy. The headquarters of ACI in Palermo is at 6 viale delle Alpi (branch offices in all the main towns). They provide a breakdown service (Soccorso ACI, ☎ 116).

**Rules of the road**. Italian law requires that you carry a valid driving licence when travelling. It is obligatory to keep a red triangle in the car in case of accident or breakdown. This serves as a warning to other traffic when placed on the road at a distance of 50 metres from the stationary car. It is now compulsory to wear seatbelts in the front seat of cars in Italy. Driving in Italy is generally faster (and often more aggressive) than driving in Britain or America. Road signs are now more or less standardised to the international codes, but certain habits differ radically from those in Britain or America. Unless otherwise indicated, cars entering a road from the right are given precedence (also at roundabouts). If a driver flashes his headlights, it means he is proceeding and not giving you precedence. In towns, Italian drivers are very lax about changing lanes without much warning. Some crossroads in small towns have unexpected 'stop' signs. Italian drivers tend to ignore pedestrian crossings. In towns, beware of motorbikes, mopeds and scooters, the drivers of which seem to consider that they always have right of way.

The police (see p.27) sometimes set up road blocks to check cars and their drivers: it is important to stop at once if you are waved down by a policeman at the side of a road and you must show them your driving licence and the car documents.

## Maps
Although detailed town plans have been included in this book, it has not been possible, because of the format, to provide an atlas of Sicily adequate for those travelling by car. The maps at the end of the book are only intended to be used when planning an itinerary. The Italian Touring Club publishes several sets of excellent maps, these are constantly updated and are indispensable to anyone travelling by car in Italy.

They include the *Grande Carta Stradale d'Italia*, on a scale of 1:200,000. This is divided into 15 maps covering the regions of Italy; Sicily is covered on one of these. They are also published in a handier form as an atlas (with a comprehensive index) called the *Atlante Stradale d'Italia* in three volumes (the one entitled *Sud* covers Sicily). These maps can be purchased from the Italian Touring Club offices and at many booksellers: in London they can be purchased from Stanfords, 12–14 Long Acre, WC2E 9LP (☎ 0171 836 1321).

The Istituto Geografico Militare of Italy has for many years been famous for its map production (much of it done by aerial photography). Their maps are now available at numerous bookshops in the main towns of Italy. They publish a map of Italy on a scale of 1:100,000 in 277 sheets, and a field survey partly 1:50,000, partly 1:25,000, which are invaluable for the detailed exploration of the country, especially its more mountainous regions; the coverage is, however, still far from complete at the larger scales, and some of the maps are out-of-date.

## By rail
Sicilian trains are generally fast and comfortable, although in some places the service is infrequent. The two main lines, Messina to Palermo, and Messina to Catania and Siracusa have a frequent service, but almost all the fast trains are through trains from the Italian mainland (Naples, Rome, Milan, etc.) and more often than not subject to considerable delays. Work began in 1981 to electrify the main lines and install double tracks. Some of the minor secondary lines on the island have recently been closed and substituted by bus connections. With careful plannning and with the help of the regional timetables (see below) it is still possible to reach many places by rail, and details of the lines have been given in the main text, although local bus services are now often quicker and more frequent than train services.

The Italian State Railways (FS; *Ferrovie dello Stato*) run various categories of trains: ES (Eurostar), international express trains (with a special supplement, approximately 30 per cent of the normal single fare) running between the main Italian and European cities (with obligatory seat reservation since no standing passengers are permitted), with first- and second-class carriages; EC and IC (Eurocity and Intercity), international and national express trains, with a supplement (but cheaper than the Eurostar supplement); *Espressi*, long-distance trains (both classes) not as fast as the Intercity trains; *Diretti*, although not stopping at every station, a good deal slower than *Espressi*; *Interregionali*, local trains stopping at most stations; and *Regionali*, local trains stopping at all stations, mostly with second-class carriages only.

**Tickets** (valid for two months after the day sold) must be bought before the journey, otherwise a fairly large supplement has to be paid to the ticket-collector on the train. **In order to validate your ticket it has to be stamped at an automatic machine in the railway station before starting the journey (there is always a machine at the beginning of each platform and sometimes half-way up the platform**). If, for some reason, you fail to do this, try to find the ticket conductor on the train before he finds you. Once the ticket has been stamped it is valid for 6 hours for distances up to 200km, and for 24 hours for distances over 200km.

The most convenient way of buying rail tickets (and making seat reservations) is from a travel agent (but only those who are agents for the Italian State Railways), as there are often long queues at the station ticket offices. Some trains charge a special supplement (see above), and on some seats must be booked in advance; when buying tickets you therefore have to specify which category of train you intend to take as well as the destination. Trains in Italy are usually crowded especially on holidays and in summer; and it is now always advisable to book your seat for long-distance journeys when buying a ticket for a Eurocity or Intercity train. There is a booking fee of 5000 lire and the service is available from 2 months to 3 hours before departure.

In the main stations the better known credit cards are now generally accepted (but in Sicily only at Palermo station) and there is a special ticket window which must be used when buying a ticket with a credit card.

**Fares and reductions**. In Italy fares are still much lower than in Britain. Children under the age of 4 travel free, and between the ages of 4 and 12 travel half price, and there are certain reductions for families. For travellers over the age of 60 (with Senior Citizen Railcards), the *Carta Res* (valid one year) offers a 30 per cent reduction on international rail fares. The Inter-rail card (valid 1 month) which can be purchased in Britain by young people up to the age of 26, is valid in Italy (and allows a reduction of 50 per cent on normal fares). In Italy the *Carta d'Argento* and the *Carta Verde* (which both cost 40,000 lire and are valid for one year) allow a reduction on rail fares for those over 60, and between the ages of 12 and 26. A *Chilometrico* ticket is valid for 3000km (and can be used by up to five people at the same time) for a maximum of 20 journeys. A *Eurodomino* ticket is valid for one month's travel in a number of European countries (for 3, 5, or 10 days). You can claim reimbursement (on payment of a small penalty) for unused tickets and sleepers not later than 24 hours before the departure of the train. Bicycles are allowed on most trains (except Eurostar trains): a day ticket costs 5000 lire on slow trains, and 10,000 lire on Intercity, Eurocity, and Espressi. A *Carta Blu* is available for the disabled, and certain trains have special facilities for them (information from the main railway stations).

**Timetables**. The timetable for the train services changes on about 26 September and 31 May every year. Excellent timetables are published twice a year by the Italian State Railways (*In Treno*; one volume for the whole of Italy) and by Pozzorario in several volumes (*Sud e Centro Italia* covers Sicily). These can be purchased at news-stands and railway stations.

**Left luggage offices** are usually open 24 hours at the main stations; at smaller stations they often close at night, and for a few hours in the middle of the day.

**Porters** are entitled to a fixed amount (shown on noticeboards at all stations) for each piece of baggage, but trollies are now usually available in the larger stations.

**Restaurant cars** (sometimes self-service) are attached to most international and internal long-distance trains. Also, on most express trains, snacks, hot coffee and drinks are sold thoughout the journey from a trolley wheeled down the train. At every large station snacks are on sale from trolleys on the platform and you can buy them from the train window.

**Sleeping cars**, with couchettes, or first- and second-class cabins, are carried on certain trains from the mainland, as well as 'Sleeperette' compartments with reclining seats (first-class only).

### By bus

In Sicily it is now easier to reach some destinations by bus rather than by train, since the buses are sometimes quicker and almost always more punctual than trains. Local buses, run by numerous different companies, abound between the main towns in Sicily. It is, however, difficult to obtain accurate information about these services outside Italy. Some information is available from Citalia, London, or from the local tourist offices (APT) in Italy. The names of the local bus companies and their town termini have been given where possible in the text. The fastest way by public transport from Palermo to Catania is by the direct bus service operated by SAIS along the motorway (service c every hour in 2 hr 40 min.) Other comfortable express coaches run direct by motorway from Palermo to Trapani and from Messina to Catania. Fares are normally comparable to rail fares and luggage is carried free of charge.

The main bus companies operating on the island include *AST*, piazza Marina, Palermo, ☎ 091/620811; piazza delle Poste, Siracusa, ☎ 0931/462711; Catania, ☎ 095/7461096. *SAIS*, via Balsamo, Palermo (☎ 091/6166028); 28 via Trieste, Siracusa, ☎ 0931/66710; Catania, ☎ 095/536168. *Segesta*, 26 via Balsamo, Palermo, ☎ 091/6167919.

### Town buses

It is almost always necessary to purchase tickets before boarding (at tobacconists, bars, newspaper kiosks, information offices, etc.) and stamp them on board at automatic machines. It is usually best to explore towns on foot as the buses in the big cities tend to be overcrowded, infrequent, and slow, but it is well worth taking a bus to the places of interest on the outskirts of towns (and details of these have been given in the text).

### Taxis

Taxis (yellow or white in colour) are provided with taximeters: it is advisable to make sure these are operational before hiring a taxi. Taxis are hired from ranks or by telephone, there are no cruising taxis. When you telephone for a taxi you are given the approximate arrival time and the number of the taxi. A small tip of about 1000 lire can be given to the driver, but is often not expected. A supplement for night service and for lugguage is charged. There is a heavy surplus charge when the destination is outside the town limits (ask roughly how much the fare is likely to be). In Sicily taxis are noticeably more expensive than in most other places in Italy, usually with a minimum charge of 10,000 lire. In Palermo horse cabs (with metres) are being re-introduced.

# Disabled travellers

Italy is catching up slowly with the rest of Europe in the provision of facilities for the disabled. All new public buildings are now obliged by law to provide access for the disabled, and specially designed facilities. In the annual list of hotels published by the local APT offices, hotels which are able to give hospitality to the disabled are indicated. Airports and railway stations now provide assistance and certain trains are equipped to transport wheelchairs. Access for cars with disabled people is allowed to the centre of towns normally closed to traffic where parking places are reserved for them. For all other information, contact the local APT offices.

# Food and wine

Sicilian food is generally excellent and better than that to be found on the Italian mainland. **Pasta dishes** include *pasta con le sarde* with fresh sardines, wild fennel, pine nuts and raisins; *spaghetti alla Norma* or *maccheroni alla Norma*, with fresh tomato, basil, fried aubergine, and grated salted ricotta cheese; *spaghetti al peperoncino* with red pepper and garlic (very spicy), *pasta all'arrabbiata* with a dry anchovy sauce. You are usually given dry roasted breadcrumbs instead of grated parmesan cheese to sprinkle on the pasta dishes with fish sauces. Pasta is also often served with courgettes or broccoli. *Pasta con la mollica* is spaghetti with capers, anchovies, green olives, garlic and roasted breadcrumbs. *Bottarga*, dried tuna fish roe, is also sometimes used as a condiment for pasta. Another interesting pasta dish is *pasta con il matarocco*, served with fresh tomatoes, garlic, basil and almonds mixed with olive oil.

A characteristic **hors d'oeuvre** dish is *caponata* which contains aubergines, tomatoes, olives, capers, celery, and onion, served cold in a vinegar and sugar dressing. The olives of Sicily are famous. Broad beans (*fave, fagioli*) chick peas (*ceci*) and lentils (*lenticchie*) are also often served (sometimes with pasta). *Fave a maccu* is a rich dish made with mashed broad beans. On the west coast of the island (Trapani and Erice) *cuscus con pesce* is a traditional Arab dish (couscous) made from coarse semolina steamed in an earthenware pan with spices and onion, to which a *zuppa di pesce* (fish stew) is added, in a tomato sauce.

The **fish** in the seaside towns and villages (and on the islands) is usually extremely good, but, as elsewhere in Italy, it is generally a good deal more expensive than meat. It is often best served simply *alla griglia* (grilled) or *arrosto* (roasted). *Zuppa di pesce* in Sicily usually consists of a variety of fish baked in a herb and tomato sauce. Shellfish is abundant, and is often served fried, in a *fritto misto di mare*. *Calamari ripieni alla griglia* are grilled whole squid filled with capers, salted anchovies, olives, garlic, pine nuts, raisins, pecorino cheese and breadcrumbs. Tuna fish (*tonno*, caught off the north coast and off the Egadi islands) and swordfish (*pesce spada*, abundant near Messina in May, June and July) are delicious cooked *alla griglia, in bianco* (in oil, water and spices) or *alla Siciliana* (with capers, red pepper and herbs). *Involtini di pesce spada* are grilled roulades of swordfish covered with breadcrumbs and oil. Sardines are cooked in a variety of ways, including *sarde a beccafico* with breadcrumbs, grated cheese, pine nuts, salted anchovies, parsley, oil, sultanas, and lemon. Meat dishes include *falsomagro*, a meat loaf.

Good **fruit** (especially oranges, mandarins, tangerines, melons, and grapes) are always available in season. Prickly pears are ripe from September to November. The **ice-creams** and **water ices** (*granite*) are famous, and can be made from roses and jasmine as well as the more traditional flavours. The

**confectionery** of Sicily is justly renowned, and ricotta cheeese, almond paste and pistachio nuts are widely used. Particularly good and decorative are the marzipan fruits (*frutti di martorana*, or *pastareale*), biscuits made with egg whites, almonds and lemon rind (*dolci di mandorla*) and *cannoli* (rolls of thin, deep fried pastry, made with red wine and Marsala, filled with ricotta, candied fruits, bitter chocolate and chopped pistachio). The *cassata alla siciliana* is a delicious light cake filled with ricotta and candied fruits. *Giuggiolena* is made with sesame seeds, honey, toasted almonds and orange rind. Biscuits are often flavoured with sesame seeds, or filled with a rich *conserva* of figs, almonds and candied fruit. The confectionery of Modica (including chocolate) is particularly good.

The local **wines** are usually excellent, and it is often advisable to accept the house wine (*vino della casa*), white and red are usually available. This varies a great deal but is normally a *vino da tavola* of average standard and reasonable price. The most famous (but not necessarily the best) Sicilian wines, widely known outside the island, are *Corvo di Salaparuta* (red and white) and *Regaleali* (red, white and rosé). The most widely consumed white wine is *Bianco d'Alcamo*. An excellent red wine is *Donnafugata*.

Good red wines include *Cerasuolo* produced around Vittoria, Ragusa and Comiso, and *Faro* still made by a few wine-growers near Messina. A white wine called *Capo Bianco* is also produced near Messina. The wine called *Etna* made from grapes cultivated on volcanic soil, can be white, red or rosé. *Ciclopi* is also found around Etna. *Mamertino Bianco* is produced near Castroreale. Near Catania the red *Terreforti* is sold, and near Siracusa, *Anapo* (white), *Eloro* and *Pachino* (red). In the west of the island, wines produced near Agrigento include *Menfi*, *Akragas* and *Belice*, and near Trapani the white *Capo Boeo* is produced. In the Palermo area *Casteldaccia* and *Partinico* (white) can be found. Famous desert wines produced in Sicily are *Marsala*, still made in large quantities around Marsala; *Malvasia* from Salina in the Aeolian Islands, bottled locally by Fenich and Caravaglio; and *Moscato* (white Muscatel) from Pantelleria. There is an annual guide to Italian wines published jointly by Gambero Rosso and Slow Food.

## Eating out

Restaurants in Italy are called *ristoranti* or *trattorie*; there is now usually no difference between the two, although a *trattoria* used to be less smart (and usually cheaper) than a *ristorante*. The least pretentious restaurant almost invariably provides the best value. Almost every locality has a simple (often family run) restaurant which caters for the local residents; the decor is usually very simple and the food excellent value. This type of restaurant does not always offer a menu and the choice is usually limited to three or four first courses, and three or four second courses, with only fruit as a sweet. The more sophisticated restaurants are more attractive and comfortable and often larger and you can sometimes eat at tables outside. They display a menu outside, and are also usually considerably more expensive. In all restaurants it is acceptable to order a first course only, or skip the first course and have only a second course. Note that fish is always the most expensive item on the menu in any restaurant.

**In each chapter in the main text a small up-to-date selection of restaurants has been given, which is by no means exhaustive. The**

**restaurants have been divided into three categories (A, B, and C) to reflect current price ranges**:

**A** luxury-class restaurants, where the prices are likely to be over 60,000 lire a head (and sometimes well over 100,000 lire a head). These are among the most famous restaurants in Sicily and they usually offer international cuisine.

**B** first-class restaurants where the prices range from 45,000 lire and above. These are generally comfortable, with good service, but are not cheap.

**C** which are simple trattorie and pizzerie where you can eat for around 35,000 lire a head, or less. Although simple, and by no means 'smart', the food in this category which often includes local specialities, is usually the best value.

Lunch is normally around 13.00 or 13.30, while dinner is around 20.00 or 21.00. Some restaurants still have a cover charge (*coperto*, shown separately on the menu), which is added to the bill (although this has officially been discontinued). Prices include service, unless otherwise stated on the menu. Tipping is therefore not necessary, but a few thousand lire can be left on the table to convey appreciation. Restaurants are now obliged by law (for tax purposes) to issue an official receipt to customers, you should not leave the premises without this (*ricevuta fiscale*).

Some of the best annual guides to eating in Italy (but only in Italian) are published by Gambero Rosso (*Ristoranti d'Italia*) and Slow Food Arcigola *Osterie d'Italia* (a guide to cheaper eating). Specialised annual guides to the restaurants (mostly in the A and B categories as described above) include the red Michelin guide (*Italia: hotel-ristoranti*); *I Ristoranti di Veronelli*, and *Alberghi e Ristoranti* (TCI).

*Pizze* (a popular and cheap food throughout Italy) and other excellent snacks are served in a *pizzeria*, *rosticceria*, and *tavola calda*. Some of these have no seating accommodation and sell food to take away or eat on the spot. Typical Sicilian snacks are *arancini di riso*, rice balls fried in breadcrumbs, filled with butter and cheese, or meat. Sicilian bread is particularly good and nutritious. In Palermo and the western part of the island it always has a topping of sesame seeds. For **picnics**, sandwiches (*panini*) are made up on request (with ham, salami, cheese, anchovies, tuna fish, etc.) at *pizzicherie* and *alimentari* (grocery shops) and *fornai* (bakeries). Bakeries often also sell delicious individual pizzas, *focacce* or *schiacciate*, bread or puff pastry topped or filled with cheese, spinach, tomato, salted anchovies, ham, etc., they also usually sell good sweet buns, rolls and cakes. Some of the best places to picnic in towns have been indicated in each section in the main text.

**Bars and cafés** (*caffè* or *pasticcerie*)are comfortable and pleasant places to sit and have a good snack, and soft drinks, wines and spirits are also available. A selection of these has been given in each section in the main text. They are open all day, and most Italians eat the excellent refreshments they serve standing up. You pay the cashier first and show the receipt to the barman in order to get served. In almost all bars, if you sit at a table you are charged considerably more (at least double) and are given waiter service (you should not pay first). However, some simple bars have a few tables which can be used with no extra charge (it is always best to ask before sitting down). Black coffee (*caffè* or *espresso*) can be ordered diluted (*alto*, *lungo* or *americano*) or with a dash of milk (*macchiato*) with a liquor (*corretto*) or with hot milk (*cappuccino* or *caffè-latte*). In summer cold coffee (*caffè freddo*) and cold coffee and milk (*caffè latte freddo*) are served.

Sicily is particularly famous for its cakes and ice-creams. A **pasticceria** (usually also a café) always sells the best cakes since they are made on the premises. Delicious local specialities are still produced (see above). Ice-creams should always be bought in a **gelateria** where they are made on the premises; bars usually sell packaged ice-cream only.

## Money and banks

In Italy the monetary unit is the Italian lira (pl. lire). Notes are issued for 1000, 2000, 5000, 10,000, 50,000, 100,000 and 500,000 lire. Coins of 50, 100, 200 and 500 lire. There are currently three sizes of 50 and 100 lire coins. Travellers' cheques and Eurocheques are the safest way of carrying money when travelling, and most credit cards are now generally accepted in shops, hotels and restaurants (and at some petrol stations). In the centre of the main towns there are automatic teller machines (ATMs) called Bancomat and also machines which change foreign bank notes.

**Banks** are usually open Monday–Friday 08.30–13.30, 14.45–15.45 (or 14.30–15.30); closed Saturday, Sunday and public holidays. They close early (about 11.00) on days preceding national holidays. The commission on cashing travellers' cheques can be quite high. Money can also be changed at exchange offices (*cambio*), in travel agencies, some post offices and main railway stations. Exchange offices are usually open seven days a week at airports and main railway stations. At hotels, restaurants, and shops money can sometimes be exchanged (but usually at a lower rate).

## Working hours and public holidays

Shops (clothes, hardware, hairdressers, etc.) are generally open 09.00–13.00 and 16.00–19.30, including Saturday, and for most of the year are closed on Monday morning. Food shops usually open at 07.30/08.00–13.00, 17.00–19.30/20.00, and for most of the year are closed on one afternoon a week. From mid-June to mid-September all shops are closed instead on Saturday afternoon. Banks are usually open Mon–Fri 08.20–13.20, 14.30–15.45. They are closed on Saturday and public holidays, and close early (about 11.00) on days preceding national holidays. Government offices usually work six days a week from 08.00–13.30 or 14.00.

The Italian national holidays when offices, shops and schools are closed are as follows: 1 January (New Year), 25 April (Liberation Day), Easter Monday, 1 May (Labour Day), 15 August (Assumption), 1 November (All Saints' day), 8 December (Immaculate Conception), Christmas Day and 26 December (St Stephen). Each town keeps its patron saint's day as a holiday.

## Health

British citizens, as members of the EU, have the right to claim health services in Italy if they are in possession of the E111 form (available from all post offices). There are also a number of private holiday health insurance policies. First aid services (*pronto soccorso*) are available at all hospitals, railways stations and airports. **Chemist shops** (*farmacie*) are usually open Mon–Fri 09.00–13.00,

15.30–19.30. On Saturdays, Sundays and public holidays a few are open (listed on the door of every chemist). In every town there is also at least one chemist open at night (opening times are shown on the door). For emergencies, dial 113.

# Crime and personal security

For all emergencies, dial 113. Pickpocketing is a widespread problem in large towns all over Italy: it is always advisable not to carry valuables in handbags and be particularly careful on public transport. Cash and documents etc. can be left in hotel safes. It is a good idea to make photocopies of all important documents in case of loss. You are strongly advised to carry some means of identity with you at all times while in Italy, since you can be held at a police station if you are stopped and found to be without a form of identification.

There are three categories of policemen in Italy: *vigili urbani*, the municipal police (who wear blue uniform in winter and white during the summer and hats similar to London policemen); *carabinieri*, the military police who have local offices in every town and village (and who wear a black uniform with a red stripe down the side of their trousers); and the *polizia di stato*, State police (who wear dark blue jackets and light blue trousers).

Crime should be reported at once. A detailed statement has to be given in order to get an official document confirming loss or damage (essential for insurance claims). Interpreters are usually provided.

# Telephones and postal information

There are numerous public telephones all over Italy in kiosks, bars, restaurants etc. These are operated by coins or telephone cards which can be purchased from tobacconists (displaying a blue 'T' sign), bars, news-stands and post offices. Telephone numbers in Italy can have from four to eight numbers. All numbers have an area code, which (since 1998) always has to be dialled, even if making a local call. Placing a local call costs 200 lire. Directory assistance (in Italian) is available by dialling 12. Numbers that begin with 167, called *numeri verdi*, are toll-free, but require a deposit of at least 200 lire. Most cities in the world can now by dialled direct from Italy (and international telephone cards are available). To make a call to Italy the full area code (ie. 091 for Palermo) now has to be used after the international code for Italy.

Stamps are sold at tobacconists as well as post offices. Post offices are open Mon–Sat 08.10–13.25, and central offices in main towns are now often open seven days a week 08.10–19.25.

# Public toilets

There is a notable shortage of public toilets in Italy. All bars (cafés) should have toilets available to the public (generally speaking the larger the bar, the better the facilities). Nearly all museums now have toilets. There are also toilets in railway stations and bus stations.

# Annual festivals

There are a number of traditional festivals in Sicilian towns which are of the greatest interest. At these times, the towns become extremely lively and, apart from the central procession or competition, numerous celebrations take place on the side, and local markets are usually held at the same time. They are particularly exciting events for children. The local APT offices will provide particulars, and some of the most important have been described in the main text. The following list groups some of them according to season.

**Spring**. Carnival celebrations at Acireale, Termini Imerese and Sciacca. *Easter week* is particularly important at Caltanissetta (Maundy Thursday), Trapani (Good Friday), Erice (Good Friday), Noto (*S. Spina*; Good Friday), Castelvetrano (Easter Sunday), Prizzi (Easter Sunday; 'dance of the devils'), Modica, Caltagirone, Adrano, Enna, Piana degli Albanesi, S. Fratello (Maundy Thursday and Good Friday; *Festa dei Giudei*) and Castroreale. *After Easter* the *Palio di S. Vincenzo* is run at Acate, and in April Modica holds the *Festa di S. Giorgio*. At Isnello, on *30 April–1 May* there is a festival in honour of the Santissimo Crocifisso. On the *first and second Sunday in May* Siracusa celebrates *S. Lucia*, and on the *third Sunday in May* the *Infiorata* is held in Noto. On *10 May* there is a festival at S. Alfio. On the *last Sunday in May* Ragusa Ibla commemorates *S. Giorgio* and Casteltermini holds the *Tataratà* festival. Also in *May S. Gandolfo* is celebrated at Polizzi Generosa, and the *Settimana delle Egadi* usually takes place at the end of May. Corpus Domini (*May or early June*) is celebrated in Cefalù with the *Festa della Frottola*.

**Summer**. On *3 June* Messina has celebrations in honour of the *Madonna della Lettera* and on *2 July* Enna honours the *Madonna della Visitazione*. At the *end of June S. Pietro* is celebrated in Modica, *S. Paolo* in Palazzolo Acreide, and the *Ecce Homo* in Sclafani Bagni. The summer solstice (*24 June*) is celebrated at Alcara Li Fusi with the pagan *Festa del Muzzuni*. The famous *Festa di S. Rosalia* takes place in Palermo from *10–15*

*July*. The *Scala* is illuminated at Caltagirone on *24–5 July*. From *2–6 August* there are festivities in honour of *S. Salvatore* at Cefalù, and on *13–14 August* the *Palio dei Normanni* is held in Piazza Armerina. Messina has processions of the *Giganti* and the Vara on *13–15 August*, and 15 August is also celebrated at Randazzo. Mistretta celebrates *S. Sebastiano* on *18 August*, and Ragusa celebrates *S. Giovanni* on *29 August*. There is an historical pageant in August at Castelbuono. On the *last Sunday* in August and the *first Sunday in September* the festival of *S. Corrado* takes place in Noto.

**Autumn and winter**. In *September* a hazelnut fair is held in Polizzi Generosa and the *Madonna della Luce* is celebrated at Mistretta. There is a pilgrimmage to the sanctuary of Gibilmanna on *8 September*, and on 8–9 September *S. Giacomo* is celebrated at Gratteri. A pistachio festival is held in *early October* at Bronte, and an autumn festival at Zafferana Etnea on *each Sunday in October*. In Siracusa in *December* the *Immacolata* festival takes place (8th) and the festival in honour of *S. Lucia* (13th). A festival is held on *26 December* in Polizzi Generosa, and on *6 January* the Epiphany is celebrated in Piana degli Albanesi. On *20 January* festivities in honour of *S. Sebastiano* take place in Siracusa and Mistretta. In the *first week in February* the *Sagra del mandorlo in fiore* is held in Agrigento. From the 3–5 February *S. Agata* is celebrated in Catania. On *19 February* there are more festivities in honour of *S. Corrado* in Noto.

## Music and theatre festivals

Music festivals are held in summer at Agrigento, Erice, Noto, Taormina and Trapani. Summer theatre festivals include those at Segesta, Siracusa, Gibellina and Catania. There is often a festival of plays by Pirandello at his birthplace near Agrigento. In Taormina in July an international film festival takes place. In November a music festival is held in the cathedral of Monreale, and in December a festival of international folk music is played on popular instruments in Erice.

## Local handicrafts

It has become much harder to find locally made handicrafts on the island in the last few decades. Baskets are still made in a style distinctive to the island and a few local basket-makers' workshops can still be found. Sicilian baskets are also some-times sold at weekly markets (and in some hardware shops or *mesticherie*). Ceramics can also sometimes be found for sale: Caltagirone still has numerous small potteries which sell their wares, and S. Stefano di Camastra is also famous for its ceramics (which are sold in the town and from the potteries on the Messina road on the outskirts). The main street of Giarre is lined with shops selling Sicilian folk art. Colourful rugs are woven in Erice. But the traditional artisans' skill is now perhaps best seen in the sweets still produced in local *pasticcerie* all over the island.

## Travelling with children

A holiday can often be marred for parents as well as children if too much serious sightseeing is attempted in too short a time. Sicily has a variety of sights which may be of special interest to children and may help to alleviate a day of undiluted museums and churches. A golden rule when allowing a break for an ice-cream is to search for a *gelateria* (rather than a bar) where the locally produced ice-creams are generally excellent.

A few suggestions are given below of places that might have particular appeal to children, listed in the order of the sections into which the book is divided. These include some important monuments which are likely to give a clear impression of a particular period of art or architecture, a few museums, and places of naturalistic interest (see pp.38/39). Local festivals, often with colourful processions etc. (listed above) should not be missed if your visit coincides with one of them. Detailed descriptions of all the places mentioned below are given in the main text (and can easily be found by reference to the index at the back of the book).

### *Province of Palermo*

**Palermo**: street markets, and puppet theatre performances; the Cappella Palatina and Palazzo dei Normanni; S. Giovanni degli Eremiti; the park (and zoo) of Palazzo d'Orleans; the Puppet museum; the park of Villa Giulia and the Botanical gardens; Palazzo Mirto; the Galleria Regionale; La Zisa; the Museo Etnografico Siciliano Pitré and Monte Pellegrino

*Sicilian puppet*

Monreale cathedral, including the roof
Excavations of Solunto
Castle of Caccamo and the ruins of Himera
Cefalù, including the Rocca and the Museo Mandralisca
Madonie Mountains
Ethnographical museum in Piana degli Albanesi and the Bosco della Ficuzza
Island of Ustica

### Province of Trapani
Trapani: the Museo Trapanese di preistoria, the Museo Regionale Pepoli, and the
    Museo delle Saline (when it re-opens)
Erice: the town, including the gardens of Villa Balio, and the Castello di Venere;
    the Museo Agro-Forestale di S. Matteo, and the Parco-zoo di Martogna
The Tonnara di Scopello, the Riserva Naturale dello Zingaro, Custonaci
Segesta (the temple and the theatre)
Egadi Islands and Pantelleria
Island of Mozia, and, in Marsala, the Museo Archeologico di Baglio Anselmi and
    the Stabilimento Florio
Ruins of Selinunte and the Cave di Cusa

### Province of Agrigento
Agrigento: the temples, the Museo Regionale and the rock sanctuary of Demeter
Site of Eraclea Minoa

### Province of Enna
Enna: the evening *passeggiata*, the numismatic collection in the Museo Alessi,
    the Castello di Lombardia, and the Rocca Cerere
Leonforte, including the Granfonte
Castle of Sperlinga
Mosaics in the Villa Romana at Casale near Piazza Armerina
Ruins of Morgantina

### Province of Ragusa
Museo Ibleo delle Arti e delle Tradizioni Popolari at Modica and the Cava d'Ispica
Castello di Donnafugata, and the ruins (and museum) of Camarina

### Province of Siracusa
Siracusa: the town of Ortygia, the Duomo, the Fonte Aretusa, the Museo Arche-
    ologico Regionale Paolo Orsi, the catacombs of S. Giovanni, the Latomia del
    Paradiso and Ear of Dionysius, the Greek theatre and the amphitheatre
Castello Eurialo and the River Ciane
Noto
Noto Antica, the ruins of Eloro, the nature reserve of Vendicari
In Palazzolo Acreide, the Casa-Museo ethnographical museum, the excavations
    of Akrai and the Santoni
Park of the Valle dell'Anapo, and the necropolis of Pantalica

### Province of Catania
Catania: Castello Ursino (when it re-opens)

Trip to the summit of Etna, the castle of Adrano, the Castello Maniace at Bronte, the castle of Aci Castello, Giarre (to see the folk art sold on the streets)

Caltagirone: the Scala, the public gardens, the Museo Regionale della Ceramica

### Province of Messina
Messina: the Museo Regionale, the Punta Faro

Taormina: the town, the theatre, the public gardens, the Madonna della Rocca, the Castello, the excavations of Naxos, the Alcantara gorge

Monti Peloritani

Castle of Milazzo, Capo Milazzo, the Aeolian Islands

Excavations of Tindari and the Nebrodi Mountains

# Museums and churches

The opening times of museums and monuments have been given in the text but they vary and often change without warning: when possible it is always advisable to consult the local tourist office (APT) on arrival about the up-to-date times. Many museums and archaeological sites in Sicily are now open seven days a week. State-owned museums and monuments are usually open 09.00–14.00, Sun & PH 09.00–13.00 and are sometimes closed on Mondays. However, they are extending their opening times and some now open in the afternoon on certain days and others stay open seven days a week. There is no standard timetable and you should take great care to allow enough time for variations in the hours shown in the text when planning a visit to a museum or monument. Some museums are closed on the main public holidays: 1 January, Easter, 1 May, 15 August and Christmas Day (although there is now a policy to keep at least a few of them open on these days in the larger cities, information has to be obtained there and then).

**Admission charges** vary, but are usually around 8000 lire for the main regional museums, 4000 lire for archaeological sites, and between 2000–4000 lire for local museums. British citizens under the age of 18 and over the age of 60 are entitled to free admission to state-owned museums and monuments in Italy (because of reciprocal arrangements in Britain). During Museum Week (the *Settimana per i Beni Culturali e Ambientali*) there is free entrance to all state-owned museums, and others are specially opened: traditionally in early December, for the last few years it has been held instead in March.

**Churches** are almost always closed for a considerable period during the middle of the day (11.30 or 12.00 to 16.00 or 17.00), although they usually open very early in the morning (at 07.00 or 08.00). Small churches and oratories are often open only in the early morning, or just for services, but it is sometimes possible to find the key by asking locally. The sacristan will show closed chapels, crypts, etc. and sometimes expects a tip. Many pictures and frescoes are difficult to see without lights which are sometimes provided (operated by lire coins); a torch and binoculars are always useful. Some churches now ask that sightseers do not enter during a service, but normally you may do so, provided you are silent and do not approach the altar in use. An entrance fee is becoming customary for admission to cloisters, bell-towers, etc. Sometimes you are not allowed to enter churches wearing shorts, or with bare shoulders.

## Useful Italian words and phrases

Although many people speak a little English, some basic Italian is helpful for everyday dealings. If you are able to say a few words and phrases your efforts will be much appreciated. See Food and wine section for relevant vocabulary.

good morning *buon giorno*
good afternoon/good evening *buona sera*
good night *buona notte*
goodbye *arrivederci*
hello/goodbye (informal) *ciao*
see you later *a più tardi*

yes/no *si/no*
okay *va bene*
please/thank you *per favore/grazie*
today *oggi*
tomorrow *domani*
yesterday *ieri*
now *adesso*
later *più tardi*
in the morning *di mattina*
in the afternoon/evening *di pomeriggio/di sera*
at night *di notte*

what is your name? *come si chiama/come ti chiami?* (informal)

my name is ... *mi chiamo ...*
I would like *vorrei*
do you have ...? *ha ...?/avete ...?* (plural)

where is ...? *dov'è ...?*
what time is it? *che ore sono?*
at what time? *a che ora?*
when? *quando?*
how much is it? *quanto è?*
the bill *il conto*
where are the toilets? *dove sono i gabinetti?*

do you speak English? *parla inglese?*
I don't understand *non capisco*
cold/hot *freddo/caldo*
with/without *con/senza*
open/closed *aperto/chiuso*
cheap/expensive *economico/caro*
left/right/straight on *sinistra/destra/diritto*

railway station *stazione ferroviaria*
bus station *stazione degli autobus*
airport *aeroporto*
ticket *biglietto*
police station *ufficio di polizia/questura*
hospital *ospedale*
doctor *medico*

dentist *dentista*
asprin *aspirina*
town council/town hall *comune*
municipality/town hall *municipio*
old town (centre) *centro storico*
café (which sells cakes) *pasticceria/e*
ice-cream parlour *gelateria*

Monday *lunedì*
Tuesday *martedì*
Wednesday *mercoledì*
Thursday *giovedì*
Friday *venerdì*
Saturday *sabato*
Sunday *domenica*

spring *primavera*
summer *estate*
autumn *autunno*
winter *inverno*

January *gennaio*
February *febbraio*
March *marzo*
April *aprile*
May *maggio*
June *giugno*
July *luglio*
August *agosto*
September *settembre*
October *ottobre*
November *novembre*
December *dicembre*

# Background information

## Historical summary

The geographical position of Sicily in the centre of the Mediterranean has made her not only the prized possession of foreign powers, but also a battleground between warring nations. But her long history of foreign domination has often been coloured by a brilliant mixture of traditions and cultures which has produced some of the most remarkable art in the Mediterranean world.

The earliest prehistoric finds on the island are the Palaeolithic cave paintings on Levanzo and Monte Pellegrino. The first Neolithic culture so far recognised in Sicily is that known as *Stentinello*, named after one of its typical fortified villages near Siracusa. The Aeolian Islands became important because of the existence of obsidian, which was much sought after by the Mediterranean peoples. In the Bronze Age the islands were on the trade route between the Aegean Islands and the western Mediterranean.

The earliest recorded inhabitants of Sicily are the **Siculi** (hence the modern name *Sicilia* for the island) in the east and the *Sicani* in the west. The *Elymni* are known to have occupied Segesta, Erice and Entella but evidence of their civilisation has so far only been found at Segesta. All these people, in the 15C–10C BC, were in close commercial touch with the Aegeo-Mycenaean peoples of Greece. Archaeological evidence has suggested that the **Phoenicians** visited the west coast of Sicily to establish trading outposts (at Mozia, S. Pantaleo, and later Palermo) even before the Greek settlers began to arrive in the 8C BC. The **Greeks** established strongholds on the east coast at Naxos (c 735 BC) and Siracusa (734), going on into the next century with Lentini, Catania, Megara Hyblaea, Zancle (Messina) and Gela. Most of these settlements were separate from the Sicel villages, although in some cases (such as Morgantina, from the mid-6C BC) the two communities merged.

The 6C BC saw the beginning of the **heroic age of tyrants** with the notorious, if shadowy, figure of Phalaris, who ruled in Akragas probably from 570–555. The brothers Cleander and Hippocrates were succeeded in Gela by Gelon, who captured Siracusa in 485. He and his father-in-law, Theron, tyrant of Akragas, soon controlled nearly all of Greek Sicily, and Gelon became the most powerful figure in the Greek world after his decisive victory over the Carthaginians at the Battle of Himera in 480. This supremacy aroused the jealousy of Athens, but a massive Athenian attack (415) on Siracusa met with fatal disaster.

In the late 5C BC **Dionysius the Elder** dominated the affairs of the island for 38 years as the most powerful tyrant in Sicilian history. The Corinthian Timoleon brought greater prosperity to the island, while **Agathocles** extended control not only over Carthaginian Sicily, but also into North Africa. He became the first King of Sicily.

His successor, Hieron II, brought Sicily under **Roman influence**, and in 264 the **First Punic War** broke out between Rome and Carthage, with Sicily as one of the main battlegrounds. Continuous destructive fighting continued until the Carthaginian surrender in 241. In the Second Punic War Sicily again found herself in an important strategic position between Italy and North Africa. In 212 Siracusa finally fell to the Roman Marcellus, and by 210 Rome controlled the whole of the island including the former Carthaginian territories in the west.

Under Roman domination the Greek cities lost some of their autonomy. Extensive rural estates were established in the interior, and luxurious villas were built (typified by the villas found at Piazza Armerina, Patti and Eloro). In the coastal towns public buildings were erected. The huge slave population on the island (increased by prisoners-of-war taken by the Romans in their battles in the east), led by Eunus in Enna and Cleon in Agrigento, revolted c 139. A second revolt (c104) led to cruel repressions by the Romans. In the early Imperial period Sicily lost importance as a Roman province.

During the 5C Sicily was the successive prey of the Vandals and the Ostrogoths, but in AD 535 it was conquered for **Byzantium** by Belisarius. The weak hold of the Eastern Emperors (although in the 7C Siracusa became the capital of the Byzantine Empire for five years) relaxed under the pressure of the Saracen invasion (827); fierce fighting for possession of the island continued for 50 years. Palermo fell to the **Arabs** in 831, Siracusa in 878. Muslim rule, accompanied by vast numbers of North African and Spanish settlers, was marked by a spirit of tolerance. Palermo in the 9C was one of the great centres of scholarship and art in the world, surpassed in size only by Constantinople in the Christian world. The fertility of the island was exploited to the full, and cotton, oranges, lemons and sugar cane were first cultivated at this time.

In 1060 the Norman **Count Roger de Hauteville** (1031–1101), with a handful of knights, seized Messina. By 1091 Roger was in control of the entire island. Norman rule was characterised by its efficiency and willingness to adapt to the Arabic, Greek and Roman traditions which already existed on the island. In 1130 Roger's son (1093–1154) was crowned King of Sicily as **Roger II**. At that time he was probably the wealthiest ruler in Europe and his court in Palermo the most opulent. Meanwhile Messina flourished as a supply base for the Crusaders.

In 1194 the crown was claimed by the **Emperor Henry VI of Swabia**, son of Barbarossa, in the name of his wife, Constance (daughter of Roger II), and the last of the Hautevilles was put to death. He was succeeded as Emperor and King of Sicily by his son **Frederick II** ('*stupor mundi*'), whose reign was marked by a prolonged struggle with the Papacy. His court in Palermo, drawing on Islamic and Jewish, as well as Christian cultures, was famous throughout Europe for its splendour and learning. The Swabian line ended with the beheading of Conradin in 1268 and the Pope invested **Charles of Anjou** with the crown of Sicily and Naples.

The hated Angevin rule was, however, soon terminated by the famous rebellion known as the **Sicilian Vespers**, which broke out at Palermo at the hour of vespers on Easter Tuesday in 1282. A French officer, who had insulted a Sicilian bride on her way to church by insisting upon searching her for concealed weapons, was immediately killed and every Frenchman in Palermo was massacred. Every Sicilian town, except Sperlinga, followed suit by massacring or expelling its French garrison, and the Sicilians summoned **Peter of Aragon** to be their king. From that day for over four centuries Sicily was ruled by Aragonese princes and Spanish and Bourbon kings, a period in which the rebellious spirit of the islanders lay dormant. By the 16C Charles V had moved the centre of power west of the Mediterranean and Sicily lost much of her strategic importance.

After Napoleon failed to invade the island, the British took control of Sicily in the first years of the 19C and established a constitution for a brief time. Then in 1848 revolution broke out against the Bourbons of Naples. In 1860 **Garibaldi** fired the imagination of the Sicilian people and led an attack against Naples, thus paving the way for Italian Unification. But hard Piedmontese rule by Cavour soon proved unpopular. The northern Italian cities took up a dominant position over the south, and the economic position of Sicily was to remain a long way behind that of the rest of Italy for a century. Violence increased in the ungovernable interior of the island. In 1931 40 per cent of Sicilians still remained illiterate.

The geographical position of Sicily meant that the Allies chose the island for their first important attack on Hitler in Europe in 1943. During the Italian administration in 1944 civil war broke out on the island. Regional administration was approved by Rome in 1946 and the first Assembly was elected in 1947. Palermo is the regional capital and Siracusa, Agrigento, Messina, Catania, Caltanissetta, Trapani, Enna and Ragusa are provincial capitals. Today the region remains one of the poorest in Italy, with the highest unemployment level in the country.

---

**Emigration**

Because of the poverty in Sicily at the end of the 19C many inhabitants of the island, especially from the villages in the interior, emigrated to northern and southern America and by 1900 Sicily was one of the chief emigration regions of the world. Some one and a half million Sicilians had left the island by the outbreak of World War I. The émigrés sent money back to their families and some eventually made enough money overseas to return. One of the most famous emigrants was Lucky Luciano (Salvatore Lucania born at Lercara Friddi in 1897) who emigrated with his family as a child to New York where he later became head of 'Cosa Nostra'. Condemned to 30 years' imprisonment in 1936, he helped the Americans during their landings in Sicily in 1943 by arranging for their reception by the local Mafia (the American secret servicemen wore yellow scarves with 'L' for Luciano printed on them in order to be recognised when disembarking). As a result the combined British and American forces occupied the island in just 38 days (known as Operation 'Husky'). In return Luciano was let out of prison by the Americans in 1946 and extradited to Italy, where he died in Naples in 1962. As a consequence of America's dependence on the Mafia during the war, it unfortunately grew in prestige and power during the subsequent decades.

After World War II many more artisans and peasants left the island to settle permanently in the Americas and Australia. Another exodus from rural Sicily began in the 1950s and early 1960s, this time mostly for a limited period to the industrial cities of northern Italy such as Turin, or to Switzerland, and later Germany. Many of these Sicilians returned in the boom years of the 1960s to build houses which, however, they were never able to finish when the economy once more suffered a decline (in numerous towns, including Gela and Palma di Montechiaro, these half-constructed houses are still abandoned shells).

In the 1960s and 1970s much ugly new building work took place around the coast of the island, including the Conca d'Oro on the outskirts of Palermo. Huge industrial plants in Gela and Augusta brought serious problems of pollution. As in the rest of Italy, almost every town, large and small, is now surrounded by ugly new buildings, and some of these towns have recently mistakenly been 'tidied up' with anonymous urban 'furnishings'. However, in the last few years there have been important signs of change in the island. Nature reserves have been created to safeguard the landscape, restoration of historic monuments has been undertaken, longer opening hours introduced for museums and more churches are being kept open. Palermo and Catania are becoming much more attractive cities and after many years of neglect they both now have enlightened local administrations. Although the problems affecting the island are generally ignored by the rest of Italy, and the Sicilian regional government remains an obstacle to many attempts by local administrators to bring about much needed changes, there is no doubt that the standard of living of many Sicilians, especially in the larger towns, has greatly improved over the last few years. These optimistic signs have gone largely unnoticed by the rest of the country. Much could be done to encourage tourism on the island where the mild climate makes it an excellent place to visit throughout the year. Sicily now has about 4,961,000 inhabitants.

## The Mafia

This century has seen the power of the Mafia on the island steadily increase. Giovanni Falcone estimated that there were more than 5000 'men of honour' in Sicily, chosen after a rigorous selection process. He saw these men as true professionals of crime, who obeyed strict rules. Through a rigid 'protection' system they have controlled Sicilian business transactions for many years.

In the 1980s a number of men in key positions, including magistrates, politicians, and members of the police force who stood up to the Mafia, were killed by them: General Carlo Alberto Dalla Chiesa, sent to Palermo as the prefect in 1982 to deal with the problem of the Mafia, was assassinated by them after only a few months in office. Rocco Chinnici, one of a group of investigating magistrates in Palermo, was murdered in 1983. The journalist Giuseppe Fava, who became known for his outspoken opposition to the Mafia through his newspaper *I Siciliani*, was killed by them in 1984. In 1991 Libero Grassi, an entrepreneur who ran a small factory in Palermo and who had spoken out against the Mafia racket in the city, was murdered by them. In the same year a courageous group of shopkeepers and tradesmen in Capo d'Orlando formed an association and stood up in court against those accused of extortion, and their example has been followed by other Sicilians.

A sentence passed in 1987, at the end of the largest trial ever held against the Mafia (the evidence for which had been collected by Giovanni Falcone), condemned hundreds of people of crimes connected with the Mafia. But this achievement in the battle against the Mafia was soon overshadowed when the anti-Mafia 'pool' of judges, created by Antonino Caponnetto in 1983 and led by Giovanni Falcone, disintegrated because of internal conflicts and a belief on the part of Falcone that his attempt to fight the Mafia was being obstructed. In 1992 this courageous Sicilian, who had raised the hopes of so many honest Italians, was assassinated together with his wife and bodyguards outside Palermo. Just a few months later his friend and fellow magistrate Paolo Borsellino was also murdered by the Mafia in Palermo. These tragic events were seen by many as a desperate blow in the battle against the Mafia and the response from Rome was to send in the army.

In 1993 the arrest of Toto Riina, the acknowledged boss of *Cosa Nostra*, after more than 20 years 'in hiding' in Palermo, closely followed by the capture of Nitto Santapaola outside Catania, the head of the Mafia in that city since 1982, was greeted, not without some scepticism, as a step in the right direction.

However, since 1992, the whole question of the power of the Mafia has been placed on a different level. In 1992 the murder by the Mafia of Salvo Lima, Christian Democrat member of the European parliament and the most powerful politician on the island, was interpreted by many as a sign that he was no longer able to guarantee judicial immunity for Mafia bosses. In 1993 Giulio Andreotti, the most famous political figure in the country over the past four decades, was accused of collaboration with the Mafia. It now looks likely that a connection between the Mafia and the national political scene up to this decade will be proved. A document published by a parliamentary commission, entitled *Mafia and politics* points the way to this conclusion, but the trial was still in progress at the time of writing.

In 1996 Giovanni Brusca, who ignited the bomb which killed Giovanni Falcone, was arrested. In 1997 many Mafia bosses were condemned (and most of them given life imprisonment) for their part in the murder of Falcone. Meanwhile, a pool of courageous magistrates in Palermo, led by Gian Carlo Caselli (a Piedmontese who asked to be transferred to Palermo), continues the struggle against the power of the Mafia. Following the example of Falcone they also make use of *pentiti*, members of the Mafia who have decided to collaborate with the law in return for reduced jail sentences. However, it is also generally recognised that without more help from the State the struggle can never be won.

## The landscape of Sicily

Sicily, the largest and most important of the Mediterranean islands (25,708 sq km), owed its ancient name *Trinacria* to its triangular shape. Its sub-tropical climate and volcanic soil produce lush vegetation in the coastal areas, with bushes of hibiscus with their huge orange, blue, red and yellow flowers, geraniums, and purple bougainvillea. There are numerous orange, lemon, and mandarin trees (*agrumi*), splendid palm trees, fig trees and hedges of prickly pear (*fichi d'India*). The characteristic agave (or aloe), which can sometimes grow to a height of 8m, takes ten years to produce a yellow flower and then dies. Fruit trees grow all over the islands, and Bronte is famous for its pistachio plantations and Agrigento for its almonds (a regional park here now protects some 300 species of almond trees). There are numerous vineyards which produce an excellent wine, as well as ancient olive trees. The wooded areas, although once far more extensive, still have a great variety of trees including oak, chestnut, beech, poplar, ilex, pine, cork, manna ash, elm, maple, yew and fir. Carob trees also flourish on the island. The hills are often covered with low bushes of broom, myrtle, euphorbia, mastic and heather. Wild flowers are particularly beautiful all over the island in spring.

In the central uplands grain is still grown, although the interior of the island used to be more fertile and intensely cultivated when Etna and the Peloritani and

Nebrodi mountains were forested so that the rivers were larger (and some of them even navigable). The cult of Ceres (or Demeter) thrived in ancient times all over the island: she is supposed to have taught the islanders to cultivate wheat. Homer mentions the fertility of the island and Cicero talks of it as the granary of Rome. Since the land has been worked for centuries it provides a particularly interesting landscape.

Physically the island is a continuation of the chain of the Apennines on the one hand, and of the Atlas mountains on the other. But it appears that far from Sicily being joined in comparatively recent history to Calabria, the Straits of Messina is actually narrower now than in former times. The island is mountainous across the north and east, with plateaux in the centre, lowering towards the south, and it has fertile coastal plains. The landscape around Enna, Caltanissetta and Piazza Armerina is particularly beautiful and well preserved. Etna, the largest volcano in Europe, dominates the eastern half and much of the centre of Sicily. The island is notorious for its earthquakes. Fumarole, macalube, or diminutive mud-volcanoes and thermal springs occur frequently. Within Sicilian waters are many smaller islands: the Aeolian or Lipari Islands to the north-east; Ustica to the north-west; the Egadi to the west; and Pantelleria and the distant Pelagian Isles to the south-west. Of the meagre rivers the largest are the Simeto, Salso and Belice; most of the smaller streams are dry in the summer. The island, since its deforestation, has suffered from a shortage of water. The surrounding sea is still rich in fish, especially in the Straits of Messina where over 140 species are known, including unusual deep-sea varieties.

## Nature reserves and beaches

Some of the most beautiful parts of the island are at last becoming protected areas. The two excellently run coastal reserves of the Zingaro on the north coast, and Vendicari on the east coast, stand out not only as areas of extraordinary beauty and interest for their scenery, vegetation and birdlife, but also as examples of the success of the efforts of the local population to preserve them from 'development'. They are both only accessible on foot. Since 1984 there have been oases around the mouths of the Simeto and Fiumefreddo, at the southern and northern borders of the province of Catania. The wooded areas of the island include the Nebrodi (a protected area since 1993) and Peloritani mountain ranges on the north coast, and the Bosco della Ficuzza, south of Palermo, one of the largest forests left on the island. Beautiful walks (and rides) can be taken in the Madonie Mountains south of Cefalù, which became a regional nature reserve in 1989. Etna, now a national park, remains one of the most fascinating areas on the island, despite the fact that its lower slopes have been covered with new buildings.

Smaller areas, but with their own particular interest, which have also been protected, where lovely countryside can be explored, include the Valle dell'Anapo and the Cava d'Ispica. The remote plateau of Pantalica is also very beautiful. A similar area, the Cava Grande at Cassibile, became a reserve in 1984. The salt marshes between Trapani and Marsala, interesting for their birdlife, are partially protected, but the most beautiful accessible countryside here is on the island of S. Pantaleo (Mozia). Capo Bianco and Torre Salsa, near Eraclea Minoa on the south coast, is another lovely stretch of coastline, purchased by the Worldwide Fund for Nature in 1991, with interesting vegetation and birdlife. On the hillside below Erice the Museo Agro Forestale di S. Matteo was opened in 1986 where a farm of some 500 hectares may be visited. The islands off the Sicilian coast are all of great natural beauty, particularly the Aeolian Islands, Marettimo in the Egadi group and Pantelleria. A well-run marine reserve protects the splendid seabed off the shore of Ustica.

The sea around Sicily has suffered from pollution this century, as it has around the rest of Italy, and much of the coastline has been spoilt by new building. The industrial zones of Augusta and Gela should be avoided by visitors at all costs. Some of the prettiest beaches can be found near Noto, at Cala Bernardo and Noto Marina. The south coast is generally the least spoilt part of the island, with good beaches especially around Porto Palo (south of Menfi, near Selinunte) and at Torre di Monterosso, south of Siculiana. Further east are the small resorts with some good beaches of Marina di Ragusa, Donnalucata, Cava d'Aliga and Marina di Modica. The rocky coast around Acireale and Taormina is popular for sea bathing. On the north coast there are fine (but crowded) beaches at the resorts of Cefalù and Mondello. There are rocky beaches on Capo di Milazzo. North of Castellammare del Golfo there is a remarkable stretch of unspoilt rocky coastline (only accessible by paths) at Cala Bianca, Cala Rossa and Baia Guidaloca, and sea bathing is allowed in the beautiful nature reserve of Zingaro on the promontory of Capo S. Vito. S. Vito lo Capo has become a seaside resort, with good beaches. The best sea bathing of all is to be found on the islands, especially the Aeolian Islands, Marittima and Pantelleria. Ustica has a particularly beautiful seabed, much explored by skin-divers.

# The art and architecture of Sicily

*by Helen Hills*

Sicily's strategic position, lying between Europe and Africa, linking the eastern and western Mediterranean and the Latin world with the Greek, resulted not only in its tumultuous history of successive invasions and conquests, but also in a unique cultural mixture which, in turn, stimulated the creation of rich and original works of art. The powers which ruled Sicily, and those which traded with it, each left their distinctive cultural imprints, and individual artists, both foreigners working in Sicily and Sicilians who had trained abroad, enriched these patterns. Yet the art history of Sicily is not simply a succession of disconnected impositions from foreign cultures; a strong local or Sicilian pride and conservatism nourished the development of insular and regional traditions which, during the most inventive periods, were fused with ideas coming from outside to create distinctive forms and styles quite peculiar to Sicily.

Sadly, the richness of Sicily's cultural heritage has not inspired the scholarly interest or political commitment it deserves. Many buildings which have survived the ravages of earthquakes, volcanic eruption and the bombardment of World War II now stand in desolate ruin, without hope of restoration, closed to the public and wasted. Paintings and sculpture have not fared much better: sales abroad, scandalous thefts, and over-restoration or poor conservation have dispersed or destroyed many irreplaceable and outstanding works. This pattern will continue so long as the necessary political will is lacking.

## Prehistoric art

Some of the finest manifestations of Palaeolithic art yet known have been discovered in Sicily. In a small cave at Cala dei Genovesi on the island of **Levanzo** are two distinct series of figures, one set incised, and the other painted, of c 8700 BC. The incised figures, of red deer, oxen, equids and other animals, are particularly vivacious. Another series of incised drawings (c 8000 BC), in one of the Addaura caves of **Monte Pellegrino**, is of particular interest because it features not only figures of animals of the kind usually depicted in Quaternary art, but human figures as well, sometimes isolated and sometimes arranged in groups and drawn with the same naturalistic liveliness as the animals.

The earliest Neolithic culture known in Sicily, the *Stentinello*, may have covered much of the island by 3000 BC. Its pottery, decorated by impressions or incisions often made with the edges of shells, is finer and more compactly decorated than similar pottery of the same period elsewhere in the Mediterranean. In some of the sites of this civilisation (Stentinello, Lipari and especially Megara Hyblaea) more spirited pottery has been found, painted with red bands or flames on a light background, recalling the early painted ware of the Greek mainland. Painted wares were followed by others with incised spirals or complicated rolled handles. Each of these styles reflects an impact from outside, either casual landings or settlements, whose local nature accounts for the regional variations. The main sources were Anatolia, the Aegean, Cyprus and Syria, but contacts with North Africa and Egypt can be inferred now and then. This rather disjointed development lasted throughout the so-called Copper Age (3rd millennium).

Examples of the pottery, idols and jewellery can be seen in the Archaeological Museums in Palermo and Siracusa.

Cultural influences from Anatolia and the Aegean created the rock-cut chamber tombs which became ubiquitous in Sicily with little variation until the 5C BC. Most of the tombs are very simple, small oval, mitten-shaped rooms but a few are more complicated architecturally with recessed doorways, pilasters and pillars in front of a prepared façade. Some fine tombs at **S. Angelo Muxaro**, in use from the 8C to the mid-5C BC, attain very grandiose dimensions and are comparable with Mycenean examples. At **Castelluccio**, near Noto, spiral motifs in relief of the 3rd or 2nd millennium BC sometimes decorate the stone slabs closing the tomb doorways, and these are the only examples of prehistoric stonecarving so far known in Sicily. As the population centres expanded in the Late Bronze and Iron Ages, so their necropoleis became larger and more conspicuous, giving rise to the thousands of tombs which honeycomb the hills at Pantalica, most of which date from the 13C to the 11C BC. Mycenean influences manifested themselves at **Pantalica** in the architecture of the so-called 'Anaktoron', or prince's palace, and in the form and decoration of pottery. However, in spite of its dolmens, strongholds, the variety of chamber tombs and Mycenean influence, Sicily does not display cultural or architectural sophistication until the arrival of the Greeks in the 8C BC.

## Hellenic Sicily
### Architecture
Early Greek settlements were focused on the south-east of Sicily, especially at Siracusa, founded 733 BC (Naxos, on the east coast, was founded in c 735 BC). At first, Greek pottery was imported, but soon a flourishing pottery industry in decorated 'red-figured' ware sprang up and architecture and graves were created in the Greek manner within Sicily. Greek Sicily was, and felt itself to be, fully Greek, not just a rude distant outpost. From the 6C BC Greek cities like Megara Hyblaea and Selinus (Selinunte) were planned in a rational way and had the characteristic Greek central square or agora, temples and cemeteries. But their most magnificent and influential monuments were the Doric temples which still stand, noble and unforgettable, in the dry Sicilian hills. The oldest of these, the temple of Apollo, or of Apollo and Artemis, built c 575 BC, at **Siracusa**, characterised by an enormous heaviness, is obviously a pioneer building. It was followed in the course of the next one and a half centuries at Himera, Akragas and elsewhere, but most grandly of all at **Selinunte** where at least nine temples were built in the long period of peace c 580–480 BC.

Sicilian Greeks were able to keep in step with old Greece through the continuous traffic between Sicily and the old Greek world; documentary evidence suggests the arrival of skilled craftsmen and architects summoned by Sicilian patrons. But distinctive Sicilian peculiarities also developed in the temples: sculpted reliefs on friezes and pediments are much rarer than in Greece and the rule that a pteron (an external colonnade) should be more closely spaced along the sides than at the ends was gradually abandoned, as at **Selinunte Temple C**, whereas the differentiation was adhered to in Greece. Aesthetic considerations often prompted these changes, for instance the unorthodox elements of the

*The ancient theatre, Taormina*

unfinished temple at Segesta were designed to give the building a squat appear-ance in keeping with its situation in a wide valley.

The most remarkable Sicilian Greek building is the temple of Olympian Zeus at **Agrigento**, the largest of all the Doric temples and never finished. Its struc-ture, plan and elevation, with its enormous engaged half columns and colossal Atlas figures, were all revolutionary. At Gela, Timoleon founded a whole new city in 339, and the fortifications on Capo Soprano, which were completed during the reign of Agathocles, were recovered from the sand in almost perfect condition in 1953–4. But the most impressive image of Greek defenceworks is provided by the Castello Eurialo at Siracusa, the strategic position of which offered exemplary solutions to the defensive problems of the 4C BC.

Most of the Greek theatres in Sicily were modified or completely rebuilt when Sicily belonged to Rome. For example, at **Segesta**, the best preserved of all the Hellenic Sicilian theatres (of the 3C BC), the unusually high scena frons with architectural decoration was probably added early in the 1C, and at Tyndaris the theatre was drastically altered by the Romans. Nevertheless, it is clear that these buildings were conceived as part of a wonderful natural stage, taking careful advantage of dramatic views and slopes of the land around.

### Sculpture

The rarity of sculpted reliefs on temples in Sicily in comparison with ancient Greece is most arresting and has not yet been convincingly explained. Of all the Greek cities in Sicily, Selinunte is the only one to have decorated its temples with sculptured metopes. These, therefore, are very important in the story of archaic sculpture. The oldest, belonging to Temple C, of the early 6C BC, are in flat relief, but others are almost in the round, and those of Temple E, dated between 460 and 450 BC, abound with life and movement.

## The Roman period
### Architecture

After Hieron II's switch away from Carthage to a partnership with Rome in 263 BC, the culture and civilisation of Sicily absorbed much from Rome. Most of the monuments of this era were public. The theatre of **Catania**, the aqueduct of **Termini Imerese**, the theatre and the naumachia of **Taormina** are representative. Only the central powers were willing to fund such expensive projects and consequently a number of similar buildings went up simultaneously in the most important towns of Sicily, as in the rest of Italy and the provinces. For instance, amphitheatres (which were sometimes converted theatres), in use until the late empire with gladiatorial games and jousting, frequently date from the Augustan age. However, the most spectacular sign of Roman wealth and luxury is the villa in the wooded valley at Casale near **Piazza Armerina**, near Enna. Probably built in the early 4C as the country retreat of Diocletian's colleague Maximian, it had nearly 50 rooms, courts, galleries, baths and corridors arranged in five complex groups and approached by an imposing entrance. Little remains of the sculpture, murals or marble architectural elements, but the mosaic pavements surpass in extent and inventiveness any others of their kind. Ranging from geometrical patterns to scenes of bathing, dancing, fishing, from theatrical performances to scenes of animal life and complicated narrative compositions drawn from Greek mythology, the mosaics create a wonderful display of trompe l'oeil effects, colours and designs. Despite their Roman imperial style, they are almost certainly the work of craftsmen imported from North Africa. Indeed, Roman Sicily did not develop a distinctive culture of its own: the marble portrait busts of local dignitaries, Roman emperors and Greek philosophers are exactly like those of Italy or Gaul.

The early catacombs in Siracusa also date from this period and the grandest of them exceed those of Rome in size and embellishment. The oldest, that of S. Lucia, was in continuous use for at least a century during the period of illegality before Constantine. There was little attempt at decoration during this period, but after the Edict of Toleration, the Siracusan Christians enlarged their underground cemeteries, and introduced new architectural and decorative elements. Higher social class was expressed by more carefully cut chambers with arched entrances and the creation of 'rotundas' in which sculpted sarcophagi were placed in groups.

## The Byzantine period

Of the years of Byzantine rule very little architecture, painting or sculpture remains and the fragmentary pieces in the Palazzo Bellomo, Siracusa and elsewhere are a sorry contrast to the long duration of the dominion. A sketchy picture of architectural developments can be constructed, however, from the few surviving churches. Up until the 6C most churches were basilican in plan, ending in one or more semicircular apses, as at S. Pietro, Siracusa. Then the eastern provinces began to favour the centralised church in variations on the Greek cross. A few of these were erected in Sicily too, but the basilica seems to have remained the most common form. Hardly any fresco painting of this period has survived, although the remains in **S. Pietro, Noto**; **S. Maria della Rotonda, Catania** and elsewhere show that painted decoration was the rule. The most important surviving frescoes, although severely damaged, are the six half-length figures of the saints covering the walls and ceiling of an oratory built in the catacombs of **S. Lucia, Siracusa**. Their style and spirit are Byzantine and their date is probably 8C. Paradoxically, Byzantine art is better represented in the Norman period.

## The Norman period
### Architecture

King Roger II de Hauteville (1093–1154; king, 1130–54) and his two successors were guided above all by a political desire not to antagonise unnecessarily any of their subjects, be they Latins, Orthodox or Muslims. As art tended to be controlled by the royal court, this tolerance manifests itself as a fascinating heterogeneous mixture of styles in the architecture, mosaics and woodwork, in the sculpture, coins and vestments of this period. Their architecture absorbed alien elements with particular grace, producing monuments of composite style, harmony and dignity. Secular, especially court, architecture, naturally inclined to Muslim models whose levels of refinement were unknown in the north. In Palermo the palaces of Favara, La Zisa and La Cuba, built or adapted to house royal and aristocratic families in splendour, show remarkable cultural heterogeneity: Muslim, Romanesque and Byzantine forms rub shoulders; Norman interlaced round arches, Muslim domes, honeycomb roofs and stilted pointed arches occur in compositions carrying Byzantine mosaics and classically proportioned columns. La Zisa is a particularly beautiful example.

The ecclesiastical architecture of the Norman period is its most celebrated achievement today. Indeed the interiors of Cefalù and Monreale cathedrals and of the Palatine chapel in Palermo are without equal in Europe. The first of these great Norman churches was Cefalù, begun in 1131 in a newly-founded bishopric and intended to reinforce monarchical, as opposed to papal, power. It is largely a northern, Romanesque church: tall, adorned with chevron patterning, and with a projecting transept and deep choir, flanked by chapels. But traditional Sicilian forms such as stilted pointed arches and columns set into angles were used.

A more complicated stylistic syncretism occurred at the Palatine Chapel in the **Royal Palace in Palermo**, built 1132–40. The ground plan is a combination of the Byzantine, centralised, inscribed cross plan and the south Italian longitudinal plan. The cupola, with its high drum and stepped squinches which oversail the wall, is of Egyptian Islamic derivation; and the wooden honeycomb ceiling of the nave, probably erected under William I (1154–66), belongs to the North African, Islamic world. Its paintings include Cufic inscriptions, Hellenistic scenes, and images traceable to Persian and Indian legends. It has been given many attributions, but it was probably executed by local Sicilians. The effect of the interior of this chapel is extraordinarily harmonious and tranquil, its richness is never strident because of the careful balancing of the colours and spatial rhythms.

**La Martorana, Palermo**, completed in 1143, is the only important church of this period which was not built for the Hautevilles, although its founder Admiral George of Antioch (d. 1151) was an important figure at Roger II's court. His Greek Orthodox religion probably explains why the plan is of the Byzantine inscribed cross type. This seems to have been especially popular for Basilian monasteries: it occurs at **Trinità di Delia** near Castelvetrano and at **S. Antonio in Palermo**.

The climax of Sicilian Romanesque architecture is **Monreale Cathedral**, built by William II as his mausoleum and as a counterpoise to the power of the Archbishop of Palermo. Like the Palatine Chapel, it is a combination of a southern Italian basilica and a Byzantine cross-in-square church, but its great size compelled the architect to do without vaults. As before, no attempt was made to fuse the Latin, Byzantine and Islamic ideas, but they are all handled on an unprecedentedly large and exhilarating scale.

It is the mosaic decoration of these buildings which contributes most to their splendour and constitutes Sicily's main claim to fame in the visual arts of the 12C. The Pantocrators in the choirs of Cefalù and Monreale with their ascetic reserve and haggard beauty attain a particularly deep spiritual intensity. The presence of Byzantine decoration in these Latin churches is explicable by the fact that they were royal foundations and the Norman kings were seeking to rival the Byzantine emperors. They were executed by important Byzantine craftsmen. Two styles are discernible: the elegant, humane, classical style of Cefalù and the Palatine Chapel; and the dynamic, late Comnenian style of Monreale (decorated 1185–90). Both styles profoundly influenced 12C Western painting, such as the Winchester Bible (c 1150–80). They are not, however, completely Byzantine. Their iconography reflects the outlook of their patrons (hence the early appearance of St Thomas Becket at Monreale). Whereas in a Byzantine church mosaic decoration consisted of an image of the world, the places sanctified by Christ's life and the feasts of the Church, in Sicily such decoration was didactic. At Monreale, for example, the Christian story from the *Fall* to the *Last Judgement* unfolds from the entrance eastwards (typically the *Last Judgement* is represented at the west end). This is the largest and most important Greek mosaic decoration of the 12C which exists anywhere.

Very few secular mosaics have survived and, of those that have, hardly any have been dated. Most of the palaces built in the Conca d'Oro by Roger and his followers probably contained mosaic decorations. The Sala Terrena at La Zisa, probably set at the beginning of William II's reign, displays beautiful interlaced roundels, pairs of peacocks and other characteristic motifs, but the Norman Stanza in the Royal Palace at Palermo far exceeds this in sumptuousness. Despite clumsy restorations, the mosaics still glimmer brilliantly in greens and golds in this evocative room.

The fall of the Hauteville dynasty, however, put an end to these developments. A court art, fostered by kings who were strangers in their country and executed by foreign artists, the mosaic work flourished and died with the Hautevilles and did not lead to the subsequent developments in mosaic art in Sicily.

## Sculpture

The largest and most impressive group of sculpture of this period is the cloister of the Benedictine monastery at Monreale, created between 1172 and 1189. Here over 200 paired colonnettes, with twin capitals treated in single compositions, display an astonishing variety of styles and subjects. Sources of the styles and iconography include Arabic, Byzantine (the mosaics of Monreale Cathedral and Byzantine caskets were drawn upon), north French, Tuscan, Lombard and Campanian; but a general stylistic harmony exists because of the dominance of the classicising style of Campania. The royal porphyry tombs, free-standing under monumental sedicula, in the cathedrals of Palermo and Monreale are equally outstanding, but very different, examples of the sculpture of this period. The unique forms of their sarcophagi were derived from antique models. Some monuments reflect the style of contemporary Byzantine sculpture, such as the relief slabs from the cathedral of Messina, now in the Museo Regionale, Messina.

## Manuscripts

A particularly fine group of illustrated manuscripts was produced at Messina under the patronage of Richard Palmer, the English archbishop of Messina (1182–95). This exceptional work provides a tantalising glimpse of the patronage of one of the highly educated foreign prelates.

# Thirteenth and fourteenth centuries

## Architecture

Unlike his predecessors, Frederick II did not endow monasteries or bishoprics; instead he devoted his building energies to creating a line of fortifications running from Germany to southern Italy and Sicily. In Sicily this line tended to favour the east coast and internally towards Enna. Castles dominated the cities of this area and fortresses were erected at strategic points inland. The most characteristic of the Swabian castles are **Castello Maniace (Siracusa), Augusta** (begun 1232) and **Castello Ursino** (begun 1234) in Catania; the contemporaneity of their construction—or reconstruction—indicates the existence of an efficient technical organisation and illustrates Frederick's personal control over the castle building programme. The castles consist of quadrangular curtain walls with corner towers, a plan and spatial form derived from Byzantine and Muslim architecture. Castello Maniace, for instance, is square with round towers at the corners. Others, like the castle at Augusta, have towers in the middle as well as at the corners. Their original internal arrangement is best seen at Castello Maniace. Here the ground floor was originally unpartitioned but was divided by square bays with rib vaults resting on robust round columns, except for the central bay, which formed a small atrium. The atrium acquired a dominant role through its swollen size and luminosity in the castles of Catania and Prato in Tuscany. The Swabian castles are remarkable above all because they encase elegant apartments built in the Gothic style, as at Castello Maniace and Castello Ursino. This reflects the fact that in addition to their military function the castles were designed to house Frederick on his journeys through Sicily. Although these 13C castles, in their remote sites, are still awe-inspiring sights, little detailed research on them has been carried out or published. Thus we know very little about **Castello di Paternò**, an austere tower of volcanic rock commanding the wide Simeto valley, or the **Castello di Garsiliato** (recorded 1240) which rises in forbidding solitude in the immense valley of Gela; indeed, many buildings generally attributed to the Swabian period could date from other periods.

Frederick II did not give much impulse to the development of religious architecture. His direct involvement was restricted to the Murgo basilica near Lentini; but the religious orders initiated some important buildings like the Badiazza near Messina, a Cistercian church, or the Franciscan foundation at Messina. The **Murgo**, founded c 1225, demonstrates the continuity of Norman architectural forms in the use of Byzantine and Islamic motifs, but its plan is typical of Cistercian buildings and it has elements in common with contemporary castles: the side aisles of the basilica strongly recall the arcades of Castello Maniace. Similar elements occur in the Badiazza, whose rib vaults are among the most beautiful of 13C buildings and whose capitals include Byzantine, Burgundian and Cistercian types. Burgundian Gothic rib vaults, responds and portal capitals also appear in another important church, **S. Maria degli Alemanni** (c 1220) in Messina. They are combined with Romanesque elements which persist in the portal and interior capitals. Among the most remarkable churches is **S. Francesco**, Messina (founded 1254) whose architectural sophistication is illustrative of the axiom that the finest achievements of Italian Gothic architecture are often obtained by the simplest forms. Its eight nave chapels create interesting effects: too shallow to disturb the spatial unity of the nave, their undecorated pointed arches give the appearance of internal buttressing (a feature which originated among the mendicants in Catalonia and southern France). Its apse is unexpectedly animated by the introduction of Gothic decoration elements not found elsewhere in the church.

With the fall of the Swabian monarchy and the break up of its central authority, 14C Sicily became tormented by factional struggles. As a result, the dominating 14C structural feature is the tower. The great feudal lords continued the well-tried building traditions established in the Swabian castles: the castle of **Naro**, for instance, reproduces the constructive system of Frederick II's castles in its use of round and quadrangular towers. Swabian forms also persisted in the castle at Mussomeli built by Manfredo Chiaramonte towards the mid 14C, and in that at Venetico, erected by the Spadafora in the first half of the 15C.

Castle building in the country was echoed in the towns by the erection of 'strong' houses, such as those of the Chiaramonte (begun 1307) and Sclafani (1329–30) at Palermo, or the tower houses of the 15C and early 16C still visible at Enna, Randazzo, Taormina and Alcamo. Of these the **Palazzo Steri** (Chiaramonte) in Palermo is the most interesting. Its lava inlay decoration and large windows belie the impression of a fortified castle given by the exterior. Inside, the painted ceiling, full of verve, dated 1377–80 and signed by three Sicilians, is the only surviving example of what may have been a widespread vernacular decoration.

## Painting

Our knowledge of 14C painting is very cloudy because of the loss of many paintings and the inadequacy of research to date. Most important paintings executed in Sicily during the 14C were by foreigners and show Sienese influence. For instance, the elegant early 14C St Peter Enthroned in the Chiaramonte Collection, outstanding for the decorative brilliance of its design, recalls the work of Lippo Memmi and has been attributed to him. The important panel of 1346, signed by **Bartolommeo da Carmogli** (fl. 1346–after 1358) in the Galleria Regionale, Palermo, which shows the *Virgin feeding Christ at the breast*, is the earliest dated example of what became one of the key symbols of Italian painting for the rest of the 14C. Its predella is also interesting. It shows kneeling members of a flagellant confraternity, four of whom wear the hooded robes with circles cut into the backs to bare the body to the scourge, reflecting the fashion of violent self-mortification.

## Sculpture

In sculpture as in painting the Sienese influence was marked in 14C Sicily. The wall tomb of Archbishop Guidotto de' Tabiati, dated 1333, in the cathedral at Messina, signed by **Goro di Gregorio** (fl. 1324–43), a Sienese, shows the weaknesses and strengths characteristic of this period: in places the composition is swallowed up by the narrative and crowded figures make a hectic impression, but in the *Annunciation* the composition is more controlled and the clear lines and careful balance of the masses are most eloquent. Throughout the Gothic period, Sicilian sculpture betrays a certain clumsiness. Figure sculpture in particular, is often coarse and shows little appreciation of the living form. Ornament and relief display the continuing influence of Byzantine work. Not until the Gagini family came down from Geneva, some time in the late 1450s, was a group of able sculptors established in Sicily.

## Fifteenth and sixteenth centuries
### Architecture

Soon after 1400, Catalan art, often combined with Gothic forms from other sources, began to make its mark in Sicily. In architecture Catalan influences appeared throughout Sicily, but especially at Trapani, Siracusa, Ragusa, Modica and Palermo. The most significant building of the period occurred at **Palermo Cathedral**, and, as the capital was in closer contact with Barcelona than other towns, orthodox Catalan style was used for the sacristy (begun 1430) and the south loggia (1440s), and for the Flamboyant window added to the archiepiscopal palace by Archbishop Simone da Bologna (1458–62); but on the whole Catalan influence in church architecture was limited to superficial details: doors and windows of typical shapes and with distinctive forms of vegetal ornament, in particular, of bands of leaves serving as capitals for a group of colonnettes, as in S. Pietro and S. Martino in Siracusa. **S. Giorgio Vecchio**, in Ragusa, is a perfect example of a Catalan Gothic façade transplanted to Sicily (compare with, for example, S. Martí Provençals, Barcelona), but usually doors and windows were plainer than comparable examples in Catalonia and Valencia. Elements associated with florid Gothic became increasingly evident during the 15C. Flowing tracery in place of a tympanum appears at S. Maria del Gesù in Palermo, in a chapel doorway, built by a family of Catalan origins, probably in the second half of the 15C. But unlike cities where Gothic had taken stronger root, these elements never produced a thoroughly Flamboyant style.

In secular architecture the **Palazzo Aiutamicristo** (c 1495) and **Palazzo Abbatellis** (1488–95, by M. Carnelivari), both in Palermo, best represent the peculiar blend of southern Italian and Spanish forms; their courtyards are closely akin to the courtyard of Palacio Velado, Avila; and the massive portal of the Palazzo Abbatellis, like a rope-bound raft, combines Castilian and Catalan designs. Secular architecture of this period reflects the metamorphosis of the ruling class. The castle-tower of the 14C, closed and defensive, hostile to the urban scene and reflecting the military power of its owner, was replaced by the 15C palace, open and outward-looking, expressive of the civil and economic power of the aristocracy. Bankers were the patrons of the Palermitan palazzi Aiutamicristo and the Afflitto, both begun in the 1490s. On the whole, 15C palace architecture tended towards the solid block marked by a strong, but not over-stressed, horizontality. This was the result of the three distinct vertical divisions: the ground floor was for the services, stalls and kitchens; the grand *piano nobile* for the owner and reception rooms; and the attic housed the servants or cadet members of the family. Other characteristics of 15C Sicilian palaces include the vaulted entrance passage, patio, sunken garden and a regular grid of rooms.

Sicilian architecture of the 15C was not sustained by humanism and remained somewhat inaccessible to Renaissance ideas; but great changes were wrought by two artists working in a mature Renaissance style who arrived in Palermo in the middle years of the century. **Francesco Laurana** (c 1420–79) had worked for Alfonso I in Naples, and was in Palermo from 1467–71 (and he may have returned later: the tomb relief of Abate Speciale now in the Galleria Regionale, Palermo, is dated 1495). His most significant work, the arch to the **Cappella Maestrantonio** in the church of S. Francesco d'Assisi, Palermo, executed in 1468, was the earliest important Renaissance work in Sicily. However, his advanced style was too aloof to take root and it was the sculptor-architect **Domenico Gagini** (fl. 1448–92)—founder of a dynasty of craftsmen which dominated Sicily for the next century—who effectively introduced the new style. Gagini, who had been trained in Genoa and worked in Naples on the triumphal arch of the Castelnuovo, arrived in Palermo in 1458/9 and stayed there until his death in 1492. Among his first documented works is the door to the church of S. Agostino (c 1470) in Palermo. It is a competent, if crudely executed, version of the style current in central and northern Italy, and soon doors of this type appeared all over Sicily, persisting long after the type had become old-fashioned in Lombardy and Tuscany. Domenico's gifted son, **Antonello** (1478–1536), carried on his tradition into the 16C. The gulf between him and local architects is well illustrated in the church of **S. Maria di Porto Salvo** (Palermo), which he began in c 1527 in a Tuscan Quattrocento style, its chapels being articulated with orthodox pilasters and round-headed arches with more or less correct mouldings. But when Antonello died in 1536, it was impossible to find an architect able to complete it in the Renaissance style and it was finished in the Gothic tradition by Antonio Scaglione, a local architect.

S. Maria di Porto Salvo is one of a most interesting group of churches, almost all near the port of Palermo, dating from the last years of the 15C and the early 16C, which demonstrate that the juxtaposition of Gothic and Renaissance forms, which is so disconcerting to us, was not regarded as inappropriate by contemporaries. At **S. Maria della Catena** in Palermo, which was probably begun soon after 1502, columns crowned by 15C Florentine-style capitals stand on late Gothic pedestals, to which they are joined by French High Gothic bases, and carry Gothic rib vaulting; and a similar combination of Gothic and Renaissance elements appears in S. Maria Nuova.

The persistence in Sicily of certain architectural forms is particularly striking in this period. The unusual rustication and diamond-cut blocks of 16C buildings such as the Giudecca, Trapani and Palazzo Steripinto, Sciacca, may derive from the prestigious rustication of the Hohenstaufen castles. However, the most obvious of these persistent architectural elements is the squinch. Inherited from Arab architecture and frequently found in Norman buildings in Sicily, the squinch was still being used in the 16C: the **Cappella Naselli** (built between 1517 and 1555) in S. Francesco, Comiso, and the remarkable **Cappella dei Marinai** in the Santuario dell'Annunziata, Trapani, are two instances out of many. In these later buildings the squinch is used with compelling conviction, not as an overworn cliché to be inserted where inspiration failed, and this raises questions about the significance it must have had for the architects.

Another Norman practice which survived into the 16C was the use of two or three superimposed columns for the pier of the crossing of a church. The most remarkable example of this occurs at S. Giorgio dei Genovesi, Palermo, built in an otherwise full Renaissance style between 1576 and 1591. These Sicilian forms have no bearing on the ideas developed in the rest of Italy.

## Sculpture

A surprising amount of late 15C and early 16C sculpture survives in churches and museums scattered throughout Sicily. Quite unlike the pattern of development in northern Italy, where ducal workshops provided focuses of development, in Sicily a single style tended to spread over the whole coastal area of the island. As in architecture, the main impetus came from **Francesco Laurana** and **Domenico Gagini**, both marble sculptors working in a style deriving from late Quattrocento Florence. Indeed, the similarity of their styles has created problems in attributing some works like the reliefs on the holy-water stoups in Palermo Cathedral and portrait busts (now in the Galleria Regionale, Palermo). **Domenico Gagini**'s style reflects that of late 15C Florence and particularly his interest in the work of Ghiberti and Buggiano, Brunelleschi's protégé. His *Madonnas* are exceptional for their suggestion of delicate movement: in his later works he departs from his early rigid frontal presentation of the image, creating a greater dynamic tension as in the figure on the tomb of Pietro Speciale in S. Francesco d'Assisi, Palermo, but on the whole his work and especially his portraits lack the sensitivity of Laurana's. Laurana executed an influential series of standing polychrome *Madonnas*, beginning with the one in Palermo Cathedral modelled on a Trecento Virgin by Nino Pisano in Trapani; others can be seen in the church of the Crocifisso in Noto and in the museum at Messina. They demonstrate Laurana's ability to fuse late Gothic and Renaissance ideas.

**Antonello Gagini** developed his father's work. He came to be considered the most significant Renaissance sculptor of Sicily and his vast amount of work reflects his popularity. The period between 1510 and 1536 was particularly busy: not only did he have his usual studio work of statues, tombs and altars, but also the vast tribuna of Palermo Cathedral, remarkable for its combination of old and new styles and ideas, and for the introduction to Palermo of stucco as a material for sculpture. Indeed, Antonello and his workshop sculpted in marble, terracotta, *mistura* (plaster and papier mâché mixed) and stucco, which meant that their work was available at a range of prices. Antonello's search for an ideal beauty, evident in the roundels in the Gancia, Palermo, of c 1500, was related to the contemporary classicising trend in Lombardy, and tended to produce rather sickly sweet Madonnas, such as the *Madonna della Scala* of 1503 in Palermo Cathedral.

Just as the ambivalence between Gothic and Renaissance forms persisted in architecture into the 16C, so it did in sculpture. A relief in the church of the Magione, Palermo, produced in the workshop of the Gagini in the late 15C or early 16C illustrates this well. Florentine Quattrocento-style figures stand between late Gothic twisted colonnettes and snuggle into shell niches below Gothic gables.

## Painting

During the early 15C, Sicilian painting was markedly Spanish in character and showed little awareness of developments in the north. The most important paintings were by foreigners and most were in a Catalan style of which the early 15C polyptych in the church of S. Martino, Siracusa, by the so-called **Maestro di S. Martino**, is representative. The only major work in an independent 'Sicilian' style is the *Triumph of Death* in Palazzo Sclafani, Palermo.

However, **Antonello da Messina** (c 1430–79) dramatically altered the character of Sicilian painting in the late 15C. As no strong Sicilian stylistic tradition existed, he turned to movements abroad: three separate foreign experiences deeply affected his work. These were a training (probably in Naples) in the Flemish style and in the technique of oil painting; the influence of Giovanni Bellini during a stay in Venice; and the influence of the work of Piero della Francesca. The first half of Antonello's career is well documented, but almost entirely devoid of extant works. He seems to have been working from 1457–65 in and around Messina. Paintings of this period are dominated by Flemish forms, but show signs of his experimentation with the representation of spatial depth that had been developing in central Italy. During his most active period, 1473–77, Flemish influences, such as the work of Robert Campion, Petrus Christus or Memling, remained keen: the interior setting, decorated drapery and the fascination with precise rendering of reflected light in both the polyptych for the church of S. Gregorio of 1473 (now in the Museo Regionale, Messina) and in the *Annunciation* of 1475 (now in the Museo Regionale, Siracusa) are good examples of this; but Italian influences make themselves felt in the column dividing the Annunciation which recalls Piero della Francesca's *Annunciations*, and in the shape of the polyptych itself. In Venice, and especially from Bellini, Antonello learned how to handle architectural space. His **Virgin Annunciate** (Galleria Regionale, Palermo) displays this new mastery in the placing and perspectival treatment of the lectern and the Virgin's hand, which give a dramatic depth and solidity to the picture.

The influence of Antonello da Messina was widespread, especially amongst his descendants and relations who included **Jacobello di Antonello** (c 1455–90), **Antonello De Saliba** (1466/7–after 1535), **Salvo de Antonio** (fl. c 1493–1525) and **Marco Costanza** (15C).

## 16C sculpture

Because of its geographical position, Messina was in closer contact with the mainland than other towns in Sicily, and during the 16C artists from Florence and Rome frequently travelled there, attracted by its political and social importance. Of these, a pupil of Michelangelo, the Florentine **Giovanni Angelo Montorsoli** (1507?–63), who came to Messina in 1547, was the most important. He established in Sicily the Tuscan manner of the mid-century in both sculpture and architecture, reinstating the use of human and monstrous figures in sculpture, which had been lost largely because of Arab influence. Montorsoli's **Orion fountain** (begun 1547), with its Michelangelesque forms, was particularly influential both in Sicily and mainland Italy, and his **Neptune fountain** (begun 1557) was hardly less so. He left behind a long line of followers at Messina, principal among whom was **Martino Montanini** whose work, exemplified by the S. Caterina statue in the church of SS. Annunziata (1558/9) at Forza d'Agro, is a frostier version of Montorsoli's.

In Palermo the influence of Tuscan Mannerism was much weaker and, except for piecemeal scatterings, is restricted to one monument. In 1570 it was decided to embellish the square in front of the Palazzo Municipale with a fountain, and in 1574 the Fontana Pretoria, by the Florentine sculptor **Francesco Camilliani** (d. 1586), originally intended for a Florentine villa, was duly inserted, with the necessary additions by Francesco's son, **Camillo** (fl. 1574–1603) and **Michelangelo Naccherino** (1550–1622). With this, Palermo tasted, albeit belatedly, the new language of Mannerist sculpture; but, unlike in Messina, no new school of sculptors formed, and the fountain remained an isolated case, even though its unusual figures were sometimes copied or adapted in later works of art.

## 16C architecture and town planning

These fountains were part of flamboyant attempts to modernise the urban environment, by opening new streets, creating vistas marked by prestigious buildings or gates, improving the water supply, and so on, with which ambitious viceroys, courting popularity, sought to link their names. Religious orders also played an important role, demonstrating their power by building churches and convents. This process of renewal of the urban fabric, which was to be most significant at Palermo, began in Messina, where **Andrea Calamech** (1514–78) and Camillo Camilliani were entrusted with much of the work. A great deal of their work has been destroyed, but what survives reveals a new sturdy monumentality. Temporary architecture, designed for special religious or political occasions, was probably very influential. In Palermo, for instance, when the road to Monreale was opened between 1580 and 1584, the new gates of Porta Felice and Porta Nuova were erected, and the latter perpetuated ideas of the temporary triumphal arch put up for Charles V's celebrated visit of 1535.

Two of the finest streets of Palermo took their names from viceroys, the via Toledo in the 1560s and the via Maqueda in the 1590s, and ten years later another viceroy built a fine Baroque octagon at their intersection, the Quattro Canti, in imitation of Rome's Quattro Fontane. Begun by the Florentine architect, **Giulio Lasso**, most of the work was completed by **Smiriglio**. Monarchical, heavenly, and local references were combined in a ponderously impressive work, which hid, as it still does today, the slums of the poor behind its proud screens.

The return to Sicily of the Messinese **Giacomo Del Duca** (fl. 1540–1600), who had worked in Rome under Michelangelo in his later years, also contributed to the new phase of late 16C architecture in Messina. His understanding of Michelangelo's late style is visible in the remarkable church of **S. Giovanni di Malta**, Messina, on which he began work with Camilliani from about 1590: the use of giant pilasters and deep triangular *guttae* had repercussions in Sicilian architecture until the 18C. His establishment of a mature late 16C Roman style in a country with very different architectural traditions is unparalleled anywhere else in Italy. The vigour and monumentality of the tradition was perpetuated by **Natale Masuccio** (fl. 1560–70), a Jesuit architect, who had trained in Rome at the turn of the century and absorbed there a mixed Tuscan-Roman style from Bartolommeo Ammanati and Giuseppe Valeriani. Their influence can be seen in his Jesuit Novitiate in Trapani (begun before 1614) and the ruins of his Monte di Pietà in Messina.

## Baroque architecture

This is one of the most exciting periods of the architectural history of Sicily. The exuberant vivacity and inventiveness, the variety and exhilarating beauty of Sicilian Baroque architecture (including vernacular architecture) are unparalleled. In the more sophisticated buildings architects familiar with current styles in Rome worked to create, not slavish copies of Roman Baroque, but vigorous interpretations of that style from within Sicilian traditions. This is best seen in the work of **Rosario Gagliardi** (?1700–70). At their best Sicilian buildings occupy positions of dignity and authority in the field of European Baroque architecture.

The earthquake of 1693 which devastated most of the towns of south and east Sicily deeply affected the development of Baroque architecture on the island

and our picture of it. Little remains of pre-1693 architecture in the earthquake zone, but that which does, such as **S. Sebastiano**, Acireale, suggests that it was highly decorated with scrolls, rustication and grotesque masks. This strange anthropomorphised architecture was rarely taken up again after 1693. The abruptness of this break and the inevitable self-consciousness of the new style makes the architecture of the east unlike that of the west where, particularly at Palermo, local traditions persisted as the most powerful force.

The new towns in the earthquake zone often enjoyed the benefits of new sites and plans. At Avolà **Angelo Italia** created a regular grid with large open piazzas, designed for safety in the event of another quake; but here and at Grammichele these new ideas were encased in a dramatic hexagon, derived from traditional military treatises. This approach, which cannot be appreciated from within the town, contrasts strongly with the ideas used at Noto where the grid arrangement of the streets was exploited to create beautiful vistas punctuated by fine buildings to be enjoyed from within the city.

The buildings around the cathedral square in Catania illustrate well the first style which evolved after the earthquake. Its main characteristics were vigorous superficial decoration and multiform rustication. **G.B. Vaccarini** (1702–68), who arrived in Catania c 1730, introduced a completely different style which was to dominate Catanese architecture for several decades. From Rome, where he had trained in the early 1720s, he brought a number of new church plans and architectural features, especially windows, which show a thorough study of the great Roman Baroque architects and of Borromini in particular. In his best buildings, such as the **Palazzo Valle** (c 1740–50) or **S. Agata**, Vaccarini stretched out from these Roman ideas and created a unified movement and play of curves unthinkable in contemporary Rome. His introduction of certain Roman church plans to Sicily was seminal, but he always developed the Roman plans to achieve new effects. S. Agata, based on S. Agnese in piazza Navona, is less centralised than its model (and its interior is lighter as a result of using stucco rather than marble). In contrast, the most active mid-18C local architect, **Francesco Battaglia** (fl. 1732–78), created in the *salone* of **Palazzo Biscari**, Catania, the most liberated Rococo decoration to be found in Sicily or southern Italy. Vaccarini's later classicising style was continued by Stefano Ittar in S. Placido and the Collegiata; but the move towards the neo-classical use of orders and decoration is most marked in Antonio Battaglia's new staircase at the monastery of the Benedettini, 1749.

The most original architect in the south-east was **Rosario Gagliardi**, engineer to the town and district of Noto. Several churches have been grouped around his documented works, whose distinctive traits can perhaps best be appreciated at **S. Giorgio**, Ragusa Ibla, of 1744. Both here and at **S. Giorgio**, Modica, the hillside site is brilliantly exploited, and underlined by the façade design, in which the tower seems to burst from the central bay, itself a solution to the Sicilian belfry façade problem. The columns, canted boldly against the curved centres, and the pediments, flicked above the doorways, exploit a freedom never tasted by the Roman followers of Bernini and Borromini (if hinted at in some Roman façades, such as Martino Longhi's SS. Vincenzo ed Anastasio) and add dynamism to the design. The interiors of Gagliardi's churches, unlike those of the Roman architects and his fellow countryman and contemporary Filippo Juvarra, do not display great commitment to spatial experimentation, but they are full of fascinating details, some of which reveal an interest in Gothic forms. In Siracusa the masterpiece of Baroque architecture is **Andrea Palma**'s (1664–1730) cathedral façade (begun in 1728) which uses broken masses within a columnar façade to create a jagged and dramatic effect.

In Palermo ecclesiastical Baroque architecture shows greater continuity with insular architectural traditions. The basilican plan remained popular and the local (Norman) tradition of columnar arcades persisted, of which **S. Giuseppe dei Teatini**, begun 1612 by **Giacomo Besio**, is the most awe-inspiring example. Greater attention was given to plans consisting of a simple hall with shallow side chapels and apses, such as **Giacomo Amato**'s (1643–1732) **S. Teresa alla Kalsa**; this plan type was readily taken up by the many confraternities which blossomed in post-Tridentine Sicily. As in Catania, centralised plans were created more frequently but spatial experimentation was less important than in Rome.

A few Palermitan churches show that their architects were familiar with Roman Baroque architecture. **Paolo Amato**'s (1634–1714) SS. Salvatore (begun 1682), an elongated oval plan, is a much more spacious and flatter version of Rainaldi's S. Maria di Montesanto; and Giacomo Amato, who was in Rome from 1670 to 1687, derived the magnificent façades of S. Teresa (begun c 1686) and La Pietà (begun 1689) from Rainaldi's S. Maria in Campitelli and S. Andrea della Valle. These bold and majestic façades also incorporate traditional Sicilian elements, such as the circular window at the centre of the design, which would never have been used on a church on the mainland. This interest in Sicily's own traditions is shown equally in Angelo Italia's exceptional (if not wholly satisfactory) little church, **S. Francesco Saverio** (1684–1710), whose pierced hexagonal chapels were derived from Guarini's churches in Messina (tragically destroyed in 1908).

One of the most fascinating and peculiar aspects of Palermitan (and, to a lesser extent, Messinese) Baroque architecture is the use of cut and polished inlaid stones, known as **_marmi mischi_**, to cover the walls in a fabulous display of motifs, sometimes religious and symbolic, sometimes purely decorative. The practice seems to have begun with the use of flat panels of coloured marble on tombs; white reliefs were subsequently introduced and the rigid geometric forms were discarded: an early example is a tomb of 1637 in S. Domenico. Particularly fine examples of the fully developed form include the Cappella dell'Immacolata (c 1650) in S. Francesco d'Assisi, and the churches of the Casa Professa and S. Caterina, which incorporate low and high reliefs and statuary in complex iconographic programmes. Small biblical scenes were frequently depicted in marble on chapel walls and altarpieces in the 18C. The technical virtuosity in the _Flight out of Egypt_ in S. Maria Miracoli is characteristic.

The exquisite stuccowork by **Giacomo Serpotta** (1656–1732) and his descendants displays similar concerns. Although indebted to earlier traditions of stucco work, the celebrated oratories of Serpotta surpass them by far in artistic sensibility and technique. In the Oratorio di S. Zita (1685–88), the walls appear to be draped in cloth, against which are set the _Mysteries of the Rosary_ and the _Victory at Lepanto_, all delicately modelled in stucco. The paintings and frescoes around which Serpotta conceived his stuccowork still exist in the Oratorio del SS. Rosario di S. Domenico (c 1710–17), showing how harmonious and elegant these interiors must have been. Giacomo Serpotta's son, **Procopio**, allowed architecture a greater importance in his compositions, as in his masterpiece, the Oratorio of S. Caterina (1719–26). Although he strove to achieve his father's elegance and perfect finish of modelling, his figures are elongated and languid and lack his father's verve and energy.

Palace architecture has suffered from disgraceful neglect in Palermo, but enough survives for us to appreciate the diversity of plans, the character of the façades and the most important features, such as doors, windows and staircases, on all of which creative energy was concentrated. Giacomo Amato's **Palazzo Cutò** (begun 1705) and **Palazzo Cattolica** (c 1720) combine innovative planning with the creation of impressive spaces and vistas. Similar theatrical effects are created by the most spectacular of Palermitan staircases at **Palazzo Bonagia** by **Andrea Giganti** (18C), probably executed in the 1760s. The interiors of 17C and 18C palaces have almost all been destroyed, but surviving examples show an imaginative gaiety rarely found outside Sicily. **Palazzo Gangi**, c 1770–90, for instance, boasts a spectacular suite of rooms culminating in the diaphonous Sala degli Specchi, whose unique ceiling is composed of a deeply coved upper shell, painted with allegorical frescoes, and a pierced lower ceiling suspended below. This creates an effect of shifting worlds, like a magic lantern.

Built by an extravagant and feckless aristocracy as retreats from the feverish capital during hot weather, the villas of Bagheria and Piana dei Colli are among the most inventive of Sicilian 18C buildings. Their simple façades, in keeping with their rustic setting, contrast with the grand and complex exterior staircases, which reflect the sophisticated life-style of the owners. Almost all these staircases are double, some are curved, as at the Villa Spina, others are jaggedly contorted, as at the Villa Palagonia. The latter was built by **Tomaso Napoli** (17C) who emerges as an outstanding architect here and at the Villa Valguernera (begun c 1709). He combined unusual forms, concave and convex curves, with ingenious and inventive planning involving the creation of many different shaped rooms, to achieve an overall effect of grace and flowing line.

It is important to remember that our picture of Baroque architecture in Sicily is very fragmentary, for two main reasons. First, in the 17C and 18C, temporary architecture and decoration, erected to celebrate church festivals and political events, were at least as important as permanent architecture. Although they are recorded in drawings and engravings, our impressions of these *apparati* are necessarily imperfect without being able to experience them in the round and bedecked with lights and colour. Second, much Baroque architecture has been destroyed. The ravages caused by the earthquake of 1693 prompted much fertile rebuilding; but much of the damage caused by subsequent earthquakes and by the bombing of World War II has never been attended to. Consequently, many 17C and 18C palaces and churches stand as empty shells, their once splendid features crumbling into meaningless rubble. This is the result of political irresponsibility and it is horrifying to see.

## Seventeenth-century painting

Seventeenth-century painting is illuminated by the contributions of two outstanding foreign artists, Caravaggio and Van Dyck. **Caravaggio** (1571–1609/10), fleeing arrest in Malta, landed in Messina in 1608/9 and executed in Sicily at least five paintings, mainly for private patrons. His first work in Sicily, the **Burial of St Lucy** (now in the Galleria Regionale, Siracusa), probably begun in early 1609, concentrates on the human aspects only of the divine drama, making an eloquent contrast between the helpless passivity, even distraction, of the mourners, and the empty but self-confident gestures of the officials. The **Adoration of the Shepherds** (1609, Museo Regionale, Messina), commissioned by the Messinese Senate as the high altarpiece of the church of S. Maria degli Angeli, is one of Caravaggio's most deeply felt and impressively simple works. Here the dignity he recognised in the poor and simple is intensely conveyed; even the resonant space accentuates the silent devotion of the shepherds.

**Van Dyck**'s (1599–1641) visit to Palermo in 1624, although cut short by his fear of the plague raging in west Sicily, produced a remarkable group of pictures of S. Rosalia (now in New York, Houston and Ponce) and his grandest Italian altarpiece, the **Madonna of the Rosary** 1624–28 (finished in Genoa) which is still in the Oratorio del Rosario in S. Domenico. Although Sicily has retained only one of Van Dyck's Sicilian paintings, his influence is frequently apparent in local 17C painting, and in the work of **Pietro Novelli** (1603–47) above all.

## Eighteenth- and nineteenth-century architecture

During the 18C neo-classical architecture gradually took root all over Sicily, but particularly in Palermo, as a result of its close links with Naples, Rome and France. **Venanzio Marvuglia** (1729–1814), a Palermitan who had become deeply imbued with neo-classicism during his stay in Rome (1747–59), was the most significant architect of this style. With his Benedictine monastery, **S. Martino delle Scale**, near Palermo (1762–76), the curvaceous middle bays and flowing lines of Palermitan Baroque palaces are shrugged off and replaced by straight lines and planes. Of great significance is Marvuglia's use of a flat impost, rather than the traditional arcade, above the columns of the nave in the Oratory of S. Filippo Neri, in Palermo, built 1769. This was in accordance with Laugier's influential idea that the ancient Greek is the only true standard in architecture. However, Marvuglia's obvious feeling for the effect of simple masses and carefully thought-out proportions and his use of characteristic Sicilian balconies in the palaces of Riso-Belmonte and Constantino in Palermo push him far from the inflexible rigidity of some neo-classicists. Sicily's antiquity was very fashionable in 18C Europe and it was a Frenchman, **Léon Dufourny**, who first used again in Sicily the Greek Doric style when he built his pavilion in the Palermo Botanic Gardens in 1787. This style was taken up all over Sicily for 19C public buildings, such as the theatre at Castelvetrano and the Ministry of Finance offices in Palermo.

## Art Nouveau

Palermo is an important centre of Art Nouveau architecture, surpassed in Italy only by Turin and Milan. Its importance reflects the concentration of upper middle-class families gravitating around the Florio financial empire whose patronage provided the mainstay of Ernesto Basile's commissions. For it was **Ernesto Basile** (1857–1932), whose father, **G.B. Basile** (1825–91), had created the heavy Corinthian Teatro Massimo, Palermo, who dominated the Art Nouveau style in Sicily. He was an able architect, keenly aware of Sicily's architectural traditions, without feeling bound to copy them slavishly. He borrowed heavily from Sicilian 15C motifs for the exteriors of his buildings, such as the **Palazzo Bruno**, Ispica, and the **Villino Florio** in Palermo. Here Carnelivari, of whose work he had made careful measured drawings, was particularly important. By contrast, Sicilian Norman motifs are the predominant source for his interiors. Basile's characteristic fusion of structural and ornamental elements is best seen today in the **Villa Igiea** (1899), Palermo, whose dining room is the epitome of Basile's fantastic medievalism. Although most of his work was for private patrons, Basile also designed the theatre in Canicattì and the Palazzo Municipale in Licata (1930s). The interest of Basile's workshops in the revival of the applied arts contributed to the spread of Art Nouveau throughout Sicily, and to Catania in particular, where a number of good examples survive in the Viale Regina Margherita. Sadly, however, many fine Art Nouveau style villas have been demolished in the last 20 years.

## Twentieth century

Twentieth-century architecture in Sicily is a dispiriting subject. Political irresponsibility has allowed ugly speculative schemes to stampede unhindered into the countryside and to smother the coastlines with blocks of flats, tourist villages and holiday villas. Awareness of Sicilian traditions and of the distinctiveness of Sicilian culture, which were for centuries such important and invigorating forces in the island's architecture, has been cast aside, and the language these new buildings speak is the same inarticulate grunting that occurs everywhere in Europe where speculative gain has triumphed over artistic and social concerns.

# Further reading

## General

Cronin, Vincent, *The Golden Honeycomb* (1954; 2nd edn. 1980)

Dolci, Danilo, *Poverty in Sicily* (translation of 1966) and *Sicilian Lives* (translation of 1981)

Grammatico, Maria and Simeti, Mary Taylor, *Bitter Almonds* (1994)

Maxwell, G., *God Protect me from my Friends* (1956); *The Ten Pains of Death* (1959)

Simeti, Mary Taylor, *On Persephone's Island* (1986)

Simeti, Mary Taylor, *Pomp and Sustenance* (1998)

## History

Ahmad, Aziz, *A History of Islamic Sicily* (1976)

Falcone, Giovanni, *Men of Honour; the truth about the Mafia* (1992)

Finley, M.I., Mack Smith, Denis, and Duggan, Christopher, *History of Sicily* (1986)

Matthew, Donald, *The Norman Kingdom of Sicily* (1992)

Norwich, John Julius, *The Normans in the South* (1967) and *The Kingdom in the Sun* (1970)

Runciman, Stephen, *The Sicilian Vespers* (1958)

Stille, Alexander, *Excellent Cadavers* (1996)

Trevelyan, Raleigh, *Princes under the Volcano* (1972)

## Art and architecture

Blunt, Anthony, *Sicilian Baroque* (1968)

Borsook, Eve, *Messages in Mosaic* (1990)

Demus, Otto, *The Mosaics of Norman Sicily* (1949)

Garstang, Donald, *Giacomo Serpotta and the Stuccatori of Palermo, 1560–1790* (1984)

Guido, Margaret, *Sicily: an archaeological guide* (1967, 1977)

Sitwell, Sacheverell, *Southern Baroque Revisited* (1967)

Tobringer, Stephen, *The Genesis of Noto, an eighteenth-century Sicilian city* (1982)

## Literature

The most famous Sicilian writer was Giovanni Verga. His masterpieces (*Mastro-Don Gesualdo, I Malavoglia* and *Vita dei Campi*) are usually available in translation (some of them were translated by D.H. Lawrence in 1925 and 1932).

Lampedusa, Giuseppe di: *Il Gattopardo (The Leopard*, translated in 1960) and *I Racconti (Two stories and a memory*, translated in 1962).

Many of the plays by the Sicilian Luigi Pirandello are usually available in translation. Another Sicilian writer was Elio Vittorini (*Conversazione in Sicilia, Uomini e no, Il Garofano Rosso*).

The Sicilian author Gesualdo Bufalino (1920–96) is known for his six novels which include *La Diceria dell'Untore* (1981) and *Le Menzogne della Notte* (1988), both translated into English.

The most important recent Sicilian writer was Leonardo Sciascia (1921–89), famous for his novels as well as his writings on the Mafia (*Il Giorno della Civetta, Il Consiglio d'Egitto, A ciascuno il Suo, Il Mare Colore del Vino, La Sicilia come Metafora*). Translations of his works in English include: *Candido, or a dream dreamed in Sicily* (1995), *To each his own* (1992) and *Sicilian Uncles; four novellas* (1986).

# THE GUIDE

## Palermo

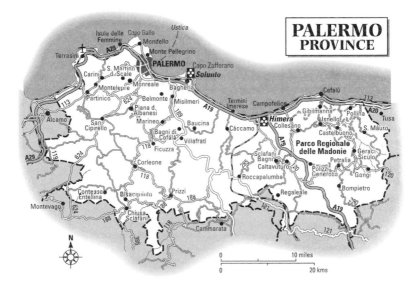

Palermo (population 730,800), the capital of Sicily and her most interesting city, is built on a bay on the north coast at the foot of Monte Pellegrino, a beautiful headland. It has a superb climate. One of the largest and most important cities in the world from the 9C to the 12C, Palermo still possesses some of the great Arab-Norman buildings erected at that time: the Cappella Palatina, La Martorana, S. Giovanni degli Eremiti, the Zisa, and, a few kilometres outside the city, the cathedral of Monreale. Numerous delightful Baroque churches and oratories survive from later centuries. The Archaeological Museum and the Regional Gallery contain outstanding collections.

The bustling streets and animated markets give the town an oriental atmosphere. The centre, suffering from depopulation, was neglected for decades after World War II and numerous decaying slum areas grew up around the bomb sites and a large proportion of the houses were in danger of collapse. This disastrous situation finally changed in 1988–90 when detailed plans to restore and renovate the centre of the city were drawn up by three distinguished architects and conservationists, together with the town planning office. These were approved by the town council in 1990–97, and conspicuous restoration work is in progress to change the face of the city and give it the careful attention it deserves. Churches and palaces are being restored and the huge Teatro Massimo has been re-opened after being closed for years. The spectacular restoration of the former church and convent of Lo Spasimo as a cultural centre is perhaps the most significant project completed to date.

Leoluca Orlando, famous for his courageous opposition to the influence of the Mafia in Palermo and his decisive actions to eliminate dishonesty and inefficiency in the local administration, was first elected mayor by direct ballot in 1993 (with a landslide majority, the largest of any of the other large towns in Italy). He was re-elected on the first ballot in 1997 for his last four-year term of office in an atmosphere of great enthusiasm, despite general indifference in the rest of Italy. The city has become much cleaner in the last few years and the gardens are better kept. The council is showing admirable attention to detail of the urban townscape, such as railings, balconies, paving, lamp-posts, fountains and litter-bins. The palaces where the government of the city, province and region are carried out have all been recently opened or re-opened to the public. Museums have longer opening hours and numerous churches are now opened by associations of young Palermitans in collaboration with the *Curia* and the town council. Numerous cafés and restaurants now have tables outside and the city is particularly animated by the younger generation on summer evenings.

However, the chaotic traffic in the city is still a major problem and nothing seems to have been done yet about noise levels and speed control. Because of the congestion, public transport functions with difficulty. To add to the problem numerous weddings take place in the churches in the centre of the city throughout the year. However, there are signs here too of an improvement, with the introduction of two mini-bus services in the historic centre, the re-introduction of a horse cab service, and the closure of via Vittorio Emanuele to traffic on Saturday evenings in the summer and certain other times of the year.

The *Conca d'Oro*, a small fertile plain enclosed by limestone hills, which surrounds the city, was once filled with dark groves of orange, lemon and carob trees, but in the 1960s and 1970s it was covered with ugly tower blocks built with the support of the Mafia.

# ■ Practical information

**Information offices**. APT Palermo, 35 piazza Castelnuovo (see map: 6 ☎ 091/583847). Subsidiary offices are situated at the railway station and the airport. These offices always have up-to-date information on opening times and what's on in the city. Azienda Autonoma di Turismo, Villa Igiea, 43 salita Belmonte (☎ 091/540122). Assessorato Regionale del Turismo (Sicilian Regional Tourist Board), 11 via Notarbartolo.

**Airport**. *Falcone Borsellino*, at Punta Raisi 32km west (motorway). ☎ 091/591698. Internal and international services. Coach services (4,500 lire) about every 30 minutes run by Prestia & Comandé to the Politeama (via Emerico Amari; map: 7), and the central railway station; the taxis are a lot more expensive.

**Railway stations**. *Centrale* (map: 16) for all state railway services (☎ 091/6165914); *Notarbartolo* (N. of map: 1), subsidiary station on the Trapani line.

**City buses** run by *AMAT* (☎ 167018378) tend to be overcrowded, infrequent and very slow because of the traffic congestion in the city centre. Tickets (1500 lire; or 5000 lire valid for 24 hours) must be purchased at tobacconists, kiosks, etc. and stamped at automatic machines on board.

There are now two excellent mini-bus circular services, both of which penetrate some of the narrower streets of the city and pass many of its most important monuments:

**Linea Giallo (yellow)**: railway station • corso dei Mille • Orto Botanico • Kalsa • via Alloro (Galleria Regionale in Palazzo Abatellis) • via Maqueda • Ballarò • corso Tuköry • S. Spirito • via Oreto • railway station.

**Linea Rosso (red)**: via Alloro (at the Galleria Regionale in Palazzo Abatellis) • Quattro Canti • Cassaro (corso Vittorio Emanuele) • cathedral • via Papireto • via S. Agostino • via Maqueda • Vucciria • Cala • piazza Marina • via Alloro (Palazzo Abatellis).

Many of the other lines serve the railway station and follow the corso, via Maqueda, or via Roma for part of their course:

From the station **no. 107** follows via Roma and its continuations north to the Giardino Inglese to terminate near the Parco della Favorita; **no. 101** also runs north along via Roma and then, via the Politeama (piazza Ruggero Settimo) it follows viale della Libertà; **no. 109** follows corso Tuköry to piazza Indipendenza (for the Palazzo dei Normanni and Cappella Palatina).

Bus **no. 108** links piazza Indipendenza and the cathedral to the Politeama; **no. 105** follows corso Vittorio Emanuele east to west from the sea front and piazza Marina up past the cathedral to piazza Indipendenza and from there it continues along corso Calatafimi.

The buses to monuments outside the centre of the town, and in the outskirts, are listed in the text below.

An **underground railway** links the railway station to the north-western suburbs via the stations of Vespri (near S. Spirito dei Vespri), Notarbartolo, Imperatore Federico (at the southern end of the Parco della Favorita), Fiera, Giachery, Francia, S. Lorenzo Colli, Cardillo and Tommaso Natale. It runs c every 25 minutes from 06.00–20.35 (ticket 1300 lire). An intermediate station near piazza Indipendenza is under construction (Palazzo Reale).

**Taxis**, as elsewhere in Sicily, are for some reason much more expensive than in the rest of Italy (minimum fare 10,000 lire).

**Horse cabs**, which were used as taxis up until a decade or so ago when they virtually disappeared from the streets, are now subsidised by the town council and are again increasing in number. They are available at certain periods of the year from 09.00–13.00, 16.00–20.00 (exc Tues, Sun & PH) at the station, the churches of S. Domenico and the Magione, piazza Marina and piazza Bellini for 50,000 lire an hour.

**Car parking** is extremely difficult in the centre of Palermo (where no major roads have yet been closed to private cars except corso Vittorio Emanuele on Saturday evenings in summer). Most 3- and 4-star hotels have parking facilities or garages (at extra cost). Pay car-parks (with parking attendant) are situated near piazza Castelnuovo, the station and via Stabile. There are some garages and ACI car-parks in and near piazza Castelnuovo (map: 6) and piazza Verdi (map: 11). If your car is illegally parked and towed away, telephone the city police (*vigili urbani*), ☎ 091/6954111.

**Country buses**. There is a wide network of services from Palermo run by various bus companies, including those listed below.

Daily services from **via Balsamo** (beside the railway station; map: 16): *SAIS* c every hour to Catania (via the motorway in 2hr 40min.), and, less frequently to Enna (in c 2hr); also to Taormina, Cefalù and Messina. *Segesta* to Trapani (via Alcamo); *Cuffaro* to Agrigento, and *Randazzo* to Piazza Armerina. From **piazza Marina** (map: 12): *Trepanum* to Segesta; *Stassi* to Erice, and *AST* to Ragusa and Siracusa. *Segesta* also run a daily overnight coach service to Rome. For services to the environs of Palermo, see chapters below.

**Maritime services**. Port: Molo Vittorio Veneto (map: 8). Overnight ferry service run by *Tirrenia* (via del Mare, beside the port; ☎ 091/6021111) to Naples, Cagliari, Tunis and Genoa. Services run by *Grandi Traghetti* (179 via M. Stabile; ☎ 091/587801) from Molo S. Lucia to Livorno, Genoa, Tunis and Malta. Hydrofoil and ferry services run by *Siremar* (120 via Crispi; ☎ 091/336631) to Ustica. There is now also a hydrofoil service run by *Snav* (☎ 167 254138) to Naples.

## Hotels in Palermo
★★★★★
*Villa Igiea* (beyond map: 3), 43 salita Belmonte, 90142. ☎ 091 543744; fax 091 547654. In a remarkable Art Nouveau building on the sea at Acquasanta, 3km north of the city in a large park with tennis courts and swimming-pool.
★★★★
*Centrale Palace Hotel* (map: 11), 327 corso Vittorio Emanuele, 90139. ☎ 091 336666; fax 091 334881.
*Grande Hotel et des Palmes* (map: 7), 398 via Roma, 90139. ☎ 091 583933; fax 091 331545. In the former Palazzo Ingham, which retains its luxurious furnishings.
*Politeama Palace* (map: 6), 15 piazza Ruggero Settimo, 90139. ☎ 091 322777; fax 091 6111589.
*President* (map: 3), 228 via Crispi, 90139. ☎ 091 580733; fax 091 6111588.
*Jolly* (map: 16), Foro Italico, 90133. ☎ 091 6165090; fax 091 6161441.
★★★
*Grande Albergo Sole* (map: 11), 291 corso Vittorio Emanuele, 90133. ☎ 091 581811; fax 091 6110182.
*Mediterraneo* (map: 7), 43 via Rosolino Pilo, 90139. ☎ 091 581133; fax 091 586974.
*Europa* (map: 2), 3 via Agrigento, 90141. ☎ & fax 091 6256323.

★★
*Sausele*, 12 via Vincenzo Errante, 300m south-west of the Stazione Centrale, 90127. ☎ 091 6161308; fax 091 6167525.
*Villa Archirafi* (map: 16), 10 via Archirafi, 90133. ☎ 091 6168827; fax 091 6168631.
★
*Letizia* (map: 12), 30 via Bottai, 90133. ☎ & fax 091 589110.
*Petit* (map: 7), 84 via Principe di Belmonte, 90139. ☎ 091 323616.
*Orientale* (map: 15), 26 via Maqueda, 90134. ☎ 091 6165727.

### Hotels in Mondello
★★★★
*Mondello Palace*, 1953 viale Principe di Scalea, 90151. ☎ 091 450001; fax 091 450657. With golf course and swimming-pool.
★★★
*Splendid Hotel La Torre*, 11 Piano Gallo, 90151. ☎ 091 450222; fax 091 450033. In a fine position by the sea (swimming-pool).
*Conchiglia d'Oro*, 9 viale Cloe, 90151. ☎ 091 450359; fax 091 450032.
★★
*Esplanade*, 22 via Gallo, 90151. ☎ 091 450003.

**Campsites** on the coast north of the city at **Sferracavallo**:
★★ *Trinacria* (☎ 091 530590), and ★ *Degli Ulivi* (☎ 091 533021).

### Restaurants in Palermo
**A** *Charleston*, 71 piazzale Ungheria; *Chamade*, 22 via Torrearsa; *Da Renato*, via Messina Marine; *Regine*, 4 via Trapani (for fish); *La Scuderia*, 9 viale del Fante.
**B** *Stella*, 104 via Alloro (in a pretty courtyard with tables outside); *A Cuccagna*, 21 via Principe di Granatelli; *Friend's Bar*, 138 via Brunelleschi; *Trattoria del Buongustaio*, 79 via Venezia.
**C** *Trattoria Lo Bianco*, 104 via Enrico Amari; *Trattoria Italia*, via dell'Orologio (also pizzeria); *I Beati Paoli*, piazza Marina (also a pizzeria, with tables outside); *Le Pergamene* (pizzeria), piazza Marina; *Casa del Brodo*, 170 via Vittorio Emanuele; *Primavera*, piazza Bologna; *'Ngrasciata*, 12 via Tiro a Segno; *Bellini*, piazza Bellini; *Peppino*, 49 piazza Castelnuovo; *Al 59*, 59 piazza Verdi; *Osteria dei Vespri*, piazza Croce dei Vespri (with tables outside); *Antica Focacceria di S. Francesco* (sandwiches), 58 via Paternostro.
Vegetarian restaurant: *Cotto e Crudo*, 45 piazza Marina.

### Restaurants in Mondello well known for fish
**A** *Chamade Mare* and *Le Terrazze*
**B** *Calogero*; *Franco*; *Il Gambero Rosso*
**C** *Da Totuccio*
Vegetarian restaurant: *Giardino dei Melograni*

### Restaurants in Sferracavallo
**B** *Al Delfino*

### Cafés and pasticcerie

| | |
|---|---|
| **Roney**, via Libertà | **Mazzara**, via Generale Magliocco |
| **Extra Bar**, piazza Politeama | **Preferita**, via Villareale |
| **Scimone**, 18 via Miceli | **Mamma Andrea**, 67 via Principe di Scordia |

There are now more and more cafés with tables outside, many of them off via Ruggero Settimo, in via Principe di Belmonte (map: 7; closed to traffic). In summer numerous cafés in the centre of the city provide music.

*Places to picnic*. Well-kept public parks near the centre of the town include the Villa Giulia (map: 16), the Giardino Inglese (map: 2) and the Parco d'Orleans (map: 14).

*Opening times* of museums and monuments have been extended but often change: for the latest list of times contact the APT. In summer, some of the most important museums and monuments are kept open on Thurs, Fri, & Sat evenings (20.30–23.30). Numerous **churches** are now kept open (usually weekdays 09.00–17.00, Sat 09.00–13.00) through a scheme (*Cento Chiese Aperte*) promoted by the local council and the *Curia* by which associations of young people act as guides and custodians. So far 24 lesser-known churches have been re-opened, although the final goal is to open 100. For information, contact the association Alba Chiara, ☎ 091/6884302.

*Theatres*. Massimo, piazza Verdi (re-opened in 1997), ☎ 091/ 6053111; Politeama Garibaldi, piazza Ruggero Settimo; Biondo, 260 via Roma. Concerts are also held at S. Maria dello Spasimo, in via dello Spasimo in the Kalsa district and in the churches of La Gancia, S. Salvatore and S. Giuseppe, and in the Sala Scarlatti of the Conservatorio, 45 via Squarcialupo.

*Puppet theatres*. Performances at the Museo Internazionale delle Marionette (see text below), 1 via Butera (☎ 091/328060), and periodically at various small theatres in the city (it is advisable to telephone in advance for information), including Cuticchio, 95 via Bara (map: 11; ☎ 091/323400; performances usually held on Sat & Sun at 17.30) and Opera dei Pupi, vicolo Ragusi (☎ 091/6113680).

Important *exhibitions* are held at the Albergo delle Povere, corso Calatafimi, as well as at the Museo Archeologico and S. Giorgio dei Genovesi.

*Markets*. The street markets of Palermo are justly famous, and should not be missed even by the most hurried visitor. The stalls are set up in the morning around 08.30 or 09.00 and they stay open all day until around 19.30. The biggest are: **Vucciria** (see map: 11), for produce (especially fish); **Ballarò** (map: 15), for produce (and some antiques); **Capo** (via S. Agostino; map: 10, 11), for clothes and produce; **Papireto** (piazza Peranni; map: 10), for antiques and bric-a-brac (although this is now in decline).

There is another food market open in the afternoon and evening in corso Scina (map: 3).

*Annual festivals*. *Festino di S. Rosalia* (10–15 July), with celebrations including theatre performances, concerts, fireworks and a street procession with the statue of St Rosalia on a huge cart drawn by horses; pilgrimage (with a torch-light procession) to the shrine on Monte Pellegrino, 3–4 September. A music festival is held for a week in November in the cathedral of Monreale.

**Police station** (*Questura*), 11 piazza della Vittoria (☎ 091/210111); office for foreigners, ☎ 091/6514330. For all emergencies, ☎ 113.

**English church** (Holy Cross; map: 7), 118 via Stabile; services in winter only.

### History

Traces of Paleolithic settlements have been found in grottoes on Monte Pellegrino. The carsic mountains which surround the plain ensured the fertility of the Conca d'Oro which was important to the inhabitants of Palermo throughout her history. *Panormus*, a Phoenician colony of the 8C–6C BC, was never a Greek city, despite its Greek name signifying 'all harbour'. It was, instead, an important Carthaginian centre, hotly disputed during the First Punic War, and not finally acquired by Rome until 254 BC. It became a municipium, and after 20 BC, a flourishing colony. After the invasions of the Vandals and Ostrogoths it was reconquered for the Byzantine emperors in 535 and remained in their possession until 831, when the Saracens captured it after a prolonged resistance.

Under Muslim rule it was made capital of an emirate (and named *al-Madinah*) and rivalled Cordoba and Cairo in oriental splendour. It became an important trading-post and cosmopolitan centre which showed tolerance towards the Christians, even though hundreds of mosques were built in the city at this time.

Taken by Count Roger de Hauteville in 1072, it again reached a high state of prosperity under his son King Roger II (1130–54), and became the centre of trade between Europe and Asia. Under the brilliant court of the Emperor Frederick II of Hohenstaufen (1198–1250), *stupor mundi*, the city became famous throughout Europe for its learning and magnificence.

The famous rebellion of the 'Sicilian Vespers' (see p.107) put an end to the misrule of Charles of Anjou in 1282. A long period of Spanish domination, which became increasingly tyrannical, led to the gradual decline of the city, despite an insurrection of 1646. By the treaty of Utrecht (1713) Sicily was allotted to Vittorio Amadeo of Savoy, who was, however, forced to exchange it for Sardinia (1718) in favour of the Neapolitan Bourbons. Under their rule the island suffered more than ever, though Ferdinand IV established his court at Palermo in 1799 during the French occupation of Naples. The city was granted a temporary constitution in 1811 while under British protection. In the 18C it was the largest town in Italy after Naples. The city rebelled against misgovernment in 1820 (when Sir Richard Church was relieved of his governorship), 1848, and in April 1860. On 27 May 1860 Garibaldi and the Thousand made a triumphal entry into the city.

Parts of the centre of Palermo were badly damaged during air raids in World War II and a few bomb sites still remain. The city was virtually governed by the Mafia in the following decades, when much illegal new building took place in the Conca d'Oro which spoiled the once beautiful surrounding area. In the 1960s and 1970s it was perhaps the most neglected city in Italy, when a vast number of houses in the historical centre were in danger of collapse, and the population of this area dwindled to some 35,000 (from 125,000 in 1951), representing a mere five per cent of the total population of the municipal area.

But an enlightened city government since 1988 has produced a period of optimism and a detailed plan to restore and revitalise the beautiful old centre of the city was finally approved in 1997 and is in the process of being carried out, with numerous restorations under way or already completed.

**Art.** The Norman domination, with its architecture showing a strongly oriental influence, has left many magnificent buildings, including the Palazzo della Zisa and Palazzo dei Normanni, the Cappella Palatina, La Martorana, and, in the outskirts, Monreale Cathedral. All these buildings also have especially remarkable mosaic decoration. Architecture and painting in the early 15C was influenced by Catalan masters, as can be seen from the south porch of the cathedral and Palazzo Abatellis.

Matteo Carnelivari was the most important architect working in Palermo at this time. Francesco Laurana, the Renaissance sculptor came to work in Palermo in the middle of the 15C. Another extremely influential sculptor here in the second half of the 15C was Domenico Gagini; his style was continued into the following century by his son Antonello.

If the dramatic 15C fresco of the *Triumph of Death* (now in the Galleria Regionale) is by a Sicilian master, it is the most important Sicilian work of this period.

Numerous splendid Baroque churches were erected in Palermo, many of them by the local architect Giacomo Amato (1643–1732). From the mid-17C to the end of the 18C the interiors of many churches were lavishly decorated with coloured marbles and mosaic inlay. The delightful stuccoes of Giacomo Serpotta (1656–1732) are best seen in the oratories of S. Cita, S. Domenico and S. Lorenzo. Pietro Novelli of Monreale was the greatest Sicilian painter of the 17C. Venanzio Marvuglia (1729–1814) produced some fine neo-classical buildings in Palermo, and the city is particularly rich in Art Nouveau architecture. There are also a number of monumental edifices in eclectic styles by Ernesto Basile (1857–1932).

**Topography.** The ancient town, bounded by two small rivers, the Kemonia and the Papireto, near their mouths on the sea, occupied an elliptical area centring on the present cathedral. Its main street (now the western half of the corso Vittorio Emanuele) was known as the Cassaro Vecchio, a name derived from Castrum or the Arabic *Kasr* (meaning 'castle'). The Saracen citadel, called *Khalisa*, grew up to the south of the harbour, in an area thought to have been occupied also by the *Neapolis*, or new town, another fortified area which was created in the Roman era nearer the port.

By the mid-16C the rivers had silted up and the harbour was reduced to its existing proportions and the plan of Palermo from then on hinged on two main thoroughfares: the Cassaro, extended to the east in 1565 and prolonged to the sea in 1581, and the via Maqueda (laid out c 1600), running roughly parallel with the coast. These bisect one another at the Quattro Canti. In the 19C and 20C the city expanded towards the north, with its focus at piazza Verdi (map: 10). In present day Palermo very few street names are written up, even though they all have an official name on the maps.

**Famous natives of Palermo** include Alessandro Scarlatti (1660–1725), the composer, Stanislao Cannizzaro (1826–1910), the chemist, and Vittorio Emanuele Orlando (1860–1952), prime minister of Italy in 1917–19 and a brilliant jurist. Though educated in Palermo, Sergius I (pope, 687–701) is now thought to have been born at Antioch.

M.W. Balfe produced his first opera *I Rivali di se stessi* in Palermo in 1830, and William Harris (c 1796–1823), the English architect, died here of malaria, contracted while excavating Selinunte. Ippolito Nievo (1831–61), the patriot-novelist, was drowned when his ship the *Ercole* disappeared without trace between Palermo and Naples. Constantine of Greece died here in 1923 (commemorative plaque at Villa Igiea).

# The centre of the city

The monumental crossroads known as the **Quattro Canti** (map: 11) was laid out in 1608–20 by Giulio Lasso at the central intersection of the four longest and straightest streets of the city. It was named piazza Vigliena after the Duke of Vigliena, Spanish viceroy in 1611. The four decorative façades bear fountains with statues of the seasons, the four Spanish kings of Sicily, and of the patronesses of Palermo (Cristina, Ninfa, Oliva and Agata). It is now a confined and busy road junction, but is still used as a meeting-place by the local inhabitants. At either end of corso Vittorio Emanuele, Porta Nuova and the sea beyond Porta Felice can be seen, while via Maqueda has a vista of the hills surrounding the Conca d'Oro.

## Piazza Pretoria

A few steps along via Maqueda to the south-east, piazza Pretoria (map: 11) is almost entirely occupied by a fountain designed by the Florentine Francesco Camilliani (1554–55) and Michelangelo Naccherino (1573). The great basin, designed for the garden of a Florentine villa, installed here in 1573, is decorated with numerous statues.

PALAZZO DELLE AQUILE (formerly Palazzo Senatorio), named after the eagles which decorate its exterior, is the town hall. It was built in 1463, enlarged in the 16C, and over-restored in 1874. On the top of the façade is a statue of St Rosalia by Carlo d'Aprile (1661). Visitors are admitted without formality when it is not in use. This was formerly the seat of the Senate which governed the city from the 14C until 1816: the senators were elected from the local aristocracy.

In the **atrium** is a Baroque portal by Paolo Amato, and a Roman funerary monument with statues of a husband and wife. At the foot of the 19C staircase is part of a 16C fountain of the *Genius of Palermo*, one of a number of allegorical statues in the city with the figure of a king, personifying civic rule, entangled in a serpent. On the **first floor**, the assembly room, which has a 16C painted wooden ceiling, is covered with numerous inscriptions relating to events which have taken place in the room, the last of which was dedicated to the memory of victims of the Mafia by Elda Pucci, a former mayor, in 1983. The other rooms, including that of the mayor, were decorated by Damiani Almeyda in 1870 and contain mementoes of Garibaldi and Napoleon.

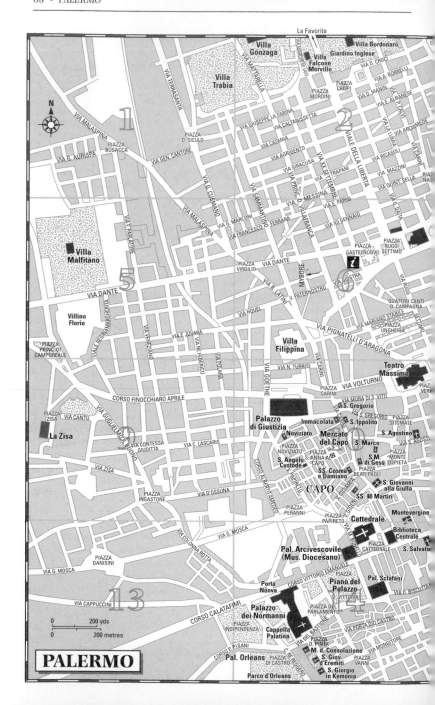

PALERMO

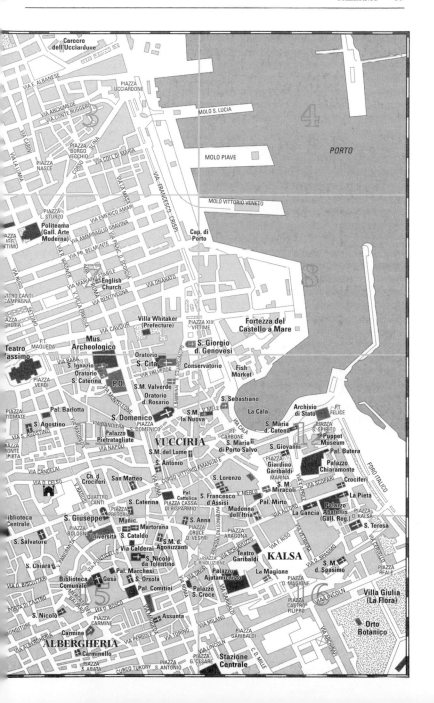

Another side of the piazza is closed by the flank and dome of the church of **S. Caterina** (1566–96).The interior (closed for restoration), especially the choir, is an elaborate example of Sicilian Baroque, with its striking effects of sculptural decoration and marble veneering (executed in the early 18C). In the right transept is a *St Catherine* by Antonello Gagini(1534). The frescoes in the cupola are by Vito d'Anna (1751).

## San Giuseppe dei Teatini

Across via Maqueda is the side of the church of S. Giuseppe dei Teatini (map: 15). The upper church, built by Giacomo Besio of Genoa (1612–45), was the scene of two popular assemblies called by Giuseppe D'Alessi during the revolt of 1647 against the Spanish governors.

In the beautiful Baroque **interior** (open 07.00–12.00, 17.00–20.00), in addition to the 14 monolithic columns in the nave, eight colossal columns of grey marble support the well-proportioned central dome. The frescoes of the nave roof are copies of the originals by Filippo Tancredi; those in the dome are by Borremans; the stuccoes are remarkable. The two large angels holding the stoups on either side of the entrance are by Marabitti.

In the fourth south chapel, with pretty marble decoration, is a statue of the *Madonna* by the school of Gagini.

In the south transept, beneath the altarpiece of *St Andrea Avellino* by Sebastiano Conca is a charming frieze of child musicians, and the altar has a bas-relief of a *Madonna amidst angels*, both by Federico Siragusa (1800).

In the choir vault are fine reliefs, with full-length figures, by Procopio Serpotta. In the chapels flanking the choir are (right) a *Crucifix* by Fra Umile da Petralia and (left) reliefs by Filippo Pennino, and an 18C statue of *St Joseph*. In the north transept, above an altar of marble mosaic (probably late 17C), is a painting of *St Gaetano* by Pietro Novelli.

Next to the church is the former Convent of the Teatini di S. Giuseppe, now occupied by the university (the building was modified in the 19C). The small Geological Museum founded here in the early 19C is now at no. 131 corso Tuköry (map: 15), and open to students.

## La Martorana and San Cataldo

Adjoining piazza Pretoria is piazza Bellini where the majestic campanile of La Martorana stands next to the three little red domes of S. Cataldo, raised above part of the east wall of the Roman city and surrounded by a few trees; it is fitting that these two beautiful churches, founded by two of Norman Sicily's greatest statesmen, should survive together in the centre of the city.

**LA MARTORANA** (map: 15; open 08.30–13.00, 15.30–dusk; Sun & PH 08.30–13.00) or S. Maria dell'Ammiraglio, is a Norman church founded c 1146 by George of Antioch, a Syrian of the Greek Orthodox faith who became admiral under Roger II. It was presented in 1433 to a convent founded in the 12C by Eloisa Martorana, wife of Goffredo de Martorana. The Sicilian Parliament met here after the Sicilian Vespers. Since 1935 it has shared cathedral status with S. Demetrio in Piana degli Albanesi, with offices according to the Greek rite.

**Exterior**. The Norman structure survives on the north and south sides, although a Baroque façade was inserted in 1588 on the north side when the Norman narthex was demolished and the atrium covered. The present entrance

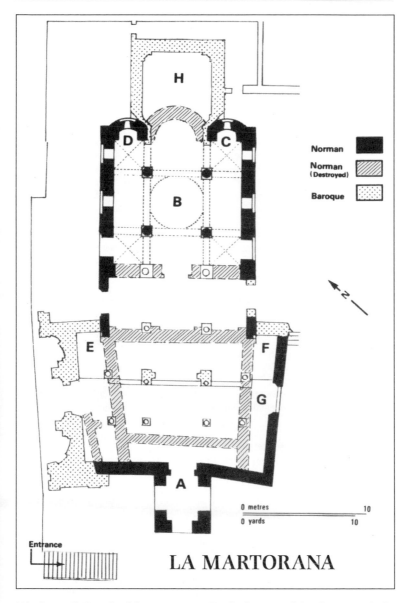

Norman

Norman (Destroyed)

Baroque

LA MARTORANA

Entrance

(**A**) is beneath the splendid 12C **campanile** which survived the alterations (only its red dome is missing).

**Interior**. The central Greek-cross plan of the tiny original church can still be detected, despite the Baroque alterations at the west end and the prolongation of the chancel in 1683. The walls at the west end are heavily decorated with

Baroque marble and frescoes which at first overpower the original mosaic decoration which remains on and around the central cupola. The **mosaics**, probably by Greek craftsmen from Constantinople, date from the first half of the 12C; *Christ and four angels* is depicted in the dome (B) and, in Arabic lettering, a quotation from a Byzantine hymn; around the drum, *Prophets and Evangelists*; on the triumphal arch, the Annunciation; in the south apse (C) *St Anne*, in the north apse (D), *St Joachim*; and in the side vaults, *four evangelists*, the *Nativity* and the *Dormition of the Virgin*. The transennae in front of the apses and the mosaic pavement are also Norman.

At the west end are two more original mosaic panels (restored; set in Baroque frames) from the destroyed portico: to the left (E), *George of Antioch at the feet of the Virgin*, and, to the right (F), *Roger crowned by Christ*. Also here are frescoes by Borremans (1717), and in the embrasure of the south portal (G) is a carved wooden door of the 12C. Above the main altar (H) is a good painting of the *Ascension* (1533) by Vincenzo da Pavia.

South-east of the church some arches survive of the cloister of the 12C **Casa di Martorana**, the Benedictine convent founded by Eloisa Martorana. Although the convent has disappeared, the marzipan fruits which used to be made by the nuns here are immortalised by the name *frutti di martorana*, and are still produced by numerous confectioners all over the island.

In the pretty pebbled courtyard with several very tall trees, opposite the campanile, is the **Cappella di S. Cataldo** (ask for the key at La Martorana). It was founded by Maio of Bari, William I's chancellor, because of his early death in 1160 the interior was never decorated. After 1787 it served as a post office and was restored in 1885. The fine exterior has blind arcading round the windows and pretty crenellations at the top of the wall. In the centre three small red domes rise, pierced by little windows. The simple plan of the interior has three aisles ending in apses and three domes high up above the central aisle. The beautiful old capitals are all different. The original mosaic floor and lattice windows survive.

## Corso Vittorio Emanuele to the cathedral

The busy **corso Vittorio Emanuele** (map: 11,14), the main street of the town, was once called the Cassaro Vecchio (from the Arab *Kasr* meaning *Castello*) because it led from the port to the royal castle. It now has numerous bookshops. On the left it passes **piazza Bologni** (map: 11,15), beautifully paved in marble, with an unsuccessful statue of Charles V by Scipione Li Volsi (1630), and some fine palaces (several of which have recently been restored).

From the far end of the piazza a detour can be made: beside Palazzo Ugo delle Favare with attractive balconies, the interesting old via Panormita leads to piazzetta Speciale where the **Palazzo Speciale** has an 18C staircase in its pretty courtyard. Further on is piazza S. Chiara where the church, with a delightful little campanile, has just been restored (the two houses opposite are in the process of a careful restoration). Via Puglia continues (with a view left down via Benfratelli to the 14C tower of S. Niccolò, at present covered for restoration), and tunnels under a massive arch to emerge in piazza S. Giovanni Decollato beside the impressive **Palazzo Sclafani** (map: 14), built by Matteo Sclafani in 1330. Part of the original façade here has attractive lava decoration around the windows. The fine portal has sculptures by Bonaiuto da Pisa. Opposite is the ruined church of S. Giovanni Decollato, with a huge ficus tree growing through its façade. The piazza beyond, known as the Piano del Palazzo, is described below.

Facing piazza Bologni (see above), across the corso, is the façade of **Palazzo Riso-Belmonte** which has at last been restored: this was once the grandest of all Marvuglia's buildings (1784) in the city. Farther along the corso is the church of **S. Salvatore** (map: 14; open 09.30–12.30, exc Tues), built in 1682 by Paolo Amato. Damaged in the war, its oval interior has been well restored. It is frequently used for weddings.

On the opposite side of the corso the narrow via Montevergini leads to the church of **Montevergini** (map: 10; open 08.30–20.00) with a fine façade (awaiting restoration) by Andrea Palma and a little campanile with an onion-shaped dome decorated with early 18C tiles, beside an 18C loggia for the nuns. The interior is to be restored: after its deconsecration in 1866 it became a school for artisans, then the seat of the Fascist party, and was later used (until 1955) as a law court. The trial of Gaspare Pisciotta, who murdered his brother-in-law, the bandit Salvatore Giuliano, took place here (see p.133). In the interior there are some vault frescoes by Borremans, and a neo-classical east end decorated by Emanuele Cordona with frescoes by Giuseppe Velasco. The sacristy also has a neo-classical vault.

Further on in the corso is the **Biblioteca Centrale della Regione Siciliana**. It occupies the former Jesuit college, and is entered by the portal of the adjacent church of S. Maria della Grotta. It owns over 500,000 volumes and many ancient manuscripts (particularly of the 15C and 16C).

Just beyond is piazza della Cattedrale, with the elaborate flank of the cathedral on the other side of a garden of palm trees enclosed by a balustrade bearing statues of saints.

## The cathedral
The cathedral (map: 10; *Assunta*; open April–Sept 07.00–19.00; Oct–May 07.00–12.00, 16.00–19.00), a building of many styles not too skilfully blended, is still a striking edifice with its sharp lights and shades and the golden colour of its stone.

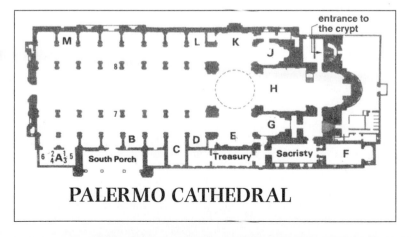

PALERMO CATHEDRAL

The present cathedral, on the site of an older basilica which did duty as a mosque in the 9C, was founded in 1185 by Walter, Archbishop of Palermo. Building continued for many centuries and in the 15C much of the exterior acquired a Catalan Gothic style. The incongruous dome was added by Ferdinando Fuga in 1781–1801. Baroque and neo-classical elements predominate in the interior.

### Exterior

The façade, turned towards the south-west on via Matteo Bonello, is a fine example of local Gothic craftsmanship (13C–14C). The doorway dates from 1352. Two powerful Gothic arches span the road to a Norman tower transformed into the campanile in the 19C. The east end, with three apses and two towers matching those at the west end, is practically original 12C work.

The usual entrance is from the garden through the great **south porch**, a splendid Catalan Gothic work of 1429 by Antonio Gambara, carefully restored in 1983–93. In the tympanum there is a delicate relief of the *Redeemer between the archangel Gabriel and Maria*. Beneath is a frieze of saints in polychrome relief. The remarkable painted intarsia decoration above the three arches, which probably dates from 1296, was rediscovered during the recent restoration work. It represents the *Tree of Life* in a complicated geometric composition showing Islamic influence. The twelve tondi are decorated with a great variety of symbolic animals (including fish, cockerels, serpents, crab, mice, camels, lions, wolves, bears, peacocks, dragons, doves and owls), as well as fruit and flowers and human figures. Intended to be read from left to right, the last tondo seems to represent the sun with the head of Christ in the centre.

Beneath the porch, the column on the left, probably preserved from the earlier mosque, is inscribed with a passage from the Koran. The fine doorway by Antonio Gambara (1426) has wooden doors by Francesco Miranda (1432).

### Interior

The aisled nave has been spoilt by Fuga's alterations. In the **south aisle** the first two chapels (A) enclose six splendid **royal tombs** including that of the first king of Sicily, Roger II (d. 1154), who was crowned in this cathedral in 1130. His daughter Constance (d. 1198) is also buried here with her husband, Henry VI (d. 1197), Emperor of Germany and son of Frederick Barbarossa. Their son, Frederick II (d. 1250), Emperor of Germany and King of Sicily, lies nearby along with his wife, Constance of Aragon (d. 1222). The Emperor died in Puglia but his body was embalmed and transported here since he had expressed the wish to be buried beside his father and grandfather. The later Aragonese royalties buried here are Duke William (d. 1338), son of Frederick II of Aragon, and (in Frederick II's sarcophagus) Peter II (d. 1342), King of Sicily.

The tombs were moved here from the choir in the 18C and have been enclosed (making it difficult to see them): four are canopied and two set in the wall. On the left in front is the porphyry sarcophagus (1) of Frederick II and Peter II; the similar tomb on the right (2) contains the ashes of Henry VI. At the back, beneath mosaic canopies (3,4), are the tombs of Roger II and his daughter Constance. The two fine porphyry sarcophagi which Roger had had installed in the cathedral of Cefalù where he wished to be buried, were later moved here. On the left (5), is the sarcophagus of Duke William. The Roman sarcophagus on the right (6) contains the body of Constance of Aragon.

In the **nave** are statues of saints from a high altar by the Gagini and (7) a canopied stoup by Giuseppe Spadafora and Antonio Ferraro (1553–55). In the fourth chapel (B), altarpiece by Pietro Novelli, and in the sixth chapel (C), reliquary urns of saints of Palermo, and, used as an altar frontal, the tomb slab of St Cosma (d. 1160). The seventh chapel (D) has a fine altar of *marmi mischi* (1713). In the **south transept** (E) there is an altarpiece by Giuseppe Velasquez and, above the altar, a bas-relief of the *Dormition of the Virgin* by Antonello Gagini (1535).

The **treasury** (open at the same times as the cathedral, except closed on Sun & PH) contains the **crown of Constance of Aragon** (wife of Frederick II), made by local craftsmen in the 12C, found in her tomb (see above) in the 18C. Also displayed here are the contents of some of the other royal tombs, 18C and 19C copes, chalices and altar frontals. There are plans to re-arrange the collection.

The **crypt** (open at the same time as the treasury but with a separate ticket), restored and re-opened in 1995, is approached through the **sacristy** which has two fine portals by Vincenzo Gagini (1568). The inner sacristy (F: usually closed) has a *Madonna* by Antonello Gagini (1503). To the left is a tower with a fine Catalan doorway and the remains of a little Arab stalactite vault. It is now necessary to cross the east end of the choir which has a *Resurrection of Christ* on the altar, high reliefs, and (in niches), statues of the apostles, all fragments of Antonello Gagini's high altar. Stairs lead down to the interesting **crypt** which preserves 23 tombs, many of them Roman sarcophagi (all of them numbered and labelled). The tomb (no. 12) of archbishop Giovanni Paternò (d. 1511) has a very fine effigy by Antonello Gagini, resting on a Greek sarcophagus. The tomb (no. 16) of the founder of the cathedral, Archbishop Walter (d. 1190), has a beautiful red green and gold mosaic border. No. 7 is a splendid large Roman sarcophagus with a scene of the coronation of a poet accompanied by the nine muses and Apollo. The tomb of Frederick of Antioch (d. 1305) has a Gothic effigy of the warrior with his helmet.

In the chapel (G) to the right of the choir is a silver coffer containing the relics of St Rosalia by Francesco Rivelo, Giancola Viviano and Matteo Lo Castro (1631). The reliefs on the walls are by Valerio Villareale (1818). In the **choir** (H) the stalls date from 1466. In the chapel on the left (J) is a large domed ciborium in lapis lazuli (1663) and the funerary monument of Bishop Sanseverino by Filippo and Gaetano Pennino (1793).

**North transept** (K). At the foot of an early 14C wooden Crucifix donated by Manfredi Chiaramonte are marble statues of the mourners by Gaspare Serpotta and Gaspare Guercio. On the altar are fine reliefs with scenes of the *Passion* by Fazio and Vincenzo Gagini.

**North aisle**. In the seventh chapel (L), there is a statue of the *Madonna* by Francesco Laurana and his pupils. In the nave (8) is a stoup attributed to Domenico Gagini (damaged) of finer workmanship than the one opposite. The second chapel (M) has an *Assumption* and three reliefs by the Gagini, once part of the high altar.

**Palazzo Arcivescovile**, across the busy via Bonello, has a portal of 1460 which survived the rebuilding in the 18C. The **Museo Diocesano** was founded here to house fragments from the cathedral and works of art from destroyed churches. It has been closed for many years. The contents include paintings by Zoppo di Ganci, Carlo Maratta, Antonio Veneziano, Gera da Pisa, Riccardo Quartararo, Antonello Riccio, Pietro Ruzzolone, Vincenzo da Pavia, Antonello Crecenzio,

Pietro Novelli, Mario di Laureto, Giuseppe Velasquez and Giorgio Vasari.

The sculpture includes works by the Gagini, Pietro da Bonitate and Gabriele di Battista.

Behind Palazzo Arcivescovile, in a lane, is the **Oratorio dei SS. Pietro e Paolo** (usually closed) which contains stuccoes by Giacomo Serpotta and Domenico Castelli (1698) and a 17C ceiling-fresco by Filippo Tancredi. The entrance can be seen from via Bonello. On the other side of via Bonello is the **Loggia dell'Incoronazione** (map: 10), erected in the 16C–17C using earlier columns and capitals. It takes its name from the tradition that the kings used to show themselves to the people here after their coronation. Behind is the Cappella dell'Incoronata, a Norman building partly destroyed in 1860.

## Palazzo dei Normanni and the Cappella Palatina

**Piazza della Vittoria**, or **Piano del Palazzo** (map 14) is occupied by Villa Bonanno, a well-kept public garden planted with palm trees in 1905. At the centre of the old city and in front of the royal palace the piazza has been used throughout Palermo's history for public celebrations. Partially protected by a roof are some remains of three Roman houses, the only buildings of this period so far found in the city. The garden adjoins piazza del Parlamento with a monument to Philip V of Bourbon, at the foot of the huge Palazzo dei Normanni. Spanning the corso is the **Porta Nuova**, a triumphal gateway celebrating Charles V's Tunisian victory (1535), reconstructed after damage by lightning in 1667 (with a conical top).

### Palazzo dei Normanni with the Cappella Palatina

Palazzo dei Normanni (or Palazzo Reale; map: 14) stands on the highest part of the old city. It was built by the Saracens, enlarged by the Normans, and later restored by the Spaniards who added the principal façade.

It has always been the palace of the rulers of the island, and here the splendid courts of Roger II and Frederick II, *stupor mundi*, held sway over Europe. Since 1947 it has been the seat of the Regional Assembly. The long façade (1616) hides the apse of the famous Cappella Palatina: at the right end is the massive Torre Pisana, part of the Norman palace.

**Admission**. When not in use the palace is open Mon, Fri and Sat (09.00–12.00 for guided tours). The Cappella Palatina is open 09.00–12.00, 15.00–17.00; Sat 09.00–12.00; Sun & PH 09.00–10.00, 12.00–13.00.

The entrance for visitors is at the back of the palace: this is reached by steps down from the left side of the piazza to the very busy and noisy via del Bastione, which skirts the great wall of the palace around to the right. From the bastions a ramp leads up to the back entrance (**A**). Here a monumental **staircase** (C; 1735) leads up to a **loggia** overlooking the fine courtyard (B; 1600). Set into the wall of the loggia is a pillar with an inscription (behind glass) in Greek, Latin and Arabic relating to a water-clock built by Roger II in 1142.

Beneath the portico of seven columns with modern mosaics, is the side entrance to the **Cappella Palatina** (for admission, see above), a jewel of Norman-Saracenic art built by Roger II c 1132–40.

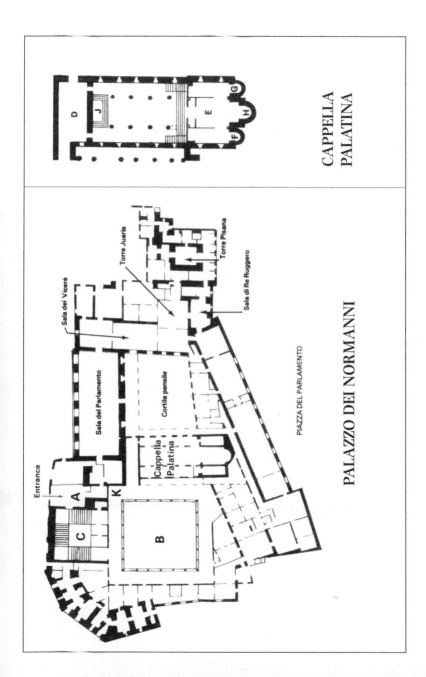

CAPPELLA PALATINA

PALAZZO DEI NORMANNI

The gracious **interior** is famous for its wonderful mosaics, one of the finest works of art of its kind in Italy. The light changes constantly: the chapel should, if possible, be visited at different times of the day. A small aisled basilica in form, with a raised choir and a cupola above the central bay, it shows the perfection reached by this style of architecture. Every detail of the decoration is exquisite.

The ten antique columns of the nave are made from granite and cipollino; the ceiling (which has been covered for many years for restoration) is a splendid Saracenic work. The ambo and paschal candlestick are good examples of the richest Norman marble decoration. The pavement and lower part of the walls are made of white marble inlaid with red, green and gold patterns, which combine in a delightful harmony of colour and design with the mosaics of glass and plaster on a gold ground above.

The **mosaics** were commissioned by Roger II and completed by his son William I at an unknown date. They follow a carefully worked out design intended to celebrate the monarchy of Roger II, and the subjects seem to have been chosen with particular reference to the Holy Spirit and the theology of light. The earliest and finest mosaics are in the east part of the chapel and are thought to have been the work of Byzantine Greeks (c 1140–50). Here the splendour of the mosaics is increased by the use of silver as well as gold tesserae.

**Sanctuary** (E). In the cupola is *Christ surrounded by angels and archangels*; on the drum, *David, Solomon, Zachariah and St John the Baptist*; on the pendentives, *Evangelists*. On the triumphal arch, an *Annunciation* is depicted. Above the right apse (F) is a *Nativity*; on the upper part of the right wall, *Joseph's Dream* and the *Flight into Egypt*; on the nave arch, *Presentation in the Temple*; in the middle of the right wall, *Baptism, Transfiguration*, and the *Raising of Lazarus*; and on the lower part of the right wall, *Entry into Jerusalem*. On the lower part of the left wall, five bishops of the Greek church (among the best preserved mosaic figures in the building), and, on the arch, three female saints. Above the left apse (G), are a *Madonna and Child* and *St John the Baptist*. In the main apse (H) is *Christ Pantocrator*, above a late 18C mosaic of the *Virgin*.

The mosaics in the **nave** were probably the last mosaics to be executed in the chapel (c 1150–71) and are Roman rather than Greek in style. They illustrate the book of Genesis in two tiers of scenes between the clerestory windows and in the spandrels of the arches. The cycle begins in the upper tier of the south wall nearest to the sanctuary, showing the first seven days of the *Creation* up to the *Creation of Eve*. The sequence continues in the upper tier of the north wall (beginning at the west end) with the *Fall* up to the *Building of the Ark*. The lower tier of the south wall (from the east end) illustrates the *Flood* up to the *Hospitality of Lot*, and continues in the lower tier of the north wall (west end) with the *Destruction of Sodom* and continues up to *Jacob's Dream* and his *Wrestling with the Angel*, which is the last scene in the sequence (nearest to the sanctuary).

In the **aisles** are scenes from the lives of Sts Peter and Paul, also executed after the mosaics in the east part of the church, possibly by local artists. The sequence begins at the east end of the south aisle with *Saul leaving Jerusalem for Damascus* and the last scene in this aisle shows *St Peter's escape from Prison*. The cycle continues at the west end of the north aisle with *Sts Peter and John healing the lame man at the temple gate*, and the last scene in this aisle, nearest to the sanctuary, shows the *Fall of Simon Magus*.

Above the recomposed Norman throne on a dias at the **west end** (J) is a 15C mosaic of *Christ enthroned between Sts Peter and Paul*. The original **narthex** (D; now the baptistery, with a mosaic font), has two beautifully carved mosaic door-ways with bronze doors. The sacristy and treasury are usually closed.

The staircase, with red marble risers, leads up to the top floor of the palace and the former **Royal Apartments** (for admission, see above), mostly decorated in the 19C. The **sala del viceré** has a series of portraits of viceroys from 1754 to 1837. The **sala della preghiera** contains a self-portrait by Anna Maria Cario-lato (1890). The **Torre Juaria** preserves part of the Norman building, with four columns. The most interesting room is the so-called **Sala di Re Ruggero** with delightful mosaics of 1140, including hunting scenes, birds, palm trees, lions and tigers. In the vault are heraldic beasts. The lower parts of the walls with marble and mosaic decoration, and the floor all survive intact. The **Sala da Ballo** has a fine view over the piazza to the sea.

Other parts of the palace, which are not usually shown, include the Sala del Parlamento decorated in 1700 by Giuseppe Velasquez where the Regional Assembly meets. The vaulted armoury, treasure-chamber and dungeons survive from the Norman period. From the observatory at the top of the Torre Pisano, Giuseppe Piazzi discovered the first asteroid (Ceres) on 1 January 1801.

Across corso Re Ruggero is **Palazzo d'Orléans** (map: 14), now the seat of the Regional President, which has a pretty park (with a small zoo) open to the public (09.00–dusk). This was the residence of the exiled Louis Philippe d'Orléans (1773–1850), eldest son of the Duke d'Orléans and King of France, at the time of his marriage in 1809 to Marie Amélie, daughter of Ferdinand IV, the Spanish King of the Two Sicilies. Their son Ferdinand Philippe (1810–42) was born here in the following year.

In piazza della Pinta (map: 14) is the little Oratorio della Compagnia della Madonna della Consolazione (S. Mercurio, propped up by a wooden scaffold). The stucco decoration in the interior has recently been attributed, as an early work, to Giacomo Serpotta.

## San Giovanni degli Eremiti

Via dei Benedettini, an extremely busy and noisy road, leads from here to the church of S. Giovanni degli Eremiti (map: 14; open 09.00–13.00, 15.00–19.00; Sun & PH 09.00–12.30; in winter 09.00–13.00 and on Mon and Thurs also 15.00–18.00). This is perhaps the most romantic building of Norman Palermo, because of its small luxuriant garden, carefully tended, which somewhat protects it from the noisy road. It was built by Roger II in 1132–48, and has now been de-consecrated. Paths lead up through the beautiful garden, with splendid palm trees, cactus and papyrus plants and flowering jasmine, overshadowed by five charming red domes, the tallest one crowning the campanile of the little **church**. In the bare interior the nave is surmounted by two domes divided by an arch (pierced by a window). At the east end are three apses and three smaller domes, the one on the left part of the campanile.

To the right is an older structure, probably a **mosque**, consisting of a rectan-gular hall with cross vaulting and once divided by a row of pillars. Adjoining this (seen from the right of the entrance to the church) is a portico of five arches, whose inner wall is now the right wall of the church, and an open courtyard.

The little **cloister** of the late 13C has twin columns bearing pointed arches which surround a delightful garden.

Next to the church, in via dei Benedettini, is the church of **S. Giorgio in Kemonia**, of ancient foundation, rebuilt in 1765. The interior has rococo and neo-classical elements and paintings by Giuseppe Tresca.

## The Gesù and the Quartiere dell'Albergheria

From the Quattro Canti (see p.67) via Maqueda (map: 11,15) leads south past the church of S. Giuseppe (described above) to via del Ponticello which branches off to the right. On the left is piazza dei SS. 40 Martiri. Here the sturdy tower (with a Catalan window) of the 15C **Palazzo Marchesi** forms the base of the campanile of the Gesù. The garden of the palace is sometimes open.

Via del Ponticello continues past a derelict and ruined building to the church of the **Gesù** (or church of the *Casa Professa*; map: 15; open 07.30–11.30), the first church to be erected in Sicily by the Jesuits (1564–1633). The splendid **interior** was beautifully decorated in the 17C and 18C with colourful marble intarsia and sculptures (especially good in the nave chapels, 1665–91). It was well restored after severe damage in the last war. The inside façade has very fine 18C sculptural decoration. In the south aisle, the second chapel has paintings of two saints by Pietro Novelli, and the fourth chapel has a statue of the *Madonna* by the school of Gagini. The presbytery also has remarkably good marble decoration.

Beside the church is the fine Baroque atrium of the Casa Professa, now partly occupied by the **Biblioteca Communale**, founded in 1760. It has over 250,000 volumes, and more than 1000 incunabula and manuscripts. Restoration is in progress here and of the churches of S. Michele Arcangelo (the cloister of which is used as a theatre) and SS. Crispino e Crispiniano.

Via Casa Professa, with a street market, continues straight on to piazza Ballarò, the centre of the colourful market known since the Arab period as the **Mercato di Ballarò** (from the Arab *Suk-el-Bahlara*), when fruit and vegetables were brought into town through the nearby Porta S. Agata. This is part of the **Quartiere dell'Albergheria**, one of the poorest districts in the city, which was devastated by bombing in 1943. The colourful stalls stand out against a background of drab houses. Beyond, the church tower of **S. Nicolò** (map: 15; covered with scaffolding) can be seen, once part of the 14C fortifications of the town.

Via Ballarò continues left through the market to piazza del Carmine, with more stalls, above which towers the fantastic dome of the church of the **Carmine** with its telamones and colourful majolica tiles (1681). The interior (closed for restoration) contains altars in the transepts by Giuseppe and Giacomo Serpotta (1683–84), paintings (in the sanctuary) by Tommaso de Vigilia (late 15C), a statue of *St Catherine* by Antonello Gagini, and a *Madonna* by the Gagini School. Behind the church in via delle Mosche, Giuseppe Balsamo was born in 1743. Under the assumed title of Count Cagliostro, he travelled all over Europe professing skills as a physician and an alchemist until he was sentenced to life imprisonment for freemasonry by the Inquisition six years before he died in 1795. His story fascinated Goethe when he was in Palermo in 1787.

Via Musco and via Mugnosi lead to the church of the **Carminello** (open 09.00–17.00; Sat 09.00–13.00), built in 1605 and decorated with stuccoes at the end of the 17C and the beginning of the 18C. Those on the entrance wall have recently been attributed to Procopio Serpotta.

The straight via del Bosco leads away from the market back towards via Maqueda past some fine, but delapidated palaces (some of which are being restored). On the corner of via Maqueda is **Palazzo Comitini** by Nicolò Palma (1771). This is the seat of the province of Palermo and admission is granted when it is not in use. The 18C rococo interior has fine frescoed ceilings, Murano chandeliers and decorative mirrors.

On the opposite side of via Maqueda (to the right) is the long façade (mid-18C) of Palazzo S. Croce, which has a fine courtyard. Just beyond is the **Assunta** (open 09.00–12.00, 16.00–18.30; Sat & Sun mornings only), a convent church built in 1625–28 and richly decorated in the 18C with stuccoes by Giacomo Serpotta (the high altar and angels) and his bottega. The vault frescoes are by Filippo Tancredi. The marble intarsia pavement dates from 1638.

Returning towards the Quattro Canti via Maqueda passes, next to Palazzo Comitini, the church of **S. Orsola** (open 09.00–13.00), built in 1662. The interior was redecorated in the late 18C. The two last chapels on either side of the nave contain stuccoes by Giacomo Serpotta (1692), and (in the left chapel) an altarpiece of *St Jerome* by Zoppo di Ganci. A fine painting of the *Madonna and Child* (as Salvator Mundi) by Pietro Novelli is kept in the sacristy.

Farther on, on the opposite side of the road is the church of **S. Nicolò da Tolentino** (open weekdays 09.00–17.00; Sat 09.00–13.00), in the centre of a district where the Jews lived freely from the 9C onwards. However, Ferdinando of Spain expelled them from the city in 1492 and the synagogue here was destroyed, on the site of which the building of the church was begun in 1609. The two altarpieces in the transepts are by Pietro Novelli. The convent (which is being restored) houses the city archives.

Just beyond, via dei Calderai diverges right from via Roma. It leads to via Giovanni da Procida where the church of **S. Maria degli Agonizzanti** is situated (open 09.00–17.00; Sat & Sun mornings only), rebuilt in 1784. The polychrome marble high altar has reliefs by Ignazio Marabitti.

## San Francesco d'Assisi and the Galleria Regionale

Corso Vittorio Emanuele leads east from the Quattro Canti towards the sea. A short way along on the left is the fine Baroque church of **S. Matteo** (map: 11; open on weekdays at 17.00, and on Sun & PH at 10.30), recently restored. It was begun in 1633 by Mariano Smiriglio. It contains stucco statues by Giacomo Serpotta and frescoes by Vito d'Anna (1754).

The corso intersects with **via Roma**, one of the main thoroughfares of the city running north from the station. Its typical paving in porphyry dates from the late 19C.

### San Francesco d'Assisi

Beyond via Roma, the narrow via Paternostro (with numerous shops selling and repairing luggage) curves right towards the attractive piazza, recently repaved, in front of the 13C church of S. Francesco d'Assisi (map: 12; open 07.00–11.00, 16.00–18.00; Sun & PH 07.00–12.30, 16.00–18.00). The **façade** has a beautiful portal with three designs of zig-zag ornamentation (1302) and a lovely rose window.

*S. Francesco d'Assisi, Palermo*

**Interior** (with inconspicuous lights in most of the chapels). The church was damaged by an earthquake in 1823 and again during air raids in 1943, after which it was well restored. The Franciscan nave of 1255–77 is flanked by beautiful chapels added in the 14C–15C. Eight statues by Serpotta (1723) decorate the west door and nave.

**South aisle**. Above the door is a fine sculpted arch of 1465; in the second chapel there is an altarpiece of *St George and the dragon* in high relief and carved roundels by Antonello Gagini (1526); in the third chapel there is a *Madonna* attributed to Antonio Gagini flanked by 15C statues of *saints*. The Gothic fourth chapel contains a beautiful 15C *Madonna* by a Catalan sculptor and the sarcophagus of Elisabetta Omodei (1498) attributed to Domenico Gagini. Beyond the side door and another Gothic chapel is the sixth chapel with three bas-reliefs by Ignazio Marabitti (including the altar frontal). The seventh chapel has interesting 14C lava decoration on the arches.

The chapel to the right of the sanctuary has a fine polychrome marble intarsia decoration (17C–18C; carefully restored after war damage). The eight figures of Sicilian saints are by Giovanni Battista Ragusa (1717). The altarpiece of the *Immacolata* in mosaic is on a design by Vito d'Anna and below is an elaborate marble altar frontal. The **sanctuary** has fine choir stalls carved and inlaid in 1520 by Giovanni and Paolo Gili. The chapel to the left of the sanctuary has good marble decoration and an 18C wooden statue of *St Francis*.

**North aisle**. Eighth chapel: a bust of *St John* in polychrome terracotta, attributed to Antonello Gagini, has been replaced by a cast (it will be exhibited in the museum when it opens). The four statuettes of the *Virtues* are attributed to Pietro da Bonitate.

By the door into the sacristy there is a tomb effigy of the young warrior Antonio Speciale attributed to Domenico Gagini (1477) with a touching inscription above it. The fifth chapel has a 14C portal with zig-zag ornamentation and remains of early frescoes on the intrados. The fourth chapel, the **Cappella Mastrantonio** has an arch superbly sculpted by Francesco Laurana and Pietro da Bonitate (1468; restored in 1992), the earliest important Renaissance work in Sicily. On the left wall of the chapel, the *Madonna and saints* has been attributed to Vincenzo da Pavia.

In the second chapel a highly venerated silver statue of the *Immacolata* (1647) is hidden by a curtain, and the remains of a fresco of *St Francis* is on the left wall. In the first chapel (light on the right), with a fine 16C portal, is a *Madonna and Child with St John*, by Domenico Gagini (with a beautiful base), and a relief of the *Madonna*.

To the left of the church is the **Oratorio di S. Lorenzo** (entrance at no. 5 via Immacolatella; closed for restoration). The interior, designed by Giacomo Amato is decorated with stuccoes illustrating the lives of *St Lawrence* and *St Francis*, perhaps the masterpiece of Giacomo Serpotta (1699–1707). Ten symbolic statues, eight vivacious little reliefs, and the *Martyrdom of St Laurence* situated above the door, the whole encircled by a throng of joyous putti, make up a well-balanced and animated composition. The modelling of the male figures above the windows is especially skilful. Some of the statuettes have been stolen and others damaged since 1991, although apparently the interior is going to be restored.

The *Nativity*, by Caravaggio (1609; almost his last known work), which was stolen from the altar in 1969, has never been found. It is thought that the Mafia was responsible for the theft and that the painting may subsequently have been destroyed. The superb 18C mahogany benches with carved supports, and beautiful mother-of-pearl inlay, are no longer here.

In via Paternostro, opposite S. Francesco, is a *foccacceria,* a snack bar founded in 1834, with a charming old-fashioned interior. The huge **Palazzo Cattolica** (no. 48) has a double courtyard by Giacomo Amato (c 1720).

## Palazzo Mirto

Via Merlo leads out of the piazza to the right of the façade of S. Francesco. At no. 2 an 18C gateway leads into Palazzo Mirto (map: 12; open daily 09.00–13.30, 16.00–19.30; Sun & PH 09.00–12.30). The main façade on via Lungarini, with a double row of balconies, dates from 1793. The residence of the Lanza-Filangeri family since the early 17C, it was donated by them, together with its contents, to the region of Sicily in 1982. The well-kept interior is interesting as a typical example of a princely residence in Palermo with 18C and 19C decorations, including a little 'Chinese' room. The contents include furniture (mostly 18C and 19C), Capodimonte porcelain and Murano glass, etc. On the ground floor, near the delightful stables (1812), the funerary stele of Giambattista and Elisabetta Mellerio (c 1820) by Antonio Canova are displayed, purchased by the region of Sicily in 1978 to prevent them being exported.

Beyond, opposite **Palazzo Rostagno** (being restored) is the Renaissance church of **S. Maria dei Miracoli** (1547; the good interior has been closed indefinitely).

## Piazza Marina

S. Maria dei Miracoli overlooks the huge piazza Marina (map: 12), which was once a shallow inlet of the sea, and reclaimed in Saracen times. Here 16C Aragonese weddings and victories were celebrated by jousting, then later, in the proximity of two prisons (the Vicaria and that of the Inquisition), public executions were held here. The centre is occupied by the **Giardino Garibaldi**, with fine palms and fig-trees, and incredible huge old banyans. The garden was tidied up and surrounded by new railings and elegant lamp-posts in 1996 and the piazza has become animated again, with several pizzerie with tables outside. **Palazzo Galletti Marchesi di S. Cataldo** is a reconstruction incorporating some windows of a Renaissance palace (in the side street) which is being restored. Palazzo Burgio di Villafiorita nearby is also in the process of restoration.

At the end is the huge **Palazzo Chiaramonte**, known as **Lo Steri** (i.e.

Hosterium, or fortified palace), which was occupied by the law courts from 1799 until 1972. The building was restored in 1984 for the University Rector (sometimes open for concerts or exhibitions).

Begun in 1307 by the Chiaramonte family, it became the palace of the Spanish viceroys. From 1605–1782 it was the seat of the Inquisition; the graffiti which survive on the prison walls provide a fascinating historical record of the persecutions. The exterior, though deprived of its battlements, retains several of its original windows. Inside are two rooms with wooden ceilings painted by Simone da Corleone and Cecco di Naro (1377–80), in Saracenic style. The inner courtyard, surrounded by a loggia with pointed arches, has two fine three-light windows on the left. In the courtyard on the right of the palazzo is the charming façade of the chapel of S. Antonio Abate.

Beyond the last side of the square is the **Cala**, a shallow basin used as a mooring for the fishing fleet, all that remains of the ancient harbour which, until Norman times, extended far into the old town. There are three churches here. On the corner by the corso is the church of **S. Giovanni dei Napoletani** (1526–1617; open only on some days, usually Tues and Thurs afternoons). The harmonious interior has a magnificent contemporary organ by Raffaele La Valle, with its choir-loft decorated with 15 panels, perhaps the work of Vincenzo da Pavia, and a *St John the Baptist* by Zoppo di Ganci.

On the other side of the corso is the late 15C church of **S. Maria della Catena** (map: 12; open 09.00–17.00; Sat 09.00–13.00), probably the work of Matteo Carnelivari(1502–34). Its name *catena* (chain) probably comes from the chain that used to close the old port: it stretched from this bank across the harbour to Castello a Mare. There is also a legend that three innocent people were condemned in 1391 and as they passed the church their chains fell from their hands. A flight of steps leads up to the three-arched porch, which, with its two corner-pilasters, provides an ingenious combination of Gothic and Renaissance styles. The delicate carving of the three doorways is attributed to Vincenzo Gagini.

The elegant interior (open 09.00–17.00; Sat 09.00–13.00) has recently been beautifully restored. In the chapel on the right, inside a 16C baldacchino, is a lovely 14C fresco of the *Madonna and Child*, discovered in the 1980s. The four statues are by the school of the Gagini. In the second chapel is a late 15C relief of the *Madonna and Child with angels* from the church of S. Niccolò alla Calza. In a chapel with a 16C relief are frescoes by Olivio Sozzi. The east end is particularly beautiful with elaborate Gothic decoration and double columns. There is a Roman sarcophagus here.

The Renaissance church of **S. Maria di Porto Salvo** (closed), was mutilated in the replanning of 1564. It was begun in c 1527 by Antonello Gagini and the interior was completed by Antonio Scaglione.

In the corner of the piazza is the **Fontana del Garraffo** (designed by Paolo Amato in 1698), recently restored and surrounded by a little garden protected by railings in a clump of trees.

The lower end of the corso, the Cassaro Morto, was virtually destroyed in 1943; the **Fontana del Cavallo Marino**, with a sea horse by Ignazio Marabitti, is now surrounded by palm trees and protected by a fence. The reconstructed **Porta Felice** (1582–1637) has no arch between the two monumental pillars so that the procession with the tall vara (or 'float') of St Rosalia could pass through it on her festival. The long 17C façade of the damaged **Palazzo Butera** stands above the terraced **Mura delle Cattive**, which are being restored.

Outside the walls is the **Foro Italico** (map: 12), a wide thoroughfare always busy with traffic, which runs along the seafront, with a splendid view of Monte Pellegrino. This was once a fashionable esplanade: part of the huge area to seaward, reclaimed by pouring in war debris has been planted with palm trees. The bandstand here is being restored.

## Museo Internazionale delle Marionette

Just out of the piazza here, at no. 1 via Butera, is the Museo Internazionale delle Marionette (map: 12; ring the bell; open daily 09.00–13.00, 16.00–19.00; except Sat afternoon, Sun & PH), founded in 1975, with a delightful collection of puppets from Sicily and Naples, as well as puppets, marionettes, glove puppets and shadow puppets from all over the world.

Sicily has long been famous for its **puppet theatres**, known as the *opera dei pupi*. The traditional performances illustrate the chivalrous episodes in the lives of the paladins of Charlemagne's court, through the various heroic deeds of Orlando, Rinaldo, Astolfo and others who pitted their strength against the Saracens, and sought to protect the fair Angelica. Each character became a familiar personality whose adventures were well known but relived with every new performance.

In the 18C and 19C the most important puppet theatres on the island were in Palermo and Catania, which differed from each other in several respects. In Palermo, the puppets were between 80cm and 1m high, weighed about 8kg and had articulated knees. Each theatre owned about 100 puppets and about 70 different backcloths. In Catania, the puppets were between 1.10m and 1.3m high, weighed about 25kg and the knee was not articulated. Each theatre owned about 50 puppets and about 500 different backcloths. Puppet shows are held in the small theatre here, usually in November and December. There are still a few puppet theatres in the town which give delightful traditional performances (for information, ask at the APT).

The museum also has beautifully displayed puppets from Africa, the New Hebrides, Vietnam, Korea, Burma, China, India, Rajastan, shadow puppets from Malaysia, Cambodia, and Java, and even Professor Jingles' Punch and Judy theatre from England. There is a room where children can play and make their own puppets.

## Santa Maria della Pietà

Via Butera continues (past a plaque on a wing of Palazzo Butera recording Goethe's stay here in a hotel on this site in 1787) to the church of S. Maria della Pietà, with a splendid Baroque **façade** by Giacomo Amato (1678–84). The **interior** (map: 12; open 08.00–12.00, 16.00–19.00) is a particularly striking example of local Baroque architecture. The delightful vestibule has stuccoes by Procopio Serpotta and frescoes by Borremans: it supports a splendid nuns' choir. Four cantorie in gilded wood decorate the nave. The fresco in the vault is by

Antonio Grano (1708). On the south side, the first altar has a painting of Dominican saints by Antonio and Francesco Manno, and the second altar a *Madonna of the Rosary* by Olivio Sozzi. The high altar has a tabernacle in lapis lazuli. On the north side, the third altar has a *Pietà* (in a good frame) by Vincenzo da Pavia and the second altar, *St Dominic* by Olivio Sozzi.

## Galleria Regionale della Sicilia

At no. 4 via Alloro is Palazzo Abatellis (formerly called Palazzo Patella; map: 12), designed in 1488–95 by Matteo Carnelivari for Francesco Abatellis, appointed 'master-pilot' (or admiral) of Sicily by the Spaniards, in a style combining elements of the Renaissance with late Catalan Gothic. Much altered internally during its occupation by Dominican nuns from 1526 until 1943, when it was damaged by bombs, the palace was freely restored in 1954 as the home of the Galleria Regionale della Sicilia, with a fine collection of Sicilian sculpture and paintings (open daily 09.00–13.30; Tues, Thurs, Fri also 15.00–19.00; Sun & PH 09.00–12.30). The exhibits are well documented and have been beautifully selected and arranged, gaining much from their appropriate surroundings.

### Ground floor

A doorway of original design leads out to the pleasant courtyard. The ground floor is devoted principally to **sculpture**. A door on the left leads into **room 1**. On display here are some 16C wooden sculptures, a 12C Arab door frame carved in wood and a painting of the *Madonna with saints* from the workshop of Tommaso de Vigilia. Beyond, **room 2**, the former **chapel** is dominated by a famous large fresco of the *Triumph of Death*, detached from Palazzo Sclafani. Dating from c 1449 it is of uncertain attribution, thought by some scholars to be a Sicilian work and by others to be by Pisanello or his school. Death is portrayed as an archer on a spectral horse, piercing the contented and successful (*right*) with his arrows, while the unhappy and aged (*left*), among whom are the painter and a pupil, pray in vain for release.

A corridor (**3**) containing Saracenic ceramics, including a magnificent majolica vase of Hispano-Moresque type (13C–14C) from Mazara del Vallo, and a fragment of a wooden ceiling (Siculo-Arabic, 12C) from Palazzo dei Normanni, leads to three rooms devoted to **late 15C and early 16C sculpture**. **Room 4** contains works by **Francesco Laurana**, principally a **bust of Eleonora of Aragon**, his masterpiece. The bust of a young boy here has recently been attributed to Domenico Gagini (c 1469), who also sculpted (with assistants) the *Madonna del Latte*. **Room 5** is devoted to the Gagini; notable are a marble statuette of the *Madonna and Child*, the Tabernacle of the Ansalone, with the *Madonna del Buon Riposo* (1528), and the head of a young boy, all by Antonello Gagini, and the *Madonna della Neve* (1516) by his workshop. In **room 6** there are architectural fragments, including carved capitals.

### First floor

The first floor is reached by a staircase from **room 6** or from the courtyard. It contains the **Pinacoteca**, with its wonderful series of **Sicilian paintings**, including 13C–14C works, still in the Byzantine manner, and later works showing the influence of various schools (Umbrian, Sienese, Catalan, and Flemish): **room 7** (left) contains the *Raising of Lazarus* and *Christ in Limbo*, two small paintings, perhaps Venetian, of the 13C; a painted 13C Crucifix; *Madonna* in mosaic in a Byzantine style (early 14C); Antonio Veneziano, *Madonna and Child*; Bartolommeo da Camogli, *Madonna dell'Umiltà* (1346). In **room 8** (left) are paintings of the late 14C and early 15C. Giovanni di Pietro, *St Nicholas*; Turino Vanni, *Madonna and saints*; Master of the Trapani Polyptych, *Madonna del Fiore*; Gera da Pisa, *Sts George and Agatha*.

Beyond a short corridor is **room 9** which contains **Sicilian paintings of the early 15C**, including several *Coronations of the Virgin* by the same unknown master, and works by the 'Master of the Trapani Polyptych'. **Room 10**. **late 15C**. Paintings and frescoes by Tommaso de Vigilia; Pietro Ruzzolone, *Crucifix*; *Coronation of the Virgin*, a polyptych from Corleone, by an unknown hand. In a little room off the hall, 16C custodia from Palermo. Beyond, in **room 11**, is a precious collection of works by **Antonello da Messina**, including his masterpiece, ***Virgin Annunciate***, and *Sts Gregory, Augustine* and *Jerome*; also, *Madonna*, attributed to Marco Basaiti.

**Room 12**, the upper half of the chapel, overlooks the *Triumph of Death* (see above), and is devoted mainly to Riccardo Quartararo, notably *Sts Peter and Paul* and *Coronation of the Virgin*. Also here is a 15C–16C *Pietà* of wood. A number of 16C works of uncertain attribution are displayed in **room 13**: these include Master of the Pentecost, *Pietà* and *Pentecost*; Andrea da Salerno's *Sts John the Baptist and John the Evangelist*; and a copy (1538) by Antonello Crescenzio of Raphael's Spasimo (formerly in the church of S. Maria dello Spasimo, see below).

**Room 14** is devoted to 15C–16C **Flemish paintings**: an *Annunciation*, in the style of the master of Flémalle; Mabuse, Malvagna Triptych of the *Virgin and Child between Sts Catherine and Barbara* (on the outside, *Adam and Eve*), a painting of extraordinary detail; works of the 16C Antwerp and Bruges schools. **Room 15** (left). Jan van Scorel, *St Mary Magdalen*; Tuscan school (dated 1563), portrait of a young man. **Room 16** is devoted mainly to works by Vincenzo da Pavia: *Deposition, St Conrad the Hermit* and two scenes from the *Life of the Virgin*. **Room 17**: Giuseppe Cesari, *Andromeda*; Mattia Preti, *Christ and the Centurion*; Pietro Novelli, *Communion of St Mary of Egypt*; Van Dyck (copy), *Madonna*, his early masterpiece; Leandro Bassano, portrait of a man; Palma Giovane, *Deposition*.

## La Gancia

Next to Palazzo Abatellis is the 15C church called La Gancia (map: 12), or S. Maria degli Angeli, entered by the side door (open 09.00–12.00, 15.30–18.00; Sun & PH 09.00–12.00). The fine exterior dates from the 15C.

In the **interior** (lights in each chapel) the wooden ceiling and fine organ (over the west door; perhaps by Raffaele La Valle) date from the transformation begun in 1672. **South side**: in the second chapel (right) are Antonello Crescenzio, *Madonna with Sts Catherine and Agatha* (signed and dated 1528, removed for restoration), Pietro Novelli (attributed), *Holy Family*; in the fourth chapel: Antonello Gagini (attributed), seated *Madonna* (the head of the Christ Child is modern); fifth and sixth chapels, inlaid marble panels with scenes of the *Flight into Egypt*: outside is a pulpit made up of fragments of sculpture by the Gagini. The chapel on the right of the choir has fine marble decoration and stuccoes by Giacomo Serpotta. On the choir-piers are two delicately carved *Annunciations* attributed to Antonello Gagini.

In the chapel to the left of the choir are more stuccoes by Serpotta, and a

*Marriage of the Virgin* by Vincenzo da Pavia (removed for restoration). **North transept**: on the wall (high up), *St Francis* by Zoppo di Ganci. **North side**: in the sixth chapel are two fine reliefs (one of the *Descent into Limbo*) by Antonello Gagini; in the third chapel, Pietro Novelli, *S. Pietro d'Alcantara* and in the second chapel, Vincenzo da Pavia, *Nativity*.

The adjoining convent is famous in the annals of the revolution of 4 April 1860 against Neapolitan rule. Its bell gave the signal to the insurgents; Francesco Riso, their leader, was mortally wounded; 13 were captured and shot; while two hid for five days in the vaults of the church, before escaping through the *Buca della Salvezza*, a hole in the wall next to Palazzo Abatellis.

The nearby Kalsa district with the church of Lo Spasimo, Villa Giulia and the Orto Botanico, are all described in the next itinerary below. **Via Alloro**, a narrow old street with some delapidated palaces, continues back from the church of La Gancia towards the centre of the city. Opposite the church Palazzo Palagonia is being restored as offices and flats. At no. 54, some way along on the left, stood **Palazzo Bonagia**, which was almost totally destroyed in the last war. The remarkable Baroque staircase in the courtyard, attributed to Andrea Giganti, survives, propped up by scaffolding behind a closed gateway.

Beyond, on the right, is the church of the **Madonna dell'Itria dei Cocchieri** (map: 12; open 8.30–15.30; Sat 09.00–13.00), once the seat of the confraternity of coachmen. It was built in 1596 and has a crypt or burial chamber with 18C frescoes (not at present open). The confraternity, dressed in coachmen's livery (examples of which are preserved in the church) still carry the statue of the *Madonna Addolorata* (also kept here) through the streets of Palermo in the procession on Good Friday. Via Alloro ends in piazza Aragona, described below.

## The Kalsa district

From the seaward end of via Alloro (see above) via Torremuzza leads past the church of the **Crociferi** or **S. Mattia** (which is covered in scaffolding and has been under restoration since 1995), by Giacomo Amato. Farther on is the façade (1686–1706) of the church of **S. Teresa**, also by Amato, and one of his best works. It is also closed for restoration. In the interior, on the south side: the first altar contains Giovanni Odazzi's *Holy Family* (1720); and the second altar Ignazio Marabitti's marble *Crucifixion* group (1780–81). The high altarpiece is by Gaspare Serenario (1746) and the two statues of female saints in the sanctuary are by Giacomo Serpotta. North side: the second altarpiece is by Guglielmo Borremans (1722) and the first altarpiece by Sebastiano Conca.

The church faces **piazza della Kalsa** (from the Arabic *khalisa*, meaning 'pure'), with a little garden. This was one of the oldest parts of the city fortified by the Arabs in 938. Here the remains of the 19C Palazzo Forcella are built on the bastions facing the sea. The **Quartiere della Kalsa** (map: 16) is a very poor district of the city, badly damaged by bombs in World War II.

Via Niccolò Cervello ends at viale Lincoln across which is the entrance to **Villa Giulia** (map: 16), or La Flora, a delightful garden laid out in 1777, with beautiful trees and flowers, much admired by Goethe in 1787. The monuments are being restored. In the centre are four *prospetti*, or niches in the Pompeian style, and a sundial fountain; towards the sea is another statue of the *Genius of Palermo*, by Marabitti.

The **Orto Botanico**, adjoining the Villa, is remarkable for its subtropical vegetation (open 09.00–12.30; Sat 09.00–11.00; closed Sun & PH; entered by the side gate). The entrance pavilion was built in the Greek Doric style in 1789 by Léon Dufourny; Marvuglia worked on the decoration and added the side wings. The botanical garden, one of the best in Europe, was laid out by Filippo Parlatore, the important Italian botanist who was born in Palermo. It was opened to the public here in 1795. It has ficus trees, bamboo, date palms, lotus trees and tropical plants from all over the world. The circular water-lily pond dates from 1796.

From beside the church of S. Teresa (see above) via S. Teresa and via dello Spasimo lead away from the sea through the Kalsa district to the former church and convent of **Lo Spasimo**, beautifully restored as a cultural centre for exhibitions, concerts and theatre performances (opened daily 09.00–24.00 by a group of young Palermitans). It has justly become the symbol of the city's 'rebirth' in the last decade. Founded in 1509, the church and convent were never completed as the area was taken over by the Spanish viceroy in a general plan of strengthening the city's defences. In 1573 the convent was sold to the Senate and the church was used as a theatre after 1582, and again at the end of the 17C. Part of the convent was used as an isolation hospital for plague vicitims in 1624, and in the 19C and 20C as a general hospital. Over the centuries the buildings have been used as warehouses, a deposit for the snow brought down from the mountains used for making ice-creams, and stores for the debris after the bombardments of World War II. After the hospital was finally closed in 1986 a remarkable restoration programme, still in progress, was begun in 1988.

Beyond the 16C cloister is the huge church of **S. Maria dello Spasimo** (roofless except for the beautiful Gothic apse vault) which has been cleaned up, leaving a few trees growing in the nave. It is used for theatre performances and concerts. In 1516 Raphael was commissioned to paint an altarpiece of *Jesus falling beneath the Cross* (which came to be known as *Lo Spasimo di Sicilia*) for this church. After an adventurous journey, during which, according to Vasari, the painting was lost at sea in a shipwreck, but subsequently refound on the shore near Genoa, it was finally installed here in 1520. However, the Spanish viceroy presented it to Philip IV of Spain in 1661 and it is now in the Prado in Madrid. The original frame by Antonello Gagini is to be re-installed here, having been found recently in a villa garden in Bagheria and restored by the Fondo per l'Ambiente Italiano.

Beyond the church is a little public **garden** with pine, eucalyptus and palm trees on the bastions, and another chapel used for exhibitions.

Just beyond the Spasimo is the huge **piazza Magione**, really a bomb site left from World War II. After years of neglect it is being carefully paved. In the centre, between two agaves, is a small memorial plaque to Giovanni Falcone, who was born in this area in 1939. It was set up by the city of Palermo in 1995 'in gratitude and admiration' for this courageous magistrate who was assassinated by the Mafia in 1992. At the beginning of via Castrofilippo is the little **Teatro Garibaldi**, built in 1861, and visited by Garibaldi himself in 1862. Once used for the performance of popular comedies, it was acquired by the Comune of Palermo in 1983 and has recently been saved from total ruin by a group of Palermitans, but is in urgent need of restoration.

## La Magione

Also on this side of the piazza is the fine Norman apse of the church of La Magione (map: 16; open 08.00–11.30, 16.00–18.30; Sun & PH 08.30–13.00) which stands in majestic isolation, painstakingly restored since the bombs in World War II devastated the neighbourhood. It was founded by Matteo d'Aiello before 1151 as the Chiesa della Trinità for the Cistercians, but transferred to the Teutonic knights in 1193 by the Emperor Henry VI as their mansion, from which it takes its name. It is a precious example of Arab Norman architecture.

The **façade** has three handsome and very unusual doorways. The beautiful tall **interior** has a fine apse decorated with six small columns. Above the 14C stone altar hangs a painted *Crucifix*. The contents include statues of *Christ* and the *Madonna and Child* by the Gagini school, a 15C marble triptych, and a tabernacle of 1528. The custodian shows the charming little Cistercian **cloister** (c 1190) around a garden; one walk with twin columns and carved capitals has survived. A room off the cloister contains a detached 15C fresco of the *Crucifixion* with its sinopia. Outside is a delightful garden of palm trees and a monumental 17C gateway on via Magione.

Via Magione leads to **via Garibaldi**, a dilapidated street with some handsome palaces and numerous balconies. Here is the huge **Palazzo Aiutamicristo**, built by Matteo Carnelivari in 1490, with Catalan-Gothic elements (doorway at no. 41; the courtyard, in a sad state of disrepair, is entered from no. 23). Here Charles V was entertained on his return from Tunis in 1535. Via Garibaldi, and its continuation corso dei Mille mark the route followed by Garibaldi on his entry into the city. At the end is **piazza della Rivoluzione**, the scene of the outbreak of the rebellion of 1848, inspired by Giuseppe La Masa. Here is another bizarre fountain of the *Genius of Palermo*. Near the 16C **Palazzo Scavuzzo** is the church of **S. Carlo** (1643–48) with an elliptical interior (closed). Beyond is piazza Aragona at the top of via Alloro (see above).

The other end of piazza Aragona leads into piazza della Croce dei Vespri, where the graves of many French victims of the Vespers were marked in 1737 by a cross (the copy here, set up in 1873, has been broken). Two sides of the piazza are occupied by the fine 18C **Palazzo Valguarnera-Ganci**, with pretty balconies, still owned by the family. The lovely courtyard with trees is an oasis for birds. Visconti used the sumptuous *Salone degli Specchi* here for the setting of the scene of the great ball in his film *Il Gattopardo*, based on the novel by Giuseppe di Lampedusa. The Art Nouveau palace in the piazza has an amusing portal and balcony.

Nearby is the church of **S. Anna**, with a fine Baroque façade begun in 1726 by Giovanni Biagio Amico, with sculptures by Giacomo Pennino and Lorenzo Marabitti, on designs by Giacomo Serpotta. The **interior** dates from 1606–36. On the west wall are two paintings by Giuseppe Albina. South aisle: the second chapel contains a 17C altarpiece of the *Holy Family* and two good paintings from the life of the *Virgin*. The third chapel has a 17C painting of *St Rosalia* with a view of Monte Pellegrino and the port. In the south transept there are frescoes by Filippo Tancredi. In the sanctuary is a 16C organ case. The convent of S. Anna della Miscricordia is being restored.

Via Roma leads back (right) to corso Vittorio Emanuele and the Quattro Canti.

## San Domenico and the Museo Archeologico Regionale

From the Quattro Canti corso Vittorio Emanuele (described above) leads towards the sea. Take via Roma left past (right) the church of **S. Antonio** (map: 11) which occupies the highest point of the eastern part of the old city. The 14C campanile was lowered in height at the end of the 16C, and the church reconstructed after the earthquake of 1823 in the Chiaramonte style of the original.

The maze of small streets below is the scene of a busy daily market known as the **Vucciria** (map: 11; the area around piazza Caracciolo, piazza Garraffello, etc.) where produce of all kinds is sold on the streets, including fish. It is one of the most colourful sights in the city. The streets here were repaved in 1997. In **piazza Garraffello**, which has a fountain, is **Palazzo Lo Mazzarino**, still owned by the family. Many of its precious contents were stolen in 1989. It has pretty balconies but is abandoned and in urgent need of repair.

The market extends along via dei Cassari passing the 18C church of **S. Maria del Lume,** designed by Salvatore Marvuglia. From piazza Garraffello via Materassai leads to the piazza in front of the 16C church of **S. Maria la Nuova** (open 09.00–17.00; Sat 09.00–13.00) with a Catalan Gothic porch (the upper storey was added in the 19C in neo-Gothic style). The fine interior contains stuccoes in the presbytery and 18C paintings. Close by, towards the sea, can be seen the well-sited late Renaissance façade of **S. Sebastiano**. In the interior (closed) there are 18C polychrome marble altars, stuccoes by Giacomo Serpotta (1692) and 18C frescoes.

Via G. Meli leads away from the sea back up towards via Roma and piazza S. Domenico, in the middle of which rises the Colonna dell'Immacolata by Giovanni d'Amico (1724–27), crowned by a *Madonna* by Giovanni Battista Ragusa.

### San Domenico

The large church of S. Domenico (map: 11; open 07.30–12.00; Sat and Sun also 17.00–19.00), rebuilt in 1640, has a tall façade of 1726 (being restored). Since the middle of the last century the church has served as a burial place for illustrious Sicilians.

**Interior**. South aisle: on the left wall of the first chapel is the funerary monument of Francesco Maria Emanuele di Villabianca by Leonardo Pennino(1802). In the second chapel, there is an altarpiece of the *Crucifixion* by Paolo Fondulli (1573); in the third chapel there is a fine marble decoration on a design by Gaspare Serpotta and a very fine **statue of St Joseph** by Antonio Gagini. Beyond is the fourth chapel with an altarpiece attributed to Rosario Novelli. The fifth chapel has the funerary monument of Enrico Amari, by Domenico Costantini (1875). The sixth chapel has a painting of *St Vincent Ferrer* by Giuseppe Velasquez (1787).

**South transept**. The altarpiece of *St Dominic* is by Filippo Paladino, and on the left wall there is a monument to Giovanni Ramondetta by Giacomo Serpotta and Gerardo Scudo (1691). In the chapel to the right of the sanctuary is a good bas-relief of *St Catherine* attributed to Antonello Gagini, a neo-classical monument by Benedetto de Lisi (1864), a relief of the *Trinity* (1477) by Rinaldo Bartolomeo, and a small *Pietà* in high relief by Antonello Gagini and a pretty little stoup. The two fine organs date from 1781; beneath the one on the right is a small Turrisi Colonna funerary monument, with a female figure by Antonio Canova.

The **sanctuary** has 18C choir stalls. The chapel to the left of the sanctuary has Gaginesque reliefs including a tondo of *St Dominic*, and the tomb of Ruggero Settimo (1778–1863), who convened the Sicilian parliament in this church in 1848. **North transept** On either side of the altarpiece by Vincenzo da Pavia are funerary monuments by Ignazio Marabitti.

**North aisle**. The tomb of Pietro Novelli, the painter (1608–47), is situated here. In the fourth chapel is an altarpiece of *St Raimondo* by Filippo Paladino; third chapel: on the left is a statue of *St Catherine* by Antonello Gagini (1528), with reliefs on the base, and on the right, a statue of *St Barbara* by his school. The second chapel has a terracotta statue of *St Catherine of Siena*, and the first chapel an altarpiece by Andrea da Trapani. On the left is a Lancellotti funerary monument by Leonardo Pennino (1870), and on the right a tomb by Valerio Villareale. The fragmentary 14C **cloister**, which was part of the first church built on this site by the Dominicans, has been restored.

Behind the church, in an area with numerous jewellery shops, in via Bambinai, is the **Oratorio del Rosario di S. Domenico** (ring for the custodian at the shop at no. 16 via Bambinai; fee). It contains an **altarpiece** by Van Dyck, representing the *Virgin of the Rosary with St Dominic and the patronesses of Palermo*. The artist painted it in Genoa in 1628 having left Palermo because of the plague. The wall-paintings of the *Mysteries* are by Novelli, Lo Verde, Stomer, Luca Giordano and Borremans. Giacomo Serpotta's graceful **stuccoes** (1720) display amazing skill. Statues of elegant society ladies represent various allegorical virtues. The black and white ceramic floor is also well preserved.

In its fine piazza the church of **S. Maria di Valverde** was built in 1635 (restored in 1997; open 09.00–17.00, Sat 09.00–13.00) by Mariano Smiriglio. It has a grey marble side portal, and a campanile rebuilt in 1723. Its sumptuous Baroque interior (1694–1716), decorated with polychrome *marmi mischi*, was designed by Paolo Amato and Andrea Palma. On the high altar is an 18C wooden statue of the *Madonna of the Rosary*.

The street continues as via Squarcialupo. The next large church on the left is **S. Cita** (or S. Zita; map: 11; open 09.00–13.30, 14.30–17.00), rebuilt in 1586–1603 (but damaged in 1943). The interior contains fine but damaged **sculptures** by Antonello Gagini (1517–27). In the apse behind the altar is a huge marble tabernacle surrounded by a magnificent arch, both superbly carved. In the second chapel on the left of the choir is the sarcophagus of Antonio Scirotta, also by Gagini; and more sculptures by the same artist are in the second chapel (Platamone) on the right of the choir. The chapel of the Rosary has splendid polychrome marble decoration (1696–1722) and sculpted reliefs by Gioacchino Vitaliano.

Adjoining the left side of the church is the **Oratorio del Rosario di S. Cita** (or Zita; now usually entered through the church, open 09.00–17.00, Sat 09.00–13.00; closed Sun & PH), reconstructed in the early 17C. It is approached through a little garden and loggia.

The stucco decoration of the exquisite **interior** is one of Giacomo Serpotta's finest: between 1685 and 1688 he worked on the nave and in 1717on the apse. On the entrance wall there is an elaborate representation of the *Battle of Lepanto* which commemorates the victory over the Turks in which the Christian fleet was protected by the *Madonna of the Rosary* (the confraternity of the Rosary had been founded just before the battle in 1571). On the two side walls are New Testament scenes in high relief representing the 15 *Mysteries of the Rosary* between numerous seated allegorical statues. The decorative frames and stucco drapes are supported by hundreds of delightful putti. The altarpiece of the *Madonna of the Rosary* (1702) is by Carlo Maratta. The ebony benches were decorated with mother-of-pearl inlay in 1702.

Nearly opposite S. Cita is the fine 14C doorway of the Conservatorio di Musica. Beyond is the isolated church of **S. Giorgio dei Genovesi** (map: 7, 8; deconsecrated and at present only open for exhibitions, but soon to be opened regularly 09.00–17.00; Sat 09.00–13.00; Sun & PH closed), a church built for the Genoese sea captains by Giorgio di Faccio in 1576–91. It has a graceful façade. The aisled interior is in the purest Renaissance style. Marble tomb-slabs (17C and 18C) cover the floor of the nave. It contains paintings attributed to Luca Giordano, Bernardo Castello of Genoa and by Palma Giovane.

Beyond lies piazza delle Tredici Vittime, where an obelisk commemorates 13 patriots shot by the Bourbons on 14 April 1860. A huge steel stele, 30m high, was set up here in 1989 to commemorate victims of the struggle against the Mafia. A fence protects recent excavations of 10C Arab buildings, and part of the Norman fortifications of the city (restored in the 16C).

To the south-east lies the Cala (see above). Across the busy via Francesco Crispi are remains of the fortress of **Castello a Mare**, used in the 12C as a prison, and from the 13C onwards as a barracks. It was partially restored in 1988–91 (and is usually open on Tues 09.00–13.00 and Wed 09.00–13.00, 14.30–18.00). Nearby there are remains of an Arab tower.

In via Cavour, on the other side of piazza XIII Vittime, is **Villa Whitaker** (1885; now used by the Prefecture), surrounded by a garden. This was one of two properties in Palermo owned by the Whitaker brothers, sons of Joseph Whitaker (1802–84) who had purchased Villa Sofia near La Favorita. They were members of the English family descended from the Inghams, famous Marsala wine merchants. This villa was built by Joshua Whitaker (brother of 'Pip' who owned Villa Malfitano) and his wife Effie, in Venetian Gothic style and the garden was planted with palms and conifers.

In front of piazza S. Domenico (see above), across via Roma, the narrow via Monteleone leads up behind the huge post office (1933) to (no. 50) the **Oratorio di S. Caterina d'Alessandria**. The oratory has been owned by the Knights of the Holy Sepulchre of Jerusalem since 1946 and is at present only open on Thurs (12.00–14.45). The interior has fine stuccoes by Serpotta's son, Procopio (1719–26). It also contains two paintings by Zoppo di Ganci, and a *Madonna and Child* by Vincenzo da Pavia above a bench inlaid with ivory and mother of pearl. The polychrome marble floor dates from 1730.

Just beyond is the church of **S. Ignazio all'Olivella** (map: 11; open 08.30–11.00, 18.00–19.00; Sun & PH 09.00–12.30), begun in 1598, with a good 17C façade. The fine **interior** has a barrel vault designed by Venanzio Marvuglia (1772) with frescoes by Antonio Manno (1790). South aisle: first chapel, Filippo Paladino, *St Mary of Egypt*; the second chapel has beautiful 17C decorations in *marmi mischi*. In the south transept, altarpiece by Filippo Paladino. The high altarpiece of the *Trinity* is by Sebastiano Conca and in the sanctuary are two statues by Ignazio Marabitti. In the north transept is an interesting altarpiece, of unusual design, of the *martyrdom of St Ignatius* by Filippo Paladino. (1613). North aisle: the fifth chapel was sumptuously decorated in 1622 and has an altarpiece of *St Philip Neri* by Sebastiano Conca (1740) and two statues by Giovanni Battista Ragusa. The third chapel is also elaborately decorated with polychrome marble and precious stones and an altar frontal in relief. The small fresco in the vault of the *Pietà* is by Pietro Novelli. In the first chapel the altarpiece of the *Archangel Gabriel* is by Pietro Novelli.

In the piazza is the façade, by Filippo Pennino, of the **Oratorio di S. Ignazio Olivella** or **di S. Filippo Neri** (open 08.30–11.00: Sun & PH 09.30–11.00). It has an interesting neo-classical interior of 1769 by Venanzio Marvuglia, with splendid columns and good capitals by Filippo Pennino. It is lit by pretty chandeliers. In the presbytery there is an elaborate sculpture with angels and cherubs by Ignazio Marabitti.

## Museo Archeologico Regionale

Adjoining the church is the former monastery of the Filippini, now the seat of the Museo Archeologico Regionale (map: 7), one of the most interesting collections in Italy, illustrating the history of western Sicily from prehistoric times to the Roman era. It is arranged around two charming 17C cloisters, but is a little bit shabby, with some of the exhibits in need of cleaning, and the labelling is poor. It is open 09.00–14.00; Tues, Wed and Fri, also 15.00–19.00; Sat & Sun 09.00–12.30.

The rooms are numbered in the text and on the plans in their logical sequence. The collection was formed at the beginning of the 19C when it belonged to the university. During the century it acquired various collections, including that of Casuccini, the most important collection of Etruscan material outside Tuscany. It also houses finds from excavations in the western part of the island, notably those of Selinunte.

### Ground floor

In the centre of the **chiostro minore** is a triton from a 16C fountain. Off this cloister (right) **room 2** is used for exhibitions. **Rooms 3** and **4** contain **Egyptian and Punic sculpture**.

In **room 3** are two Phoenician sarcophagi of the 5C BC found near Palermo. In the centre of **room 4** is a male torso of the 6C BC: on the wall, the *Pietra di Palermo*, a black diorite slab whose hieroglyphic inscription records the delivery of 40 shiploads of cedarwood to Pharaoh Snefru (c 2700 BC); Punic inscription to the sun god Baal-Hammon, on white stone from Lilybaeum; male figure (4C BC) of Egyptian type.

The pretty **chiostro maggiore** (**5**) has palms and flower-beds and a papyrus pool in the centre. In the arcades are Roman fragments: in niches: Zeus enthroned (**6**), derived from a Greek type of 4C BC, and a colossal statue of the emperor Claudius (**8**), both restored by Villareale; also an interesting funerary stele with three portrait busts (40–30 BC). On the right: sarcophagi, cippi and stelae. At the far end, **room 9** has Greek inscriptions, the majority

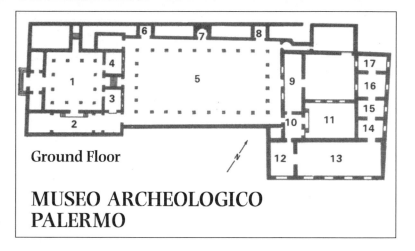

**Ground Floor**

# MUSEO ARCHEOLOGICO PALERMO

from Selinunte. **Room 10** contains stelae from Selinunte, and a dedicatory inscription to Apollo from Temple G. Steps lead down to **room 11** in which fragments of Temple C have been gathered; part of the entablature has been assembled. **Room 12** contains a cornice of lion head **water-spouts** from the Doric temple of Victory at Himera (2nd quarter of 5C BC), discovered by Pirro Marconi in 1929–30.

**Room 13** contains the famous **metopes of Selinunte**, the most important treasures of the museum. These sculpted panels once decorated the friezes of the temples at Selinunte, and they show the development in the skill of the local sculptors from the early 6C BC to the end of the 5C BC. On either side of the entrance are three delicate female heads and fragmentary reliefs from Temple E. Beneath the windows are six small **Archaic metopes**, sculptured in low relief, from an early 6C temple, perhaps destroyed by the people of Selinunte themselves to repair their citadel, in the time of Dionysius the Elder (397–392 BC). They represent scenes with *Demeter and Kore* (one with a quadriga), three deities, a winged sphinx, the *Rape of Europa*, and *Hercules and the Cretan bull*. Facing the windows is a reconstruction, incorporating original fragments, of a frieze and cornice with three triglyphs and three fine **Archaic metopes** from **Temple C** (early 6C), representing a *quadriga*; *Perseus, protected by Athene, beheading the Gorgon*; and *Herakles punishing the pigmies Cercopes*. Also on this wall are parts of two metopes from **Temple F**, with scenes from the *gigantomachia* (5C BC). Opposite the entrance, four splendid **Classical metopes** from **Temple E** (early 5C) show *Herakles fighting an amazon*, the *wedding of Zeus and Hera*, the *punishment of Actaeon*, who is attacked by dogs in the presence of Artemis and Athene overcoming a titan.

**Rooms 14–17** contain the Casuccini collection of **Etruscan antiquities** from Chiusi. Particularly interesting are the urns and tombs in high relief, a number of panels with delicately carved bas-reliefs (many with traces of painting), and a magnificent oinochoe of bucchero ware (6C BC) portraying the story of *Perseus and Medusa*, perhaps the finest vase of its kind in existence.

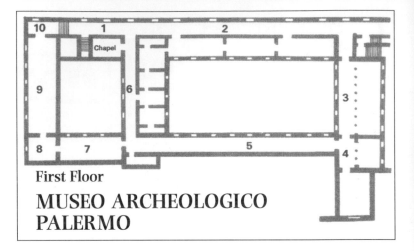

First Floor
# MUSEO ARCHEOLOGICO PALERMO

### First floor

The first floor is reached from the small cloister. The long **north gallery** (**rooms 1 and 2**) displays **finds from Greek and Roman sites in western Sicily**, arranged topographically. Selinunte, Lilybaeum, Randazzo, the Lípari Islands and Marsala are especially well represented. Between the cases, containing vases, terracottas, bronzes, etc., are sepulchral stelae from Marsala painted with portraits of the deceased, and sections of lead water-pipes, showing junction points and stop-cocks, from the Cornelian aqueduct at Termini Imerese. **Room 3** contains terracotta figures, mainly from Gela, Himera, and Palazzolo Acreide. In **room 4** are more terracottas and a 5C kylix fished from the sea off Termini Imerese. The long **south gallery** (**5**) contains some of the 12,000 terracotta votive figures found in the sanctuary of Demeter at Selinunte which demonstrate their chronology by the evolution of their design. The **west gallery** (**6**) contains some of the more important recent finds from sites in Palermo (fine vases).

A few steps lead up to **room 7** with **large Roman bronzes**. The famous **ram** is a superb sculpture dating from the 3C BC, probably modelled on an original by Lysippos and formerly one of a pair. Up until 1448 it was in the Castello Maniace in Siracusa; in the 18C it was admired by Jean Houel and Goethe in the Palazzo Reale in Palermo. The second ram was destroyed in the 19C. The very fine *athlete fighting a stag* is a Roman copy of a 3C BC original. It decorated a fountain at Pompeii, and was donated to the museum by Francesco I. **Room 8** is devoted to **Greek sculpture**: in the centre is a satyr filling a drinking cup, a Roman copy from Torre del Greco of a Praxitelean original. Further items displayed here are a portrait of Aristotle, a Roman copy of an original of c 330 BC; a herm of a bearded Dionysus, another Roman copy; beautiful **5C reliefs and stelae**, and a fragment of the frieze of the Parthenon.

**Room 9** contains Roman sculpture: a Roman matron; a priestess of Isis (from Taormina); reliefs of vestal virgins, and Mithras killing the bull; and a sarcophagus of the 2nd half of the 2C. On the floor is a mosaic pavement (3C AD). Beyond a vestibule (**10**), with Roman fragments, is the landing at the head of the stairs. Nearby is a small chapel (usually closed), which is part of the 17C convent.

The **second floor** (opened on request) surrounds the Chiostro Maggiore. It contains a superb collection of **Greek vases** (see p.372 for vase types). At the top of the stairs to the right is the **short gallery** with proto-Corinthian pottery of the 7C BC. In the central wall case is a 6C plate with horses and a fragment of an amphora with elaborately dressed figures. In the second central case is a 6C oinochoe from Selinunte and various aryballi.

### Long gallery

The long gallery has a splendid series of Attic black-figure vases (580–460 BC). Among the lekythoi with figures on a white ground is one (second central case) showing the sacrifice of Iphenegea, signed by Douris. In the third central case is a large krater with a quadriga and dionysic scenes, and two amphorae with Hercules. In the fifth central case is a red-figure stamnos with Hercules and the hydra (480–460 BC).

In the room at the end (right) red-figure vases are displayed, including a kylix decorated by Oltos, a hydra with the judgement of Paris and a bell-shaped krater with dionysic scenes. Another room displays mosaic pavements (1C BC–4C AD), mostly from piazza Vittoria in Palermo.

The wall-paintings here include five from the 1C BC from Solunto and a fragment (1C AD) from Pompeii. The room at the end of the next long corridor contains Italiot vases (4C–3C BC), many with reliefs and traces of painting from Puglia, Campania and Sicily. The last long gallery contains the collection of prehistoric and Early Bronze Age material which comes mainly from north-west Sicily. Here are displayed casts of the fine incised drawings (late Palaeolithic) of hooded figures and animals from Cave B at Addaura on Monte Pellegrino. Nearby are the bones of elephants, rhinoceros and hippopotami found in via Villafranca, Palermo.

The pretty via Bara, in front of the museum, leads past one of Palermo's puppet theatres and a recently well-restored house to piazza Verdi (described below). From here via Maqueda leads back to the Quattro Canti.

## Sant'Agostino and the Quartiere del Capo

From the Quattro Canti via Maqueda runs gradually uphill to the north. It passes a large bomb site where remains of the 14C church of S. Croce and a few neighbouring buildings were demolished in 1981: plans for this important area owned by the church in the centre of the city are uncertain. On its far side is **via S. Agostino** which is given over to a street market (clothes, household goods, food, etc.). On the right is **Palazzo Barlotta di S. Giuseppe** with interesting details in a mixture of styles. At the end of the modern via Gaetano Donizetti the restored dome of the Teatro Massimo (described below) can be seen.

Beyond, on the right, hidden behind the stalls, is the flank and bell-tower of the church of **S. Agostino** (map: 11; open 07.00–12.00, 16.00–17.30). The unusual tall side portal (restored) is attributed to Domenico Gagini. The beautiful façade, on via Maestri dell'Acqua, has a late 13C portal decorated with lava mosaic and a beautiful 14C rose window. The hall **interior** was decorated with gilded stuccoes by Giacomo Serpotta and assistants from 1711, including numerous cherubs, statues and lunettes over the side altars. South side: second altar, 17C *Flight into Egypt*; third altar, Olivio Sozzi (attributed), *St Nicholas of*

*Tolentino*; fifth altar, two frescoes of the 16C and 14C (and a Byzantine icon). The pretty organ dates from the 18C. North side: fourth altar, Zoppo di Ganci, *St Thomas of Villanova* and stories from his life (removed). On the left of the second altar is a monument to Francesco Medici, with his bust (1774; surmounted by a cockerel) by Ignazio Marabitti. The pretty 16C cloister, with tall pulvins above its capitals, surrounds a little garden. The fine Gothic entrance to the chapterhouse was exposed here in 1962 and restored.

Opposite the church is the crumbling façade of the church of the Congregazione dei Diecimila Martiri.

Via S. Agostino, now a little wider, continues uphill past the church dedicated to the **Crocifisso di Lucca**, with another very ruined but interesting façade dating from the early 17C. Just beyond on the left is a little piazza in front of the former church of **S. Marco** with a handsome façade dating from the early 16C. It has been restored as an old people's home run by nuns (and two of the bells have been hung in the windows). The next crossroads is the centre of the **Mercato del Capo**, a colourful food market. The **Quartiere del Capo** (map: 10), historically one of the poorest areas of the city, has a maze of narrow streets.

Via Porta Carini, with stalls selling fish, fruit and vegetables, leads right to three churches. **S. Ippolito Maritire** (1583) has a façade of 1728. It is being restored. It has pretty columns, a chapel off the south aisle with numerous ex votoes, and in the north aisle, a 14C Byzantine fresco of the *Madonna* (very damaged). The 18C paintings include the high altarpiece of the *martyrdom of St Ippolito* by Gaspare Serenario.

Opposite is the **Immacolata Concezione** built in 1612. The interior, one of the most beautiful in the city, was elaborately decorated in the course of the 17C with polychrome marble, sculptures, singing galleries and marble intarsia altars. On the gilded stucco ceiling is a fresco by Olivio Sozzi.

Beyond S. Ippolito is the church of **S. Gregorio**, built in 1686–88. It contains some interesting wooden statues. At the end of the street is the **Porta Carini**, the only one of the three gateways to have survived at the northern limit of the old city, although it was reconstructed in 1782.

From the crossroads of the Mercato del Capo (see above) via Cappuccinella continues through the food market and piazza S. Anna al Capo in a very rundown area of the city. In via Quattro Coronati (right) is the little church of the **Quattro Coronati** built in 1674. At the next crossroads, via Matteo Bonello and via del Noviziato lead right to the church of the **Noviziato dei Gesuiti**, in an unattractive area behind the huge law courts. Built in 1591, the interior preserves some fine 18C stuccoes and *marmi mischi* decoration, as well as an effigy of *St Stanislaus* by Giacomo Pennino (1725).

In the other direction, via Matteo Bonello leads to the church of **S. Angelo Custode** (on the corner of via dei Carettieri), preceded by an outside stair. It dates from the early 18C. To the west is the wide and busy via Papireto across which is piazza Peranni, with an antique and bric-à-brac market.

Via Carettieri (see above) returns down to the Mercato del Capo in via Beati Paoli which leads right to piazza Beati Paoli. This is named after a group of bandits who operated in this area in the 17C. The church of **SS. Cosma e Damiano** was built after the plague of 1575 and that of **S. Maria di Gesù** was founded in 1660 (it contains a large 18C vault fresco, restored in 1884). Via Beati Paoli continues past the church of **S. Giovanni alla Guilla**, rebuilt in 1669 and badly damaged in World War II. On the right vicolo Tortorici leads into piazza SS. 40 Martiri with the church of **SS. Quaranta Martiri alla Guilla** (open 09.00–17.00; Sat 09.00–13.00), founded by some Pisan nobles in 1605 and rebuilt in 1725. It contains frescoes by Guglielmo Borremans.

From via Beati Paoli via S. Agata alla Guilla leads steeply uphill past Palazzo S. Isidoro (with a fine Mannerist portal) to join corso Vittorio Emanuele near the cathedral, while the interesting old via del Celso, in which the church of S. Paolino has recently been converted into a **mosque**, forks left for via Maqueda.

# The nineteenth-century city

> **Bus no. 101** from the railway station follows via Roma as far as the Politeama and then viale della Libertà north past the Giardino Inglese to piazzale de Gaspari near La Favorita.

At the north end of via Maqueda is **piazza Verdi** (map: 10, 11), laid out at the end of the 19C, now one of the most central squares in the city. It is dominated by the **Teatro Massimo**, a huge Corinthian structure begun by Giovanni Battista Basile and finished by his son Ernesto (1875–97). Among the historic late 19C opera theatres in Europe its stage is exceeded in size only by that of the Paris Opera and the Vienna opera house. It was inaugurated in 1897 with Verdi's *Falstaff*. Having been closed since 1973, it was finally re-opened for concerts in 1997. Large contributions towards its restoration came from local companies. In the piazza in front of the theatre are two decorative little kiosks, also designed by Basile and recently restored.

From the piazza, via Maqueda is continued north by via Ruggero Settimo, which has numerous cinemas, shops and cafés, to the double piazza Ruggero Settimo and piazza Castelnuovo. The huge **Politeama Garibaldi** (map: 7) is situated here, a 'Pompeian' theatre (1874, by Giuseppe Damiani-Almeyda) crowned by a bronze quadriga by Mario Rutelli.

In part of the building the **Gallery of Modern Art** is housed, founded in 1910, with 19C and 20C works, mostly by artists from Sicily and southern Italy (open 09.00–13.00; Wed also 15.30–17.30; closed Mon), including Domenico Morelli, Antonio Mancini, Giovanni Boldini, Corrado Cagli, Carlo Carrà, Felice Casorati, Gino Severini.

To the east, in via Roma, is the **Grande Albergo e delle Palme** (formerly Palazzo Ingham). Here Richard Wagner stayed with his family and completed *Parsifal* in 1882. The building was modified in 1907 by Ernesto Basile.

Viale della Libertà (map: 2), a wide avenue (one-way south) laid out in 1860, with trees and some pretty Art Nouveau houses, leads north. Beyond the double piazze Mordini and Crispi and the Excelsior Hotel, the road narrows. On the left it passes a statue of Garibaldi in a garden recently renamed after Giovanni Falcone and his wife Francesca Morvillo, who were assassinated by the Mafia in 1992. Opposite is the larger **Giardino Inglese** (map: 2), a delightful well-kept public garden, designed at the end of the last century. It is bordered on the far side by via Generale Dalla Chiesa which commemorates General Carlo Alberto

Dalla Chiesa who was assassinated by the Mafia here in 1982 (plaque), along with his wife and chauffeur, after just five months in office as Prefect of Palermo.

Further east towards the sea is the **Ucciardone** (map: 3), built in 1837–60, and now a maximum security jail. A special wing was added in the late 1980s to house a number of huge collective trials which resulted in the conviction of hundreds of people for crimes connected with the Mafia. Two of the courageous judges who collected evidence for these trials, Giovanni Falcone and Paolo Borsellino, were assassinated by the Mafia in Palermo, together with their bodyguards, in 1992. Further east is the modern port of Palermo.

Across via Notarbartolo viale della Libertà passes (left; no. 52) the head office of the Banco di Sicilia with the **Museo Archeologico della Fondazione Mormino** (open 09.00–13.00, Mon & Fri also 15.00–17.30), which contains good archaeological material, a numismatic collection and a philatelic collection (1860, from Naples and Sicily).

Viale della Libertà ends in the circular piazza Vittorio Veneto. From here via d'Artigliera (right) leads shortly to piazza dei Leoni at the south entrance (c 4km from the Quattro Canti) to La Favorita, described below.

## The Zisa, the Convento dei Cappuccini and the Cuba

Since these monuments are outside the central area of the city they are best reached by car or bus. For the Zisa, take **bus no. 124** (infrequent service) from via Mariano Stabile; near the Zisa there is an inconspicuous request stop in via Mulini beside the church of the Annunziata and four little trees. On the return to the centre the bus runs along via Volturno and terminates in piazza Verdi.

For the Cappuccini, take **bus no. 327** from piazza Indipendenza. For the Cuba, Cubula and Villa Tasca, **bus no. 389** runs from piazza Indipendenza along corso Calatafimi.

### La Zisa

The palace of La Zisa (map: 9) is open 09.00–13.00, 16.00–19.00; Sun & PH 09.00–12.30.

Its name comes from the Arab, *el aziz* (or magnificent) and it is the most important secular monument of Arab-Norman architecture to survive in Sicily, purely Islamic in inspiration.

La Zisa was one of a group of palaces built by the Norman kings in their private park of Genoard (used as a hunting reserve) on the outskirts of Palermo. It was begun by William I c 1164–65 and completed by his son. After years of neglect, it was beautifully restored in 1974–90. The structure had to be consolidated throughout, but the unity of its remarkable design of geometrical perfection (on three floors) has been preserved. It is now surrounded by a railing beside a humble piazza while beyond rise the tower blocks of the city, although there are long-term plans to recreate the garden and park which used to surround it.

The palace is known to have been used by Frederick II, but it was already in disrepair in the late 13C. It was fortified by the Chiaramonte in the 14C. By the 16C it was in a ruined state and was drastically reconstructed by the

Spanish Sandoval family who owned it from 1635 to 1806. It was expropriated by the Sicilian government in 1955 but then abandoned until part of the upper floors collapsed in 1971. A remarkable restoration programme was begun in 1974 and it was finally opened to the public in 1990.

The fine **exterior** has a symmetrical design, although the two-light windows on the upper floors were all destroyed in the 17C by the Sandoval, who set up their coat of arms on the façade and altered the portico.

In William's day the sandstone was faced with plaster decorated in a red and white design. The small pond outside, formerly part of a garden in Arab style, collected the water from the fountain in the ground floor hall, which was fed by a nearby Roman aqueduct. A damaged inscription in Cufic letters at the top of the east façade has not yet been deciphered.

The beautiful **interior** of the palace, on three floors, can be visited. The exceptionally thick outer walls (1.9 metres on the ground floor), the original small windows and a system of air vents (also found in ancient Egyptian buildings) kept the palace protected from the extremes of heat and cold. The rooms were all vaulted: the square rooms with cross vaults and the oblong rooms with barrel vaults. Amphorae were used in the structure of the vaults in order to allow for the foundations of the floors above. Some of the vaults have had to be reconstructed in reinforced concrete. The pavements (very few of the original ones remain) were in tiles laid in a herring-bone pattern, except for the ground floor hall which was in marble. The miniature stalactite vaults (known as *mouqarnas*) which decorate niches in some of the rooms and the intrados of many of the windows are borrowed from Arab architecture.

On the **ground floor** are explanatory plans and a display illustrating the history of the building. A model in plexiglass shows where it had to be reconstructed (after its partial collapse in 1971) and where iron girders have been inserted to reinforce the building.

The small rooms here were originally service rooms or rooms used by court dignataries. The splendid central **hall**, used for entertainments, has niches with stalactite vaults derived from Islamic architecture. Around the walls runs a mosaic freize which expands into three ornamental circles in the central recess. The Norman mosaics (which recall those in the Sala di Re Ruggero in the Palazzo Reale), show Byzantine, Islamic, and even Frankish influences. A fountain gushed from the opening surmounted by the imperial eagle in mosaic and flowed down a runnel towards the entrance to be collected in the fish pond outside. A majolica floor survives here and the faded frescoes were added in the 17C. The little columns have beautiful capitals. On the inner side of the entrance arch is a damaged 12C inscription in large stucco letters.

Two symmetrical staircases used to lead up to the **first floor** (replaced by modern iron stairways). Here the living rooms are connected by a corridor along the west front. Numerous fine vaults survive here and a series of air vents (see above). Egyptian Muslim objects, including metalwork, ceramics, and wooden lattice work, which served as windows, are displayed in some of the rooms, as well as amphorae found in the vaulting. On the **top floor** is a remarkable central hall with columns and water channels which was originally an open atrium surrounded by loggias, used in the summer. The small rooms on either side were probably a harem. From the windows there is a view of the hills surrounding the Conca d'Oro beyond modern tower blocks. There are plans to recreate the garden and park around the palace.

To the north of the Zisa, in via dei Normanni, is the church of **Gesù, Maria e S. Stefano** which incorporates a Norman chapel built at the same time as the palace. Nearby is a huge furniture factory closed down in 1987 which is being restored by the comune and is used as an auditorium and exhibition centre, known as the **Cantieri Culturali della Zisa**.

In piazza Zisa is the 17C church of the **Annunziata**, with Sandoval funerary monuments.

## Villa Malfitano

From the Zisa, via Whitaker and via Serradifalco lead north to **Villa Malfitano** (map: 5) (being restored), built for Joseph (Pip) and Tina Whitaker by Ignazio Greco in 1887. This was the centre of English society in Palermo at the beginning of the century, and here the Whitakers were visited by Edward VII in 1907 and by George V and Queen Mary in 1925. Pip Whitaker, descendant of the famous Marsala wine merchants, was owner and excavator of Mozia (see p.166) and the house was left by his daughter on her death in 1971 to the Joseph Whitaker Foundation and it is sometimes used for exhibitions. It is surrounded by a magnificent **park** (nearly 7 ha; open daily except Sun & PH 09.00–13.00) of rare trees and plants collected by the owners, including yuccas, bamboos, white judases, and a giant ficus magnoloides.

To the south, at no. 38 viale Regina Margherita, is the **Villino Florio**, one of Ernesto Basile's best works (1890). It has been partially reconstructed after a fire in 1962. A number of Art Nouveau houses are situated in via Dante.

To the south is the **Convento dei Cappuccini** (open 09.00–12.00, 15.00–17.00), famous for its catacombs in which the bodies of wealthy citizens, bishops, friars, children, etc. were interred until 1881. A friar conducts visitors to the macabre underground passages with about 8000 bodies, some naturally mummified.

From piazza Cappuccini via Pindemonte leads (right) to via La Loggia where the scant ruins of the Norman **Palazzo dell'Uscibene** (or Scibene, formerly Mimnermo) are found, built at the time of William II as a summer residence for the archbishops of Palermo. A hall with niches decorated with stucco shells has all but disappeared.

Outside Porta Nuova (map: 14) Corso Calatafimi begins, which leads to Monreale. On the left is a huge charitable institute built in 1735–38 by Casimiro Agretta; the church façade is by Marvuglia (1772–76).

On the corner is a fountain of 1630 (recently restored), the only one to survive of the many which used to line the road. Opposite is the vast **Albergo dei Poveri** (map: 13), an interesting building by Orazio Furetto (1746–72), recently restored and now used for important exhibitions.

## La Cuba

There follow a series of barracks including (on the left) the Caserma Tuköry (no. 100; c 1km from the gate) where excavations since 1989 have revealed part of a huge Punic necropolis (no admission), with tombs dating from the 6C BC. Here, separated from the barracks by a wall with a charming modern mural, is the entrance to **La Cuba** (open 09.00–13.00; Mon & Thurs also 15.00–18.00; first and third Sun of month, 16.00–18.45).

This was a Norman palace built by William II (1180) in imitation of the Zisa. The name comes from the Arab, *kubbeh*, meaning dome. A copy of the Arabic inscription at the top of the outer wall and a model of the Cuba are displayed in a restored stable block. The interesting building (recently restored) is now roofless and a few trees grow inside the walls. It was once surrounded by water, today replaced by a little garden. In one part are remains of a hall with miniature stalactite vaults, typical of Arab architecture, and delicate reliefs, and a small cupola decorated with stuccoes.

Further on in the corso, opposite a Standa department store and behind no. 575, a short road leads right to the remains of the 18C **Villa di Napoli** (now derelict). Here is the entrance to the delightful orchard which still surrounds the **Cubula**, although ugly new buildings have engulfed the square in the last decade or so. The gate is unlocked by the custodian who lives at the house beside the villa on the left; a path leads to the little pavilion with its characteristic red dome, built by William I. It is the only one to survive of the many which used to decorate his private park in this area (see above).

Across the busy viale della Regione Sicilia, in the south-western part of the city, the corso passes close to the **Villa Tasca** which has a privately owned **garden** (admission only by previous appointment), remarkable for its araucarias and palms. Part of the garden can be seen from the nursery here.

## La Favorita, Piana dei Colli and Monte Pellegrino

For **La Favorita** take **bus no. 107** from the railway station to piazzale de Gasperi and from there the **no. 615** for the **Museo Pitrè**. For **Piana dei Colli**, take bus no. 619 from piazzale de Gasperi. For **Mondello**, take the **bus GT** from piazza Verdi and viale della Libertà; and the **no. 615** from piazzale de Gasperi. For **Monte Pellegrino**, take the **no. 812** from piazza Sturzo and the **no. 603** from piazza Vittorio Veneto, via Arenella and Addaura (terminating at Mondello).

### La Favorita

La Favorita (see map p.105) is a large area of woods and gardens at the foot of Monte Pellegrino. It is a public park (nearly 3km long), traversed by a one-way road system and contains a hippodrome and other sports facilities. On viale del Fante bounding the west side of the park are the Stadio Comunale (right) and the Istituto Agrario (left).

Just beyond piazza Niscemi is the main entrance (c 7km from the Quattro Canti) to the formal **Parco della Favorita**, an estate bought by Ferdinand of Bourbon in 1799, and laid out by him in the taste of the early 19C. The **Palazzina Cinese** (being restored), a charming building in a Chinese style by Venanzio Marvuglia was occupied by Ferdinand and Maria Carolina in 1799–1802 during their enforced exile from Naples. The collection of English prints was a gift from Nelson, who in 1799 shared the neighbouring town house of the Palagonia family with the Hamiltons.

Nearby is the **Museo Etnografico Siciliano Pitrè** (open 09.00–13.00, 15.30–18.30; closed Fridays), which was founded in 1909 by Giuseppe Pitrè. It contains an outstanding collection illustrating Sicilian life through its customs, costumes, popular arts (painted carts, ex-votos, etc.), musical instruments, implements and objects of common use.

## Piana dei Colli

In the Piana dei Colli, the area between Monte Pellegrino and Monte Castellaccio (see map opposite), numerous villas were built in the 18C as summer residences by the Palermitan nobility. They are notable for their ingenious design (often with elaborate outside staircases). In this century many of them have been engulfed by new buildings or left to decay, although in recent years there has been more interest in their preservation.

In piazza Niscemi (see above) is the 18C **Villa Niscemi**, acquired by the Comune of Palermo in 1987. The park is open daily (08.00–19.00), and the villa on Sun & PH 09.00–12.30. Across via Duca degli Abruzzi is the small early 18C **Villa Spina** which also has its own park. Nearby is **Villa Lampedusa**, built in 1770 and now in a state of abandon. This was bought by the Principe di Lampedusa, Giulio Tomasi c 1845, and described in *Il Gattopardo* by his great-grandson Giuseppe Tomasi.

Further west, off via Nuova is **Villa Pantelleria** (c 1730), now the seat of the Centro Internazionale di Musica, Cultura e Arte Popolare 'Django Reinhardt'. In the district of S. Lorenzo is the **Convitto Nazionale** (now used by the Red Cross), the grandest of this group of villas, built in 1683. Near here is the district of 'Z.E.N.', which contains a 1960s housing estate that used to be notorious for its social problems. Off via S. Lorenzo is **Villa Amari** built in 1720 by Count Michele Amari di S. Adriano (now abandoned) and **Villa Boscogrande** (1756).

Across via Tommaso Natale is the well-preserved **Villa De Cordova**.

In the district of Resuttana, nearer the Parco della Favorita, is **Villa Terrasi** with early 18C frescoes by Vito d'Anna. Also in this district is the **Villa Sofia** which was purchased by Joseph Whitaker in 1850. He, and one of his numerous sons, also called Joseph, but nicknamed Pip (who married Tina in 1883), created a splendid garden here famous for its palms. The house is now occupied by a hospital, and only a few palms, yuccas and Turkey oaks survive in the grounds.

At Acquasanta, on the coast, reached by via Imperatore Federico from the south entrance of the Favorita, is the **Villa Igiea** (see map opposite; reached by buses from the centre of Palermo), now a 5-star hotel in a large park. A remarkable Art Nouveau building, it was built as a sanatorium by the Florio at the end of the 19C and transformed into a hotel in 1900 by Ernesto Basile.

Nearby is **Villa Belmonte**, a neo-classical building by Venanzio Marvuglia (1801).

## Mondello

From the north end of the Parco della Favorita (see above) a road runs through the suburb of Pallavicino and beneath the western slope of Monte Pellegrino, reaching the shore among the numerous villas of Mondello. This is one of the most noted bathing resorts in Sicily, whose sandy beach extends for 2km from Monte Pellegrino to Monte Gallo.

A garden city was laid out here by a Belgian society in 1892–1910, although the bay has been filled with new buildings since World War II. At its north end

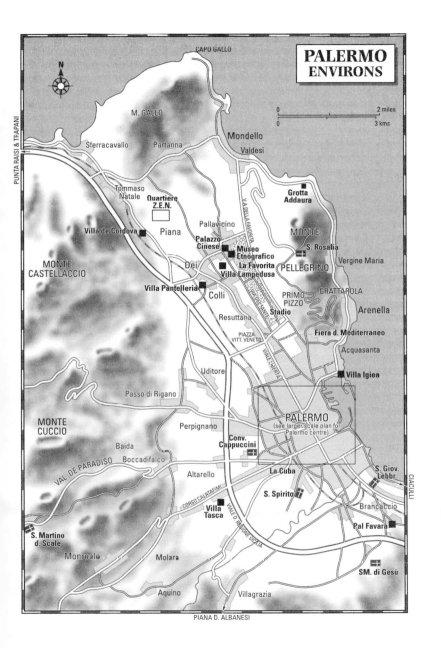

is the old fishing village of Mondello which has a medieval tower. At the south end is Valdesi from which Lungomare Cristoforo Colombo returns towards the centre of Palermo following the rocky coast at the foot of Monte Pellegrino via Vergine Maria, Arenella and Acquasanta. Inland from Mondello is Partanna, now part of the same comune, where the unusual Villa Partanna survives from 1722–28. Above the beautiful headland **Capo Gallo** rises (527m) vertically from the sea (and is now a protected area).

## Monte Pellegrino

Between the Mondello road and the sea is Monte Pellegrino (606m), described by Goethe as the most beautiful headland in the world: it rises sharply on all sides except the south. The rock, in places covered with trees and cacti, has a remarkable golden colour. Almost certainly the ancient 'Heirkte', the headland was occupied by Hamilcar Barca in the First Punic War and defended for three years (247–244 BC) against the Romans. In the **Addaura Caves** on the north slopes prehistoric rock carvings have been discovered since 1952 (for admission apply to the Soprintendenza Archeologica, next to the Museo Archeologico in Palermo, ☎ 091/6961319). The incised human and animal figures date from the Upper Palaeolithic period: they include an exceptionally interesting scene of uncertain significance with 17 human figures.

The direct approach from Palermo is from piazza Generale Cascino, near the fair and exhibition ground called the *Fiera del Mediterraneo*. From here via Pietro Bonanno, crossing and recrossing the shorter footpath, mounts towards the Santuario di S. Rosalia. A flight of steps mounts and zig-zags up the 'Scala Vecchia' (17C) between the Primo Pizzo (344m; left), with the prominent Castello Utveggio, built as a hotel in 1932 (its terrace provides the best view of the city) and the Pizzo Grattarola (276m).

A small group of buildings marks the **Santuario di S. Rosalia** (428m; open 08.00–12.30, 14.00–19.00), a cavern converted into a chapel in 1625, containing a statue of the saint, by Gregorio Tedeschi, and her coronation, by Nunzio la Mattina. The water trickling down the walls is held to be miraculous and the grotto is filled with an extraordinary variety of ex-votos. This was the hermitage of St Rosalia, daughter of Duke Sinibald and niece of William II. She died here in 1166, and is supposed to have appeared to a man on Monte Pellegrino in 1624 to show him the cave where her remains were, since she had never received a Christian burial. When found, her relics were carried in procession through Palermo and a terrible plague, then raging in the town, miraculously ceased. She was declared patron saint and the annual procession in her honour, with a tall and elaborate carriage drawn by animals, became a famous spectacle.

A steep road on the farther side of the adjoining convent climbs up to the summit, from which there is a wonderful view extending from the Aeolian Islands to Etna. Another road from the sanctuary leads to a colossal 19C statue by Benedetto De Lisi of St Rosalia on the cliff edge.

# The southern districts of the city

For S. Spirito **bus no. 108** (terminating at the Ospedale Civico); or underground from the railway station to the first stop, piazza Vespri. For Ponte dell'Ammiraglio and S. Giovanni dei Lebbrosi, any bus which follows corso dei Mille from Porta Garibaldi near the railway station.

From the station corso Tuköry leads west to Porta S. Agata (follow the signs for 'Policlinico/Ospedale'). Here via del Vespro forks left; beyond the Policlinico and just across the railway are the flower stalls and stonemasons' yards outside the cemetery of **S. Orsola**, in the midst of which is the church of **S. Spirito** or **dei Vespri** (which is a 15–20 minute walk from the station, open 08.00–14.00).

This fine Norman church (1173–78) was founded by Walter, Archbishop of Palermo. It has a pretty exterior with arches and bands of volcanic stone and lattice-work windows. The interior has a restored painted wood ceiling and a painted wooden crucifix of the 15C.

At a traditional festival on the Tuesday after Easter on 31 March 1282 at the hour of vespers a French soldier offended a young Sicilian girl in front of this church: her husband retaliated by killing the soldier and the crowd immediately showed their sympathy by massacring the other French soldiers present. Their action sparked off a rebellion in the city against the Angevin overlords and by the next morning some 2000 Frenchmen had been killed. The revolt spread to the rest of the island and in the following centuries the famous '**Sicilian Vespers**' came to symbolise the pride of the Sicilians and their struggle for independence from foreign rule. The revolt also had important consequences on the course of European history, as from this time onwards the political power of Charles of Anjou, who had the support of the Papacy, dwindled and he lost his ambition to create an Empire.

From Porta Garibaldi near the station, corso dei Mille (map: 16) leads south to the Oreto; this ancient thoroughfare was used by Garibaldi and his men on their entrance to the city. Just across the river is the **Ponte dell'Ammiraglio**, a fine bridge built by George of Antioch in 1113, and extremely well preserved. Since the river has been diverted it is now surrounded by a well-kept garden and busy roads. Here the first skirmish between the Garibaldini and the Bourbon troops took place on 27 May 1860.

A short way beyond is piazza Scaffa. On the left of the corso, hidden behind crumbling edifices (and now approached from no. 38 via Salvatore Cappello), is **S. Giovanni dei Lebbrosi**, one of the oldest Norman churches in Sicily. It is surrounded by a well-kept garden of palms; the custodian lives next to it, ring at the gate (16.00–18.45; Sun & PH 07.30–12.00). Traditionally thought to have been founded by Roger I in 1072, it was more probably erected at the time of Roger II when it became a leper hospital. The fine interior has been restored.

From piazza Scaffa (see above) via Brancaccio leads south through the unattractive suburb of Brancaccio. Via Conte Federico continues to the **Castello del Maredolce** (or **Flavia**), which is now in ruins and almost totally engulfed by tower blocks. The palazzo, once surrounded on three sides by an artificial lake,

*S. Giovanni dei Lebbrosi, Palermo*

was built by the emir Giafar in 997–1019, and was later used by the Norman kings and Frederick II. A chapel was built here by Roger II.

To the south across the motorway is the ruined 18C church of S. Ciro near which the Grotto dei Giganti yielded finds of fossil bones. A road leads from here to the suburb of **Ciaculli**, where a huge property once controlled by the Mafia boss Michele Greco, has been turned into a park of great botanical interest. Greco, known as *il Papa*, was found guilty of some 100 murders and is now in prison. Among the citrus trees which flourish here is a mandarin which bears fruit exceptionally late (February–March). The vegetation and landscape of the park is typical of the Conca d'Oro which once surrounded Palermo.

Beyond ugly new suburbs and the ring road and motorway (at present very difficult to find by car) the church of **S. Maria di Gesù** is situated, preceded by a terraced graveyard. The church has been restored; if closed, ring the bell at the convent. The simple chapel of 1426 was enlarged laterally in 1481 and a presbytery was added, with two fine Gothic arches. Here are the arcade and colonnettes of the tomb of Antonio Alliata, by Antonello Gagini (1524), and a monument to a lady of the Alliata family, by the workshop of Domenico Gagini (1490–1500). In a chapel off the nave is a wooden statue of *St Francis*, by Pippinico; a Baroque niche contains a wooden statue of the *Madonna* (late 15C).

The atrium, the funerary chapel of the Bonet family, has a wooden ceiling from the late 12C. The main doorway, with a frieze of the *Apostles*, dates from c 1495, and is from the workshop of Domenico Gagini. Outside the presbytery is the Gothic **Cappella La Grua**; the frescoes, probably by a Spanish artist of the late 15C, have been removed for restoration and will be returned to the main church.

**Monte Grifone** (832m), the hill overlooking Palermo from the south-east, may be reached either from S. Maria di Gesù or from S. Ciro (see above). On its northern slope is the ravine of the Discesa dei Mille (descent of the Thousand), above which an obelisk (337m) marks the site of Garibaldi's encampment of 26 May 1860.

# Monreale

In the pleasant little town of Monreale, the cathedral is one of the most famous Norman buildings in Sicily, extremely important for its superb mosaics.

## ■ Practical information

*Information office*. Azienda Autonoma del Turismo, Villa Igiea, Palermo (☎ 091/540122).

*Getting there from Palermo*. Monreale is 8km south-west of Palermo. **Bus** no. 389 from piazza Indipendenza (see Palermo map: 13; frequent service in 20–30 minutes). By **car** it is approached by corso Calatafimi from Porta Nuova (see Palermo map: 13).

*Hotels*. ★★★ *Carrubbella Park Hotel*, 233 via Umberto I (☎ 091/6402188; fax 091/6402189). In the hill-resort of S. Martino delle Scale, ★★ *Ai Pini* (☎ 091/418198).

*Restaurant*. *Taverna del Pavone*, 18 vicolo Pensato (**C**). Outside the town, in contrada da Lenzitti, *La Botte* (**B**).

## The Cathedral

Monreale grew up around William II's great church. On a hill (310m) overlooking the Conca d'Oro, it is now a small town with fine views.

In piazza Vittorio Emanuele is the north side of the Cathedral (dedicated to the Assumption; open 08.00–12.00, 15.30–18.00), the last and most beautiful of the Norman churches in Sicily, built to contain one of the most remarkable mosaic cycles ever produced. Begun c 1174 by William II and already near to completion by 1183, it was one of the architectural wonders of the Middle Ages.

The **façade**, facing the adjoining piazza Guglielmo, flanked by two square towers (one incomplete) and approached by an 18C porch, has a fine portal with a beautiful bronze **door** signed by Bonanno da Pisa (1186). The splendid apse, decorated with interlacing arches of limestone and lava, can be seen from via del Arcivescovado (see below). The entrance is beneath the portico along the north side built in 1547–69 by Gian Domenico and Fazio Gagini, with elegant benches. Here the portal has a mosaic frieze and a fine bronze **door** by Barisano da Trani (1179).

The **interior** (102m by 40m), remarkably simple in design but glittering with golden and coloured mosaics, gives an immediate impression of majesty and splendour. It is the conception of the Cappella Palatina carried out on a magnificent scale. Beyond the rectangular crossing, surmounted by a high lantern, with shallow transepts, is a deep presbytery with three apses, recalling the plan of Cluniac abbey churches. The stilted arches in the nave are carried on 18

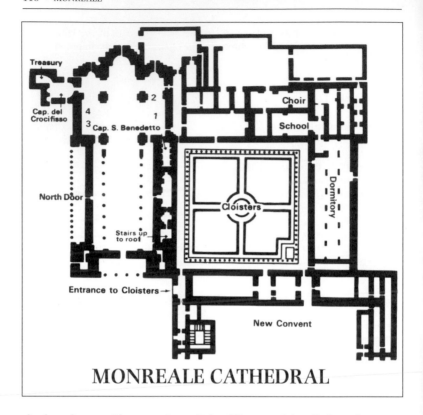

**MONREALE CATHEDRAL**

slender columns with composite capitals, of Roman origin, all of granite except the first on the south side, which is of cipollino. The ceiling of the nave was restored after a fire in 1811; that of the choir bears the stamp of Saracenic art. The handsome marble slabs decorated with mosaic on the lower part of the walls were installed in the 19C.

The magnificent series of **mosaics** have recently been beautifully restored (the numerous coin-operated lights are essential to see the exquisite details). It is not known whether Greek or local craftsmen trained by Greek mosaicists were involved in this remarkable project, and the exact date of its completion, thought to be around 1182, is uncertain. The large scenes chosen to illustrate the theme of *Christ's Ascension* and the *Assumption of the Virgin* fit an overall scheme designed to celebrate the Norman monarchy and to emphasise its affinity with Jerusalem. All the scenes bear detailed inscriptions in mosaic.

Above the arcade in the **nave** the Genesis cycle in a double tier begins, starting on the upper tier at the eastern end of the south side with the *Creation* and continuing round the western wall and along the northern side to end (on the lower tier) with the *Dream of Jacob* and *Jacob wrestling with the Angel*. In the **crossing** and **transepts** the story of Christ is illustrated from the *Nativity* to the *Passion*. The piers in the transept are covered on all sides with tiers of saints.

In the **aisles** scenes show the *Ministry of Christ*. On either side of the **pres-**

**bytery** are scenes from the life of *St Peter and Paul*, whose figures are represented in the side apses. In the **main apse** is the mighty half-length figure of *Christ Pantocrator*, the most imposing of all such figures in Sicily. Below is the enthroned *Madonna with angels and apostles*, and lower still, on either side of the east window, figures of saints including *Thomas Becket*, made within ten years of his martyrdom; Henry II of England was William II's father-in-law. Above the original royal throne (left; restored) *William II receives the crown at the hands of Christ*; above the episcopal throne (right; reconstructed) *William offers the cathedral to the Virgin*. The floor of marble mosaic dates in its present form from 1559.

**Chapels** The transept south of the choir contains the porphyry sarcophagus of William I (**1**; d. 1166) and that of William II (**2**; d. 1190) in white marble (1575). Here is the **Cappella di S. Benedetto** (1569), with a relief of the saint by Marabitti (1760). On the north of the choir are the tombs (**3**; reconstructions of 1846) of Margaret, Roger and Henry, the wife and sons of William I, and an inscription (**4**) recording the resting-place (1270) of the body of St Louis when on its way back from Tunis; his heart remains buried here.

The **treasury** (admission fee), which contains precious reliquaries, is entered through the splendid 17C Baroque **Cappella del Crocifisso**, by whose entrance is a marble tabernacle by the school of the Gagini. At the south-western corner of the nave is the entrance (admission fee) to the **roof** which is well worth visiting. Stairs (180 steps) and walkways lead across the roof above the cloisters and round the apses of the cathedral. The view of the Conca d'Oro and the coast is now marred by modern high-rise buildings; the plain was described by Augustus Hare at the end of the last century as a 'vast garden of orange and olive trees'.

On the south side of the church are the lovely **cloisters** (open 09.00–13.00, 16.00–19.00; Sun & PH 09.00–13.00); a masterpiece of 12C art, with pointed arches borne by twin columns of every imaginable design, with delicate and varied capitals. Many of the colonnettes are decorated with mosaics or reliefs; the seventh from the north-western corner is signed on the capital. In the south-western corner a single column in a little enclosure of its own forms a charming fountain. The northern wall is pierced by a doorway and eight two-light windows with a decoration of limestone and lava like that of the apse. The south walk is surmounted by a fine Norman wall (possibly predating the cloisters) of the

*The cloisters of Monreale Cathedral*

ruined dormitory of the monastery, built for Cluniac Benedictines.

A pleasant public garden is entered on the right of the façade of the new **convent** (1747), now a school. South of the cloister there is a grand staircase with two large paintings: *St Benedict distributing bread, symbolising his Rule, to all the monastic and knightly orders*, the masterpiece of Pietro Novelli (1635) who was born at Monreale in 1608, and the *Discovery of a treasure revealed by the Virgin to William II in a dream*, by Giuseppe Velasquez (1797). The **Belvedere** behind, with traces of the old monastic wall and exotic plants, has a lovely view of the Oreto valley.

In **piazza Vittorio Emanuele**, surrounded by palm trees, is a fountain with a triton by Mario Rutelli. The restored 18C town hall occupies part of the Norman palace (remnants of which can be seen from behind). In the council chamber is a *Madonna with two saints* (terracotta), attributed to Antonello Gagini (1528), and an *Adoration of the Shepherds*, by Mathias Stomer (17C). Behind is via Arcivescovado, from which the magnificent exterior of the east end of the cathedral can be seen. The choir school here incorporates some arches and windows of the Norman palace which originally had an entrance to the cathedral. The medieval districts here (where the houses are decorated with numerous plants), and between via Cassara and via Roma, are worth exploring.

The little town also possesses some fine Baroque churches. The **Chiesa del Monte** in via Umberto I contains stuccoes by Serpotta and his school and the *Madonna of the Constellation*, by Orazio Ferraro (1612). Higher up, on the left, is the **collegiata**, with large 18C paintings in the nave by Marco Benefial, a 17C Crucifix (on the external wall of the presbytery), and a stucco *Crucifixion* by Omodei (16C; on the high altar). Higher still is the Madonna delle Croci, with a fine view. In the other direction, in via Roma, is the 18C **Collegio di Maria**, and, at the end of via Pietro Novelli, the church of **S. Castrense**, with a pretty 18C interior with stuccoes by the school of Serpotta and a high altarpiece by Antonio Novelli (1602).

## San Martino delle Scale

The road between Monreale and S. Martino delle Scale ascends to Portella S. Martino. Here a path climbs up through a pinewood to (c 20 minutes) the **Castellaccio** (766m), the south-western summit of Monte Cuccio, a splendid view-point. The castle was a fortified monastery built by William II as a hospice for the convent of Monreale. It then passed to the Benedictines, and was badly damaged by Manfredi Chiaramonte in the 14C. Towards the end of the 18C it was abandoned and fell into ruin until in 1899 it was purchased by the Club Alpino Siciliano.

**S. Martino della Scale** (500m) is a hill-resort in pinewoods. The huge Benedictine **Abbey of S. Martino**, possibly founded by St Gregory the Great, was rebuilt after 1347 by Archbishop Emanuele Spinola and the Benedictine Angelo Sisinio, and enlarged c 1762 by Venanzio Marvuglia. It is now occupied by a college. The church (closed 12.30–16.30), dating from 1561–95 (with part of the 14C masonry in the north wall) contains carved choir-stalls by Benvenuto Tortelli da Brescia (1591–97); *St Benedict* and the *Madonna with Saints Benedict and Scholastica*, are both by Pietro Novelli; six altarpieces by Lo Zoppo di Ganci; and *St Martin*, by Filippo Paladino. The fine organ in the apse was made in 1650 by Raffaele la Valle. The sacristy contains vestments of 16C–18C, paintings attributed to Annibale Carracci and Guercino and a reliquary by Pietro di Spagna.

The carved doorway into the convent dates from the 15C, and nearby is a stoup dated 1396. In the convent, at the foot of the splendid grand staircase (1786) by Marvuglia, is a group of *St Martin and the beggar*, by Marabitti. A statue of *St Benedict*, by Benedetto Pompillion, stands in the graceful monastic cloister (1612; altered and enlarged in the 18C). The Oreto fountain is by Marabitti (1784). The refectory ceiling is frescoed by Novelli (*Daniel in the Lions' den*).

**Baida** is an isolated hamlet backed by a crescent of hills that rise in Monte Cuccio to 1050m. The Convento di Baida (for admission ring at no. 41 via del Convento) was built in 1377–88 by Benedictine monks, expelled by Manfredi Chiaramonte from the Castellaccio (see above), on the site of a 10C Saracen village (*baidha*, white). The foundation was already in decline in 1499 when Giovanni Paternò took it over as a summer residence for the archbishops of Palermo; in 1595 it passed to the Observantine order. The church, its original Gothic façade pierced by a portal of 1507, preserves a fine 14C apse, and a statue, by Antonello Gagini, of St John the Baptist; traces of the 14C cloister remain.

# Bagheria and Solunto

Bagheria, although surrounded by very ugly suburbs, is still worth visiting for its villas, in particular the Villa Palagonia. Solunto, close by, is a beautiful archaeological site in a very fine position on the coast.

## ■ Practical information

*Information office*. APT Palermo, ☎ 091/583847.

*Getting there from Palermo*. Bagheria is about 14km from Palermo, and Solunto 18km from Palermo. **Bus** services run by AST from Palermo (piazza Lolli and the railway station) to Bagheria. A few **trains** a day on the Messina line stop at Bagheria (14km in c 10 min.) and 'S. Flavia–Solunto' (16km in c 15 min.). The Palermo–Bagheria line was the first to be opened on the island in 1863. By **car** Bagheria and Solunto are best approached from Palermo by the coastal road via Ficarazzi (and not by the motorway).

*Restaurant*. In Bagheria: *Don Ciccio* (**C**), 87 via del Cavaliere. **Ice-creams** at *Gelateria Anni Venti*, 13 via Mattarella. Solunto is a lovely place to **picnic**.

### Bagheria
Bagheria (population 47,100) was a country town famous for its 18C Baroque villas amidst orange groves and vineyards. It has been suffocated by uncontrolled new buildings in the last 30 years, when it became notorious (together with Altavilla and Misilmeri) as a centre of Mafia activities. The villas are suffering from neglect, and only two of them are now usually open to visitors.

The conspicuous **Villa dei Principi di Cattolica**, a fine building of c 1737, is now in an ugly setting. It houses the Pinacoteca Civica di Bagheria, which has a large collection of paintings by Renato Guttuso (1912–87), a native of Bagheria, and other contemporary artists. It is at present closed for restoration (☎ 091/943352). In the garden is the bright blue marble tomb of Guttuso by Giacomo Manzù.

Near the villa, beyond a railway crossing (right), is the start of the long corso Butera which passes the fine **Palazzo Inguaggiato**, attributed to Andrea Giganti (1770) before reaching the piazza in front of the 18C cathedral. At the far end of the corso **Villa Buttera** can be seen, built in 1658 by Giuseppe Branciforte (façade of 1769). In the grounds, now engulfed by modern buildings, the *Certosa* (ruined) was built to house a collection of wax figures of historical characters dressed in the Carthusian habit.

In front of the cathedral is the beginning of corso Umberto which ends in the untidy piazza Garibaldi beside (left) a garden gate (guarded by two monsters) of **Villa Palagonia** (ring for the custodian; open 09.00–12.30, and for three hours in the afternoon before dusk). The garden, and vestibule and hall on the first floor may be visited. The fine building was erected in 1705 by Francesco Gravina, Prince of Palagonia (and his architect Tommaso Maria Napoli). His eccentric grandson Ferdinando Gravina Alliata lived in rooms decorated in a bizarre fashion, including the hall with its ceiling covered with mirrors set at strange angles (now very damaged) and its walls encased in marble with busts of ladies and gentlemen. The oval vestibule has frescoes of *Four Labours of Hercules*.

The villa is famous for the grotesque statues of monsters, dwarfs, strange animals, etc. set up on the garden wall by Ferdinando (their effect now sadly diminished by the houses which have been built just outside the wall). At the time these carved figures were not to everyone's taste; when Goethe visited the villa in 1787 he was appalled by them.

Opposite is the entrance gate to the avenue which leads up to **Villa Valguarnera** (not visible from here and closed to the public). Built by Tommaso Napoli c 1713–37, this is the most handsome of the Bagheria villas. The statues above the parapet are by Marabitti. It is in very poor condition, and most of its contents were stolen in 1988, but there are signs that it may at last be restored.

Off via IV Novembre is **Villa Trabia** (mid-18C), perhaps by Nicolò Palma, with a façade of 1890. It is surrounded by a neglected park. Near the railway station is the early 18C **Villa Cuto**, which is sometimes shown by appointment on guided tours (☎ 091/905438).

## Solunto

The solitary ruins of Solunto are in a beautiful position on the slope of Monte Catalfano (374m) close to the sea.

### History

The ancient town of *Solus* is thought to have replaced a Phoenician settlement in the vicinity of the same name (perhaps at Cozzo Cannita where traces of walls have been found) which was destroyed in 397 by Dionysius of Siracusa. Solus was built in the 4C BC on an interesting grid plan similar to the urban layout of some Hellenistic sites in Asia Minor. It fell to the Romans, who named it *Soluntum*, in 254 BC and had been abandoned by the beginning of the 3C AD. It was discovered in 1825 and still much of the site remains to be excavated.

The archaeological site and museum are open daily 09.00–two hours before sunset; Sun & PH 09.00–12.30. The entrance is through a small **museum** with good plans of the site, and Hellenistic capitals, two female statues, architectural fragments, etc. A Roman road, beside terraces of prickly pear, mounts the side of the hill past via delle Terme (with the remains of **baths**) and bends round to the right into the wide **via dell'Agora**. This, the main street, traverses the town to the cliff edge overlooking the sea; it is crossed at regular intervals by side streets with considerable remains of houses on the hillside above. Beyond via Ciauri and via Perez is the stepped via Cavallaro on which are some of the columns and architrave of the so-called **gymnasium** (restored in 1866), really a sumptuous house. This stretch of via dell'Agora is beautifully paved in brick.

The next stepped road, via Ippodamo di Mileto, links the main hill to another small hill towards the sea. Here on the slope of the hill above is the so-called **Casa di Leda** on three levels: above four small shops on via dell'Agora, is an oblong cistern and courtyard with a fountain off which are rooms with mosaic and tiled floors and traces of red wall-paintings. Further up via Ippodamo di Mileto there are more interesting houses.

Further on in via dell'Agora, beyond a large **sanctuary** (on the corner of via Salinas), the road widens out into the large **agora** with brick paving in front of nine rectangular exedrae along the back wall thought to have been used as shelters for the public. On the hillside above are traces of the **theatre** and a small **bouleuterion** probably used for council meetings. The hillside higher up may have been the site of the **acropolis**. Via dell'Agora next passes a huge public **cistern**, still filled with water, part of a complex system of storage tanks (many vestiges of which are still visible), made necessary by the lack of spring water in the area.

On the edge of the cliff, looking towards Capo Zafferano, in via Bagnera is a small Roman villa with mosaics and wall-paintings.

The view along the coast towards Cefalù, of the Aeolian Islands and Etna, is magnificent. In the foreground are the medieval castle of Solanto and the bay of Fondachello with the villas of Casteldaccia (famous for its wine) amid luxuriant vegetation on the slopes behind.

The return to the entrance can be made by taking via Ippodamo di Mileto (see above) which passes a second museum building under construction.

At the foot of Monte Catalfano a few orange groves survive but a lot of new building has taken place in recent years in the fishing village of **Porticello** (with an important fish market open in the very early morning). **Capo Zafferano** is an isolated crag of sheer eroded rock of great geological interest. On the cape dwarf palms and (in spring) wild orchids grow.

# Termini Imerese, Caccamo and Himera

Termini Imerese is a town of some interest. Since it is near the motorway it is a good centre for visiting places in the eastern part of the province of Palermo, including the Madonie mountains (see p.124). Caccamo is a little hill town dominated by a huge castle with a number of interesting churches. Remains of the ancient city of Himera include an important Doric temple, and scant remains of a sacred area and houses on the top of a hill. The archaeological museum is at present closed.

# ■ Practical information

*Information offices*. APT Palermo, ☎ 091/583847. In Caccamo, Associazione Culturale Jridos, 19 via Termitana, ☎ 091/8148171.

*Getting there from Palermo*. Termini Imerese is 37km from Palermo; Caccamo is 10km south of Termini Imerese; and Himera is 49km from Palermo. **Train** services on the main Palermo–Messina line run about every hour from Palermo to Termini Imerese (in c 20 minutes). **Buses** run by SAIS from Palermo (via Balsamo) to Termini Imerese. Randazzo bus services from Palermo and Termini Imerese to Caccamo. By **car** Termini Imerese and Himera are easily reached by the Palermo–Messina motorway (A19), with exits at Termini Imerese and Buonfornello (for Himera).

*Hotels*. In Termini Imerese: ★★★★ *Grand Hotel delle Terme*, 2 piazza Terme (a spa hotel), ☎ 091/8113557, fax 091/8113107. Near Himera: ★★★★ *Polis Himera*, on the main road (SS 113) at Buonfornello, ☎ & fax 091/8140566. At Buonfornello ★★ **campsite** Himera, ☎ 091/8140175, fax 091/8159206.

*Restaurants*. Caccamo has three simple trattorie (**C**). Termini Imerese has restaurants of all categories and the *Bar del Centro* has good biscuits and sweets.

## Termini Imerese

Termini Imerese (population 26,000) is built on the slopes of a hill (113m) and divided into an upper and lower town. Much new building has taken place here in the last few decades, including ugly tower blocks. The town has recently been provided with a commercial port.

### History

*Thermae Himerenses* received its name from the two neighbouring Greek cities of Thermae and Himera. It was captured by the Carthaginians after their sack of Himera in 408 BC and the inhabitants of the destroyed city of Himera were resettled in Thermae. In 307 BC it was ruled by Agathocles (361–289 BC), a native of the town and the first and most ferocious of the Greek tyrants of Siracusa. Its most prosperous period followed the Roman conquest. Its thermal mineral waters were praised by Pindar.

Outside the town are conspicuous remains of a Roman **aqueduct** built in the 2C AD to bring water to the town from a spring 7 kilometres away. In the **upper town** there is a spacious main square, with an old-fashioned men's club. From the belvedere behind the cathedral there is a fine view of the coast and the modern port.

The 17C **cathedral** (which has been undergoing extensive restorations since 1986) has a façade dating from 1912. The four statues (see below) have been replaced here by copies. Beneath the tower (right) is a fragment of a Roman cornice (in poor condition). The interior has huge columns and capitals. The third north chapel has a pretty tiled floor. Here are sculptures by Giuliano Mancino and Bartolomeo Berrettaro (followers of the Gagini), including a statue of the *Madonna*, bas-reliefs, and four statues of saints (1504–06) from the façade. The chapel also has two 17C funerary monuments. In the sanctuary is a *Crucifix*, painted on both sides, by Pietro Ruzzolone (1484). In the chapel to the left of the choir are reliefs by Marabitti and Federico Siragusa. In the fourth south chapel is a marble oval relief of the *Madonna del Ponte* by Ignazio Marabitti.

The 17C **Palazzo Comunale** is approached by an outside staircase. Just out of the piazza is the **Museo Civico** (open Wed, Thurs, Sat & Sun 09.00–13.00, 16.00–19.00; Tues & Fri 09.00–13.00; closed Mon). It was founded in 1873 and restored in 1990. On the ground floor are prehistoric finds from Termini; red- and black-figure vases from Himera; coins; and Roman capitals, a bust of a lady (c 115 AD), statues, inscriptions, architectural fragments, and glass. The last room contains Arab-Norman material and a Renaissance doorway. On the first floor is a chapel frescoed in the 15C by Nicolò da Pettineo, paintings (16C–19C) and a natural history collection.

In via Mazzini which leads out of piazza Duomo are the **Chiesa del Monte** (sometimes open in the afternoon), burial place of local dignatories since the 16C (containing 16C and 17C Sicilian paintings), and **S. Maria della Misericordia** (usually closed), with a beautiful triptych (*Madonna with Saints John and Michael*), ascribed to Gaspare da Pesaro (1453).

Viale Iannelli leads west from piazza Duomo to the church of **S. Caterina** (often closed) whose frescoes of the life of the saint are probably by Nicolò and Giacomo Graffeo (15C–16C; much damaged) of Termini. From here there is a pretty view of the sea beyond groves of citrus fruit trees.

In the **public gardens** laid out in 1845 with some fine palms, pines and ficus trees, are remains of a Roman public building, known as the *Curia*, dating from the 2C AD. A bronze plaque dedicated to the magistrates Giovanni Falcone and Paolo Borsellino, killed by the Mafia in 1992, was set up here in 1993.

From behind the cathedral there is a good view down to the pretty tiled dome of the church of the **Annunziata**. A road winds down from here to the **lower town** and, on the site of the Roman baths, the **Grand Hotel delle Terme**, begun in 1890 on a design by Giuseppe Damiani Almeyda). The thermal waters (43°C) still in use here provide natural steam baths and swimming-pools.

## Caccamo

Caccamo (population 8600) is a little town of ancient origins in a fine position above olive groves in the hills (521m). There is a tradition that the Carthaginians took refuge here after their defeat at Himera in 480 BC. The castle was one of the major Norman strongholds on the island, and, never captured, it remained the residence of the dukes of Caccamo up until this century.

At the entrance to the town is the impressive 12C **castle** (for admission enquire at the tourist office in via Termitano opposite the War Memorial). It was enlarged by the Chiaramonte in the 14C, and several times restored. It was sold to the region of Sicily in 1963 by the De Spuches family. Extensive restoration work was begun in 1986 and is finally near completion: the interior is to be used by the comune for conferences and exhibitions. The interior courtyard has a pretty pavement, and there is a good view from the terrace of unspoilt countryside and the artificial lake of Rosamarina created by a dam built in 1993 (which, however, submerged a bridge which had been built in 1307 to connect the town with Palermo). The main tower of the castle was 70 metres high but was toppled in an earthquake in the 19C. The empty interior has been heavily restored.

From the main road (Corso Umberto I) steps and narrow streets lead down to **piazza del Duomo**, an attractive and unusual square with a fine view over the valley. Above the raised terrace, with a balustrade decorated with four statues of the town's patron saints, is the Monte di Pietà (the palace is now used for exhibitions) flanked by the twin façades of two churches. The one on the right is dedicated to the **Anime del Purgatorio**. It contains charming gilded stuccoes at the east end and an 18C organ. The custodian shows the burial chapel below, also beautifully decorated with stuccoes (but in urgent need of restoration), with the crumbling, but fully-clothed, skeletons of past inhabitants of the town.

The **Duomo** (ring if locked) has a good 17C façade. Founded in 1090, it was altered in 1477 and 1614. There is a lovely relief (1660) of *Saint George* above the door by Gaspare Guercio. The tall campanile was built above a 14C tower of the castle.

In the **interior** St George features in a number of fine works of art. In the **south aisle** is a 15C triptych with *St George* and a charming processional statue of the saint with his dragon. In the south transept the architrave of the door into the sacristy has delicate carvings of the *Madonna and Child with angels* and *Sts Peter and Paul* attributed to Francesco Laurana. The tondoes of the *Annunciation* and relief of the *Madonna and Child* are by the Gagini school. The rich **treasury** and **sacristy** are shown on request. They contain 16–19C church silver, as well as a precious collection of vestments, and Flemish paintings. In the chapel to the right of the sanctuary is a statue of the *Madonna and Child* by the Gagini school. By the high altar is an unusual font (1466) with four large heads. In the **sanctuary** are two polychrome wooden statues: *St John the Baptist* by Antonino Siragusa (1532) and *St Lucy* (16C), both recently restored. An exquisite silver processional statuette of St Rosalia is also kept here. On the high altar are three very fine alabaster carvings (16C–18C).

In the **north transept** are two painted terracotta sculptures: a *Madonna and Child* by the Gagini school and a *Pietà* group by the early 15C Sienese school. The altar here has 16C and 17C reliquary busts and an early 18C neo-classical carved and gilded altar frontal. In the **north aisle** an altar decorated with *marmi mischi* has a 14C painted *Crucifix*, and the first altarpiece of the *Miracle of St Isidore* is a fine painting by Mattia Stomer (in need of restoration). A sedan chair and armour belonging to the De Spuches family is also kept in this aisle.

There are good views of the castle from the old streets behind the Duomo. In the other direction via Cartagine leads to the deconsecrated church of San Francesco and, beyond, the church of **SS. Annunziata**, its Baroque façade flanked by two earlier towers. Inside is a carved 16C organ case, and the east end has stuccoes by the Serpotta school. The church of **S. Benedetto alla Badia** (1615) was attached to a former Benedictine convent. The charming interior has a splendid majolica tiled pavement in the nave and choir, once attributed to Nicolò Sarzana, but now thought to date from before 1701. There are also fine wrought-iron grilles. The two graceful female figures in stucco on either side of the sanctuary are by the school of Serpotta.

**S. Maria degli Angeli** (1497; ring at the convent) has a fine relief of the *Madonna and Child* over the door. Inside its original wooden ceiling is preserved (with 15C paintings of Dominican saints) and a statue of the *Madonna* by Antonello Gagini.

# Himera

Beyond a huge industrial plant (partly abandoned), including an important Fiat factory, which occupies the low coastal plain east of Termini Imerese in the locality of Buonfornello is the site of Himera (open daily 09.00–two hours before sunset). It is near the 'Buonfornello' exit of the motorway and on the bank of the Fiume Grande (or Imera Settentrionale), but is very poorly sign-posted. On the right of the road, just across the busy railway line are remains of a temple. On the hillside above the road is a conspicuous modern museum, and the site of the ancient city is on the top of the hill.

### History

This was a colony of Zancle (now Messina), founded in 648 BC near the mouth of the River Imera and at the head of the valley which provided access to the interior of the island. It was the westernmost Greek colony on the north coast of Sicily, and the scene of the famous defeat of the Carthaginians by Theron of Agrigento and Gelon of Siracusa in 480 BC. This was important as it was their first decisive defeat in the Mediterranean: their leader Hamilcar was killed and his ships were burned on the beach. However, the Carthaginians returned under Hannibal, nephew of Hamilcar, in 409 BC and utterly destroyed the city. The inhabitants who survived the battle were moved to Thermae (now Termini Imerese). Himera was the home city of Stesichorus (born c 630 BC), the lyric poet.

On the right of the main road (just across the railway line; beware of trains) are the ruins of a **Doric temple**, peripteral and hexastyle, probably built around 470 BC. This is the only building which remains here of a sanctuary probably dedicated to Athena, on the banks of the River Imera. It is still known as the 'Temple of Victory', although some scholars no longer believe it was built to celebrate the victory over the Carthaginians. In any case it seems to have been burnt and destroyed by the Carthaginians in 409 BC.

Only the basement and lower part of the columns and part of the cella walls survive. It measured 22 x 55m and had 14 columns at the sides and 6 in front. The cella had a pronaos and opisthodomus in antis. In the Middle Ages the site was built over and it was only rediscovered in 1823 and excavated by Pirro Marconi in 1929–30 when the splendid lion head water-spouts from the cornice were taken to the Archaeological Museum in Palermo.

Off the main road, just beyond, a byroad (left; signposted) leads up to the museum and the areas of the city excavated since 1963. The **museum** (closed in 1998) was built in 1984 to house finds from the site. The material is well displayed and labelled in a building of strikingly modern design, and there are good plans etc. of the site. The first section displays finds from the temples in the sacred area on the hill top, including a votive deposit with fragments of metopes. The second section has material from the city and necropoli, including ceramics, architectural fragments and votive statues. There is also a section devoted to finds from recent excavations in the surrounding territory, including Cefalù and Caltavuturo.

Just above the museum are excavations ('restored' in 1986) of part of the city. Steps continue up to a plateau on the edge of the hill overlooking the plain towards the sea. Here is the **_Area Sacra_** with a temenos enclosing the bases of an altar and four temples (7–5C BC). There are also traces of houses here. The view extends along the coast as far as Solunto, and in the other direction the village of Gratteri, nestling in the Madonie mountains (see p.126), can be seen.

Away from the sea are more excavations of houses beside an olive grove. Three necropoli have been identified in the surrounding area. There are long-term plans to protect the extensive site in an archaeological park.

# Cefalù

Cefalù (population 18,000) is an extremely pleasant little town. Its picturesque streets near its old port are clustered beneath an isolated rock. It has a remarkable urban structure and one of the finest Norman churches in Sicily. In its well-kept cobbled streets many buildings have recently been restored. It has numerous cafés and restaurants. Because of its excellent beaches Cefalù has become a resort in recent years and much new building has taken place on the outskirts.

## ■ Practical information

*Information office*. Azienda Autonoma, 77 corso Ruggero (corner of via Amendola), ☎ 0921/421050, 421458.

*Getting there from Palermo*. Cefalù is 67km from Palermo. **Railway station**, via Gramsci, 500m south-west of corso Ruggero. **Trains** on the Palermo–Messina line c every hour from Palermo in 50–60 min. **Buses** (SAIS) from Palermo (once a day). **Car parking** (free) in piazza Colombo on the seafront (corso Ruggero is closed to traffic). ACI car-park, with an hourly tariff, in via Verga.

*Hotels*. The nearest to the old centre are: ★★ *La Giara*, 40 via Veterani (☎ & fax 0921/22518); *Riva del Sole*, 25 viale Lungomare Colombo (☎ 0921/421320; fax 0921/421984). ★ *Locanda Cangelosi*, via Umberto I (☎ 0921/421591).

The large modern ★★★ hotels on the beaches to the west near S. Lucia and east near Caldura, many with swimming-pools and tennis courts, include: *Kalura* (☎ 0921/421354; fax 0921/423122) and *Le Calette* (☎ 0921/424144; fax 0921/423688).

*Campsites*. on the coast west of the town at Contrada Ogliastrillo (★★★): *Costa Ponente* (☎ 0921/420085) and (★★) *Sanfilippo* (☎ 0921/420184).

*Restaurants.* Numerous restaurants all over the town. **A** Al Giardino, lungomare Giardino; *Al Porticciolo*, 66 via di Bordonaro. **B** *Osteria del Duomo*, 5 via Seminario; *Vecchia Marina*, 73 via Vittorio Emanuele. **C** *Kentia*, 15 via Nicola Botta; *Nasca* 3, 1 via Bellini (corner of via Roma). Pizzerie: *Da Nino* and *Al Gabbiano-da Saro* on the lungomare.

*Cafés and pasticcerie*. Two (with tables outside) in piazza del Duomo, and *Dolce Delizia* in via Matteotti.

*Places to picnic* on the 'Rocca' hill above the town, on the bastion of Capo Marchiafava, or on the sea front near the port.

*Hydrofoil services* in June–Sept to the Aeolian Islands (three times a week): information from the tourist office. Local buses from the railway station to Gibilmanna and the small towns in the Madonie mountains.

*Annual festivals*. S. Salvatore 2–6 August. *Frottola* on Corpus Domini (end of May or early June), with decorated floats and religious processions. Music festivals in summer.

### History
Founded at the end of the 5C or early 4C BC, its name *Cephaloedium* comes from the head-like shape of the rock which towers above. In 307 BC it was taken by Agathocles of Siracusa. In 857 it was conquered by the Arabs. In 1131 Roger II rebuilt the town on the sea, and constructed the magnificent cathedral which became head of a powerful bishopric.

**Corso Ruggero** (closed to traffic) leads through the little town. At the beginning on the right is the former hotel Barranco next to the sandstone façade of **Maria SS. della Catena** (1780; closed) preceded by a high portico with three statues. On the right of the façade are a few large blocks from the old walls (late 5C BC) on the site of the Porta Terra, the main entrance to the old town. The corso continues past (right) vicolo dei Saraceni (signposted for the *Tempio di Diana*) beyond which begins a path up to the Rocca (described below), and then runs slightly downhill. On the left is the restored **Osteria Magno** (used for exhibitions) with a good 13C triple window high up on its façade and (in via Amendola) windows decorated with black lava.

On the left are a series of nine picturesque, straight, parallel streets which lead downhill to corso Vittorio Emanuele, with a view of the sea beyond. They were laid out by Roger II in 1130. The corso continues past the tall, plain façade of the 16C church of the Annunziata (closed). To the right opens the little piazza in front of the 15C church of the Purgatorio (formerly S. Stefano Protomartire) with outside stairs and a decorative portal.

Beyond on the right opens the piazza with palm trees which slopes up to the **DUOMO**, a splendid edifice begun by Roger II in 1131, and intended as his burial-place, but still unfinished at the time of his death in 1154. It was consecrated in 1166 by which time it was probably completed. It is in a particularly effective setting with the formidable cliff (or *Rocca*) rising immediately behind it. Excavations during restoration work have revealed Roman remains on this site. It is preceded by a raised terrace surrounded by a balustrade with statues (this gate is closed; entrance from the south door).

The unusual **façade** is flanked by two massive towers with fine windows. Above the narthex built by Ambrogio da Como in 1471 a double row of blind arcades can be seen. The beautiful exterior of the south side and transept are visible from via Passafiume. The building has been the object of controversial restorations in recent years.

The basilican **interior** (open 08.00–12.00, 15.30–20.00; entrance from the south side; visitors in shorts or bare shoulders are forbidden entry) has 16 ancient columns with Roman capitals supporting stilted Gothic arches. The open timber roof of the nave bears traces of painting (1263). The stained-glass windows high up in the nave were installed in 1985–90. The crossing is approached through an arch borne by huge columns. In the sanctuary is a 15C painted Cross attributed to Tommaso de Vigilia.

The presbytery is decorated with exquisite **mosaics** carried out for Roger II in a careful decorative scheme, reflecting Greek models. They are the best preserved and perhaps the earliest of their kind in Sicily. The apse, vault, and possibly the lunettes of the side walls are thought to be the work of Greek craftsmen. In the apse is the splendid colossal figure of *Christ Pantocrator* holding an open book with the Greek and Latin biblical text from John 8:12 ('I am the Light of the world, he who follows me will not walk in darkness').

On the curved apse wall below are three tiers of figures: the Virgin in prayer between four archangels, and the Apostles in the two lower registers. In the vault of the presbytery are angels and seraphims and on the walls below are (left) prophets, deacon martyrs, and Latin bishop saints, and (right) prophets, warrior saints, and Greek patriarchs and theologians. These standing figures were probably carried out c 1164 by Greek or possibly local craftsmen.

The south aisle and transepts were 'restored' (i.e. stripped of their Baroque decoration) in the 1970s. In the chapel to the right of the sanctuary is a statue of the *Madonna* by Antonello Gagini. On the left pilaster of the sanctuary, high up in a niche, is a statue of the annunciatory angel (the Madonna and niche on the right pilaster have been removed). In the neo-classical chapel to the left of the sanctuary is an elaborate 18C silver altar.

The redesigned marble and mosaic episcopal and royal thrones were dismantled in 1985: these, together with the 12C font with lions, are at present stacked in pieces in the south aisle.

From the north aisle is the entrance to the charming **cloister** (closed indefinitely for restoration) which had three galleries of twin columns with charming capitals (including *Noah's Ark* and the *Trinacria* symbol) supporting Gothic arches. There is a fine view of the cathedral and the rock behind.

In **piazza del Duomo** is Palazzo Maria, with medieval traces, and the 17C Oratorio del Santissimo Sacramento beside the neo-classical Palazzo Legambi. Opposite is Palazzo Vescovile (1793), next to the 17C Seminario Vescovile with a hanging garden. Opposite the Duomo is the huge former monastery of S. Caterina, restored and enlarged in the 18C and in 1857, and drastically restored a few years ago as an exhibition centre.

Via Mandralisca leads down to the **MUSEO MANDRALISCA** (open daily 09.00–12.30, 15.30–18.00), the exterior of which has also been restored. The cellar of the palace, with huge terracotta jars for storing oil, can be seen from the road.

The palace was the residence of Enrico Pirajno, Baron Mandralisca (1809–64) and contains his remarkable collection left by him to the city as a museum (now owned by a private foundation). The Baron was a member of the first Italian parliament and had a special interest in archaeology (he took part in excavations on Lípari and near Cefalù) and natural history. He also endowed a local school.

On the **ground floor** is a mosaic from Cefalù (1C BC). Stairs lead up to the **first floor**. **Room 1** contains a famous vase from Lípari showing a vendor of tuna fish (4C BC) and a numismatic collection dating from the Greek period up to the last century (some 400 pieces are exhibited, but about 100 were never recovered after a theft in 1989). The collection is particularly important for its coins from Lipari, Cefalù and Siracusa. **Room 2** has Veneto-Cretan paintings and other 15C–18C works.

In **Room 3** is the famous **portrait of a man** by Antonello da Messina (c 1465–72), the jewel of the collection and one of the most striking portraits in Sicily. Mandralisca apparently bought this small painting from a pharmacy in Lípari, where he discovered it in use as part of a cupboard door. The sitter, with his enigmatic smile, has never been identified. The influence of the Flemish school of painting is evident in this exquisite work. Also displayed here is a sarcophagus in the form of an Ionic temple which dates from the 2C BC. **Room 4** has Mandralisca's remarkable collection of c 20,000 shells. **Room 5** has archaeological material, including Italiot vases from Lípari (320–300 BC), and a well-preserved kylix.

The **second floor** contains more archaeological finds, and miscellaneous objects including a 19C dinner service, arms, reliquaries, paintings (*Madonna and Child* attributed to Antonello da Saliba), and an ornithological collection. Mandralisca's important library, which has been added to over the years, is also kept here.

Corso Ruggero continues down to end at via Porpora which leads right to a restored square tower in a gap between the houses. Outside the tiny postern gate a fine stretch of the megalithic walls (5C BC) built onto the rock can be seen here. In the other direction via Carlo Ortolani di Bordonaro leads past (right) piazza Francesco Crispi with the church of the Madonna del Cammino. Here modern steps lead up to a 17C bastion (Capo Marchiafava) where a 14C fountain has been placed (good view). Via Ortolani continues down towards the sea and ends beside a terrace overlooking the little **port**, with picturesque old houses on the sea front.

From here via Vittorio Emanuele leads back past the church of the Badiola (12C–17C), next to its convent (the old portal survives on the corner of via Porto Salvo). Opposite is the 16C Porta Pescara with a lovely Gothic arch through which the sea can be seen. It is now used to display fishermen's tackle and nets. Beyond, the discesa Fiume, with wide steps curving down past a few trees, leads to a medieval **Lavatoio** (restored in the 16C and in 1991), a public fountain. A spring, famous since antiquity, it was converted into an Arab bath-house.

From corso Ruggero and vicolo dei Saraceni steps and a path lead up (in c 1 hour) to the **Rocca**; the summit (278m) commands a fine view. Here the so-called Temple of Diana has walls made out of huge polygonal blocks and a carved architrave over the entrance. It was probably a sacred edifice built in the 5C–4C BC over an earlier cistern. Stretches of castellated walls can also be seen here as well as numerous cisterns and ovens. Although it has recently been restored, virtually nothing remains of the original castle where Charles of Salerno was imprisoned.

# The Madonie Mountains

The Madonie Mountains have extensive woods and fine views. The small hill towns here, particularly Polizzi Generosa, Petralia Soprana and Castelbuono, are of great interest.

The **Madonie Mountains** lie between the Imera Settentrionale to the west and the Pollina river to the east. The Pizzo Carbonara (1979m) is the second highest mountain on the island (after Etna). This area of some 40,000 ha was at last protected as a nature reserve known as the **Parco Naturale Regionale delle Madonie** in 1989. The vegetation in the upland plains and mountains includes beech trees, chestnuts, oaks, poplars, ilexes, cork trees and ancient olive trees. A rare species of fir, only found here and in the Nebrodi mountains, with small cylindrical cones, was saved from extinction in 1969. Manna is still extracted from the bark of Manna ash trees around Pollina and Castelbuono. Apart from these extensive woods the landscape has spectacular rock formations and there are splendid views. There is still some pastureland where sheep and cattle are grazed. The museum in Castelbuono provides a fascinating history of the flora and fauna of the Madonie.

## ■ Practical information

*Getting there*. The northern part of the Madonie can be visited from Cefalù and the byroads which lead inland from the main coastal road between Palermo and Messina. The southern part of the area is best approached from the Palermo–Catania motorway ('Scillato' and 'Tre Monzelli' exits). The roads within the park are generally good and well signposted. **Bus services** are run by SAIS (☎ 091/6166028) from Palermo and Cefalù to most of the hill towns and villages.

*Excursions*. Marked trails provide beautiful routes for walkers, riders and cyclists with mountain bikes. The road which runs through the centre of the park across the Piano Zucchi (1085m) and up to Piano Battaglia (1646m), which lies below the Pizzo della Principessa (1975m), one of the highest of the range, provides a good view of the landscape, even though an unattractive ski resort has been built at Piano Battaglia.

*Information offices*. The main office of the Ente Parco delle Madonie is at Petralia Sottana, 16 corso Paolo Agliata (☎ 0921/680201). There is a subsidiary office at Isnello (☎ 0921/662795). A tourist office is situated in the Centro Civico (☎ 0921/671124) at Castelbuono. At Polizzi Generosa, information can be obtained from the Vigili Urbani in piazza Umberto.

### Hotels
**Gibilmanna**. ★★ *Bel Soggiorno*.
**Isnello**. ★★★ *Piano Torre Park*, località Piano Torre (☎ 0921/662671; fax 0921/662672), with restaurant. *Vincenza Manzella*, 36 via Roma (rooms to let), ☎ 0921/666279.

**Castelbuono.** ★★★ *Milocca*, in contrada Piano Castagna (☎ 0921/671944; fax 0921/671437). ★★ *Villaggio dei Fauni*, in località S. Guglielmo (☎ 0921/671592).

**Sclafani Bagni.** *Agriturismo* accommodation: *Fontana Murata*, contrada Fontana Murata, Valledolmo (☎ 0921/542080), with restaurant.

**Polizzi Generosa.** *Agriturismo* accommodation: *Il Pavone*, contrada S. Nicola; (☎ 0921/649751); *La Sorgente di Iside*, contrada Chiaretta (☎ 0921/688277); and *Il Tipico*, contrada S. Nicola (☎ 0921/688302), with restaurant.

**Petralia Sottana.** ★★ *Madonie*, 81 corso Paolo Agliata (☎ & fax 0921/641106).

**S. Mauro Castelverde.** *Agriturismo* accommodation: *Flugy Ravetto*, località contrada Ogliastro (☎ 0921/74128), with restaurant.

**Gangi.** *Agriturismo* accommodation: *Tenuta Gangivecchio*, località Gangivecchio (☎ 0921/644804; fax 0921/689191), with restaurant.

*Alpine refuges*

**Castelbuono.** *Francesco Crispi*, località Piano Sempria (☎ 0921/672279).

**Isnello.** *Lo Scoiattolo*, località Piano Zucchi (☎ & fax 0921/662831); *Luigi Orestano*, località Piano Zucchi (☎ 0921/662159); *Ostello della Gioventù* (Youth Hostel), Piano Battaglia, località Mandria Marcate (☎ 0921/649995).

**Petralia Sottana.** *Giuliano Marini*, Piano Battaglia (☎ 0921/649994).

### Restaurants

**Gratteri** *Trattoria Sapienza* (**C**).

Between **Collesano** and **Campofelice di Roccella** *Mari e Monti* (**B**) in contrada Pizzillo.

**Castelbuono** *Romitaggio S. Guglielmo* (**C**), about 5km outside the town beyond S. Guglielmo; *U Trappitu* (**C**); *Vecchio Palmento*, 2 via Failla (**B**); *Nangalarruni*, 5 via Alberghi (**C**).

**Polizzi Generosa** *Itria*, 3 via Itria (**B**); *Pizzeria Il Pioniere* (**C**).

### Cafés and pasticcerie

**Isnello** *Pasticceria Bontempo*. **Castelbuono** *Fiasonaro*, piazza Margherita and *Pinsino*, salita al Monumento. They make their own biscuits, and, in winter, a rich cream and chocolate cake called *testa di turco*.

### Annual festivals

**Gibilmanna:** pilgrimage on 8 September.

**Gratteri:** Festa di S. Giacomo on 8–9 September.

**Isnello:** Festa del SS. Crocifisso di S. Maria Maggiore (30 April–1 May), with a procession of the Crucifix and a *frittella* festival.

**Collesano:** *Festa del Casazza* in the Easter period when the life of Christ is re-enacted.

**Castelbuono:** *Arruccata di li Ventimiglia* in August (a historical pageant).

**Sclafani Bagni:** Procession of the *Ecce Homo* on last Sunday in June.

**Polizzi Generosa:** Festa di S. Gandolfo in May; hazelnut fair in September; and festivities on 26 December when a huge bonfire is lit in front of the ruined church of La Commenda.

# Hill towns in the northern district of the Madonie

## Gibilmanna

The sanctuary of Gibilmanna is in a beautiful position looking towards the sea, on the slopes of the Pizzo S. Angelo (1081m), with woods of olives, cork trees, pines and chestnuts. Its name is derived from the Arab *Gebel*, meaning mountain and *manna* which used to be extracted from the Manna-ash trees in the locality, and used for medicinal purposes. There was a sanctuary here before 857 and in 1535 it became a Capuchin convent: it is still a famous centre of pilgrimmage on the island. The church, rebuilt in the 17C, has, however, been altered many times and its external appearance dates from this century. The interior preserves an 18C Baroque altar, and a fresco of the *Madonna* and a Crucifix from an earlier church. The wooden tabernacle on the high altar is by Pietro Bencivinni (1700).

An interesting **museum** (open daily 09.00–13.00, 15.00–17.00; April–Sept 09.30–12.30, 15.30–19.00) was opened in part of the Capuchin convent in 1993 to preserve works of art from convents and churches in this area of the island. These include 16C–18C paintings, church vestments, statuettes (in wax and wood), ex votos, a rare early 18C wooden organ with cane pipes, and an ethnographical collection illustrating monastic life. On the nearby Cozzo Timpa Rossa (1006m) there is an observatory (1952) run by the Istituto Nazionale di Geofisica.

**Gratteri** is a little hill town (657m) facing west with a fine distant view along the coast. The Chiesa Madre is closed for restoration, and S. Giacomo, approached by a wide flight of steps, has a pretty east end with a dome, lantern and stuccoes.

## Isnello

Isnello is a pleasant little town (570m). The **Chiesa Madre** has 16C frescoes by Antonino Ferraro, 17C stuccoes by Giuseppe Li Volsi, and a carved wooden choir and organ loft dating from the early 17C. A marble ciborium is attributed to Domenico Gagini (1492). The *Deposition* is by Zoppo di Ganci. The little church of **S. Michele** has a painted wooden ceiling, a wooden Crucifix by Fra' Umile da Petralia, a painting of *Martyrs* by Zoppo di Ganci, and a 15C fresco of *St Leonard*. The church of the Rosario (closed) contains a painting of the *Madonna of the Rosary* attributed to the Flemish school. The church of the **Annunziata** (being restored) contains a *Nativity* by Zoppo di Ganci.

Steps lead up from the piazza by the Chiesa Madre to the church of **S. Maria Maggiore** (key at no. 4 via Purgatorio) near the ruins of the castle and beneath a rock called the Grotta Grande. It has a pretty campanile. The charming interior has a decorative organ loft at the west end, and a 15C–16C Cross, unusual in its iconography and painted on both sides, hangs from the centre of the nave ceiling. Off the north side, the Cappella del Crocifisso contains a processional Cross. Above the high altar is a *Madonna and Child* of the Gagini school (1547). There is also a charming little statue of the *Madonna* as a baby, lovingly preserved in a glass case. There is a fine view of the town from the door.

**Collesano**. This little medieval town (population 4500) has several interesting churches including the Duomo (S. Maria la Nuova) which contains a painted

Crucifix of 1555, a fine carved tabernacle of 1489 by Donatello Gagini, and a *Madonna with angels* by Zoppo di Ganci. In S. Maria la Vecchia is a statue of the *Madonna* by Antonello Gagini.

## Castelbuono

Castelbuono is a pleasant little hill town (population 9900) in a fold of hills (423m) covered with chestnut woods. Of Byzantine origins it became the seat of the Ventimiglia princes of Geraci in the 14C.

The road leads up past a 16C fountain with bas-reliefs and a statue of Venus to piazza Margherita, with another 16C fountain. Here the **Matrice Vecchia** (usually closed) of 1350 is preceded by a loggia. It contains a marble ciborium attributed to Giorgio da Milano (late 15C), a huge polyptych on the high altar attributed to Pietro Ruzzolone, and statues and frescoes of the 16C. The crypt has frescoes of the *Passion of Christ*.

Also in the piazza is a building owned by the Ventimiglia family in the 14C–16C and used as a prison from the 18C up to 1965. Exhibitions are now held here and it has a local tourist office. A road continues uphill past the town hall to the **castle** (closed since 1996) built by the Ventimiglia in 1316. Off the courtyard (being restored) is the Cappella di S. Anna (c 1683) with white stuccoed putti on a gold ground by the school of Serpotta. Relics of the saint are preserved here in a 16C silver urn, and the chapel possesses a treasury. The castle will be used for exhibitions. Behind the castle the terrace has a view of the Madonie and the little hill town of Geraci Siculo.

From the Matrice Vecchia a road (signposted) leads up to a piazza with palm trees and a memorial surrounded by cannon used in World War I. Here is the **Matrice Nuova** begun at the beginning of the 17C (and rebuilt in 1830). It contains a painted Cross attributed to Pietro Ruzzolone, stucco altars, and a 16C triptych.

Another road leads up to the right of the Matrice Nuova to the church of **S. Francesco**, which has a pretty white and gold interior decorated in the 18C, with an organ and monks' choir above the entrance. It also has decorative chandeliers and charming little confessionals dating from 1910. Off the right side of the sanctuary, entered through a lovely late 15C doorway carved by the school of Laurana, is a pretty octagonal chapel with twisted columns. Here are tombs of the Ventimiglia family, including one dated 1543 and one 1687. The two 15C frescoes were detached from the Franciscan convent. The attractive 18C cloister (awaiting restoration) of the convent is entered between two marble columns left of the church façade.

In via Roma the former Convent of S. Venere now houses the **Museo Minà Palumbo** (open 09.00–13.00; Mon 16.00–19.00). It is named after the naturalist Francesco Minà Palumbo, a native of Castelbuono. His collections, which he carefully catalogued, provide a fascinating documentation of the Madonie. The exhibits include fossils, a botanical and natural history section, minerals, archaeological finds (including prehistoric material), examples of glass produced here from the late 16C to the end of the 18C, and examples of paper produced in the town between 1822–46. There is also an interesting display illustrating the extraction of manna (used for medicinal purposes as a laxative) from the trunks of Manna-ash trees in the Madonie (a local industry which survives here).

In the hill town of **Pollina** (730m) the church has works by Antonello Gagini. A theatre was built on the hillside here in 1979 (summer theatre festival).

## Hill towns in the southern district of the Madonie

### Sclafani Bagni

Sclafani Bagni is a small remote fortress-village on a precipitous crag (813m) with superb views. The medieval **town gate** bears the coat of arms of the Sclafani (Matteo Sclafani, count of the town in 1330, constructed its defences). Higher up the **Chiesa Madre** contains a splendid Roman sarcophagus, with Bacchic scenes, two statues (*the Madonna* and *St Peter*) by the school of Gagini, an organ (being restored) by Della Valle (1615), and a processional statue of the *Ecce Homo*. Above, steps lead up to the scant remains of the Norman **castle**, with an excellent view. In the lower part of the town is the church of **S. Giacomo** on the edge of the hillside, with charming stuccoes in the interior in very poor condition. The church of **S. Filippo** (also in need of restoration) contains a ceramic pavement, a 17C wooden processional Crucifix in a tabernacle, and two popular statues made out of waxed canvas (1901).

The thermal sulphur **baths** in a 19C building below the town were closed down in 1994. Up until the 1970s the Portella di Cascio (401m) at the base of the rock, formed part of the 72km circuit used for the annual Targa Florio motorcar race, first run in 1906. A 'Madonie' race still takes place here in March.

The famous Regaleali wine is produced by the Tasca d'Almerita family in the district of Sclafani Bagni, at **Regaleali**, many kilometres south of the town on the southern border of the province of Palermo (best reached from Vallelunga in the province of Caltanissetta). The cellars are open to the public and wine and local produce can be purchased.

**Caltavuturo** is a 16C town with stepped streets. It lies in a superb position in cultivated uplands (635m) beneath outcrops of red rock and the ruined fortress taken from the Saracens by Roger I.

### Polizzi Generosa

Polizzi Generosa (917m) is in a beautiful position at the head of the Imera valley. It is a delightful little town which received its name 'Generosa' from Frederick II in 1234. It once boasted 76 churches within its walls, and many of them now belong to local confraternities (who have the keys).

From the small piazza Umberto, where all the main roads converge, via Cardinale Rampolla (with pretty stone and brick paving) leads up to the **Chiesa Madre** with a charming 16C porch and two very worn statues of *St Peter* and *St Paul*. A Gothic portal has been exposed beside the Renaissance doorway. In the south aisle is a painting of the *Madonna of the Rosary* by Zoppo di Ganci. At the end of the aisle, a chapel on the right (closed by a grille) contains some particularly fine sculptures, including the sarcophagus of Beato Gandolfo da Binasco (recomposed) by Domenico Gagini; reliefs by the Berrettaro family, and a fragment of the *Last Supper* by Domenico Gagini and his workshop. In the sanctuary are two precious large triptychs: the one on the right with the *Madonna enthroned amidst angels* is attributed to the 'Maitre au feuillage en broderie' (early 16C), and the one on the left (with the *Visitation*) dates from the 16C. In the Cappella Ventimiglia (left of the sanctuary) are interesting funerary monuments and in the left transept are 18C statues. The font (with a pagan base) at the west end dates from 1488. The decorative organ was made in the 18C.

Beside the Chiesa Madre is **S. Gandolfo la Povera** (1622) with a high altar-piece of *St Gandolfo* by Zoppo di Ganci. The road continues up to the church of S. Francesco, founded in 1303, now used as an auditorium. On the left is piazza Castello with the ruins of the so-called castle of the Regina Bianca. In the walled Casale garden here two rare fir trees (of the Nebrodi type) survive. A little museum (open only on Sundays) in the piazza illustrates the natural history of the Madonie Mountains. Below S. Francesco is the church of **S. Nicolò de Franchis** (locked) founded in 1167 by Peter of Toulouse, with a bellcote. Nearby is **S. Margherita** (or the Badia Vecchia), a 15C church. It has delicate white and gold stucco decoration. The barrel vault and sanctuary have 19C pictorial decorations, including a copy of Leonardo's *Last Supper*.

Another road from piazza Umberto leads up to the remains of the circular **Torre di Leo**, named after a family who purchased it in 1240 next to the church of **S. Pancrazio Dei Greci** (locked), recently restored, which contains a painting by Zoppo di Ganci. From its terrace (when the gate is open) there is a wonderful view of the mountains.

The main street of the little town, corso Garibaldi, also starts in piazza Umberto. It leads past the centrally-planned church of **S. Girolamo** (deconsecrated and kept locked) by Angelo Italia. Next to it is the former **Collegio Dei Gesuiti**, a large building now occupied by the town hall and prefecture. The fine interior courtyard with loggias on two levels and a single balcony on the top storey has recently been restored. In the morning visitors are allowed up to the top storey where an open balcony has a fine view over the roofs of the town (and the ruined church of the Commenda below). The corso continues past a flight of steps (right) which lead up to the large **Palazzo Carpinello** with a long, low façade. The corso ends at a terrace known as the **Belvedere** which has a magnificent view: the motorway from Palermo to Catania is reduced to a winding stream in the distant valley below, while to the east rise the Madonie mountains. The ancient church of **S. Maria Lo Piano** here, seat of the Teutonic Knights, contains 17C paintings. Via Malatacca leads down from the corso towards **S. Antonio Abate** (closed), which has a red Arabic dome crowning its campanile (once a minaret). Inside is another painting by Zoppo di Ganci. It is worth taking a look at the one-storey houses in the Arab district here.

## Petralia Sottana

Petralia Sottana is a town (population 3800) on a hillside (1000m) enclosed by the mountains. The attractive corso Paolo Agliata passes S. Maria della Fontana (16–17C) and the 18C church of S. Francesco before reaching piazza Umberto I (with a view of the Imera valley). The Chiesa Madre, which has a pretty campanile, was rebuilt in the 17C. It contains a fine sculpted altarpiece of 1501, and a 17C statue of the *Madonna and Child*. Above the town on the road for Petralia Soprana is the church and convent of the SS. Trinità with a marble ancona by Gian Domenico Gagini (1542).

## Petralia Soprana

In a beautiful position on a hillside (1147m) above pinewoods is Petralia Soprana, one of the most interesting and best preserved little towns in the interior of the island. *Petra* was important in the Roman era, and in 1062 it passed into the hands of Count Roger. During the 19C and early 20C rock-salt mines were in operation here, one of which is still in use. The exteriors of the attractive old stone houses have not been covered with plaster as in numerous other Sicilian towns.

In the central **piazza del Popolo** is a large war memorial by Antonio Ugo (1929) and the neo-Gothic town hall (1896). Via Generale Medici leads up past (left) the fine façade of S. Giovanni Evangelista (1770; closed) to piazza Fra Umile with a bust commemorating Fra Umile da Petralia (Pintorno: 1588–1639), the sculptor, famous for his Crucifixes which adorn many churches in Sicily, who was born here. On the right is the 18C Oratorio delle Anime del Purgatorio with a bellcote and very worn portal. Further up is piazza dei Quattro Cannoli with a pretty 18C fountain and palace.

Beyond on the right a wide flight of steps leads down to the **Duomo**, consecrated in 1497, which has a delightful 18C portico. At one end is a squat tower and at the other is the 15C campanile with a two-light window in which two quaint statues of *St Peter* and *St Paul* have been placed. The gilded and white stucco decoration in the interior was carried out in 1859. On the north side the first altar has a fine painted statue of the *Madonna and Child*, and the fourth altar a marble statue of the *Madonna* (*della Catena*). The fifth altar has a high relief of the *Pietà* with symbols of the *Passion*. In the chapel to the left of the sanctuary is an 18C gilded wooden altarpiece. The realistic Crucifix in the sanctuary is the first work of Fra Umile da Petralia (c 1624). The polychrome statues of *St Peter* and *St Paul* are by the Neapolitan sculptor Gaetano Franzese (1764), and the large painting of their martyrdom is by Vincenzo Riolo. On the fifth altar on the south side is a beautiful *Deposition*, attributed since its recent restoration to Pietro Novelli or the school of Ribera. Above the duomo is the 18C domed circular church of S. Salvatore (closed), which was built on the site of a Norman church. It contains 17C–18C statues.

From the other side of piazza del Popolo (see above) via Loreto leads uphill past a pretty courtyard, several nice small palaces, and the 16C church of S. Michele (recently restored) with a miniature bellcote and fountain on its west front. The street ends in the piazza (paved with pebbles) in front of the attractive façade of **S. Maria di Loreto**. The façade of 1750 is by two local sculptors named Serpotta and the two little spires on either side are decorated with coloured stones. It is preceded by a wrought-iron gate of 1881. The beautiful interior has a carved high altarpiece attributed to Gian Domencio Gagini or Antonio Vanello (with a *Madonna* attributed to Giacomo Mancini). It also contains paintings by Vincenzo Riolo, 18C–19C statues, and a fine sacristy of 1783. On the right a lane (via Belvedere) leads out under an arch to a terrace beside the apse of the church, with an excellent view which extends as far as Etna on a clear day.

On the edge of the hill, below corso Umberto, is the church of **S. Teodoro** (closed), founded by Count Roger and rebuilt in 1759. An interesting sarcophagus decorated with animal carvings was discovered here in 1991.

**Geraci Siculo** (1077m) has a ruined castle (1072), which was the seat of the Ventimiglia before they moved to Castelbuono. The church of S. Maria della Porta contains a *Madonna and Child* by Domenico Gagini and his workshop (1475).

**Gangi** is a few kilometres east of the boundary of the Madonie park. It was the birthplace of Giuseppe Salerno, known as 'Lo Zoppo di Ganci', whose *Last Judgement* adorns the church. Attached to the castle is a Renaissance chapel attributed to the Gagini family (early 16C). The town was notorious as a stronghold of the Mafia until the late 1920s when one of their most famous leaders, the 'Queen of Gangi' (who dressed as a man), was arrested by Cesare Mori, the police officer sent to Sicily by Mussolini to deal with the Mafia. At the same time some 100 inhabitants of the little town were convicted as members of the Mafia.

# South and west of Palermo province

This section covers minor towns and villages widely scattered over the large province of Palermo. The most interesting town is Piana degli Albanesi which has been inhabited by Albanians since the 15C. The Bosco della Ficuzza is one of the best preserved forests on the island, and the Bagni di Cefalà a remarkable Arab bath-house. On Monte Iato and near the remote village of Contessa Entellina interesting excavations are in progress.

## ■ Practical information

*Information office.* APT Palermo, ☎ 091/583847.

*Getting there from Palermo.* Piana degli Albanesi is 24km south of Palermo. Buses (*Prestia e Comandè*) run several times a day from via Balsamo and piazza Stazione in Palermo.
**By car.** S. Giuseppe Iato, 25km from Palermo, is just off the new fast *superstrada* from Palermo to Sciacca. Partinico, 28km from Palermo, is on the main road to Trapani, and the places nearer the coast are in the vicinity of the Palermo–Trapani motorway. The southern part of the province is traversed by two roads to Agrigento, the main road via Lercara Friddi, and the secondary road via Corleone, which has some fine scenery and very little traffic.

### Hotels
There are a number of typical resort hotels (mostly ★★★) on the coast at **Isola delle Femmine, Carini, Cinisi** and **Terrasini.** Otherwise this area has very few hotels (and all of them are very simple).
*Agriturismo* accommodation near **Partinico**: *Fattoria Monostalla* and *Il Pescheto*, in contrada Pacino (☎ 091/8783005).
There are two alpine refuges in the **Bosco della Ficuzza**: *Alpe Cucco*, at Godrano (1080 m), ☎ 091/8208225; and *Val dei Conti* (710m), ☎ 091/8464114.
### Restaurants
**Montelepre.** *Monte d'Oro* (**C**).
**Torretta** (10 km from Montelepre). *U zu Caliddu* (**C**) in contrada Piano dell' Occhio.

**Belmonte Mezzagno.** *Trattoria Italiano*, 80 via John Kennedy.
**Villafrati** (near Bagni di Cefalà). *Mulinazzo* (**B**), contrada Mulinazzo on the main road (N121).

# The western part of the province

## Piana degli Albanesi

Piana degli Albanesi (once *dei Greci*; 720m) is the most interesting of the 15C Albanian colonies (population 6100) in Sicily. The inhabitants still use their native tongue, are Catholics of the Byzantine-Greek rite and wear traditional costume for weddings, etc. The most characteristic ceremonies take place at Easter and the Epiphany. Here Garibaldi planned the tactics that led to the capture of Palermo. Piana is known for its excellent bread, cheeses and *cannoli*.

In the pleasant main street, via Giorgio Kastriota, is the cathedral church of **S. Demetrio** (usually open 10.00–12.30). On the west wall is a 19C painting of *St Nicholas* by Andrea d'Antoni (a pupil of Giuseppe Patania). On the north wall of the church is a small Byzantine *Madonna and Child*. The statues are attributed to Nicolò Bagnasco, and the damaged apse frescoes are by Pietro Novelli. The iconostasis was decorated with paintings in 1975.

The main street leads uphill to the piazza beside the church of the **Madonna Odigitria** (usually closed), on a design by Pietro Novelli. Just out of the square is the church of **S. Giorgio**, the oldest church in the town built in 1495. On the south side is a mosaic by the local artist Tanina Cuccia (1984) and a painting of *St Philip Neri* by Giuseppe Patania. The iconostasis has 20C paintings. On the north side is a fresco of *St Anthony Abbot* by Antonio Novelli and a charming equestrian statue of *St George*, fully armed. Other churches of interest include S. Vito (18C, with statues) and SS. Annunziata (with a fresco by Pietro Novelli).

At the lower end of the main street, a stable block (no. 207) has been converted into a library, cultural centre and an interesting **Ethnographical Museum**, arranged by the local inhabitants in 1988 (open 09.30–12.30; Sun & PH 10.00–13.00; Tues, Thurs, & Sat also 15.30–18.30; closed Mon). The delightful exhibits illustrate the peasant life of the community, and some of the traditional costumes (and 18C jewellery) worn by the women of Piana are preserved here.

A few kilometres south of the town is **Portella della Ginestra**, where there is a memorial to the peasants massacred here while celebrating a traditional May Day festival in 1947. Eleven people were killed and 59 wounded by Mafia gangs led by Salvatore Giuliano from Montelepre (see below). This was later understood as an attempt by right-wing activists, in collusion with the Mafia, to combat Communism and advocate independence for the island (both the right wing and the separatists had just lost votes in the local elections).

South-east of the town is the **Lago di Piana degli Albanesi**, a pretty reservoir formed in 1923 by an impressive dam between two high mountains (Kumeta and Maganoce, 1200m and 900m), across the Belice river.

## Monte Iato

S. Giuseppe Iato has recently been much in the news as a centre of the Mafia. On Monte Iato excavations (not yet regularly open to the public; for information, ☎ 091/8573988) have brought to light remains of the ancient city of **Jetae** (the Roman *Iaitas*), a town which flourished from the 4C BC until it was destroyed by Frederick II in the 13C.

Outside **S. Cipirello**, a very rough road (which is to be resurfaced) leads up through lovely countryside to the top of the hill where the site has recently been enclosed and provided with a small museum. The best preserved remains date from the Hellenistic period. From the entrance gate it is a walk of about 20 minutes to the top of the hill with the theatre (late 4C BC, reconstructed in the 1C AD), which could seat 4000, a temple of Aphrodite (c 550 BC), and a large villa on two floors with a peristyle and 25 rooms. The agora has also been partially uncovered. There are splendid views from this isolated spot. Excavations here over the past 25 years have been carried out by the University of Zürich. In the Museo Civico in S. Cipirello (usually open 09.00–13.00) there are finds from the site, including statues.

## Partinico

Partinico (population 29,500) is an agricultural town associated with the name of Danilo Dolci.

**Danilo Dolci** (1924–1997) was a remarkable man from Trieste, who trained as an engineer and architect and also wrote poetry. After a visit to Sicily he became deeply involved in the plight of Sicily's poverty-stricken population and moved here in 1955 to open his principal centre (known as Mirto, an excellent local school). In 1952 he opened *Borgo di Dio*, an orphanage, nearby on the coast at Trappeto. He set up the first free radio station on the island, and organised the building of a dam over the River Iato south-west of Partinico to form the Lago di Poma. This was run by a local co-operative and finally provided water for the local inhabitants and greatly improved agricultural production in the area. His books *Banditi a Partinico* (1955) and *Inchiesta a Palermo* (1956; translated into English in 1959 under the title *Poverty in Sicily*, with an introduction by Aldous Huxley), exposed the devastating effect of the power of the Mafia in Sicily. Often known as Sicily's Gandhi, he used non-violent means to improve the condition of the Sicilian poor, but his Utopian realism came up against the opposition of Italian politicians and he had to face several trials. He was particularly admired abroad: in 1997 his death in poverty passed virtually un-noticed in most of Italy.

In piazza Duomo is a fountain of 1716. The Biblioteca Comunale nearby has an archaeological collection (open Mon–Fri 08.00–14.00, 15.00–19.00) with finds from Monte Iato and Rocca d'Entella, and a local ethnographical collection. From the Duomo corso dei Mille leads to a neo-classical bandstand (1875) near the 17C church of S. Leonardo with works by the school of Novelli. Opposite is the church of the Carmine (1634).

In the hill town of **Montelepre**, where much ugly new building has taken place, the bandit Salvatore Giuliano reigned over a large part of the province, with the support of the Mafia for seven years before he was murdered here in 1950 by his brother-in-law, Gaspare Pisciotta, at the age of 27. His body was shown to the press in a courtyard in Castelvetrano with the story that he had been tracked down and killed there by the authorities. He remained a mythical figure in the imagination of many Sicilians until 1960, when his connection with the Mafia and local police was revealed, as well as his part in the massacre of peasants at Portella della Ginestra (see above). A remarkable film by Francesco Rosi, *Salvatore Giuliano* (1961), tells his true story.

On the coast between Mondello, a suburb of Palermo, and the gulf of Castellammare there are a few holiday resorts. These include **Isola delle Femmine**, facing an island of the same name. It is now surrounded by an industrial zone which has polluted the sea, and hampered its development as a tourist resort. **Carini** (population 20,500) gave its name to the gulf here. It has interesting stalactite caverns, and its fine 16C castle has been acquired by the state in an attempt to save it from ruin. Beyond Punta Raisi airport and Monte Pecoraro (910m) is the lovely gulf of Castellammare which stretches away to Capo S. Vito (see p.153), with a striking background of mountains. Despite a lot of new building it still has some olive groves and plantations of orange trees.

**Terrasini** has a huge holiday centre. The town has a particularly good Museo Civico (open 09.00–12.30; May to Sept also 16.00–19.00) at present divided into three buildings (there is a project to rehouse the collections in Palazzo D'Aumale built in 1835). At no. 12 via Calarossa is the natural history section (with an important ornithological collection); the archaeological section is arranged in the town hall (with finds from a Roman ship of the 1C AD found offshore in 1963); and the ethnographical section, with a remarkable large collection of painted Sicilian carts, is in Palazzo Leone in via Della Chiesa.

## The southern part of the province

**Belmonte Mezzagno**, founded in 1752, has a theatrical church built in 1776. The valley of the ancient River Eleutheros has been filled with new buildings but some persimmon plantations survive here. Above the plain is the ruined castle of **Misilmeri**. It takes its name from the Arab *Menzil el Emir* (village of the Emir). Here in 1068 Count Roger de Hauteville defeated the Saracens, thus paving the way for the Norman domination of Sicily.

The castle of **Marineo** stands at the foot of an oddly shaped rock. The castle (partly abandoned and partly inhabited) was reconstructed in 1559 by Matteo Carnelivari.

## *Bosco della Ficuzza*

Ficuzza is a village dominated by the **Palazzina Reale**, a handsome building in sandstone with numerous chimneys and two clocks (now used by the Forestry Commission; for admission ☎ 091/8463655). It was built by Venanzio Marvuglia in 1803 as a hunting-lodge for the Bourbons, whose huge estate surrounded the lodge. Behind it extends the **Bosco della Ficuzza**, a splendid forest of oak, chestnut and ilex, which is the most extensive and interesting wooded area of its kind left on the island, noted for its fine trees, plants and wildlife. Although once much more extensive, it now covers some 4000 ha. Several rough roads and paths traverse the woods, although much of it is fenced off for protection. Above the woods rises the mountain wall of calcareous rock called the **Rocca Busambra** (1613m), which dominates the plain for many kilometres around. It is wooded at its foot but, above the sheer rock face, its summit provides pastureland. Numerous birds nest here, including the golden eagle.

The *Gorgo del Drago*, the source of the River Frattina, is a lovely green oasis in the barren countryside, with yellow and red rocks.

## Bagni di Cefalà

The Bagni di Cefalà, is a remarkable bath-house dating from the 10C–11C, considered the most interesting Arab edifice left on the island (open daily 10.00–13.00; Sun & PH also 16.00–19.00; closed Mon). The baths have a splendid barrel vault and a pretty arch with two capitals and columns at one end. The water used to bubble up here at 33°C, but since 1989 the spring has been dry, and the baths, in use up until a few years ago, have lost much of their character after their recent restoration. The cufic inscription on a frieze of tufa which runs around the top of the outside wall has virtually disappeared. From here the castle of **Cefalà Diana** is very prominent on a rocky outcrop to the south.

**Baucina** was founded in 1626. The church has a wooden Crucifix by the school of Salvatore Bagnasco. **Ciminna** has a number of interesting churches including the Chiesa Madre with 17C stuccoes by Scipione and Francesco Li Volsi and a painting of *St John the Baptist* by Paolo Amato.

The little hill town of **Mezzojuso** (534m) has Arab origins. Settled by Albanians in the 15C, several of its churches still have services according to the Greek rite. A monastery here has a restoration laboratory for antique books.

**Vicari**, above the fertile valley of the S. Leonardo, has a ruined castle built by Count Roger, with views of extraordinary beauty.

**Lercara Friddi** (660m) was founded in 1605 and was important in the 19C and early 20C for its sulphur mines. A number of 18C churches survive here.

On the southern border of the province, in the hills above the Platani valley is **Castronuovo di Sicilia** where the churches contain 18C stuccoes by Antonio Messina, and the Chiesa Madre has works by the Gagini.

The medieval town of **Prizzi** is near a lake beneath curious outcrops of rock appropriately known as *Imbriaca* (or drunken). An interesting traditional 'dance of the devils' takes place in the town on Easter Sunday. Excavations on the Montagna dei Cavalli in the vicinity have revealed 4C–3C BC remains thought to belong to the ancient city of *Hippana*.

The little town of **Palazzo Adriano**, is a late 15C Albanian colony, with its main monuments in piazza Umberto I.

**Bisacquino**, with good mountain views, was an Arab citadel and then a medieval fortress town. The Olivetan abbey of **S. Maria del Bosco**, has a church (1676–1757) attributed to Vanvitelli, to be restored following serious damage in the Belice earthquake in 1968. It contained a terracotta of the Della Robbia school, two large cloisters (one of the 16C), and a fresco of the *Miracle of the Loaves* (in the refectory).

## Contessa Entellina

Contessa Entellina (524m; population 2100) is a charming mountain village, colonised by Albanians in 1450. Nearly half the population had to be rehoused after the Belice earthquake in 1968. It takes its surname from Entella, a town of the Elymi which is to the north-west on a high isolated rock which stands out above the surrounding hills. On the extensive plateau, excavations are in progress of the city: so far the fortifications have been identified, part of the medieval rocca, and a building of 4C–3C BC. At the foot of the hill were the necropoli. A small antiquarium was opened here in 1996: for admission to the excavations and museum, ☎ 091/8355556, or 091/8355065.

At **Monte Adranone** (1000m), on the provincial border with Agrigento, excavations were begun in 1968 of the ancient city of *Adranon*. This was an indigenous settlement occupied by a Greek city in the 6C BC, probably founded by Selinunte. It was destroyed at the end of the 5C by Carthage. The Carthaginian settlement was conquered by Rome in 263 BC and the site abandoned. Beside the small Antiquarium is part of an Iron Age necropolis including the so-called Tomba della Regina with an interesting entrance. Tombs of the 5C and 4C BC have also been found here. Other remains include walls and the south gate, a sanctuary, and part of the acropolis to the north-east.

## Corleone

Corleone is a town (population 11,400) nestled in the hillside, but now surrounded by ugly buildings. In recent years it has been notorious for its Mafia gang, whose boss Totò Riina ruled *Cosa Nostra* for many years until he was arrested in 1993, after more than 20 years 'in hiding' in Palermo. However, an enlightened local administration since 1994, together with most of its citizens, have courageously attempted to correct this image, symbolised by the renaming of the central piazza after Falcone and Borsellino.

The town of Saracen origin has a Lombard colony established here by Frederick II in 1237. Traces of its importance as a medieval town can be seen in the old centre which preserves some fine palace doorways in its narrow streets. The **Chiesa Madre** (if closed, ring at the inconspicuous north door approached from the road on the left of the outside steps through a gate) contains some interesting wooden statues (16C–17C), wooden stalls by Giovanni Battista Li Volsi, and paintings (on the transept altars) by Fra Felice da Sambuca, and (first north chapel) by Tommaso de Vigilia (*Adoration of the Magi*). The public gardens, laid out in 1820, are well kept. There is an archaeological collection in Palazzo Provenzano (open 09.00–13.00).

# Ustica

Ustica is a pretty island which is the summit of a huge submerged volcano. It has an area of just over 8.6 sq km, and its highest hills rise to c 240m above sea-level. Some 36 miles from Palermo it has 1200 inhabitants. Its rocky shore has numerous grottoes and it is particularly remarkable for its beautiful seabed with a great variety of vegetation and fish. In 1987 the first marine reserve in Italy was established around the coast of the island (although State-owned, it is very efficiently run by the comune of Ustica) and it is much visited by skin-divers. The pleasant little village above the port is well kept, and only crowded in the summer months. The shore of the island has been well preserved, but the local architecture has all but disappeared and been replaced by anonymous little villas, as in many other parts of Italy. One road encircles the island.

# ■ Practical information

*Information offices*. Visitors' Centre of the office of the marine reserve (*Centro Accoglienza*), piazza Umberto I (☎ 091/8449456). Comune di Ustica, ☎ 091/8449045.

## Getting there
**Maritime services to Ustica**. From Palermo daily car ferry in 2 hr 20 min., and hydrofoils in 1 hr 15 min. (more expensive, but several services a day) run by *Siremar*, 120 via Crispi, Palermo (☎ 091/336631). From 1 June–30 September hydrofoil service from Naples four times a week in 4 hours (going on to Favignana and Kelibia in Tunisia).
**Summer boat excursions**. The local fishermen organise 2-hour trips around the island 4–6 times a day (tickets, 15,000 lire, are sold at the Centro Accoglienza of the marine reserve). The trip includes visits to grottoes and time for swimming.

The marine reserve boat, which has a glass keel, also takes small groups of 20 around the coast (4 times a day, 20,000 lire) on a trip which lasts about 1 hr 30 min. and gives the opportunity of observing the marine life on the seabed.

**Transport on the island**. Mini-bus service every half hour from the port around the island. It is sometimes still possible to hire a donkey (there are plans to increase their number on the island).

## Hotels
★★ *Stella Marina*, ☎ 091/8449014; fax 091/8449325; ★ *Clelia*, ☎ 091/8449039; fax 091/ 8449459. Rooms to let at Carmela Tranchina, ☎ 091/8449340 (and others). All the other hotels are only open from April or May to September, including the ★★★★or ★★★★★: *Grotta Azzurra*, ☎ 091/8449048; fax 091/8449396. Numerous school parties visit the island in May, and from June–September it can be difficult to find a hotel room.

## Restaurants
In the village: **A:** *Mamma Lia*, 1 via S. Giacomo. **B:** *Giulia*, via Calvaria; *Ariston*, 5 via della Vittoria; *Stella Marina* and *Le Terrazze*, via Colombo; *Baia del Sole* at contrada Spalmatore.
*Pasticceria*. Bar Centrale, piazza Umberto I.

*Flora and fauna*. The vegetation includes cultivated fields of wheat and low vineyards, as well as almonds and fruit trees, with hedges of prickly pear. Capers and lentils are also produced on the island. Very few woods remain (the island was once covered with trees). Ustica has interesting migratory birdlife, including peregrine falcon, kestrels, storks, heron, razorbills and cormorants. There is no natural water source on the island, but a plant has been installed to treat the sea water for domestic use.

*Fishing*. About 30 professional fishermen live on the island. Although much fishing with explosives took place offshore in the 1960s this has now been prohibited, and the catch is increasing as a result. *Cernia* (a type of sea perch) abound in the rocks, as well as hake, red mullet and lobsters. Swordfish are caught in the spring. As a result of a scheme in collaboration with the marine reserve the local fishermen also organise boat trips for visitors (see above).

**Swimming**. The coast provides excellent swimming, although in some areas of the marine reserve swimming is not allowed. Guides can be hired at the Visitors' Centre for snorkelling and skin-diving.

**Walks**. There are two pretty walks along well-kept paths. One leads up from the village to the hill of Culunnedda (with a radar station). It follows the side of the hill overlooking the cultivated plain of Tramontana. Above the *macchia*, where wild broom flowers in Spring, there are woods of pines and eucalyptus. The other walk starts at the Torre S. Maria (archaeological museum) and skirts the south coast as far as the disused lighthouse at Punta Cavazzi, on the western tip of the island.

### History

The name of Ustica from the Latin 'ustum' (burnt) is derived from the colour of its black volcanic rock. Excavations have proved that it was inhabited in prehistoric times and in the Roman era. It declined under the attacks of Barbary pirates who defeated all attempts to colonise it in the Middle Ages. It remained deserted for many centuries until in 1762 it was repopulated from the Aeolian Islands and Naples by the Bourbons because of its position on the trade route between Naples and Palermo. At this time three towers were constructed to defend the island.

In this century (up until 1961) it was used as a place of exile and as a prison: Carlo and Nello Rosselli and Antonio Gramsci were held here as political prisoners under the Fascist regime. In September 1943 Italian and British officers met in secret on the island to discuss details of Italy's change of sides. The name of the island is connected with a DC 9 air disaster in 1980 when a civil aircraft on its way from Bologna to Palermo exploded over the sea between the island of Ponza and Ustica, leaving 81 people dead. The cause of the explosion has never been solved, although all the evidence points to a military missile directed against a Libyan fighter aircraft, and there has been an international cover-up of this scandal. A radar station was built immediately after the disaster in the centre of the island, probably in an attempt to divert attention and to suggest that this area of the sea was not covered by radar instruments. The establishment of the marine reserve in the last decade, efficiently run by professional management and a group of well-informed local guides, has brought renewed prosperity to the island.

The little **village** above the port of Cala S. Maria was laid out on geometric lines by the Bourbons in the 18C. A road winds up to the pretty piazza (also reached by steps from the port) which is planted with ficus trees. To the right of the church via Calvaria leads uphill to the via Crucis where on the left a charming path continues up to the **Rocca della Falconiera** (157m) a defensive tower built by the Bourbons which is to be used for exhibitions (the fort is also reached by car along a narrow road paved with pebbles in 1995). The tower is on the site of a settlement of the 3C BC, also inhabited in Roman times. This has been excavated in the tufo on three levels, and the most conspicuous remains include a staircase and some 30 cisterns used to collect the rainwater, and a number of tombs. There are fine views above the lighthouse which protects the eastern tip of the island and the rocky point known as the Punta Omo Morto, a nesting-place for numerous birds. To the south-west a necropolis of 5C–6C AD has been identified.

On the other side of the village the **Torre S. Maria**, another Bourbon tower once used as a prison, has been restored and an **archaeological museum** was opened here in 1997 in the fine vaulted rooms. The finds from the island, including Bronze Age objects from the village at Faraglioni, and underwater finds, are well displayed in charming old-fashioned show-cases. Near the tower are remains of a 16C Benedictine convent and interesting old houses known as the *centro storico*, with stables, built around courtyards (some of them recently carefully restored by the local inhabitants).

On the northern tip of the island, at **Faraglioni**, excavations begun in 1989 discovered a large prehistoric village (14C–13C BC), probably settled from the Aeolian Islands, with some 300 houses built in stone. The defensive walls are among the best fortifications of this period known in Italy. The site is not yet open regularly to visitors.

On the west coast, between Cala Sidoti and Caletta is the central zone of the **Riserva Naturale Marina**, a protected area marked by red buoys where fishing is prohibited and boats have to keep offshore. Swimming is allowed only at the extreme northern and southern ends of the reserve (limited access). The delightful little **aquarium** here has a fine display of Mediterranean sea plants and fish. Above is the interesting Bourbon **Torre della Spalmatore**, with fine vaulted rooms, which is owned by the marine reserve who have restored it. It is to be used as a museum and cultural centre. From the tower the view is spoilt by a tourist village built in the 1970s (only open in summer). Just to the south is a disused **lighthouse** at **Punta Cavazzi** which may become a scientific laboratory for marine research. A buoy in the sea here marks an **underwater archaeological itinerary** for skin-divers where a number of finds from various wrecks have been left in situ.

# *Trapani*

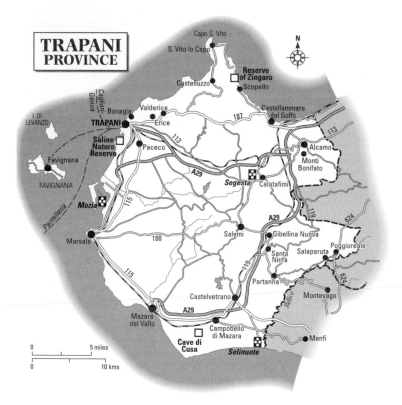

Trapani, the most important town on the west coast of the island (population 73,000), lies below the headland of Mount Erice, with the Egadi Islands usually visible offshore. Its old district occupies a scimitar-shaped promontory between the open sea to the north and the port and salt-marshes to the south, but from inland the town is approached through extensive modern suburbs laid out on a dreary chessboard pattern. The old centre, now a pedestrian precinct, has elegant shops and an air of opulence, and the corso is given distinction by its interesting monumental buildings. Trapani has a number of unusual churches (not all of them open) by the local architect Giovanni Biagio Amico (1684–1754). The collection of decorative arts in the Museo Pepoli is one of the best on the island, and attests to the traditional skill of the native sculptors, silversmiths and jewellers (particularly famous for their works in coral).

Trapani is the capital of a particularly interesting province, including, in the immediate environs, the beautiful little hilltown of Erice, the promontory of Capo S. Vito stretching north beyond the splendid headland of Monte Cofano, and, to the south, the lovely island of Mozia and the town of Marsala. The classical sites of Segesta and Selinunte, also in its province, can easily be reached from Trapani. It is also the port for the Egadi islands and Pantelleria. The ancient industry of extracting salt from the marshes has recently been revived and documented in a museum. For decades a province in economic decline, there have been signs in recent years of an increase in the production of wine and olive oil, as well as salt. Trapani itself is notorious as one of the most important centres of Mafia activity on the island.

# ■ Practical information

*Information offices*. APT Trapani, 27 via S. Francesco d'Assisi (☎ 0923/545511). Information office, piazza Saturno (☎ 0923/29000).

### Getting there
**Railway station** in piazza Umberto. Trains from Palermo, Marsala and Castelvetrano. **Bus services** run by *Autoservizi Segesta* from Palermo terminate in piazza Marina. **Car parking** on lungomare Dante Alighieri, in piazza Vittorio Veneto, or in via Mazzini (near the railway station). **Airport** at Birgi, 18km south. Services to Palermo, Pantelleria, Rome, etc. (and sometimes to Milan in summer). There are plans to introduce flights to Tunis. Bus from the bus station in piazza Malta.

**Town buses** from the centre of the town to the Museo Pepoli (Nos 1, 10 and 11). The corso may be reached by buses from the station or Villa Margherita which terminate in piazza Generale Scio (near the Museo di Preistoria, at the end of the promontory).
**Buses for the province** run by AST (departures from via Malta). For Erice services from the bus station in via Malta and from via Fardella.
**Maritime services**. Ferries from Molo della Sanità to Tunis and Cagliari weekly. To Pantelleria daily ferry (in 4–5 hr) and hydrofoils (*Snav*). Boats (*Siremar*) and hydrofoils from via Ammiraglio Staiti daily to the Egadi Islands (boats in c 50 min.; hydrofoil in 15–20 min.).

### Hotels
★★★★ *Crystal*, 17 via S. Giovanni Bosco (☎ 0923/20000; fax 0923/25555).
★★★ *Nuovo Albergo Russo*, 4 via Tintori (☎ 0923/22166; fax 0923/26623); *Vittoria*, 4 via Francesco Crispi (☎ 0923/873044; fax 0923/29870).
★★ *Moderno*, 20 via Genovese (☎ 0923/21247; fax 0923/23348).
★ *Messina*, 71 corso Vittorio Emanuele (☎ 0923/21198).
   Two kilometres north of the centre, in the comune of Erice on the coast at S. Cusumano, ★★★ *Astoria Park*, lungomare Dante Alighieri (☎ 0923/562400; fax 0923/567422). Better accommodation (★★★ and ★★) is to be found at Erice, on the hill above the town (14km), see p.149.
**Youth hostel**. *Ostello della Gioventù G. Amodeo* (run by the APT of Trapani) at the foot of the hill of Erice on the Martogna road. Another youth hostel is open (in summer only) in via delle Pinete, Erice.

**Campsites** at S. Vito lo Capo and Lido Valderice, see p.154.

## Restaurants

**A** *Da Peppe*, 54 via Spalti; *del Porto*, 45 via Ammiraglio Staiti; *Meeting*, 321 via Fardella; *Ristorante Paolo*, via Firenze; *Taverna Paradiso*, lungomare Dante Alighieri.

**B** *Cantina Siciliana*, via Giudecca; *Da Bettina*, via S. Cristoforo; *Trattoria del Corso*, corso Italia; *Ristorante I Lumi*, corso Vittorio Emanuele; *La Carbonella*, via Fardella.

**C** *Calvino*, 71 via Nunzio Nasi (pizzeria).

The *Trattoria del Sale* at the Museo del Sale (località Nubia) 5km south of the town (described below) serves good meals if ordered in advance (☎ 0923/867442).

**Cafés and pasticcerie**. *Bar Novecento*, via Fardella and *Colicchia*, via delle Arti. A good place to **picnic** is in the gardens of Villa Margherita.

## Annual festivals

Passion procession on Good Friday of the *Misteri*, 20 groups of remarkable figures in wood and paste carved in the 17C–18C, by local artists, including Andrea Tipa. A music festival, the *Luglio Musicale Trapanese* is held in the Villa Margherita in July.

### History

*Drepana* or *Drepanon*, which occupied the promontory in ancient times, was the port of Eryx (see p.149), but was raised to the status of a city when Hamilcar Barca transferred part of the population of Eryx here in 260 BC. It was captured for the Romans by Catulus in 241. It acquired strategic importance as the maritime crossroads between Tunis, Anjou and Aragon in the 13C; King Theobald of Navarre died of typhoid here contracted near Tunis (1270), and here on the 'Scoglio del Malconsiglio', a rock at the extreme end of the cape, John of Procida is supposed to have plotted the Sicilian Vespers with his confederates. Edward I of England, who landed at Trapani on his return from the crusades in 1272, received the news of his accession to the throne here. The city was specially favoured by Peter of Aragon, who landed at Trapani as the saviour of Sicily in 1282, and by Charles V. Nunzio Nasi (1850–1935), a native, who represented Trapani in parliament for 40 years. In 1940 and again in 1943 the city suffered many air raids and naval bombardment, the district of S. Pietro being razed to the ground. Floods caused by the lack of adequate drainage since the construction of new buildings at the foot of Mount Erice afflict the east end of the city; in 1976 16 people were drowned.

From the large piazza Vittorio Emanuele (1869), planted with palm trees, and with a monument to the king by Giovanni Duprè (1882), viale Regina Margherita skirts the north side of **Villa Margherita**, a lovely garden of tropical trees laid out in the late 19C, to **piazza Vittorio Veneto**, the modern centre of administration. Here the early 20C buildings include the fine post office (1924). Restoration is in progress of the old **Castello di Terra**, a castle which has been reconstructed during the centuries and which was converted into a

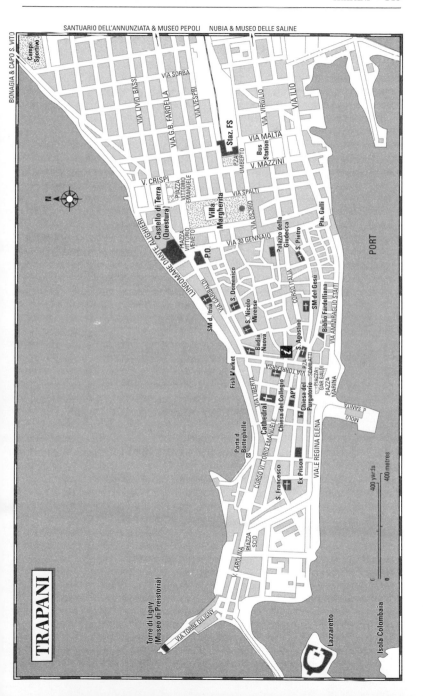

barracks in the 19C. The outer walls have survived, but a modern building is being built inside them to house a police station. The streets to the north give access to the sea front, with a good view of the old city on its promontory.

Via Garibaldi leads towards the old centre past the 18C Palazzo Fardella Fontana, with an elaborate window above its portal, and the 18C Palazzo Riccio di Morana decorated with stuccoes. The 17C church of **S. Maria dell'Itria** has a façade completed in 1745. Inside is a sculptural group of the *Holy Family* by Andrea Tipa. Beyond is the 19C red-brick Palazzo Staiti opposite the 18C Palazzo Milo.

The salita S. Domenico (with steps and pretty cobbles) leads up to the church of **S. Domenico** (often closed), with a blind 14C rose window. The interior contains a remarkable wooden Crucifix (thought to date from the 14C) in an 18C chapel by Giovanni Biagio Amico in the north aisle. Near the entrance is a fresco fragment of the 15C. The sanctuary preserves the sarcophagus of Manfred, son of Frederick III of Aragon. A chapel behind has fresco fragments (14C and 15C), recently discovered. The Baroque frames, pulpit and organ are interesting.

Nearby, downhill to the south, is the church of **S. Nicolò Mirense** (usually closed), which has a little garden. Inside is a 16C marble tabernacle on the east wall and in the left transept a striking sculptural group of *Christ between the two thieves*, a realistic 18C work in wood and paste by a local sculptor. Via delle Arti and via della Badia lead back to via Garibaldi where the 17C façade of **S. Maria del Soccorso** (or the **Badia Nuova**) is situated, with a fine interior decorated in pink and grey marble and elaborate organ lofts. A short way back along via Garibaldi is the church of the **Carminello** (or S. Giuseppe; usually closed), with an 18C portal with bizarre twisted columns. It was built in 1699 and the statue in the apse of *St Joseph and the young Christ Child* is a charming 18C sculpture by Antonio Nolfò (an earlier version of the statue, probably used for processions, is kept in the sacristy). A wooden Crucifix is attributed to Giacomo Tartaglio.

From the Badia via Torrearsa leads right, past the 16C church of the **Carmine** with a fine exterior with tall pilasters and a high cornice to the sea front beyond a pretty market building of 1874. Fish is sold under the portico and produce sold in the piazza around a fountain with a statue of *Venus*. Via Torrearsa leads in the other direction to **Palazzo Senatorio**, used as municipal offices, built in 1672, which has an eccentric theatrical façade with statues on the upper part.

From here the handsome wide **corso Vittorio Emanuele** leads towards the end of the promontory. On the right is the **Chiesa del Collegio dei Gesuiti**, built c 1614–40 by Natale Masuccio, with a Baroque façade by Francesco Bonamici (1657). The interior, with stuccoes by Bartolomeo Sanseverino, has been closed for restoration for many years. The sacristy has beautifully carved cupboards in walnut by Pietro Orlando (18C). Beyond the monumental former Collegio dei Gesuiti (now a school) is the **Cathedral of S. Lorenzo** (1635), which has a very unusual façade, built by Giovanni Biagio Amico in 1743, preceded by a portico. On the south side (fourth altar) is a Crucifixion attributed to the local 17C artist Giacomo Lo Verde, and on the north side (second altar) is a painting of *St George* by Andrea Carreca and (fourth altar) a fine painting of the *Deposition* (showing Flemish influence).

In front of the cathedral via Giglio leads to the church of the **Purgatorio** (closed) with a fine tiled dome and elaborate façade by Giovanni Biagio Amico. Nearby in via S. Francesco is a building (being restored) built in the 17C as a prison, with four caryatids on its façade, and, further on, on the opposite side of via S. Francesco, the church of the **Immacolatella** (recently restored but not yet open), with a delightful apse by Giovanni Biagio Amico (1732). At the end of via S. Francesco the church of **S. Francesco** (13C–17C) can be seen, with a green dome next to a fine doorway.

The corso continues past (left) the 18C Palazzo Berardo Ferro, which has a courtyard, and then Palazzo Alessandro Ferro (1775), decorated with a clock and busts in medallions. Beyond on the right is the little Porta delle Botteghelle (13C), outside of which the defensive fortifications which protected the town from the sea can be seen. The corso, now at the narrowest part of the promontory (the sea can be seen at either end of the side streets), becomes less interesting. Some 800m further on (buses to piazza Generale Scio), via Torre di Ligny bears right and ends at the **Torre di Ligny**, a fortress built in 1671 by the Spanish Viceroy, on the tip of the promontory. It has been well restored to house the **Museo Trapanese di Preistoria** (open daily 09.30–12.30, 16.00–19.00), beautifully arranged on two floors, with excellent views from the windows.

The province of Trapani is one of the richest areas on the island for prehistoric finds. Among the exhibits are stone artefacts and pebble-tools from the Lower Paleolithic period; finds from caves (including tombs in the Grotta dell'Uzzo); material from Tunis (Upper Paleolithic); and Neolithic artefacts in ossidian and flint. An important section is dedicated to the incised drawings (Upper Paleolithic) and cave paintings (Neolithic) from the Cala dei Genovesi cave on the island of Levanzo (see p.163). Numerous fossils and animal remains (elephants, etc.) are displayed, found in caves on Monte Cofano and Capo S. Vito. In the upper room are underwater finds, including ceramics from North Africa and Spain, amphorae and a bronze helmet of 5C–4C BC. When there is no wind, admission is sometimes granted to the balcony on the roof of the fort from which there is a fine view.

From beside the Torre di Ligny there is a view across the bay to the **Isola Colombaia**, which was the base of the Roman siege operations in 241 BC. An Aragonese castle here, the **Castello di Mare**, was restored in later centuries, and in 1714 the octagonal lantern was added by Giovanni Biagio Amico. It was used as a prison up until the 1960s and there are plans to restore it as a museum (and connect it to the mainland by a wooden bridge). The boulevards which run alongside the harbour return to the town past (on the left) the so-called *Palazzo*, a 14C building several times enlarged.

Near the south end of via Torrearsa (see above) is the restored Templars' church of **S. Agostino**, with its 14C rose window and portal (now used as a concert hall). The Saturn fountain here is on the site of a 14C fountain. Nearby is the **Biblioteca Fardelliana** in the former church of S. Giacomo, with a fine Mannerist façade. Opened to the public in 1830, it contains some important manuscripts, and 90,000 volumes (open 10.00–13.00, 16.00–19.00; Sat 09.00–13.00). In the rebuilt district of S. Pietro is **S. Maria del Gesù** (closed), a church with a transitional 16C façade and a Renaissance south doorway bearing an *Annunciation* in a Catalan-Gothic style. The fine simple interior, golden in colour, contains a decorative niche with a very beautiful *Madonna and*

*Child* in enamelled terracotta by Andrea della Robbia under a marble baldacchino by Antonello Gagini. Further east in the former Jewish district is the unusual **Palazzo della Giudecca**, its embossed tower and 16C windows recalling the Plateresque style of Spain.

At the landward end of the town (c 4km from the centre; bus nos 1, 10 and 11) is the SANTUARIO DELL'ANNUNZIATA (sanctuary of the Madonna di Trapani), founded in 1315 and rebuilt in 1760. Little remains of the 14C structure except the west front with a rose window which overlooks a well-kept little garden with palm trees. The campanile dates from 1650. The entrance is through the north door on the main road. The unusual grey and white interior (open 07.00–12.00, 16.00–19.00) was redesigned in the 18C by Giovanni Biagio Amico. Off the right side the **Cappella dei Pescatori** is situated, a beautiful little chapel built in 1481, perhaps an adaption of an earlier chapel. On the left of the presbytery is the **Cappella dei Marinai**, another attractive chapel built in the 16C in a mixture of styles. From the sanctuary, which has a pretty apse, two fine 16C doorways lead into the **Cappella della Madonna**; here another arch, with sculptures by Antonino Gagini (1531–37) and a bronze gate of 1591 (by Giuliano Musarra), gives access to the inner sanctuary containing a highly venerated statue of the *Madonna and Child*, a very fine work by Nino Pisano or his bottega, known as the *Madonna di Trapani*. Below it is a tiny silver model of Trapani by Vincenzo Bonaiuto, who also made the silver statue in the Cappella di S. Alberto, on the right of this chapel. The sacristy has fine 18C cupboards.

## Museo Regionale Pepoli

In the former Carmelite convent, entered on the right of the façade of the church, is the Museo Regionale Pepoli (open 09.00–13.30, Tues and Thurs also 15.00–18.30; Sun & PH 09.00–12.30). This includes a municipal collection formed in 1827, a group of paintings which belonged to General Giovanni Battista Fardella, and a large collection donated by Count Agostino Pepoli in 1906. The museum was opened here in 1914 (and re-arranged in 1965). The exhibits are beautifully arranged and well labelled, but some rooms can be kept closed when there is a lack of custodians. The entrance is through the paved 16C–17C cloisters, with palm trees. The rooms are un-numbered but described below in their logical sequence.

**Ground floor. Room I** contains architectural fragments and Arab funerary inscriptions (10C–12C), and a wooden ceiling salvaged from a chapel. **Room II** contains a sculpted portal by Bartolommeo Berrettaro; a **stoup** of 1486 from the *Annunziata*, resembling those in Palermo Cathedral; and works by the Gagini, notably a figure of *St James the Great*, by Antonello (1522). In the room on the left is a macabre guillotine.

The grand staircase (begun in 1639 and decorated in the 18C) leads up to the **first floor** where **rooms III–XI** are devoted to paintings of the Neapolitan and local schools. **Room III**, Master of the Trapani Polyptych, *Madonna and Child with saints* (from the church of S. Antonio Abate; removed for restoration), Roberto di Oderisio, *Pietà* (c 1380). In **room IV** are three paintings by Il Pastura (Antonio del Massaro). **Room VI** contains *St Francis receiving the Stigmata*, attributed to Titian, and works by the local painters Andrea Carreca

(1590–1677) and Giacomo Lo Verde. **Rooms VII–XI** display 17C Neapolitan works.

In the corridor there is a portrait of Nunzio Nasi by Giacomo Balla and cases of wooden figurines by Giovanni Matera (1653–1718) illustrating the *Massacre of the Innocents* in 16 tableaux. The bronze head of an old man is by Domenico Trentacoste. Also to be found here are 19C scenes of the *Adoration of the Magi* and *Nativity* by Andrea Tipa in wax alabaster, coral, etc., a late 17C salt cellar; 18C–19C Sicilian coral jewellery and a 17C chalice.

In **rooms XII–XXI** is a superb **collection of decorative arts**, most of them made by local craftsmen in the 17C–19C, including silversmiths, jewellers and sculptors. Particularly remarkable are the charming **crêche figures**, the best by Giovanni Matera (1653–1718), and *Nativity* scenes.

At the end of the corridor there are some elaborate 17C objects in coral, a skill for which Trapani is particularly famous, notably a *Crucifixion* and a candelabra by Fra Matteo Bavera; 16C silver works from Nuremburg and exquisite jewellery made in Trapani. **Room XXI** contains majolica, made locally, and from Faenza and Montelupo. The archaeological collection in **rooms XXIII–XXIV** contains finds from Erice, Selinunte and Mozia, and coins of the 5C BC. At the top of the stairs, in the first corridor, are majolica tiled pavements, including one with a splendid scene of tuna fishing (the *mattanza*). The small prints and drawings collection (not usually on view) includes works by Stefano della Bella and Jacopo Callot. The flag of *Il Lombardo*, the ship sailed by Garibaldi and the 'Thousand', is also owned by the museum.

## The salt-pans of Trapani

On the secondary road from the port to Marsala (which runs to seaward of the railway and the main N115 road) the *saline* of Trapani can be seen, the salt-pans where a number of windmills (some with sails), which used to be used to refine the salt, survive. There are two nature reserves run by the Worldwide Fund for Nature here. At **Nubia**, on the edge of the sea c 5km south of Trapani, the **Museo delle Saline** was opened in 1988 (it is temporarily closed for restructuring). This illustrates the ancient industry of extracting salt which still takes place here and in a number of other salt-pans in the marshes between Trapani and Marsala. Piles of salt, protected by tiles, can usually be seen in the area. The museum is housed in a 17C building which was used as a store and dormitory for the workers. In the centre of the building is a windmill once used for refining the salt (this process

*The salt-pans of Trapani*

is now carried out at a refinery). The exhibits illustrate the various stages in extracting the salt, an industry which from the 15C up to the beginning of the 20C was extremely important to the local economy.

From February to March sea water is pumped by a mill (seen from the window) from a canal into the beds, and then into salt-pans which decrease in depth to allow the salinity of the water to increase. When the sun has evaporated the water from the last pan the harvest begins in July. The salt is then piled up and protected from humidity by tiles. Particularly good fish are caught in the pans in December, and there is interesting birdlife in the marshes which became a protected area in 1991. A restaurant here is usually open if booking is made in advance (see p.142).

# Erice

Erice is a silent little medieval town (population 350) in a remarkable position perched on top of an isolated calcareous hill (751m), high above the sea. It is often shrouded in mist (and chilly in winter) which contributes to its feeling of isolation from the rest of the world. It was famous in ancient times for its important sanctuary of Venus; white doves sacred to the goddess still inhabit the town. The view to the north of **Monte Cofano**, one of the most beautiful promontories on the coast of Sicily, is unforgettable. The reddish colour of its sheer rock face changes according to the weather and time of day. To the south-west there is another remarkable view of Trapani and the Egadi Islands, and, on a clear day, Cape Bon in Tunisia.

The grey stone houses of Erice (mostly dating from the 14C to 17C), hidden behind their high courtyard walls, and the beautifully paved streets, unusually clean and deserted, give the town an austere aspect. Some of the charming courtyards have little gardens. The perfect triangular shape of the town makes it difficult to find one's bearings, despite the fact it is so small. It has particularly good hotels, restaurants, and *pasticcerie*. The resident population is diminishing rapidly, and many of its houses are now occupied only in the summer months by residents of Trapani or Palermo who come here on holiday to escape the heat: the number of inhabitants in August rises to about 5000. A number of churches in the town, including the Chiesa Madre, are now open regularly.

## ■ Practical information

*Information office*. Azienda Autonoma, 11 viale Conte Pepoli, ☎ 0923/869388.

*Getting there*. Three roads ascend the hill from Trapani. The most spectacular leaves the east end of the town at Raganzili (via Martogna) beside the disused cableway station and ascends in 14km. It passes beneath the cableway and begins to climb through pine woods, with fine views of Trapani and the Egadi Islands. Higher up it rounds the wooded hill to reveal Monte Cofano and Capo S. Vito in the distance. It then traverses an upland plain with a few vineyards and a picturesque group of abandoned farmhouses on a promontory. It passes the turn for the Museo Agro Forestale di S. Matteo, described at the end of this chapter. It then joins the road from Valderice and traverse thick woods before entering Erice.

Another road (constructed by the Bourbons in 1850) forks left from the N187 outside Trapani and climbs via the cemetery to the summit (10.5 km). The longest road (17km) forks off from the N187 at Valderice.

**Bus** from Trapani in c 40 minutes (the cableway at the end of via Fardella at Raganzili has been out of action for some 30 years: there are long-term plans to re-activate it).

**Car parking** outside Porta Trapani (in August a car-park is open near the youth hostel with a minibus service).

### Hotels

★★★ *Moderno*, 67 via Vittorio Emanuele, with restaurant, ☎ 0923/869300; fax 0923/869139; *Elimo*, 75 via Vittorio Emanuele, ☎ 0923/869377; fax 0923/869252.

★★ *Edelweiss*, 5 cortile P. Vincenzo, vicolo S. Domenico (☎ 0923/869420).

**Youth hostels**. *Ostello della Gioventù G. Amodeo* at the foot of the hill on the Martogna road; *Ostello della Gioventù, C.S.I.*, via delle Pinete (open in summer only).

### Restaurants

**B** *Moderno*, 67 via Vittorio Emanuele; *Monte S. Giuliano*, 7 via S. Rocco; *Elimo*, 75 via Vittorio Emanuele. **C** *La Pentolaccia*, 17 via Guarnotti; *La Vetta da Mario*, via Fontana.

**Cafés and pasticcerie**. Two cafés in via Vittorio Emanuele are run by Maria Grammatico (the second in a charming house, beautifully furnished). They have excellent home-made almond pastries. There are two more *pasticcerie* near S. Domenico: *Antico Pasticceria del Convento* and *Silvestro*.

**Places to picnic** in Villa Balio or in the pinewoods below the walls (off viale delle Pinete), or at the Museo di S. Matteo.

**Annual festivals**. Procession of the *Misteri* on Good Friday. Festivals of medieval and Renaissance music (in summer) and of international folk music played on popular instruments (first Sunday in December).

### History

*Eryx*, an Elymian city of mythical origin, was famous all over the Mediterranean for the magnificent temple of the goddess of fertility, known to the Romans as Venus Erycina. On this splendid site, naturally defended and visible for miles around it was a noted landmark for navigators from Africa. An altar was first set up here by the Sicani and the sanctuary became famous during the Elimian and Phoenician period. In 415 BC the inhabitants of Segesta took the Athenians to see its rich treasury. Captured by Pyrrhus in 278 BC it was destroyed in 260 by Hamilcar. The Roman consul L. Junius Pullus took the hill in 248 and was besieged by Hamilcar, who was himself blockaded by a Roman army, until the Punic cause was lost by the naval victory of Catulus. The cult of Venus Erycina reached its maximum splendour under the Romans and the sanctuary was restored for the last time by Tiberius and Claudius. The Saracens called the place *Gebel-Hamed*, which Count Roger, who had seen St Julian in a dream while besieging it, changed to *Monte S. Giuliano*, a name it kept until 1934. The city thrived in the 18C when the population was around 12,000.

A local industry which survives here is the weaving of lovely brightly coloured cotton rugs which are made and sold in the shops in viale Conte Pepoli, near S. Domenico, and at 9 via Vittorio Emanuele. A ceramics factory operates below the town on via Martogna (the wares are also for sale here).

The entrance to the town is by **Porta Trapani**, beyond which via Vittorio Emanuele climbs steeply uphill. Just to the left is the CHIESA MADRE (Assunta), which has a beautiful fortified Gothic exterior. The porch dates from 1426. The splendid detached **campanile** was built as an Aragonese look-out tower in c 1315 by Frederic III, several years before the foundation of the church. The **interior** (open 09.30–13.00, 15.00–17.15) received its impressive neo-Gothic form, with an elaborate cream-coloured vault, in 1852. The side chapels have pretty tiled floors. The apse is filled with a huge marble altarpiece by Giuliano Mancino (1513). In the sanctuary, through a small tondo on the left wall, a fresco fragment of an angel can be seen, the only part of the 15C decoration of the church to have survived. In a chapel on the left the 16C painting of the *Madonna of Custonaci* (the venerated patron of Erice) was replaced in 1892 by the present copy when the original was taken to the sanctuary of Custonaci on the coast. The next chapel, with a pretty dome, dates from 1568. Another chapel on this side has early 19C paintings. In a chapel on the right side is a *Madonna* by Domenico Gagini (1469), with a finely carved base.

Via Vittorio Emanuele continues steeply uphill past several old shop-fronts and characteristic courtyards. At a fork via Vittorio Emanuele continues left past the huge old ruined Gothic church of S. Salvatore beside a lovely old narrow lane which leads downhill (and has a distant view of the sea). To the right via Bonaventura Provenzano ends at a house with a Baroque doorway and window near the church of **S. Martino** (open 15.00–18.00), with another Baroque portal, and an interesting 15C statue of the *Madonna* in the interior. Just before reaching piazza Umberto, beside a charming café in a 19C palace, a flight of steps leads down left to the monumental doorway with four columns of S. Rocco (closed). The last building in the corso houses a *Circolo*, an old-fashioned private club.

The central **piazza Umberto** is the only large open space in the town. A pretty palace is now used by a bank, and a long 19C building houses the town hall and the **Biblioteca and Museo Comunale Cordici** (open 08.30–13.30; or on request), named after the local historian Antonino Cordici (1586–1666). The library was founded in 1867 with material from the suppressed convents of the city. It now has c 20,000 volumes. In the entrance hall is a beautiful relief of the *Annunciation* by Antonello Gagini, one of his finest works (1525), and a number of inscriptions. Upstairs in the well-arranged charming small **museum** are interesting local archaeological finds (including a small Attic head of *Venus*, 5C BC); a 15C well-head; 16C–18C church vestments; a painting of *St Mary Magdalene and Martha* by the local 17C artist, Andrea Carreca; and a wooden Crucifix by Pietro Orlando (also 17C).

Via Guarrasi leads ahead out of the piazza and immediately on the left a stepped lane (via Argentieri) leads down across via Carvini into via Vultaggio which continues to wind down past the 17C church of **S. Francesco di Paola**

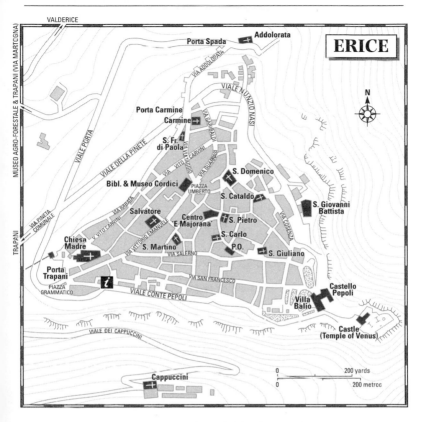

(open 10.30–12.30) with a classical façade. The delightful interior was restored in 1954 by an American benefactor. It has white stucco decoration in very low relief on the walls and the barrel vault, a worn tiled pavement in the sanctuary, fine woodwork, and popular votive statues.

Lower down on the right is the 14C Palazzo Militari with Gothic traces next to the Gothic church of the Carmine (closed). Here is **Porta Carmine**, with a worn headless statue in a niche, on its outer face.

The magnificent **walls** here, which stretch from Porta Spada to Porta Trapani, protected the only side of the hill which has no natural defences: on all the other sides the sheer rock face made the town one of the most impregnable fortresses on the island. The walls are constructed on huge blocks of rough stone which probably date from the Elimian period, above which can be seen the square blocks added by the Carthaginians. The masonry in the upper parts, with stones of smaller dimension, date from the 6C BC. The defences were strengthened in the Roman era and in the Middle Ages, and six postern gates and 16 medieval towers survive. Inside the gate the stepped via Addolorata leads down past a well-preserved stretch of the walls, with a distant view ahead of Monte Cofano, to the church of the **Addolorata** (or S. Orsola; closed), surrounded by a little garden. It has an interesting 15C–16C plan. The 18C sculptures of the *Misteri* are kept here, which are taken in procession through the streets of Erice on Good Friday. In this remote and picturesque corner of the town is the Norman **Porta Spada**.

From Porta Carmine (see above) via Rabatà (which has lost its traditional paving) leads back to Porta Trapani following the walls (less well preserved here) where there are a number of postern gates. Tiny narrow alleyways lead up left to via Carvini and piazza Umberto.

From piazza Umberto (see above), in front of the museum, via Antonio Cordici leads up out of the piazza past a few shops to piazza S. Domenico where there is a pretty Baroque palace. The former church of **S. Domenico**, with a classical porch, has been restored as a lecture hall for the Centro Majorana (see below). From the right side of the church via S. Cataldo leads downhill (and right) past a neo-Gothic electricity tower to the bare façade of **S. Cataldo** (open for services only) on the edge of the old town. It was founded before 1339, and rebuilt in 1740–86. It contains a stoup of 1474 by the workshop of Domenico Gagini, and a painting by Andrea Carreca.

Further downhill and to the right, beyond a less picturesque part of the town, is the church of **S. Giovanni Battista** (deconsecrated, opened on request by the religious community here) on the cliff edge, with a 15C dome whose pretty shape recalls Arab architecture, and an ancient side doorway. It contains a statue of *St John the Evangelist* by Antonello Gagini, and of *St John the Baptist* by Antonino Gagini. There is a good view from via Cusenza.

From piazza S. Domenico (see above), via Guarnotti leads up right to the church of **S. Pietro** (open for services) with an 18C portal. The beautiful white interior by Giovanni Biagio Amico (1745) has a worn tiled pavement. Beside it is an arch over the road and on the right (at no. 26) a convent has been restored as the headquarters of the **Centro Internazionale di Cultura Scientifica Ettore Majorana**. Founded in 1963, this has become a famous centre of learning where courses are held for scientists from all over the world.

Via Guarnotti continues past the former convent and orphanage of S. Carlo next to the bare façade of the church of **S. Carlo** (open 10.30–12.30). It has a pretty majolica floor, and on a side altar there is a statue of the *Madonna del Soccorso* with a tiny relief of *St Michael Archangel* on the base. The nuns' choirs are protected with carved wooden screens. On the right is the post office and downhill on the left is a pleasant raised piazza with a statue in front of the church of **S. Giuliano** (deconsecrated, used by a religious community), with an elegant 18C campanile. The road continues down past two very old shop fronts and crosses via Porta Gervasi (with a view left of the church of S. Giovanni Battista with its dome, see above). A ramp leads up right to **Villa Balio**, delightful public gardens (with ilexes and box hedges) laid out in 1870 by Count Agostino Pepoli on the summit of the hill, with wonderful views. It has a monumental entrance with a double staircase on via S. Francesco. Above is the **Castello Pepoli** (still privately owned by the Pepoli; no admission), a Norman castle reconstructed in 1875–85 by Count Pepoli, with a 15C tower restored in 1973. The excellent view from the terrace on the left takes in Monte Cofano, the sea coast, and S. Giovanni Battista on the side of the hill. Below the abandoned neo-Gothic *Torretta* in trees can be seen, also built by Count Pepoli.

A ramp leads down from the gardens beside the castle to viale Conte Pepoli, on the southern edge of the hill, which continues left to end beside the 17C steps up to the **Castello 'di Venere'** (opened daily by volunteers 08.30–13.30, and sometimes in the afternoon), on the edge of the rock. Above the entrance to the castle is the coat of arms of Charles V and a Gothic window. In the disappointing interior, the ruined Norman walls surround the sacred area which was once the site of the famous Temple of Venus (see above), many fragments of which are embedded in the masonry of the castle. A few very worn Roman fluted column drums can be seen here and the so-called *Pozzo di Venere*, once thought to be a piscina, was probably a silo. A mosaic pavement discovered in 1932 has disappeared. The view is breathtaking.

On the hillside below the town the interesting **Museo Agro Forestale di S. Matteo** was opened in 1986 (open daily 08.00–14.00; Sun & PH 09.00–17.00). It is reached from the Raganzili road (described at the beginning of this chapter). About 3km below Erice a signposted turn leads in c 500m to the gates of the estate owned by the forestry commission.

A rough road (c 1km) continues to the museum in the lovely old Baglio di S. Matteo, arranged in rooms around the courtyard. The exhibits include wine- and olive-presses, farm carts, saddle and tack, agricultural implements and household objects. There is also a natural history section.

The beautifully kept farm of c 500 ha may also be visited, where work horses (a Sicilian breed known as 'S. Fratello', until recently threatened with extinction) are raised. The site is spectacular with fine views towards Capo S. Vito, and the vegetation includes dwarf palm trees, cypresses, fruit trees and woods (experimental replanting is carried out). A path leads past a little palaeochristian oratory below ground level. A smithy and carpentry shop operate on the estate. A huge reservoir to collect rainwater is conspicuous on the hillside. Further downhill (only 1km from Trapani) is the charming little **Parco-zoo di Martogna** where wildfowl and Tibetan goats are kept.

# San Vito lo Capo & Castellammare del Golfo

This chapter covers the coastal areas north-east of Trapani, including S. Vito lo Capo on the northernmost tip of the island and the town of Castellammare del Golfo on its wide gulf. One part of this coast has been protected as a beautiful nature reserve (the Riserva Naturale dello Zingaro), which can be explored on foot.

## ■ Practical information

*Information office*. APT Trapani, ☎ 0923/29000.

*Getting there*. A road (38km) runs along the coast north from Trapani to S. Vito lo Capo. It continues around the point but terminates at the northern entrance to the Zingaro nature reserve. Castellammare del Golfo, 37km from Trapani, can only be reached by the road across the base of the peninsular via Valderice. The picturesque village of Scopello and its old tunny fishery are reached along a byroad (10km) from Castellammare.

## Hotels

**S. Cusumano**. ★★★ *Astoria Park Hotel*, lungomare Dante Alighieri, ☎ 0923/562400; fax 0923/567422.

**Bonagia**. ★★★★ *La Tonnara di Bonagia*, piazza Tonnara, ☎ 0923/431111; fax 0923/592177.

**S. Vito lo Capo**. ★★★ *Capo S. Vito*, 29 via Tommaso, ☎ 0923/972122; fax 0923/972559. ★★ *Egitarso*, 54 via Lungomare, ☎ 0923/972111; fax 0923/972062; *Miraspiaggia*, 44 via lungomare, ☎ 0923/972355; fax 0923/972009; *Riva del Sole*, 11 via Generale Arimondi, ☎ & fax 0923/972629. Near **Valderice**. ★★★ *Baglio S. Croce*, on the main road (SS 187), 6 km east of Valderice (☎ 0923/89111; fax 0923/891192).

**Castellammare del Golfo**. ★★★ *Al Madarig*, 7 piazza Petrolo, ☎ 0924/33533; fax 0924/33790.

**Scopello**. ★ *Pensione Torre Bennistra*, 9 via Armando Diaz, and 19 via Natale di Roma (☎ 0924/541128)

## Campsites

**Bonagia**. ★ *Lido Valderice*, ☎ 0923/573086

**S. Vito lo Capo**. ★★★★ *El Bahira*, località Makari (Salinella), ☎ 0923/972577. ★★★ *La Fata*, via Mattarella, ☎ 0923/972133. ★★ *Soleado*, 40 via del Secco, ☎ 0923/972166

**Castellammare del Golfo** (open mid June–Sept). ★★★ *Baia di Guidaloca*, on the bay of Guidaloca, ☎ 0924/541262; *Lu Baruni*, località Barone, ☎ 0924/39133; *Nausicaa*, località Forgia, ☎ 0924/33030. ★★ *Ciauli*, località Ciauli, ☎ 0924/39049.

## Restaurants

**S. Vito lo Capo**. B *Alfredo*, contrada Valanga; *Thàam*, 32 via Duca degli Abruzzi; *Sicilia in Bocca*, 24 via Savoia.

**Castellammare del Golfo**. C *Da Totò*, 121 via Marconi.

**Scopello**. C *Torre Bennistra*, 9 via Armando Diaz.

## The road from Trapani to Capo San Vito

At the foot of Mount Erice is **S. Cusomano** where the windmill of a salt-pan is being restored, near a tuna fishery. Ships are protected from the low islands offshore here by a lighthouse. Pizzolungo is an unattractive place with marble quarries. At **Bonagia** there is a picturesque tuna fishery which has been restored as a hotel. Beside the pretty little fishing port are hundreds of rusting anchors and a fine tall tower. On the plain here numerous small holiday houses have been built.

**Custonaci** has a sanctuary with a venerated painting of the *Madonna*, and a number of marble quarries. On the outskirts, a rough road (signposted *Grotte Mangiapane*) leads past an old quarry to a tiny abandoned borgo built inside a huge cave at the foot of the beautiful Monte Cofano. On either side of the paved street are little houses with courtyards, bread ovens, etc, and high above the cave serves as a second roof.

Surrounded by barren hills is **Castelluzzo**, with one-storey houses and palm trees. It has a picturesque main street which leads downhill, and outside the town are plantations of almonds and olive trees on the plain which descends to the seashore. There is a fine view of the beautiful headland of Monte Cofano, with Erice in the distance. On the main road is the interesting little 16C domed Cubola di S. Crescenzia, derived from Arab models.

## San Vito lo Capo

S. Vito lo Capo at the tip of the cape has been developed as a seaside resort (population 4000) with good beaches. Laid out on a regular plan in the 18C–19C, most of the houses are decorated with colourful plants. The unusual church, a square fortress, was a 13C sanctuary which was fortified by order of Charles V in 1526 to defend it against pirate raids. On the eastern side of the beautiful promontory of Monte Monaco is a disused tuna fishery overlooking the Gulf of Castellammare. A deserted road (signposted Calampiso) continues high above the shore across bare hills through an African landscape, with dwarf palm trees and giant carobs, where broom and wild flowers blossom in spring. Beyond the holiday village of Calampiso (hidden below the road) the right fork continues to an unsurfaced road which ends at the northern entrance to the **Riserva Naturale dello Zingaro** (described below).

## Castellammare del Golfo

Castellammare del Golfo is a port (population 14,500) which was important for its tuna fisheries in the Middle Ages. It was notorious for its Mafia connections in the 1960s and 1970s. The old centre has a particularly interesting plan with numerous long, straight, parallel streets sloping down at an angle to the sea. The 18C Chiesa Madre has a 17C majolica statue of the *Madonna*. The 14C castle (signposted), at the end of the promontory, is approached over a narrow bridge with a view of the port on the left. A road (signposted *Porto Turistico*) descends to the harbour at the foot of the castle headland, with its colourful houses and boats and a number of trattorie. On the other side of the cape, the seaboard has been planted with palm trees.

## Scopello

A byroad follows the coast north of Castellammare for Scopello. Paths lead down to Cala Bianca, Cala Rossa and Baia Guidaloca, beautiful bays on the rocky coast, where the sea is particularly clear.

Scopello is a tiny picturesque village. From the little piazza (with a large drinking trough) an archway leads into the old paved courtyard with a few trees of an 18C *baglio* surrounded by one-storey houses, a number of them now used as cafés or restaurants.

Below the village is the **Tonnara di Scopello** an important tuna fishery from the 13C up to the middle of this century. It is well seen on the sea below the road, beside fantastically shaped rocks on which ruined defense towers are situated. The buildings have been beautifully preserved (now private property, but visitors are welcome from 09.00–19.00). A footpath leads down to the sea front where hundreds of anchors are piled up beside the picturesque old buildings and a little cove. The life of the fishermen who used to live here was vividly described by Gavin Maxwell in *The Ten Pains of Death* (1959).

## The Zingaro nature reserve

The coast road soon ends at the southern entrance to the **Riserva Naturale dello Zingaro**, a beautiful nature reserve (open daily, sunrise to sunset), the first of its kind in Sicily. Local protest in 1981 succeeded in blocking the construction of a road here, which was begun in 1976 and was to have connected Castellammare to S. Vito lo Capo, and open up the area to development. Now these 6km of unspoilt coastline can be explored on foot along marked paths, and there are six beaches where you can swim. The well-preserved landscape is particularly beautiful and interesting for its birdlife. No motorised transport of any kind is allowed inside the park, and the guardians and keepers use mules to carry out their work. The museum, about 500m from the Scopello entrance, is open 09.00–16.00 in winter, and 08.00–21.00 in summer: it illustrates the peasant life of the area. The Grotta dell'Uzzo, also in the reserve (about 5km from the Scopello entrance), was inhabited in the Paleolithic era. There is another entrance to the park on its northern border, approached by the road from S. Vito lo Capo, see above. In 1996 some 1300 ha of *macchia* were burnt in a fire but the vegetation is expected, in time, to regenerate itself.

# Segesta

Segesta, with its famous temple, is one of the most evocative Greek sites on the island, in an isolated spot surrounded by beautiful countryside. The nearby town of Alcamo has an unusually large number of interesting 18C churches.

## ■ Practical information

*Information office*. APT Trapani, ☎ 0923/29000.

*Getting there*. The road (N113) and motorway between Palermo and Trapani (exit at Segesta, 29km from Trapani or 75km from Palermo) run close to the site. There is a railway station (Segesta Tempio) a 20-minute walk from the site on the Palermo–Trapani line (but only one train a day stops here from Palermo, and one from Trapani).

*Hotels*. There are no **hotels** near the site. In Alcamo, ★ *Miramare*, 72 corso Medici, ☎ 0924/21197.

*Refreshments*. There is a **café** by the entrance which serves snacks, and has a well-supplied book and gift shop, but the site is a wonderful place to **picnic.**

A classical **drama festival** is held in summer at the theatre.

The temple and theatre of Segesta are two of the most magnificently sited classical monuments in existence. From the old road, the view of the famous temple on a bare hill in deserted countryside backed by the rolling hills west of the Gaggera is unforgettable. It has been admired by travellers for centuries. The theatre is on a second, higher hill to the east. The site has been enclosed, but is open daily 09.00–dusk.

*The temple of Segesta*

## History

Segesta, also originally known as *Egesta*, was the principal city of the Elymians, who are now thought to have come from the eastern Mediterranean, probably Anatolia. It was rapidly Hellenised, and was in continual warfare with Selinunte from 580 onwards. Its mint was one of the most important on the island. It sought the alliance of Athens in 426. After the destruction of Selinunte in 409 Segesta became a subject-ally of Carthage, and was saved by Himilco (397) from the attacks of Dionysius of Siracusa. In 307, however, Agathocles sacked the city, and changed its name to *Dikoeopolis*. It resumed its old name under the protection of Carthage, but treacherously murdered the Carthaginian garrison during the First Punic War, after which it became the first city in Sicily to ally itself to Rome. It declined during the Arab period and was abandoned by the late 13C.

The ancient city which covered the slopes of Monte Barbaro is still largely unexcavated, and the site of the necropolis has not yet been identified. Sporadic excavations have taken place since the end of the 18C, when the temple was first restored. The theatre was excavated in 1822. An important sanctuary at the foot of Monte Barbaro was discovered in 1950. Excavations since 1989 have been in progress on top of the hill near the theatre. The attractive countryside in the vicinity, with vineyards and some lovely old farmhouses and pine, eucalyptus and olive trees, has been spoiled by the intrusion of the motorway (raised on stilts) from Palermo to Trapani. The pretty viaducts of the railway offer a striking contrast in scale. The distant view of the temple of Segesta is now marred by the two motorway tunnels directly below the elevation on which it stands. The sustaining wall of the theatre stands out on the skyline of Monte Barbaro.

From the car-park a path (flanked by two posts on which the Fascist symbol survives) and steps lead up past agave plants to the **temple**, beautifully situated on a low hill (304m) on the edge of a deep ravine formed by the Pispisa river, across which is a hillside covered with pinewoods. It is one of the grandest existing monuments of Doric architecture, and since it has no cella, scholars are still in doubt whether it represents an unfinished temple or was instead an open peristyle used by a cult. It is thought to have been constructed by a Greek architect c 424–416 BC. It is peripteral and hexastyle with 36 unfluted columns (c 9m high, 2m wide at base) on a stylobate 58m by 23m. The high entablature and the pediments are intact. The bosses used for manoeuvring the blocks of the stylobate into position remain. Refinements include the curvature of the entablature and the abaci. The building is inhabited by birds, but the sound of the motorway in the distance now disturbs this wonderfully romantic spot.

A road (1km; closed to cars; shuttle bus every half hour) climbs up Monte Barbaro to the theatre from the car-park. A prettier and more interesting approach (with spectacular views back down the hill of the temple) is by the path which roughly follows the road (a steep climb of 20–30 minutes) At the foot of the hill conspicuous excavations of part of the walls (and gate) of the ancient city can be seen. Above a sheepfold, yellow signs mark various excavations including an upper line of walls (2C BC) and a cave dwelling (re-used in Roman times; protected by a wooden roof). Beside the car-park near the top of the hill are two enclosures, the higher one has remains of medieval houses built over public buildings from the Hellenistic era and the lower one has a monumental Hellenistic edifice, reconstructed in the Roman period. A path continues towards the theatre with a fine view of the temple below. On the right is an enclosure with a ruined church (12C–15C), and on the summit of the hill remains of a 12C–13C castle and, on the other side of the hill, a 12C mosque (destroyed by the owners of the castle in the 13C).

The **theatre** is in a wonderful position near the summit of Monte Barbaro (415m). It looks towards the gulf of Castellammare beyond Monte Inici (1064m), while inland to the east rise more high mountain ranges. It is one of the best preserved ancient theatres in existence, built in the mid-3C BC or possibly earlier. With a diameter of 63m and two rows of seats, it could hold 3200 spectators. The exterior of the cavea was supported by a high polygonal wall, which is particularly well preserved at the two sides. Beneath the cavea a grotto with late Bronze Age finds was discovered in 1927 by Pirro Marconi. The theatre has been damaged by the sight and sound of the motorway in the valley below.

In contrada Mango at the foot of Monte Barbaro to the east near the Gaggera river is a large Archaic **sanctuary** (not fully excavated), of great importance. The temenos measures 83 x 47m. It is thought to date from the 7C BC. A huge deposit of pottery sherds dumped from the town on the hill above has also come to light here. The rough footpath (c 3km) is no longer practicable.

The nearest town to Segesta is **Calatafimi** (population 8400), which suffered damage in the Belice earthquake of 1968. The town was frequently visited by Samuel Butler in 1893–1900, author of *Erewhon*, who travelled extensively in southern Italy. South-west of the town (signposted Pianto Romano, off the N113) an obelisk commemorates Garibaldi's victory here on 15 May 1860. A cypress avenue leads to the monument by Ernesto Basile (1892) on which Garibaldi's words are inscribed, on reaching the hill after his disembarkation from Marsala (*Qui si fa l'Italia o si muore*; 'here we will create Italy or die'). There are fine views from the hilltop.

## Alcamo

At the eastern extremity of the province of Trapani is the agricultural town (population 43,200) of **Alcamo**, with numerous fine 18C churches. Founded at the end of the 10C, it derives its name from the Arab *Alqamah*. It was the birthplace of the 13C poet Cielo or Ciullo, one of the earliest masters of Italian literature.

In piazza Bagolino (car-park) the terrace has a panorama of the plain stretching towards the sea. Beyond the 16C Porta S. Francesco (or Porta Palermo) corso VI Aprile leads into the town. On the left is the church of **S. Francesco d'Assisi**, founded in 1348 and rebuilt in 1716. It contains a beautiful marble altarpiece attributed to Giacomo Gagini (1568), statues of *St Mark and Mary Magdalene* by Antonello Gagini and a 17C painting of the *Immacolata* by Giuseppe Carrera. The corso continues past the former church of S. Tommaso (c 1450) with a carved Gothic portal. Opposite, next to a convent, is the church of **SS. Cosma e Damiano** (closed), a domed centrally planned building of c 1721 by Giuseppe Mariani. It contains two stucco statues by Giacomo Serpotta and two altarpieces by Guglielmo Borremans.

The corso crosses via Rossotti with a view left of the castle and right of S. Salvatore. The well-preserved **Castello dei Conti di Modica** was built c 1350. On a square plan with four towers, it is being restored and there are long-term plans to open a local ethnographical museum here. **S. Salvatore** stands next to the monastery of the Badia Grande. It contains allegorical statues by Bartolomeo Sanseverino (1758), a follower of Serpotta. The vault fresco and high altarpiece are by Carlo Brunetti (1759–60). The statue of *St Benedict* is by Antonino Gagini (1545). Nearby is the church of the Annunziata, a Catalan-Gothic building in ruins (without a roof).

The corso continues past the former church of the Madonna del Soccorso (15C) with a portal attributed to Bartolomeo Berrettaro to the CHIESA MADRE. Founded in 1332, it was rebuilt in 1669 by Angelo Italia and Giuseppe Diamante, with a fine dome. In the interior are columns of red marble quarried on Monte Bonifato. The frescoes in the vault, cupola and apse are by Guglielmo Borremans. **South side**: in the second chapel is a Crucifix by Antonello Gagini (1523); in the fourth chapel a late 16C sarcophagus with portraits of two members of the De Ballis family; in the fifth chapel there is a marble relief by Antonello Gagini. In the chapel to the right of the choir is the *Last Supper* by Giuseppe Carrera (1613). In the adjoining chapel (right) are two fine Gothic arches and a beautiful fresco fragment of the *Pentecost* (1430). In the chapel to the left of the choir is a wooden statue of the *Madonna* (1721) by Lorenzo Curti. On the altar of the north transept, the statue of *St Peter* is by Giacomo Gagini (1556).

The inner door of the sacristy (beyond the wooden door in the north aisle) is decorated with carvings of fruit attributed to Bartolomeo Berrettaro. **North side**: in the third chapel there is a high relief of the *Transition of the Virgin* by Antonello Gagini; in the first chapel there is a painting of the *Madonna* by Giuseppe Renda (late 18C). Opposite the Chiesa Madre is the former church of S. Nicolò di Bari with a fine portal of 1563.

The corso continues to piazza Ciullo, the centre of the town. On the corner is **S. Oliva**, built by Giovanni Biagio Amico in 1724. It was restored in 1990 after a fire in 1987 destroyed the 18C frescoes and stuccoes in the vault of the nave.

The lovely interior has altars beautifully decorated with marble. On the fourth south altar is a statue of *St Oliva* by Antonello Gagini (1511). The high altarpiece is by Pietro Novelli and on the left wall is a marble tabernacle by Luigi di Battista (1552). On the north side are 18C statues and a marble group of the *Annunciation* by Antonino and Giacomo Gagini (1545). The **Chiesa del Collegio** (1684–1767) has a theatrical façade on piazza Ciullo. It contains 18C stuccoes and altarpieces. Corso VI Aprile continues from piazza Ciullo past 18C and neo-classical palaces to the church of **SS. Paolo e Bartolomeo** (1689) with a splendid interior decorated by Vincenzo and Gabriele Messina and Antonino lo Grano. The oval *Madonna del Miele* dates from the end of the 14C or beginning of the 15C.

In via Amendola is the church of the **Rosario (S. Domenico)** which contains a fresco attributed to Tommaso de Vigilia. Beyond the castle (see above) and the large piazza della Repubblica is the church of **S. Maria del Gesù** (1762). Beneath the portico is a portal attributed to Bartolomeo Berrettaro (1507). It contains a 16C altarpiece of the *Madonna and saints* with the counts of Modica, and a statue of the *Madonna and Child* attributed to Bartolomeo Berrettaro or Giuliano Mancino. In via Caruso is the **Badia Nuova** (or S. Francesco di Paola) rebuilt in 1699 by Giovanni Biagio Amico. The pretty interior has stucco statues by Giacomo Serpotta and an altarpiece of *St Benedict* by Pietro Novelli.

On **Monte Bonifato** (825m), south of the town, planted with conifers and pine trees, a ruined Norman castle of the Ventimiglia is situated, with the chapel of the Madonna dell'Alto (superb view). The medieval *Fontanazza* here is a huge reservoir or thermal edifice.

# The Egadi Islands and Pantelleria

The Egadi Islands, consisting of Favignana, Levanzo and Marettimo, lie 15–30km off the west coast of Sicily. They are reached by boat and hydrofoil from Trapani. The inhabitants (4800) were once famed as skilled fishermen; fish are now far less abundant. Oil wells were sunk in the sea here a few years ago despite local efforts to preserve the sea from pollution. The sea between Favignana and Marsala is of great interest to underwater archaeologists. The varied birdlife includes migratory species from Africa in the spring. The islands, much visited by skin-divers, were declared a marine reserve in 1988.

## ■ Practical information

*Information offices*. APT Trapani (☎ 0923/29000); 'pro Loco', piazza Matrice, Favignana (☎ 0923/921647).

*Maritime services from Trapani*. Daily ferries from Molo Sanità to Favignana (in 50 min.) and to Levanzo in 1hr 20min. Once a week in 2hr 40min. to Marettimo. Hydrofoils (several times a day) from via Ammiraglio Staiti in 25 min. to Favignana and Levanzo, and once a day in 55 min. to Marettimo. The ferries are cheaper than the hydrofoils. Several companies operate the services including *Siremar*, ☎ 0923/921388, 0923/540515; *Volaviamare*, ☎ 0923/872499 and

*Ustica Lines*, ☎ 0923/21754. In bad weather it is the boats which get suspended as the moorings at the ports are poor: unless there are very high seas the hydrofoils usually operate.
**Bicycles** can be hired on Favignana.

### Hotels
**Favignana**. ★★★ *Approdo di Ulisse* (open June–November), località Calagrande, ☎ 0923/922525, fax 0923/921511. ★★ *Aegusa*, 11 via Garibaldi (at the port), ☎ 0923/922430, fax 0923/922440. ★ *Egadi*, with an excellent restaurant, 17 via Colombo (at the port), ☎ & fax 0923/921232.
**Levanzo**. ★★ *Pensione dei Fenici*, 18 via Calvario, ☎ 0923/924083. ★ *Paradiso*, via lungomare, ☎ 0923/924080.
**Marettimo** has no hotels, but rooms can be rented in private houses.
Favignana and Levanzo also have rooms to rent.

### Campsites
**Favignana** ★★★★ *Miramare*, località Costicella, ☎ 0923/921330.★★★ *Egad*, località Arena, ☎ 0923/921555. Free camping is often allowed on Levanzo and Marettimo.

### Restaurants
**Favignana**. B *Egadi*, 17 via Colombo. *La Tavernetta*, piazza Matrice. C *La Bettola*, piazza Castello and *Il Nautilus*, via Amendola.
**Marettimo**. C *Il Pirata, Il Veliero*, and *Il Timone*.
***Cafés and pasticcerie*** in **Favignana** *Giacomino*, off the corso; and *Albatros* in the corso.

***Annual festival*** called the *Settimana delle Egadi* is usually held at the end of May.

#### History
These islands were the ancient *Aegades* or *Aegates*, off which Lutatius Catulus routed the fleet of Hanno in 241 BC in one of the most famous Roman victories over Carthage. In the middle of the 16C the islands were given to the Genoese Camillo Pallavicini, from whom they were purchased in 1874 by the Florio.

## Favignana
Favignana, 17km from Trapani, is the biggest island of the group (19 sq km) and the seat of the comune (population 3800). The island has a slightly run-down atmosphere, with a number of its cube-like houses half restored, half built, or for sale. The boats and hydrofoils dock at the little port, filled with numerous picturesque fishing boats.

At Favignana is the **Stabilimento Florio**, a huge old tuna fishery built in 1859 by Giulio Drago for the Pallavicini: the **tuna fisheries** of Favignana used to be the most important in the Mediterranean, and the tuna caught in the sea here was renowned for its excellent quality. The catch in a good year in the 19C could sometimes number as many as 10,000 fish. Before the fishery was built the fish were salted: here, instead, they were hung up by the tail and then cut in pieces to be smoked, cooked or canned. Every piece of the fish was utilized, including the bones which were boiled up to make glue or fishmeal. The industry thrived up until 1874 when Drago ceded his contract to the Florio when they bought all three Egadi islands from the Pallavicini family.

The Florio, a family from Calabria, who settled in Palermo, became important ship owners and were great entrepreneurs on the west coast of Sicily especially in the period preceding World War I. They ran this factory up until 1937, but by 1977 it had been closed down because of competition from the tuna fishing in the Atlantic. The fine buildings are now owned by the region of Sicily and restoration is to begin in 1998 (partly financed by the EU): there are plans to use them to house a restaurant, theatre, auditorium, museum, artisans' workshops and a marine research centre.

In the deep channel between Levanzo and Favignana the traditional method of tuna fishing known as **la mattanza** has been practiced in spring according to a precise ritual since ancient times. A complicated series of net traps are anchored to the bed of the sea some 40–50m below the surface. When a sufficient number of tuna fish are caught in the first trap the head fisherman (known as the *Rais*) orders one side of the net to be lifted so the fish pass into the next trap, and so on until they reach the *camera della morta* (death chamber). When there are around 100 fish here the area is encircled by boats, with the boat belonging to the *Rais* in the centre, and the nets slowly hauled in. The fish tend to dive when in danger so that during this operation they often collide with each other and hit their heads: by the time the net reaches the surface (the whole operation takes about an hour) many of them are wounded and stunned. They are then harpooned and pulled into the boats.

The catch has drastically declined in recent years due in part to modern fishing techniques, polluted water, and disturbance of the water by motorboats and hydrofoils. However, the spectacle still usually takes place between 15 May and 15 June if the fish are sighted. Almost the entire catch is now sold to Japanese buyers.

The little medieval **town**, where most of the inhabitants live, and where all its shops are situated, was refounded in 1637 by the Pallavicini. Palazzo Florio, a large Art Nouveau palace, surrounded by a few trees, near the port, was built in 1876 for Ignazio Florio by Giuseppe Damiani Almeyda. It is now used as a police headquarters. Nearby is a smaller 19C palace used as the town hall, with a statue in front of Ignazio Florio. The little church of S. Antonio da Padova is being restored. Via Vittorio Emanuele, the main street, leads to piazza Matrice where there is a pleasant church with a green dome and the tourist office. The castle nearby has been transformed into a modern prison. Numerous shops sell smoked tuna fish and *bottarga* (dried smoked tuna roe): locally produced tuna fish products are still sold in a house near the cemetery.

The rest of the island is flat and has a rather bare landscape, mostly used as pastureland. Very little interesting local architecture survives. The best swimming is at the rocky bay of Cala Rossa, on the north coast; there are more crowded sandy beaches on the south coast between Grotta Pergiata and Punta Longa. In the eastern part of the island are numerous disused tufa quarries (the white tufa found here is particular to the island and provides an excellent building stone and used to be exported throughout Sicily). The small quarries are now mostly planted with trees or used as orchards, although one quarry still operates to supply the local market. Near the cemetery several wells with huge wooden water wheels of Arab origin survive, once used for irrigation. At Punta Marsala there is a view of Marsala and (on the left) the low green island of Mozia. A tourist village built in the 1970s at Punta Fanfalo has been totally abandoned.

The prettiest part of the island is to the west beyond Monte S. Caterina (where a Norman castle is now used by the armed forces). On the south coast at Punta Longa is a tiny port and fishing village.

**Levanzo** (10 sq km), 15km from Trapani, has no springs and supports a population of just 200 (it has virtually no cars). It also has an austere, barren landscape and a few beaches. It is famous for its prehistoric caves, notably the **Grotta del Genovese**, which has the most interesting prehistoric wall paintings in Italy, discovered by chance in 1950. The cave paintings date from the Neolithic period, and the incised drawings from the Upper Paleolithic period. A footpath leads across the island from the port to the cave (which can also be reached by boat; enquire for directions at the port, or the custodian, ☎ 0923/924032).

Between Favignano and Levanzo and Trapani are the little islands called **Le Formiche**, one of which has a large old tuna fishery, now a centre for helping young people in difficulty.

**Marettimo** (12 sq km) is the most isolated of the Egadi Islands, 38km from Trapani. It is wild and mountainous, rich in springs and beautiful grottoes and is the best preserved of the three islands. With a little Arab-like village, it has a population of just 800 (and no cars). Samuel Butler suggested that this was the island described as Ithaca in the Odyssey, and the islets of Le Formiche were the rocks hurled by Polyphemus at Ulysses (see p.316).

## Pantelleria

Far away to the south-west, about 110km from the Sicilian mainland (and only 70km from Tunisia) lies Pantelleria (population 7500), the largest island (83 sq km) off the Sicilian coast. It has beautiful wild scenery and interesting volcanic phenomena including hot springs (the last eruption was in 1891). Its central conical peak rises to a height of 836m. The sea bathing is exceptionally good. It is a sanctuary for migratory birds. Capers, figs, and sweet raisin grapes called *zibibbo* are cultivated here despite the lack of spring water, and it is especially famous for its wine *moscato di Pantelleria* (the *moscato passito* is a white desert wine). The cube-like white-washed houses, called *dammusi*, with thick walls and domed roofs, are Arabic in origin.

## ■ Practical information

*Information offices*. Pro-loco, via S. Nicola (☎ 0923/911838); APT Trapani (☎ 0923/27273).

### Getting there

**Maritime services**. Car ferries daily from Trapani (Molo della Sanità) in c 5hr run by *Siremar*, ☎ 0923/540515, and hydrofoils in c 2hr 30 min. run by *Ustica Lines*, ☎ 0923/21754. **Air services** from Trapani (twice a day in 30 min.) and from Palermo once a day in 1hr 20 min. (and from Rome). Connecting bus from the airport to the town of Pantelleria. Airport, ☎ 0923/841222. **Cars** and mopeds may be hired at the port.

### Hotels

★★★ *Port Hotel*, 6 via Borgo Italia, ☎ 0923/911299, fax 0923/912203.
★★ *Miryam*, 1 corso Umberto, ☎ 0923/911374, fax 0923/911777. Rooms to let available locally.

### Restaurants

**A** *I Mulini*, contrada da Tracino; **B** *Il Cappero*, 31 via Roma (at the port); *La Nicchia*, contrada Scauri Basso; *Trattoria di Bugeber*, contrada Bugeber.

#### History

Archaeological evidence has proved the island was inhabited in the Neolithic era. Later a Phoenician settlement, it was taken by the Romans in 217 BC, and called by them *Cossyra*. After its conquest by Roger I in 1123 it remained a Sicilian possession. During World War II it was used as a base for harrying allied convoys; reduced by heavy bombardment during May 1943 it was taken from the sea on 11 June with 11,000 prisoners, allied casualties being reported as 'one soldier bitten by a mule'. It has been used as a place of exile for political prisoners. It now has Italian and US military installations. Mafia activities here have threatened to spoil the island in recent years, which has become a fashionable place to have a summer villa.

The port of Pantelleria had to be rebuilt after World War II. In località Mursia 58 prehistoric tombs known as *sesi*, were discovered by Paolo Orsi in the 19C. These large domed tumuli were built in blocks of lava. Only 27 have survived, notably the *Sese Grande*, the others have either fallen into ruin or been engulfed by new buildings.

The beautiful inland crater lake of **Bagno dell'Acqua** (or the *Lago di Venere*) is about 6km from the port. It is fed by a hot water spring and is 500m in diameter and 2m above sea-level. The fine rocky coast is best seen from a boat (which can be hired at the port). Some of the best swimming on the island can be had at the *Arco dell'Elefante*.

# Mozia, Marsala and Mazara del Vallo

This chapter covers the west coast of Sicily from Trapani to Mazara del Vallo. The salt marshes between Trapani and Marsala (now a partially protected area), have interesting birdlife. Some salt-pans are still worked here, and the landscape is characterised by piles of salt protected by tiles and windmills once used for refining the salt. The coastal plain is reminiscent of North Africa, dotted with white cube-shaped houses, palms and monkey puzzle trees. Between Marsala and Mazara del Vallo the plain is densely cultivated with olives, low vineyards and market gardens (tomatoes are grown in the greenhouses). The beautiful island of Mozia has interesting Phoenician remains, and Marsala, on the site of a Carthaginian city and famous for its wine, is well worth a visit.

# ■ Practical information

*Information offices*. APT Trapani, ☎ 0923/29000, and APT information office in Marsala, 100 via XI Maggio, ☎ 0923/714097.

*Getting there from Trapani*. Mozia is 23km, Marsala 31km and Mazara del Vallo 53 km.
**Buses** (*AST*) run from Trapani (via Malta) to Marsala and Mazara del Vallo. The landing-stage for Mozia is c 1km away from Ragattisi where the bus between Trapani and Marsala stops. Buses from Marsala (piazza del Popolo) run to Mozia, Trapani, Palermo, Mazara del Vallo, Castelvetrano and Agrigento.
**Railway** from Trapani to Marsala in c 40 min, to Mazara del Vallo in c 1 hr (the trains continue to Castelvetrano, see p.175). The trains stop at Ragattisi, the nearest station to the landing-stage for the boat to Mozia (a walk from the station of about 1km).
**By car**. The main road (N115) between Trapani and Marsala bears heavy traffic and has numerous traffic lights; it is worth taking the prettier secondary coastal road here. This leaves Trapani on the seaward side of the railway and passes the salt marshes and the turn for Nubia, with the interesting Museo delle Saline (c 5km south of Trapani), described on p.147. It then passes close to the island of Mozia (turning, signposted for Mozia on the island of S. Pantaleo at the station of Ragattisi). Car parking in Marsala, on lungomare Boeo, or outside Porta Nuova or Porta Garibaldi.
**Maritime services** in July–Sept from Marsala (Molo Dogana) for the Egadi Islands and Pantelleria.

### Hotels
On the outskirts of **Marsala**. ★★★ *Cap 3000*, 161 via Trapani, ☎ 0923/989055, fax 0923/989634; *President*, 1 via Nino Bixio, ☎ 0923/999333, fax 0923/999115.
**Mazara del Vallo**. ★★★ *Hopps*, 29 via Hopps, ☎ 0923/946133, fax 0923/946075.

### Restaurants
**Marsala**. B *Delfino*, 672 lungomare Mediterraneo (1km south of the town); *Garibaldi*, 35 piazza Addolorata; *Capo Lilybeo*, 40 lungomare Boeo; *Villa Favorita*, 27 via Favorita (on the southern outskirts). C *Belvedere*, via Vaccari; *Aloa*, via Mazzini; *De Gaetano*, piazza Mameli; *Enzo e Nino*, via XI Maggio.
**Mazara del Vallo**. A *Papaya*, 95 corso Umberto I; *Il Pescatore*, 191 via Castelvetrano, and numerous trattorie **C** mostly on the waterfront.
*Cafés and pasticcerie*. **Marsala** *Enzo e Nino* (*Tiffany*), via XI Maggio; *De Gaetano*, via Rapisardi; *Grand Italia* (*Pace e Messina*), 3 piazza della Repubblica.
*Places to picnic*. The island of **Mozia** is a delightful place to picnic; in Marsala, on the sea front near Capo Boeo.

## Mozia on the island of San Pantaleo

The island of S. Pantaleo, just 1km offshore, famous as the site of the Phoenician town of Mozia, is one of three islands in the beautiful shallow lagoon, known as **Lo Stagnone**, protected from the sea by the Isola Longa. The lagoon (2000 ha) has an average depth of just over 1m, and is abundant in fish (now threatened by the polluted water). Since at least the 15C salt has been extracted from the marshes and, after a period of decline, the industry is showing a slight revival. Pyramidal heaps of salt roofed with red tiles line the shore, and a few salt-crushing windmills survive.

*Getting there.* On the edge of the lagoon (signposted from the coastal road), in front of the island of S. Pantaleo, beside a hut there is a car-park (2000 lire). You walk to the end of the dyke in order to be seen by the boatman on the island who operates a ferry in c 10 minutes (5000 lire round trip) at any reasonable hour, usually 09.00–13.30; 15.00–17.00 (or 15.00–19.00 in summer). There is a splendid view from the water's edge of the island of S. Pantaleo with its pine trees, just to the left of which can be seen the island of Favignana. Behind S. Pantaleo there is a view of Levanzo, and to the left in the distance is Marettima. On the far right the headland of Erice is prominent beyond salt-pans and wind-mills and piles of salt.

On the **island of S. Pantaleo** (2.5km in circumference) are the remains of the Phoenician **Mozia** (or *Motya*). It is an oasis of luxuriant vegetation, a sanctuary for birds, with sweet-smelling plants, palm trees and pinewoods. The ruins are unenclosed and the views are delightful. Admission daily 09.00–13.00, 15.00–17.00 (19.00 in summer).

Sandwiches and drinks are available at a custodian's house and it is a lovely place to picnic.

### History

Mozia was founded in the mid-8C BC by the Phoenicians as a commercial base. By the mid-6C BC the island was entirely surrounded by defensive walls, 2400m long and over 2m thick. In his determination to wipe out the Carthaginians from the west of the island, Dionysius I of Siracusa brought a huge army here in 398 BC. During the fierce battle which ensued the tyrant's fleet was trapped in the lagoon; he brilliantly resolved the situation by constructing a 'road' of logs nearly 4km long, along which his ships were dragged to the open sea where he finally defeated the enemy. By the following year the Carthaginians had moved their headquarters to Lilybaeum.

The island was owned by Joseph (Pip) Whitaker (1850–1936), a distinguished ornithologist and member of the famous family of Marsala wine-merchants. He began the excavations here around 1913, and since the death of his daughter Delia in 1971 the island has been the property of the Joseph Whitaker Foundation (167 via Dante, Palermo, ☎ 091/6820522). Excavations continued up until around 1993. Just three families now live on the island. The low vineyards here used to produce an excellent wine (since 1971 the grapes have been sold on the mainland). Restoration is in progress (partly funded by the EU) of the museum buildings.

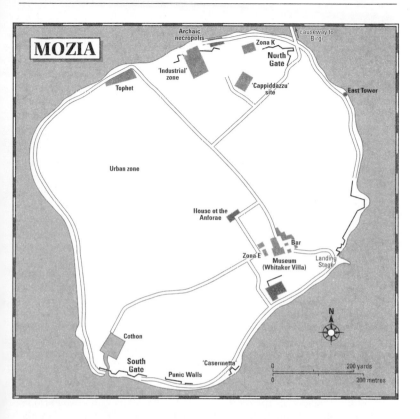

The boat crosses the lagoon with a view left of the island of Favignana and right of Mount Erice beyond the salt-pans. It docks near a stretch of the fortifications of the Punic city. A path leads to a group of houses and, beside a bronze bust of Whitaker, the crenellated Whitaker villa. It is appropriately used as a **museum**, but is only partially open during restoration work. It was founded in 1925, and some of the showcases brought at that time from Edinburgh and Belfast are still used. The material, delightfully displayed, comes from excavations at Mozia, Lilybacum and Birgi, carried out by Whitaker and (in the last few years) by the Italian State. It includes Phoenician ceramics, the earliest dating from the 8C BC, and Greek ware including proto-Corinthian and Corinthian vases and Attic black- and red-figure vases. Other finds from the island include Phoenician glass, alabaster and jewellery. Among the sculptural fragments is a metope from the North Gate showing two lions attacking a bull, distinctly Mycenaean in style (end of 7C or beginning of 6C BC), and a marble crater with bas-reliefs (Augustan period). The very fine **marble statue of a young man** (perhaps a charioteer, or a magistrate) in a tight-fitting tunic was found on the north-east side of the island in 1979. This remarkable work is thought to be by a Greek master and to date from c 440 BC.

Nearby is a small building used up until the 1970s for wine-making. During reconstruction work in 1995 remains of houses (called *Zona E*), dating from 7C–4C BC, were found beneath the pavement: the excavations can now be viewed from a walkway.

The excavations on the island are discreetly signposted along various paths which start from the museum. In front of the museum a path leads towards the lagoon to the **House of the Mosaics**, surrounded by a fence and rich vegetation, with bases of columns and interesting pebble mosaics showing a panther attacking a bull, a griffin chasing a deer, etc. (4C–3C BC). A longer path, flanked by bushes, leads from the custodian's house across the southern part of the island to the waterfront at the south-east corner, beside the **Cothon** and **South Gate**. This small basin (50 x 40m) within the walls is thought to have been an artificial dock used for repairing ships. A paved canal with ashlar walls of the 6C BC, thought to be its seaward entrance, has also been excavated. A path leads along the edge of the south shore past an enclosure near a clump of pine trees where excavations have unearthed a building probably used for military purposes (and known as the *Casermetta*). There are fine views across the lagoon of the piles of salt on the mainland, and of the Egadi Islands.

The path continues along the water's edge past the landing-stage and the impressive **fortifications** (late 6C BC), the best preserved stretch on the island. The **East Tower** preserves its flight of steps. Beyond some recent excavations (protected by a roof) is the imposing **North Gate**, with a treble line of defences. It defended a **causeway**, now just submerged (but up to a few years ago practicable for a horse and cart) which was built in the late 6C BC to link the island to the mainland (and a necropolis at Birgi). It is 7km long and just wide enough for two carts to pass each other. There is a fine view of Erice from here, beyond the low islands of the lagoon. A path leads inland through the north gate to **Cappiddazzu**, probably a sacred area. Above the level of the path is an edifice with mosaic remains. To the right is a field with low vines and two enclosed areas, the farthest of which, on the edge of the sea, is the **Archaic necropolis** with tombs dating from the 8C–6C BC. Nearby a fence surrounds an 'industrial area', known as *Zona K*, with interesting kilns, similar in design to some found in Syria and Palestine. The most recent excavations have taken place here (when the remarkable Greek statue, now in the museum, was found).

The largest enclosure is the **Tophet**, a Punic sacrificial burial ground dedicated to the goddess Tanit and to the god Baal Hammon, where child sacrifices were immolated (replaced after the 5C BC by animal sacrifices). The tombs are protected by low roofs. Excavations here produced cinerary urns, votive terracotta masks, and stelae (some with human figures). From the Tophet a path, marked by low olive trees, leads back through a vineyard in the centre of the island towards the museum. It passes (right) an enclosure with remains of the **Casa delle Anfore**, so-called because a huge deposit of amphorae was found here. Nearby are four conspicuous white pylons once used for generating electricity for the island.

Boats can sometimes be hired (enquire on the island) to visit the lovely **Stagnone lagoon**, with its three small islands, including the large Isola Longa (admission only with special permission), which has luxuriant vegetation and some abandoned salt-works.

# Marsala

Marsala (population 80,800) is a pleasant town with a 16C aspect, and an attractive open sea front on Capo Boeo, the site of the Carthaginian city of *Lilybaeum*. It gives its name to a famous dessert wine still produced here in large quantities from the vineyards along the coast, and stored in huge *bagli*. It is the most important wine-producing centre on the island.

### History

*Lilybaeum*, founded by the Carthaginians in 396 BC, near the headland of Capo Boeo, the western extremity of Sicily, and peopled from Mozia (see above), was their strongest bulwark in Sicily, and succumbed to the Romans only after a siege of ten years (250–241). As the seat of the Roman governor of Sicily it reached its zenith. Cicero called it *civitas splendidissima*. In 47 BC Julius Caesar pitched camp here on his way to Africa. A *municipium* during the Augustan age, it was later raised to the status of *colonia*. It kept its importance as an avenue of communication with Africa during the Saracen dominion under the name Marsa Alí or *Mars-al-Allah*, the harbour of Ali or God, but declined after 1574 when Don Juan of Austria (illegitimate son of Charles V) almost completely blocked its port to protect it from Barbary pirates.

The wine trade was founded by John Woodhouse in 1773 when he made the first shipment of the local white wine to Liverpool, conserving it on its month-long journey by adding alcohol. Marsala became popular in England as an alternative to madeira and port. In 1798, after the Battle of the Nile, Nelson placed a large order of Marsala for his fleet. In 1806 Benjamin Ingham and his nephew Whitaker also took up trading in Marsala with great success; by 1812 they were exporting the wine to North America. Production on an even grander scale was undertaken by Vincenzo Florio (d. 1868), one of Sicily's most able businessmen. In 1929 the establishments of Woodhouse, Ingham Whitaker and Florio were taken over by Cinzano, and merged under the name of Florio. The house of Florio continues to flourish along with many other companies, including Pellegrino and Rallo (all of which welcome visitors).

Garibaldi and the 'Thousand' landed here on 11 May 1860, being unobtrusively assisted by two British warships which were there for the protection of the wine merchants. Marsala was heavily damaged in 1943 by allied air attacks.

The town is entered by the monumental **Porta Garibaldi**, formerly the 'Porta di Mare', reconstructed in 1685. On the left is the church of the **Addolorata**, with a fine circular domed 18C interior, and a venerated popular statue of the *Madonna* wearing a black cloak. Municipal offices occupy a restored 16C military building, behind which is the market square. Via Garibaldi continues to the central piazza della Repubblica with the idiosyncratic **Palazzo Communale** (the town hall) which has original lamps on its upper storey. Opposite on via XI Maggio, is the flank and dome of the 17C church of **S. Giuseppe**. The exterior has been restored but the lovely interior with a fine organ is in urgent need of attention.

The **CATHEDRAL** (S. Tommaso di Canterbury) has a Baroque front completed in 1957. The first church on this site was built in 1176–82 and dedicated to St Thomas Becket. A new building, begun in 1607 and completed in 1717 was ruined when the dome collapsed in 1893, and it was partly rebuilt in the 20C. The pleasant interior, with pretty tiled floors in the side chapels, has interesting 17C paintings and sculptures.

**South side**: in the first chapel there is an unusual statue of the *Assunta* and two reliefs on the side wall, all by Antonino Gagini. The delicately carved tomb slab dates from 1556. In the second chapel there is a 15C statue of the *Madonna*, and a tomb with the effigy of *Antonio Grignano* (d. 1475) attributed to Domenico Gagini. In the third chapel is an elaborate statue of the *Madonna dell'Itria*, and the tomb of Giulio Alazzaro with an amusing effigy, both by Antonino Gagini. The fifth chapel has a 15C Crucifix and an expressive popular statue, fully dressed, of the *Virgin in mourning*. In the south transept is a good altarpiece of the *Presentation in the Temple* by Antonello or Mariano Riccio, and the tomb of Antonio Lombardo, who donated the tapestries to the cathedral (now in a museum, see below). In the chapel to the right of the sanctuary is an unusual statue of the *Madonna* (wielding a club), attributed to Giuliano Mancino, and a tomb with an effigy of Antonio Liotta (d. 1512), also attributed to Mancino. On either side of the sanctuary are two statues, one of *St Vincent Ferrer* attributed to Giacomo Gagini and one of *St Thomas the Apostle* by Antonello Gagini. In the apse is a 17C painting of the *Martyrdom of St Thomas* in a good frame. In the chapel to the left of the sanctuary is a beautiful gilded marble altarpiece of the *Passion* begun in 1518 by Bartolomeo Berrettaro and finished by Antonello Gagini (1532; four of the panels have been set into the walls).

**North side**: in the sixth chapel is a charming polychrome wooden statue of the *Madonna del Carmelo*, and in the second chapel is another wooden statue of the *Madonna* (1593), and two frescoed ex-votos with scenes of Marsala. A 17C silver statue of *St Thomas of Canterbury*, formerly outside the choir, has been removed for safety.

Behind the Duomo, in via Giuseppe Garraffa is the little **Museo degli Arazzi** (open 09.00–13.00, 16.00–18.00 except Mon), opened in 1985 to display eight precious tapestries given to the cathedral in 1589 by Antonio Lombardo, archbishop of Messina (1523–95) born in Marsala and buried in the cathedral. He became ambassador to Spain, and the very fine tapestries depicting the *Capture of Jerusalem* (made in Brussels between 1530 and 1550) are known to have come from the Palazzo Reale of Philip II in Madrid. They are displayed on three floors: since their careful restoration they have to be kept in darkened rooms.

Via XI Maggio runs off piazza della Repubblica (see above). The convent of S. Pietro, with a massive pointed tower, is now used as the town library. A street on the left leads towards the former church of the **Carmine**, now used to house the municipal archives. The pretty detached campanile was designed by Giovanni Battista Amico. The interesting former convent, founded in the late 14C (partly reconstructed in 1837) with an 18C cloister was beautifully restored in 1996. Temporary exhibitions are at present held here.

Nearby, in a pretty square with a Baroque fountain is the former church of **S. Cecilia**, which has a Baroque façade, where concerts are held. In via XI Maggio, just before Porta Nuova (which is being restored), is the façade (left) of Palazzo

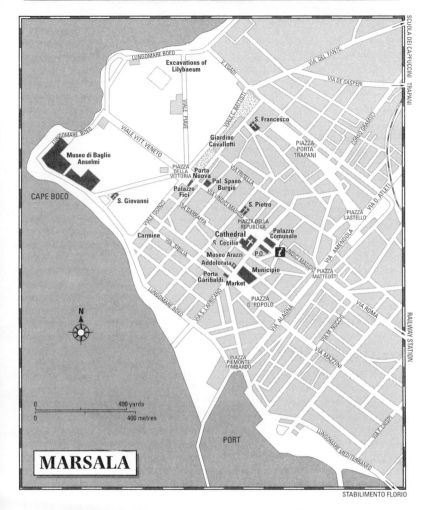

Fici (in poor repair) with a tall palm tree in its delightful Baroque courtyard. Opposite is the 19C–20C Palazzo Spanò Burgio (no. 15).

Outside the gate is the entrance (right) to the **Giardino Cavallotti**, lovely public gardens with huge ficus trees, magnolias and ornamental araucarie. Between piazza della Vittoria and the sea front extends **Cape Boeo**, an open area (closed to traffic, and protected from new buildings) with lawns and trees. Some picturesque old *bagli* on the seafront are still used as warehouses for wine barrels, others have been converted into restaurants, and one of them houses the Archaeological Museum (see below).

Capo Boeo was the site of **Lilybaeum**, the excavations of which are reached by steps from viale Piave, or by a path from Porta Nuova (open 09.00–13.00,

14.00–18.00 except Sun & PH). In a well-restored house are diagrams of the site, which includes a **Roman villa** (surrounded by a fence and covered for protection) dating from the 3C AD, which was built over in the Arab period. Around the impluvium are four mosaics of wild beasts attacking each other (thought to represent circus animals), probably the work of African craftsmen. There are remains of baths and other rooms with mosaics, including a head of Medusa, the symbol of Trinacria, the four seasons, etc. Nearby are more recent excavations including part of the walls, a necropolis, a Roman road, a Roman vomitorium, etc. A hypogeum with painted walls where Crispia Salvia was buried in the 2C AD has also been discovered.

On the tip of the promontory is the **Baglio Anselmi**, a former Marsala distillery and wine cellar, which has been restored as the MUSEO ARCHEOLOGICO DI BAGLIO ANSELMI (open daily 09.00–13.00; Wed and Sat, also 16.00–19.00; Sun & PH 09.00–13.00), with a very interesting collection. From the entrance hall the spacious courtyard of the baglio can be seen, planted with palm trees; the museum is arranged in two huge vaulted warehouses. The display begins in the hall on the left (and on the left wall), with **prehistoric** material from the Marsala area, in particular from **Mozia**. Beyond, two showcases have **Phoenician** finds from the tophet of Mozia. In the centre of the rooms are two cases of exquisite **Hellenistic gold jewellery** found in Marsala. The finds from the Phoenician necropoli of **Lilybaeum** are displayed chronologically with explanatory diagrams and photographs, and include ceramics, funerary monuments, sculptures, terracottas, and *Tanagra* figurines. On the end wall are fragments of funerary monuments, stele and edicole with carved inscriptions or paintings (3C–2C BC) from Mozia and Lilybaeum. Also here are fragments from a large mausoleum in local stone covered with a fine layer of white and polychrome stucco (its hypothetical form has been reconstructed in a drawing). A small room displays epigraphs. On the right wall of the hall are finds from **Roman Lilybaeum** (3C–4C AD), and in the centre of the room a model of the excavations on Cape Boeo. In show cases are fragments of wall paintings, a hoard of coins, lamps and a fragment of a female statuette of the 3C AD. In the centre, two mosaics (5C AD and 3C AD) and an *opus sectile* pavement from the 4C AD. The display ends with photographs of Palaeochristian finds, and a case of ceramics including Siculo-Norman ware. The last case illustrates the discovery of a Norman wreck offshore in 1983, with a few finds from the boat.

The other splendid hall on the right contains the **Punic ship**, discovered by Honor Frost in 1971 off the Isola Longa, in the Stagnone lagoon north of Marsala (see above), and subjected to a long and delicate process of restoration under her supervision. The well-preserved poop was recovered from the seabed and the rest of the hulk, 35m long, was carefully reconstructed in 1980. Manned by 68 oarsmen, it is thought to have been sunk on its maiden voyage during the First Punic War. It is unique as the only warship of this period so far discovered; it is not known how the iron nails resisted the corrosion of the sea. The ship has been partly reconstructed around the original wood which is conserved beneath a huge tent which makes viewing awkward. Drawings illustrate the original appearance of the ship. At the end of the room are two cases of objects found on board, including remains of ropes, a sailor's wooden button, a bone needle used for making nets, corks from the amphorae, a brush and a few ceramic fragments. The underwater finds include numerous amphorae.

Nearby is the conspicuous little church of **S. Giovanni** (kept locked, enquire for the key at the tourist office), covering the so-called Grotto of the Sibyl which was probably the shrine of a Roman water-cult (recently restored).

On the road which continues along the sea front, lined with palms (but with ugly modern buildings on the left) is the former **Baglio Woodhouse** (the entrance is marked by two round towers in front of a jetty and next to a chapel built by the English). In the harbour only the base remains of the monument commemorating the *Landing of the Thousand*, by Ettore Ximenes, which was destroyed in World War II. The road passes a number of old *bagli*, and, beside two tall palm trees, is the huge **Stabilimento Florio** (see above; open to visitors Mon–Thurs at 15.00, and on Fri at 11.00). The monumental buildings were designed in 1833–35 by Ernesto Basile around a huge inner courtyard planted with trees. Visitors are shown the historic cellars and invited to taste the wine (free of charge). In the small museum a letter is preserved from Nelson, Duke of Bronte to John Woodhouse in 1800 with an order for Marsala for his fleet. In the grounds are the tombstone of John Woodhouse, and the neo-classical villa built by Benjamin Ingham.

North of the town, in the **Scuola dei Cappuccini** are remains of a huge Punic-Roman necropolis (open in summer). To the south, on N115, the former Baglio Amodeo, one of the oldest Marsala warehouses, is surrounded by a beautiful garden and is open as a restaurant (Villa Favorita).

Some 10km outside the town, in the contrada Biesina, the **Museo di Villa Genna** contains an interesting local collection of artisans' tools, etc. (admission only by appointment).

## Mazara del Vallo

Mazara del Vallo, at the mouth of the Mazaro, is the most important fishing town in Italy (population 49,000). It has a pleasant waterfront and busy harbour. The town, built in golden-coloured tufa, has a distinctly Arab flavour; since 1968 the ancient *Casbah* of the city in the Pilazza district has been repopulated by Tunisians. Much unregulated new building has taken place on the outskirts in the last few decades. It was damaged by an earthquake in 1980. In 1998 a remarkable bronze statue of a young satyr dating from the classical period was recovered from the seabed offshore.

### History

Mazara was an emporium of Selinunte and fell with it in 409 BC. It was held by the Carthaginians until 210 BC when it came under Roman rule. Here in 827 the Saracens, called in by the governor Euphemius to abet his pretensions to the Imperial purple, gained their first foothold in Sicily. There followed the most important period in the town's history, when it became the main city in the Val di Mazara. It was finally captured by Count Roger in 1075; and here the first Norman parliament in Sicily met in 1097.

The **Cathedral** was founded in 1093 and rebuilt in 1690–94. Above the west door, which faces the sea, is a 16C sculpture of Count Roger on horseback. The interior contains a *Transfiguration* in the apse by Antonello Gagini (finished by his son Antonino, 1537). The two statues of *St Bartolomeo* and *St Ignazio* are by Ignazio Marabitti. In the south aisle is a sculpted portal by Bartolomeo Berrettaro. In the vestibule of the chapter-house are two Roman sarcophaghi. Off the north side is a chapel with a 13C painted Cross, and in the chapel of the Madonna del Soccorso is a Byzantine fresco in a niche of *Christ pantocrator*.

Between the cathedral and the sea front is a **public garden** with fine trees on the site of the Norman castle, a ruined wall of which faces the busy piazza Mokarta at the end of the main corso Umberto I. On the other side of the cathedral is the 18C **piazza della Repubblica**, with a statue by Marabitti (1771) and the handsome **Seminario Vescovile** (1710) with a double portico. Here a **Diocesan Museum** (open Sat & Sun 10.00–12.00) was arranged in 1993, which contains the tomb of Giovanni Montaperto (1495) by Domenico Gagini, paintings, vestments, etc. The precious cathedral treasury displayed here includes a processional Cross from Salemi dated 1386, by a Pisan artist, and another Cross attributed to Giovanni di Spagna (c 1448), as well as numerous 18C reliquaries and church silver.

Via S. Giuseppe leads to the church of **S. Caterina** decorated in 1797 by Giuseppe Testa, with a statue of the saint by Antonello Gagini (1524). On the other side of piazza della Repubblica via XX Settembre leads to piazza Plebiscito with the 18C church of **S. Ignazio** and the **Collegio dei Gesuiti** (1675–86). This now houses the municipal library and archives and the **Museo Comunale** (open weekdays 08.30–14.00) which has Roman finds from the area and two interesting sculpted elephants which bore the columns outside the west porch of the Norman cathedral. A section dedicated to the history of the local fishing industry is also to be opened here.

The **harbour** lies at the mouth of the River Mazaro which is normally filled with the fishing fleet during the day (except on Saturdays). This is the most interesting part of the city (with the Tunisian district around via Porta Palermo and via Bagno). A short way upstream stands the little Norman-Byzantine church of **S. Nicolò Regale** with a crenallated top (recently restored; usually open on Sundays). The Lungomazaro continues along the river past the fish market to the bridge from which there is a splendid view of the boats. Further upstream are caves, formerly inhabited. The *marrobbio*, a curious tidal movement of the sea, probably due to variations in the atmospheric pressure near the mouth of the river, now rarely occurs.

The church of the **Madonna dell'Alto**, erected in 1103 by Giulitta, daughter of Count Roger, is 2km outside the town.

# Selinunte and Castelvetrano

Selinunte is one of the most impressive classical sites in Sicily since it was never subsequently built over: there are temples and the extensive remains of the acropolis. The nearest little town, Castelvetrano, has a small archaeological museum. The quarries used to build the temples of Selinunte survive nearby at Cave di Cusa and are still an extraordinary sight in a lovely peaceful spot.

## ■ Practical information

***Information office*** of APT Trapani at Selinunte, by the car-park and entrance to the east group of temples, ☎ 0924/46251.

### Getting there

**Railway** from Trapani to Castelvetrano 121km in 2–3 hr via Alcamo diramazione; a bus service has replaced the branch line from Castelvetrano to Selinunte, 14km in 25 min.

**Buses** from Castelvetrano to Selinunte (the stop near the disused railway station is a 5 min. walk from the east group of temples).

The most interesting route by **car** from Trapani is along the coastal road via Mozia and Marsala (see p.165); there is also a motorway (longer) all the way from Trapani via Segesta and Salemi to Castelvetrano.

### Hotels

**Selinunte** (Marinella). ★★★ *Alceste*, 21 via Alceste, ☎ 0924/46184, fax 0924/46143.

**Castelvetrano.** ★★ *Zeus*, 6 via Vittorio Veneto, ☎ 0924/905565, fax 0924/905566.

**Campsites** on the coast at Selinunte ★ *Athena*, ☎ 0924/46132 and *Il Maggiolino*, ☎ 0924/46044.

### Restaurants

At Marinella on the coast at Selinunte: **B** *Alceste Hotel* (see above); *Lido Azzurro*, 51 via Marco Polo. **C** *Pierrot*, 108 via Marco Polo.

Selinunte is a wonderful place to **picnic** (tables are also provided in the shady river valley off the road between the east group of temples and the acropolis).

There is an **annual festival** in Castelvetrano called *Aurora* on Easter Sunday morning, with a traditional procession, etc.

## Selinunte

The extensive ruins of the ancient city of Selinunte are on the edge of the sea (with superb views along the coast to the east).

On the coast the simple fishing village of **Marinella** has been developed as a little resort. The beautiful coast beyond, around the mouth of the Belice river (and as far as Porto Palo), with its sand dunes, has recently been preserved as a nature reserve (the Riserva Naturale Foce del Fiume Belice). It is also interesting for its flora and fauna.

The ancient town with its acropolis occupied a terrace above the sea, between the River Selinon and the marshy depression now called Gorgo di Cottone or Galici, and possessed a harbour at the mouth of each valley. An important group of temples lay to the east of this site, and a necropolis to the north. The sandy soil is overgrown with wild celery, mandrake, acanthus and capers. This is perhaps the most impressive of the Greek cities of Sicily, since the ruins have never been built over in modern times. However, the site has been damaged by the recent construction (despite the protest of the local inhabitants) of a huge dyke, with tunnels, beside Temple E. The site (270 ha) has now been enclosed in an attempt to discourage clandestine excavations and preserve the area from new buildings. A new entrance and ticket office have been built together with a car-park near the east group of temples. However, an elaborate new ticket office behind a glass wall below the dyke and nearer the car-park is at present closed.

**Admission** daily 09.00–dusk. The visit, best started early in the morning, takes at least 2–3 hours.

### History
Selinunte was colonised from Megara Hyblaea, probably as early as 651 BC. It takes its name (*Selinous*) from the wild celery (Greek, selinon), which still grows here in abundance. Its most prosperous period was the 5C BC, when the great temples were built and the city was laid out on a rectangular plan. After the battle of Himera Selinunte allied itself with Siracusa against Carthage, and in 409 BC the Carthaginians, summoned to the help of Segesta, the mortal enemy of Selinunte, sent an army of 100,000 under Hannibal, son of Gisco, which took Selinunte by assault before the allied troops of Agrigento and Siracusa could arrive. The city was sacked and destroyed, and a later settlement led by Hermocrates, a Siracusan exile, was dispersed by Carthage in 250, and the population resettled at Lilybaeum. It is thought, however, that the utter destruction of every building, scarcely a single column being left upright, must have been due to earthquakes, rather than to the hand of man.

### Excavations of the site
The site was rediscovered in the 16C; but systematic excavations were begun only in 1822–3 by the Englishmen William Harris and Samuel Angell, after a fruitless dig had been made in 1809–10 by Robert Fagan, British consul-general in Sicily. Harris and Angell found the famous metopes of **Temple C**, but Harris died of maleria contracted while excavating here. In 1956–8 12 streets were excavated, and in 1973 excavations were begun to the north, on the site of the ancient city. There have been recent excavations also in the area of the Temple of Malophoros. A bronze statue (Phoenician, 12C–11C BC) of *Reshef* (kept in the Museo Archeologico in Palermo), found in the vicinity, is the first archaeological confirmation that the Phoenicians traded here before the foundation of Carthage.

### *The temples*
The temples are distinguished by letters as their dedications are still under discussion. They were the only temples in Sicily to have had sculptured metopes; many of these beautiful works are displayed in the archaeological museum in Palermo. All except Temples B and G are peripteral and hexastyle and all are orientated. The measurements given in the text refer to the temple stylobates. Many architectural fragments bear remains of *intonaco* (plaster), and throughout the site are underground cisterns, built to collect rainwater. Beside most of the temples are sacrificial altars.

The main road from Castelvetrano, before entering Marinella, passes (right) a huge ugly dyke (apparently designed to isolate the temples from the few modern buildings of Marinella) beside a roundabout (and the information office) at the entrance to the site (which includes the east group of temples and the acropolis). Beyond the temporary ticket office is the car-park for the east group of temples (behind a row of palm trees here there is another ticket office, at present closed, which is a modern building constructed in the dyke).

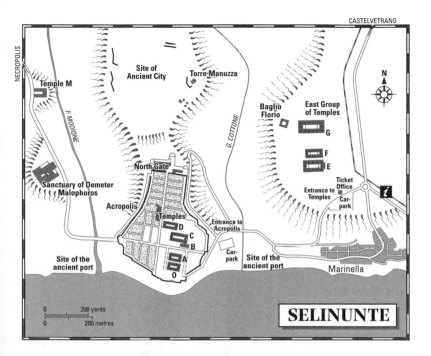

## The east group of temples

The east group of temples consists of the ruins of three large temples. Beside the modern dyke and tunnel is **Temple E**, which measures 67.7 x 25.3m, and was probably dedicated to Hera or Aphrodite. It is a Doric building of 490–480 BC; four of its metopes discovered in 1831 and now in the Palermo archaeological museum attest the beauty of its sculpture. Toppled by an earthquake, its colonnades were reconstructed in 1958. It is possible to visit the interior of the temple.

**Temple F**, the oldest on this hill (c 560–540 BC), totally ruined, had a double row of columns in front and 14 at the sides. It may have been dedicated to Athena or Dionysius. Part of one column rises above others which are now only a few metres high.

The furthest north is **Temple G**, probably dedicated to Apollo or Zeus; octastyle in form, it ranks second in size (110 x 50m), after the Olympieion at Agrigento, among Sicilian temples. Its columnar arrangement (8 x 17) is matched only by the Parthenon. It was laid out before the end of the 6C and left incomplete in 480. It is now one huge heap of overgrown ruins with only one column alone still standing, and it is very difficult to 'enter' the temple, although a well-paved path leads round the exterior. The columns, over 16m high with a base diameter of 3.4m, were built up of drums, each weighing c 100 tons, from the quarries at Cusa. As each drum was placed in position it was caused to revolve around a central pivot, until, by the attrition of sand inserted for the purpose, it rested absolutely truly on the drum beneath. The fact that many of

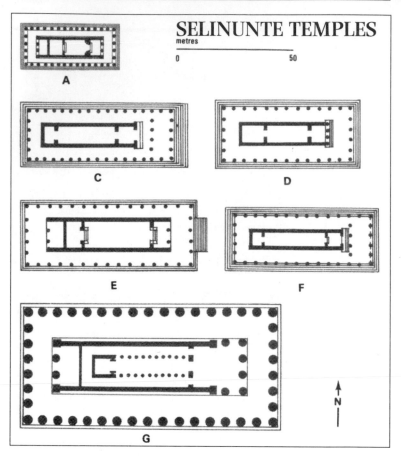

**SELINUNTE TEMPLES**

metres

0 — 50

A

C

D

E

F

G

N

the columns are unfluted implies that the temple was never completed. The cella, preceded by a pronaos of four columns, had three aisles, the central aisle being open to the sky. At one end are huge blocks from the quarries; the fallen capitals give some idea of the colossal scale of the building. The enormous stylobate is in itself a marvel of monumental construction.

There is a fine view of the plain filled with olive plantations and the large farmhouse (*Baglio Florio*) which is eventually to become a **museum**. The handsome spacious building was well restored some years ago.

### Acropolis

From the first car-park a road continues downhill across the Gorgo di Cottone (site of one of the ancient harbours) and up to the **Acropolis**, where there is a second car-park. From here a path continues up between the sea and massive double **walls**, in which five towers and four gates have been located, which date from around 307–306 BC. Beside the custodian's house is an abandoned house called the *Casa del Viaggiatore* by a group of palm trees, which is being restored.

In front of the custodian's house is a plan of the site beside the stylobate of **Temple O**, whose superstructure has entirely disappeared, and, beyond, the stylobate of **Temple A** (40 x 16m; 36 columns), with some fluted drums. The cella was one step higher than the pronaos and the adytum one higher still. Between the cella and pronaos two spiral staircases led up to the roof. Fragmentary ruins of a propylaea exist to the east. **Temples A** and **O**, built in 490–480 BC, and identical in form and dimension, were the latest and probably the most perfect of the Selinuntine temples. In front of Temple O a sacred area has been excavated, thought to date from after the destruction of the city in 409 BC.

*Metope from Temple E at Selinunte (Museo Archeologico, Palermo)*

The complicated ruins of the acropolis are traversed by two principal streets at right-angles, with lesser streets running parallel. The site is particularly peaceful, with numerous birds, and well worth exploring in detail. To the north are the remains of the great **Temple C**, on the highest point of the knoll, and the most conspicuous monument on the acropolis. It measured 63.7 x 24m, and dates from the early 6C. It was probably dedicated to Apollo; the famous metopes in the Palermo archaeological museum were found here in 1823. The colossal columns (6 x 17), some of which were monolithic, are nearly 2m in diameter at the base, except for the corner-columns which are even thicker; they fell during an earthquake in Christian times, burying a Byzantine village that had grown up in the 5C (Crosses are carved on some of the architectural fragments). The north colonnade was re-erected in 1925–7. Part of the sacrificial altar remains. To the south of the temple is a **megaron** (17.6 x 5.5m), dating from 580–570 BC. In the east corner of the temenos a **stoa** has been excavated which was probably built at the same time as the acropolis walls (late 6C). To the right is the small **Temple B**, a prostyle aediculum with pronaos and cella.

The path leads left, following the east–west thoroughfare of the city, passing in front of the pronaos of Temple A. Near a solitary ancient ilex tree is a crude little mosaic pavement which has the representation of the Punic goddess Tanit.

The wide main northern thoroughfare of the city (the north gate can be seen at its end) leads away from the sea. It leads past the stylobate of **Temple D** (570–554 BC) which flanks the road: it carried 34 columns, and measures 56 x 24m. Some of its blocks still have their bosses. Beyond, by a small pine tree is a row of modest constructions, thought to have been shops, each with two rooms, a courtyard, and stairs up to the living quarters on the first floor. Nearby are the foundations of the **Temple of the small Metopes**, so-called because it is thought the six small metopes, now in the Palermo Museum, belong to it; it had a simple cella and adytum and measured 15.2 x 5.4m.

Just before the North Gate there is a good view east of the splendid Temple E (see above) on its hill. The **North Gate**, one of the main gates of the city, is well preserved. Outside it is a sophisticated defence system once thought to date from the time of Hermocrates, but probably constructed by Agathocles in 307–306 BC. The fortifications include three semicircular towers, and a second line of walls c 5m outside the earlier ones which were reinforced after their destruction by Hannibal in 409 BC using material from the acropolis including capitals. The imposing remains are explained in a diagram at the site.

A sandy path continues through the low *macchia* to the most recent area of excavations of the **ancient city** (not yet open to the public), near another well-restored farmhouse. The city was orientated north-south and recent research has suggested it may originally have extended beyond the (later) perimeter wall to the north, and into the valleys of the Cotone and Modione rivers. Another area of the city farther north, on the sand-covered hill of Manuzza, may have had a slightly different orientation. Farther north was a necropolis (probably on the site of a prehistoric burial-place).

Outside the North Gate (see above), to the west, can be seen the excavations on the right bank of the Modione. These can most easily be reached by the rough road (c 1km, used by the custodians) which branches off from the main cross-roads near Temple C. Here the interesting **Sanctuary of Demeter Malophoros** consists of a sacred area enclosed by walls. It is now approached by a propylaea (late 5C) and portico. In the centre is a huge sacrificial altar, and beyond, the temple (a megaron), thought to have been built c 560, with a Doric cornice. Nearby are the scant remains of two other sacred precincts, one of them dedicated to **Zeus Meilichios** with two altars, where numerous stelae carved with a male and female head were discovered. More than 5000 terracotta figurines have been found in the vicinity. Another temple is being excavated to the south. Near a spring, some 200m north, a sacred edifice has recently been excavated and called **Temple M**. This may, in fact, be an altar or a monumental fountain of the 6C BC. The necropolis proper extends for some kilometres to the west: several tombs and heaps of bones are still visible. It has recently been suggested that this necropolis did not belong to the city of Selinunte.

## The Cave di Cusa

Off the road between Selinunte and Castelvetrano a pretty byroad (signposted) leads through extensive olive groves and vineyards to **Campobello di Mazara**, a wine-producing centre (population 11,800), with a Crucifix in its church by Fra Umile da Petralia. From here a road (signposted) leads south towards Tre Fontane on the coast. At a crossroads by the ruins of the Baglio Ingham (a little beyond which, in a field on the left, lies a column drum abandoned on its way to Selinunte) a right turn continues past a sewage plant to end at the **Cave di Cusa**, the ancient quarries used for the construction of the temples of Selinunte. The entrance, guarded by a custodian, is open daily from 09.00 to dusk.

The **quarries** have not been worked since the destruction of Selinunte in 409 BC and no excavations have ever been carried out here. Ancient olive trees grow among the peaceful ruins, and the beautiful site, inhabited by birds, is surrounded by olive and orange plantations and vineyards. The quarries (which are only about 120 m wide) extend for some 2km, and the fact that the site is not yet enclosed and there are no labels, make it one of the most romantic spots left in Sicily, especially on winter days when it is totally deserted. It is well worthwhile taking time to explore the site where the various processes of quarrying can be studied, from the first incisions in the rock to the empy spaces left by the removal of completed drums for columns. A block, still attached to the rock, seems to have been intended for a capital. Around each column carved out of the rock a space of c 50cm allowed room for the stonemason. Close together stand four drums which have been carved for the whole of their length and await only to be detached at their bases. The large cylindrical masses of stone (c 3 x 2m ) were probably intended for Temple G. It is thought that wooden frames were constructed around the columns and they were transported to Selinunte, about 18km away, on wheels of solid wood strengthened by iron bands and pulled by oxen or slaves.

## Castelvetrano

Castelvetrano is a town (population 32,000) in the centre of a wine- and oil-producing area, which is also known for its cabinet-makers. To the south the view falls away across the cultivated plain towards the sea and the ruins of Selinunte. The simple architecture of many of the houses, with internal courtyards, is interesting, although the town was damaged in the Belìce earthquake of 1968. The body of the bandit Salvatore Giuliano (see p.133) was 'found' here in 1950.

The centre of the town is the cramped and oddly shaped **piazza Garibaldi**, which is planted with trees. The **Duomo** (usually entered by the side door in piazza Umberto I) is a 16C church with an unusual flowery portal. The central roof beam has preserved its painted decoration. Two triumphal arches are bedecked with white stuccoes of putti, festoons and angels, by Antonino Ferraro and Gaspare Serpotta (who also executed the four saints in the nave). In the presbytery there is gilded decoration by Antonino Ferraro and an *Assumption* by Orazio Ferraro (1619). The chapel to the right of the sanctuary has a wooden Crucifix of the 16C, and the chapel to the left of the sanctuary, a marble Gaginesque statue, and, on the wall, a painting attributed to Pietro Novelli. Off the left aisle, the Cappella della Maddalena has fine decoration, especially in the dome, by Tommaso Ferraro. The detached campanile dates from the 16C. On the corner of piazza Umberto I is an elaborate fountain (1615) with a statue of a nymph by Orazio Nigrone.

The church of the **Purgatorio**, which has a decorative 18C façade (now used as an auditorium), and the neo-classical **Teatro Selinus** (1870; by Giuseppe Patricolo) are both situated in piazza Garibaldi. Via Garibaldi leads downhill past via Francesco la Croce, on the corner of which is the Biblioteca Comunale.

Here the **Museo Civico** (open 08.30–13.00, 15.00–dusk; Sun & PH 08.30–13.00) was re-opened in 1997. On the ground floor is an unusual little room, well designed in an intimate arrangement to display the interesting bronze statuette known as the *Ephebus of Selinunte* (5C BC), which has finally been returned here after its theft in 1962 (and recovery in 1968). It was found in a tomb at Selinunte in 1882, and during its recent restoration certain defects in the original casting were detected; a somewhat enigmatic work, it is thought to be a local product of c 480–460 BC. The small collection includes some other finds from Selinunte: a red-figure krater with four satyrs (470–460 BC); Corinthian ware; terracottas; coins; and a stele from the sanctuary of Malophorus. The statue of the *Madonna and Child* by Francesco Laurana and his bottega (c 1460) comes from the church of the Annunziata (the majestic head is especially fine). Upstairs is the quaint miscellaneous municipal collection, which includes bones from a Punic tomb discovered in 1929.

From the top of via Garibaldi, via Fra Pantaleo leads downhill south-east to piazza Regina Margherita, where there is a little public garden and two churches. **S. Domenico**, which has a plain façade, contains a riot of Baroque terracotta stuccoes by Antonino Ferraro (late 16C), and unusual funerary monuments. The east end was damaged in the Belice earthquake in 1968.

On another side of the piazza is the church of **S. Giovanni Battista** with an elaborate façade and a green cupola. The interesting interior (also damaged in the earthquake) is closed during restoration work. It contains a good statue of its patron by Antonello Gagini, 1522, and three 17C paintings, formerly attributed to Gherardo delle Notti. In viale Roma is a private collection of Sicilian carts.

About 3km west of the town is the church of the **SS. Trinità di Delia**. It is reached by taking the road downhill from piazza Umberto I and continuing straight ahead (signposted 'Trinità di Delia'), leaving the Trapani/Agrigento road on the left. After c 1km, at a fork, the road (unsignposted) continues left past a gravel works and straight on (signposted 'Lago di Trinità'). It passes a small eucalyptus wood and then follows the white wall of the farm, which incorporates the church. The key is kept at the modern house on the right. The chapel, dating from the 11C–12C, is a very fine building derived from Arab and Byzantine models. It was beautifully restored in 1880, and contains 19C family tombs. The crypt beneath is entered by an outside stairway. In the churchyard in a little wood is a romantic tombstone by Benedetto Civiletti, erected by the Saporito family. Beneath the hill is the large dammed Lago Trinità.

## The Valle del Belice

The Belice valley east of Castelvetrano, on the provincial border with Agrigento, was badly damaged in 1968 by an earthquake in which 531 people died and thousands were made homeless. Reconstruction was scandalously slow and tens of thousands in the area lived in temporary shelters for many years (and many people have not yet been properly rehoused). Legal proceedings are in progress for embezzlement of the funds destined for the area, etc. Where new towns have been built (such as Gibellina Nuova) they tend to have a design which shows little consideration for the needs of the local population.

The worst-hit place was the old town of **Gibellina** (400m), below a ridge of sulphur-bearing hills, which was abandoned after its total destruction. It is not clear why it was decided to 'cover' the ruins with cement as a work of 'Land Art' by the sculptor Alberto Burri. During a summer festival open-air theatrical performances are held here.

The inhabitants were moved some 20km west to the new town of **Gibellina Nuova** (population 5000), built since 1968 on the plain near the motorway and railway station of Salemi in an unattractive site, unpleasantly hot in summer. It is approached by a colossal concrete 'star' over the motorway.

The architecture of the new town is disappointing and numerous modern sculptures have been set up in its streets in highly questionable taste (and many of them are now deteriorating). The new church collapsed without warning (and without the help of an earthquake) in 1994, thankfully before it had been inaugurated. The town has a sad atmosphere and seems to have nothing to do with the traditional farming culture of the area. The Museo Elimo has local Elymnian and Greek archaeological material, and there is a local Ethnographical Museum.

On the eastern border of the province was the old town of **Poggioreale** (also destroyed in the earthquake), to the east of which excavations in 1970 revealed part of a town and its necropolis (with 7C and 6C BC tombs). **Salaparuta** was also abandoned after the earthquake and a new town partially reconstructed. A famous wine is produced in this district, known as *Salaparuta*.

**Partanna** is an agricultural centre (population 12,000) which was also badly damaged in 1968. It preserves a Norman castle (rebuilt in the 17C), in the courtyard of which is a damaged coat of arms sculpted by Francesco Laurana who visited here in 1468. The Chiesa Matrice has been partially reconstructed after it was almost totally destroyed in the earthquake. It contains stuccoes by Vincenzo Messina, an organ by Paolo Amato, and a statue of the *Madonna* by the bottega of Laurana.

North of Castelvetrano is **Salemi**, probably the site of Halicyae, a town of the ancient Sicani or Elymians. Here Garibaldi, three days after landing at Marsala, assumed the function of dictator in Sicily in the name of Vittorio Emanuele II. The town was badly damaged in the earthquake of 1968 when a third of the population (population 12,400) were housed in huts on the edge of the town. The cathedral and Cappuccino monastery were destroyed.

The church of the Collegio (near the summit of the hill), with its twisted Baroque columns either side of the entrance, was given cathedral status. The imposing castle of the mid-13C has fine vaulted rooms. The Collegio dei Gesuiti was restored to house the **Museo Civico** (open 08.00–14.00, 16.00–18.00; Sun & PH 10.00–13.00, 16.00–18.00). It contains sculptures attributed to Domenico and Antonello Gagini and Francesco Laurana, and a section on the Risorgimento. On the outskirts of the town is the interesting early Christian basilica of S. Miceli, with mosaic pavements.

# Agrigento

**AGRIGENTO PROVINCE**

Agrigento (population 56,300), once one of the most prosperous of the Greek cities on the island, preserves a remarkable series of Doric temples of the 5C BC, unequalled except in Greece itself. The medieval and modern city, on the site of the ancient acropolis, crowns a narrow ridge overlooking a valley which stretches towards the distant sea, and in the midst of which, on a second lower ridge, stand the classical ruins.

The beautiful 'Valle dei Templi' is now disturbed by a network of busy roads, and the ugly high buildings of the modern city have encroached on the valley. Long-term plans to preserve the archaeological zone as a national park have still not been finalised and illegal new building has even been allowed to take place in this area. To date 600 buildings have been erected in the zone where all building is prohibited, and 1500 in a protected zone. For many years the demolition of these illegal buildings has been proposed but has so far been successfully opposed by most of the local inhabitants, and the authorities have shown little inclination to impose their will, although three unfinished villas close to the Temple of Concord were finally demolished in 1995. Unregulated new building in the modern town caused a disastrous landslide in 1966. Agrigento is the capital of one of the poorest provinces in Italy, and to add to its problems it has a serious lack of water. See map on p.188-189.

# ■ Practical information

*Information offices.* Azienda Autonoma, 15 via Cesare Battisti (☎ 0922/ 20454), with its headquarters at 73 via Empedocle. APT Agrigento, 255 viale della Vittoria.

### Getting there

**Railway stations.** Agrigento Centrale is the terminus for all trains (from Palermo, Caltanissetta, etc.). There is a subsidiary station at Agrigento Bassa, 3km north.

**Car parking.** There are car-parks near the archaeological museum, and at the Posto di Ristoro near the temples. In the upper town parking is extremely difficult, although space is sometimes available in piazza Fratelli Rosselli or viale della Vittoria. A multi-storey car-park is to be opened shortly in via Empedocle.

**Buses.** Small buses traverse the upper town along via Atenea. Nos 1, 2 and 3 run from piazza Marconi to the Valle dei Templi (request stops at the museum and, lower down, for the temples at the Posto di Ristoro). Buses run from piazza Marconi to the birthplace of Pirandello, and Porto Empedocle, and from piazza Fratelli Rosselli to Palermo, Catania, Sciacca and Gela. Bus no. 2 from piazza Marconi and the Valle dei Templi continues to S. Leone on the sea.

### Hotels

★★★★ *Villa Athena*, ☎ 0922/5962888, with restaurant, in a beautiful quiet position in the Valle dei Templi. Also near the temples, ★★★ *Colleverde*, 21 via dei Templi, ☎ 0922/29555.

**In the upper city.** ★★★ *Del Viale*, 12 via del Piave, ☎ 0922/20063 and *Pirandello*, 5 via Giovanni XXIII, ☎ 0922/595666; ★★ *Belvedere*, 20 via S. Vito, ☎ 0922/20051 and *Bella Napoli*, 6 piazza Lena, ☎ 0922/20051.

**Outside the centre of the city** (not practical without a car). ★★★★ *Baglio della Luna*, contrada Maddalusa, ☎ 0922/511061, with restaurant. ★★★ *Grand Hotel Mosè*, contrada Angeli, Villaggio Mosè, ☎ 0922/608388.

**Campsites.** ★★★ near the sea at S. Leone (7km): *Internazionale S. Leone*, ☎ 0922/416121 and *Nettuno*, ☎ 0922/416268.

### Restaurants

**A** *Hotel Athena*, at the hotel (see above); *Le Caprice*, via Panoramica; *Taverna Mosé*, contrada S. Biagio. **B** *L'Ambasciata di Sicilia*, 2 via Giambertoni (off via Atenea); *La Francescana*, via Atenea. **C** *La Forchetta*, piazza S. Francesco; *Trattoria Atenea*, via Atenea.

At **S. Leone**, on the coast, 7km outside the city: **A** *Trattoria del Pescatore*, 20 via Lungomare, and **B** *Leon d'Oro*, viale Emporium, and *Trattoria Caico*, 35 via Nettuno.

**Cafés and pasticcerie.** *Saieva*, viale della Vittoria; *La Preferita*, via Atenea; *Patti*, piazza Aldo Moro. Delicious sweets, made by nuns, can be purchased at the convent next to the church of S. Spirito, see below.

Good places to **picnic** in the Valle dei Templi.

**Theatre.** The **Teatro Pirandello** in the upper town was re-opened in 1994.

*Annual festivals.* The *Sagra del mandorla in fiore*, an international festival of folklore, is held at the temples around the first week in February when the almond blossom is in flower. For one week in July there is often a festival of plays by Pirandello at his birthplace near Porto Empedocle (see p.199).

### History

Agrigento, the *Akragas* of the Greeks and the *Agrigentum* of the Romans, claims Daedalus as its legendary founder, but seems almost certainly to have originated in a colony from Gela (581 BC). From 570 to 555 the city suffered under the tyranny of Phalaris, though the bull-cult (of Moloch?) which he introduced was more likely Rhodian than Carthaginian, and the story (related by Pindar) that he sacrificed his enemies by hurling them alive into a red-hot brazen bull is probably apocryphal. Under the wise rule of Theron (489–472), in alliance with his son-in-law Gelon of Siracusa, the soldiers of Akragas defeated the Carthaginians at Himera (480), captured that city, and so extended their wealth and power that Pindar (who lived in the city) described Akragas as 'the fairest city of men'. Its population was then about 200,000. Its breed of horses was renowned, and the racing chariot found on many coins minted here may derive from their constant successes at the Olympic Games. Conflict with Siracusa led to defeat in the field, after which Theron's dynasty gave place to a republican government. In 406 the Carthaginians, under Hannibal, son of Gisco, and Himilco, took the city and burned it after a siege of eight months. Timoleon conquered the Carthaginians (340) and rebuilt the city, but it was taken by the Romans in 261 and again in 210, and remained in their possession till the fall of the Empire. It fell into Saracen power in 827, and was delivered in 1087 by Count Roger, who founded the bishopric.

The present town occupies the acropolis of the Greek city. The name of *Girgenti*, abandoned in 1927, was derived from Kerkent, a Saracen corruption of Agrigentum. The most famous native of Akragas was Empedocles (c 490–430), 'a poet, a physician, a patriot, and a philosopher'. His contemporary Acron, the physician, succeeded in stopping the Athenian plague of 430 BC, through the invention of fumigation. Luigi Pirandello (1867–1936), the dramatist (see p.199) and Leonardo Sciascia (1921–89), the writer (see p.207), were born in the district.

## The medieval and modern city

The old part of the town occupies the summit of Monte Camico (326m); its modern suburbs extend along the ridge to the east below the Rupe Atenea, and the city is expanding down the hillsides to the north and south. Three connected squares effectively divide the centre of the town; the area to the west contains the old city. To the north is the huge **piazza Fratelli Rosselli** (250m) where the roads from Palermo and Enna enter the city; here is the circular post office. To the south is **piazzale Aldo Moro**, with a garden, and farther south still, and at a lower level, lies **piazza Marconi** with the **central station**; opposite, at a confused intersection, the straight tree-lined Viale della Vittoria runs for over 1km along the edge of the ridge below modern buildings; while via Crispi descends to the Valle dei Templi.

**Via Atenea**, the long main street of the old town leads west from piazzale

Aldo Moro. Via Porcello (right) and the stepped Salita S. Spirito lead steeply up to the abbey church of **S. Spirito** (if locked, ring for the custodian at no. 2 or 11 salita S. Spirito, offering expected, or at the convent), founded c 1290 for Cistercian nuns. The nuns still make exquisite sweets (*frutti di martorana*, marzipan fruits, *kus-kus*, with pistachio and cocoa, marzipan shells filled with pistacchio, etc.) which may be purchased here. A Gothic portal survives and inside are good stuccoes (c 1693–95), by Serpotta and his school. The statue of the *Madonna* enthroned is by the workshop of Domenico Gagini.

Part of the **convent** was restored in 1990 to house part of the **Museo Civico** (open 09.00–13.00 except Sun & PH), formerly in piazza Luigi Pirandello (see below), with a miscellany of objects, poorly labelled. It is approached through an over-restored cloister, and up a modern flight of stairs. The two rooms on the top floor (with views of the sea) contain a local ethnographical collection (agricultural implements, domestic ware, etc.) On the floor below archaeological material and remains of frescoes are displayed. Steps lead down to the *stanza della Badessa* in a tower with a Gothic vault and a painted 15C Crucifix. Another room has architectural fragments including a carved marble doorway and a Crucifix. The fine dormitory has good vaulting and an exhibition of international folk costumes, as well as a collection of butterflies and shells. On the ground floor a chapel with a Gothic vault has a crèche, with charming domestic scenes, made by a local craftsman in 1991. The chapter-house (now used for marriages) is also shown. The paintings (not yet exhibited) include works by Pietro Novelli, Luca Giordano and Fra Felice da Sambuca.

Further on in via Atenea is the unfinished façade of S. Rosalia beside the **Purgatorio** or S. Lorenzo (containing elegant statues by Giacomo Serpotta). The lion to the left of the church sleeps above the locked entrance to a huge labyrinth of underground water channels and reservoirs, built by the Greek architect Phaiax in the 5C BC. Beyond the neo-Gothic exchange building the street widens at the undistinguished piazza Nicola Gallo, once the centre of the old city, with a private club in a neo-classical building. Beyond the church of S. Giuseppe, at the top of the rise, via Atenea descends to piazza del Municipio (now renamed piazza Luigi Pirandello). On the right is the Baroque façade of S. Domenico; occupying the former convent (mid-17C) are the town hall and the fine **Teatro Pirandello** (restored and re-opened).

To the right of S. Giuseppe (see above) via Bac-Bac leads to the stepped via Saponara (signposted for S. Maria dei Greci). From here it is a steep climb up the salita Eubernatis and salita S. Maria dei Greci to (right; inconspicuous entrance) **S. Maria dei Greci** (usually open 08.00–12.00, 15.00–dusk except on Sun & PH afternoons), preceded by a charming little courtyard with a palm tree and a cypress. The custodians live at no. 8 salita S. Alfonso and no. 1 salita S. Maria dei Greci (offering expected). This small basilica was built with antique materials, on the site of a Doric temple, perhaps that of Athena begun by Theron in the 5C BC. The interior preserves fragments of charming 14C frescoes. Parts of the temple may be seen here, and in a passage (entered from the churchyard; unlocked on request by the custodian) below the north aisle are the stumps of six fluted columns on the stylobate.

The alleys on the north side of the church join via del Duomo. The **Duomo** (S. Gerlando), though altered at the east end in the 17C is basically a 14C building with an unfinished **campanile** (to the south-west) that shows in its Gothic

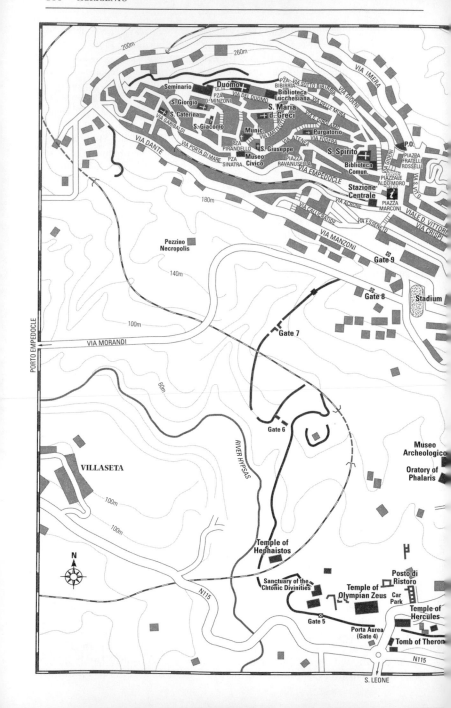

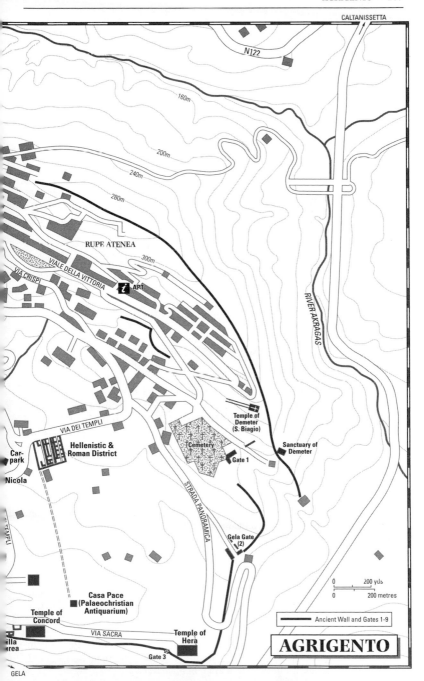

CALTANISSETTA

N122

160m

200m

240m

280m

RUPE ATENEA

300m

VIALE DELLA VITTORIA

VIA CRISPI

*i* APT

RIVER AKRAGAS

VIA DEI TEMPLI

Car-
park

Nicola

TEMPLI

Hellenistic &
Roman District

Cemetery

STRADA PANORAMICA

Temple of
Demeter
(S. Biagio)

Sanctuary of
Demeter

Gate 1

Gela Gate
(2)

Casa Pace
(Palaeochristian
Antiquarium)

Temple of
Concord

illa
rea

VIA SACRA

Temple of
Hera

Gate 3

GELA

0          200 yds
0          200 metres

■ Ancient Wall and Gates 1-9

**AGRIGENTO**

windows a mixture of Arab-Norman and Catalan influences. The north aisle was dislodged in the disastrous landslide of 1966, and the church, normally entered by the side door at the top of a double flight of steps, has been closed for restoration since 1993.

**Interior**. A single round arch divides the nave into two parts; to the west the tall polygonal piers support an open painted roof of 1518, to the east a coffered ceiling of 1603. At the end of the south aisle is the chapel of the Norman St Gerland (who refounded the see after the Saracen defeat), with a silver reliquary by Michele Ricca (1639). Opposite, in the north aisle is the tomb of Gaspare de Marino, by Andrea Mancino and Giovanni Gagini (1492), and other Baroque funerary monuments, and fragments of 15C frescoes. A curious acoustical phenomenon (*il portavoce*) permits a person standing beneath the cornice of the apse to hear every word spoken even in a low voice near the main doorway, though the reverse is not true.

The **Seminario** (17C–18C) has an arcaded courtyard, off which (shown on request) is a Gothic hall with a double vault, remains of the Chiaramonte Steri (14C).

In via del Duomo is the long façade of the **Biblioteca Lucchesiana**, in a fine building founded here in 1765 as a public library by the bishop of Agrigento. Its treasures number 40,000 volumes (including Arab MSS. still housed in the original presses of 1765).

## The Valle dei Templi and the ancient city

The ancient city of Agrigento, encircled by a wall, occupied the angle between the rivers Hypsas and Akragas (now the Fiume di S. Anna and the Fiume di S. Biagio) which meet near the coast to flow into the sea.

### Plan of visit and opening times

The museum and all the main ruins are linked by road. On foot at least a whole day should be allowed for the visit. Those with less time should not miss the **museum**, the **temples** on the Strada Panoramica and the **Temple of Zeus**.

The Temples of Concord, Hera and Herakles are still unenclosed, but there are plans to introduce a ticket for these temples also (and the ticket office will be moved to the beginning of the via Sacra). The **Temple of Zeus** and the **Hellenistic** and **Roman District** are open every day 08.30–17.00 (19.30 in summer). The museum is open every day 09.00–13.00; and also usually Wed, Thurs, Fri & Sat 14.30–17.30; Sun & PH 09.00–13.00.

The temples should, if possible, be seen at several different times of the day, especially in the early morning and at sunset; and at night when floodlit. In early spring, when the almond trees are in bloom, they are particularly beautiful. Butterflies are in the valley in abundance.

## The Temples of Herakles, Concord and Hera

Viale Crispi (bus) descends from the modern city past the Hellenistic and Roman District and the museum (see below) to (c 3km) the car-park and café, known as the *Posto di Ristoro*, near the main temples.

Here the via Sacra (closed to cars) branches off to the left. It traverses the ridge on which the temples of Herakles, Concord and Hera are built. Beyond the Temple of Concord it leads through delightful countryside, here undisturbed, with beautiful groves of almonds and ancient olive trees.

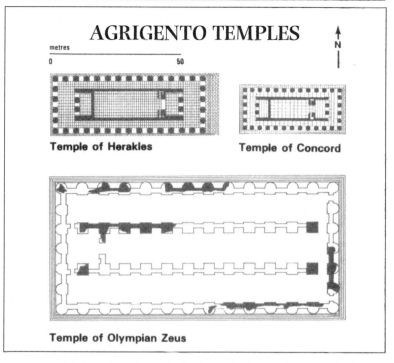

# AGRIGENTO TEMPLES

metres
0 — 50

↑ N

**Temple of Herakles**

**Temple of Concord**

**Temple of Olympian Zeus**

At the beginning on the right a footbridge leads above a deep sepulchral street to the **Temple of Herakles**, a heap of ruins showing traces of fire, with nine columns upright, eight of them re-erected in 1922–3 by the munificence of Captain Alexander Hardcastle. This is probably the oldest visible temple of Akragas (built c 500 BC). It was peripteral and hexastyle (67 x 25m) and had 38 columns (6 x 15), 9.9m high and 2m in diameter, and a cella (perhaps roofless) with pronaos and opisthodomus in antis. Anciently it was famed for its statue of Hercules, which Verres attempted to steal, and for a painting of the infant Hercules strangling the serpents, by Zeuxis. Beyond, on the via Sacra is the **Villa Aurea** (now used as offices, admission only with special permission) surrounded by a luxuriant and beautifully kept garden.

In the forecourt is a bust of Captain Alexander Hardcastle set up in 1984 as a memorial to him. This eccentric Englishman repaired the villa in 1921 and, with his brother Henry, a parson, lived here until Alexander's death in 1933. The Captain provided substantial funds to restore and excavate the ancient city, supporting the work of Pirro Marconi. He also took an interest in the modern city, and provided an aqueduct from there to the temple valley. In gratitude the Italian government made him a *commendatore* of the *Corona d'Italia* and the Home Office allowed him to wear the insignia. The Villa now contains an antiquarium (material from the Pezzino Necropolis, and excavations in contrada Mosè), and in the garden are tombs and underground cisterns.

Further up on the left is a **Palaeochristian necropolis**. Here are Christian tombs cut in the surface of the rock, as well as extensive **catacombs** (closed) with subterranean passages extending below the road. In the field here are two tholos tombs thought to date from the 5C BC.

The road continues up to the so-called **Temple of Concord**, the best preserved of all the Greek temples except the Theseion at Athens, which it recalls in its majestic symmetry and rich colour. For preservation reasons, it is sadly no longer possible to enter the building, and it has been disfigured by a rusting scaffolding fence for many years. The name occurs in a Latin inscription found here, but has no real connection with the temple (although a tradition persists among the inhabitants of Agrigento that the temple should be visited by a husband and wife on their wedding day).

The building, which probably dates from about 430 and was only slightly harmed by the Carthaginians, stands on a stylobate of four steps (39.3 x 16.9m) and is peripteral and hexastyle with 34 Doric columns (6 x 13), 6.8m high including the capitals, with a diameter of 1.4m at the base. The intercolumniations of the façades become narrower towards the sides (to accommodate the corner metopes); this is one of the earliest instances in Sicily of this refinement in temple design. The cella has a pronaos and an opisthodomus, both in antis. From the east end of the cella two spiral staircases mount to the architrave. The complete entablature survives at both ends.

The excellent state of preservation of the temple is explained by the fact that it was converted into a church by S. Gregorio delle Rape (i.e. of the turnips), bishop of Agrigento, in the 6C AD. It was restored in the 18C, but the arches of the nave remain in the cella walls. The material of this and of the other temples is easily eroded oolitic limestone, formerly protected by white stucco made of marble dust, and brightly painted above the capitals, and now burnt by the sun to a rich tawny gold.

From the temple the pretty building of the Villa Athena hotel can be seen, which has a neo-classical loggia beside two palm trees. A little gate on the road gives access to the **Casa Pace,** an attractive little house restored to house a **Palaeochristian Antiquarium** (officially open at the same time as the temples, but if closed ask at the custodian's hut by the Temple of Concord). The exhibits illustrate the history of the three early Christian churches so far found in Agrigento (one outside the walls at the eastern edge of the temple ridge, one built inside the Temple of Concord and one excavated beside the Hotel Villa Athena). Finds include a finely carved sarcophagus (5C AD), left unfinished. Upstairs are photographs and plans of the necropoli excavated in the area. From the Antiquarium a path leads across pretty countryside to the Roman and Hellenistic District (see below).

The lovely road, now more peaceful, continues parallel to the ancient city **walls**; in the inner face there are many Byzantine tomb recesses. There is a view on the left of the cemetery, to the right of which S. Biagio can be seen (see below) beside a clump of trees. On the skyline, radio masts mark the Rupe Ateneo. Three ugly unfinished houses in the fields here were demolished in 1995, the first sign that the valley may one day be preserved.

Above the road, c 1km farther east, stands the much ruined but picturesque **Temple of Hera**, called the Temple of Juno Lacinia, from a confusion with a temple dedicated to Hera on the Lacinian promontory at Croton. It resembles the Temple of Concord in form, but is slightly smaller and older (c 450 BC). Since a

*Temple of Concord, Agrigento*

landslide in 1976 threatened its stability the entrance has been fenced off. The stylobate, on a massive artificial platform, measures 38 x 16.8m. Of its 34 columns (6 x 13), 6.4m high with a base-diameter of 1.3m, nine have fallen. Traces of a fire (which probably occurred in 406) are still visible, and the work of the Roman restorers was ruined by an earthquake. To the east is the sacrificial altar; to the west an ancient cistern.

Looking west there is a good sight of the outer face of the wall, in some places carved out of the natural rock, clinging to the brow of the hill. Nearby are the scant remains of **Gate Three**, and, outside the walls, an ancient roadway (with deep ruts) can still be seen. In the other direction, at the foot of the hill, are numerous roads.

## The Temple of Olympian Zeus

At the *Posto di Ristoro* (see above) is the entrance (admission see above) to the Temple of Olympian Zeus and the excavations which extend to the westernmost edge of the temple ridge. The custodians of the ancient monuments of Agrigento have their office here: they are helpful and informed. Enquire here for admission to areas found closed or for the key to sites normally kept locked (see the text).

Beside the entrance is the vast, complicated heap of ruins of the **Temple of Olympian Zeus**, or **Olympieion**, thought to have been begun by the Carthaginian prisoners taken at Himera, and left unfinished in 406: its destruction, due in part to the Edict of Olympia (6C AD), and in part to earthquakes, was completed by quarrying in the 18C, much of the stone going into the foundations of Porto Empedocle.

This huge Doric temple (110.1 x 52.7m, virtually a double square), is the largest Doric temple known, and is unique in form among Greek temples. It was built of comparatively small stones (each capital was composed of three blocks) and then covered in stucco. It is heptastyle and pseudoperipteral, i.e. the seven columns at each end and the 14 on each side were engaged in the walls, being rounded externally and presenting a square face towards the interior. In between the semi-columns, 16.7m high and 4m thick at the base, were 38 colossal telamones set on the outer wall; their exact arrangement is still under discussion (see below). In the east pediment a Gigantomachia was represented, and in the west pediment the capture of Troy. The cella was divided into three aisles, separated by square pillars (to support the vast roof).

Little remains in position except the stereobate, which alone, however, is sufficient to convey an impression of the immensity of the monument. Part of the north wall survives (note the outer face), and the foundations of the aisle pillars. To the east, beyond the wall which (curiously) 'blocked' what is thought to have been the entrance, are the foundations of the altar platform. All around the temple is a heap of ruins, amid which lies a copy of a **Gigante** (7.6m high), one of the telamones; the original 19C reconstruction is displayed in the Archaeological Museum. The U-shaped incision visible on many stones is believed to have facilitated their being raised by ropes. Near the south-eastern corner, below one of the colossal fallen capitals, is a small temple of archaic date with a cella divided by piers. The **agora** of the ancient city is thought to have been to the east (near the car-park).

## Sanctuary of Chthonic Divinities

To the west is a complicated area of excavations including remains of houses, and traces of an L-shaped portico which enclosed a sanctuary and a tholos on a spur beside **Gate Five**, its carriageway obstructed by masonry, which apparently fell in Greek times. It was probably a double gate defended by a tower. On the other side of the gate are various shrines that together formed the **Sanctuary of the Chthonic Divinities**, which were entirely enclosed by a precinct wall, a portion of which is visible on the west side. Here is the misnamed **Temple of Castor and Pollux**. The four columns bearing a portion of the architrave, which have been used as the picturesque symbol of Classical Sicily, are a reconstruction of 1836 now known to incorporate elements from more than one building on this site.

Superimposed ruins show the existence of shrines dedicated to the cult of the earth-goddesses as early as the 7C BC. Of this period are the structures on the north side, notably the pairs of altars, one circular and one square. To the south of these, remains exist of two unfinished temples of the 6C; the third is that formerly misascribed to Castor and Pollux, which was probably of the same plan as the Temple of Concord; and a fourth was built, just to the south, in Hellenistic or Roman times. Many of the fallen column-drums belong to the last temple and the well-preserved altar east of the platform.

Beyond the custodians' house is an **Archaic Sanctuary**, recently excavated on the edge of the hill. From here two columns of the Temple of Hephaistos (or Vulcan) can be seen on the hill across a delightful fertile little valley where there are orange trees. The pretty footpath from here to the temple is now difficult to find; the temple is therefore best reached from the main road (see below). The ugly via Morandi on stilts and high-rise buildings of the modern town of Agrigento are conspicuous from here. Beneath the viaduct of the via Morandi the **Pezzino necropolis** (admission from via Dante) has been excavated.

## The Museo Regionale Archeologico

On the main road, about 1km uphill from the *Posto di Ristoro* (see the plan), is the Museo Regionale Archeologico (for admission see above; inconspicuous car-park off the road just above the museum), one of the finest museums in Sicily, spaciously arranged in a building of 1967. It is approached through a garden and the 15C cloisters of the convent attached to the church of S. Nicola (see below). In the cloisters is a long bench carrying an inscription to Herakles and Hermes found in the Agora zone of the city.

**Room I** contains Early and Late Bronze Age material from sites near Agrigento, including a small Mycenaean amphora (probably found at Porto Empedocle), and painted vases. Also, prehistoric objects found in Agrigento beneath the classical area.

**Room II** contains objects from Gela (6C–7C BC), including Corinthian and Rhodian ware (note the head of a bull), as well as locally made vases; votive statuettes from Licata (late 4C BC).

**Room III** displays a superb collection of **vases**, including a group of outstanding Attic vases, from the mid-6C BC to the early 3C BC. The following description follows the cases in sequence from the top of the steps left in a clockwise direction around the four halls (see p.372 for the nomenclature of vases). On the walls are photos of some of the most famous vases found in Agrigento and now in other museums. **Case1**: Attic black-figured vases, including a fine amphora; **Case 2**: red-figured kraters; **Case 3**: Attic red-figured vases including a lekythos with Nike sacrificing (460–450 BC), and a krater with Dionysiac scenes (c 440 BC); **Case 4**: krater showing Perseus and Andromeda in polychrome on a white ground, a rare example of c 430 BC, and a stamnos (440–430 BC) showing a sacrifice to Apollo; **Case 5**: a small red-figured krater with a bull being led to sacrifice, and several kraters and stamni with banqueting scenes (some by the 'Painter of Lugano', c 400 BC); **Case 6**: Hellenistic vases. At the end of the hall, fine marble statue of a warrior (damaged); belonging to the Early Classical period, this may have adorned part of the pediment of the Temple of Herakles (c 480 BC). **Case 7** contain vases (4C BC) from Campania. **Cases 8** and **9**: vases from Apulia (4C BC); **Case 10**: Attic red-figured vase of the first half of the 5C BC, including two kraters by the 'Harrow Painter', and a krater showing the burial of a warrior; **Cases 11** and **12**: black-figured Attic vases of the end of the 6C BC, including a lekythos with Herakles and the hydra; and a large amphora with four gods and a quadriga by the 'Painter of Dikaios'.

**Room IV** contains architectonic fragments including a remarkable variety of lion-head water spouts from various buildings (including the Temple of Herakles and the Temple of Demeter). **Room V** Statuettes and heads in terracotta, notably, female votive statues; (**Case 45**) askos, the mule of Dionysos (late 6C BC, from Favissa), and the mask of a negro of the same date; two cases of moulds; (**Case 51**) head of Athena with a helmet (c 490 BC); (**Case 55**) head of a kouros (500 BC). On the end wall are delicate bas-relief friezes, including some showing the telamones. Beyond the steps which descend to Room VI, **Case 59** on the balcony displays the head of a kouros (?) of c 540 BC, and a female bust of the end of the 6C BC. Other cases here contain finds from the area near the Temple of Herakles, including architectonic fragments in terracotta.

Steps descend to **room VI**, devoted to the Temple of Zeus. Here the remarkable **Gigante** (7.6m high) is displayed, one of the telamones from the temple, which was recomposed from fragments in the 19C; along the wall are three colossal **telamone heads**. The blocks of stone were originally covered with plaster. Plans and models suggest possible reconstructions of the temple, and the controversial position of the telamones. The recent discovery of a leg attached to a block of stone of one of the statues has shown that their feet must have been further apart than is indicated here. **Room VII** contains fragments of wall paintings (recomposed) and mosaics (including three in small tesserae of animals) from the Roman District. **Room VIII** (inscriptions) and **room IX** (coins) are opened only on special request.

**Room X** is reached from the balcony (Room V). In the first part three statuettes are displayed: the *Ephebus of Agrigento*, a statuette of Apollo, or the river-god Akragas (c 480 BC), a fragment of a female kneeling statue of Aphrodite (2C–1C BC) and a fragment of a male torso. In the second part material found in the bouleuterion is displayed, including coins. A corridor, overlooking a little garden with two Roman statues, has panels illustrating the political history of Akragas. **Room XI**, has finds from various necropoli, notably that at contrada Pezzino, the oldest one in Agrigento and the one that has produced the richest finds (early 6C–3C BC). The miniature vases were found in children's tombs. At the end of the room, the fine alabaster sarcophagus of a child, with charming childhood scenes (ended by illness and death), a Hellenistic work of the 2C BC, was found near Agrigento. Nearby is another Roman sarcophagus. From the window here recent excavations can be seen.

**Room XII** has an introductory display of prehistoric material, and finds from Sciacca; in **room XIII** there are objects from the province of Agrigento, including finds from the Grotto dell'Acqua Fitusa and from S. Angelo Muxaro. The fragments of ochre are thought to have been used to colour vases. Material from Eraclea Minoa is displayed in **room XIV**, and Greek and Roman helmets; busts from Licata; bronze cooking utensils, etc. **Room XV** contains a splendid red-figured krater from Gela (5C BC). In perfect condition, it displays the battle of the amazons. Photographs on the walls show other vases, now in the Gela museum. **Room XVII** has finds from Caltanissetta (notably a fine red-figured krater showing horsemen of 450–440 BC).

The exit from the museum is left past **room XVIII** (opened only on special request), which houses the contents of the **treasury of the cathedral**: especially noteworthy are two reliquaries of Limoges-enamelled copper, a portable altar-stone with Byzantine enamels (13C), an ivory crozier, and a *Madonna* attributed to Guido Reni.

Outside the museum is the entrance to an area of **excavations**. The **bouleuterion** (or *ekklesiasterion*) was built in the 4C–3C BC and transformed into an odeon in the Imperial era. It was used for the meetings of the *boulé*, a political ruling body. It could hold some 300 people; the participants are thought to have stood. The narrow divisional rows are carved into the rock. In one corner is the so-called **Oratory of Phalaris**, a prostyle building in antis, probably a late-Hellenistic shrine, which was transformed into a Gothic chapel. A footbridge crosses an area with remains of late-Hellenistic houses, and Imperial Roman buildings (mosaics).

The early 13C church of **S. Nicola** has a curious façade made up of a Gothic doorway in strong relief between antae with a Doric cornice (the material probably came from a Roman edifice nearby). It is kept locked and only opened for weddings, but can usually be visited by appointment with the custodian, ☎ 0922/26672. The architecture of the interior, reconstructed in 1322, and altered in 1426, is interesting. In the second chapel (right; a contribution is requested for the lighting) there is a magnificent **sarcophagus**. With great delicacy and purity of style it portrays four episodes in the story of Hippolytus and Phaedra; it derives from Classical Greek models but is thought to be a Roman work of the 2C–3C AD. The front panel shows Hippolytus with his male companions and numerous horses and dogs, and the side panel illustrates Phaedra with female companions. The angle figures are particularly skilful, as well as the delicate frieze at the top and bottom of the scenes. The last two sides do not appear to have been completed, possibly because the sarcophagus was placed in the corner of a building. In 1787, when it was in the Duomo, it was much admired by Goethe as the best preserved Classical relief carving he had seen. The church also contains a venerated wooden Crucifix, a statue of the *Madonna and Child* by the Gagini school, and an unusual stoup with a grey marble hand, which bears two dates (1529 and 1685). From the terrace there is a fine view of the valley of the temples.

On the opposite side of the main road is the entrance to the enclosure (behind a green fence) with the conspicuous remains of the **Hellenistic and Roman District** (for admission see above) of the city. Here an area of c 120 sq m has been excavated, exposing four cardines, running north and south, with their complex of buildings sloping downwards from east to west in a series of terraces. The district was first developed towards the end of the 2C BC and its civic life lasted probably to the 4C or 5C BC. The drainage system is elaborate and traces of stairs show that buildings were of more than one storey. Houses, of sandstone blocks, are built around a peristyle, or with an atrium; many of their rooms have good pavements (the best, which include the *Casa della Gazella* and the *Casa del Maestro Astratista*, are covered for protection).

Beside the entrance excavations are in progress and an ancient **road** (reached by steps beneath a modern foot bridge) can be followed through delightful countryside to join the via Sacra near the Temple of Concord (see above). This was the *cardine* which led from the city to the temple ridge.

### The Rock Sanctuary of Demeter
From viale Crispi opposite the Hotel Della Valle, a road to the left crosses a main road and continues to the cemetery. Here a gate on the left (signposted) is officially open at the same time as the temples (but is often kept locked). Beyond it an unsurfaced road can be followed on foot for c 200m to the edge of the cliff. On the hillside above is **S. Biagio**. This Norman church was built on the cella of a small temple begun after the victory at Himera in 480, and dedicated to Demeter and Persephone. The pronaos and stylobate of the temple protrude beyond the apse of the church. To the north are two large round altars. The temple was approached by the ancient track with deep wheel ruts, still clearly visible, mounting the side of the hill. On the rock face a marble plaque records excavations here by Alexander Hardcastle (see p.191).

On the edge of the cliff the line of the **walls** can clearly be seen from the Rupe Atenea (see below), above S. Biagio, to the Temple of Hera; beyond, the view extends along the temple ridge and to the sea. Just outside the walls and below the cliff edge is the entrance gate to the **Rock Sanctuary of Demeter**. The long, steep flight of steps was constructed in the rock face in the twentieth century; they lead down through a delightful garden to the sanctuary. Beside two natural caverns in the rock (in which numerous votive busts and statues dating from the 5C–4C BC were found) is a tunnel which carries a terracotta aqueduct from a spring far inside the hill. In front is a complicated series of cisterns on different levels and remains of what may have been a monumental fountain. The sanctuary was formerly thought to antedate the foundation of the city by some two centuries, but some scholars now believe it was constructed in the 5C BC.

From the cemetery (see above) another unsurfaced road (signposted) leads along the wall of the cemetery to (200m) an interesting wedge-shaped **Bastion** that guarded the vulnerable spot where a valley interrupts the natural defence line. To the north is **Gate One**. Captain Alexander Hardcastle (see above) was buried in the cemetery beside a 'window' in the wall: he was responsible for excavating the ancient walls here.

The **Rupe Atenea** (351m), a rocky hill, the highest part of the town, now crowned with masts and aerials, was part of the acropolis of Akragas. It is reached by road (unsignposted) from above the hospital through an unattractive part of the town. It is now military property and has little interest since the ruins of a large ancient building found here are inaccessible. The wide view is marred by modern buildings on all sides.

Viale Crispi continues downhill from the Hotel Della Valle (see above), and the Strada Panoramica forks left passing near the **Gela Gate** (**Gate Two**) which guards a steep defile, and continues to the Temple of Hera (described above). Those on foot can continue along the via Sacra to rejoin the main road at the *Posto di Ristoro*.

Just below the *Posto di Ristoro* the main road (the ancient road to the sea) descends through the rock on the site of the **Porta Aurea** (**Gate Four**). This was the main gate of Akragas built over in Byzantine times. Just before the roundabout on the high ground to the left is a Roman funerary monument, miscalled the **Tomb of Theron**, a two-storeyed edifice with a Doric entablature and Ionic corner-columns. It stands on the edge of a huge Roman cemetery (1C BC–5C AD) which extends eastwards below the line of the walls (here much ruined by landslides).

## Temples of Asklepios and Hephasitos

The Gela road runs east from the roundabout beneath the temple ridge and walls, past a park of 4 ha which has recently been designated to protect the almond trees here, which include some 300 varieties. The **Museo Vivente del Mandorlo** is run jointly by the province and the university. The first unsurfaced road on the right (signposted) leads through another field of almonds to a farm beside the little **Temple of Asklepios** on the bank of the S. Biagio river (near a medicinal spring). Excavations are in progress here and the site has recently been enclosed (it is closed for restoration but is usually unlocked on request at the custodian's office, at the entrance to the Temple of Olympian Zeus, see above). This is a small Doric temple in antis with a pronaos, cella and false opisthodomus. In spite of its size, it shows the advanced techniques of construction (including convex lines) associated with the (contemporary) Parthenon. The stairway is preserved between the cella and pronaos. This is the temple mentioned by Polybius in his account of the Roman siege of 262 and it contained the statue of *Apollo* by Myron whose adventures are chronicled by Cicero.

From the roundabout (see above) the Porto Empedocle road leads (c 500m) to the bottom of a little valley where, just before a bridge, an unsurfaced road (unsignposted) forks right. This should be followed as far as the high railway viaduct. From here steps (signposted) lead up past plants of agave and aloe to the **Temple of Hephaistos** (or **Vulcan**), beyond a charming field of almonds near a branch railway line and right beside a primitive farmhouse. The temple, hexastyle and peripteral, was built c 430 BC and two columns remain upright. The cella was partly built over a small archaic temple of the early 6C. A marble stone beneath the stylobate on the south side records excavations here in 1930 by Alexander Hardcastle. From here the irregular line of **walls** is pierced by **Gates Six**, **Seven**, **Eight** and **Nine**.

# Porto Empedocle and the Isole Pelagie

Near Porto Empedocle is Luigi Pirandello's birthplace. The Isole Pelagie are remote islands nearer Tunisia than Sicily.

## *Porto Empedocle*

Porto Empedocle, is an ugly industrial town (population 17,700) with cement works, and a fishing port (in decline), now engulfed by high-rise buildings. It is the port for the Pelagie islands. On the inner mole, built in 1749–63, partly of stone from the temples of Agrigento, is a massive tower. On the western outskirts a Roman villa, the **Villa Romana di Durrueli**, dating from the 1C AD, has been excavated. Nearby at Punta Grande are the **Scala dei Turchi**, remarkable white rocks of limestone and sandy clay which have been eroded by the sea into fantastic shapes.

Just outside Porto Empedocle is **Caos** where the **birthplace of Luigi Pirandello** (1867–1936) is now a delightful small museum. Admission daily 09.00–12.00, 15.00–17.00 (or 19.00 in summer). Under a wind-blown pine (damaged in a storm in 1997), the ashes of the dramatist and novelist are buried according to his wishes beneath a 'rough rock in the countryside of Girgenti'. There is usually an open-air festival of his plays here in July.

### *Luigi Pirandello*

Luigi Pirandello became famous as a playwright after World War I, making his name in 1921 with the first performance of *Sei personaggi in cerca d'autore* (*Six characters in search of an Author*). He was a theatre director in Rome from 1925 to 1934, the year in which he was awarded the Nobel prize for literature. In his writings he conveys an idea of man suffering from solitude, disillusioned by his ideals. With a strong element of irony he suggests that his characters frequently reveal the necessity of 'wearing a mask'. He was a prolific writer, and was widely acclaimed in his lifetime: one of his most famous novels was *Il Fu Mattia Pascal*, (*The Late Mattia Pascal*), published in 1904.

# The Isole Pelagie

## ■ Practical information

*Information offices*. APT Agrigento, ☎ 0922/401352. Pro loco on Lampedusa, ☎ 0922/971390.

### Getting there

**By sea** from Porto Empedocle. Car ferries run every day (*Siremar*, ☎ 0922/6070150) to Linosa and Lampedusa. In summer *Ustica Lines* run hydrofoil services twice a day, ☎ 0922/970003.

**By air**. There are flights from Palermo to Lampedusa and in summer flights from Milan and Rome also usually operate.

### Hotels

**Lampedusa**. ★★★ *Baia Turchese*, ☎ 0922/970455; *Le Pelagie*, ☎ 0922/970211; *Medusa*, ☎ 0922/970126; *Guilgia Tomasino*, ☎ 0922/970879. **Linosa**. ★★★ *Algusa*, ☎ 0922/972052.

**Campsites** on Lampedusa. ★★ *La Roccia*, ☎ 0922/970055 and ★ *Lampedusa*, ☎ 0922/970720.

### Restaurants

**Lampedusa**. B *Gemelli*, 2 via Cala Pisana; *Lampedusa Invoca*, 38 via Mazzini.

The Isole Pelagie lie about 205km south-west of the Sicilian mainland (and 113km from Tunisia). They consist of three flat and barren islands, **Lampedusa**, **Linosa** and **Lampione**, off which there is good fishing (especially noted for sardines and anchovies). They fell to the allies without resistance in June 1943; Lampedusa surrendered to an English airman who landed by accident, having run out of petrol.

**Lampedusa** is the largest of the three islands with an area of 20 sq km and 4500 inhabitants. Although it has a beautiful coast with excellent swimming, its beaches are not as clean as they might be, and it has some unattractive new buildings and noisy traffic. The **Isolotto dei Conigli**, just offshore, has been declared a nature reserve (sea turtles can still sometimes be seen here). Lampedusa has important US and Italian military installations; the Libyans made an unsuccessful attack in 1986 when two missiles fell 2.5km short of the island.

**Linosa**, 42km north of Lampedusa, has an area of 5.3 sq km and 452 inhabitants. Volcanic in origin, it is the most fertile of the islands and has colourful houses. It has been used as a place of exile for Mafia detainees. You are not allowed to bring your car to the island in summer.

**Lampione**, with an area of just 1.2 sq km, is uninhabited.

# Sciacca and Eraclea Minoa

Sciacca, although surrounded by ugly buildings, is a small town of interest with a local ceramic industry. Eraclea Minoa is an ancient site in a wonderful position on the sea.

## ■ Practical information

***Information offices***. In Sciacca: Azienda Autonoma, 84 Corso Vittorio Emanuele (☎ 0925/21182). Azienda Autonoma delle Terme, 2 via Agatocle (☎ 0925/961111). APT Agrigento, ☎ 0922/401352.

***Buses***. Frequent services from Agrigento and Palermo to Sciacca.

### Hotels
**Sciacca**. ★★★ *Grande Albergo delle Terme*, via delle Nuove Terme, ☎ 0925/23133 and *Garden*, via Valverde, ☎ 0925/26299.
North of Sciacca at **contrada Monte Kronio**, ★★★ spa hotel (open April–Nov) *Grand Hotel S. Calogero*, ☎ 0925/21005.

### Campsites
By the sea **near Sciacca**. ★★ *Baia Makauda*, ☎ 0925/997001, and ★ *Gioventù*, ☎ 0925/991167.
At **Siculiana Marina** (★), *Canne*, ☎ 0922/815255; *Herbesso*, ☎ 0922/817221.
**Near Menfi** ★★★ *Geser Club*, in contrada Torrenove, ☎ 0925/74666 and ★ *La Palma* in contrada Fiori, ☎ 0925/77232.

### Restaurants
**Sciacca**. **A** *Al Caminetto*, 67 via da Garaffe. **B** *Hostaria del Vicolo*, 10 vicolo Sammaritano.
**Eraclea Minoa** is a beautiful place to **picnic**.

***Annual festival***. Carnival procession in Sciacca with allegorical floats, etc.

## Sciacca

Sciacca (population 40,000) is a spa town known since Roman times, when it was the *thermae* of Selinunte. It has been engulfed by new buildings, and many of its monuments are in poor repair. A local ceramic industry flourished here in the 16C and 17C, and a few artisans' workshops survive in the town.

In the centre of the town beside part of its old fortifications is the unusual **Porta S. Salvatore** (1581), a fine work by local stonemasons. Beside it is the eccentric façade of the **Carmine** with a half finished neo-classical lower part and an asymmetrical 13C rose window. The dome, with green tiles, dates from 1807. The church contains a good painting of the *Transition of the Virgin*, the last work of Vincenzo da Pavia, completed by Giampaolo Fondulo in 1572.

A short way up via Geradi (left) is the **Steripinto**, a small fortified palace in the Gothic Catalan style. It is interesting for its façade, with diamond-shaped stone facing, erected in 1501 by Antonio Noceto. Opposite the Carmine, on the other side of via Incisa, is the north portal, sculpted in 1468 by Francesco Laurana and his workshop, of the church of **S. Margherita** (closed many years ago). It contains polychrome stuccoes by Orazio Ferraro. Beyond is the Gothic portal of the former church of S. Gerlando and the abandoned Ospedale di S. Margherita. Opposite are the late-Gothic Palazzo Perollo-Arone and the 15C Torre di Pardo, both ruined by modern alterations.

Corso Vittorio Emanuele continues into the central **piazza Angelo Scandaliato** planted with trees and with a long terrace from which there is a view of the old houses rising in terraces above the fishing harbour. Here is the huge former **Collegio dei Gesuiti** (now the town hall), begun in 1613, with a fine courtyard. The corso continues to the dilapidated piazza Duomo where the **Duomo** (called the *Basilica*) has statues by Antonino and Gian Domenico Gagini on its façade. It was rebuilt in 1656 by Michele Blasco, and the vault fresco is by the local artist Tommaso Rossi (1829). It has some good sculptures including a statue of the *Madonna* of 1457, a marble ancona with reliefs by Antonino Gagini, and (on the high altar) the *Madonna del Soccorso* by Giuliano Mancino and Bartolomeo Berrettaro.

The corso continues to **piazza Friscia** which has pretty 19C public gardens with tropical plants, in a pleasanter part of the town. Via Agatocle leads right past a new theatre to the edge of the cliff. Here is the **Nuovo Stabilimento Termale**, a pink spa building in Art Nouveau style built in 1928–38. The sulphureous waters (32°C) are used in thermal swimming-pools (open June to October) and mud bath therapy. The Grand Hotel was built next door in 1952.

From piazza Friscia via Valverde leads up to the gardens in front of the church of **S. Maria delle Giummare** (or Valverde), its façade tucked in between two castellated Norman towers; the restored chapel in the left tower has an interesting interior. The elaborate 18C rococo decoration in the main church is the work of Ferraiolo. The vault was frescoed by Mariano Rossi (1768). Also in the upper town is **S. Nicolò La Latina**, a simple 12C church. Above is the ruined **castle** of the Spanish Luna family. Their feud with the Perollo clan in 15C–16C became notorious under the name of *caso di Sciacca* (the Sciacca affair); it was resolved only after the population of the town had been reduced to almost half its size.

Three churches are situated in piazza Noceto, with the 16C Porta S. Calogero, including **S. Michele** (1614–20), which contains an 18C cantoria, a Gothic wooden Crucifix, and a 16C marble bas-relief.

## The environs of Sciacca

North-east of Sciacca is **Menfi** (population 13,000), a town laid out on a regular plan in 1698, with the houses arranged around courtyards off the main streets, many of which were made uninhabitable by the Belice earthquake (see p.182) in 1968. A new town has been built on the higher ground above. On the coast, beyond woods, is the fishing village of **Porto Palo**. There are good beaches on the unspoilt coast here which adjoins the nature reserve around the mouth of the Belice river in the province of Trapani (which extends to Marinella and Selinunte, see p.175).

North of Menfi is **S. Margherita di Belice** where the country house described by Lampedusa in *Il Gattopardo*, called *Donnafugata*, was destroyed together with most of the town in the 1968 earthquake. To the east **Sambuca**

**di Sicilia** (population 7000) has an old centre which preserves its Islamic layout (near piazza Navarro). The church of the Concezione has a 14C portal and the church of the Carmine contains 19C stuccoes and a statue of the *Madonna* attributed to Antonello Gagini. In Palazzo Panitteri there is a museum of 19C wax models. The Chiesa del Collegio and Cappuccini have works by Fra Felice da Sambuca (1734–1805). To the north, on the provincial border with Palermo, are the excavations of Adranone and Contessa Entellina, described on p.135-6.

**Caltabellotta**, north-east of Sciacca, is a little town (population 5200) in a beautiful situation in a commanding position (849m). Here the peace ending the war of the Sicilian Vespers (see p.107) was signed in 1302. The Norman church (usually locked) has statues by the Gagini. In 1194 the castle sheltered Sibylla of Acerra, widow of King Tancred, and her infant son who reigned for a few months as William III, shortly before they were imprisoned by the new king of Sicily, Henry VI. The church of the Salvatore, below the rock face, has a late Gothic portal. On the outskirts is the hermitage of S. Pellegrino (17C–18C; now derelict). Below Caltabellotta is the little town of **S. Anna**, founded in 1622.

**Villafranca Sicula**, founded in 1499, was also damaged in the Belice earthquake. **Burgio** is an agricultural town with a local ceramics industry founded in the 16C and a bell-foundry. A castle survives here and in the church there is a *Madonna* by Vincenzo Gagini.

**Monte Kronio** (or **Monte S. Calogero**; 388m) has caves with interesting steam vapours, known since Roman times, and now a little spa. The sanctuary of S. Calogero (1530–1644) has a statue of the saint by Giacomo Gagini.

On the Agrigento road east of Sciacca is the '**Castello incantato**' (well signposted), a park with olive and almond trees where thousands of heads were sculpted in wood and stone by a local sculptor Filippo Bentivegna (d. 1967). In an area cultivated with olives, vineyards, strawberries and citrus fruit plantations (protected from the wind by net screens), is **Ribera**, a town (population 18,000) founded in 1627 by Luigi, Prince of Paternò, and named in honour of his Spanish wife, Maria de Ribera. It was the birthplace of Francesco Crispi (1818–1901), the statesman who was Garibaldi's Secretary of State, and supported his landing in Sicily in 1860. He was a deputy in the first national parliament and twice prime minister of Italy (in 1887 and 1893).

## Eraclea Minoa

The excavations of Eraclea Minoa, are in a magnificent isolated position on the sea at the mouth of the ancient Halykos (now the Platani). The road follows the lovely meandering river valley and climbs the low hill past vineyards. Beyond the turning for the seaside village an unsurfaced road continues for the last 500m. Here part of the town **defences** can be seen, which were improved in the 4C (when the length of the walls was increased to c 6km). Above the dirt road on the left are the foundation of a circular Greek tower and a section of well-preserved wall (ending in a square Roman tower). The continuation of the walls has been lost in landslides. A splendid view extends along the wooded shore and white limestone cliffs to **Capo Bianco**, beyond the river. The beautiful coastline here, which includes **Torre Salsa**, which has interesting flora and fauna (where sea turtles survive), was saved from development in 1991 when part of it was purchased by the Worldwide Fund for Nature.

The **main entrance to the excavations** of Eraclea Minoa is beside the ruins of Hellenistic houses. **Admission** daily, 09.00 to dusk. No refreshments are available, but it is a beautiful place to picnic.

### History
The name suggests an origin as a Minoan colony; a legend that Minos pursued Daedalus from Crete and founded a city here was reiterated by Diodorus who records that Theron Akragas found the bones of Minos at Minoa. A colony of Selinunte was founded on this site in the 6C, and the name Heracleia was probably added later in the century by Spartan emigrés. The Halykos formed the boundary between the Greek and Carthaginian territories in Sicily. The town thrived during the 4C when it was resettled by Timoleon, but it seems to have been uninhabited by the end of the 1C BC. The first excavations took place in 1907 (and were resumed in 1950–61).

A small **Antiquarium** (open 09.00–15.00 or 16.00) houses finds from Eraclea Minoa, and has instructive plans of the area so far excavated. A path leads on through the beautifully kept site where the visible remains (excavations in progress) date mainly from the 4C. The **theatre** was built at the end of the 4C. The soft sandstone has been covered in perspex for protection. On the hillside in front was the site of the **city**. Under cover is the so-called **governor's house**: part of the wall decoration and mosaic pavement survives. Also here is a little altar for sacrifices (under glass). Outside excavations have revealed three levels of destruction; the level of the Archaic city is at present being uncovered. The second line of the walls (built when the eastern part of the town was abandoned) is visible nearby. A path (or steps) lead up to the top of the hill above the theatre and a paved path leads over the hillside to the line of **walls** to the northeast, with square towers built in the 4C BC.

Near Eraclea is the little town of **Montallegro**, rebuilt in the 18C below its abandoned predecessor on the hill (a grotto here has produced finds from the Early Bronze Age to the Copper Age). To the north is Cattolica Eraclea, founded in 1610.

**Siculiana**, on a low hill between Eraclea Minoa and Agrigento, has a prominent domed church (1750–1813). The castle dates from 1350. Much new building has taken place on the plain. A byroad leads down to the pretty coast (with good beaches) beside the **Torre di Monterosso**. There is a Worldwide Fund for Nature reserve open to the public here.

# The northern part of Agrigento province

This section covers small towns scattered over the province of Agrigento in remote country traversed by the Platani river. Sulphur was mined in the hills here up until the middle of this century.

***Information office***. APT Agrigento, ☎ 0922/401352.

**Aragona** (population 10,000), founded in 1606, has an interesting street plan. Almonds and pistachios are cultivated in the surrounding fields. Nearby are the

**Vulcanelli di Macalube**, tiny conical volcanoes, only 0.5–1m high, filled with salty bubbling mud.

**Raffadali** is a town of 14,200 inhabitants, where the church contains a Roman sarcophagus depicting the *Rape of Proserpine*. A prehistoric necropolis on the hill of **Busone** has yielded finds including a number of statuettes of a female divinity made from pebbles. **Joppolo Giancaxio** is a pretty village in a fine position with an 18C castle and church.

**S. Angelo Muxaro**, surrounded by rugged farming country, is possibly the site of the ancient *Kamikos*. Prehistoric tombs pepper the hillside. Those near the foot of the road which mounts to the village date from the 11C–9C BC; the higher domed tombs were used in the 8C–5C BC. Across the Platani river is **S. Biagio Platani** where an interesting festival takes place at Easter.

Above the narrow Platani valley with odd-looking sulphurous hills is **Castel-Termini**, which has an interesting festival on the last Sunday in May known as the *Tataratà*. This was once a sulphur mining town.

The **sulphur mines** in central Sicily (in the provinces of Agrigento and Caltanissetta), which were worked throughout the 19C, gave Italy a world monopoly of sulphur by 1900. Some 16,000 miners were employed by 1860, and in the 300 or so mines in operation, steam engines were used in only four of them, and horses in only ten. In all the other mines sulphur was extracted manually from an average depth of 60m, and many of the workers, known as *carusi* were children under 14. It was not until 1934 that legislation was introduced forbidding employers to use women and boys under 16 as miners. The appalling working conditions endured by these Sicilians influenced many native writers, including Sciascia (see below). The last mines in the province of Agrigento were closed down in 1988, and those at Cozzo Disi and Ciavolotta may become museums. The mines in the province of Caltanissetta were abandoned in the 1970s. There are models of the mines in the interesting Museum of Mineralogy in Caltanissetta (see p.211).

**Sutera**, in the province of Caltanissetta, rises above the left of the road at the foot of the gypseous outcrop of Monte S. Paolino (819m; surmounted by a chapel).

The ruined Chiaramonte castle of **Mussomeli** also in the province of Caltanissetta, stands on an impregnable crag. In 1976, at the age of 83, Genco Russo died here; he was considered one of the most famous Mafia bosses of his time.

**Cammarata** is a little medieval town and **S. Stefano Quisquina** (population 5800), another pleasant little town where the Chiesa Madre has an altarpiece of the *Resurrection of Lazarus* by the Carracci school. The Santuario di S. Rosalia on a hill to the east, has frescoes by the Manno family.

**Bivona** (population 5000), where peaches are cultivated, also has a number of fine churches. **Cianciana** is a little town founded in 1640.

# The eastern part of Agrigento province

This section describes minor towns which have some 17C–18C churches of interest, but which are now surrounded by ugly outskirts. Racalmuto was the birthplace of Leonardo Sciascia.

**Information office.** APT Agrigento, ☎ 0922/401352.
**Restaurants. Licata. B** *Logico,* 5 via Brigadiere d'Acquisto. **Canicattì. B**
*Papillon,* 20 via La Carruba; *Zaliclò,* 172 viale della Vittoria.

Above lonely country planted with almond trees, olives and vineyards, is **Palma
di Montechiaro** (population 25,000), founded in 1637 by the prince of
Lampedusa, ancestor of novelist Giuseppe Tomasi di Lampedusa. The town,
notorious for its poverty and its Mafia connections, is surrounded by hundreds
of half-constructed houses (now abandoned concrete shells), begun by
emigrants in the 1960s. The conspicuous Chiesa Matrice is a fine building
(1666–1703) by Angelo Italia which is approached by a scenic flight of steps.
The 17C Lampedusa palace, now owned by the comune, has been partially
restored and is sometimes open in summer at weekends.

> ### Giuseppe Tomasi di Lampedusa
> Lampedusa (1896–1957) wrote his famous novel *Il Gattopardo* (*The
> Leopard,* translated into English in 1960) at the end of his life and it was
> published posthumously. The book recounts the life of his great-
> grand-father Giulio Tomasi (1815–1885), renamed Don Fabrizio Salina in
> the novel, who reacted with instinctive resignation to the turmoil produced
> by the landing of Garibaldi on the island in 1860. It had enormous success
> and was made into a film by Visconti in 1963. Lampedusa was born in
> Palma di Montechiaro, however, the palace of Donnafugata he describes in
> his novel *Il Gottapardo* is not that of Palma di Montechiaro but a palace in S.
> Margherita Belice, which was destroyed in the earthquake of 1968. His
> family were princes of Lampedusa and dukes of Palma di Montechiaro.
> Another villa (built in 1770), which was bought by his great-grandfather
> around 1845, also described in the book, survives on the Piana dei Colli
> outside Palermo. Lampedusa also wrote *I Racconti,* translated in 1962 as
> *Two Stories and a Memory.*

A plain (now disfigured with new buildings) surrounds Licata, an unattractive
town (population 41,200), suffering from economic decline. It occupies the site of
Phintias, the city founded by the tyrant of the same name from Gela (see below).
In the **Palazzo del Municipio** (1935), designed by Ernesto Basile, antique reliefs
and a 15C triptych are preserved; also a *Madonna* by Domenico Gagini (1470).

The corso leads past Palazzo Canarelli, which is decorated with grotesque
heads. Beyond (left) is **S. Francesco**; its fine convent (now a school) was reconstructed in the 17C and the marble façade added in 1750 by Giovanni Biagio
Amico. Behind, piazza S. Angelo is surrounded by pretty 18C buildings.

The 17C church of S. Angelo has a façade and cupola attributed to Angelo
Italia. The corso ends at the duomo where a chapel in the south transept, elaborately decorated in 1600–1705, preserves a wooden Crucifix which narrowly
escaped destruction at the hands of the raiding Turks in 1553. The church of
**S. Domenico** in corso Roma has two paintings by Filippo Paladino.

The 16C Badia del Soccorso houses the **Museo Archeologico** which
contains local archaeological material from the prehistoric and Greek periods,

including Hellenistic votive statuettes, ceramics and red-figure vases from a necropolis of the 5C BC.

Off the mouth of the Salso (the ancient Himera), Attilius Regulus defeated the Carthaginian fleet in 256 BC, but in 249 a convoy of Roman transports for Africa was driven ashore by the Carthaginians in a tempest. Landings were effected here by the 7th Army in 1943.

**Ravanusa** was founded in 1621. Nearby on **Monte Saracino**, excavations have revealed a prehistoric site, Hellenised at the end of the 7C BC. **Campobello di Licata** was founded in 1681.

There is a castle of the Chiaramonte family (1275; enlarged in 1488) in **Favara**, which has been damaged and 'restored'.

The little town of **Racalmuto** (from the Arabic *Rahal-maut*), in lovely countryside, was the birthplace of Leonardo Sciascia. Another inhabitant was Pietro d'Asaro (1597–1647), called *il Monocolo*, whose paintings can be seen in the churches of the town.

---

### Leonardo Sciascia

Sciascia (1921–89), one of the greatest Italian writers of this century, was born in Racalmuto. He left his library to the town, where he lived for most of his life, and a foundation was inaugurated here in his memory in 1994. He is also fittingly commemorated, by a life-size bronze statue (1997), on the pavement in the main street near the Chiesa Madre, by a local artist. His simple white marble tomb slab surrounded by jasmine is in the little cemetery nearby. He is famous for his novels, including *Il giorno della civetta* (1961) (*The day of the owl*), *A ciascuno il suo* (1966) (*To each his own*), *Il Consiglio d'Egitto* (*The council of Egypt*) and *Todo modo* (1974) (*One way or another*), written in a particularly simple and direct style. In some perceptive articles and essays he also wrote about the problems which afflict the island, and exposed the insidious power of the Mafia and corruption in politics long before these two evils of Italian society were generally recognised in public. Sciascia was extremely reserved and often pessimistic, but had a particularly high moral standing in Italy in the 1970s as an intellectual figurehead.

---

**Canicattì** (population 34,500) is a market town of some importance and a railway junction. Notorious for its remoteness, it has come to be synonymous with *Timbuctoo* in the Italian language. It is surrounded by fertile hills clad with olives and almonds, and to the north are disused sulphur mines (see p.205). The little town of **Naro** stands on a hilltop (520m), once defended by battlemented walls (1263). It has early 17C churches and a Chiaramonte castle (13C–14C).

**Serradifalco** gave a ducal title to Domenico Pietrasanta (1773–1863), author of an important work on Sicilian antiquities.

# Caltanissetta

Caltanissetta is a pleasant provincial capital (population 62,500), with 17C and 18C works in its churches and an interesting local archaeological museum. Its prosperity seems, however, to have declined in recent years. It is given an old-fashioned air by the two 'shoe-shines' who still work on the pavement in the centre of the city. The town is much in the news because numerous important trials against the Mafia are being held here.

## ■ Practical information

***Information offices***. APT Caltanissetta, 109 corso Vittorio Emanuele (☎ 0934/ 530411); information office, 20 viale Conte Testasecca (☎ 0934/ 21089).

### *Getting there*
**Railway stations**. *Centrale*, piazza Roma, with services via Canicattì to Agrigento, Gela, Ragusa and Siracusa. The station of **Caltanissetta Xirbi**, 7km north, is on another line between Palermo, Enna and Catania.

**Buses**. Frequent services (usually faster than the trains) from piazza della Repubblica for Palermo and Catania (SAIS); for piazza Armerina (ASTRA) and for towns in the province.

**Parking** is difficult, there is a 1hr limit in corso Umberto. Space sometimes available in via Francesco Crispi and via Kennedy.

### Hotels

★★★★ *S. Michele*, via Fasci Siciliani, ☎ 0934/553750; fax 0934/598791.
★★★ *Plaza*, 5 via B. Gaetani, ☎ & fax 0934/583877; *Ventura*, contrada Gurra Pinselli (on the Agrigento road), ☎ 0934/553780.

### Restaurants

**B** *Il Vicolo*, 7 vicolo Duomo; *l'Altro Mondo*, via Nicolò Palmieri; *Cortese*, 166 viale Sicilia. **C** *La Cantinola*, 140 corso Vittorio Emanuele; *Delfino Bianco*, via Scovazzo; *l'Oca Bianca*, 37 via Moncada.

**Café and pasticceria**. *Romano*, corso Umberto.

Villa Cordova is a pleasant place to **picnic**.

**Theatre**. The Teatro Comunale Margherita re-opened in 1997. Teatro Baufremont, salita Matteotti, for concerts and prose.

**Annual festival** on Maundy Thursday, when the *Misteri* are carried in procession. At present they are kept in the church of S. Pio X in via Napoleone Colajanni.

### History

The name of the town was for many years thought to have been derived from that of the ancient Sikel city of *Nissa*, with the Arabic prefix *Kal' at* (castle). Excavations in 1989 on Monte S. Giuliano (or *del Redentore*) yielded 7C–6C BC finds. The site was then abandoned until the Roman period. After its conquest by Count Roger in 1086 it was given as an appanage to his son Jourdain, and passed subsequently into the hands of Corrado Lancia (1296) and the Moncada family (1406). The province was an extremely important centre of sulphur mining from the 18C up until the early 20C (the last mines were closed down in the 1970s), and potassium salt was also extracted in the area.

In the central **piazza Garibaldi** is an amusing fountain with two monsters spraying a hippogryph by Michele Tripisciano (1860–1913), a talented local sculptor, whose statues also decorate corso Umberto I, the town hall and the public gardens. Here is the façade of the **Duomo** (1570–1622), which was damaged in the last war. In the pretty interior, decorated with white and gold stuccoes, the vault-painting is Guglielmo Borremans' masterpiece (1720). In the second south chapel is a wooden statue (covered with silver) of the *Immacolata* (1760). In the chapel to the right of the sanctuary is a charming wooden statue of the archangel *Michael* by Stefano Li Volsi, and two marble statues of the archangels by Vincenzo Vitaliano (1753). The high altarpiece is by Borremans, and the organ dates from after 1653. In the north transept is a painting by Filippo Paladino, and in the second north chapel is a Crucifix attributed to Fra' Umile da Petralia.

*The Duomo of Caltanissetta*

The church of **S. Sebastiano**, opposite, has an unusual façade (1891), painted bright red, and a blue campanile. At the east end is a fine 17C wooden statue of the titular saint. The last side of the piazza is closed by a large former convent which now houses the town hall (with statues by Tripisciano) and the Teatro Margherita, re-opened in 1997 after restoration.

Beside the town hall corso Umberto I leads up to a statue of Umberto I (wearing a flambuoyant hat) by Tripisciano, outside the church of **S. Agata**, also painted red, and preceded by an outside staircase. It was built on a Greek-cross plan in 1605. In the interior is fine marble intarsia decoration, especially on the two side altars. The north altar (with a delightful frontal with birds) is surmounted by a relief of *St Ignazio* by Ignazio Marabitti. The little chapel in the north-west corner has frescoes by Luigi Borremans. The high altarpiece (*Martyrdom of St Agatha*), a good work by Agostino Scilla (1654), is flanked by statues by Salvatore Marino (1753), and above are putti by Marabitti. The first north chapel has frescoes by Borremans (including an *Assumption* in the vault, and a *Nativity* on a side wall).

Off the right side of corso Umberto is the grand Palazzo Moncada (1635–38), left unfinished. A street on the left side of the duomo leads downhill to via S. Domenico which continues to the church of **S. Domenico** with a delightfully shaped Baroque façade fitting an awkward site. The stuccoes inside have recently been repainted in bright blue (the pastel shades in the nave instead date from 1961). The fine painting of the *Madonna of the Rosary* is by Filippo Paladino (1614). The painting of *St Vincent Ferrer* by Guglielmo Borremans (1722) has been removed to the Museo d'Arte Sacra.

From here the 14C church of **S. Maria degli Angeli** (closed) can be reached in ten minutes. Sadly ruined, it preserves its west door. Beyond a warehouse, on a fantastic rock, stand the shattered ruins of the Castello di Pietrarossa, residence of Frederick III of Aragon.

To the south, near the station, in via Napoleone Colajanni, is the **Museo Civico** (admission 09.00–13.00 except Sun & PH), with a particularly interesting archaeological collection from sites in the province. There are long-term plans to move it to a new building. **Room 1**. Objects from tombs at Gibil Gabib, including fine kraters (many with animal illustrations), and black- and red-figure vases; figurines found recently on Monte S. Giuliano (on the northern outskirts of

Caltanissetta), the earliest portrayal of the human figure so far discovered in Sicily. Dating from the Early Bronze Age, they are thought to have been used in a prehistoric sanctuary. The Arabic finds date from 996 to 1020 AD.

**Room 2** displays material from Sabucina (see below), dating from 1270–1000 BC; red-figure kraters and a lekythos on a white ground (c 500 BC); a child's doll and shell necklace; a unique votive model of a Greek temple in terracotta (6C BC) from Sabucina. **Rooms 3** and **4** display finds from Capodarso and Mimiani, including a bronze helmet of the 6C BC. On the floor below is a sculpture gallery, with notable works by Michele Tripisciano (see above).

Near the public gardens the Seminario Vescovile houses a small **Museo d'Arte Sacra** (usually closed) with 17C and 18C vestments and two paintings by Borremans. At no. 73 viale della Regione is a **Museum of Mineralogy** (open 09.00–14.00, except Sun & PH), with a collection of some 3000 minerals, and scale models of sulphur mines, some 300 of which existed in the provinces of Caltanissetta and Agrigento (see p.205).

## Environs of Caltanissetta

South of Caltanissetta is the site of the ancient city of **Gibil Gabib** (open on weekdays with permission from the Soprintendenza). The name is dervied from the Arab *Gebel Habib*, and it was discovered in the 19C. A necropolis here has yielded finds from three periods of occupation: 7C BC, 6C BC and the 4C BC.

The **Abbazia di S. Spirito**, also outside Caltanissetta, is a basilica founded by Roger and his wife Adelasia (probably between 1086 and 1093), and consecrated in 1153. It was attached to a fortified building, parts of which now form the sacristy. The church has a fine treble apse, recently restored. The charming small interior (ring at the door on the right marked *Abbazia*, 11.00–12.00 17.00–18.00) contains a large font below an interesting painted Crucifix dating from the 15C. On the walls are three detached 15C frescoes which have been restored. The striking 17C fresco of *Christ in benediction* was repainted in 1974. On the arch of the apse is the dedication stone (1153), and nearby is a little Roman cinerary urn (1C AD), with rams' heads, birds and a festoon. A 17C sedan-chair, with its original fittings, which used to be used as a confessional, has been removed to the priest's house (shown on request).

Off the Enna road, beneath Monte Sabucina, is the site of **Sabucina** (admission with permission from the Soprintendenza, ☎ 0934/554964). The approach road climbs up past several disused mines, and there is a view up to the right above an overgrown mine of the line of walls of Sabucina, just below the summit of the hill. After 2km the asphalted road ends beside recent excavations of a necropolis and the new circular museum building (still closed). An unsurfaced road continues downhill for another 500m to a gate by a modern house at the entrance to the site, in a fine position with wide views. Monte Sabucina was first occupied in the Bronze Age. A thriving Iron Age village was then settled by the Greeks in the 6C BC. The city declined after the revolt of Ducezio in 450 BC. The long line of Greek fortifications with towers and gates were built directly onto the rock. Sacred edifices can also be seen here. The rich material from the necropoli is displayed in the Museo Civico at Caltanissetta (see above).

East of Caltanissetta is the forbidding Terra Pilata, a sterile upland of white clay affording a fine retrospective view of Caltanissetta. The River Salso is crossed by **Ponte Capodarso**, a graceful bridge built in 1553 by Venetian engineers. Nearby is the archaeological zone of **Capodarso**, an ancient city which had disappeared by the beginning of the 3C BC. Part of the walls and necropolis survive. Finds from the site are kept in the museum in Caltanissetta (see above).

# Gela

Gela is an important port and now the fifth largest town in Sicily (population 79,000). Its superb Greek fortifications testify to its ancient importance, and it has one of the best archaeological museums on the island. The huge petrochemical plant which has dominated the east side of the town since the 1960s faced serious accusations of pollution in 1979; not only the sea but also the air in the town suffer from its proximity. Yet another enquiry is under way to determine the level of damage which has been caused. Uncontrolled new building in the 1960s and 1970s, in the wake of the false prosperity brought to the city by the refinery, has rendered Gela perhaps the ugliest city on the island. Many of these houses, left half-finished, have now been abandoned, although some, built without permission, were demolished in 1993. In 1983 5000 inhabitants occupied the town hall destroying documents in protest against the chaotic local administration. Business is controlled by a mafia racket which results in numerous murders between rival Mafia clans every year. However, in the last few years there have been some signs of an improvement in the life of the city.

## ■ Practical information

*Information offices*. Azienda Autonoma, via Bresmes (☎ 0933/913788). APT information office, via Palazzi (corner of via Francia), ☎ 0933/823107.

*Railway station* on the Siracusa, Ragusa, Canicattì, Agrigento line.
*Buses* from the bus station next to the railway station.

*Hotel*. ★★★ *Motel Agip*, località Giardinelli (on the SS 117), ☎ 0933/911144.

*Restaurant*. **B** *Casanova*, 89 via Venezia. Capo Soprano, with the famous Greek fortifications is a lovely place to **picnic**.

### History
The modern city, known until 1927 as Terranova, was founded by Frederick II in 1230, on the site of Gela, a colony of Rhodians and Cretans established in 689 BC. Gela soon rose to importance, and sent out a colony to Akragas in 582.

It had an important influence on the Hellenisation of the local settlements in the interior of the island. The site of the city corresponded roughly to the area of the medieval town and the present historical centre. Under Hippocrates (498–491) the city reached its greatest prosperity, but Gelon, his cavalry-commander and successor, transferred the seat of government and half the population to Siracusa in 485. Aeschylus died at Gela in 456. In 405 the town was destroyed by the Carthaginians, but Timoleon refounded it in 339. The new city was larger than the earlier one and received a new circle of walls. Phintias, tyrant of Akragas, transferred its inhabitants in 282 to his new city at the mouth of the Himera (see Licata, p.206), and Gela disappeared from history. Hieron I of Siracusa and the ancient comic poet Apollodorus were among the distinguished natives of Gela.

## Archaeological Museum

At the east end of the town is the fine Archaeological Museum (open daily 09.00–12.30, 16.00–19.00, except the last Mon of the month), with a beautifully displayed collection. It contains some of the painted vases for which Gela is best known, and which are exhibited in most of the archaeological museums of Europe.

**Ground floor**. Near the entrance, displayed in a case on its own, is the foot of a black-figure Attic kylix with an inscription to Antifemo, one of the founders of the Greek colony. **Section I** is dedicated to the **acropolis area** (east of the modern city) which was inhabited from prehistoric times up to the 5C BC. Finds from a sacred area dedicated to Athena (with two Doric temples built in the 6C–5C BC) include terracottas, bronzes, architectural fragments, votive statues, the head of a horse, a charming little statuette in stone of a girl holding a wreath (6C BC), and a lovely marble basin dating from 338 BC. **Section II** displays later material from the acropolis (4C–3C BC) when it was an artisans' district. There is also material salvaged from an Archaic Greek ship found off the coast of Gela in 1988, finds from a warehouse, and from an urban sanctuary dedicated to Hera. **Section III** is devoted to **Capo Soprano**, now at the western extremity of the modern city, where there was a residential area and public edifices were erected in the late 4C BC, including (in case 22) a small altar of the 6C BC, showing Hercules slaying Alkyoneus. The last section has an exhibition illustrating the production of various potteries, some with dedicatory inscriptions on their bases.

Upstairs, on the balcony, is **Section IV** where more than 50 amphorae (7C–4C BC) attest to the importance of Gela's commerce with other centres in the Mediterranean. **Section V** is dedicated to sanctuaries found outside Gela, most of them dedicated to Demetra and Kore, with numerous votive statuettes and Corinthian ware. **Section VI** displays material from the prehistoric to Hellenistic era from the surrounding territory. Roman and medieval material found during the restoration of the Castelluccio (see below) is displayed in **Section VII**. Also temporarily on display here are a magnificent hoard of c 1000 **silver coins**, minted in Agrigento, Gela, Siracusa, Messina and Athens, between 515 BC and 485 BC, and one of the most important collections in existence. Discovered in Gela in 1956, the coins were stolen in 1976, but about half of them were subsequently recovered (only a small selection is at present displayed here).

Downstairs is **Section VIII** which contains the 19C **Navarra collection,** one of the most important private collections in Sicily of ancient vases (with a fine group of Attic black- and red-figure vases, and Corinthian ware from the 8C–6C BC). Also here is the smaller Nocera collection and two cases of finds from the necropolis. In Case F no. 3 is an Attic lekythoi on a white ground showing Aeneas and Anchise (460–450 BC) and Case G has an exquisite Attic red-figure lekythoi, by the Nikon painter.

Outside the museum (same admission times as the museum, but with a separate ticket) is the entrance to the **Molino a Vento Acropolis**, which now overlooks the oil refinery. This was part of Timoleon's city on a terraced grid plan with shops and houses (c 339–310 BC), above the ruins of a small sacred enclosure. In the garden on the site of the **acropolis** of the earliest city, stands a single (re-erected) column of a temple probably dedicated to Athena (6C BC), and the basement of a second earlier temple also dedicated to Athena. This area had been abandoned by 282 BC. Excavations in the area have been temporarily suspended.

The corso traverses the long untidy town, but the most pleasant way of reaching Capo Soprano and the Greek fortifications (which are over 3km from the museum) is along the sea front. The remarkable **Greek fortifications** (open 09.00–dusk every day) of Capo Soprano have been excellently preserved after centuries beneath the sand: they extend for several hundred metres, and reach a height of nearly 13m. They were first excavated in 1948. The walls were begun by Timoleon in 333 BC and completed under Agathocles. Their height was regularly increased to keep ahead of the encroaching sand, a danger today removed by the planting of trees. In the lovely peaceful site close to the sea, with eucalyptus and acacia trees, a path (right) leads past excavations of battlements to a circular medieval kiln (under cover). From here there is a view of the coast.

The path follows walls (partly under cover) and foundations of the brick angle towers to the west gate, and then descends to the best stretch of walls: the lower course is built of sandstone, while the top is finished with plain mud bricks (being restored). Here also a little postern gate in the walls can be seen, dating from the time of Agathocles (filled in with mud bricks soon after it was built), as well as a well-preserved drain. Steps lead up past a little house which contains photographs of the site and then another path leads back past the abutment wall to the entrance.

About 500m from the fortifications (signposted *Bagni Greci*), now engulfed by modern apartment blocks, are remains of **Greek baths** (4C). They are protected by a roof, but are always open, surrounded by a little garden behind a railing. The hip baths are provided with seats.

## Environs of Gela

On the coast west of Gela is **Falconara** with its 15C castle in an oasis of palm trees around a large fountain (a custodian lives near by). Beyond are cotton fields and market gardens (protected from the wind by cane fences).

Inland from Gela is **Butera**, perched on a flat rock, with fine views towards the sea. Much new building has recently taken place here and the castle has been restored.

**Mazzarino** was founded by the princes of Butera, whose palace survives. Its churches preserve Branciforte funerary monuments and paintings by Filippo Paladino. At **Riesi** Giuseppe di Cristina, considered one of the most powerful Mafia bosses of his time, was killed in 1978. Nearly 10,000 people were present at his funeral.

On the Caltagirone road is the **Castelluccio**, a castle restored in 1996 (shown by a custodian), in a remarkable site on a small mound sticking sharply up in the fertile Gela valley (surrounded by extensive plantations of artichokes). On the approach road there is a little war memorial to the battle of 1943 which followed the landings of the American assault forces on the beaches in the Gulf of Gela. It is appropriately sited beside two 'pill-box' defences. Monte Disueri is situated in the district where there is a prehistoric necropolis.

# *Enna*

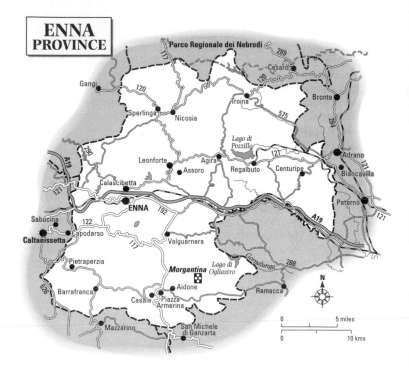

Enna, known as the *Belvedere della Sicilia* because of its wonderful position on the gentle slope of a precipitous hill (931m), is the most interesting inland town (population 29,300) on the island. The most impregnable stronghold in Sicily, it was for centuries the only town in the interior. The view of the medieval hill town of Calascibetta from Enna is exceptional. The evening *passeggiata* here (a social occasion which still takes place in numerous small towns all over Italy when the inhabitants stroll through the town), when via Roma is closed to traffic, is a remarkable spectacle. Much ugly new building has taken place in recent years on the southern edge of the hill and in the valleys beneath, even though the town is the capital of one of the poorest provinces in Italy. Enna is a good centre for visiting the famous mosaics in the Roman villa near Piazza Armerina, and the excavations of Morgantina (see p.226). The secondary roads in the province often traverse spectacular countryside, and small towns of interest include Leonforte, Sperlinga and Nicosia (see below).

# ■ Practical information

*Information offices*. APT Enna, 413 via Roma (☎ 0935/528228).
Azienda Autonoma, 6 piazza Colajanni, ☎ 0935/26119.

### Getting there
**Railway station**, in the valley, 5km from the town centre, on the Palermo–Catania line.
**Buses**. Bus station, viale Diaz. Services run by SAIS to Catania (via the motorway in 1hr 20min.), Palermo, Taormina and Messina, Caltanissetta and Agrigento, Caltagirone, Piazza Armerina (in 45min.), Nicosia, Leonforte, Adrano, and Paternò.
**Parking** in piazza Prefettura and piazza Umberto I.

### Hotels
★★★ *Grande Albergo Sicilia*, 5 piazza Colajanni, ☎ 0935/500850.
On the Lago di Pergusa, 9km south of Enna: ★★★ *Riviera*, via Autodromo, ☎ 0935/541267. ★★ *Miralago*, via Nazionale, contrada Staglio, ☎ 0935/541272.

### Restaurants
**B** *Tiffany*, 467 via Roma. **C** *Da Marino*, near the Castello.
Places to **picnic** in the Castello di Lombardia.

*Theatres*. Teatro Garibaldi for concerts and prose. Open-air performances in summer in the Castello di Lombardia.

*Annual festivals*. The religious ceremonies in Holy Week culminate with a procession on Good Friday. On 2 July, festivities in honour of the *Madonna della Visitazione*.

### History
The city occupies the site of *Henna*, a Siculian stronghold subjected to Greek influences perhaps from Gela as early as the 7C BC. The legendary scene of the rape of Proserpine (see below), and the centre of the cult of Ceres or Demeter, her mother, to whom Gelon erected a temple in 480 BC, it fell by treachery to Dionysius I of Siracusa in 397. In 135 BC the First Servile War broke out here under the slave Eunus, and the town was taken in 132 by the Roman army only after two years' siege. The Saracens, who took it in 859 by crawling in one by one through a sewer, named it *Kasr Janna* (Castrum Ennae); and it was not captured by the Normans until 1087. From then on the town was known as Castrogiovanni until in 1927 it became the chief town of a new province. Some damage was caused by bombing in 1943.

The short via S. Agata leads into **piazza Vittorio Emanuele**, the centre of the city, planted with trees and illuminated with pretty lamp-posts. On the north side is the bold flank of **S. Francesco**, with its fine 16C tower. On the left is piazza Crispi which has an excellent view across the valley to Calascibetta, and,

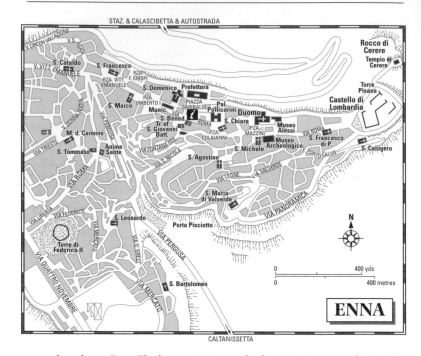

on a clear day to Etna. The bronze statue on the fountain is a copy of Bernini's *Rape of Proserpine*. Via Roma, the principal street, continues uphill traversing a series of piazze. In piazza Umberto I, with trees and more decorative lamp-posts, is the neo-classical municipio (town hall), which incorporates the Teatro Garibaldi. The Baroque façade of **S. Benedetto** (or S. Giuseppe) decorates piazza Coppola, off which is the 15C tower of **S. Giovanni Battista** with Gothic arches, and crowned by an Arabic cupola, beside an incongruous modern building.

On the north side of via Roma the tower of the **Prefettura** (1939) rises from piazza Garibaldi. **S. Chiara**, in piazza Colajanni, is a war memorial and burial chapel. Two majolica pictures (1852) decorate the tiled pavement, one celebrating the advent of steam navigation, and the other the triumph of Christianity over Mohammedanism. The bronze statue of Napoleone Colajanni (1847–1921), in the piazza outside, is by Ettore Ximenes.

The view to the south-west takes in the Torre di Federico II (see below) surrounded by new tower blocks. Here **Palazzo Pollicarini** retains one or two Catalan-Gothic features. Via Roma continues up towards the duomo past several narrow side streets on the left which lead to the edge of the hill.

The **Duomo**, founded in 1307 by Eleonora, wife of Frederick II of Aragon, and damaged by fire in 1446, was slowly restored in the 16C. The strange front with a 17C bell-tower, covers its Gothic predecessor. The transepts and the polygonal apses survive in their original form (they can be seen from the courtyard of the Museo Alessi, see below). The south door is also partly original.

The interesting **interior** has dark grey basalt columns with splendid bases, carved with grotesques, and Corinthian capitals (1550–60; the work of various artists including Gian Domenico Gagini who carved the symbols of the Evangelists on the first two at the west end). The nave ceiling is by Scipione di Guido, who probably carved the stalls as well. On either side of the west door are 16C statues of the *Annunciation*. The two stoups in the nave date from the 16C, and at the east end of the nave are richly carved 16C organ lofts. The altarpieces on the south side are by Guglielmo Borremans (the painting of *Saints Lucilla* and *Giacinto* on the second altar is particularly good). In the presbytery are five paintings of New Testament scenes by Filippo Paladino (1613). The late 15C painted Crucifix was restored in 1990. In the chapel to the right of the sanctuary is 18C marble decoration and a painting of the *Visitation* attributed to Filippo Paladino. There are more works by Borremans in the north transept and on the fourth north altar. The Renaissance font is preceded by an interesting screen.

The very fine **MUSEO ALESSI** (open 09.00–13.00, 16.00–19.00 except Mon) was re-opened in 1987 in a building behind the east end of the duomo. It is named after Canon Giuseppe Alessi (1774–1837), a native of Enna, who left his remarkable collection to his brother intending that he should donate it to the church. The church instead had to buy it in 1860 and it was first opened to the public in 1862. It is beautifully arranged. In the **basement** are church vestments of the 17C and 18C. On the **ground floor**: the *Sala Alessi* has interesting small paintings collected by Alessi, together with his portrait. The other room has paintings from various provenances, including a *Pietà* with symbols of the *Passion* (late 15C), *St John the Baptist* and *St John the Evangelist*, attributed to Antonello Crescenzio (*Il Panormita*); the *Mystical Marriage of St Catherine* by Antonio Spatafora (1584); a striking 16C *Madonna and Child*, and *St Peter the fisherman* by the school of Ribera. In the **corridor** are works by 19C local painters.

On the **first floor** the **treasury** of the duomo is exhibited, with splendid 16C and 17C works, one of the richest on the island. In the large room the 16C pieces include a monstrance by Paolo Gili (1536), and four reliquaries by Scipione di Blasi (1573). There are fine views from the windows of the valley and Calascibetta. In the room beyond is a cupboard made in 1750. The room at the other side of the stairs contains 18C and 19C silver and two large paintings by Zoppo di Ganci. In the little adjoining room is a precious gold crown, encrusted with jewels and enamels, made for a statue of the *Madonna* in 1653 by Leonardo and Giuseppe Montalbano and Michele Castellani, and a beautiful 16C jewel in the form of a pelican.

The **gallery** has the remarkable **numismatic collection** made by Alessi, one of the most important in Sicily. The Greek, Roman and Byzantine coins are arranged topographically and include many in bronze used in everyday transactions. A section of Roman coins is arranged chronologically. Alessi's charming archaeological collection (with some of his original labels) is also displayed here. It includes missiles (glandes) used in the Servile war, bronzes, pottery, etc. In the last room the Egyptian Ushebti figurines (664–525 BC), which also formed part of the Alessi collection and were presumably found in Sicily, are of the greatest interest.

Across piazza Mazzini the pretty 15C **Palazzo Varisano**, with attractive ceil-ings, houses the **Archaeological Museum** (or **Museo Varisano**; open daily 09.00–13.30, 15.00–19.30). The collection is beautifully displayed and includes finds from: Calascibetta and Capodarso (7C BC local products), including the prehistoric rock tombs of Realmese; Enna (Greek, Roman, and medieval ceramics, including an Attic red-figure krater); Cozza Matrice (where the necropolis was in use from the Bronze Age up to the 5C BC) and prehistoric material from the lake of Pergusa. There is also a collection of coins (not yet on display); interesting Hellenistic objects from Rossomanno (and an unusual bronze belt or necklace of the 6C BC); and material from Assoro, Agira, Cerami and Pietraperzia.

Via Roma continues up to the **Castello di Lombardia** (or *Cittadella*; open daily 08.00–18.30), built by the Swabians and adapted as his residence by Fred-erick III of Aragon. One of the best preserved medieval castles on the island, six of the 20 towers remain. Outside is a World War I memorial by Ernesto Basile (1927). On the left, steps lead up to the entrance to the castle. The first courtyard is filled with a permanent open-air theatre used in summer. Beyond the second court, planted with trees, the third has remains of a church, and (beneath a roof) tombs carved in the rock. Here is the entrance to the **Torre Pisana**, which can be climbed by a modern flight of stairs. The view from the top takes in Etna, Centuripe on top of its hill and the lake of Pozzillo. In the other direction the edge of the lake of Pergusa can be seen and Calascibetta.

At the edge of the hill, beyond the castle, are the unenclosed remains of the **Rocca Cerere**, where traces of antique masonry may mark the site of the Temple of Demeter. High steps lead up to the summit with a view of Etna straight ahead. To the left the lake of Pozzillo and Centuripe can be seen, and Calascibetta.

The **lower town** is reached by following the other branch of via Roma, which takes a sharp turn to the south below piazza Vittorio Emanuele. On the right are the churches of **S. Tommaso**, with a 15C tower and a marble altarpiece by Giuliano Mancino (1515), and the **Carmine** (behind S. Tommaso), with another 15C campanile and a curious stair-tower. On the left, near the south-west end of via Roma, rises the octagonal **Torre di Federico II**, surrounded by a public garden, a Swabian work recalling the towers of Castel del Monte (it can sometimes be climbed on request).

The **Lago di Pergusa**, 9km south of Enna, is the only natural lake on the island. Its sheet of brackish water (182 ha), now polluted and drying up, has no visible outlet. The vegetation on the shores, as well as the birdlife, have been virtually destroyed since the 1950s. Although it has been developed as a resort, access to the lake is limited since it is encircled by an incongruous motor racing track. According to legend the lake occupies the chasm through which Pluto carried Proserpina off to Hades:

> ...Not that faire field
> of *Enna*, where Proserpin gathring flours
> Her self a fairer Floure by gloomie *Dis*
> was gatherd, which cost *Ceres* all that pain
> To seek her through the World;
> (Milton, *Paradise Lost*)

On a hill above the lake (signposted) excavations (not open to the public) were begun in 1878 of the necropolis, city and walls of **Cozzo Matrice**.

About 10km south-west of the lake in località **Gerace**, a Roman villa with polychrome mosaics was discovered in 1994: the excavations have apparently since been covered over.

# Calascibetta, Leonforte and Centuripe

These small hill towns are situated in beautiful countryside with panoramic views, in the province of Enna. They have interesting works of art and Leonforte is particularly charming.

## ■ Practical information

*Information office*. APT Enna, ☎ 0935/528228.
*Hotel*, near **Troina**, ★★★ *La Cittadella dell'Oasi*, località S. Michele, ☎ 0935/653966.

## Calascibetta
Calascibetta is a town perched on a flat-topped hill (691m) opposite Enna. It is particularly picturesque when seen from a distance (and provides one of the most delightful views from Enna). The narrow main street (keep left) leads up to the **Duomo** which is to be re-opened after restoration. Its 16C column bases are similar to those in the Duomo at Enna. There is a good view from the terrace.

A one-way street leads back down to piazza Umberto where the signposted road to Enna leads downhill past the church of the **Cappuccini**, on the edge of the hill. It contains a splendid large altarpiece of the *Epiphany* by Filippo Paladino, in a huge wooden frame.

The **Realmese** necropolis (unenclosed), north-west of Calascibetta, is well signposted. Here some 300 rock tombs (850–730 BC) have been found.

The road between Calascibetta and Leonfonte undulates through farming country with some orange groves.

Near the railway station of **Pirato** is a lovely old abandoned country villa. There is a view ahead of the distant hills, and views back of Enna. The road begins to climb past some old pink farmhouses (mostly abandoned) and olive trees. On the approach to Leonforte there is a good view across the valley of the little town with the conspicuous Palazzo Baronale preceded by its defensive wall, and, at the bottom of the hill in trees, the back wall of the *Granfonte*.

## Leonforte
Leonforte (603m) is a delightful little town founded in 1610 by Nicolò Placido Branciforti, where in 1833 John Henry Newman nearly died of fever. Via Porta Palermo leads to corso Umberto, just before which, below the road to the left, is the **Duomo** (17C–18C), with a striking façade in a mixture of styles. It contains numerous interesting wooden statues.

A very short steep road can be followed on foot downhill past the church of S. Stefano to the church of the Carmelo beside the delightful **Granfonte** (built in

1651 by Nicolò Branciforte) an abundant fountain of 24 jets (it can also be reached by car from via Porta Palermo). The water is collected in a stream which follows a picturesque lane downhill. Beside it is the gate of an overgrown botanical garden, with palms and orange trees. From here the defensive walls and turret in front of the Palazzo Baronale can be seen.

Just beyond the duomo is piazza Branciforte with the impressive façade of the 17C **Palazzo Baronale**, and, at the end, a stable block built in 1641 (the town used to be famous for horse-breeding). The well-proportioned corso leads gently up through a pretty circular piazza. Beyond, a side street (left) leads to the church of the **Cappuccini**. It contains a huge high altarpiece of the *Calling of St Matthew* by Pietro Novelli (in a large dark wooden frame). On either side are niches with Gaginesque statues. A finely carved arch (1647) precedes the Branciforte funerary chapel, with the sumptuous black marble sarcophagus (1634) of Caterina di Branciforte, supported on four lions.

## Assoro

To the east of Leonforte is Assoro, another interesting little town. Occupied in the Greek and Roman period, it was taken by the Arabs in 939, and by the Normans in 1061. The road leads up past the campanile of the former church of S. Caterina to piazza Umberto I, with a view from its terrace. The side façade of Palazzo Valguarnera (see below) is connected by an arch to the porch of the **Chiesa Madre** (S. Leone), which has a square bell-tower. It is entered by a Catalan doorway and has an unusual interior with twisted columns and a carved and painted wooden roof, and early 18C stucco decoration. In the raised and vaulted presbytery is a fine marble ancona (1515) with statues and reliefs, and two early 16C Valguarnera funerary monuments on the side walls. Over the nave hangs a painted Crucifix (late 15C). The high altar has three Gothic statues. To the left of the presbytery is a double chapel, the first with Gothic vaulting and bosses, and the second with Baroque decoration. Here is a carved processional Crucifix attributed to Gian Domenico Gagini, and two 17C sarcophagi. In the nave are some particularly interesting 16C polychrome gilded wooden statues.

The main façade of the duomo faces piazza Marconi, and the front of **Palazzo Valguarnera**, situated here, has a balcony with grotesque heads. The Baroque portal of an oratory is also in the square.

## Agira

The little town of Agira is perched on a conical hill (670m). The ancient *Agyrion* was a Sicel city colonised with Greeks by Timoleon (339 BC). Traces have been found here of Roman houses with mosaic pavements, a temple on what must have been the acropolis and necropoli of the 4C–3C BC. Diodorus Siculus, the historian, who lived in the Augustan era was born here: in his description of Timoleon's city he declares the theatre was the most beautiful in Sicily after that of Siracusa. It was the scene of the miracles of the apocryphal St Philip of Agirò, possibly a Christianised form of Herakles, the tutelary deity of the town. The town is now of little interest, and the churches are usually kept closed (the largest of which is S. Antonio da Padova, with a dome, built in 1549, in the lower town). On the road to Regalbuto, outside Agira (left; well signposted) is a Canadian Military Cemetery (490 graves) in a clump of pine trees on a small hill, beautifully kept.

The partly wooded shores of the pretty artificial lake of **Pozzillo** are used as pastureland. The lovely countryside has almond trees, prickly pear and agave.

North of Agira is **Troina**, on a steep ridge, the highest town (1120m) in Sicily. Its early capture by the Normans (1062) is recalled by Norman work (1078–80) in the Chiesa Matrice, which has a good 16C campanile. Parts of the Greek walls remain, and the Belvedere has a fine view.

At **Regalbuto** the church has a campanile crowned by a spire. The little town has some fine 18C buildings and a public garden. Beyond bare red and ochre hills on the left there is a splendid view ahead of Etna (with its subsidiary crater on the left). The plain is filled with bright green citrus fruit plantations, many of them protected by 'walls' of olive trees, and Centuripe can be seen on its hill to the right.

## Centuripe

Centuripe, a small town occupying a commanding position (719m) astride a ridge facing Etna, was aptly named *il balcone della Sicilia* by Garibaldi when he arrived here in 1862. The approach road winds up past citrus groves and olives and then crosses barren hills with a few almond trees. There are views of Adrano and Biancavilla on the lower slopes of Etna. Outside Centuripe the terraced hillside shows how they were once cultivated.

The key point in several Sicilian campaigns, the town was destroyed for rebellion by Frederick II (1233) and reconstructed in 1548 after a further sack by Charles I of Anjou. Its capture by the Allies in 1943 decided the Germans to abandon Sicily. Once called *Centorbi*, it was the birthplace of the physician Celsus (fl. AD 14–37).

The town centre, now surrounded by ugly new buildings, is the piazza near the 17C pink and white Duomo. On the edge of the cliff a pine avenue leads to the remains of a monument possibly of Roman (2C AD) origin (locally known as *Il Corradino* in allusion to the Swabian Corrado Capace, who is supposed to have built a castle here). There are fine views. A new museum, built to display the local Hellenistic and Roman finds, has never been opened.

In the valley (Vallone Difesa), east of the town, excavations beneath and near the church of the Crocifisso have revealed an important Augustan edifice, known as the *Sede degli Augustali*. On Monte Calvario (contrada Panneria) is a Hellenistic house, and to the north-west in Vallone dei Bagni, is a large Roman thermal edifice with five huge niches.

On the road to Adrano, near the Ponte del Maccarone, a huge aqueduct (31 arches) constructed in 1761–6 can be seen. Adrano is described, together with Etna on pp.310–311.

# Nicosia and Sperlinga

These remote small towns in the province of Enna are in particularly spectacular countryside. Nicosia has interesting churches and the lovely little town of Sperlinga has a splendid castle.

## ■ Practical information

*Information office*. APT Enna, ☎ 0935/528228.

*Hotel*. Near Nicosia: ★★★ *Pineta* in località S. Paolo, ☎ 0935/647002, fax 0935/646927.

## *Nicosia*

Nicosia (700m) was a place of some importance in the Middle Ages. The local dialect betrays the Lombard and Piedmontese origins of its early colonists. The town is now surrounded by ugly buildings, and its monuments are in poor repair. It was damaged by a landslide in 1757, by an earthquake in 1968 and a flood in 1972.

**Piazza Garibaldi** is at the centre of the town, with the Palazzo di Città by Salvatore Attinelli (early 19C), and the elegant portico of the CATHEDRAL (S. Nicola). The decorative 14C west door is in extremely poor repair; the entrance is by the south door. The imposing campanile, struck by lightning some years ago, has been partially rebuilt.

In the **interior** the vault was decorated by the Manno brothers in the early 19C. On the west wall is the organ by Raffaele La Valle. On the south side, in the second bay is a *Martyrdom of St Placido* by Giacinto Platania, and in the third and fifth bays, the *Immacolata* and *Holy Family* both by Filippo Randazzo. The pulpit is attributed to Gian Domenico Gagini. In the south transept is a Gaginesque statue of the *Madonna della Vittoria*. Over the crossing, in the octagonal vault, surrounded by 17C paintings by Antonio Filingelli, is a huge statue of *St Nicholas* by Giovanni Battista Li Volsi, a very unusual sight. In the chapel to the right of the high altar, is a venerated wooden Crucifix by Fra Umile di Petralia, carried in procession through the town on Good Friday. In the presbytery the carved stalls are by Stefano and Giovanni Battista Li Volsi (c 1622; with a relief showing the old town of Nicosia). In the chapel to the left of the high altar is delightful polychrome marble decoration, and in the north transept, a statue of *St Nicholas* by Filippo Quattrocchi, and the funerary monument of Alessandro Testa by Ignazio Marabitti. On the north side are statues by Giovanni Battista Li Volsi (fifth and second bays), and a font by Antonello Gagini. Above the nave vault (access difficult) the original 15C painted wooden ceiling is preserved.

Opposite the south door of the duomo is the fine 18C **Palazzo Vescovile**. From behind the east end of the duomo via Francesco Salomone leads up past **Palazzo La Motta Salinella** (right) which has an amusing façade, and the ruined convent of S. Domenico. Ahead is an isolated carved portal in front of a modern building, and on the right (behind two palm trees) the 18C portal of S. Giuseppe (in poor repair and closed) with two statues.

Via Ansaldi continues up to the former convent of S. Vincenzo Ferreri (1555), with an interesting closed balcony at the top of its façade for the nuns. It contains frescoes by Guglielmo Borremans.

Further uphill to the left is **S. Maria Maggiore** built in 1767. The campanile crashed to the ground in 1968 and in 1978 the bells were rehung on a low iron bracket beside the façade. Next to the interesting west door several houses built into the rock face can be seen. The interior contains a huge marble ancona at the east end, finished by Antonello Gagini in 1512, a statue of the *Madonna* in the north transept, and two statues by Li Volsi. There is a view from the terrace of the modern buildings of the town, and the church of S. Salvatore perched on a rock. Via Carlo V and via del Castello climb up behind S. Maria Maggiore to the ruins of the Norman **castle**.

From piazza Garibaldi (see above) via Fratelli Testa leads down past the closed churches of **S. Calogero** (with a good ceiling and works by Filippo Randazzo) and S. Antonio Abate. On a rocky outcrop at the top of the hill the portico and campanile of **S. Salvatore** can be seen, rebuilt in the 17C. Via Testa ends at via Li Volsi with (left) the church of the **Carmine** which contains two statues of the *Annunciation* attributed to Antonello Gagini. At the top of via Li Volsi, which is lined with trees, the Baroque façade of Palazzo Speciale can be seen, propped up by concrete pillars.

In the church of **S. Michele** (just east of the town) is a 16C font and two wooden statues by Giovanni Battista Li Volsi.

The landscape is particularly beautiful east of Nicosia, with frequent glimpses of Etna in the distance. In the rugged countryside at the foot of the Nebrodi mountains (described on p.364) the fields are dotted with *pagliari*, conical huts of straw and mud.

## Sperlinga

To the west of Nicosia is **Sperlinga**, the only Sicilian town which took no part in the 'Vespers'. It is a delightful little place laid out beneath its conspicuous castle rock. The road enters the town past the 17C church of S. Anna and on the right yellow signs indicate grottoes used as houses up until a few years ago. They are preserved as a little museum (approached by steps up the salita del Municipio by a very tall palm tree; the key is with Signora Siracusa at no. 15).

Further along the main road, a road (signposted right) leads up past the large 17C duomo to a car park just below the entrance

*The castle of Sperlinga*

to the medieval **castle** (open 09.00–12.00; if closed apply at the town hall), built on the sheer rock face. Two grottoes are used as local ethnographical museums with tools, pots, baskets, agricultural implements, etc. Steps lead up across a small bridge (on the site of the drawbridge) through the double entrance. Restoration work is in progress, and a little church is being rebuilt. Stables, carved out of the rock in the Middle Ages, were later used as prisons. In one room are old photographs of Sperlinga, some taken during the occupation in 1943 by Robert Capa (1913–53). From a terrace a flight of high steps hewn out of the rock leads up to the battlements from which there are wonderful views.

# Piazza Armerina and Morgantina

Piazza Armerina, a pleasant little town, has given its name to the Roman Villa nearby which has some of the most extensive and most beautiful Romans mosaics known. The excavations of the ancient city of Morgantina are surrounded by wonderful countryside with superb views, and the deserted and peaceful site is one of the most memorable places on the island.

## ■ Practical information

*Information offices*. APT Enna, ☎ 0935/528228; with offices at Piazza Armerina, 13 via Generale Muscarà, ☎ 0935/684814, and (in summer) at Aidone, ☎ 0935/86777. Azienda Autonoma in Piazza Armerina at 1 via Cavour, ☎ 0935/680201.

**Buses** (SAIS) from Enna to Piazza Armerina (in 45min.) and to Aidone in 1hr.

### *Hotels*
**Piazza Armerina**. ★★★ *Villa Romana*, 18 via De Gasperi, ☎ 0935/682911.
Near the **Roman Villa**. ★★ *Mosaici da Battiato*, ☎ & fax 0935/685453 (with restaurant).

### *Restaurants*
Outside **Piazza Armerina**. **B** *Al Fogher*, and *Bellia*, both on the N117 bis in contrada Bellia.
Near the **Roman Villa** (contrada Paratore). **B** *La Ruota*, and **C** *Mosaici* (in the hotel, see above).
**Picnic places** in the Villa Garibaldi, or in the Parco Ronza, north of the town. There is no café or restaurant at **Morgantina**, but it is a wonderful place to **picnic** (in summer vans usually sell sandwiches in the car-park).
*Pasticceria* in Piazza Armerina: *Giuseppe Restivo*, 21 via Mazzini.

**Annual festival** in Piazza Armerina on 13–14 August, the *Palio dei Normann*i.

## Piazza Armerina
Piazza Armerina is a pleasant well-kept little town with dark cobbled streets and interesting Baroque monuments. It was little known to travellers before the discovery of the Roman villa nearby at Casale, but, with 22,300 inhabitants, it

now rivals Enna as the most important centre of the province. Here in 1295 Frederick of Aragon summoned the council that decided to contest his brother's attempt to cede Sicily to Charles II of Anjou. To the north of the town are thick woods, the result of a scheme, initiated in 1926, to cover the area with pine, eucalyptus, cypress and poplar trees (replanting is now taking place). The Parco Ronza has picnic areas and a little wildlife enclosure.

A number of streets converge on the central **piazza Garibaldi**, with its five palm trees. Here is the 18C Palazzo di Città next to the church of the Fundrò (or S. Rocco), with a carved tufa doorway. Between them via Cavour leads up past a former electricity station, restored as the seat of the Pretura. Further uphill is the former convent of S. Francesco (now a hospital) with an elaborate balcony high up on the corner.

The road continues past the 17C Palazzo del Vescovado (in very poor condition) to piazza del Duomo, at the top of the hill, with a pretty view from its terrace. Here is a statue to Baron Marco Trigona (1905), who was responsible for financing the rebuilding of the **Duomo** in 1627. The façade was added in 1719 and the dome in 1768. The fine campanile (c 1490), survives from an earlier church.

The entrance is by one of the side doors. In the **interior** the crossing and transepts decorated in white and blue are unusually light and spacious. On the high altar is a copy of a venerated Byzantine painting, the *Madonna delle Vittorie* preserved behind in a 17C silver tabernacle. It is said to have been given by Pope Nicolas II to Count Roger. Three of the 17C paintings in the sanctuary are by Zoppo di Ganci. In the little chapel on the left of the sanctuary (above the door of which is a painting of the *Martyrdom of St Agata* by Iacopo Ligozzi) is a Cross, painted on wood, attributed to a Provençal artist (1485).

The altarpiece in the north transept of the *Assumption* of the Virgin is by Filippo Paladino. The organ is by Donato del Piano (1760). The font is surrounded by a Gaginesque portal in mottled beige marble, decorated with monsters' heads, which survives from the earlier church. An equestrian statuette of *Roger* and a reliquary by Simone d'Aversa (1392–1405) are among the cathedral's treasures, which may one day be exhibited in a museum.

Also in the piazza is the fine brick façade of the large 18C **Palazzo Trigona** (recently restored).

The picturesque via Monte leads downhill through an interesting part of the town, while via Floresta leads down past the back of Palazzo Trigona with its Renaissance loggia (partly blocked up and altered) and ends in piazza Castello. Here is the overgrown 14C **castle** and four pretty small 17C palaces. The road continues down past the college of the Gesuiti, the charming façade of S. **Anna** (18C), and the 17C façade of S. **Ignazio di Loyola** (preceded by an outside double staircase) to end in piazza Garibaldi.

To the east of the centre, in piazza Umberto I, is S. **Giovanni dei Rodi** (now used by a youth club; enquire locally for the key). This plain 13C chapel of the Knights of St John is lit by lancet windows. Nearby are the eccentric façade of S. Stefano and the Teatro Garibaldi (1905). Downhill are the fine public gardens in Villa Garibaldi near the 16C church of S. Pietro. On the rise to the south the **Chiesa del Carmine** preserves a campanile and cloister of the 14C–15C.

To the north of the town, is the Norman church of S. **Andrea** (open on Sun; at other times enquire locally for the key). Dating from 1096 the austere interior contains 13C–15C frescoes, including one of the *Crucifixion* of the titular saint.

West of the town, reached from the road to Casale, a rough track climbs the Piano Marino (or Amerino) to the little church of **S. Maria di Platea** where the Byzantine *Madonna delle Vittorie* (see above) was found. Nearby are the ruins of a castle, traditionally thought to have been founded by Count Roger. The views are delightful.

At **Montagna di Marzo**, north-west of Piazza Armerina, recent excavations have revealed a sanctuary of Demeter and Kore, in use from the 6C–3C BC. Votive statuettes and coins have been found here.

## The Roman villa at Casale

The famous **Villa Romana** lies 5.5km south-west of the Piazza Armerina, in the contrada of **Casale**, off N191. The road from Piazza Armerina (signposted) leads under a high road viaduct and then along a pretty valley. It passes the church of S. Maria del Gesù, with a double portico, beside the cemetery, and ends near a large car-park (fee; there is limited free parking farther on by the souvenir stalls at the entrance).

**Admission** daily 09.00–13.00, 15.00–18.00 (although there are plans to change the hours to 09.00 till dusk). The site is beautifully kept.

### History

This luxurious country mansion must have belonged to one of the wealthiest men in the Roman Empire, who may possibly have been Diocletian's co-Emperor Maximian (Maximianus Herculeus).

It lay in a wooded and secluded site at the foot of Monte Mangone; the nearest Roman town was Philosphiana (Soffiana), 5km south. In richness and extent the villa is comparable to that of Hadrian at Tivoli or Diocletian's Palace at Split (Spalato), but while enough remains of the walls to give an idea of the elevation, it is the extent of the polychrome mosaics covering the floors that makes the building unique.

The **villa**, which consists of four distinct though connected groups of buildings on different levels, appears to date in its entirety from the early 4C, and to have succeeded a more modest 2C dwelling. The mosaics are of the Roman-African school (probably 4C AD). The buildings seem to have been kept in a habitable state up to the Arab invasion. From c 1000 they were occupied until their destruction by William the Bad (c 1160), when they were abandoned to a few cottagers, and soon obliterated by a landslide. The buried ruins remained unnoticed until 1761 and it was not until 1881 that any but spasmodic excavations were put in hand; in 1929 and again in 1935–39 the work was continued, and finally, from 1950, with official assistance, the main structure of the building was exposed, under the direction of Vinicio Gentili; the slaves' quarters and the outbuildings still remain to be explored. The mosaics have had to be extensively restored after damage from a flood in 1991.

Most of the site has been protected against the weather by a plastic shelter, its shape designed to give an idea of the original villa. This description follows the order in which it is possible to view the rooms from platforms and elevated walkways; the plan is numbered in the same order. The plan shows the layout of the

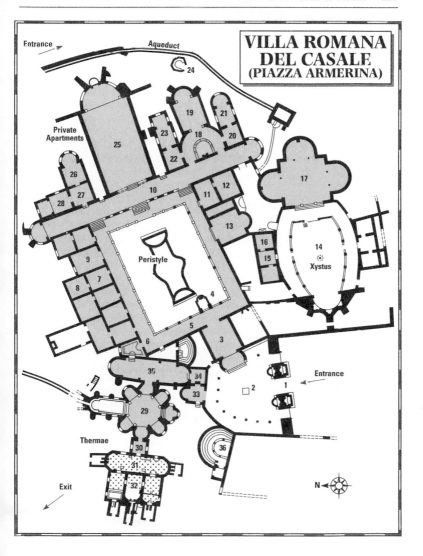

villa without the protective structure; for clarity, however, the parts enclosed have been shaded.

From the ticket office a modern path leads right round the outside of the building to the main **entrance** (1) of the villa, recalling in its massive form the Roman triumphal arch. It had two fountains on each face, fed probably from a reservoir in the attic story. The **atrium** (2) is a huge polygonal court surrounded by a portico of marble columns. To the right is the villa proper, with the **tablinum** (3) leading to steps which descend into the **peristyle**, a quadriporticus of ten columns by eight, interrupted on the east side by an arch. It has been laid out as a garden, and in the centre is a large fountain. Immediately opposite the entrance is an aediculum (4), the shrine of the patron deity of the house, decorated with a mosaic showing an ivy motif. The peristyle walks are paved with mosaic, divided by geometrical borders into panels, in which animal heads are framed in laurel wreaths.

Off the west walk opened a small court giving access to the **small latrine** (5), a sumptuous construction whose brick drain, marble hand-basin, and pictorial decoration attest the standards of imperial Roman comfort. From here it is possible to look down into the **Salone del Circo** (35; this was the narthex of the thermae, described below), so called from the scenes of the Roman circus depicted in its mosaic floor, the most extensive of their kind known. The obelisk has been identified as the obelisk of Constantius II in the Circus Maximus in Rome which received this form in AD 357. Steps lead up past a vestibule (6; this was formerly another entrance to the thermae). Its coloured mosaic, a mother with a boy and girl and two slave-girls carrying bathing necessities and clean clothing, is doubly interesting for the style of dress, and because it probably represents the imperial household in a family scene.

The majority of the **rooms on the north side of the peristyle** have geometrical mosaics, several of them damaged by Norman structural alterations. Representations of the Seasons figure in one (7); another (8) shows fishing scenes with amorini. The most interesting is the one called the *Piccola Caccia* (9), where a number of hunting scenes are depicted in great detail.

From the east walk steps ascend to the **ambulacrum** (10), a corridor (64m long) running the width of the building to isolate the private apartments and closed at either end by an exedra. An arcade overlooked the peristyle. The corridor (reached from the walkway by a little curving stair) is paved throughout with a wonderful series of **hunting scenes** (*Venationes*), one of the finest Roman mosaics known. By the stair is a dignified figure robed in Byzantine splendour, protected by two 'bodyguards' holding shields, perhaps a portrait of Maximian himself. In the exedrae are personifications of two Provinces, flanked by wild beasts, representing perhaps two opposing points of the Mediterranean, since the landscape between them is divided in the centre by a sea full of fish on which large galleys sail, which are transporting exotic animals. The hunting scenes are remarkable for the number of species of wild animals and for the accuracy with which they are depicted in action (the mosaics of the leopard on the antelope's back, and the tigress rescuing her cub are particularly skilful).

At the south-east corner of the peristyle steps lead back up to an ante-room (11), and, beyond, the **Sala delle dieci ragazze** (12), whose late mosaic (4C) shows ten girls performing gymnastic exercises, wearing 'bikinis'. In one corner is part of an earlier geometric pavement which was ruined by damp. Adjacent is a **summer living-room** (13) with a damaged mosaic representing the Orphic myth; again the animals are lovingly depicted.

Steps descend from the building, and, outside, a path skirts the apse of the triclinium (see below) to enter the **xystus** (14; uncovered), a large elliptical court surrounded on three sides by a portico and closed at the west end by a wide exedra. **Rooms 15 and 16** (to the north) are adorned with mosaics of vintage and fishing scenes. From the east end, with charming mosaic decoration, steps lead up to the **triclinium** (17), a room 12m square with deep apses on three sides. The theme of the central pavement is the *Labours of Hercules*, the violent episodes

being combined into a
single turbulent composi-
tion. Ten of the labours
can be distinguished,
those missing being the
Stymphalian Birds and
the Girdle of Hippolyte. In
the apses the *Glorification
of Hercules, Conquered
Giants* and *Lycurgus and
Ambrosia* are depicted.
The tonal shading of the
figures is remarkable.

*Detail of the 4C mosaics at the Roman villa outside
Piazza Armerina*

A path (signposted for
the exit) leads round the
outside of the triclinium
and back towards the
main building following the line of the aqueduct and past a small latrine (24) to
enter the **private apartments**. The original approach was through the semicircular **atrium** (18; with a mosaic of cupids fishing), divided by a tetrastyle
portico into a nymphaeum and an ambulatory. On either side a vestibule leads
into a bed-chamber, while the centre opens into a **living-room** (19), whose
walls were decorated with marble; the mosaic shows Arion surrounded by
Naiads and marine creatures and is the best known representation of this myth.
The **south vestibule** (20), decorated with nursery scenes leads into a **bed-
chamber** (21) in which the mosaic shows scenes of drama; the musical instruments and the indication by Greek letters of musical modes are of unusual
interest. Off the **north vestibule** (22), with its stylised tableau of Eros and Pan,
is a **bed-chamber** (23) with scenes of inexperienced young hunters, those in
the centre already amusingly routed by their quarry.

Steps lead down past the large **basilica** (25; covered and seen only through
windows), the throne room in which guests were received. The apse is decorated
with marble intarsia. Steps lead up on the right to the **northern group of
private apartments** which consists of a chamber (26) with a decorative
mosaic depicting a variety of fruit, and an antechamber (27) with a large
mosaic of Ulysses and Polyphemus. The adjoining chamber (28) has a perfectly
preserved floor in *opus musivum* with a faintly erotic scene in its 12-sided centre
panel.

It is now necessary to return down the same steps and follow the path which
leads round the outside of the buildings to a group of pine and cedar trees. Here
can be seen remains of the **Thermae** (partly covered). The **frigidarium** (29),
an octagon with radiating apses of which two served as vestibules, four as
apodyteria, and two, larger than the rest, as plunge baths, was covered with a
dome. The mosaics show robing scenes and, in the centre, marine myths. Those
in the adjoining room (30; seen through a grille), depicting the massage of
bathers by slaves, suggest its use as an aleipterion, a function consistent with its
position between the cold baths and the **tepidarium** (31) and **calidaria** (32)
which lie beyond (both uncovered).

The aediculum (33), designed for a statue of *Venus*, was the original entrance to the baths. The vestibule (34) was the entrance to the long narthex (35), which can now only be viewed from the peristyle (described above). In both these the partial disappearance of the floor has exposed the hypocaust beneath.

Near the atrium (2) of the villa are the remains of the **great latrine** (36; originally entered on the west side), the marble seats of which are lost.

A path leads back from the baths to the exit by a modern café (and steps lead back up right to the entrance and car-park).

## Aidone

The little town of Aidone (889m) lies 10km north-east of Piazza Armerina surrounded by lovely woods of pine and eucalyptus trees. It is built of local red stone.

In the upper part of the town, in a restored 17C Capuchin convent, is an Archaeological Museum (open daily 09.00–13.00, 15.00–19.00), with a well-displayed collection of finds from Morgantina (see below). The entrance is through a charming little church with wooden statues. On the ground floor room 1 contains Bronze and Iron Age finds from the Cittadella, the area of Morgantina occupied before the Greek era. This includes material from huts inhabited by the Morgetica colony. An elaborate spiral staircase leads up to room 2 which continues the display from Cittadella, with Corinthian and Attic ceramics, antefixes with gorgons' heads (6C BC), a large red-figure krater by the Euthymides painter, an Attic Corinthian krater with birds and lekythoi. Room 3 contains a fine collection of ceramics from the agora zone of Serra Orlando (including a plate with three fish), and from the houses excavated on the west and east hills (including statues). There are also numerous votive statuettes and very fine large busts of Persephone (3C BC) from the three sanctuaries of Demeter and Kore so far found in the district. Another room on two levels has a delightful display of household objects, cooking utensils, agricultural implements, toys, masks, etc. found at Morgantina.

## Morgantina

The extensive and extremely interesting remains of the ancient city of Morgantina (open every day, 09.00–13.30, 15.00–dusk, although there are plans to change the opening hours to 09.00 till dusk) lie some 4km beyond Aidone and its lovely eucalyptus woods, in beautiful deserted countryside, dotted with farms, with pastureland for cattle and sheep. The approach road forks left from the main road before entering Aidone and continues east for 2km. A good paved road (1km) curves left at a fork (signposted) where there are spectacular views. On the right, behind a green fence and under a plastic roof, is a **sanctuary of Demeter and Kore** (4C BC), still being excavated. Beyond is a car-park beside olive trees, just below which is an attractively restored old house now used as a ticket office. There are long-term plans to open a path from here via the west hill to the main site, but at present you walk down the rough stone road for some 800m to reach the entrance to the excavations.

### History

The huge site (c 20ha) occupies the long tufa ridge of **Serra Orlando** to the west and the conical hill of **Cittadella** (578m) to the east; they are separated by a deep valley. The city was in the centre of a rich agricultural plain near the source of the River Gornalunga. A colony of the Sikels, called

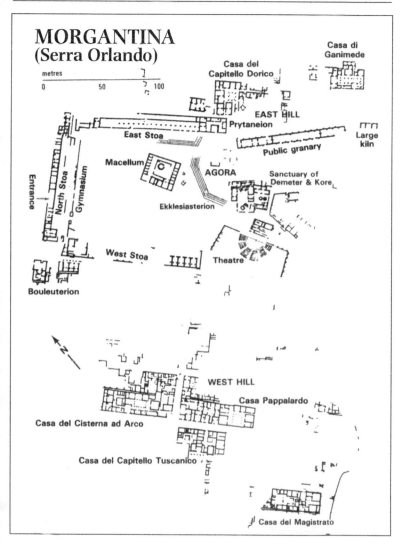

# MORGANTINA
## (Serra Orlando)

metres

0    50    100

Casa di
Ganimede

Casa del
Capitello Dorico

EAST HILL

Prytaneion

East Stoa

Large
kiln

Public granary

Macellum

AGORA

Sanctuary of
Demeter & Kore

Entrance

North Stoa

Gymnasium

Ekklesiasterion

West Stoa

Theatre

Bouleuterion

WEST HILL

Casa Pappalardo

Casa del Cisterna ad Arco

Casa del Capitello Tuscanico

Casa del Magistrato

*Morgeti* was founded c 850 BC on the Cittadella, on the site of an Early Bronze Age settlement. Signs of Greek occupation here date from the 6C BC, but the Cittadella was abandoned after its sack by Ducetius in 459 BC. The new city was built on Serra Orlando, and it probably reached its zenith in the reign of Hieron II (269–215 BC). Having sided wrongly in the Second Punic War, it was given in 211 by the victorious Romans to their Spanish mercenary Moericus. By the time of Augustus it had lost importance. The site was identified in 1955 by Princeton University, and excavations by them continue here every year.

The main excavations consist of the area of the agora laid out in the 3C BC and the houses on the two low hills to the east and west of the agora. The entrance, by a group of cypresses, to the **agora** is through the **north stoa**, with remains of the **gymnasium**. A number of Hellenistic lava millstones have been placed here. This area of the **upper agora** was also enclosed on the west and east side by a stoa. At the extreme right-hand corner, at the foot of the hill, are remains of shops and a paved street near the **bouleuterion**, where the Senate met. In the centre of the upper agora, surrounded by grass, is the large rectangular **macellum**, added in 125 BC, a covered market with shops, around a tholos. The long **east stoa** (87m) consisted of a narrow portico. A monumental fountain (under cover) with two basins has been excavated at its north end, and at its extreme south end is the so-called **prytaneion**. In the centre of the piazza is a monumental three-sided flight of steps, 55m wide, which descends to the lower polygonal **agora**. These are thought to have served as an **ekklesiasterion** for public assemblies. Beside the steps is a **sanctuary of Demeter and Kore** with two round altars (under cover). Behind this, built into the hillside, is the **theatre**. To the right, beyond a long terracotta conduit, are shops in the hillside, part of the west stoa (see above).

In front of a conspicuous ruined house in the centre of the site, a rough lane leads up along the fence (with fine views) in c 15 minutes to the **west hill**, with a residential district. It passes the large so-called *Casa del Magistrato* with 24 rooms, on the slope of the hill near the walls (well preserved here outside the fence). It follows the outer wall of the house and continues to the top of the hill where a number of houses have been excavated, separated by roads on a regular grid-plan. Here the *Casa del Capitello Tuscanico* has some good floors; across the street, near a large olive tree, is the *Casa Pappalardo*, a luxurious house with more mosaics. To the north, partly covered by a building for protection, is the *Casa della Cisterna ad Arco*, with a cistern beneath a low arch, and several mosaics. On the north side of the hill (near the approach road to the site) new excavations are in progress of another house (covered for protection).

On the other side of the sanctuary of Demeter and Kore (see above), at the foot of the east hill is the large oblong **public granary**, with a small pottery kiln (under cover), and, at the other end (by the fence), a larger kiln for tiles and bricks with elaborate ovens (also under cover). From the ekklesiasterion a stepped street zig-zags up the **east hill** to the *Casa del Capitello Dorico*, just below the summit. Beyond an old farmhouse on the extreme right, in a little group of almond trees, is the *Casa di Ganimede* built c 260 BC, and destroyed in 211 BC, with two columns and mosaic fragments in two little huts (seen through glass doors). The Ganymede mosaic is particularly interesting as one of the earliest known cut-stone tesserae mosaics, which also incorporates natural pebbles. There is a fine view of the agora and, on a clear day, of Etna to the east. A lane leads back past the farmhouse and down towards the exit.

To the east of the site the hill of the **Cittadella** (reached from here by a rough road in c 3km) can be seen, which was separately fortified. On the summit is a long narrow temple of the 4C BC. Here a hut village of the *Morgeti* (850–750 BC) was excavated, and rock hewn tombs of Siceliot type yielded considerable finds of pottery. Parts of the **walls** (7km in circumference) of Serra Orlando and the west gate can be seen near the approach road to the site.

# Ragusa

The upper town of Ragusa (population 68,800) is an elegant provincial capital laid out after the earthquake of 1693. It occupies a ridge (502m) that runs from west to east between two deep gorges, and has expanded across the river gorge to the south, where high bridges now connect it to the modern town. Beyond a declivity at its east end, on an isolated spur below, is **Ragusa Ibla**, a beautiful quiet old town, one of the best preserved in Sicily. It is connected to the upper town by a steep winding road (and steps), and has exceptionally fine Baroque palaces and churches.

## ■ Practical information

*Information office*. APT Ragusa, 33 via Capitano Bocchieri, Ragusa Ibla (☎ 0932/621421).

### Getting there
**Railway station**. Piazza del Popolo, in the newest part of the upper town; subsidiary station of Ragusa Ibla at the bottom of the hill of Ibla on N194. On

the line between Gela, Modica, Noto and Siracusa, it has services to Siracusa in c 2hr.
**Buses**. Bus no. 3 runs every half hour from the upper town (corso Italia) to Ibla (piazza della Repubblica and piazza Pola). No. 1 from the main railway station to Ibla. Country buses from piazza del Popolo run by *AST* and *Etna Trasporti* to Catania, Siracusa, Enna and Agrigento (via Gela). Services in summer to Camarina and other places on the sea.
**Parking**. In the upper town: via Natalelli, or piazza Libertà; in Ibla, piazza Duomo.

### Hotels
In the upper town. ★★★★ *Rafael*, 40 corso Italia, ☎ 0932/654080, fax 0932/653418; *Mediterraneo Palace*, 189 via Roma, ☎ 0932/621944, fax 0932/623799. ★★★ *Montreal*, 14 via S. Giuseppe, ☎ & fax 0932/621133. For Marina di Ragusa, see p.248.
*Agriturismo* accommodation 8km south of Ragusa: *Eremo della Giubiliana*, ☎ 0932/669119.
There are **campsites** on the coast at S. Croce Camerina and Marina di Ragusa, see p.248.

### Restaurants
In Ibla: **B** *Il Barocco, Il Saracino*, and *Antica Macina*. **C** *La Rusticana*.
For fish restaurants at Marina di Ragusa, see p.248. *Agriturismo* restaurant *Eremo della Giubiliana*, see above.
Places to **picnic** in the public gardens (Giardino Ibleo) in Ibla.

***Annual festivals***. *Festa di S. Giorgio* on the last Sunday in May in Ibla; *Festa di S. Giovanni* in the upper town on 29 August.

### History
Ragusa Ibla occupies the site of the Siculian *Hybla Heraea*. The county of Ragusa, created in 1091 by Roger for his son Godfrey, was united in 1296 by Manfredi Chiaramonte with that of Modica. After the earthquake of 1693 a new town arose to the west, and the two became separate communities from 1865 to 1926 when they were re-united as a new provincial capital. The area is known for its asphalt mines. Oil was found here in 1953, and there used to be oil wells scattered about the upper town. Drilling now takes place offshore, and the oil is piped from Marina di Ragusa to Augusta. The province has accused the oil companies of pollution and this remains one of the poorest areas on the island.

### The upper town
The centre of the well-kept upper town of **Ragusa** is piazza S. Giovanni around the monumental cathedral of **S. Giovanni**, with its wide façade preceded by a theatrical terrace (with cafés beneath) and surrounded by a small garden. It was begun after 1694 by Mario Spada of Ragusa and Rosario Boscarino of Modica, and has a pretty campanile. At its east end is the elegant 18C **Casa Canonica**. Across corso Italia is the **Collegio di Maria Addolorata**, with a handsome façade of 1801 next to its convent.

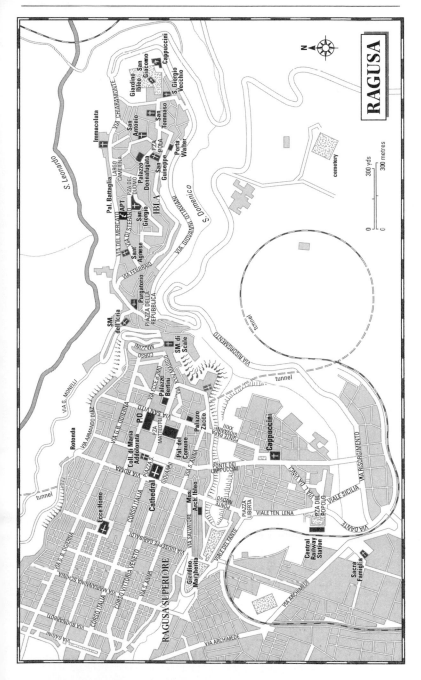

*The cathedral of Ragusa*

**Corso Italia**, the handsome long main street, lined with trees, descends very steeply to the edge of the hill above Ibla (see below). Uphill, above the Duomo, it crosses via Roma (which to the right ends in a rotonda with a view of Ibla). Via Roma leads left towards Ponte Nuovo (1937), which crosses the torrente S. Domenica high above the public gardens of Villa Margherita where there is a good view (left) of Ponte dei Cappuccini (1835) and Ponte Papa Giovanni XXIII (1964) beyond. Across the bridge is piazza Libertà, with buildings erected in the Fascist era.

Just before the bridge (right, below a Standa department store) steps lead down to a building beneath the road viaduct which houses the **Museo Archeologico Ibleo** (open every day 09.00–14.00, 15.00–17.30; Sun & PH 09.00–13.00, 15.00–17.30). The beautifully displayed collection has finds from the province, from prehistoric to Roman times. The **first section** is devoted to prehistory. The Bronze Age civilisation of *Castelluccio* is particularly well documented. Here also material belonging to the Thapsos culture (1400–1270 BC) is displayed.

The **second section** (cases 5–14) displays finds from Camarina, from the Archaic to the Classical period. Case 6: Two black-figured amphorae, one with a scene of wild boars and lions, and one showing Hercules and the lion; reconstructed necropolis of Passo Marinaro; finds from the necropolis (cases 9 and 10) include small red-figured vases of the 5C BC and a lekythos with a white ground. A statue of a kore was found in the Temple of Athena. Three levels of excavations have been reconstructed here. Case 13 contains terracotta statuettes of Demeter found in a deposit near a pottery oven (active from the end of the 5C to the beginning of the 3C BC).

**Third section**, dedicated to indigenous centres inhabited by the Siculi (Archaic to Classical period). Cases 14–18 contain finds from Monte Casasia and Licodia Eubea ware; in Case 15 is a rare Ionic kylix with an inscription in the native language. Cases 17–18 display finds from the necropolis of Castiglione, north of Ragusa. Case 20 displays finds from the necropolis of Rito, including an Attic kylix with animals outside and a running warrior inside attributed to the circle of the 'Griffin bird painter' (c 550 BC).

**Fourth section** (Hellenistic centres). A potter's oven from Scornavacche has been reconstructed, and the terracotta figurines (cases 22–24) are particularly noteworthy. **Fifth section** (Roman and late Roman cities). Finds from Caucana, and mosaics from S. Croce Camerina (with Christian motifs) are displayed here. Case 26 contains Roman glass. The **sixth section** displays various material acquired from private collections.

From piazza S. Giovanni (see above) corso Italia descends steeply past (right; no. 90) the fine 18C **Palazzo Lupis** to piazza Matteotti. Here is the huge **Palazzo del Comune** (1880; enlarged 1929) opposite the monumental post office (1930), which has colossal statues on the top of the building. Corso Italia next crosses via S. Vito in which, on the right, is the fine Baroque **Palazzo Zacco** (in poor repair). Farther down corso Italia is the late 18C **Palazzo Bertini** (no. 35) with three huge grotesque heads.

The corso ends at via XXIV Maggio, with two palaces well sited at the corner, which narrows and becomes steeper as it begins the descent to Ragusa Ibla, now seen in its magnificent position on a separate spur. At the foot of an elegant little Baroque palace, a small tabernacle recalls a cholera epidemic here in 1838; in front, wide steps descend to an interesting group of houses with courtyards, overlooking the valley. The road continues down past (left) the pretty via Pezza, which runs along the hillside, and via Ecce Homo which climbs uphill to the left, past a handsome little Baroque palace.

Via XXIV Maggio ends at the balcony beside the campanile of S. Maria delle Scale where there is a superb bird's-eye view of Ragusa Ibla, with its beautifully coloured roof tiles which have been carefully preserved. Many fragments of the 15C structure of the church of **S. Maria delle Scale** survived the rebuilding of 1693. Outside, beneath the campanile is part of a Gothic doorway and the remains of an outside pulpit. Inside (usually closed) is an elaborate Gothic arch decorated with sculptures and (over a side altar) a relief (very ruined) of the *Dormition of the Virgin* in coloured terracotta, by the Gagini school (1538).

## Ragusa Ibla

Ibla can be reached from here by the zig-zag corso Mazzini or on foot by various flights of steps, described below. The Discesa S. Maria continues down straight ahead. On the road is a relief of the *Flight into Egypt* (15C–16C), probably once part of a votive tabernacle. Across the road another flight of steps continues under the road, and then a walkway leads left in front of some houses. Just after rejoining the road, steps immediately to the left continue downhill and pass under the road twice before reaching the delightful **Palazzo Nicastro** (or *Vecchia Cancelleria*), erected in 1760 with tall pilasters, a decorative doorway, and windows with large balconies. To the left is the bell-tower and little dome decorated with majolica tiles of the 18C church of **S. Maria dell'Idria**.

The salita Commendatore continues down past (left) the 18C **Palazzo Cosentini**, with splendid Baroque pilasters, capitals, and more fantastic balconies. Its main façade is on corso Mazzini which now continues right to **piazza della Repubblica** at the foot of the hill of **Ragusa Ibla**, a beautifully preserved little town, with peaceful streets, which lends itself to exploration on foot. It is, however, suffering from depopulation and many of the old houses have been abandoned.

To the left of the closed 17C church of the **Purgatorio** via del Mercato leads up round the left side of the hill with a view of Palazzo Sortino Trono above the road. Further on it continues left past the old abandoned market building and has splendid views over the unspoilt valley, but this route instead follows the more peaceful (and nicely paved) via XI Febbraio which forks right for the centre of Ibla. On a bend there is a view left of the hillside covered with characteristic dry-stone walls. Via S. Agnese continues left, and then steps lead up to the wide via Tenente Di Stefano near the church of S. Agnese beside a low 19C palace in a pretty group of houses. It continues uphill and soon narrows with a good view ahead of the 19C dome of the cathedral. On the left are the seven delightful balconies of **Palazzo La Rocca**, beautifully restored as the seat of the APT of Ragusa. It has an interesting double staircase in black *pece* stone, and a little garden with citrus trees overlooking the unspoilt hillside.

The road continues round the the side of the duomo into **piazza del Duomo**, where there is a row of six palm trees. It slopes up to the magnificent three-tiered golden **façade** of the cathedral of **S. GIORGIO** which rises above a flight of steps surrounded by a 19C balustrade. The church was built by Rosario Gagliardi in 1744. The neo-classical dome (hidden by the façade; it can be seen from the road behind or from the extreme left side of the piazza) dates from 1820.

The contemporary **interior** (entered by one of the side doors) is lit by the delightful **dome** which rises above its high drum with windows between the coupled columns. The stained glass dates from 1926. In the south aisle, above the side door (and behind glass), is an equestrian statue of *St George*; in the third altar is Vito d'Anna's *Immacolata* and in the fourth altar, *Rest on the Flight into Egypt* by Dario Guerci. In the north transept is *St George and the dragon*, also by Dario Guerci. In the sacristy is a lovely stone tarbernacle with the equestrian statue of *St George* between saints *Ippolito* and *Mercurio*, with ruined reliefs below. Above the side door in the north aisle is a silver reliquary urn. By the west door is a stone statue of *St George* by the school of Gagini. The organ in the nave is by the Serassi brothers.

**Palazzo Arezzi**, in the piazza, has a delightful balcony over a side road. At the lower end of the piazza is a charming little fountain and the handsome Palazzo Veninata (early 20C). The fine neo-classical **Circolo di Conversazione** (c 1850), which preserves an interesting interior, houses an exclusive club recently opened to women members. Next to it is **Palazzo Donnafugata** with its delightful little wooden balcony, from which it was possible to watch the passersby in the road below without being seen. The palace contains a private art collection formed in the mid-19C by Corrado Arezzo de Spuches (admission only with special permission) and a little theatre built in the late 19C (150 seats; recently restored) where public performances are sometimes held.

The wide corso XXV Aprile continues to piazza Pola, with the splendid tall Baroque façade of the church of **S. Giuseppe** (1590, probably by Gagliardi). In the oval domed interior there are pretty galleries once used by the nuns. The interesting pavement is made with black asphalt, mined locally. The altars are made of shiny painted glass.

In the centre of the dome is a painting of the *Glory of St Benedict* by Sebastiano Lo Monaco (1793). Above the high altar, in an elaborate frame, the *Holy Family* by Matteo Battaglia is situated. The side altarpieces, including a *Holy Trinity* by Giuseppe Cristadoro, are in poor condition. Beside the church is the palace which served as the town hall up until 1926 (now used as a post office).

Corso XXV Aprile continues to wind downhill past the closed church of the Maddalena and the high wall of **S. Tommaso** which has a pretty bell-tower. In the interior is an interesting font in black asphalt (1545). Just beyond, beside the church of St Vincent Ferrer (propped up with scaffolding) is the entrance to the **Giardino Ibleo** (open 08.00–20.00), delightful public gardens laid out in 1858, with a splendid palm avenue and beds of lilies. It contains several small churches.

Beyond the colourful campanile of St Vincent Ferrer is the locked church of S. Giacomo, founded in the 16C with a façade of 1902. At the end is the church of the **Cappuccini**, now the seat of a restoration laboratory and of the Museo Diocesano (closed). It contains a very fine altarpiece with three paintings by Pietro Novelli. The beautifully kept gardens have fountains and views of the hills, and, beyond the War Memorial, the church of S. Giorgio can be seen on the skyline, with the large church of the Immacolata on the right.

In an orchard below the balustrade ancient tombs can be seen excavated in the rock. Outside the entrance to the gardens, in via Normanni, is the 15C Gothic side portal of the church of **S. Giorgio Vecchio** (in very bad condition), with a relief of *St George*, behind a little garden. The church was destroyed in the earthquake of 1693.

From piazza Pola (see above), with a view of the top of the façade of S. Giorgio and its dome, via Orfanotrofio leads past the church of S. Antonio (closed) with remains of a Gothic portal next to a little Baroque side doorway. Just beyond is the 18C **Palazzo di Quattro** with a balcony along the whole length of its façade. It has a pretty entrance and courtyard with a handsome double staircase (shown on request by the cabinet-maker who has his workshop here).

A road descends on the right past S. Teresa to reach the Immacolata (closed), with a fine campanile. It contains interesting works in *pece* stone. In piazza Chiaramonte its Gothic portal can be seen in a little garden of orange trees. The narrow via Chiaramonte leads up past the campanile to the back façade of **Palazzo Battaglia** (no. 40), a very original building. Beyond the arch on the left the main façade can be seen on via Orfanotrofio, beside the church of the Annunziata. Just uphill from Largo Camerina, via Conte Cabrera leads back past more interesting palaces, to piazza del Duomo.

A road leads out of the other side of the piazza, under the arch of Palazzo Arezzi, to (left) the salita Ventimiglia (steps) which lead down to the closed church of the Gesù. The interior has stuccoes and frescoes by Matteo Battaglia (1750). Behind the church is the **Porta Walter**, the only one of the five medieval gates of Ibla to have survived.

# Modica

Modica (population 50,000) is an unusual town divided into two parts, Modica Bassa and Modica Alta, with decorative palm trees and elegant Baroque buildings, many of them built when it was still a powerful county ruled by Spanish counts. Like many towns in this corner of Sicily it had to be rebuilt after the earthquake of 1693. The lower town occupies a valley at the confluence of two torrents, which were channelled and covered over in 1902 after a disastrous flood. On the steep spur between them the upper town rises in terraces above the huge church of S. Giorgio.

# ■ Practical information

**Information offices**. APT Ragusa, 33 via Capitano Bocchieri, Ragusa Ibla (☎ 0932/621421). Pro-Loco, Modica (☎ 0932/762626; in summer 0932/ 905803). Pro-Loco, Ispica, 21 via Bellini. Pro-Loco, Scicli, 4 via Castellana.

### Getting there
**Railway station**, Beyond via Vittorio Veneto, 600m west of corso Umberto I. On the line from Gela via Ragusa, Modica and Noto to Siracusa. Services to Siracusa in c 1hr 30min.
**Buses**. Services run by *AST* to Ragusa, Siracusa, Catania, etc.
**Parking** is very difficult in the upper town; in the lower town on corso Umberto I or viale Medaglie d'Oro.

**Hotel**. ★★★ *Motel di Modica*, 1 corso Umberto I, ☎ 0932/941022, fax 0932/941077.
**Campsite** (open in summer) on the coast at Marina di Modica: ★ *Di Vita Vera*, ☎ 0368/3806979.

**Restaurants**. Modica is famous for its excellent cuisine. **B** *Le Due Torri* (or *Fattoria delle Torri*) in Modica Alta (near S. Teresa); **C** *La Rusticana* in Modica Bassa.
**Cafés and pasticcerie**. In Modica Alta: *Colombo*; in Modica Bassa: *Bonaiuto*, *Bonomo*, and *Iacono*. *Di Lorenzo* (245 corso Umberto I) sells delicious local sweets including *mpanatigghi* (light pastry filled with mincemeat, chocolate, and spices), *cedrata* (honey and citron rind), and *cobaita* (honey and sesame seeds), and chocolate.

**Annual festivals**. Traditional processions during Easter week. The *Festa di S. Giorgio* in April, and the *Festa di S. Pietro* at the end of June, with a fair.

### History
The site of Modica was occupied by the Siculi. The county of Modica, one of the most powerful fiefs of the Middle Ages, passed from the Chiaramonte in 1392 to the Spanish Cabrera family. In the 15C it ruled over Ragusa, Vittoria, Comiso and the whole of the present-day province of Ragusa. After 1704 it came through Spanish connections to the seventh Duke of Berwick and Alba. At the end of the last century Modica was the fourth largest town in Sicily. It was the birthplace of the poet Salvatore Quasimodo (1901–68), who won the Nobel prize for literature in 1959. His father worked as a railwayman here.

**Modica Bassa**, the lower town (300m), is traversed by **corso Umberto I** which is unusually wide since it occupies the bed of a river torrent covered over in 1902. It is lined with handsome 18C and 19C palaces, and there is a splendid view of the monumental church of S. Giorgio (described below) half-way up the hillside between the lower and upper town. On the extreme right, on top of a bare rock face, a round tower surmounted by a clock can be seen, which is all that remains of the castle of the counts of Modica.

A monumental flight of steps, decorated with statues of the apostles, leads up to the church of **S. Pietro**, rebuilt after the earthquake of 1693. Nearby, off via Clemente Grimaldi, is the inconspicuous entrance (usually kept locked) to a grotto used until recently as a storeroom. Here three layers of frescoes were discovered in 1989, the earliest of which may date from the 11C. They decorated an ancient church which has been given the name of **S. Nicolò Inferiore**.

In the centre of the town, at the former confluence of the two rivers, the corso forms a fork with via Marchesa Tedeschi, which is also unusually wide since it is on the site of a riverbed. Here is the town hall, next to the church of **S. Domenico** which contains a 16C painting of the *Madonna of the Rosary*. On the other side of the corso, in via De Leva, is a fine Arab Norman doorway in a little garden, probably once part of a 13C palace. In via Marchesa Tedeschi is the church of **S. Maria di Betlem** (closed) which incorporates a beautiful chapel built in the 15C by the Cabrera. The elaborate crèche in the north aisle, with 60 terracotta statuettes, was made in Caltagirone in 1882.

On the other side of the town hall (see above) corso Umberto I continues past piazza Matteotti where there are decorative palm trees. Here the 15C church of the **Carmine** contains a marble group of the *Annunciation* by the Gagini school.

The corso ends at viale Medaglie d'oro above which in via Mercè is the church of S. Maria delle Grazie next to its huge former convent, the **Palazzo dei Mercedari**, restored as the seat of the Museo Civico and the Museo delle Arti e delle Tradizioni Popolari. On the ground floor is the **Museo Civico** (open daily 09.00–13.00, except Sun & PH), which has an archaeological collection formed at the end of the last century. It was catalogued and opened in 1960 by the local scholar Franco Libero Belgiorno (1906–71), after whom it has been named since it was re-arranged here in 1990. The display is chronological, from the Neolithic era onwards, with finds from Cava d'Ispica and Modica. A bronze statuette of Hercules dating from the 4C BC has been removed for restoration.

On the top floor, in lovely vaulted rooms of the old convent, is the **Museo Ibleo delle Arti e delle Tradizioni Popolari**, a private museum opened on request. This fascinating local ethnological collection of artisans' tools and utensils is displayed in reconstructed workshops (a smithy, shoemaker's shop, basketworker's store, a laboratory for making sweets, a cartwright's office, a saddlery, a carpenter's workshop, etc.) Local artisans will come to give demonstrations of their skills by appointment. A local farmhouse has also been faithfully reconstructed. There is a collection of Sicilian carts.

The huge church of **S. GIORGIO** is reached from corso Garibaldi which runs parallel to corso Umberto I. Some 250 steps (completed in 1818) ascend to the church which was rebuilt in 1643 and again after 1693. The **façade** is one of the most remarkable Baroque works in Italy. It has five original doorways and a very tall, central bell-tower. It is attributed by most scholars to Rosario Gagliardi (1702–38); the upper storey was added in the 19C.

In the **interior**, with double side aisles, the apse is filled with a huge polyptych attributed to the local painter Bernardino Niger (1573). The silver high altar was made in 1705. In the south aisle is a 16C painting of the *Nativity* and (on the second altar) an *Assumption* by Filippo Paladino (1610). At the end of the south side is a 14C silver reliquary urn. In the chapel to the right of the presbytery is a popular equestrian statue of *St George*. In the chapel to the left of the presbytery is a statue of the *Madonna* by Giuliano Mancino and Berrettaro. The fine Serassi organ dates from 1886–88.

On the left side of S. Giorgio is the 18C **Palazzo Polara** from which there is a fine view of the lower town and the hillside beyond. Uphill behind S. Giorgio, on corso Francesco Crispi, is the Baroque **Palazzo Tomasi-Rossi**, which has pretty balconies.

Roads and lanes continue steeply uphill to **Modica Alta** which is well worth exploring. Its main street, the corso Regina Margherita, has handsome 18C and 19C palaces. At the highest point of the hill stands its most important church, **S. Giovanni**, preceded by another monumental flight of steps. Its façade was erected in the Baroque style in 1839. In another part of the upper town, within a prison enclosure (but visible from the outside), is the elaborate doorway of 1478 of the ruined church of **S. Maria di Gesù**.

# Environs of Modica

## The Cava d'Ispica

The Cava d'Ispica lies 11km east of Modica (signposted). It is a deep gorge 13km long which follows a river (now usually dry) with beautiful plants and trees. The sides of the canyon are honeycombed with prehistoric tombs and medieval cave-dwellings; here the presence of man can be traced from the earliest times to the most recent, although the valley was greatly damaged in the earthquake of 1693. Beside the entrance is a hut used as an office by the Soprintendenza alle Antichità of the region (☎ 0932/826004), and the site is being enclosed. It is open daily 09.00–13.30, 15.00–18.30. Just below the entrance are extensive Christian catacombs known as *Larderia* (4C–5C AD). They extend for some 36m inside the rock.

Across the main road is the little church of **S. Nicola** (unlocked on request) which contains very damaged traces of late-Byzantine frescoes. A path near here leads along the dry riverbed to the prehistoric tomb of **Baravitalla**, dating from the Castelluccio period (1800 BC), and a Sicel tomb with a design of pilasters on its façade. Nearby traces of a hut village have been uncovered.

From the entrance (see above) a gravel road (c 400m) leads past numerous caves, including some on more than one storey, ruined by the earthquake. Outside the enclosure an overgrown path continues along the splendid valley, with luxuriant vegetation, for some 13km. It passes numerous rock tombs and dwellings, including the so-called *Castello* on four floors. At the far end is the **Parco della Forza**, best approached from Ispica, see below.

## Ispica

South-west of Modica, in pretty countryside typical of this region of the island, with low dry-stone walls between fields of pastureland and crops, and small farmhouses built of the local grey stone, is the little town of Ispica (population 14,800). It was rebuilt on its present site after the earthquake of 1693 destroyed the former town on the floor of the valley, and it has fine 18C and 19C buildings. It was known in the Middle Ages as Spaccaforno, but re-adopted its old name in 1935. The chalk eminence on which it stands is pierced with tombs and cliff dwellings. These can be seen in the **Parco della Forza** (open 09.00–13.30, 15.00–18.30), which is at the south end of the Cava d'Ispica (see above). It has interesting vegetation and various cisterns, catacombs, etc., and a remarkable tunnel known as the *Centoscale*.

In the little town, the church of **S. Maria Maggiore** is an attractive building by Vincenzo Sinatra with 19C stuccoes and frescoes by Olivio Sozzi (1763–65), who is buried here. **Palazzo Bruno di Belmonte**, an Art Nouveau building by Ernesto Basile (1910) has been restored as the town hall. The church of the **Annunziata** is filled with stuccoes carried out in the mid-18C, attributed to Giuseppe Gianforma.

## Scicli

A pretty byroad leads from Modica across an upland plain with low stone walls and carob trees. Before descending to Scicli, it passes the site of the old medieval town marked by the ruined church of **S. Matteo**, which was once its cathedral. Remains survive of its façade of 1762.

Scicli (population 25,000) has occupied the floor of the valley, surrounded by rocky cliffs, since the 14C. Prosperous under Saracen and Norman rule, it is another charming Baroque town rebuilt after the 1693 earthquake, with numerous churches. Here the annual festival of the *Madonna delle Milizie* is celebrated in May, which commemorates the battle between the Normans and Saracens. In piazza Italia, planted with trees and surrounded by some neo-classical buildings, is the 18C **Duomo**. It contains a papier mâché *Madonna dei Milici* which is carried in procession in May. Opposite is the Baroque **Palazzo Fava** which has attractive balconies, on the corner of via S. Bartolomeo, which opens out in front of the well-sited church of **S. Bartolomeo**, in front of a rock face. The pleasantly coloured façade, crowned with a cupola, was built at the beginning of the 19C by Salvatore d'Alì. It contains a crèche by Pietro Padula (1773–75).

Via Nazionale leads uphill and on the right, at the end of a short street, is the corner of **Palazzo Beneventano**, with remarkably eccentric Baroque details (in very poor repair). Off the other side of via Nazionale is the prettily paved via Mormino Penna where there are a few trees. Here is the town hall (1906) next to the elegant church of **S. Giovanni**, with a fine façade. Via Penna winds on past **S. Michele** with a well-designed side door, past Palazzo Spadaro and the church of S. Teresa.

Via Nazionale continues to piazza Busacca, planted with palm trees, with a 19C statue by Benedetto Civiletti, of the philanthropist Pietro Di Lorenzo (d. 1567). Here is the church of the **Carmine** (1751–69), beside its convent with a decorative balcony. Beyond, to the right, is the church of **S. Maria della Consolazione**, with another good façade. Beyond, surrounded by a rocky cliff, in an interesting old part of the town, is the church of **S. Maria la Nuova**. The neoclassical façade dates from 1816. In the interior, decorated with stuccoes, is a high altarpiece of the *Birth of the Virgin* by Sebastiano Conca. The presbytery was designed by Venanzio Marvuglia. A silver statue of the *Immacolata* dates from 1844, and there is a Gaginesque statue of the *Madonna*.

# Comiso and Vittoria

These small towns in the province of Ragusa have fine Baroque buildings. Comiso is of particular interest.

## ■ Practical information

**Information office.** APT Ragusa, ☎ 0932/621421. In Comiso, Pro-Loco information office, 26 via Ferreri.

### Hotels
**Comiso.** ★★★ *Cordial*, contrada Deserto, ☎ & fax 0932/967866.
**Vittoria.** ★★★ *Grand Hotel*, via Vico II Carlo Pisacane, ☎ & fax 0932/863888. For hotels on the coast at Scoglitti, see p. 00.

### Restaurants
**Chiaramonte Gulfi.** B *Maiore*, 12 via Martiri Ungherese; *Le Mole*, contrada di Chiara.
**Vittoria.** B *Opera*, 133 via Carlo Alberto.
**Monterosso Almo.** B *Le Due Palme*, contrada Calaforno.

## Comiso

The pretty Baroque town of Comiso (population 27,000) is dominated by the domes of the Chiesa Matrice and SS. Annunziata. Some ugly new buildings have been built here in recent years, but the main streets preserve their handsome paving made out of the local stone which has the appearance of marble. The town became a centre of pacifist and disarmament demonstrations after 1983 when a NATO nuclear missile base was installed on the old airfield north of the town. This was dismantled in 1991 as a result of the treaty signed between the Soviet Union and the USA in 1987. The author Gesualdo Bufalino (1920–96) was born here.

Three palm trees stand outside the church of the **Annunziata**, which has a lovely blue dome, rebuilt in 1772–93. The light interior has stucco decoration in blue, grey and white. It contains a wooden 15C statue of *St Nicholas* on the first south altar, and a Crucifix attributed to Fra Umile da Petralia in the south transept. On the second north altar is a painting of the *Transition of the Virgin* by Narciso Cidonio (1605). The font is a fine work by Mario Rutelli (1913). The organ is by the Polizzi brothers of Modica.

Via Papa Giovanni XXIII leads downhill in front of the church, and via degli Studi leads right to piazza del Municipio with its amusing fountain (1937). The waters of the **Fonte di Diana** were said to refuse to mix with wine when poured by unchaste hands; in Roman days they supplied a bath-house, with a mosaic of Neptune, the remains of which are visible beneath the town hall. Just out of the piazza rises the huge church of **S. Maria delle Stelle**, the Chiesa Matrice, also with a dome. The fine façade is attributed to Rosario Gagliardi. The interior has a vault painted in the 17C attributed to Antonio Barbalunga. Below its terrace is piazza delle Erbe, with a fountain, on to which faces the handsome **market**, with a raised portico, built in 1867. It has been restored as the seat of the

Biblioteca and Pinacoteca, entered from the delightful courtyard, which has a fountain. The collection of paintings includes 19C portraits.

From via Giovanni XXIII a road leads shortly (right) to the church of **S. Francesco** (if locked, ring at the convent), founded in the early 14C. The present church was built in 1478, and the very interesting **Cappella Naselli** (1517–55) was added at the east end by Gaspare Poidomani, using a fascinating pastiche of architectural styles. Arab-Norman squinches support the dome, and classical details are incorporated in the decoration. It contains the funerary monument of Gaspare Naselli, attributed to Antonello Gagini. At the west end is a wood choir loft of the 15C. The 15C **Castello Feudale** of the Naselli family, at the entrance to the town, was altered in 1575 (closed).

## Environs of Comiso

**Chiaramonte Gulfi** was founded by Manfredi Chiaramonte for the inhabitants of Gulfi, a Saracenic town destroyed in 1299 by the Angevins. The town is famous for its salami and cured hams. It has numerous churches and fine views. Remains of the castle survive. At the foot of the hill, at Scornavacche, remains have been found of a Greek colony, with numerous potteries.

East of Chiaramonte Gulfi is the little town of **Giarratana**, rebuilt on lower ground after the earthquake of 1693. Its three Baroque churches stand close together. Nearby is **Monterosso Almo** (691m). In the large central piazza are the church of S. Giovanni Battista, attributed to Vincenzo Sinatra, and neo-classical palaces. Via Roma leads down to the Chiesa Madre, with a neo-Gothic façade, which contains a 12C stoup. Opposite is the church of S. Antonio Abate which has 16C paintings.

## Vittoria

Vittoria is a prosperous agricultural town (market garden produce and flowers), and centre of the wine trade (population 50,000). It was named after the daughter of the viceroy Marcantonio Colonna in 1607. It is built on a plain overlooking the Ippari, a little river sung by Pindar, bordered by pine forests. Much illegal new building has taken place here in recent years.

In the main square the elegant neo-classical **Teatro Comunale** (1869–77) stands next to the church of the **Madonna delle Grazie**, which has an attractive façade of 1754. The **Chiesa Madre**, with an unusual façade (18C–19C), contains paintings by the school of Pietro Novelli. There are number of Art Nouveau palaces in the town, and Palazzo Traina is in the Venetian Gothic style.

North-west of Vittoria is **Acate** (population 6700), known as Biscari up until 1938, surrounded by olives and vineyards. In the central piazza Libertà, surrounding a garden, is the huge 18C Castello dei Principi di Biscari and the Chiesa Madre, rebuilt in 1859. The *Palio di S. Vincenzo* is celebrated here after Easter.

# Donnafugata and Camarina

This section describes the southern part of the province of Ragusa, with the elaborate 19C castle and garden of Donnafugata and the excavations of the Greek city of Camarina. The itinerary also takes in the south-eastern coast of the island.

## ■ Practical information

*Information office*. APT Ragusa, ☎ 0932/621421.

*Hotels*
**Scoglitti (Vittoria)**. ★★★ *Agathae*, via Eugenio Montale, ☎ 0932/980730, fax 0932/871500.
**Marina di Ragusa**. ★★★ *Terraqua*, 35 via delle Sirene, ☎ 0932/615600 & fax 0932/615580.
*Campsites* by the sea:
**S. Croce Camerina**. ★★★ *Baia dei Coralli*, ☎ 0932/918192.
**Marina di Ragusa**. ★★★★ *Baia del Sole*, ☎ 0932/239844.

*Restaurants*
**Castello di Donnafugata**. **C** *Trattoria del Castello*.
**Scoglitti (Vittoria)**. **B** *Sakalleo*, 12 piazza Cavour.
**Marina di Ragusa**. Good fish restaurants (**B**) including *Alberto* and *Da Carmelo* and *Fumia*.
**Marina di Modica**. **A** *Le Alghe;* **B** *Serrauccelli*
**Pozzallo**. **B** *Porto Isola*, contrada Raganzino; *Trattoria dello Stadio*, 22 via dello Stadio.

## Castello di Donnafugata

A pretty byroad leads south-west from Ragusa through lovely countryside with numerous farms to the Castello di Donnafugata, acquired by the comune of Ragusa in 1982 and opened to the public in 1991 (09.00–12.30, except Mon). It has its own railway station (one or two trains a day stop here, from Ragusa in 20 min.); the Ragusa–Comiso line was diverted to the south in 1893 especially for the owner of the castle.

On the site of a 17C building, the present castle was constructed by the politician Baron Corrado Arezzo De Spuches (1824–95). It is a huge country villa, built in an eclectic style, with a Venetian Gothic loggia. Its delightful setting survives, with its farm surrounded by beautiful countryside. In the exotic **garden**, with splendid huge ficus trees, are a stone labyrinth entered over a miniature drawbridge guarded by a stone soldier, a coffee-house, a little neoclassical temple above a grotto and an amusing little chapel (no admission).

Nineteen of the 122 rooms of the **castle** are shown, most of them in poor repair, the most interesting of which is the *Salone degli Specchi*. The contents include some paintings of the Neapolitan school and a spinet. The *Donnafugata* described in Lampedusa's book *Il Gattopardo* was near S. Margherita di Belice (see p.202).

*The castle of Donnafugata*

## Camarina

The excavations of Camarina are signposted from the little town of **S. Croce Camerina**, which has some Art Nouveau palaces. Near the sea are market gardens (many covered with plastic greenhouses) and huge old carob trees. The road passes several enclosures with excavations (if closed, usually unlocked on request at the museum) before reaching the **Museo Regionale** (open 09.00–13.30, 15.00–18.30).

Camarina was a Siracusan colony, founded c 598 BC, which suffered alternate sack and repopulation by Gela, Siracusa and Carthage. It was finally destroyed by the Romans in 258 BC, but there are signs of occupation in the Republican and Imperial eras and of a late Arab Norman settlement.

The **museum** is housed in a restored 19C farmhouse built above the remains of a Temple of Athena. A room displays underwater finds made offshore where six shipwrecks have so far been identified. These include a Greek bronze helmet (4C BC), and objects from Punic and medieval boats. In 1991 a hoard of some 1000 bronze coins was found from the treasure chest of a Roman cargo ship which sank offshore in 275 AD.

Outside in the courtyard, beneath a porch are sandstone sarcophagi and a circular stone tomb. Beyond part of the cella wall of the temple can be seen. Another building contains a plan of the site and explanatory diagrams, and Bronze Age finds from the area. Material from the 6C BC includes a beautiful Corinthian black-figure vase with a hunting scene. In another building the foundations of the temple, dating from the early 5C BC, have been exposed (it was re-used as a church in the Byzantine era). A room on two floors has a splendid display of amphorae (mostly Corinthian and Carthaginian), c 1000 of which were found in the oldest necropolis of Camarina known as Rifriscolaro.

The various excavated areas, overlooking the sea, include fragments of the walls, part of the street layout and houses with three or four rooms opening on to a courtyard (built after 405 BC) and part of the agora. A necropolis has yielded a great number of tombs (mostly dating from the early 6C). Traces of the port have been found on the River Hipparis. There are plans to unite the entire area of excavations in one enclosure.

# The south coast between Camarina and Pozzallo

On the coast to the north of Camarina is **Scoglitti**, the resort of Vittoria (see p.247). It overlooks the Gulf of Gela, a long shallow bay whose beaches provided the chief landing-place for the American assault forces on 10 July 1943. The land, watered by several rivers, is now intensively cultivated with fields of cane, olives, oranges, market garden produce and vineyards.

**Caucana**, a large harbour town mentioned by Procopius, where the fleet of Belisarius put in on the way to Africa, has been excavated (signposted) near **Punta Secca**, a simple little resort on Capo Scalambri, with its lighthouse.

**Marina di Ragusa** is a resort which grew up in the 1950s, with palm trees along the sea front. A fast superstrada connects it to Ragusa (see p.235). Oil is drilled offshore and piped from here to Augusta (see p.287). There are good views ahead of the coastline. The reedy sand-dunes around the mouth of the Irminio river near Playa Grande are now part of a nature reserve. The landscape in the area is dominated by numerous plastic greenhouses.

**Donnalucata** is a pretty little resort (with an open fish market on the beach). Near Cava d'Aliga there is an unspoilt sandy bay. Inland the landscape is dotted with huge carob trees and hedges of prickly pear. Market garden produce is cultivated here together with olives and almonds. Among the characteristic low stone walls are some handsome country houses built of golden stone.

    **Marina di Modica** is a little resort known for its fish restaurants.

**Pozzallo** is a small port with a prominent square tower built in the 15C by the Cabrera (reconstructed after 1693), and a popular sandy beach. On the outskirts is an industrial plant. The beaches here are hidden behind tree-covered dunes where cane fences control the sand. To the east is Pachino on the south-eastern tip of the island in the province of Siracusa, described on p.281.

# *Siracusa*

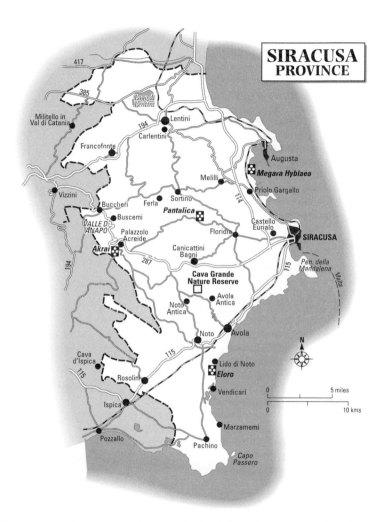

**SIRACUSA PROVINCE**

417

385

*Lago di Lentini*

Militello in
Val di Catania

Lentini

194

Carlentini

Francofonte

Augusta

Megara Hyblaea

Melilli

Priolo Gargallo

Vizzini

Buccheri   Ferla   Sortino

Buscemi

*Pantalica*

114

*VALLE D:
ANAPO*

Palazzolo
Acreide

Castello
Eurialo

Floridia

SIRACUSA

*Akrai*

287

Canicattini
Bagni

Pen. della
Maddalena

194

**Cava Grande
Nature Reserve**

115

Avola
Antica

Noto
Antica

N

Noto   Avola

115

Cava
d'Ispica

Lido di Noto
*Eloro*

Rosolini

Vendicari

0        5 miles

Ispica

0        10 kms

Marzamemi

Pozzallo

Pachino

*Capo
Passero*

Siracusa, usually known as Syracuse in English, is the successor (population 140,000), of the once magnificent *Syracusae*, which rivalled Athens as the largest and most beautiful city of the Greek world. It was one of the most delightful cities of Europe when the lovely promontory of Ortygia was its centre, but after World War II the unattractive modern town expanded in a disorderly way onto the mainland and became more and more detached from the district of Ortygia. At the same time the coastline was ruined by industrial plants and new buildings which polluted the sea to the north and south. Although Ortygia suffered from depopulation up until a few years ago, there are at last signs that this beautiful and peaceful area of the town, which has many monuments of great interest, is again becoming the heart of the city, and it now has numerous good restaurants and a lively atmosphere in the evenings. The principal ruins of the Greek city, including the famous theatre, survive in Neapolis, somewhat protected from the modern city by a park. The splendid archaeological collection was re-opened in a fine new building in 1988. Cicero noted that Siracusa knew no day without sun, and it has a mild marine climate throughout the year. See Siracusa maps 1 and 2 on pp.256 and 263.

## ■ Practical information

**Information offices**. APT Siracusa, 45 via S. Sebastiano (map 2; 2; ☎ 0931/ 67710); the information kiosk at the entrance to the archaeological zone of Neapolis is also usually open (☎ 0931/60510). Azienda Autonoma (map 1; 4), 33 via Maestranza, Ortygia. ☎ 0931/65201.

**Railway station** (map 2; 6). Services via Catania and Taormina to Messina (with some through trains to Rome); to Gela via Noto, Modica and Ragusa.

**Buses**. The city buses tend to be infrequent and only a few of them are useful to visitors. No. **1** from Riva della Posta (Ortygia) via corso Umberto, the railway station, corso Gelone, and viale Teracati for the main archaeological zone of Neapolis. No. **4** from Ortygia via corso Umberto and corso Gelone to viale Teocrito (for S. Giovanni and the Museo Archeologico). No. **2** from Riva della Posta (Ortygia) via corso Umberto and via Agatocle to via Montegrappa (for S. Lucia). No. **11** every 40 minutes from Riva della Posta (Ortygia) via corso Gelone to Castello Eurialo and Belvedere (and the youth hostel).

**Country buses** run by *AST* from piazza delle Poste (☎ 0931/462711) daily to Catania, to Palermo (in 3hr 15min.), and to Palazzolo Acreide. Services run by *SAIS* from piazza Marconi to Catania (in c 1hr), Catania airport, Palermo and Enna; to Noto (in c 1hr) and Pachino. Daily express service run by *SAIS* (terminal at 28 via Trieste, ☎ 0931/66710) for Rome via Catania and Messina (in 12hr 30 min.).

**Parking** is difficult. For the archaeologial zone, there is limited parking in viale Augusto (map 2; 2). For Ortygia, there is a small car-park in the middle of Ponte Umbertino (map 1;1), on the passeggio Adorno above the Foro Vittorio Emanuele II or on the lungomare di Levante (map 1; 4; car-park under construction).

**Maritime services**. Capitaneria di Porto, piazzale 4 Novembre. The main quay is at Molo Zanagora (map 1; 3) where trips round the harbour are organised.

### Hotels
★★★★ *Grand Hotel*, 12 viale Mazzini (map 1; 3), ☎ 0931/464600, fax 0931/464611, with restaurant.
★★★ *Domus Mariae* (map 1; 4), 76 via Vittorio Veneto, ☎ 0931/24854, fax. 0931/24859; *Grand Hotel Villa Politi* (map 2; 4), 2 via Politi (being restored), ☎ 0931/412121, fax 0931/36061.
★ *Gran Bretagna* (map 1; 3) , 21 via Savoia, ☎ 0931/68765.
*Agriturismo* accommodation outside the city: *Il Limoneto* (Adele Norcia),

☎ 0931/717352 (with restaurant), 9km from the centre, off the SS 124; and *Villa Lucia* (Lucia Palermo), ☎ 0931/721007, near the Porto Grande.
**Youth hostel**, 45 viale Epipoli, at Belvedere, 7km north-west of the town, ☎ 0931/711118.
**Campsites**. The nearest site is the ★ *Agriturist Rinaura*, 5km south of the town on SS 115 in località Rinaura, t 0931/721224. In summer ★★ sites are open on the coast to the south: *Fontane Bianche*, ☎ 0931/790333 and at Avola, *Sabbiadoro*, ☎ 0931/822415.

### Restaurants
**A** *Scalora*, 6 via Tripoli; *Grand Hotel*, 12 viale Mazzini (on the top floor).
**B** *Minosse*, via Mirabella; *Archimede*, via Mario Gemmellaro (also a pizzeria); *Don Camillo*, 96 via Maestranza; *Finanziera*, via Euripide. Outside Siracusa: *Il Limoneto* (*agriturismo* accommodation, see above).
**C** *Da Mariano*, 9 vicolo Zuccolà (off via Capodieci); *La Foglia*, 39 via Capodieci (vegetarian); *Orto di Epicuro*, largo della Gancia.
Snack bar (pub) open only in the evening: *Il Sedano Allegro*, via delle Vergini.
**Cafés and pasticcerie**. *Pasticceria Brancato*, 219 via Grotta Santa. In Ortygia: *Marciante*, 39 via Maestranze; *Caffè del Duomo*, piazza del Duomo; two bars in via Landolina; and *Bar Dock*, via dei Mille (beside Ponte Umbertino).
   Places to **picnic** on the sea front in Ortygia. In the environs, on the River Ciane or at the Castello Euriaio. Delicious snacks can be bought at the bakeries in Ortygia, or the rosticceria *Bianca* in via Roma (corner of via Minerva).

**Markets**. *La Fiera*, a large general market is held on the outskirts of the town in via Algeri (north of map: 4, near the sea) on Wednesdays. A daily market (exc Sun) is held in the morning in Ortygia in the streets near the Temple of Apollo (map 1; 3; around the former market building). There is another daily market (except Wed) at S. Panagia (north of map 2; 2).

**Theatres**. Biennial classical drama festival in the Greek Theatre (even years) in May and June. The Teatro Comunale has been closed for restoration for many years. Concerts are held in the auditorium of S. Pietro al Carmine.

**Sea bathing**. There is good swimming off the rocky coast of the peninsula of the Maddalena (or Plemmirio) south of the Porto Grande (especially at Murro di Porco and Terrauzza). There is a sandy beach (with a lido) at Arenella and Sparano. There are also good beaches further south near Noto at Calabernardo and Noto Marina.

**Annual festivals**. *S. Lucia*, 13 December, procession from the cathedral to the church of S. Lucia; *S. Lucia 'delle Quaglie'* is celebrated on the first and second Sundays in May (commemorating a miracle of the saint which took place here in 1642). A traditional procession takes place on 8 December (Immacolata).

**Topography**. Ancient Siracusa at the height of its power included five districts: Ortygia, the island now occupied by the older part of modern Siracusa, which lies between the Great Harbour, 640ha in area, extending south to the headland of Plemmyrium, and the Small Harbour on the north; **Achradina**, occupying the area immediately adjoining on the mainland, **Tyche**, called after a Temple of Fortune, to the north-east of Achradina; **Neapolis** (new town), to the north-west of Achradina; and **Epipolae** (upper district), stretching to the outer defences, inland on the north and west. Ortygia was a fortified citadel (linked to the mainland by a causeway c 550 BC); Achradina represented the commercial, maritime and administrative centre, and Neapolis the social centre; Tyche was a residential area, while Epipolae was sparsely populated. The ancient buildings were built of an oolitic limestone quarried from the latomiae, now covered with luxuriant gardens.

### History

This part of the coast of Sicily had a number of important Bronze Age sites. The Corinthian colony under Archias (734 BC), which drove out the Sicel (or perhaps Phoenician) inhabitants of Ortygia, increased so rapidly in power and wealth that, within a century of its foundation, it was able to found three sub-colonies at Akrai, Kasmenai and Camarina. Internal dissensions were put down by the firm government of Gelon, tyrant of Gela (c 485–478) who in 480, in alliance with Theron of Akragas, defeated the Carthaginians at Himera. Hieron I (478–c 467) helped the Cumaeans to overcome the Etruscan fleet (474) and welcomed to his court the poets Aeschylus, Pindar, Simonides and Bacchylides; but Thrasybulus, by misrule, brought about his downfall and the establishment of a republic (466).

The increasing power of the republic provoked the jealousy of Athens, which despatched a hostile expedition (415) under Alcibiades and Nicias. Alcibiades was soon returned to Athens under political arrest, but escaped and deserted to Sparta. The Athenian operations were almost successful, as they tried to enclose the city within a double wall and blockade it by sea. But a reinforcement from Sparta under Gylippus (despatched by the renegade Alcibiades), together with the courage of the Siracusans under Hermocrates and Athenagoras, saved the city. Athenian reinforcements under Demosthenes were themselves blockaded and their fleet destroyed in the Porto Grande. A frantic attempt to escape led in 413 to the final defeat of the Athenian army on the Assinaros, and those who survived were put to death in the latomiae.

In 405, Siracusa, again threatened by Carthage, was led by Dionysius the Elder, who built the Castello Eurialo, defeated Himilco (397), and made Siracusa the most powerful city of Sicily and sovereign of the Western Mediterranean. Under his less successful son Dionysius II (367–343) the Carthaginians again threatened the city, but it was saved from both tyrants and its enemies by the successful hero Timoleon of Corinth, who briefly re-established a democracy and died an ordinary citizen (336). Agathocles, a man of humble birth but strong personality, took power in 317, carried the war against Carthage into Africa (310), and left Siracusa once more in a position of hegemony. Pyrrhus, king of Epirus, liberated the city from a Carthaginian siege and, on his departure from Sicily, left the whole island clear for Hieron II (276–215), who wisely allied himself with Rome. His successor, Hieronymus, reversed this policy, and the city fell to Marcellus after a two-year siege (c 214–212). The task of the besiegers was aggravated by the ingenious inventions of Archimedes, who was accidentally killed during the sack of the town while quietly pursuing his studies. The Roman booty included innumerable works of art, which gave the first impetus to the appreciation of classical art in Rome, and, according to Cato, were the earliest factors in the decline of the true Roman spirit. Under Roman occupation Siracusa was governed both by Verres, who further despoiled it, and Cicero, the accuser of Verres. St Paul stayed at Siracusa for three days on his way from Malta to Rhegium in the Alexandrian ship *Castor and Pollux* (Acts xxviii, 11–12).

After the Roman period, the power of Siracusa declined rapidly, though the Emperor Constans II resided here in 662–68. It was destroyed by the Saracens in 878, and freed for a time by George Maniakes (1038–40), the general of Basil II of Byzantium, who drove the Saracens off the island. The temporary importance Siracusa regained in 1361–1536 as the quasi-independent seat of the Camera Regionale was not maintained and in 1837, having rebelled unsuccessfully against the Bourbons, it even ceded for a time to Noto its rights as a provincial capital. After the conquest of Libya the port expanded again, and during World War II it was a target first for the Allied air forces, and, after its capture on 10 July 1943, for German aircraft.

The most famous Siracusans of ancient times, besides Archimedes (287–212), are Theocritus (fl. 270 BC), the father of idyllic poetry, and Moschus (fl. 200 BC), another pastoral poet. Plato visited the city in c 397, and probably returned several years later on the invitation of Dionysius II to advise him on how to rule his kingdom. Corax of Siracusa and his pupil Tisias founded the Greek art of rhetoric in the 5C. The plot of Shakespeare's *Comedy of Errors* hinges upon the supposed enmity of Siracusa and Ephesus. Elio Vittorini (1908–66), the writer, was born in Siracusa.

*The bronze ram (3C BC) from the Castello Maniace, Siracusa (now in the Museo Archeologico, Palermo)*

## Ortygia

The beautiful promontory of Ortygia is joined to the mainland by two bridges. This charming old town, best explored on foot, has delightful streets of Baroque houses with pretty balconies and numerous trees. When the modern centre of Siracusa moved to the mainland, Ortygia faced serious problems of depopulation, but there have been signs in the last few years of a return here, and it is

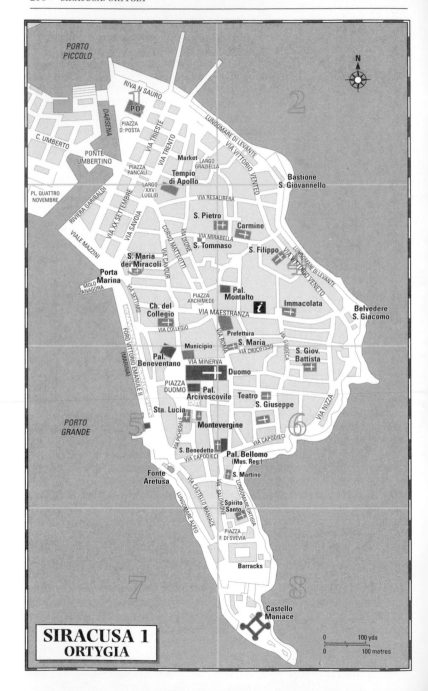

SIRACUSA 1
ORTYGIA

slowly becoming a fashionable place to live again. Numerous buildings are in the process of restoration and it has a great many characteristic restaurants and 'pubs' open at night for the younger generation. Several hotels have also been re-opened here in the last few years and it is the nicest place to stay in Siracusa.

From **Ponte Umbertino** (formerly called Ponte Nuovo) numerous small boats can be seen and part of the fishing fleet moored in the channel. The monumental **post office** by Francesco Fichera (1934) has an interesting interior with neo-classical and Art Nouveau decorations. Piazza Pancali with ficus trees leads to **largo XXV Luglio** (map 1; 3). The old covered **market-place**, a fine building of 1889–1900, is now used for exhibitions, and a daily market, where fresh fish is also sold, is held in the surrounding streets every morning. Nearby is a small area of interesting narrow streets once the old casbah district, centred on **largo della Graziella**.

The remains of the **Temple of Apollo** (map 1; 3) are in largo XXV Luglio, surrounded by lawns, papyrus plants and palm trees. It is the earliest peripteral Doric temple in Sicily, built of sandstone c 575 and attributed to the architect Epicles.

Some scholars identified it with the Artemision recorded by Cicero, but the inscription to Apollo cut in the steps of the stereobate seems conclusive. It was freed in 1938 from overlying structures, and two monolithic columns and part of the cella walls remain intact. Fragments of its polychrome terracotta cornice are preserved in the Museo Archeologico.

Via Savoia leads to the waterfront overlooking the Porto Grande, near the elaborate Camera di Commercio building. Here is the **Porta Marina**, a plain 15C gateway with a plaque in the Spanish Gothic style. The long promenade by the water's edge, planted with splendid ficus trees, called the **Foro Vittorio Emanuele II**, is known locally as the *Marina*. There is a lovely view across the harbour to the wooded shore on the headland of the ancient Plemmyrium. Within the gate to the left (in the street of the same name) is the attractive little church of **S. Maria dei Miracoli** (usually closed), with a fine doorway resting on little lions, with a sculptured lunette, and a worn tabernacle in the Gothic-Catalan style. The interior has a pretty 14C chancel, and a painting of *St Corrado the Hermit* attributed to Giovanni Maria Trevisano.

Ahead via Ruggero Settimo emerges on a terrace above the trees of the Marina, and via del Collegio leads away from the sea skirting the tall flank, with its Corinthian pilasters and overhanging cornice, of the **Chiesa del Collegio** (1635–87; being restored), whose incomplete façade recalls that of the Gesù in Rome. The interior contains altars from the former Jesuit college in Palermo, moved here in 1927–31. The church faces via Cavour, off which parallel streets run down towards the sea.

To the right is **piazza del Duomo**, where there are some fine Baroque buildings. To the left the **town hall** occupies the former Seminario (begun in 1628 by Giovanni Vermexio). Here a small **museum** (open 09.00–13.00, except Sun) in two rooms has an instructive display illustrating the building and history of Ionic temples, and fragments of unusual Ionic columns with a band at the base, which was supposedly intended to bear sculpted reliefs. The custodian also shows excavations beneath the building where foundations of an Ionic temple, probably dedicated to Artemis, were found in 1963. Begun c 530 BC, it was probably never completed and some of the stones were used in the construction of the Doric temple of Athene nearby (see below). Here, too, various levels of occupation may be seen, from a dwelling of the 8C BC (the oldest Greek structure in Siracusa) to a 17C funerary crypt.

Across via Minerva is the **Duomo** (map 1; 5,6; S. Maria del Piliero or delle Colonne; closed 12.00–16.00) reconstructed by Bishop Zosimus in the 7C from the ruins of the Doric **Temple of Athene**, erected in the 5C BC, probably to celebrate the victory of Himera. It became the cathedral of Siracusa later in the 7C, and was again rebuilt after the earthquake of 1693 when the Norman façade fell. In via Minerva 12 columns of the splendid temple, with their architrave and triglyphs, punctuate the medieval north wall of the church, their cornice replaced by battlements. The **façade** of the cathedral, a graceful Baroque composition erected in 1728–54, was designed by Andrea Palma. The marble statues of Sts Peter and Paul flanking the steps are the earliest known works of Ignazio Marabitti; he also sculpted the statues (1754) on the façade. The entrance is through an elaborate vestibule.

The **interior** was stripped of its Baroque decoration in 1909–27, reducing the **nave** arcades to the plain massive piers formed by opening eight arches in the side walls of the cella. The ceiling dates from 1518. The stained glass is by Eugenio Cisterna (1862–1933). The stoups are by Gaetano Puglisi (1802). On the west wall two columns from the opisthodomos of the cella are preserved, and 19 columns of the peristyle are incorporated in the aisles, those on the north side being engaged.

**South aisle**. First chapel (A): There is a font of antique marble with a Greek inscription (found in the catacombs of S. Giovanni), resting on seven miniature bronze lions (13C); on the wall are fragments of mosaics which survive from the earlier church. In the second chapel (B; 1711), closed by bronze gates, the work of Pietro Spagnuolo (1605), is a statue of *St Lucy* by Pietro Rizzo (1599; shown only on certain religious festivals and carried in procession on 13 December) and supported on a coffer attributed to Nibilio and Giuseppe Gagini, all of silver. The two marble medallions are attributed to Ignazio Marabitti. The third chapel (C), closed by wrought-iron gates (1811), was designed in 1650–53, probably by Giovanni Vermexio. The frescoes in the vault are by Agostino Scilla (1657). The altar frontal bears a beautiful relief of the *Last Supper* by Filippo della Valle (1762). Above is a ciborium by Luigi Vanvitelli (1752).

At the end of the aisle, in the **Cappella del Crocifisso (D)**, is a painting of *St Zosimus* attributed to Antonello da Messina, and a fine painting of the seated *St Marcian*, by an early 16C painter. In the sanctuary is a Byzantine Cross and 13 panels from a polyptych by the school of Antonello. Other works of art which are to be exhibited here include two paintings by Marco Costanzo (*St Jerome and the Annunciation*).

The bronze candelabra in the **chancel** (E) date from 1513. In the Byzantine apse (F) of the **north aisle** is a *Madonna della Neve* by Antonello Gagini.

The end of the pronaos wall of the temple with its column can be seen here. The noticeable irregularity of the pillars is due to an earthquake in 1542. In the north aisle (G) are three statues with fine bases: *St Lucy* by Antonello Gagini; *Madonna and Child* by Domenico Gagini; and *St Catherine of Alexandria* by the school of the Gagini.

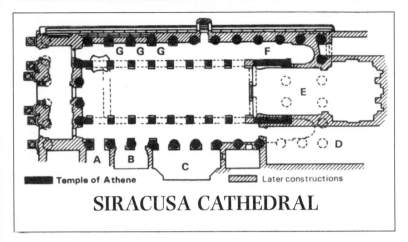

**SIRACUSA CATHEDRAL**

■■■ Temple of Athene    ▨▨▨ Later constructions

Excavations beneath the cathedral carried out by Paolo Orsi in 1912–17 revealed details of an archaic temple, demolished to make way for the later temple, and, at a lower level, pre-Greek huts of the 8C BC. Beside the steps of the Duomo more excavations (which may subsequently be covered over) are in progress, dating from the 10C–9C BC, with sporadic finds also from the Byzantine period up to the 18C.

Beyond the **Palazzo Arcivescovile** is the **Biblioteca Alagoniana** (not open regularly to the public; 13C Greek, Latin and Arabic manuscripts), which has a pretty hanging garden with palm trees behind a balustrade.

On the other side of the piazza, opposite the town hall, is **Palazzo Beneventano del Bosco**, a fine building by the local architect Luciano Alì (1778–88). It has a particularly attractive courtyard. Next to it is the curving pink façade of Palazzo Gaetani e Arezzo, and, beyond, the building of the 'Soprintendenza ai Beni Culturali e Ambientali' which used to house the Museo Archeologico (see below), and still contains a superb coin collection (not at present on view). At the end of the piazza, with a balcony on the corner, is Palazzo Impellizzeri and the church of **S. Lucia alla Badia** (closed), which has a lovely façade begun c 1695, probably by Luciano Caracciolo (the upper storey was added in the mid-18C). Just out of the piazza is the church of **Montevergine** (also closed) with a façade by Andrea Vermexio.

From the piazza via Picherale, passing the former Hotel des Etrangers (which may eventually be restored), which incorporates part of the medieval Casa Migliaccio, leads down to a charming terrace in a quiet spot on the waterfront surrounding the **Fonte Aretusa** (map 1; 5), which was one of the most famous fountains of the Hellenic world. The spring of the water nymph Arethusa was celebrated by Pindar and Virgil. It now flows into a pond (built in 1843), planted with papyrus and abounding in fish and inhabited by ducks, beside a splendid old ficus tree. The myth relates that when Arethusa was bathing in the River Alpheus near Olympia the river god fell in love with her. To escape from him she plunged into the Ionian sea and is supposed to have re-appeared here. Although the goddess Artemis transformed her into a spring, Alpheus pursued her and mingled the river water with that of the spring (in ancient times it was believed that the river in the Peloponnesus was connected across the sea with the fountain of Arethusa). A fresh-water spring, called the Occhio della Zillica, still wells up in the harbour. The spring of Arethusa diminished after the erection of the Spanish fortifications, and was mixed with salt water after an earthquake. Nelson claimed to have watered his fleet here before the battle of the Nile. There are walkways along the attractive sea front (closed to cars).

The end of the promontory, beyond piazza Federico di Svevia with its barracks, has been closed to the public. The **Castello Maniace** (map: 16), now belongs to the comune and is in need of restoration. Visitors are only admitted with special permission (although it is sometimes shown at 18 on Sunday; for information ask at the Soprintendenza ai Beni Culturali e Ambientali in piazza Duomo). The castle was built c 1239 by Frederick II but named after George Maniakes, supposed in error to be its founder. The keep, c 52 sq m, with cylindrical corner-towers, has lost a third of its original height. On either side of the imposing Gothic doorway are two consoles, formerly bearing splendid bronze rams, one of which is in the Museo Archeologico in Palermo. Overlooking the harbour are the remains of a large three-light window. Beneath the castle is the so-called Bagno della Regina (unlit staircase), an underground chamber of uncertain date, probably a reservoir.

Via Salomone and via S. Martino return past (right) the church of **S. Martino**, founded in the 6C, with a doorway of 1338. The interior (being restored), dating from Byzantine times, contains a fine triptych by a local 15C master.

At the end of the street (left) stands the church of **S. Benedetto** (usually locked), with a huge canvas by Mario Minniti, a local painter. Adjacent is **Palazzo Bellomo** (map 1; 6), where the **GALLERIA REGIONALE** is appropriately housed in a building combining elements of its Swabian construction (c 1234) with alterations of the 15C. The collection is well displayed and labelled. It is open daily 09.00–13.30, Sun & PH 09.00–12.30. The **vestibule** has a stellar vault with decoration recalling that of the Castello Maniace. A polychrome marble and glass inlaid panel with two lions and a palm tree dating from the 12C is displayed here. The staircase in the courtyard is a good example of the Catalan style; a second court with two palm trees, to the north, containing the offices, formed part of the Benedictine monastery and dates from 1365. The walls are covered with 15C–18C coats of arms.

The collection of **sculpture** is displayed on the **ground floor**. **Room 1** (right) contains sculptural fragments including Byzantine fragments (7C–9C). **Room 2** (right; sometimes closed), contains a fragment of a portal (11C–12C); a charming 14C altarpiece of the *Annunciation, Adoration of the Magi* and the *Crucifixion*, and an 11C stoup. In **room 3** (off the left side of the courtyard), is the tomb of Giovanni Cardinas, perhaps by Antonello Gagini; a monument to Eleonora Branciforte (1525) by Giovanni Battista Mazzola; the *Madonna of the Bullfinch*, attributed to Domenico Gagini; a carved tomb-slab of Giovanni Cabastida (d. 1472) and other interesting sculptures. In the loggia behind are two carriages (17C and 18C).

An attractive outside staircase leads up to the **first floor** and the **Pinacoteca**. **Room 5** (to the right) contains a beautiful *Annunciation* (1474) by Antonello da Messina, brought from Palazzolo Acreide, and transferred to canvas; Pere Serra (attrib.; 14C–15C), *Madonna and Child enthroned with saints*. In **room 6** (left) is the *Burial of St Lucy*, a superb work by Caravaggio (1608), from S. Lucia (see below); *Madonna* and three panels by Lazzaro Bastiani; Master of the Retable of St Lawrence (early 15C), *St Lawrence* and stories of his life. **Room 7** incorporates a pretty window of the palace. It displays 16C works including Marco Costanzo (attributed; c 1496), *Trinity and saints* and a tiny illuminated *Book of Hours* by the Flemish school. **Rooms 8** and **9** display more 16C works, including an album of drawings by Filippo Paladino (c 1544–1614) and an *Immacolata* by Guglielmo Borremans.

A charming collection of **Sicilian decorative arts** is displayed in **rooms 10–17**. This includes 18C statuettes, marble intarsia panels and ecclesiastical objects. In **room 10** is a silver navicella reliquary of St Orsola (1785). The other rooms contain Sicilian presepio figures including a crib by Emanuele Moscuzza (1806 -58), church vestments, 18C costumes, furniture and 19C terracotta figurines by Bongiovanni Vaccaro. Old plans of Siracusa are displayed in the last room.

Via Roma, with delightful overhanging balconies, leads away from the sea front (there is a pretty palace on the corner) north past the Teatro Comunale (which is being restored). On the corner of via Crocifisso is the church of **S. Maria della Concezione** (1651) which has a fine interior with a tiled floor. On the vault is a fresco by Sebastiano Lo Monaco, and the altarpieces on the north side and on the first south altar are by Onofrio Gabrielli. Its former monastery is being restored.

**Piazza Archimede** (map 1; 3) was laid out in 1872–78 in the centre of Ortygia, where there is a fountain by Giulio Moschetti. Palazzo Lanza is on the south side and the courtyard of the Banca d'Italia on the west side preserves medieval elements. Off the square, reached by via dei Montalto, is the façade of **Palazzo Montalto** in the Gothic Chiaramonte style of 1397; it has been propped up with concrete bastions. From the car-park behind, the shell of the building, with a fine loggia is visible.

The interesting via Maestranza leads east from the square towards the sea, past several good Baroque palaces and the church of the **Immacolata** (or S. Francesco) with an attractive little convex façade. It has a fine late 18C interior, with 12 small paintings of the apostles in the apse. On either side of the pretty Baroque east end two Gothic portals have been exposed. A number of narrow roads here called *Giudecca* recall the Jewish district of the city. At no. 110 via Maestranza is the 18C Palazzo Rizza. ViaVittorio Veneto, lined with smaller 17C–18C Spanish palaces continues left. It emerges on the sea by the church of **S. Filippo** (closed) next to the fine restored Gothic **Palazzo Interlandi**. There is a view from here of the Bastion of S. Giovannello.

Via Mirabella (with Palazzo Bongiovanni on the corner) leads away from the sea front past the Carmine which preserves part of its 14C structure. Opposite the former church of the Ritiro, with a façade attributed to Pompeo Picherali (c 1720), is being restored. Nearby is the church of S. Pietro (open only for concerts), a small aisled basilica founded in the 4C–5C, and altered in Byzantine times. It preserves a fine Gothic doorway. Via Vittorio Veneto ends near the post office and the bridges which lead back to the mainland.

## The mainland: Achradina and Tyche

The buildings of interest described below are widely scattered around the unattractive modern town; to cover the distances between them a bus is recommended where possible (listed above).

The part of the town on the mainland adjoining Ortygia corresponds to the ancient **Achradina**. From piazza Pancali buses run across the bridge along corso Umberto to the **Foro Siracusano** (map 2; 6), a huge and busy square with a Pantheon war memorial (1936), and fine trees. Here are some remains of the ancient Agora; recent excavations have revealed other parts of the Agora near corso Umberto and corso Gelone (where dwellings of the late 8C BC have also come to light, the earliest so far found in Siracusa).

From piazza Marconi, via Crispi forks right to the station, while via Elorina (left) leads to the so-called **Ginnasio Romano** (map 2; 6: usually closed), a complex ruin surrounded by lawns and palm trees. A portico surrounded on three sides, an altar, a temple and a small theatre. The portico on the north side, and part of the high temple podium remain. The orchestra of the theatre is now under water; a few of the lower steps of the cavea are visible. The buildings, all of Imperial date, probably formed part of a serapeum.

From the north-east corner of the Foro, the ugly viale Diaz leads towards borgo S. Lucia. On the left are two excavated sites, the first (straddled by a brown modern block of flats) includes a small bath-house of Byzantine date, possibly the **Baths of Daphne** in which the Emperor Constans II was assassinated in 668. The second, just beyond, behind railings marks the **Arsenale Antico**, where the foundations can be seen of the mechanism used by the Greeks to drag their ships into dry dock. In a simple house at no. 11 in via degli Orti di S. Giorgio, a figure of the Virgin is supposed to have wept in 1953 (plaque in piazza Euripide; the shrine of the *Madonna delle Lacrime* is described below). The long, narrow riviera Dionisio il Grande continues north, seaward of the railway, through the district of S. Lucia.

A long way north-east (bus no. 2) is the large piazza, surrounded by an avenue of ficus trees, in front of the church of **S. Lucia** (map 2; 3). The façade, which collapsed without warning in the 20C, has been faithfully reconstructed. It was begun in 1629 on a plan by Giovanni Vermexio, and completed in the 18C (perhaps by Rosario Gagliardi), on the spot where St Lucy (?281–304), patron saint of Siracusa, was martyred. The portal, the apses and the base of the campanile are Norman work and the rose window is of the 14C. Outside is the chapel of S. Sepolcro (see below), which has a pretty exterior.

Inside the church, in a chapel off the left side, are two ancient Crucifixes (one T-shaped). A superb painting of the *Burial of St Lucy* by Caravaggio, which belongs to the church, is displayed in the Museo Regionale (see above).

A tunnel from the church leads past the entrance to the **catacombs**, which are closed indefinitely. These are the oldest in Sicily and the most extensive in existence, after those in Rome. Caverns in the limestone existed here before the Christian era; there are Christian remains of the 2C and fragmentary Byzantine paintings. The tunnel emerges in S. Sepolcro (also closed for restoration), a domed octagonal chapel by Giovanni Vermexio, partly below ground. This was the burial-place of St Lucy and from here her body was taken to Constantinople in 1038 (the empty tomb remains behind the altar). The 17C statue of the saint

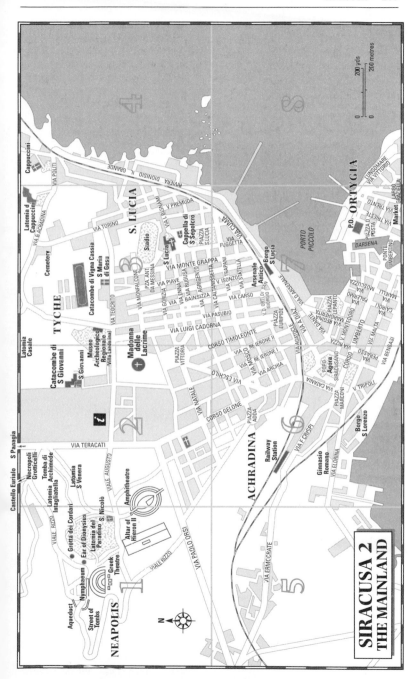

SIRACUSA 2
THE MAINLAND

NEAPOLIS

Aqueduct
Nymphaeum
Street of Tombs
Greek Theatre
Grotta dei Cordari
Ear of Dionysius
Latomia del Paradiso S. Nicolò
Altar of Hieron II
Amphitheatre

Castello Eurialo   S Panagia

Necropoli Grotticelli
Tomba di Archimede
Latomia Intagliatella
Latomia S Venera

VIALE RIZZO
VIALE AUGUSTO
VIALE RIZZO
VIA PAOLO ORSI

TYCHE

Latomia d Cappuccini
Cappuccini
VIA POLITI
VIA E ACRADINA
VIA A ACRADINA
Cemetery
Catacombe di Vigna Cassia
S Maria di Gesù
Latomia Casale
Museo Archeologico Regionale (Villa Landolina)
Catacombe di S Giovanni
S Giovanni
VIA TERACATI
VIA TEOCRITO
VIA TORINO

Madonna delle Lacrime

S. LUCIA

Stadio
S Lucia
Cappella di S Sepolcro
PIAZZA S LUCIA
VIA BIGNAMI
V PREMUDA
VIA FUGGETTA
PZA. ANT. DA MESSINA
VIA MONFALCONE
VIA MONTE GRAPPA
VIA GORIZIA
VIA PIAVE
VIA ENNA
VIA RAGUSA
VIA AGRIGENTO
VIA TRAPANI
VIA BAINSIZZA
VIA CATANISSETTA
VIA ISONZO
VIA STATELLA
VIA CARSO
VIA PASUBIO
VIA LUIGI CADORNA
CORSO TIMOLEONTE
PIAZZA VITTORIA
PIAZZA EURIPIDE
VIA MOSCO
VIA RE IERONE II
VIA RE IERONE I
VIA ARCHIA
VIA ESCHILO
CORSO GELONE
VIA NATALE
PIAZZA ADDA

ACHRADINA

Railway Station
Ginnasio Romano
VIA ELORINA
VIA F CRISPI
Borgo S Lorenzo
PIAZZA MARCONI
FORO Agorà SIRACUSANO
PIAZZA DELLA POSTA
CORSO UMBERTO
VIA CATANIA
VIA AGACIDE
VIA MALTA
VIA BENGASI
VIA TRIPOLI
V. TRIPOLI

Arsenale
Borgo S Lucia
C.D ORT. DI S GIORGIO
VIA DEI DI G
VIA AL DI AFALME
VIA DANTE
VIA REGINA MARGHERITA
PIAZZA LEPANTO
VIA MOSCUZZA
VIA PALERMO
VIA CAROU
VIA MAFIELI
VIA VITTORIO EMANUELE
VIA MONTEORO
PIAZZA GIOVANNI

ORTYGIA
P.O. ORTYGIA
DARSENA
PORTO PICCOLO
PONTE UMBERTINO
PIAZZA PANTE
PIAZZA TREPTE
Market
LARGO GRAZIELLA
LUNGOMARE VIA VITTORIO
VIA TRENTO
VIA TRIESTE

IL GRANDE
RIVIERA DIONISIO

VIA CALIMA

N

0   200 yds
0   200 metres

is by Tedeschi; a 16C silver statue by Pietro Rizzo is kept locked in the Duomo (but displayed here for eight days in December).

## Museo Archeologico Regionale Paolo Orsi

The area of the city immediately to the north corresponds to the ancient **Tyche**. About 500m north-west of S. Lucia, on viale Teocrito (bus no. 4 from Ortygia via corso Gelone), are the gardens of the **Villa Landolina**, in a small latomia (stone quarry), which surround the new building, opened in 1988, of the **Museo Archeologico Regionale Paolo Orsi** (map 2; 2, 3). It is one of the most interesting archaeological collections in Italy, especially representative of the eastern half of Sicily and one of the finest museums in Europe. The material from excavations made by Paolo Orsi, the director of the collection from 1895–1934, is outstanding. It is beautifully displayed in a handsome functional building by Franco Minissi. It was designed in 1967 and kept low in order to preserve the character of the gardens of the Villa Landolina, but since then it has been surrounded by ugly new buildings which tower above it (including the sanctuary of the Madonna delle Lacrime, see below). It is open 09.00–13.00, except Monday.

The garden, with splendid palm trees and some olives, pines, cypresses and orange trees, and some antique remains, was used as a Protestant cemetery. Among the 19C British and American tombstones (reached by the upper path which encircles the garden) is that of August von Platen (1796–1835), the German poet.

Beyond the entrance hall the centre of the building has an introductory display illustrating the history of the museum. The Museo Civico of Siracusa, which opened in 1811 under the supervision of Saverio Landolina, became a national museum in 1878. Paolo Orsi, the famous archaeologist, was director of the collection which was displayed in a building in piazza Duomo in Ortygia until it was moved here.

The display is divided into three sections: Prehistory (A), Greek colonies in Eastern Sicily (B), and sub-colonies and Hellenized centres (C). On the upper floor the Hellenistic and Roman material is eventually to be displayed.

### Section A: prehistory

An introductory display illustrates the geology of Sicily, and in particular the Monti Iblei region. The fauna of the island is described including dwarf elephants (with their fossil bones and two models). The strictly chronological display in this section begins with the **neolithic period**, represented by the **Stentinello** culture, an Agrarian civilisation, characterised by fortified villages and the use of impressed pottery. It is particularly well represented on the east side of the island around Etna and Siracusa. Four moated villages have been identified at Stentinello, Matrensa, Megara Hyblaea and Ognina. Plain, unglazed pottery with impressed decoration, and tools made out of ossidian from Lipari are exhibited from **case 14** onwards. **Cases 38–44** have Bronze Age finds from S. Ippolito (near Caltagirone), Valsavoia, Messina and Milazzo.

The display which relates to the important Bronze Age site of Castelluccio (between Noto Antica and Palazzolo Acreide), including brown painted pottery and interesting carved door slabs from rock-cut tombs begins with **case 45**. The pottery reveals trading links with Egypt and the Aegean, and shows Minoan-

Mycenaen influences. A ramp leads up to **cases 61–81** with Middle Bronze Age material from **Thapsos** on the Magnisi peninsula. The necropolis was excavated by Paolo Orsi, but the inhabited area (1500–900 BC) has only recently been excavated. Finds include imported pottery (from Mycenae, Cyprus and Malta) and a splendid display of large impasto storage jars. Material from other coastal settlements of the Thapsos culture are also exhibited.

**Cases 82–89** Material from **Pantalica**, the most important Late Bronze Age site in Sicily, which was naturally defended. This seems to have been inhabited by the Sicels who are thought to have migrated here from the Italian peninsula c 1300 BC, and whose culture remained virtually unchanged until the arrival of the Greeks. There is a splendid display of the characteristic red impasto vases, with shiny glaze, and numerous bronze artefacts. Other centres of this date are illustrated, including material from the necropolis of Madonna del Piano at Grammichele (the tombs have been reconstructed), and (**cases 112–125**) bronzes from Mendolito di Adrano. The finds from the Marcellino valley near Villasmundo (**cases 131–135**) include interesting pottery; the examples of imported Greek ware represent the earliest known examples (8C BC) so far found on the island. The last **cases (136 and 137)** in this section contain finds from Polizzello and **S. Angelo Muxaro**, with local and imported pottery.

### Section B: Greek colonisation
This period begins in the mid-8C when colonists from Corinth, Rhodes, Crete and the Chalcides arrive on the island. With the defeat of Carthage at Himera in 480 BC the Greek supremacy in the Mediterranean was established, and the great victory over Athens at Siracusa in 413 BC symbolised the importance Sicily attained in the Greek world. Finds are displayed from the earliest Greek colonies on the island: **Naxos**, founded c 734 BC (**cases 138–140**), Mylai, Zancle and Katane. The finds from **Lentini** include a fine kouros (late 6C BC). A large section is dedicated to **Megara Hyblaea**. The pottery includes imported Greek ware and local products. The highly interesting archaic sculpture includes a Greek marble statue (c 560–550 BC), thought to be a funerary monument, with an inscription on the leg to the physician Sambrotidas, son of Mandrokles, and a headless statue of a mother goddess suckling twins (mid-6C BC).

It is now necessary to go out into the central rotonda and re-enter the pavilion (still Section B) beside the splendid headless statue of **Venus Anadyomene**. This is an Imperial Roman adaption of a Hellenistic original of the 2C BC, remarkable for its anatomical perfection. It was found in Siracusa in 1804 by Saverio Landolina, and greatly admired by Guy de Maupassant when he visited Siracusa in 1885 (he left a vivid description of it). The section dedicated to **Siracusa** begins here. Finds from Ortygia are arranged topographically, and include material from recent excavations in piazza della Vittoria (**Case 226**), where a sanctuary of Demeter and Kore of the late 5C and early 4C BC has been found. There are numerous votive statuettes and a polychrome bust in terracotta (**Case 185**). Numerous pottery types are displayed. Finds from necropoli near Siracusa include those from contrada Fusco, with proto-Corinthian ware (725–700 BC) and a fine bronze statuette of a horse, in the geometric style (**Case 188**; late 8C BC). The Temples of Apollo and Athena are reconstructed in model form and terracotta fragments from them are exhibited. The frieze of seven lion-faced gargoyles comes from the Temple of Athena. The marble figure was part of its acroterion. The display of finds from sanctuaries outside the urban area include an archaic limestone head from Laganello (near the Ciane spring).

### Section C: sub-colonies and Hellenised centres

To enter section C: sub-colonies and Hellenised centres it is necessary to go out into the central rotonda and back towards the entrance. The display begins with material from **Eloro (case 226)**, including votive terracottas. Finds from **Akrai** include statues, one of a female deity, and another of a male figure enthroned (7C–6C BC). **Kasmenai** is represented by a high-relief in limestone of Kore holding a dove (570–560 BC), and ex-votos. The finds from **Camarina** include a horse and rider (6C BC), used as part of the decoration of the roof of a temple. A marble torso by a Greek artist (c 500 BC) and a terracotta goddess enthroned (late 6C BC) come from **Grammichele**. There are numerous examples of local pottery and imported Greek ware. A votive deposit found recently at **Francavilla di Sicilia** includes a remarkable series of reliefs in terracotta (470–460 BC). A lovely little clay miniature altar bears a relief of the 6C BC showing a lion attacking a bull **(case 280)** from Centuripe. The bronze statuette **(case 281)** known as the *Ephebus of Mendolito* from Adrano dates from c 460 BC.

The last section is devoted to Gela and Agrigento. Finds from **Gela** include architectural terracottas, cinerary urns and sarcophagi. The vases from Gela, include **(case 297)** an amphora with an onomachia, signed by Polygnotus (440 BC); part of a cup signed by Chachyrylion (520–510 BC); lekythoi depicting the struggle of Thetis and Peleus and of Aeneas with Anchises (black-figured; 6C); lekythos with a Nike, signed by Duris (470–460 BC); a bronze dish with relief of horses (from the necropolis at Gela, 7C BC). Also, a fragment by the 'Painter of Panaitos', and fine bronze kraters. The finds from **Agrigento** (mostly made by Paolo Orsi) include votive terracottas and busts of Demeter and Kore. Three rare wooden statuettes of archaic type dating from the late 7C BC, were found by a sacred spring at Palma di Montechiaro **(case 309)**.

To the south is the vast circular sanctuary of the **Madonnina delle Lacrime**, begun in 1970 to enshrine a miraculous sculpture of the *Madonna*. This mass-produced figure of the Virgin is supposed to have wept for five days in 1953 in a house in Achradina (see above). The church (by Michael Andrault and Pierre Parat), where the miraculous image is preserved, incorporates some remains of catacombs. The huge conical spire (90m high) towers above the high buildings of the city. In the crypt below, typical of pilgrimmage shrines, are numerous ex-votos. There are plans to clean up the exterior and create a park.

Adjoining it to the south, in **piazza della Vittoria**, extensive excavations begun in 1973 during the construction of the church of the Madonnina delle Lacrime, have revealed a group of Hellenistic and Roman houses, a Sanctuary of Demeter and Kore (late 5C BC or early 4C BC), and a monumental fountain of the 5C BC. These are visible from outside the fence. Several hundred terracotta votive statuettes found here are now exhibited in the Museo Archeologico Regionale (see above).

Off viale Teocrito, just to the west of the Museo Archeologico, via S. Giovanni leads right. Here, amidst modern buildings are the ruined CHURCH AND CATACOMBS OF S. GIOVANNI (map 2; 2; open 09.00–12.00, 14.00–17.00 or 18.00 except on

Tues). The façade is preceded by three arches constructed of medieval fragments. To the right is the entrance and ticket office, beyond which is the entrance (right) to the catacombs and (left) to the ruined church and crypt. Guides are available on request.

The **catacombs** were probably in use from the 3C to the end of the 6C. They are among the most interesting and extensive in Italy outside Rome: there are thousands of loculi. From the *decumanus maximus*, or principal gallery, adapted from a disused Greek aqueduct, smaller passages lead to five domed circular chapels, one with the rock-cut tombs of seven nuns, members of one of the first religious houses established after the persecutions in Siracusa, and one with a sarcophagus with a Greek inscription.

On the left of the entrance a delightful little garden with palms and cacti and flowering shrubs now occupies the ruins of the roofless **church** which was built into the western portion of an old basilica. Once the cathedral of Siracusa, it was reconstructed by the Normans in 1200, and reduced to ruins in 1673 by an earthquake. A fine 14C rose window survives, as well as its 7C apse.

Steps lead down to the **crypt**, in the form of a Greek cross, with three apses, which was the site of the martyrdom of St Marcian (c 254 AD): the sanctuary was transformed into a basilica at the end of the 6C or the beginning of the 7C and was probably destroyed by the Arabs in 878. The visible remains (which include faded frescoes) date from a Norman reconstruction. The fine Byzantine capitals, with symbols of the Evangelists, are thought to have been re-used from the earlier basilica. In one apse are traces of 4C and 5C frescoes from a hypogeum. The column against which the saint was martyred and his tomb, surrounded by some of the earliest catacombs, can be seen. An altar is said to mark the site of St Paul's preaching in Siracusa.

The **Latomia Casale** (no admission), a few minutes north of S. Giovanni, has luxuriant vegetation. To the east of Villa Landolina is the **Vigna Cassia** with 3C catacombs (also closed). To the north-east, near the sea (bus no. 4 from corso Umberto) are the **Latomia dei Cappuccini** (map 2; 3), to the right of the former Capuchin convent. These have been closed indefinitely because of landslides, but can be seen in part from the road outside. One of the most extensive of the ancient quarries (see below), they are now overgrown by luxuriant vegetation. Adjacent is the Villa Politi, the hotel where Churchill stayed on his holidays in Siracusa. From piazza dei Cappuccini, in front of the 17C church (recently restored), is a view of Ortygia.

Viale Teocrito leads west from the Museo Archeologico past a small private **Papyrus Museum** (no. 66). This illustrates how papyrus was produced in ancient times and preserves a collection of ancient papyruses, and artefacts from Egypt made out of papyrus. There is also a section dedicated to the production of papyrus (which still grows at the Fonte Ciane, see p.272) outside Siracusa. The most interesting place to see how paper is made from papyrus (by hand, without using glue) is at 15 via Capodieci (Flavia Massara) in Ortygia.

Viale Teocrito leads into Neapolis. At the end of viale Augusto (500m) is the entrance to the archaeological zone.

## Neapolis: the archaeological zone

Take **bus no. 1** from the town centre. map 2; 1 and 2 on p.263. Off viale Augusto the Casa del Quartiere Ellenistica, surrounded by a piece of wasteland, is used by the comune for small exhibitions. Beside a splendid giant magnolia tree and a group of huge ficus trees is the little church of **S. Nicolò** (map 2; 1). Here the funeral service of Jourdain, son of Count Roger, was held in 1093. It has been restored but is kept locked. Below it outside part of an aisled **piscina** can be seen, a reservoir used for flushing the amphitheatre (see below), to which it is connected by a channel.

A short road (closed to cars, but crowded with tourist booths), overlooking the Latomia del Paradiso on the right and the Altar of Hieron on the left, continues to the ticket office and entrance to the **archaeological area** (map 1; 1), enclosed in a public park. The monuments were pillaged in 1526 to provide stone for the Spanish defence works. A single entrance gives access to the **Latomia del Paradiso** and the **Greek Theatre** (map 1; 1: open daily 09.00– two hours before sunset).

A path leads through the beautiful garden with tropical fruit trees on the floor of the **Latomia del Paradiso**, the largest and most famous of the huge deep quarries excavated in ancient times, and since then one of the great sights of the city. They are now all covered with luxuriant vegetation because of their sheltered positions. Their extent testifies to the colossal amount of building stone used for the Greek city; following the northern limit of Achradina from here to the Cappuccini near the sea, they also served as a defensive barrier. They were used as prisons and according to Thucydides some 7000 Athenians were incarcerated here. Part of the rock face is now protected with scaffolding; this is the only latomia at present open to the public.

The right-hand path reached by steps from the ticket office ends at the **Orecchio di Dionisio** (ear of Dionysius), an S-shaped artificial cavern, 65m long, 5–11m wide, and 23m high, in section like a rough Gothic arch. Its name was given to it by Caravaggio in 1586, who referred only to the shape of the entrance; but, because of the amazing acoustic properties of the cavern, it has given rise to the legend that Dionysius used the place as a prison and, from a small fissure in the roof at the upper end, heard quite clearly the whispers of the captives at the lower end. It is now filled with the strange echoes of the song made by the doves who nest here. Once your eyes get accustomed to the dark you can walk to the far wall.

In the north-west wall of the latomia the **Grotta dei Cordari** is situated, named after the ropemakers who used to work here, a picturesque cavern supported by huge pillars and covered with maidenhair ferns and coloured lichens. Access has been prohibited since 1984 because of its perilous state (its partial disintegration has been caused by the infiltration of water, pollution from the air, and traffic vibrations).

Another path leads to the **Greek Theatre** (map 1; 1), the most celebrated of all the ruins of Siracusa, and one of the largest Greek theatres known (138m in diameter). Archaeological evidence confirms the existence on this spot of a wooden theatre as early as the 6C BC, and here it was that Epicharmus (c 540–450 BC) worked as a comic poet. In c 475 BC Hieron I constructed a small stone theatre with a trapezoidal orchestra, in which Aeschylus probably produced his Persae shortly afterwards. The semicircular form was adopted c 335 BC, when the theatre was enlarged under Timoleon by excavating deeper into the hillside; it was again enlarged under Hieron II (c 230 BC) by extending the cavea upward. Under the Romans the scena was altered and in the late Imperial period the orchestra was flooded for the production of naumachiae.

The peace of this wonderful monument is now spoiled by the noise of traffic: when performances are held during the classical drama festival here (in even years in May and June) the road below (viale Agnello) has to be closed.

The existing cavea, with 42 rows of seats in nine wedges, is almost entirely hewn out of the rock. This is now believed to represent Hieron II's auditorium of 59 rows, less the upward extension which has been quarried. The extent of Timoleon's theatre before Hieron's excavations is marked by the drainage trench at the sixth row, above the larger gangway. Around the gangway runs a very worn frieze bearing, in large Greek characters, the names of Hieron (II), Philistis (his queen), Nereis (queen of Gelon II), and Zeus Olympius, which served to distinguish the blocks of seats. The foundations of the scena remain, successive alterations making it difficult to identify their function, except for the deep recess for the curtain. The trapezoidal shape of the earlier theatre can clearly be seen as a deep trough in the orchestra. The view from the upper seats was especially good in the early morning (the hour at which Greek drama was performed). Above the theatre were two porticoes (to provide shelter from the weather).

Steps at the far end of the theatre, or a path near the entrance (which passes behind the little two-storeyed house perched on a rock) lead up to the rock wall behind the theatre. Here there are recesses for votive tablets and a grotto (or nymphaeum) in which the abundant aqueduct, which traverses Epipolae, ends. The view of the port is spoilt by the spire of the Madonna delle Lacrime. At the left-hand end of the wall the **Street of Tombs** (via dei Sepolcri) begins, rising in a curve 146m long. The wheel ruts in the limestone were made by carts in the 16C serving the mills which used to occupy the cavea of the theatre. The Byzantine tombs and Hellenistic niches in its rock walls have all been rifled. Its upper end (no admission) crosses the rock-hewn **Acquedotto Galermi**, where the water comes from the Bottiglieria spring, 20km away. Immediately to the west of the theatre a **Sanctuary of Apollo Temenites** has been discovered. A smaller, and probably older theatre lies to the south-west.

Across the road from the ticket office (see above) is a good view of the foundations of the huge **Altar of Hieron II**, hewn out of the rock. The public have not been admitted since 1983 for preservation reasons. The altar, built between 241 and 215 BC, was used for public sacrifices. It was 198m long and 22.8m wide (the largest altar known), and was destroyed by the Spaniards. To the west is an Augustan portico.

Near S. Nicolò (see above) is the entrance (somewhat hidden by souvenir stalls) to the **Amphitheatre** (admission with the same ticket as for the Latomia del Paradiso and the Greek Theatre) approached past stone sarcophagi from cemeteries in Siracusa and Megara Hyblaea. An imposing Roman building probably of the 1C AD, partly hollowed out of the hillside, in external dimensions (140 x 119m) the amphitheatre is only a little inferior to the one in Verona. The perfection of the masonry is probably attributable to a Siracusan architect. Beneath the high parapet encircling the arena runs a corridor with entrances for the gladiators and wild beasts; the marble blocks on the parapet have inscriptions recording the ownership of the seats. In the centre is a rectangular depression, probably for the machinery used in the spectacles. The original entrance was at the south end, outside which a large area has been exposed, including an enclosure thought to have been for the animals, and a large fountain. Also here, excavations have revealed an earlier roadway and the base of an Augustan arch.

There is a view of the archaeological park from **viale Rizzo** (map 2; 1) above: in the foreground is the theatre and the Latomia del Paradiso, beyond, the Altar of Hieron and the amphitheatre, and in the distance the Porto Grande and Ortygia (obscured by modern tower blocks).

A short way to the north of the church of S. Nicolò (see above) is the beautiful garden of the **Latomia di S. Venera** (closed indefinitely after landslides), in whose walls are niches for votive tablets. Above it are the **Necropoli delle Grotticelli**, a group of Hellenistic and Byzantine tombs, one of which, with a Doric pediment, is arbitrarily known as the 'Tomb of Archimedes'. The recent excavations here can be seen from the fence along the main road, via Teracati.

# Environs of Siracusa

The Castello Eurialo is one of the most important Greek military sites known and is still a very impressive sight. The romantic little Ciane spring where papyrus grows is a lovely peaceful spot.

## ■ Practical information

*Information office*. APT Siracusa, ☎ 0931/67710.

### Getting there
For the **Castello Eurialo**, take bus no. 11 (every 40min.) for Belvedere from Ortygia (riva della Posta) via corso Gelone.
The **road** (8km) leaves Siracusa north of the archaeological zone of Neapolis: at first, signposted to Catania, it leads through the ugly modern city. In the suburbs the road (signposted for Belvedere) forks left.

For the **Olympieion and River Ciane**. Bus no. 24 in summer from corso Gelone via via Elorina for the Olympieion. **Boat** for the source of the Ciane from the bridge over the Ciane on the main road (SS 115) organised by Signor Vella (☎ 0931/69076).

By **road** (c 3km) the Olympieion is reached from the Noto road which crosses first the Anapo and then the Ciane rivers. The Ciane is reached by a (signposted) road off the main road to Canicattini Bagni.

Both Castello Eurialo and the source of the River Ciane are lovely places to **picnic**.

## Castello Eurialo
The Castello Eurialo is at the western limit of the ancient city on the open, barren plateau of Epipolae. The approach road crosses the great **Wall of Dionysius** which defended the Epipolae ridge. Begun by Dionysius the Elder in 401 BC after

the Athenian siege, it was finished by 385; it had a length of 31km. Just before the main Belvedere road crosses the walls, a path (50m) leads right (near a house and water deposit) to the **Latomia del Filosofo** (or Bufalaro), so-called from the legend that Philoxenus of Cythera was confined here for expressing too candid an opinion of the verses of Dionysius. The quarry was probably used for the construction of the walls and the castle.

The main road winds up towards **Belvedere**; just after the signpost for the town, a narrow road (signposted) leads right for the **Castello Eurialo** (or *Euryelos*, meaning broad-based; open every day 09.00–one hour before sunset).

### History

Built on the highest point (172m) of the plateau of **Epipolae**, it commanded the western extremity of ancient Siracusa (as the view shows), at the most delicate point in the wall of Dionysius. These impressive ruins are the most complete and important Greek military work extant. The castle was begun by Dionysius the Elder in 402–397, and probably altered by Agathocles in 317. Archimedes is thought to have strengthened the defences in the late 3C, but his work was left unfinished because of the sack of the city in 212. A huge oil refinery now dominates the coast from Panagia to the Magnisi peninsula.

Three ditches precede the west front; the outermost (**A**) is near the custodian's house. Between the second (**B**) and the third (**D**) are the ruins of an outwork (**C**), whose walls have partly collapsed into the second ditch. On the left, steps lead down into the **innermost ditch** (**D**), the principal defence of the fortress which

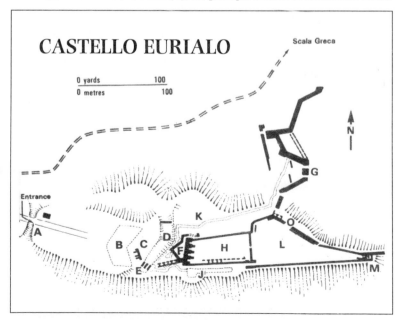

gave access to a labyrinth of casemates and passages to all parts of the fort. On the right the three piers of the drawbridge (E) are prominent. There are 11 entrances from this main ditch to the gallery parallel with it; from here three passages lead east; the longest, on the north (K; 174m long; closed since 1983) connects with the Epipolae Gateway (G; see below). The construction of the long gallery was accelerated by means of vertical shafts which were afterwards closed, but could be used as a means of escape in case the enemy occupied the castle.

The dark corridor to the south leads to a ditch (J) outside the south wall of the castle. At the end, steps (which were concealed from the enemy) lead up to the outer ward (L) of the **castle** proper, which consisted of a keep (H) with an irregular outer ward (L) on the east. In these parts of the castle the barracks and cisterns were located. On the north-east side of the outer ward was the main entrance (O) from the town; on the south-east rose a tower (M) connected with the south wall of Dionysius.

From here there is a good view of the **Epipolae gateway** (G) below, a 'pincer' type defence work on the spur of the north **wall of Dionysius** (described above), which can be seen, broken at intervals by towers and posterns, stretching towards the sea. It was united to the keep by a complicated system of underground works, notable for their ingenious provisions for shelter and defence.

An arch leads back towards the entrance into the **keep** (H), an irregular quadrilateral, which has five prominent square towers on the west side and a pointed bastion in front. The towers were probably battlemented and decorated with lions' head gargoyles. On the left a few steps lead down to a path which follows the edge of the site back to the entrance.

## The Olympieion and the River Ciane

The Olympieion or **Temple of Zeus** is on the right bank of the Ciane. On the approach its two columns can be seen among trees on the skyline of a low hill, the **Polichne**, a point of great strategic importance, invariably occupied by the besiegers of Siracusa. About 1km after the bridge over the Ciane, at the top of the rise, a road (right; signposted) leads in less than 1km (keep right) to the temple in a cypress grove. Built in the 6C, just after the Temple of Apollo (see section on Ortygia), it is the second oldest Doric peripteral temple in Sicily. It was hexastyle and peripteral with 42 monolithic columns, two of which remain standing on part of the stylobate. There is a view of the promontory of Ortygia.

The source of the **River Ciane** is reached by a turning off the Canicattini Bagni road. After crossing the Anapo, a byroad (left; signposted) leads for 3km through a fertile valley with orange and lemon groves and magnificent old olive trees (and some 'pill-box' defences left over from World War II). Beyond a tributary of the Ciane, a road (signposted) continues left to end in a grove of eucalyptus and cypress trees beside the romantic spring (the ancient 'Cyane'), overgrown with reeds and thick clumps of Egyptian papyrus. This plant grows in no other part of Europe, and is traditionally said to have found its way here as a gift from Ptolemy Philadelphus. In fact, it was probably introduced at the time of Hieron II, or later, by the Arabs. The name of the spring (in Greek, blue) describes the azure colour of its waters, but a myth relates how the nymph Cyane, who tried to prevent Pluto from carrying off Persephone, was changed into a spring and condemned to weep forever.

Beyond the bridge a path follows a fence along the reeds to the large pool, inhabited by numerous waterfowl. The spring called **Testa della Pisma**, and the smaller **Pismotta** spring, both also have pools planted with papyrus.

## Plemmyrium and the coast to the south

The ancient district of Plemmyrium was on the headland opposite Ortygia on the great harbour of Siracusa. Here was the headquarters of Nicias after his defeat on Epipolae by Gylippus, in the famous battle between Athens and Siracusa in 415 BC. It is now called the **Pennisola della Maddalena**, and has plantations of citrus fruits. There is good swimming off its rocky coast.

Neolithic settlements have been found further south on the offshore islet of **Ognina** where Neolithic and Early Bronze Age pottery finds suggest that it may have been a Maltese trading outpost. There is a pretty little port here and sea bathing at Capo Sparano, just to the north.

The bay to the south, the **Fontane Bianche**, used to be one of the best bathing beaches on the island; it has now been spoilt by illegal new building work. Nearby is **Cassibile**, where a huge Bronze Age necropolis and hut village yielded extremely interesting finds, now in the archaeological museum in Siracusa. In an olive grove near here on the afternoon of 3 September 1943, Generals Bedell Smith and Castellano signed the military terms of surrender to the Allies of the Italian army. Several 'pill-boxes' survive along the road and on the bed of the river. At the mouth of the Cassibile, the ancient *Kakyparis*, the Athenian general Demosthenes, covering the rear of Nicias' forces during the retreat from Siracusa, was cut off and forced to surrender (see above). There are wonderful old olive trees, carobs, almonds and citrus fruit plantations in this area.

# Noto

Noto (population 21,700) is the most charming and best preserved of the 18C Baroque cities of Sicily. It was built after the earthquake of 1693 when the former town of Noto (now Noto Antica, see below, 14km away) was abandoned. It is an excellent example of 18C town planning, and its architecture is exceptionally homogeneous. Many of the fine buildings, with theatrical exteriors, including numerous churches and convents, were built between 1715 and 1780 by Rosario Gagliardi, his pupil Vincenzo Sinatra and Paolo Labisi. The fragile local white tufa has been burnt to a golden brown by the sun. After years of neglect by the local administration many of its major buildings, threatened with collapse, are now being slowly restored (although part of the dome of the cathedral crashed to the ground in 1996, when the building was empty, and it still remains a broken shell). Noto lends itself to exploration by foot.

## ■ Practical information

*Information office* of the APT of Siracusa, piazza XVI Maggio (☎ 0931/573779).

### Getting there
**Railway station**, 1.5km south of the public gardens, on the Siracusa–Gela line (trains from Siracusa in c 35min.)

**Buses** (*AST* and *SAIS*) from Siracusa to largo Pantheon c every hour in 45 min. Services run by *Caruso* from Noto to Noto Marina on the coast.
**Parking** outside Porta Reale. There is limited space in piazza XVI Maggio (except on Sun & PH when the corso is closed to traffic).

### Hotels
★ *Stella*, 44 via Maiore (corner of via Napoli), ☎ 0931/835695.
Rooms to let: *L'Arca* (Antonio Bongiorno), via Rocco Pirri. About 500m outside the town on the road to Noto Antica: *Al Canisello* (Valeria Mazzone), 1 via Cesare Pavese, ☎ 0931/835793, with the possibility of camping also; and *Ambra* (Rosaria Currenti), 14 via Giantommaso, ☎ 0931/835554.

### Restaurants
C *Il Barocco*, via Cavour; *Trattoria del Carmine*, via Ducezio; *Il Giglio*, piazza Municipio; *Rosso e Nero*, Porta Reale.
**Cafés and pasticcerie**. *Corrado Costanzo*, 7/9 via Silvio Spaventa; *Mandolfiore*, 2 via Ducezio; *Il Caffè Sicilia*, corso Vittorio Emanuele; *La Vecchia Fontana*, piazza Immacolata.
Places to **picnic** in the public gardens outside Porta Reale. Snacks (*focacce*) can be bought at the Trattoria del Carmine in via Ducezio and Trattoria Piero in piazza XVI Maggio.

**Concerts** are given in several churches in the town, including the courtyard of the convent of S. Domenico. The International Classical Music Festival is held here in July and August. Theatre and concert seasons at the Teatro Comunale (Jan–June).

**Annual festivals**. Festivities in honour of *S. Corrado* on 19 February, the last Sunday in August, and the first Sunday in September. The procession of the *S. Spina* takes place on Good Friday, and other religious ceremonies during Easter week. The *Infiorata* is held on the third Sunday in May, when via Nicolaci is carpeted with fresh flowers.

### History
After the earthquake of 1693, which severely damaged Noto Antica, this new site was chosen in 1702 by a majority of the inhabitants. It is known that Giuseppe Lanza (Duke of Camastra), Giuseppe Asmundo, Giovanni Battista Landolina, and the Jesuit Angelo Italia, all played a part in planning the new city. In 1837–65 Noto displaced Siracusa as provincial capital. Since 1986 many buildings in the town have been propped up by scaffolding, and closed. The funds which have been allotted to the city by the government, the Region and UNESCO (the town was declared part of the UNESCO heritage in 1996), are at last being used to repair the easily eroded tufa and to carry out urgent restoration work.

At the east end of the town are the **public gardens** where the thick evergreen ficus trees form an impenetrable roof over the road. **Porta Reale**, erected by Orazio Angelini, for the visit of Ferdinand II in 1838, leads into the **corso** from which the town rises to the right and falls away to the left; by skilful use of open spaces and monumental flights of steps a straight and level street, 1km long, has been given a lively skyline and a succession of glimpses of the countryside. Many of the pretty little side streets at the beginning of the corso on the left are still cobbled. On the right a grandiose flight of steps leads up to **S. Francesco dell' Immacolata** by Vincenzo Sinatra, which has a good façade and a pretty white stucco interior (open 09.30–12.30, 15.00 or 16.00–18.00 or 19.00). The huge convent of **S. Salvatore** (now a seminary) faces via Zanardelli with a fine long 18C façade and attractive tower (possibly designed by Rosario Gagliardi).

S. Francesco, Noto

Opposite is the church of **S. Chiara** (usually open on Sunday morning) with an oval interior by Gagliardi (1730–48), and a *Madonna* by Antonello Gagini. The **Museo Civico**, which has been closed for many years, is to be arranged in part of the convent. The contents include Bronze Age pottery from Canicattini, Castelluccio and Licodia Eubea, and Bronze Age weapons (including volcanic glass, used as a fine-cutting instrument) from Castelluccio and Noto. The finds from Eloro include the reconstruction of part of a Sanctuary of Demeter (in use from the 6C–3C BC), with votive statuettes attached to the outside wall by a coat of stucco. There is also a collection of Roman and Byzantine coins. Material from Noto Antica includes ceramics, sculptural fragments, and the damaged sarcophagus of Niccolò Speciale (d. 1444) by the workshop of Andrea di Francesco Guardi (also attributed to Antonio Gagini). A bronze panther dates from the Norman period, and the head of a saint in hardwood from the 15C. There is a plan of the city made in 1783. Modern works include sculptures by Giuseppe Pirrone.

Beyond, in the centre of the city, the huge façade of the cathedral above a fine staircase, looks down on **piazza Municipio** with its symmetrical horseshoe hedges of ficus. The **cathedral** (S. Nicolò) was built in several stages throughout the 18C, probably with the intervention of Gagliardi and Vincenzo Sinatra. Part of the dome, which was rebuilt in the 19C, collapsed in 1996 and has not yet been repaired. The building has been closed ever since.

Beside the Duomo is the Bishop's Palace and **Palazzo Landolina**, once the residence of this important local family. Beyond the Bishop's Palace is the basilica of **S. Salvatore** (closed for restoration). The façade was designed by Andrea Gigante of Trapani and probably built by Antonio Mazza (1791). The pretty polychrome interior, with a vault painting by Mazza, contains 18C paintings by Giuseppe Velasquez, and an organ of 1778 by Donato del Piano.

On the south side of the piazza, facing the Duomo, is **Palazzo Ducezio** (the town hall; being restored), a splendid building begun as the Casa Senatorio in

1742 by Vincenzo Sinatra. The continuous raised classical portico is beautifully proportioned. The upper floor was added in 1951. Inside is a vault painting by Antonio Mazza. On the other side of the corso there is a view up via Corrado Nicolaci to the façade of the church of Montevergine (described below). In the corso is the **Chiesa del Collegio** (S. Carlo al Corso), with a tower façade (being restored) probably by Gagliardi (1730; restored by Vincenzo Sinatra in 1776). It has a pretty white stucco interior (recently restored and open 09.30–12.30, 15.00 or 16.00–18.00 or 19.00).

Beyond, the long façade of the former **Collegio dei Gesuiti** (now a school) stretches as far as piazza S. Domenico (or piazza XVI Maggio), with the **Teatro Vittorio Emanuele** (1851; recently restored and open 09.00–12.00, 16.00–18.00). Here, in a delightful little garden with tall palms and monkey-puzzle trees, the fountain is surmounted with an 18C statue of Hercules. In the pavilion behind is the APT information office. Above to the left is the charming convex façade (being restored) of **S. Domenico** (1737–56) by Gagliardi, perhaps his most successful building in the town. In via Bovio above is the former convent of the **Casa dei Crociferi** by Paolo Labisi (1750), finished by Vincenzo Sinatra. It has been restored as law courts.

From piazza S. Domenico (piazza XVI Maggio) the corso continues to **Palazzo Zappata** (covered for restoration). To the left via Ruggero Settimo leads past a small palace (recently restored) to the pretty **via Ducezio** which runs parallel to the corso to the south. It is closed at the west end by the fine concave Baroque façade (with Rococo details) of **S. Maria del Carmine** (open 09.30–12.30, 15.00 or 16.00–18.00 or 19.00), a late work by Gagliardi with a charming interior. At the other end of the street, on via Viceré Speciale, is the church of **S. Maria dell'Arco** (1730), also by Gagliardi with an elegant portal, and a decorative stucco interior (open 09.30–12.30, 15.00 or 16.00–18.00 or 19.00) with two stoups from Noto Antica. Nearby is an interesting Art Nouveau house. Via Aurispa, parallel to via Ducezio on the south, is another pretty street with simpler buildings and the church of **S. Maria Rotonda**, which has a Baroque façade.

From S. Maria dell'Arco via Viceré Speciale, beautifully paved between two rows of steps, mounts to the splendid rear façade of the town hall (see above). To the left is **Palazzo Rau della Ferla**, which has a pretty façade and a courtyard covered with jasmine. Part of the palace houses the most noted *pasticceria* in the town. At the end the impressive wall of the Collegio dei Gesuiti can be seen, which a road now follows uphill back to the corso, straight across which via Corrado Nicolaci continues uphill towards the church of Montevergine. Via Nicolaci is overlooked by the delightful Baroque balconies of the huge **Palazzo Nicolaci** (Villadorata; 1737–65), once the residence of Don Giacomo Nicolaci, a patron of the arts. He donated part of his huge library to the important Biblioteca Comunale, which, since 1982, has been housed in a wing of the palace. There are plans to open the palace to the public when it has been restored. The façade of **Montevergine** is attributed to Vincenzo Sinatra. It contains paintings by Costantino Carasi.

The church is on the handsome **via Cavour**, another attractive 18C street, with views of the countryside at either end. It leads west past **Palazzo Battaglia** (1735), on the corner of via Rocco Pirri, in which a charming little market-

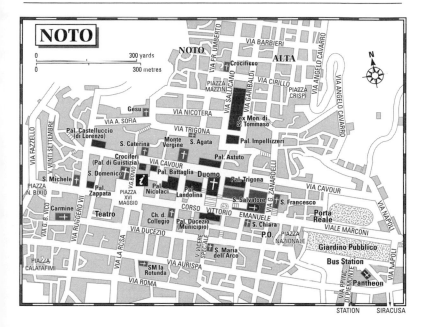

place, with a loggia supported on iron pillars surrounding a fountain, has been restored. Via Cavour continues west past the former **Oratorio di S. Filippo Neri** (1750) and the church of **S. Caterina** (attached to the oratory, on via Fratelli Ragusa). Beyond, near the end of via Cavour, is the large neo-classical **Palazzo di Lorenzo (Castelluccio)** owned by the Knights of Malta. Opposite is a basket-maker's workshop.

Via Cavour returns to Montevergine, to the right of which is the beautiful **Palazzo Astuto** (late 18C; possibly the work of Vincenzo Sinatra or Paolo Labisi) which once housed the Museo Astuziano, a very fine private museum dispersed in the mid-19C. Further on, on the right, is the fine **Palazzo Trigona** (1781; restored by Bernardo Labisi), part of it renovated as a congress centre. The Sala Gagliardi here has been restored as an exhibition room and as an auditorium. At the far end of the façade the street has a view downhill of the side façade of S. Salvatore.

Via Mariannina Coffa (partly stepped) leads uphill to the upper part of the town known as **Noto Alta**. This simpler district was laid out on a different plan and orientation from the lower monumental district with its four long, straight, parallel streets running from east to west. There is a view of the battlemented former Convento di S. Antonio di Padova on the top of the hill. The road continues left past **Palazzo Impellizeri S. Giacomo** (1752) with a balcony along the whole length of the first floor. Part of the palace is now used to house the state archives. Here can be seen the corner and bell-tower of the former **Ospedale Trigona** (being restored). Via Trigona leads past the former convent to the deconsecrated church of **S. Agata** (closed), attributed to Gagliardi and finished by Paolo Labisi. It contains stuccoes by Labisi and paintings by Costantino Carasi. Opposite is **S. Annunziata e Badia**, another church dating from 1720 and currently being restored. Just beyond, approached by a double staircase, is **S. Maria del Gesù**, next to its convent.

Via Trigona leads back to the huge former **Monastero di S. Tommaso** (1720), with an attractive façade and double staircase. It is now used as a prison, and the prison buildings (being restored) extend as far as piazza Mazzini, on the summit of the hill, at the centre of Noto Alta. Here is the church of the **Crocifisso** (open 09.30–12.30, 15.00 or 16.00–18.00 or 19.00; closed Mon), by Gagliardi (1715), which contains a number of works of art from Noto Antica, including (in the right transept) a beautiful statue of the *Madonna della Neve* signed by Francesco Laurana (1471), and two huge Romanesque lions. The Cappella Landolina (recently restored), contains paintings by the school of Costantino Carasi. On the high altar is an 18C reliquary designed by Gagliardi which contains part of a venerated Crucifix from Noto Antica. A relic of the Holy Thorn also belongs to the church (only shown on Good Friday).

The lower town is reached from here by returning down the street to via Cavour and taking the stepped via Gioberti down past S. Salvatore to the corso.

# Environs of Noto

The little ruined town of Noto Antica, destroyed by earthquake in 1693, is a very unusual sight in lovely countryside. The oasis of Vendicari is one of the most beautiful areas left on the coast of the island. The Cava Grande del Cassibile is a well-preserved river gorge with lovely vegetation. Eloro is an interesting Greek site in a fine position on the sea.

## ■ Practical information

*Information offices*. APT Siracusa, ☎ 0931/67710 and APT information office in Noto, ☎ 0931/573779.

There is no **public transport** to most of the places described below, and the **railway line** from Noto to Pachino has been substituted by a bus service (operated by *SAIS*).

### Hotels
★★★ hotels on the coast at Noto Marina, include *Helios*, località Pizzuta, ☎ 0931/812366.
*Agriturismo* accommodation near **Castelluccio**: *Il Carrubo*, contrada Castelluccio, and at **Vendicari**: *Il Roveto* (Giuseppe Loreto), ☎ 0931/66024.
At **Portopalo:** ★★ hotel: *Vittorio*, ☎ 0931/842181.
### Campsites at Portopalo
★★★ *Capo Passero*, località Vigne Vecchie, ☎ 0931/842333. ★★ *Captain*, località Isola delle Correnti, ☎ 0931/842595.

### Restaurant. Near **S. Corrado di Fuori**, *Il Falco* (**C**).

## Noto Antica

The road from Noto to Noto Antica (12km, signposted for Palazzolo Acreide) leads uphill to the left from the public gardens. It traverses Noto Alta with pleasant streets of low Art Nouveau houses.

The little town of **S. Corrado di Fuori** has more pretty early 20C houses. Outside the town, in the Valle dei Miracoli with luxuriant vegetation, is the hermitage of S. Corrado Confalonieri who lived here in the 14C. The 18C sanctuary contains a painting of the saint by Sebastiano Conca. The road continues across a fine upland plain with old olive trees. It then descends to cross a bridge decorated with four obelisks.

The byroad (left) for Noto Antica is lined with early 20C Stations of the Cross on the approach to the large sanctuary of **S. Maria della Scala** (open 09.30–12.30, 15.00 or 16.00–18.00 or 19.00), next to a seminary, which has a pleasant façade (1708) with three statues and a balcony.

The road now descends to cross another bridge in a ravine before reaching **Noto Antica**, abandoned since the earthquake of 1693 and now utterly deserted. The scant ruins, mostly reduced to rubble, are almost totally overgrown and provide an eery romantic sight. This was a settlement that long antedates its legendary foundation by the Sicel chief Ducetius in 448 BC, and was the only Sicilian town that resisted the depredations of Verres. The last stronghold of Muslim Sicily, it gave its name to the Val di Noto, one of the three areas into which the Arabs divided up the island. It fell to the Normans in 1091. A flourishing medieval city, it was the birthplace of Matteo Carnelivari, the architect. After the terrible earthquake of 1693 the inhabitants decided to move their city to its present site (see p.274).

The entrance is through the monumental **Porta della Montagna** (restored) with remains of the high walls on either side. A rough road continues through the site of the town for c 2km. It leads up past a round tower and along the ridge of the hill. The conspicuous wall on the left (the highest one to survive) belonged to the Chiesa Madre. After 1km, beside a little monument, the right fork continues (and the road deteriorates) to end beside the **Eremo della Madonna**, a little deserted chapel, with a good view of the surrounding countryside. There are usually custodians who act as guides here in the morning.

Some distance to the west is the remote prehistoric village of **Castelluccio** (c 18C–14C BC), which has given its name to the most important Early Bronze Age culture of south-east Sicily. The rock-tombs had carved portal slabs (now in the archaeological museum at Siracusa).

## Cava Grande del Cassibile

The **Cava Grande**, on the banks of the River Cassibile, where huge plane trees grow, was declared a nature reserve in 1984. There is spectacular scenery in this gorge some 250m deep and nearly 10km long. Thousands of tombs (11C–9C BC) have been identified here (finds in the archaeological museum in Siracusa). The easiest approach to the gorge is via Villa Vela, a pleasant little village with some Art Nouveau villas on the road between Noto and Palazzolo Acreide. It can also be approached on foot, from the belvedere at the end of the very windy road to **Avola Antica**, destroyed in 1693.

## Avola

Avola (population 32,100) is a prosperous agricultural town and one of the most important centres of almond culture in Italy. It has expanded in a disorderly way around its interesting centre which retains the hexagonal plan on which it was built after 1693 by Fra Angelo Italia. In the centre is piazza Umberto I where the **Chiesa Madre** (S. Nicolò) is situated, which contains an 18C organ by Donato del Piano. Four smaller piazze open off the outer edge of the hexagon, one of which, piazza Vittorio Veneto, has a fountain with three amusing 20C lions by Gaetano Vinci. The 18C churches include **S. Antonio Abate** and **S. Annunziata** (with a façade by Giuseppe Alessi) and there are a number of good Art Nouveau buildings. The church of the **Cappuccini**, outside the hexagonal centre, in piazza Francesco Crispi, has a good 17C altarpiece.

## The coast from Noto Marina to Porto Palo

Noto Marina (or **Lido di Noto**) is a little resort on the sea, which with **Calabernardo** has some of the best beaches on the east coast of the island. The beautiful landscape here has huge old olive trees, carobs, almonds and citrus fruit trees. The Asinaro river, which reaches the sea near Calabernardo, is the ancient Assinaros, where Nicias' retreating Greeks, trying to reach Heloros, were overtaken while drinking at the river and killed after the great battle between Siracusa and Athens in 415 BC.

## Eloro

Near the mouth of the Tellaro river, on a low hill, in lovely countryside, are the remains of **Eloro** (*Helorus;* open daily 08.00–14.00), one of the first cities to be founded by Siracusa, probably at the beginning of the 7C BC. The excavations are in a lovely deserted position by the sea and there is a good view inland of the Pizzuta column (see below), with Noto beyond green rolling hills. The view along the unspoilt coastline extends to the southern tip of the island.

The road passes the basement of a temple perhaps dedicated to Asklepios. To the right of the road, in a large fenced enclosure sloping down to the canal, are a Sanctuary of Demeter with a larger temple and a monumental stoa. A theatre has been partially excavated nearby. To the left, beyond the custodian's house, is another enclosure of recent excavations. An ancient road continues to the walls and north gate. Outside the walls a Hellenic Sanctuary of Demeter was found; it has been reconstructed in the Noto Museum.

The so-called **Pizzuta**, a column over 10m high, can be reached by returning to the approach road beyond the railway bridge. From the road for the tourist village of Eloro, a rough road leads right through an almond and olive grove past the column. This was once thought to be a monument to the Siracusan victory (see above), but it is in fact a funerary memorial of the 3C BC.

## Villa del Tellaro

From the main road, just by the bridge across the Tellaro, a road leads inland towards a farmhouse (conspicuous to the right of the road) in the locality of Caddeddi, less than 1km from the main road. Beneath the farmhouse a Roman villa of the second half of the 4C AD, known as the **Villa del Tellaro**, was discovered in 1972. The farmer shows some of the splendid polychrome mosaics, reminiscent of those at Piazza Armerina, but the best ones have been removed for restoration and will probably not return here but will be exhibited in the museum in Noto. There is a distant view of Noto lying in the hills.

## Vendicari

The stretch of coast south of the River Tellaro is now the remarkable nature reserve of Vendicari (open daily 09.00–dusk; for information ☎ 0931/462452). This beautiful marshy area of the coast (1500ha; closed to cars), of the greatest interest for its wildlife (an oasis for migratory birds), has been protected since 1984 after local opposition succeeded in halting the construction of a vast tourist village here. It was one of the first coastal areas on the island to become a reserve. Information is given at the entrance about the itineraries and regulations, and guides are available. It is an excellent place to picnic.

From the main road, beyond the railway, a poorly surfaced road continues for c 1km past lemon groves to the entrance. At the south end is the 18C farmhouse of **S. Lorenzo lo Vecchio**, with remains of a Hellenistic temple transformed into a Byzantine church. On the edge of the shore are ruins of a Norman tower, and a tuna fishery which closed down in 1943.

The landscape from here to the southern tip of the island is less pretty. In the shallow bay by the fishing village of **Marzamemi**, excavations begun in 1959, brought to light 14 ancient shipwrecks (four Greek, five Roman and five Byzantine ships).

**Pachino** (population 21,000) is a wine-producing centre. Beyond almond and olive trees near the sea and an inland lagoon is the untidy fishing port of **Portopalo**. There is a disused tuna fishery on the sea front next to an 18C palace. The landscape is ruined by numerous plastic greenhouses. The lighthouse stands on **Capo Passero**, the ancient *Pachynus*, the south-east horn of Sicily. A Roman necropolis has been excavated here, and the island of Capo Passero is of great interest for its vegetation. The southernmost point is the little **Isolotto delle Correnti**, 6km south-west of the cape. Sea turtles and pelicans used to be seen frequently on the shore here.

**Rosolini**, an inland town (population 17,400) between Pachino and Noto, was founded in 1713. A rock-hewn basilica of early Christian date lies beneath the Castello del Principe (1668) amid extensive catacombs (now used as a garage).

# Palazzolo Acreide

Palazzolo Acreide is the successor (population 9100) to the Greek city of *Akrai*. A pleasant little town, its finest buildings were built after the earthquake in 1693. It also has some interesting 19C and early 20C palaces. It has important Greek remains on the outskirts.

## ■ Practical information

*Information office*. APT Siracusa, ☎ 0931/67710.

**Buses** run by *AST* from Siracusa to Palazzolo Acreide (piazza del Popolo) about every hour in 40min.

**Hotel.** ★★★ *Senatore*, largo Senatore Italia, ☎ 0931/883443, fax 0931/883444.

### Restaurants

**B** *La Trota*, 5km outside the town on N287. **C** *La Polveriera* and *Zio 'Nzino. Agriturismo* restaurants: *Casa Bianca* (Sebastiano Cavalieri), contrada Pianette; and *Giannavì* (Fratelli Maltese), contrada Giannavì.
At Buccheri: **C** *U Lucale*, 14 via Dusmet.

**Annual festival** of S. Paolo on 29 June.

#### History

Akrai was a sub-colony founded from Siracusa in 663 BC. In a treaty between Rome and Hieron II in 263 BC, Akrai was assigned to Diodorus Siculus of Siracusa. Its period of greatest splendour followed, and its main monuments, including the theatre, were built at this time. It had a conspicuous Christian community, and was destroyed in the 9C by the Arabs. The name 'Palazzolo' was probably added some time in the 12C. It was governed from 1374 for two centuries by the Alagona family. It was damaged by earthquake in 1693 and bombed by the Allies in 1943 (with 700 casualties).

Just outside the town is the **Cimitero Monumentale**, an unexpected site, with elaborate funerary monuments erected in the mid-19C. In the lower town are the Duomo next to **S. Paolo**, with a good façade perhaps by Vincenzo Sinatra. In the interior are two late 19C carved thrones used for transporting a 16C statue of the saint and his relics in procession. The charming sacristy dates from 1778, with a pretty vault and its original furniture.

In piazza Umberto I, nearby, is the red 18C Palazzo Zocco, which has a decorative long balcony. A road leads downhill from the piazza towards the edge of the town and the church of the **Annunziata**, with a lovely 18C portal decorated with four twisted columns and vines and festoons of fruit. In the white interior, covered with stuccoes, is a fine high altar in *pietre dure*. The *Annunciation* by Antonello da Messina, now in Palazzo Bellomo in Siracusa, was commissioned for this church in 1474. From piazza Umberto I via Garibaldi leads uphill past Palazzo Caruso (no. 127), with monsters' heads beneath its balcony. Further uphill, after a flight of steps, is Palazzo Ferla with four good balconies. The Museo Archeologico in via Gaetano Italia has been closed for many years.

The centre of the busier and more attractive upper part of the town is piazza del Popolo. Here is the 18C church of **S. Sebastiano**, which has a theatrical façade and a portal by Paolo Labisi. In the interior is a painting of *St Margaret of Cortona* by Vito d'Anna (fourth north altar). The town hall dates from 1808. In corso Vittorio Emanuele the 19C Palazzo Judica has an eccentric façade with vases on its roof.

Off the parallel via Carlo Alberto, entered through a courtyard, is the **Casa-Museo** (open daily 09.00–13.00; ring the bell), a delightful local ethnographical museum created by the late Antonino Uccello and displayed in his 17C house. It was acquired by the region of Sicily in 1983. The interesting material from the provinces of Siracusa and Ragusa includes farming utensils and implements, household objects, puppets, terracotta statuettes, etc., beautifully displayed. An oil-press and a press used for making honey are also preserved here.

At the top of the road is S. Michele, propped up with scaffolding. Via Acre continues uphill to the church of the **Immacolata** with a convex façade, difficult to see, as the church is now entered through the courtyard at the east end (ring at the central door, at the house of the custodian of a school). It contains a very fine statue of the *Madonna* by Francesco Laurana.

## The ruins of Akrai

Above the Immacolata a road continues up to the entrance to the Greek remains of Akrai (open daily 09.00–dusk), the first colony founded by Siracusa (663 BC). It is a beautifully kept site, although part of it is at present inaccessible. Excavations began here in 1824, and were continued in this century. The small **theatre**, built in the late 3C BC, is well preserved. The scena was altered in Roman times, and in 600 AD a mill with round silos was built over the ruins. Nearby is an altar for sacrifices. Behind the theatre is the **bouleuterion**, a tiny council chamber (connected to the theatre by a passageway). From here (through a locked double gate) there is a good view of the recent excavations of the ancient city. There is a long stretch of the Decumanus constructed in lava (altered by the Romans), and parts of another road at right-angles which passes close to a circular **temple**. Probably dedicated to Persephone, it is thought to date from the 3C BC. It was covered by a cupola with a circular opening in the centre, supported on girders of terracotta (no longer in situ, but preserved); the holes for them are visible in the circular walls, and the pavement survives. Excavations continue here in the area thought to have been the Agora.

The rest of the enclosure consists of a depression between two **latomie**, or stone-quarries, showing traces of a Heroic cult and of later Christian occupation. On the face of the smaller latomia, nearest to the path, niches can be seen (formerly closed with commemorative plaques carved with reliefs and inscriptions) and an interesting funerary bas-relief of c 200 BC, showing two scenes, one Roman, with a warrior sacrificing, and one Greek, with a banquet scene. Further on (at present kept locked) are extensive Byzantine **catacombs** carved into the rock (some of them adapted by the Arabs as dwellings). The larger family chapels are decorated with unusual lattice-work transennae. From the other path the larger latomia can be seen, and near the theatre a monumental gateway. Beyond a locked gate is the basement of a **Temple of Aphrodite**.

A *strada panoramica* (above the entrance gate) circles the top of the Acropolis, with traces of its fortification walls. It gives a splendid idea of the site, and has wide views.

On request, at the entrance gate, a custodian will accompany you (in your car) to visit the so-called **Santoni**, interesting statues of Cybele, carved in a rock face. The road goes down the hill to the Ragusa road, off which a paved byroad (left) ends beside a gate (unlocked by the custodian). Steps continue down past 12 remarkable life-size statues dating from around the 3C BC representing the goddess Cybele, hewn out of the rock (protected by wooden huts). The goddess is shown between the two dioscuri on horseback; with Marsyas, Hermes and other divinities; with her daughter Persephone; seated and flanked by two little lions; etc. They are extremely worn, and were wilfully disfigured in the 20th century. There was a sanctuary here near a spring on the road to the necropolis across the valley from the city. It was reached via the **Templi Ferali**, on the east side of the hill, in a vertical cliff. These temples of the dead, containing Greek inscriptions and votive niches survive, but it is not at present possible to visit them.

### Environs of Palazzolo Acreide

East of Palazzolo Acreide, on the fast road to Siracusa is **Canicattini Bagni**, now surrounded by new buildings. Founded in 1678 it has interesting early 20C houses decorated in the local stone. Nearby the **Grotta Perciata** is the largest cave so far discovered in Sicily, where prehistoric artefacts have been found.

Across the Anapo valley north of Palazzolo Acreide is the attractive little hill town of **Buscemi**, rebuilt after 1693. The main road runs uphill past its four impressive churches. S. Antonio di Padova has an 18C façade which incorporates ten splendid large columns on its curving front (with three bells hung across the top). Higher up is S. Sebastiano, and then the neo-classical 19C church of S. Giacomo. At the top of the town is the well sited 18C Chiesa Madre. A number of artisans' workshops in the town can be visited (signposted).

On the barren **Piana di Buccheri** (820m), with views to Monte Lauro (986m), the highest point of the Monte Iblei, and of Etna to the north, some pinewoods have recently been planted.

**Buccheri** (820m) is another 18C town. The road passes S. Maria Maddalena, built in the 18C, which contains a statue of *Mary Magdalen* by Antonello Gagini (1508). From piazza Toselli a steep flight of steps rises to the towering façade of S. Antonio (covered with scaffolding).

# The Valle dell'Anapo and Pantalica

The Valle dell'Anapo is a beautiful well-preserved valley. Above it, in spectacular deserted countryside is the necroplis of Pantalica, where thousands of tombs carved in the rock can still be seen. This is the most important prehistoric site in Sicily.

## ■ Practical information

*Information office*. APT Siracusa, ☎ 0931/67710. Offices of the Forestry Commission in Buccheri, ☎ 0931/873093; in Siracusa, ☎ 0931/462452; and in Sortino, ☎ 0931/953695.

### Getting there

The Valle dell'Anapo is 36km from Siracusa and Pantalica is 56km from Siracusa. They are reached **by car** on the N124 via Floridia, and then on the byroad right for Ferla; the road from Siracusa via Sortino has not been completed. The only public transport available from Siracusa is the **bus** to Sortino which is at least 5km from Pantalica.

Both the Valle dell'Anapo and Pantalica are wonderful places to **picnic** (food should be bought in Ferla). Picnic places with tables are provided in the Valle dell'Anapo.

The plateau above the Anapo valley to the south has pretty countryside with some attractive farmhouses and low stone walls. Many of the fields are now uncultivated: in one district there are numerous small farmhouses, all of identical design, built by the Fascist government of Mussolini. The barren landscape is dominated by huge carobs and olives. In the area are Byzantine tombs and caves showing evidence of Neolithic and Bronze Age occupation.

Near Cassaro on the floor of the Anapo valley is a car-park and a hut owned by the Forestry Commission, at the entrance (signposted) to the **Valle dell'Anapo** (open every day 09.00–16.30; summer 09.00–20.00). This beautiful deep limestone gorge, a protected area since 1988, is run by the Forestry Commission. A map of the paths in the area is available at the hut. No private cars are allowed but a van takes visitors for 8km along the rough road on the site of the old narrow-gauge railway track (and its tunnels) which used to run along the floor of the valley (on the Siracusa–Vizzini line).

The interesting vegetation includes ilexes, pines, figs, olives, citrus fruit trees and poplars. The only buildings to be seen are those once used by the railway company. Horses are bred here, and may one day be used to transport visitors by carriage along the road. Careful replanting is taking place where fires have destroyed the plants. Picnic places, with tables, are provided. The van stops in the centre of the valley from where there is a good view of the tombs of the necropolis of Pantalica (see below) high up at the top of the rock face. There is another entrance to the valley from the Sortino road (approached from Solarino), where another van accompanies visitors along the valley for some 4km before joining this road.

## Pantalica

On the Ferla road is the site of the little town of **Cassaro** which moved after the earthquake of 1693 up to the top of the cliff face (seen above the road). On the approach to Ferla are terraces planted with orange trees, prickly pear and pomegranate, some of which have been allowed to grow wild. **Ferla**, is a pretty little town traversed by one long main street which slopes steeply uphill past its four Baroque churches (three of them being restored) and interesting early 20C houses.

Half-way up the main street is the turning (right; signposted) for Pantalica. The lonely road leads for 12km along a ridge through beautiful remote farming country and pine woods to the remarkable prehistoric necropolis of **Pantalica** (marked by a yellow sign), in totally deserted countryside. All around can be seen rock tombs carved in the cliffs. The huge unenclosed site is traversed by the road (which ends here) and footpaths (signposted from the road). The deep limestone gorges of the Anapo and Cava Grande almost encircle the plateau of Pantalica, occupied from the 13C to the 8C BC. In this naturally defended site Siculi from the Italian mainland settled c 1270 BC. Their way of life remained virtually unchanged up until the arrival of the Greeks in the second half of the 8C BC. The cliffs of the vast necropolis, the largest and most important in Sicily, are honeycombed with 5000 tombs of varying shapes and sizes. Each cell was the tomb of a family, and there appears to have been an arrangement of the cells in groups. The objects discovered in them, including fine pottery, are displayed in the archaeological museum in Siracusa.

The city disappeared after the foundation of the Greek colony of Akrai (see p.282) in 663 BC, and some of the tombs were converted into cave-dwellings

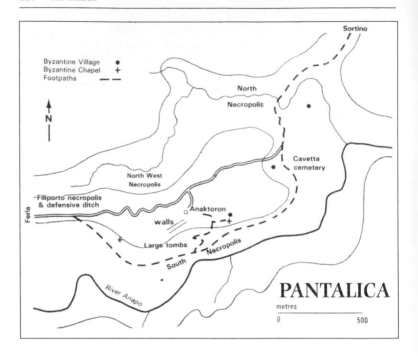

Byzantine Village ●
Byzantine Chapel +
Footpaths ── ──

N

Sortino

North
Necropolis

Cavetta
cemetery

North West
Necropolis

Filiporto necropolis
& defensive ditch

Ferla

Anaktoron

walls

Large tombs

South Necropolis

River Anapo

**PANTALICA**

metres

0          500

during the barbarian invasions, and were later inhabited by Christians. An easy footpath (signposted Villaggio Bizantino) at the beginning of the road leads to a tiny Byzantine oratory carved in the rock (with traces of fresco) known as **S. Micidiario**, and the **southern necropolis**.

Off the road, further on, a track leads up to the top of the hill and the so-called '**Anactoron**', a megalithic palace dating from the late Bronze Age, the foundations of which survive (35 x 11m). Nearby are short sections of wall and a defensive ditch, the only remains of the city, recently identified with the legendary *Hybla* whose king allowed the Megarian colonists to found Megara Hyblaea (see p.288). Far below the Anapo valley (described above) can be seen, with a white track following the line of the old railway. Further on, downhill, near the end of the road a signpost indicates the **Cavetta** cemetery (9C–7C BC), and another Byzantine village. A path leads towards the **northern necropolis** (beyond the stream in the valley). The road ends abruptly and the road from Sortino (see above), which has never been completed, can be seen across the valley. There is a view of Sortino in the distance.

On the main road between Ferla and Siracusa is **Solarino**, founded in 1759 with a handsome neo-classical palace. From here **Sortino** can be reached, which was rebuilt after the earthquake of 1693, and has some interesting 18C churches and palaces. This byroad, 6km before reaching Sortino, passes an entrance to the Valle dell'Anapo (see above). Near Solarino is **Floridia** (population 19,400), founded in 1628, with more 18C churches. The Madonna delle Grazie was built by the Spaniards to celebrate the victory over the Austrians in 1720.

# Megara Hyblaea and Lentini

Megara Hyblaea is an important Greek site on the sea, which has been surrounded in the 20C by an ugly industrial area with oil refineries. Lentini is another important site which has been spoilt by its unattractive surroundings.

## ■ Practical information

*Information office*. APT Siracusa, ☎ 0931/67710.

*Getting there*. Megara Hyblaea is 16km from Siracusa and can only be reached by car. Lentini is on the railway line between Siracusa and Catania.

The shores of the **Gulf of Augusta**, once lined by the ancient cities of Siracusa, Thapsos and Megara Hyblaea are now a jungle of oil refineries, and oil tankers are anchored offshore. The industrial zone which grew up in the 1950s extends for 30km from here to Priolo and Augusta, and has the largest concentration of chemical plants in Europe. The 42 industries here employ tens of thousands of workers. The pollution of the sea has caused the death of marine life, and because of the contaminated air the inhabitants (over 1000) of Marina de Melilli were evacuated in 1979 and the houses razed to the ground. Local protest has led to legal proceedings against those responsible for the pollution.

### History

Capo S. Panagia has been identified with ancient *Trogilus*. Fossils exist in the limestone caves and, in the over-lying clays, there are remains of Neolithic habitation. The low-lying peninsula of **Magnisi**, was the ancient **Thapsos**, under whose northern shore the Athenian fleet anchored before the siege of Siracusa. It is almost an island (2km long and 700m wide), since its only connection with the mainland is a sandy isthmus 2.5km long and little more than 100m wide at one point. The fleet of Marcellus also moored near here during the Roman siege of Siracusa. Finds from its vast necropolis have given name to a Bronze Age culture (see the archaeological museum in Siracusa) and interesting domed rock tombs line the shore west of the lighthouse. Two Mycenaean vases were found here in 1974.

The inhabited area, where the most recent excavations have taken place, shows three periods of occupation: c 1500–1400 BC, characterised by round huts; c 1300–1200 BC, where the square houses are of the Mycenean type (a bronze bar with figures of a dog and fox, unique in prehistoric Sicily, and thought to be of Aegean origin, was found here); and a final period c 1100–900 BC, with finds of remarkable pottery (now in the archaeological museum in Siracusa).

## Megara Hyblaea

Near the large port of **Priolo**, a fast motorway (signposted *Zona industriale* and *Catania via Litoreale*) branches off towards the sea through a jungle of industrial plants. Yellow signposts indicate the way to the excavations of the ancient city of Megara Hyblaea (admission 09.00–14.00; Sun & PH 09.00–13.00.

### History

Founded by the Megarians of Greece towards the end of the 8C BC, it was destroyed by Gelon in 483. A second city was founded by Timoleon in 340 BC, which in its turn was obliterated by the Romans in 214. In c 630 BC Pammilus was invited from Megara in Greece by the settlers to 'found' Selinunte. Excavations of the site were begun by the French School in Rome in 1949, and they still supervise digs here most years. The site was surrounded by oil refineries in the 1950s which still pollute the air.

The excavations are approached by a byroad which runs alongside a citrus fruit plantation behind a wall of cypresses. The road continues right (signposted *scavi*) and here in a group of pines is a stretch of **Archaic walls** (6C BC) with four semicircular towers (a fifth has been destroyed). The walls can be followed on foot for some 250m as far as the **Archaic west gate**. A number of tombs have been placed near the walls, salvaged from excavations of the two necropoleis which are now covered by industrial plants. The third necropolis was located in the vicinity of these walls. Further on, below ground level, is an oblong construction with seven bases for columns. Excavated in 1880, it is of uncertain significance. Just before the little bridge over the railway is a car-park; excavations were carried out near here in 1982 to prevent the laying of an oil pipe across the site. Cars can continue over the narrow bridge along a rough road past some abandoned farmhouses.

The road passes over the second line of **Hellenistic walls** built around the Hellenistic town (they follow a line of cypresses, see below). To the left of the road here the **Hellenistic north gate** of the city has been identified near the remains of Archaic walls. The road ends at the custodian's house in a pretty little garden. The well-restored farmhouse here may one day be used as a small museum to house the finds, including a tomb with a decorative frieze, although the most important Archaic sculptures excavated here are now in the Siracusa archaeological museum.

A path leads across a field to the main area of excavations: the complicated remains include buildings from both the Archaic and Hellenistic periods (the red iron posts indicate the Archaic areas, and the green posts the Hellenistic buildings). There are plans to restore and label the site. At the intersection of the two main roads is the Agora, near which are a sanctuary, interesting **Hellenistic thermae** with good pavements, and a poorly preserved small **Doric temple** of the 4C (protected by a roof). The main east–west road leads from the Agora to the narrow **Hellenistic west gate** in the walls (with two square towers) along the line of cypresses. Near the gate, on a lower level to the south, are ovens and houses of the Archaic period. The main north–south road ends at the **Hellenistic south gate**, a 'pincer' type defence work.

## Augusta

Augusta, the most important oil port in Italy (see above), now has 34,700 inhabitants. It stands on a rocky islet connected with the mainland by a long bridge. To the east and west are two capacious harbours, the Porto Xifonio and the Porto Megarese, the latter with two old forts (1595). Augusta was founded by Frederick II in 1232 as a refuge for the inhabitants of Centuripe and Montalbano. In 1269 it was sacked by Philip and Guy de Montfort. It was taken by the

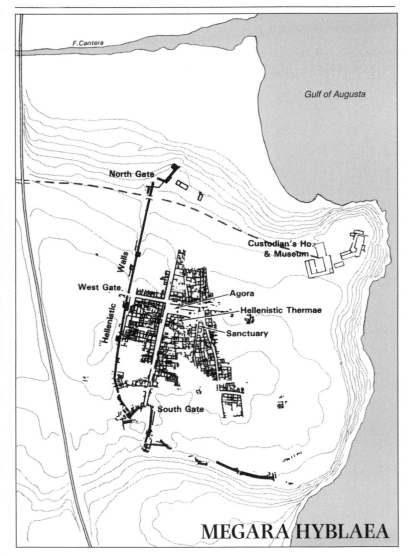

MEGARA HYBLAEA

French in 1676 after the defeat in the bay of a Dutch fleet under De Ruyter by Admiral Duquesne. De Ruyter was mortally wounded in the action and died a few days later at Siracusa. Augusta was totally destroyed by the earthquake of 1693, and the modern town suffered severe damage from the air in World War II. Another earthquake hit the town and the provinces of Siracusa, Catania and Ragusa in 1990, leaving 13,000 people homeless.

On the coast to the north is the ruined castle of **Brucoli**, erected by Giovanni Bastida in 1468. *Trotilon*, one of the oldest Greek settlements on the island, probably stood on the bay of Brucoli which now has a vast holiday village.

## Carlentini and Lentini

Inland between Augusta and Catania, lying close together, are the towns of Carlentini and Lentini. **Carlentini** (population 11,700) was founded in 1551 by Charles V as a summer residence for the people of Lentini. It is now an undistinguished town, surrounded by orange plantations, which was very badly damaged in an earthquake in 1990 (many of the inhabitants are still housed in temporary accommodation, on the road to Agnone Bagni).

A poorly signposted road leads to the site of the Greek city of **Leontinoi** (open daily 09.00–14.00), founded by the Chalcidians of Naxos, in 730–728 BC, on the site of an earlier Sicel settlement. In the 6C BC Panaetius set himself up as tyrant of Leontinoi, the first such ruler in Sicily. In the early 5C it was taken by Hippocrates of Gela, and soon afterwards succumbed to the Siracusans. In 427 BC it despatched the orator Gorgias (480–c 380) to invoke the assistance of Athens against her tyrants. Hieronymus, the last native tyrant of Siracusa, was assassinated at Leontinoi in 215 BC.

The excavations are in a nicely planted and well-kept site. A path leads down from the entrance to the elaborate **south gate**. Across the valley steps lead up to a path which follows the walls to the top of the hill, from which there is a fine view of the site and the surrounding hills. The site of the prehistoric settlement, with a **necropolis** (6C–4C BC), and hut village, are not at present open to the public.

**Lentini** is an unattractive agricultural centre (population 31,700). The medieval town was destroyed in the earthquake of 1693, and the modern town was again badly shaken in 1990. The locality is famous for its oranges. The **Chiesa Madre** preserves an icon thought to date from the 9C. The churches of S. Luca and S. Trinità have interesting 16C paintings. The **Museo Archeologico** (poorly signposted; open daily 09.00–14.00) has a well-arranged collection of local finds including three fine calyx-kraters, and a reconstruction of the south gate of the ancient city.

South-west of Lentini is **Francofonte** (population 14,200), a hill town, also damaged in 1990, where the town hall occupies the 18C Palazzo Palagonia adjoining the medieval castle.

# Catania

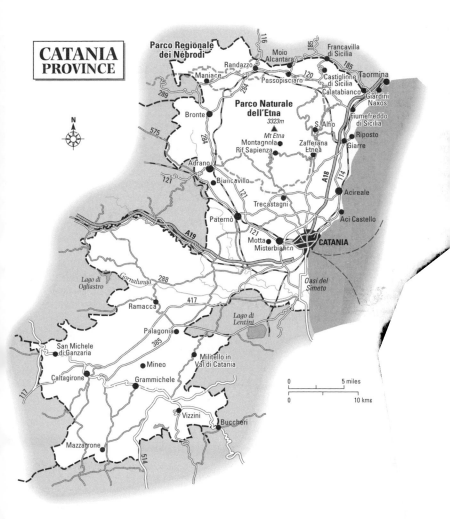

Catania, the most important town (population 376,000) in Sicily after Palermo, stands at the southern foot of Etna, whose eruptions have destroyed it several times. The spacious homogeneous appearance of the centre, with long straight streets of imposing Baroque churches and palaces, dates from the reconstruction which followed the earthquake of 1693. The black lava on which it stands has been used for the paving of the streets and as the material of almost all the buildings. The most prosperous city on the island, Catania was known in the 1960s as the 'Milan of the South', but the life of the city deteriorated drastically in the 1970s and 1980s due to chaotic local administration, and it became one of the strongholds of the Mafia on the island. However, since 1993, when the mayor was elected directly by the citizens, life in the city has improved noticeably, the crime rate has been drastically reduced, new parks are being created on the outskirts, and the streets are cleaner. The enlightened city administration was reconfirmed in the local elections held in 1997. In summer numerous musical events are organised and the centre of the town has become livelier at night with cafés and restaurants staying open late for the younger generation. **See map on pp.296-297.**

## ■ Practical information

*Information offices*. APT Catania (map: 6), 10 via Cimarosa, ☎ 095/7306211 (open every day 09.00–18.00). Information offices also at the railway station and the airport (and at the port in summer).

### Getting there
**Railway stations. Centrale** (map: 8), for all services, on the line to Palermo via Enna and on the coastal line between Siracusa and Messina (with some through trains to Rome). **Circumetnea Station**, corso delle Provincie, off corso Italia (map: 4), for the line around the foot of Etna.

**Airport** at Fontanarossa, 5km south. International and national services. Air Terminal, 105 corso Sicilia (map: 7). *Alibus* every 20min. (from 05.00–24.00) ʿrom the station with stops at corso Martiri, corso della Libertà, corso Sicilia and ʾazza Stesicoro.

ʿes. Nos **129** and **136** traverse the city from the station via via Etnea; for the ʿrt, see above. No. **241** for Ognina; no. **27** for La Plaia (and in summer 'D' ʿpiazza Verga and via Etnea for the beaches).

ʿ excellent network of **country buses** (nearly all of which terminate at the ʿay station) serve the surrounding areas. There are long-distance coaches by *SAIS* from 181 via d'Amico (map: 8) about every hour via the motorway ʿalermo (in 2hr 40min.) and Messina (in 1hr 30min.); less frequently via the ʿtorway for Enna (in 1hr 30min.) and Caltanissetta (in 1hr 30min.); for Siraʿa in c 1hr; Taormina (in 45min.–1hr); Agrigento (2hr 30min.); Noto (2hr ʿmin.). Services run by *AST* from piazza Giovanni XXIII outside the station ʿap: 8) to Gela, Caltagirone, and the province of Ragusa.

Buses run by *Etnatrasporti* (185 via d'Amico) to Piazza Armerina (2hr ʿ0min.) and Aidone. For towns at the foot of Mount Etna, see p.307. Long-ʿistance daily coach service to Rome (run by *SAIS*) in 11hr.

**Maritime services**. In summer there are usually boat services (run by *Navitalia*) for the Aeolian Islands via Naxos and Messina.

**Parking**. Multi-storey car-park in piazza Grenoble (map: 7). Garages in the centre charge reasonable tariffs.

### Hotels
★★★★ *Excelsior* (map: 4), 39 piazza Giovanni Verga, ☎ 095/537071, fax 095/7158939; *Central Palace* (map: 7), 218 via Etnea; ☎ 095/325344, fax

095/7158939; *Jolly Trinacria* (map: 3), 13 piazza Trento, ☎ 095/316933, fax 095/316832.

★★★ *Moderno* (map: 10), 9 via Alessi, ☎ 095/326250, fax 095/326674; *Villa Dina* (map: 2), 129 via Caronda, ☎ & fax 095/447103.

★★ *Gresi*, 28 via Pacini (map: 6) , ☎ 095/322709; *Royal*, 337 via Antonio di Sangiuliano (map: 10), ☎ 095/313448, fax 095/325611; *Centrale Europa*, 167 via Vittorio Emanuele (map: 11), ☎ 095/311309, fax 095/317531; *Savona*, 210 via Vittorio Emanuele (map: 11), ☎ 095/326982, fax 095/7158169.

On the northern outskirts of the city (for those with a car):

★★★ *Nettuno*, 121 viale Ruggero di Lauria (on the lungomare for Ognina), ☎ 095/7125252, fax 095/498066. ★★★★ and ★★★ hotels also at Aci-Castello and Acireale, see p.315.

**Campsites**. Ognina ★★ *Jonio*, 2 via Villini a Mare, ☎ 095/491139. Lido di Plaia, on the southern outskirts of the city: ★★ *Villaggio Turistico Europeo*, 91 viale Kennedy, ☎ 095/591026; ★ *Internazionale La Plaja*, 47 viale Kennedy, ☎ 095/340880 and *Villaggio Souvenir*, 71 viale Kennedy, ☎ 095/341162.

### Restaurants

**A** *Da Rinaldo*, 59 via Simili; *Enzo*, 26 via Malta; *Hotel Poggio Ducale*, 5 via Paolo Gaifami. **C** *Il Gabbiano*, via Giordano Bruni; *La Casalinga*, 19 via Biondi, *Da Peppino*, 43 via Empedocle, *Da Turi*, 18 piazza Bove; *Don Saro*, 129 viale Libertà. Outside the centre and at Ognina: **A** *Costa Azzurra*, 2 via de Cristoforo; *La Siciliana*, 52 viale Marco Polo; and *Selene*, 24 via Mollica.

**Cafés and pasticcerie**. *Verona-Bonvegna*, via Asiago; *Savia* and *Spinella*, via Etnea (opposite Villa Bellini), *Mantegna*, via Etnea, *Ethel*, via Milano.

Villa Bellini is a pleasant place to **picnic**.

**Theatres**. Massimo Bellini (map: 11), piazza Bellini, for opera and concerts. Teatro Stabile Verga, 35 via dello Stadio, for plays. Other theatres include Musco, Metropolitan and Ambasciatori. Concerts are also held at the Metropolitan, where, from October–May the 'Associazione Musicale Etnea' give concerts, and there is a jazz festival in November–April. In summer concerts are given in many of the Baroque churches of the city, and (open-air) in Villa Bellini. A festival is held in summer at *Le Ciminiere* (Centro Culturale Fieristico) near the station (beyond map: 8), with music, dance and theatre. A popular outdoor music festival has been held in the city in July since 1995. **Puppet shows** by Fratelli Napoli, via Madonna di Fatima (☎ 095/416787).

**Markets**. A large daily food market is held in piazza Carlo Alberto (map: 7) and a general market in the surrounding streets (including via S. Gaetano alle Grotte). In the streets south of piazza Duomo and via Garibaldi (including via Gisira; map: 14) there is another daily food market (where fresh fish and meat are also sold) and a general market.

**Annual festivals**. The Festa di St Agatha is celebrated on 3–5 February with a traditional procession and dances.

**History**

Catania was perhaps a Sicel village when the first Greek colony (Chalcidians from Naxos) established itself here in 729 BC, and, as *Catana*, it soon rose to importance. Charondas (7C or early 6C) here drew up a written code of laws which was eventually adopted by all the Ionian colonies of Sicily and Magna Graecia; the poet Tisias of Himera, called Stesichorus, died here (c 540); and Xenophanes, the pantheistic philosopher, adopted Catanian citizenship (c 530). Hieron of Siracusa took the city in 476 and exiled the inhabitants to Leontinoi, refounding the town with celebrations for which Aeschylus wrote his *Women of Aetna*; the exiles returned and drove out his Doric colonists in 461. In 415 it was the base of the Athenian operations against Siracusa, but it fell to Dionysius in 403, when the citizens were sold as slaves. After the defeat of the Siracusan fleet at the Cyclopean Isles by Mago the Carthaginian it was occupied by Himilco. Catania opened its gates to Timoleon in 339 and to Pyrrhus in 278, and was one of the first Sicilian towns to fall to the Romans (263). Its greatest prosperity dated from the time of Augustus who rewarded it for taking his part against Pompey.

In early Christian days Catania was the scene of the martyrdom of St Agatha (238–253), the patroness of the city. In the Middle Ages it was wrecked by an earthquake (1169), sacked by Henry VI (1194), and again by Frederick II (1232), who built the castle to hold his rebellious subjects in check. Constance of Aragon, his empress, died here on 23 June 1222. The 17C saw the calamities of 1669 and 1693, the former the most terrible eruption of Etna in history, the latter a violent earthquake. The lava flows which reached the town in 1669 can still be seen from the ring road. In 1943 Catania was bombarded from the air and from the sea.

**Natives of Catania** include Vincenzo Bellini (1801–35), the composer; Giovanni Verga (1840–1922), the novelist; Mario Rapisardi (1844–1912), the poet; Giovanni Pacini (1796–1867), the composer; and Luigi Capuana (1839–1915), the writer. The writer Federico de Roberto (1866–1917) lived most of his life in Catania, and died here. Frederick III of Aragon died in Catania in 1377.

## Piazza Duomo

The old centre of the city is the well-proportioned **piazza Duomo** (map: 11). In the middle stands a fountain with an antique lava elephant (which has since become the symbol of Catania) and an Egyptian obelisk that was once perhaps a turning-post in the Roman circus, set up here in 1736 by Giovanni Battista Vaccarini, a native of Catania, who became the official municipal architect in 1730. It is modelled on the monument by Bernini in piazza Minerva in Rome. The square is surrounded by 18C edifices, mostly by Vaccarini.

The **Duomo** (map: 11; closed 12.30–17.00), dedicated to St Agatha, was founded by Count Roger in 1094 and rebuilt after the earthquakes of 1169 and 1693. The granite columns on the lower storey of its Baroque **façade** (by Vaccarini, 1736–58; covered for restoration) come from the Roman theatre. The **cupola**, by Battaglia, dates from 1804. The **north door**, with three statuettes, is attributed to Gian Domenico Mazzola (1577). The structure of the mighty black lava 11C **apses** can be seen from no. 159 via Vittorio Emanuele.

In the **interior** during restoration work in the 1950s, the foundations of the 11C–12C basilica were revealed beneath the nave. The fine antique columns (of late Imperial and Byzantine date) in the transepts and three apses have also been uncovered. **South side**. Against the second pier is the tomb of Vincenzo Bellini (see below), by Giovanni Battista Tassara; its sole inscription is a well-known phrase from his opera *La Sonnambula*. The second and third altarpieces are by Borremans.

**South transept**. A doorway by Giovanni Battista Mazzola (1545) leads into the Norman **Cappella della Madonna** which preserves a huge Roman sarcophagus, with the figures (very worn) finely carved in the round, thought to come from Smyrna. It contains the ashes of Frederick II (d. 1337), Louis (d. 1355), Frederick III (d. 1377) and other illustrious members of the House of Aragon. Opposite is the beautiful tomb of Queen Constance of Aragon (d. 1363), wife of Frederick III, with contemporary scenes of Catania. The sculptured fragment above the door dates from the 15C. The other chapel in the south transept is the **Cappella di S. Agata** (seen through a grille) which contains a marble altarpiece (*Coronation of the saint*); the tomb (right) of the Viceroy Fernandez d'Acuña (d. 1494), a kneeling figure attended by a page, by Antonello Freri of Messina; and (left) the treasury, with a rich collection of relics of St Agatha, including her reliquary bust by Giovanni di Bartolo (1376). These are exposed only on the saint's festival (12 February, 17 August, and, in procession, on 4 and 5 February).

The stalls in the **choir**, finely sculpted by Scipione di Guido of Naples (1588), represent the life of St Agatha and the adventures of her corpse.

**North transept**. The Norman **Cappella del Crocifisso** is approached through an arch designed by Gian Domenico Mazzola (1563). In the **sacristy** is a fresco painted in 1675 showing the destruction of Catania by the lava flow from Etna in 1669.

The **municipio** (town hall), begun in 1695, was finished by Vaccarini in 1741. The vista on the south side of piazza Duomo is closed by the fine **Porta Uzeza** (1696) which leads to a little public garden and beyond to the harbour. The streets behind the marble fountain (1867) are lined with a colourful daily market, where meat and fish are sold.

*The 18C elephant fountain in piazza Duomo, Catania*

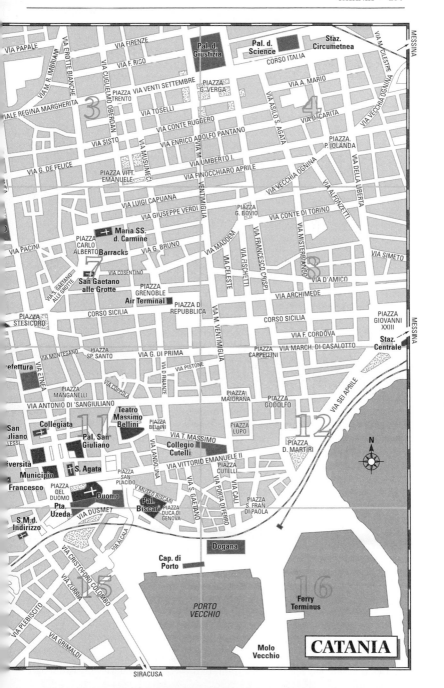

## Via Crociferi, San Nicolò and Castello Ursino

From piazza Duomo the handsome long, straight via Vittorio Emanuele II, which contains a number of Baroque church façades, leads west. In piazza S. Francesco (map: 10) a large votive deposit of 6C BC pottery came to light in 1959. Facing the Baroque façade of **S. Francesco**, is a palace which contains a small flat (across the courtyard to the left and up an old flight of steps) which houses the **Museo Belliniano** (open 09.00–13.00; Sun & PH 09.00–12.30). This delightful little old-fashioned museum was opened in 1930 to commemorate the great composer Vincenzo Bellini (1801–35), who was born here and lived here for 16 years. The charming rooms have retained their character and are crowded with mementoes, including his harpischord (in the alcove where he is meant to have been born), several pianos and his death mask. The music library (open to students) preserves the original scores of *Adelson e Salvini, I Capuleti ed i Montecchi* and *I Puritani*, besides fragments of all the remaining operas. On the upper floor of the same palace a museum was opened in 1994 dedicated to the graphic works of the sculptor Emilio Greco (1913–95), born in Catania.

From piazza S. Francesco, beyond the arch of S. Benedetto (1702) begins **via Crociferi**, the prettiest 18C street in Catania (totally closed to traffic), lined with Baroque churches, convents and palaces, many of them approached by a short flight of steps. Recent excavations here have revealed remains of the Roman city. **S. Benedetto** (left) has a good façade and vestibule of 1762. The pretty interior (entrance in via S. Benedetto; open Thurs 06.30–12.00, 15.30–18.00; Sun & PH 09.00–10.00 and 17.00–18.00) has an elaborate nuns' choir, a frescoed barrel vault by Giovanni Tuccari (1726), and a good pavement. **S. Francesco Borgia** (usually closed) has a dome frescoed by Olivio Sozzi: the church and the large Jesuit college (with four courtyards) are the work of Angelo Italia (1754). On the right **S. Giuliano** was begun in 1738 and continued by Vaccarini (who is responsible for the façade). In the fine elliptical interior is a 15C painted Crucifix. Next to it is a Baroque palace (no. 30) with a garden of banana trees.

**Via Antonio di Sangiuliano**, a handsome street lined with oleanders, with splendid views downhill of the sea, leads uphill to the highest part of the city and the church of **S. Nicolò** (map: 10). It faces a little crescent of houses which may have been designed by Stefano Ittar. This is the largest church in Sicily (105m long, transepts, 42m), begun in 1687 by Giovanni Battista Contini, and rebuilt in 1735 by Francesco Battaglia, probably to the design of Antonino Amato. The dome was designed by Stefano Ittar. The striking façade with its gigantic columns was left uncompleted in 1796.

The simplicity of the **interior** (open 09.00–13.30; Sun & PH 09.00–12.30; Tues & Thurs also 15.00–18.00) emphasises its good proportions. The meridian line on the floor of the transept dates from 1841 (recently restored). The choir stalls are by Gaetano Francese and Nicolò Bagnasco. Only the beautiful case remains of the huge organ (2916 pipes) which has been dismantled. Its builder, Donato del Piano (d. 1775), lies buried beneath. Goethe mentions its wonderful sound when he heard it here in 1787. The chapels at the east end have been made into war memorials.

Next door is the remarkable **convent** the largest in Europe after that of Mafra in Portugal. It has been undergoing a careful restoration for some years. When Patrick Brydone saw it in 1770 he thought it was a royal palace, only to discover it 'was nothing else than a convent of fat Benedictine monks, who wanted to assure themselves a paradise in this world, if not in the other'! It is now used by two university faculties (sometimes shown on request by the porter, Monday–Friday). It was almost entirely rebuilt after 1693 to the design of Antonino Amato and his son Andrea; the rich detail of its Baroque ornamentation combines well with its simplicity of line. The first court is overlooked by the splendid façade with delightful windows and balconies. Excavations here have found prehistoric fragments as well as Greek and Roman remains, including a lava road. In one of the cloisters there is a beautiful (enclosed) garden with a majolica neo-Gothic tabernacle, and another has a graceful arcade. The monumental neo-classical staircase (1794) was designed by Antonino Battaglia. The impressive long corridors have fine vaults.

The remainder of the conventual complex (entered to the right of the church), is occupied by the **municipal library**, one of the most valuable in Sicily, and the Ursino Recupero Library. The monastic library, with its original bookcases and majolica floor of 1700 also survives. Outside the convent wall, to the left of the church façade (surrounded by railings), some remains of Roman baths can be seen, well below ground level.

Via Gesuiti, with herringbone paving in large blocks of lava (typical of the side streets of the city), descends from S. Nicolò past modest houses. Via Rotonda branches off to the right. Here (behind railings) can be seen remains of Roman baths and the primitive domed church of **S. Maria della Rotonda**. Many of the adjacent houses have been converted from another bath-house. Via S. Agostino continues back down to via Vittorio Emanuele II past the Odeon (described below).

At no. 266 via Vittorio Emanuele is the inconspicuous entrance to the **Teatro Romano** (map: 10; open daily 09.00–13.00, 15.00–dusk; Sun & PH 09.00–13.00), now overlooked by houses. This is a Roman building on the site of the theatre where Alcibiades harangued the men of Catania to win them to the cause of Athens (415 BC). The building is of lava, practically all of the marble facing having disappeared. The underground passageways which gave access to the cavea are very well preserved. The cavea has nine wedges of seats in two main tiers; the diameter was 86m, the depth of the orchestra 29m. The orchestra is permanently under water since there is an underground stream here. From the top of the cavea a path leads round to the small **odeon**, a semicircular building used for the rehearsals of the chorus and for competitions. Concerts are now given here in the summer. One colonnade of the **Foro Romano** (no admission) remains near piazza S. Pantaleone, to the south-west.

On the other side of via Vittorio Emanuele II at no. 8 via S. Anna (map: 10), is the **Museo Verga**. (open 09.00–13.00; Tues, Thurs & Fri also 15.00–18.30; closed Sun & PH). On the second floor, approached by the stairs on the left, this spartan apartment belonged to the parents of the writer Giovanni Verga (1840–1922). Verga lived and died here and some of the original furnishings have been preserved in his study, library and bedroom (with his clothes in the cupboard!). The house was bought and restored by the region of Sicily and opened to the public in 1984. The library is open to students and there are photocopies of the autograph works which belong to the museum (now kept at the university for conservation reasons). These include the manuscripts of his most famous works.

---

**Giovanni Verga**

Verga is considered by many critics to be the greatest Italian writer after Manzoni. He is famous for his naturalistic fiction, which gives a dramatic picture of the tragic social conditions of everyday Sicilian life using a simple and direct language and style. His first great success was *Storia di una Capinera* published in 1871. His masterpieces include *Vita dei Campi* (a collection of short stories, including *Cavalleria Rusticana*), *I Malavoglia* and *Mastro Don Gesualdo.* By 1884 he was acclaimed as the greatest living Italian writer. He made contact with Emile Zola and remained a life-long friend of the writer Luigi Capuana, also born in Catania. Although his fame diminished towards the end of his life, his eightieth birthday was publicly celebrated in Catania with Luigi Pirandello as orator, and he was nominated senator in the same year.

---

Via S. Anna leads to the busy via Garibaldi. To the west the Baroque **Porta Garibaldi** (1768) can be seen, which closes the vista some 1km away. In the other direction is **piazza Mazzini**, charmingly arcaded (but at present propped up with scaffolding) with 32 columns from the Roman basilica (beneath S. Agostino).

Via Auteri, in a dilapidated poor district of the city, with a daily street market, leads south to piazza Federico di Svevia, where low houses surround the **Castello Ursino** (map: 14) built for Frederick II by Riccardo da Lentini. This was partly destroyed by the lava of 1669, which completely surrounded it, hardening into a natural esplanade.

The castle was restored after 1837 and now houses the **Museo Civico**, in which material taken from the monastery of S. Nicolò was augmented by the archaeological treasure collected by the Prince of Biscari (see below) in the 18C. Although exhibitions are held here, the museum has been closed since 1988. The arrangement will probably change and the description given below will no longer be accurate when the museum finally re-opens after much needed restoration.

From the **hall** (see below) is the entrance (right) to **room 1** which contains architectural fragments from the Roman theatre. **Room 3**, a fine vaulted hall, displays Roman and Hellenistic sculpture: (in the centre) *sleeping nymph* (2C–3C AD); *Eros riding a dolphin*; torso of a Roman emperor; (at the end of the room) fragment of a commemorative column with reliefs of horsemen (1C AD); heads of *Aphrodite* and Roman portrait busts. **Room 4**. Funerary reliefs; statuette of *Dionysius* (4C BC); two heads of *Zeus* (copies of 4C and 5C BC works); fine archaic head of 6C–5C BC from Lentini (possibly belonging to the torso in the archaeological museum in Siracusa); and mosaic pavement with the months of the year.

The **entrance hall** exhibits arms and armour (removed while extensive excavations are being carried out beneath the floor). **Room 12** contains 18C portrait busts, many copies of Roman works and a series of dignitaries of Paternò. The octagon tower (**room 13**), with a fine vault, contains more 18C sculpture, and a statuette of *Aphrodite* in basalt and onyx. **Room 14** contains a fine 14C tombstone of a woman, and of a young knight (16C); the bust of an abbot, by Vitto

Maria Amico (18C); a 16C bust of a gentleman; a statuette of *St John the Baptist* by Domenico Gagini. Sculptural fragments from Catanian churches, including 14C and 15C funerary monuments, and a Romanesque font, are displayed in **room 10**. **Room 9** contains cinerary urns and Roman portrait heads (including women of the Trajan era). In **room 7** are inscriptions and Roman mosaics of 2C AD; and the head of a boy (3C). The second octagon tower (**room 8**) displays Christian frescoes of Old and New Testament subjects and Byzantine candle-holders. A fine courtyard contains sculptural fragments and sarcophagi.

From the courtyard steps ascend to the **first floor**. **Room 15** (Salone dei Paramenti) contains paintings: Gherardo delle Notti, *Derision of Christ*; Ribera (attributed), *Deposition*; Pietro Novelli, *St Christopher*; Domenico Feti, *Melancholy*; Van Dyck (attributed), *St Sebastian*; Simon de Worbrecht, *Adoration of the Magi* (signed and dated 1585). **Room 16** houses the interesting collection of Baron Zappalà Asmundo: Domenico Morelli, *Death of Tasso* (sketch); portraits by Mancini; Lorenzo di Credi, *Madonna and Child*; Giuseppe Sciuti, *Visit of the Nurse*; Spanish school, *portrait of a lady*; Sebastiano Guzzone, *shepherd boy*. In this room two precious violins of Amati are exhibited, and ceramics, including Sicilian and Capodimonte ware. **Room 18** contains engravings, many of old Catania. The museum also contains a prehistoric collection, Greek ceramics, 17C bronzes and 18C costumes.

Near the submerged railway line just out of the piazza is the simple little church of **S. Maria dell'Indirizzo** (map: 14). Behind it, in the courtyard of a school with a palm tree (seen from behind the railings) are the remains of Roman baths and a tiny domed Greek-cross building in black lava. Via Gemelli with a Baroque palace leads back through the market to piazza Duomo.

*Castello Ursino, Catania*

## The district east of the Duomo

Via Vittorio Emanuele II leads east out of piazza Duomo (map: 11) between the north side of the cathedral and the Baroque church of **S. Agata** (open 08.00–11.00), another work by Vaccarini (1748–67; the Rococo interior was completed after his death). Beyond in a little piazza on the right is the church of **S. Placido** (usually closed) with a façade of 1769, attributed to Stefano Ittar, and a pretty interior.

Via Museo Biscari is named after the huge **Palazzo Biscari**, the most impressive private palace in Catania. The best view of the exterior is from via Dusmet. Here in the 18C the Prince of Biscari, Ignazio Paternò Castello, collected for his famous museum, part of which is preserved in the Museo Civico (see above). In the lovely Rococo Salone della Musica concerts are occasionally held.

On the other side of via Vittorio Emanuele II via Landolina leads to the splendid **Teatro Massimo Bellini**, 1873–90). The narrow streets in this area, which were once a run-down part of the city, have recently become popular with the younger generation since lots of 'pubs' are now open here in the evening. Via Vittorio Emanuele II continues towards the sea passing the **Collegio Cutelli** (left), with a remarkable round courtyard designed by Vaccarini (1779). Piazza dei Martiri has a statue of St Agatha on top of a column from the ancient theatre. Here a wide terrace overlooks the harbour.

## Via Etnea

From the north side of piazza Duomo (map: 11) begins the handsome **via Etnea**, nearly 3km long, the main street of the city (closed to private cars south of Villa Bellini), with the most elegant shops (especially clothes and books) and some cafés. Its wide lava pavements are always crowded. It rises to a splendid view of the peak of Mount Etna in the distance.

Beyond the town hall is the distinguished piazza dell'Università, laid out by Vaccarini. The **university** (map: 11) was founded in 1434 by Alfonso V of Aragon as the first university in Sicily, and rebuilt after the earthquake of 1693; the court was begun by Andrea Amato and finished in 1752 by Giovanni Battista Vaccarini. Just beyond is the **Collegiata**, a royal chapel of c 1768 by Stefano Ittar.

Some way further on via Etnea runs through the huge **piazza Stesicoro** (map: 6,7), the heart of modern Catania, with a monument to Bellini by Giulio Monteverde (1882). Overlooking the piazza is the 18C church of S. Biagio. In the centre are the scant ruins of the **amphitheatre** in black lava, thought to date from the 2C AD. The external circumference was 389m, and the arena was one of the largest after the Colosseum in Rome. There were 56 entrance arches. The visible remains include a corridor, part of the exterior wall, and fragments of the cavea supported on vaults; the rest of the structure still exists in part beneath the surrounding edifices. Its destruction had already begun under Theodoric when it was used as a quarry; Totila made use of the stone in building the city walls in 530, and Count Roger stole its decorative elements to embellish his cathedral in 1091. In 1693 the municipality used the area as a dump for the ruins of the earthquake.

Nearby, in piazza della Borsa are remains of the 18C church of **S. Euplio** covering a 3C Roman hypogeum. It was partially restored in 1978 after its destruction in 1943 (for admission to the crypt apply at the town hall).

Via Manzoni (map: 10), which leads out of the south side of the square parallel to via Etnea is interesting for its numerous well-stocked haberdashery shops and old-fashioned children's clothes shops. Beyond the top end of the square behind S. Biagio is the church of the **S. Carcere**, flanked by a strong defence wall. Incorporated into the Baroque façade is a doorway, with grotesque animal heads, which dates from 1236; it was formerly in the façade of the cathedral. In the interior (open Thurs & Sat 16.00–19.00; Sun & PH 09.30–12.00)

the prison of St Agatha, with a Roman barrel vault, is shown by the custodian.
Via Cappuccini continues uphill to via Maddalena where the church of **S. Agata la Vetere** (map: 6) which has been closed since the earthquake in 1990 stands opposite the church of the **Purità** (or the *Visitazione*), with a curving façade by Battaglia (1775) next to its handsome convent.

A little to the north is the church of **S. Domenico** (map: 6; open before 09.30 and 17.00–18.30; ring at the convent next door). It contains a beautiful *Madonna* by Antonello Gagini (1526), and a painting of *St Vincent Ferrer* by Olivio Sozzi (1757). Some way to the west, in via Castromarina, in a poor district of the town, a tiny **mosque** (map: 5; open 11.00–13.00; Fridays also 17.00–19.00) was built in 1980.

From piazza Stesicoro on via Etnea (near the lone policeman who attempts to regulate the traffic) via S. Gaetano alle Grotte with its daily market leads to the little church of **S. Gaetano alle Grotte** which dates from 1700. The former church, built into a volcanic cavern beneath in 1262, is now usually kept closed (but is sometimes shown by the custodian; donation expected). Photographs in the upper church of the contemporary frescoes help visitors identify them on the much ruined walls below, where the ancient altar survives. The main produce market occupies **piazza Carlo Alberto** (map: 7) overlooked by the fine palace occupied by the Lucchesi-Palli barracks (in the court an antique cella is traditionally held to be the tomb of Stesichorus) next to the huge church of the Carmine.

Via Etnea continues north past the post office. Steps lead up to the charming **Villa Bellini** (map: 2, 6), a fine public garden laid out c 1870, which is crowded on sunny days. It contains a bust of Bellini and a monument to Giovanni Pacini (1796–1867), another Catanese musician. At the north end of the garden a gate leads out to viale Regina Margherita, part of the modern east–west artery of the city, c 5km long.

Further north is a fine **Botanical Garden** (map: 2; open weekdays 09.00–13.00). The main entrance is on via Etnea; but the usual entrance is on via Longo. It is particularly famous for its cacti plants. Via Etnea ends at **Parco Gioeni**, on a lava-flow, opened to the public in 1997 as part of a scheme to create a number of parks on the outskirts of the city. To the east of via Etnea near piazza Lincoln, on via Raffaello Sanzio, land which was formerly owned by a Mafia boss was sequestered and a park opened here in 1994 (named after Giovanni Falcone).

About 500m west of the Botanical Garden, surrounded by tall, modern apartment blocks, is the church of **S. Maria di Gesù** (map: 1), founded in 1442 and built in 1465. To the left is the pretty exterior of the Cappella Paternò which survived the earthquake of 1693. It is entered from the north aisle of the church through a doorway by Antonello Gagini (1519) with a *Pietà* in the lunette above. Inside is a fresco (transferred to wood) of the *Madonna with St Agatha and St Catherine*, by Angelo de Chirico (signed 1525). Above the main altar of the church is a Crucifix by Fra Umile di Petralia, and in the last north chapel, a *Madonna with four angels in adoration* by Antonello Gagini.

In the other direction viale Regina Margherita and its continuation viale XX Settembre, run east beyond via Etnea into piazza Giovanni Verga, a vast square dominated by the **Palazzo di Giustizia** (map: 3; 1952) and the focus of a new and fashionable district. Further east, in corso Italia, **Palazzo delle Scienze** (map: 4; 1942) houses the geological and volcanological collections of the university. The corso, passing close to the **Stazione Circumetnea**, terminates at the sea in piazza Europa, with a shrine on top of a mound of lava. Via Lungomare leads from here through new housing to Ognina. In the other direction the main road leads south towards the main railway station past **Le Ciminiere**, with its tall chimneys, which was built at the end of the last century as a sulphur refinery. It has been restored as a cultural centre with exhibition halls and space for theatrical performances and concerts in the summer.

# Mount Etna and its foothills

This chapter describes the famous volcano, Mount Etna, and the excursions to just below its summit. It also takes in the fertile territory on the lower slopes of the mountain (the best scenery is on the north side), and the lava-built towns at its foot, including Adrano and Randazzo. Other places of particular interest are the Castello Maniace near Bronte, and Acireale on the coast.

### Etna

Mount Etna, to the north-west of Catania, the highest volcano (c 3330m) in Europe and one of the largest in the world, forms a circular cone nearly 40km in diameter. From a distance it appears almost perfectly regular in shape (and the great width of its base detracts from its height), even though the terminal cone with its crater rises from a truncated cone 2801m high on whose sides are about 200 groups of subsidiary craters. The smaller craters have been formed by lateral eruptions (one in 1971 opened three more craters) and are nearly always arranged along a regular line of fracture. Eruptions from the central crater are rare although its depth varies constantly (914m in 1874, 161m in 1897, 244m in 1916).

On the south-east side is the Valle del Bove, an immense chasm, 19km in circumference, bounded on three sides by sheer walls of tufa and lava, in places 900m high. During the eruptions of 1978–79, 1986 and 1992 the lava flowed into this huge natural reservoir, thus avoiding the towns on the south-east slopes. In 1981 Etna was designated a protected area in an attempt to preserve its unique vegetation and prohibit more new buildings; its southern slopes were covered in the 1960s and 1970s by holiday villas. In 1987 some 50,000ha of the mountainside were at last declared a national park.

The **ascent of Etna**, although now easy and commonplace, is an experience which should not be missed, both because of the volcanic phenomena and the superb view. The extent of a visit is subject to the current volcanic activity, and the visibility determined by cloud conditions and the direction of the smoke from the main crater. There are splendid views of the lava fields on the approach roads to the Rifugio Sapienza and Piano Provenzana. Higher up it is usually possible to see smoking and gaseous fissures, and explosions from the main crater. There is often a strong smell of sulphur and much of the mountainside is covered by yellow sulphur patches. The view, beyond the mountain's hundreds of subsidiary cones and craters, can extend across the whole of Sicily, the Aeolian Islands and Calabria. The spectacle is unique owing to the enormous difference in height between Etna and the surrounding hills.

There are organised excursions from the Rifugio Sapienza on the southern slopes and from Piano Provenzana on the northern slopes, both of which can be reached easily by car or bus. The summit of the volcano can also be explored by foot from both these points, and there are some spectacular walks which are signposted on the lower slopes of the mountain. Near the top there is almost always a very strong wind and the temperature can be many degrees below freezing: a warm jacket, sturdy shoes and a hat are in order (shoes and jackets can be hired at the Rifugio Sapienza, or at the *piccolo rifugio* higher up on the Montagnola).

## History

Etna, called *Aetna* in ancient times and *Mongibello* (from *Monte* and *Jebel*, the Arabic word for mountain) by the Sicilians (often simply *La Montagna*), probably originated from a submarine eruption in the gulf which is now occupied by the plain of Catania. Some 130 eruptions have taken place in historical times. In ancient Greece the volcano was held to be the forge of Vulcan or of the Cyclopes, or the mountain from beneath which the imprisoned Titan, Enceladus, forever struggled to free himself. Empedocles, the philosopher, scientist and statesman from Agrigento who lived in the 5C BC, was said to have thrown himself into the crater to create the belief that he was a god.

Among early eruptions that of 475 BC was described by Pindar and Aeschylus, while that of 396, whose lava reached the sea, is said to have prevented the Carthaginian general Himilco from marching on Siracusa in the 5C BC. Hadrian climbed Etna to see the sunrise and the conical shape of the mountain reflected on the island. In 1169, 1329 and 1381 the lava again reached the sea, twice near Acireale, the third time (1381) at Catania.

The most famous of more recent eruptions took place in 1669 when an open cleft extended from the summit to Nicolosi and part of Catania was overwhelmed. The Monti Rossi were formed at this date. Since 1800 there have been over 30 eruptions, the one in 1923 being the most destructive of the 20th century. The British statesman William Ewart Gladstone ascended the volcano in 1838 and left a graphic account in his journal. In 1847 Edward Lear wrote: 'From Catania we saw Etna and went up it; a task, but now it is done I am glad I did it; such extremes of heat and cold at once I never thought it possible to feel.'

In 1908 a huge pit of lava opened in the Valle del Bove. In 1911 there were two eruptions on the north side, creating a cleft 5km long and about 170 temporary craters. In 1923 lava began to flow from the cleft of 1911. The eruption of 1947 threatened Passopisciaro, and that of 1950–51 menaced Rinazzo and Fornazzo before the lava halted. The 1971 eruption destroyed the observatory and the second stage of the cableway on the summit, as well as vineyards and some houses near Fornazzo. The lava-stream cut several roads, and stopped just above S. Alfio. Eruptions on the western slopes at a height of 1600m and 2850m took place in 1974–75. In

1978–79 four new cones erupted and the lava flowed into the Valle del Bove; the town of Fornazzo was again threatened. Nine people were killed by an explosion on the edge of the main crater itself in 1979. An eruption in 1981 caused considerable damage around Randazzo, crossing the main road for Linguaglossa. In the spring of 1983 activity started up on the opposite side of the mountain above Nicolosi and Belpasso (in the area of the 1910 lava flow). The main road up the southern slopes from Nicolosi was damaged and the cableway above the Rifugio Sapienza. After several months dynamite was exploded in an attempt to divert the lava stream.

In 1984 an earthquake damaged the little town of Zafferana Etnea and in 1986 eruptions took place on the south-east side near Milo, but no damage was caused as the lava flowed into the Valle del Bove. In 1987 two people were killed by an explosion on the edge of the main crater. In 1991–92 eruptions took place for four months and threatened the town of Zafferana Etnea again. Dynamite was exploded and huge blocks of reinforced concrete dropped from helicopters in an attempt to arrest the flow and divert it into the Valle del Bove. Although the concrete blocks had no effect, the lava halted within one kilometre of Zafferana Etnea.

**Vegetation**. The soil at the foot of Etna is extraordinarily fertile as a result of enormous quantities of lava having poured out of the craters at various dates (156,000 cubic metres in 1908; 28,317,000 cubic metres in 1669; 31,148,000 cubic metres in a prehistoric flow near Randazzo). In the cultivated zone (*pedemontana*) oranges and lemons are grown behind low, black, lava walls, on which poinsettias and bougainvillea grow wild. The higher slopes of the mountain were forested up until the 19C, but now they are planted with groves of walnuts, cherries, apples, pistachio, almonds and vineyards. Broom flourishes on many of the lava-flows. At 1300m forest trees grow, especially oaks, chestnuts, pines and beeches. Reafforestation (mostly chestnut trees) is taking place. Above 2000m extends the 'desert zone', with some junipers and the *spino santo* (*Astragalus aetnensis*), which collects little heaps of earth round it, affording protection to a few violets in spring and crocuses in autumn. An unusual lichen flourishes in the hot vapour of the large fumarole near where the observatory used to stand. Animal life is scarce. The heat of the rocks and the hot vapours of the terminal cone cause the snow to melt partly even in winter. In certain depressions with a northern aspect the snow used to be preserved for refrigeration purposes throughout the summer by covering it with volcanic ash, and it was transported on mule-back in the eastern part of the island.

## The southern approach ~ Etna Sud

## ■ Practical information

*Information offices*. The offices of the Parco Regionale dell'Etna are in Nicolosi (via Etnea 107, ☎ 095/914588). SITAS information offices at the Rifugio Sapienza (☎ 095/914209) and at Nicolosi (45 piazza Vittorio Emanuele, ☎ 095/911158). Mountain guides, ☎ 095/7914755.

**Getting there**
The journey (34km) by **car** from Catania to the Rifugio Sapienza (1910m) and back may be made easily in a day. The visibility is usually best in the early morning, as the summit is often shrouded in clouds later on in the day. The night can also be spent at the Rifugio Sapienza where night excursions can be arranged in order to see the sunrise.

Every day a **bus** (run by AST) departs at 8am from piazza Stazione in Catania and takes about 2hr to reach the Rifugio Sapienza. In July and August a second service is run by AST, leaving piazza Stazione at 11.15 for Nicolosi where a connecting bus continues to Rifugio Sapienza. A bus returns to Catania from the Rifugio Sapienza every day at 16.00.

There are a number of **walks** along marked footpaths which start from the road up to the Rifugio Sapienza, including the nature trail to Monte Nero degli Zappini. There are also walks from Zafferana Etnea towards the Valle del Bove.

## The ascent from the Rifugio Sapienza

The **organised excursion** from Rifugio Sapienza takes about 2hr. Tickets (58,000 lire) which include the cableway, bus ride and guide are purchased at the cableway station near the Rifugio Sapienza. From Rifugio Sapienza a cableway which operates 09.00–16.00 every day (enclosed cabins which can each accommodate up to six people) climbs in 15 minutes to a height of 2600m; from there small buses (which can each take about 16 people) continue to the site of the Torre del Filosofo (2900m) where guides meet you and lead you up an easy path to a height of about 3000m.

**Ascent by foot**. Before undertaking the climb alone advice must be obtained about weather conditions, etc. at the SITAS offices at the Rifugio Sapienza, or in Catania (64 via Vecchia Ognina) or Nicolosi (where guides are available to accompany walkers). The easiest and most usual approach from Sapienza follows the track used by the small buses. About 4hr should be allowed for the return trip from the refuge. The most spectacular time for the ascent is before dawn.

**Hotels**
**Nicolosi**, ★★★ *Gemmellero*, 160 via Etnea, ☎ 095/911373, fax 095/ 911071; *Biancaneve*, 163 via Etnea, ☎ 095/911176, fax 095/911194.
**Mountain refuge**. *Rifugio Sapienza*, ☎ 095/911062.
**Campsite**. **Nicolosi**, ★★ campsite *Etna*, via Goethe, Pineta Monti Rossi, ☎ 095/914309.

**Restaurant**. **Nicolosi**, **C** (pizzeria) *Le Tartarughe*, 45 via Marconi.

The **Strada dell'Etna** was opened in 1934 by Vittorio Emanuele III from Catania. It is well signposted beyond Nicolosi. **Nicolosi** (990m; population 5400) is one of the best centres for visiting Etna. To the west are the craters of the **Monti Rossi** (949m), which represent one of the most important subsidiary groups of craters (over 3km round), formed in 1669.

Beyond Nicolosi the well-engineered road (partly re-aligned since damage in 1983) climbs through lava-beds and some woods, where many houses have been built. It crosses the lava flows of 1886 and 1910; the names of the craters on either side of the road are indicated. Walks off this road are also signposted. A loop road (left) leads to the winter-sports fields of **Serra La Nave** (1750m), where much new building has taken place near the pinewoods. Several ski-lifts were destroyed in the eruptions of 1983. From here there is one of the closest and best views of the summit, the line of the cableway, and some of the more recent lava-streams. The university **observatory** here can sometimes be visited.

The main road continues to the **Casa Contoniera** (1882m), a small group of restaurants and cafés (and an information office). A little higher up (1910m) the road ends at a huge car-park (invaded with tourist booths and cafés) beside the **Rifugio Sapienza**, a mountain refuge. Always open, it has sleeping accommodation, a restaurant and guides. In the desert of hardened volcanic lava (or clinker) nearby several extinct volcanoes can be explored easily on foot.

A cableway ascends from here up the slopes of the **Montagnola** (2507m), a crater of 1763 through a desert of lapilli devoid of trees with splendid views of the sea and port of Catania. It takes 15 minutes to reach the *Piccolo Rifugio*. This is the site of the second cableway station and the old observatory, both destroyed in the eruption of 1971. Here walking shoes and warm jackets can be hired for a small sum, and the four-wheel-drive vans are boarded to continue up (in 10min.) to the site of the small Torre del Filosofo (2926m), a tower, said to have been the home of Empedocles, but more probably a Roman memorial commemorating Hadrian's ascent, which was also ruined in recent eruptions. A little wooden hut here has a bar and shop. Guides take small groups up an easy path (in 10min.) to a height of about 3000m (about 300m below the main crater at the summit). Although at present you are not allowed any nearer to the main crater, from this distance you can usually see (and hear) volcanic activity.

Another road (narrower and in places poorly surfaced) descends from the Rifugio Sapienza down the thickly wooded eastern slopes of the mountain and across numerous lava-flows to Zafferana Etnea (see below).

## The northern approach ~ Etna Nord

### ■ Practical information

*Information office*. Linguaglossa: Pro-Loco, piazza Annunziata, ☎ 095/643094.

### *Getting there*
Excursions run by *Circumetnea* (from piazza Teatro Massimo, Catania) by train and bus to Linguaglossa. For Piano Provenzano in January–April a ski-bus run by *FCE* (*Ferrovia Circumetnea*) leaves Catania on Sun and PH at 07.00 for Piano Provenzana (in 1hr 30min.), returning at 15.30. From May–October excursions are organised to below the crater from the Piano Provenzano refuge by *STAR* (233 via Roma, Linguaglossa, ☎ 095/643180).

*Hotel*. **Linguaglossa**. ★★ *Happy Day*, 9 via Mareneve, ☎ & fax 095/643484.

*Pasticceria* in the church square.

**Linguaglossa** (550m; population 5500) is the best centre for excursions on the northern slopes of Etna. The pleasant little town has a number of late 19C and early 20C houses. The 18C church has its doorways and windows decorated with lava and elaborate lamps on its façade.

The mountain road, known as the *Mareneve*, which climbs towards the summit of Etna, begins here. It leads up through the **Pineta di Linguaglossa**, ancient pinewoods of great interest to naturalists, to the ski-fields of **Piano Provenzana** (1800m), the main ski resort on Etna, with a refuge, and five ski-lifts (1800m and 2300m). From here excursions by four-wheel-drive vans are organised to below the summit. It is also possible to walk up the cone from here in c 3hr (the easiest way is to follow the track used by the excursion vans).

Another mountain road descends from Piano Provenzana following the eastern slope of the mountain passing beneath the Citelli refuge (1741m; closed after damage in 1983), to Fornazzo.

## The foothills of Etna

## ▨ Practical information

*Information offices*. APT Catania, ☎ 095/7306233. **Randazzo** Pro-Loco, piazza Municipio.

### Getting there
The **road** which encircles the foot of Etna traverses spectacular countryside, with rich vegetation. There are numerous plantations of pistachio trees, prickly pear and vineyards. There are lovely ever-changing views of Etna (although the summit is often hidden by cloud in the afternoon) and its volcanic outcrops, and the fertile land is densely cultivated. The road on the east side of the mountain is very windy and slow, while the stretch between Linguaglossa and Adrano is much faster.

**Railway**. The *Circumetnea*, opened in 1898, provides a classic rail trip. From Catania (corso delle Provincie; map: 4) to Randazzo in c 2hr, continuing less frequently to Giarre in c 1hr more; from there the direct return (poor connections) may be made by the main Messina–Siracusa line.

Frequent **bus** service from Catania to Paternò and Adrano.

### Hotels
**S. Giovanni La Punta**. ★★★★ *Villa Paradiso dell'Etna*, 37 via Viagrande, ☎ 095/7512409, fax 095/7413861, with restaurant.
**Zafferana Etnea**. ★★★ *Airone*, 67 via Cassone, ☎ 095/7081819, fax 095/7082142; *Primavera dell'Etna*, 86 via Cassone, ☎ 095/7082348, fax 095/7081695. ★★ *Del Bosco*, 75 via Cassone, ☎ 095/7081888, fax 095/7081791.
**Milo**. ★★★ **campsite** *Mareneve*, 30 via del Bosco, ☎ 095/7082163.
**Paternò**. ★★ *Sicilia*, 391 via Vittorio Emanuele, ☎ 095/853604, fax 095/854742.

### Restaurants
**S. Giovanni La Punta**. **A** *Villa Paradiso dell'Etna*, 37 via Viagrande; **B** *Il Giardino di Bacco*, 3 via Piave.

**Castello Maniace** is a lovely place to **picnic** (where there is also a café and a restaurant).

**S. Alfio**. **C** *Casa Perrotta*, località Perrotta.

**Randazzo**. **B** *Trattoria Veneziano*, 8 via Romano.

**Trecastagni**. **B** *Uliveto*, 4 via Perni.

*Cafés and pasticcerie*

**Randazzo** *Santo Musumeci*, piazza S. Maria; **Bronte**, *Bar il Tartufo*, for pistachio ice-cream and confectionery.

*Annual festivals*

**Zafferana Etnea** autumn festival on October Sundays with local specialities sold on the streets.

**Randazzo** festival on 15 August.

**Bronte** pistachio festival in early October.

**S. Alfio** festival on 10 May.

## The eastern and southern foothills

**Zafferana Etnea** (600m) is the main town on the east side of Etna. It was damaged by earthquake in 1986, and a lava-flow in 1992 reached the outskirts of the town (this can now be visited: it is at the end of a signposted road, where a statue was set up as a thanks offering to the Madonna). Climbs towards the Valle del Bove can be made from here.

To the north is **S. Alfio** near which is a famous giant **chestnut tree** known as the *Castagno dei Cento Cavalli*, because its branches were reputed to be able to shelter 100 horses with their riders. It is one of the largest trees to survive on the island, with a circumference of over 60m and it is hundreds of years old. The area was once a forest of chestnuts, and some chestnut woods survive here. The numerous lovely old farmhouses in the district built out of lava have now almost all been abandoned. The fruit from the apple orchards in the district is sold on the streets in the autumn.

To the south at **Trecastagni** the Chiesa Madre is perhaps the purest Renaissance building in Sicily, thought to be the work of Antonello Gagini. The Chiesa del Bianco has a good 15C campanile.

Nicolosi, the most important centre for exploring the southern slopes of Etna, is described above.

At **Paternò** (population 46,100) much new building sprawls at the base of a 14C castle. The austere tower built of volcanic rock commands the wide Simeto valley. It was restored in 1900, with a fine hall and frescoed chapel (key at the municipio). From the terrace there is a good view. Frederick II of Aragon died near Paternò while journeying to Enna. The churches of S. Francesco and S. Maria della Valle di Giosafat retain Gothic elements.

East of Paternò is the village of **Motta S. Anastasia** perched on a rock, with a fine 11C Norman castle which preserves its crenellations. The unusual name of **Misterbianco**, a town now surrounded by industrial suburbs, is from a Benedictine monastery, the *monastero bianco*, destroyed, with the town, in 1669.

North of Paternò is **Biancavilla** where the best oranges in Sicily are produced: beside the extensive orange plantations are fields of olive trees and hedges of prickly pear.

**Adrano** (560m), with 35,000 inhabitants, represents the ancient *Adranon*

*The Ponte dei Saraceni near Adrano*

founded by Dionysius the Elder. Overlooking the huge Giardino della Vittoria (with superb trees) is the former monastery of **S. Lucia**, rebuilt in the 15C–16C, and now a school, flanked by the towering façade of its church (1775), with a pretty oval interior.

The imposing black lava **castle** was built in 1070 by Count Roger. The interior, with a delightful local **museum**, has been closed for restoration since 1995. The archaeological section includes prehistoric material from Stentinello and Castelluccio (ground and first floors). On the second floor the later finds from Mendolito (see below) include a hanging Ascos and bronze figurine, *Il Banchettante* of the 6C BC. In a little Norman chapel, with an apse fresco, is a collection of coins from ancient Adrano. The third floor has paintings, most of them in very poor condition.

Next to the castle is the **Chiesa Madre** preceded by an unfinished portico which was to have supported a bell-tower but which was left unfinished in 1902–03 (there is a photograph of the project inside the church). The interior, of Norman origin, incorporates 16 basalt columns possibly from a Greek temple. High up above the west door is a fine polyptych of the 16C Messina school in a good frame. The painted Crucifix of the 15C was damaged by restoration in 1924. In the transepts are four panels (two saints and the *Annunciation*) by Girolamo Alibrandi. In the pretty sacristy is a fine painting of the *Last Supper* (in a good frame) by Pietro Paolo Vasta.

Off a byroad below the town (signposted *Strada per il Ponte dei Saraceni*) a poorly surfaced road between low lava walls leads in c 1.5km past citrus plantations and lovely small, old farmhouses to the Simeto river spanned by the impressive 14C **Ponte dei Saraceni**, an extremely well-preserved bridge. It has four unequal arches decorated with black lava and the path over the top is still traversable. In this beautiful peaceful spot there is a view of Etna and a waterfall on the rocky bed of the Simeto. Nearby (not signposted) are a few remains of the walls and south gate of the ancient Sicel town of **Mendolito**.

Remains of Greek **walls** can be seen in fields outside Adrano to the east (in contrada Cartalemi). A huge experimental solar energy plant, financed by the EU, was opened north of Adrano in 1981, in contrada Contrasto.

*j*, a town of 19,800 inhabitants, is an important centre for the
pistachio trees (90 per cent of the pistachios produced in Italy are
*e*). The fruit is harvested every two years at the end of August and
*ig* of September. Pistachios are used in the local cuisine for pasta dishes
*l* as for sweets and ice-creams. Recent new building on the outskirts of
*ite* has obscured its characteristic battlemented church steeples.

To the north, in a little wooded valley on the Saraceno, a tributary of the Simeto,
CASTELLO MANIACE or **Abbazia di Maniace** is situated (open every day 09.00–
13.30, 14.30–19.00). The house and estate were presented to Admiral Horatio
Nelson in 1799 by Ferdinand IV (later King Ferdinand I of the Two Sicilies). Nelson
was bestowed with the dukedom of Bronte in gratitude for his help the year before
when the king had fled from Naples on Nelson's flagship during the Napoleonic
invasion. Nelson never managed to visit Maniace, but the title and estate passed,
by the marriage of Nelson's niece, to the family of Viscount Bridport who sold the
property in 1981 to the comune of Bronte. A very impressive careful restoration is
in progress of the extensive buildings, some of which may be used as a local
museum. There is also a restaurant and café in the outbuildings.

A convent was founded here in 1173 by Margaret of Navarre, mother of
William II, on the spot where the Byzantine general George Maniakes defeated the
Saracens in 1040, with the help of the Russian Varangian Guard and Norman
mercenaries, among whom there may have been the Scandanavian hero Harold
Hardrada. In the courtyard is a stone Cross memorial to Nelson. The 13C **chapel**,
with a good portal, has a Byzantine *Madonna and Child*, two charming primitive
reliefs of the *Annunciation*, and two 15C paintings. In the **barn**, where the roof
has been restored, there are walkways above excavations of an older church. The
**house** retains its appearance from the days when it was the residence of
Alexander Hood who lived here from 1873 until just before World War II: it has
lovely tiled floors (beautifully restored) and English wallpaper.

The delightful **gardens**, also designed by Hood (with palm trees, planted in
1912, magnolias, cypresses and box hedges), can also be visited. The vast estate
with plantations of fruit trees was broken up and sold off in 1981. The Scottish
writer William Sharp (who also published under the pseudonym Fiona Macleod)
died here in 1905 and is buried beneath an Iona cross in the **cemetery** (shown
on request).

## The northern foothills

Between Bronte and Randazzo the landscape is barren, with numerous volcanic
deposits. The countryside, studded with little farmhouses built of black lava, is
used for grazing and the cultivation of vineyards. There is a large lava-stream of
1832 near **Maletto**, whose sandstone cliff (1140m) is the highest sedimentary
rock on Etna (views). The low vineyards in this region produce an excellent red
and white wine (*Etna rosso* and *Etna bianco*).

## Randazzo

Randazzo (765m), above the Alcantara valley, is a lava-built town of great
antiquity (population 11,700), which has never in historic times suffered
volcanic destruction. Its medieval history resolves itself into a rivalry between
the three churches of S. Maria, S. Nicolò, and S. Martino, each of which served

as cathedral for alternate periods of three years. The parishioners (of Greek, Latin and Lombard origin) of each church spoke different dialects until the 16C. It was damaged from allied bombs when, in August 1943, the Germans made it the strong-point of their last resistance in the island.

**S. Maria**, the present cathedral, is a 13C church (attributed without foundation to Leone Cumier), with fine black lava apses and a three-storeyed south portal (approached by two flights of steps) in the Catalan-Gothic style of the 15C. The dome is attributed to Venanzio Marvuglia and the black and white tower was badly restored in 1863. The terrace, beyond the sacristy and canonica above a 16C portico, looks out over the Alcantara valley.

The interior (1594) has fine black columns and capitals, one of which serves as an altar. Over the south door is a small painting with a view of the town attributed to Girolamo Alibrandi (15C); over the north door is a fragment of a fresco of the *Madonna and Child* (13C). The church contains six paintings by Giuseppe Velasquez (on the first north altar, the fourth and fifth altars in the north and south aisles, and on the right wall of the sanctuary). The second north and second south altarpieces are by Onofrio Gabrieli. The third south altar is by Jean van Houbraken, of the 17C Messina school. The treasury (closed) contains a chalice given to the church by Peter I of Aragon.

Via Umberto I leads past the southern flank of S. Maria past a little natural history museum (with an ornithological section and a collection of shells) to piazza Municipio where the **Palazzo Comunale** (recently restored) occupies a 14C convent reconstructed in 1610. The lovely cloister has columns of lava. From here the narrow, pretty via degli Archi leads beneath four arches to **S. Nicoló** which dates mainly from the 16C–17C (damaged in 1943). The apse, however, is original (13C). In the north transept is a seated statue of *St Nicholas* (with two small reliefs below) by Antonello Gagini signed and dated 1523. In the south transept is a 16C painted Crucifix and four delicately carved bas-reliefs of the *Passion* by Giacomo Gagini. Outside is an 18C copy of a curious antique figure of a man, thought to symbolise the union of the three parishes (see above). Nearby is Palazzo Clarentano (1509) and a medieval arch tunnels beneath houses back towards the corso.

Via Umberto I continues to the district of S. Martino, with evident signs of shell fire from the last war. The damaged church of **S. Martino** preserves its fine 14C campanile (covered for restoration). The façade has 15C reliefs of saints and martyrs. In the interior are black lava columns and in the south transept a statue of the *Madonna and Child* by the school of Gagini (which retains part of its polychrome decoration). In the north aisle is a triptych by a local painter influenced by Antonello da Messina. The marble font is by Angelo Riccio da Messina (1447). In front of the church is the little 13C **castle** which was rebuilt in 1645 and used as a prison up until 1973. It has been restored and the **Museo Vagliasindi** was opened here in 1998. The collection includes some fine vases from a neighbouring Greek necropolis (5C–2C BC), including a red-figure Oinochoe of the 5C, as well as coins and jewellery. A collection of puppets is also to be displayed here. Just beyond is Porta S. Martino (1753) in the walls.

To the east of **Passopisciaro**, near a huge lava-flow of 1981, oaks and chestnuts are now being replaced by vineyards and olive trees. Some of the prettiest scenery in the Etna foothills can be seen here, with numerous handsome old russet-coloured houses (many of them now abandoned), and excellent views of the volcano and, to the north, the wooded mountains beyond the Alcantara.

An attractive little Byzantine Arab building locally called La Cuba can be seen to the north in the beautiful valley of the Alcantara. It is reached by taking the Malvagna road from the little horticultural centre of **Moio Alcantara**. After the cemetery the first turning on the right (unsignposted) leads to the tiny ruined chapel which survives in a field just to the right of the road amidst olive trees (before the road reaches the local stadium).

**Castiglione di Sicilia**, an ancient city of 4700 inhabitants, in a fine position perched on a crag (621m), was once a stronghold of Roger of Lauria (see below). The Duomo at the top of the town is closed for restoration. Below it is the church of S. Antonio (open all day), with an ingenious façade and campanile, in a charming little piazza. Inside it preserves delightful intarsia work (1700) and four octagonal paintings by Giovanni Tuccari. In the sanctuary is an elaborate wooden confessional supporting a pulpit and a simple painted organ loft.

Below the town off the Randazzo road (well signposted for the *Cuba Bizantino*) is another abandoned Byzantine Arab building surrounded by vineyards. It is approached along a narrow country road beyond a railway line. Built of lava probably in the late 8C it has an interesting plan and although very ruined the vault survives.

There are oaks and chestnuts near **Linguaglossa**, an important centre for excursions on Etna (described above). At **Rovittello** there is a golf course. **Piedimonte Etneo** is another pleasant little town surrounded by fine citrus fruit plantations, and with views of Taormina and Castel Mola. Nearer the sea is **Fiumefreddo di Sicilia** (population 9200) amid plantations of oranges. For the coastal oasis at the mouth of the River Fiumefreddo, see below.

## Acireale and its coastal environs

Acireale (population 47,100) is a pleasant, prosperous town in a good position above the sea (161m). It is in the midst of a fertile valley of Etna, intensely cultivated with citrus trees. The town, which has been visited as a spa for many years, stands on seven streams of lava. It is interesting for its Baroque buildings, some of which date from the 17C; others were erected after the earthquake of 1693. Acireale and several neighbouring villages derive their name from the Aci, the mythical river which came into being on the death of Acis, the shepherd beloved by Galatea and killed by Polyphemus.

## ■ Practical information

***Information office***. Azienda Autonoma, 177 corso Umberto, ☎ 095/604522. Acireale Terme, 47 via delle Terme, ☎ 095/604508.

***Buses*** to Catania and to Nicolosi and the foothills of Etna.

### Hotels
**Acireale**. ★★★★ *Aloha d'Oro*, 10 via Alcide De Gasperi, ☎ 095/604344, fax 095/606984; *S. Tecla*, 100 via Balestrate, ☎ 095/604933, fax 095/607705.

★★★ *Delle Terme*, 20 via Alcide De Gasperi, ☎ 095/601166, fax 095/601182 and *Teclina*, 100 via Balestrate, S. Tecla, ☎ 095/604933, fax 095/607705.
★★ *Maugeri*, 27 via Garibaldi, ☎ & fax 608666.
**Aci Castello**. Large ★★★★ and ★★★ hotels at Aci Trezza and Cannizzaro, including (★★★★) the *Catania Sheraton*, 45 via Antonello da Messina, Cannizzaro, ☎ 095/271557, fax 095/271380, with restaurant (**A**) *Il Timo*, and ★★★ *Eden Riviera*, 57 via Litteri at Aci Trezza, ☎ 095/277760, fax 095/277761.
**Campsites** on the sea: ★★ *La Timpa*, 25 via Floristella, ☎ 095/7648155; *Panorama*, 55 via S. Caterina, ☎ 095/605987.

### Restaurants

**Acireale**. **B** *La Brocca*, 49 corso Savoia; *Il Panoramico*, viale dello Ionico (on the Giarre road); *La Grotta (da Carmelo)*, 46 via Scalo Grande at S. Maria la Scala.
**Aci Trezza**. **A** *Galatea*, 146 via Livorno; **C:** *Baci e Abbracci dei Vicerè*, 59 via Litteri (pizzeria).
**Aci Castello** (Cannizzaro). **A** *Selene*, 24 via Mollica; *Il Timo* (in the Catania Sheraton hotel, see above).
**Pasticceria**. **Acireale** *Giuseppe Castorina*, corso Umberto and corso Savoia.

**Annual festival**. The carnival of Acireale (in February or March) is one of the most famous in Italy.

At the south end of the town, near the railway station (opened in 1866) are the sulphur baths of **S. Venera** in a park; the waters have been used since Roman times. The spa building of 1873 stands near the modern Hotel Delle Terme.
The main corso Vittorio Emanuele leads up to piazza Vigo, where the church of S. Sebastiano has a fine 17C façade in the Spanish style with numerous statues and a delightful frieze of putti with garlands. The balustrade and statues are by Giovanni Battista Marino (1754). On the other side of the piazza with fine palm trees and two charming little kiosks, is the large classical **Palazzo Pennisi di Floristella**, which once housed a famous numismatic collection (now owned by the region of Sicily and moved to Siracusa). Beyond, the main streets of the town meet at the long piazza Duomo. Here is the huge 17C **Palazzo Comunale** which has splendid balconies supported on monsters, and the church of **SS. Pietro e Paolo**, with a fine early 18C façade and campanile. The 17C **Duomo** has a neo-Gothic façade which was added at the beginning of this century by Giovanni Battista Basile. Inside at the east end are 18C frescoes by the local painter Pietro Paolo Vasta.
Opposite, via Cavour leads to the church of **S. Domenico**, which has another elaborate façade beside the large 17C **Palazzo Musmeci** with an unusual curving façade and pretty windows. At no. 17 via Marchese di S. Giuliano, opposite a charming little Baroque palace, is the **Biblioteca** and **Pinacoteca Zelantea** in a fine building of 1913/14. The Accademia was founded in 1671, and the library in 1716. It now has some 100,000 vols and is one of the most important on the island. The Pinacoteca (usually open on Mon & Wed 09.00–12.30) contains paintings and engravings by local painters from the 17C onwards and a Roman bust, thought to be a portrait of Julius Caesar (1C AD). It also has an eclectic collection including shells, wigs, a carriage and archaeological finds. In this area there are some fine early 18C buildings.

At the north end of the town is the **Belvedere**, a public garden laid out in 1848, which has a good view. Nearby is the little neo-classical church of **S. Maria dell'Indirizzo**, by Stefano Ittar.

A pleasant walk follows via Romeo from the cathedral and the picturesque strada delle Chiazzette to **S. Maria la Scala**, a little fishing village with a port. In the summer boat trips are organised from Stazzo south to the Faraglioni and Aci Castello.

### Environs of Acireale

To the south of Acireale is **Aci Trezza** which was described by Giovanni Verga in *I Malavoglia*.

ACI CASTELLO (population 18,600), now surrounded by ugly buildings, has a pretty little quay with colourful fishing boats beneath its **castle** (open daily 09.00–13.00, 15.30–18.00) on a splendid basalt rock of extremely interesting geological formation which sticks sharply out of the sea. It was covered with lava in the eruption of 1169. It was rebuilt by Roger of Lauria, the rebel admiral of Frederick II (1297). Frederick succeeded in taking it by building a wooden tower of equal height alongside. A long flight of steps built in the lava lead up to a beautifully kept little cactus garden. Here is the entrance to the small **Museo Civico**, with interesting mineralogical, palaeontological and archaeological material, including underwater finds (well labelled). Across the bright green sea there is a fine view of the **Isole de' Ciclopi** (or **Faraglioni**), the largest of which is the **Isola Lachea** (or Isola di Aci), remarkable basalt rocks of volcanic origin. These were said to be the rocks which the blinded Polyphemus hurled at the ships of Ulysses.

Further south, now a suburb of Catania, is **Ognina**, on a little bay, perhaps the Portus Ulixis of the *Aeneid*, half-filled with lava in the 15C.

To the north of Acireale the pretty shore is known as the *Riviera dei Limoni*; citrus fruit plantations continue along the coast all the way to Taormina. Outside Mangano is the fertile lava-stream of 1329.

**Giarre** (population 27,300) is traversed by the wide main road, still paved in lava, where ceramics and Sicilian folk art are sold. The town has unexpectedly grand eclectic buildings and a huge 18C church. In the north-east corner of the province, near Marina di Cottone, is an oasis at the mouth of the **River Fiumefreddo**, a protected area since 1984. Papyrus and other aquatic plants grow at the source of the river. **Calatabiano** is dominated by a medieval castle, which is not built on lava, despite the legend that Himilco was diverted here by a lava-stream from his direct march on Siracusa (396 BC).

# Caltagirone and environs

Caltagirone, in the province of Catania, is one of the most important inland towns of the island (population 38,500). The old town, with pleasant Baroque and Art Nouveau buildings, is built on three hills (608m), to which it owes its irregular plan and narrow streets and its medieval name *Regina dei Monti*. It has been noted throughout its history for its ceramic ware, and numerous artisans' workshops are still active here. The use of majolica tiles and terracotta finials is characteristic of the local architecture.

# ■ Practical information

*Information office*. Azienda Autonoma del Turismo, 3 via Volta Libertini (off via Emanuele Taranto), ☎ 0933/53809.

### Getting there
**Railway station**. Piazza della Repubblica, built in 1975 about 500m from the public gardens. On the Catania–Gela line, it has services to Catania in c 2hr.
**Buses** from the railway station to Catania and Piazza Armerina (*AST*); to Palermo and Gela (*SAIS*), to Catania (*Etna Trasporti*) and to Ragusa and its province (*Ditta Pitrelli*).
**Parking** in via Roma (some free spaces; others with an hourly limit).

### Hotels
★★★ *Villa S. Mauro*, 10 Porto Salvo, ☎ 0933/26500, fax 0933/31661.
★★ *Monteverde*, 11 via delle Industrie, ☎ 0933/53682, fax 0933/53533. *Agriturismo* accommodation: *Testa Crispino*, contrada Angeli, on the Niscemi road (☎ 0933/25317).

### Restaurants
**C** S. *Giorgio*, viale Regina Elena; *La Baita*, 117 viale Milazzo; *La Scala*, scala S. Maria del Monte; *Non solo Vino*, 1 via Vittorio Emanuele.
Outside the town at Bosco S. Pietro, contrada Corvaccio (**C**) *La Quercia*.
**Pasticceria** in via Luigi Sturzo.
The public gardens are a pleasant place to **picnic.**

The Politeama **theatre** has been closed for many years for restoration.

*Annual festivals*. The *Scala* is illuminated with oil lamps on 24–25 July, when there is a also a ceramics fair, and the procession of S. Giacomo. Processions etc. during Easter week and an exhibition of terracotta whistles. There are also various events at Christmas.

There are some 120 **ceramic workshops** in the town which sell their products. Many of them are around piazza Umberto and on the *Scala*.

### History
Traces of one or more Bronze Age and Iron Age settlements have been found in the area. The Greek city, together with other centres in central and southern Sicily, came under the influence of Gela. The present name is of Arabic origin (*kal at*, castle and *gerun*, caves). The town was conquered by the Genoese in 1030 and destroyed by the earthquake of 1693. A bombardment of July 1943 caused more than 700 casualties. The sculptor Antonuzzo Gagini (c 1576–1627) died at Caltagirone, where his son Gian Domenico was probably born.

The politician and priest Don Luigi Sturzo (1871–1959) is a much honoured native of the town. He advocated local autonomy and he improved social conditions here while he was mayor. He was a founder of the national *Partito Popolare* in 1919, and remained secretary of the party until 1923. This was the first Catholic political party, a forerunner of the Christian Democrat Party which came into being in 1942 and was to remain at the centre of Italian political life for most of the 20th century.

In the central piazza Umberto I a bank occupies a building of 1783 by Natale Bonaiuto. The **cathedral** was completely transformed in 1920. In the south aisle are altarpieces by the Vaccaro, a 19C family of local painters, and in the south transept an unusual carved Crucifix attributed to Giovanni de' Mattinari (1500). Beyond is the **Corte Capitaniale**, a delightful one-storey building decorated in the 16C–17C by Antonuzzo and Gian Domenico Gagini (in very poor repair). In piazza del Municipio is the neo-classical façade of the former Teatro Comunale, which serves as an entrance to the **Galleria Luigi Sturzo**, an unusual monumental building inaugurated in 1959. The **Municipio** has a fine façade of 1895.

Adjacent to the piazza rises the impressive long flight of 142 steps known as the *Scala*. It has colourful majolica risers, predominantly yellow, green and blue, on a white ground. They were designed by Giuseppe Giacolone in 1606, and altered in the 19C. It is a tiring climb (past numerous little ceramic workshops) up to **S. Maria del Monte**, once the mother church. The Baroque façade is by Francesco Battaglia and Natale Bonaiuto. The campanile, by Venanzio Marvuglia, is one of the very few bell-towers which can be climbed in Sicily. A little spiral staircase, which gets narrower and lower as it reaches the top, leads to the bell-chamber, from which there is a fine view. The church owns a *Madonna* attributed to the workshop of Domenico Gagini. Higher up is the former church of S. Nicola and there are interesting medieval streets in this area.

From near the foot of the steps via Luigi Sturzo leads past the church of **S. Maria degli Angeli** with a 19C façade, behind which the façade of **S. Chiara** can be seen, by Rosario Gagliardi (1743–48), which contains majolica decorations. Further uphill is **Palazzo della Magnolia** (no. 76), an elaborate Art Nouveau house. Just beyond, the 19C façade of **S. Domenico** faces that of **S. Salvatore** by Natale Bonaiuto (1794). It has a pretty white and gold octagonal interior with a Gaginesque *Madonna*. A modern chapel contains the tomb of Luigi Sturzo (1871–1959; see above). Via Sturzo continues uphill past the former **ospedale delle Donne**, an interesting building, recently well restored and now used for exhibitions of contemporary art. The road ends at **S. Giorgio**, rebuilt in 1699, which contains a beautiful little *Trinity*, attributed to Roger van der Weyden (a fragile painting in poor condition). From the terrace (left) there is a fine view of the countryside.

From piazza del Municipio (see above) the pleasant corso Vittorio Emanuele passes several fine palaces, and the Art Nouveau post office (still in use) on the way to the basilica of **S. Giacomo**, rebuilt in 1694–1708; at the side a pretty flight of steps ascends through the base of the campanile. In the interior, above the west door, the marble coat of arms of the city is by Gian Domenico Gagini. In the north aisle is a blue-and-brown portal (formerly belonging to the baptistery), and a blue-and-gold arch in the Cappella del Sacramento by Antonuzzo Gagini. In the north transept is the charming little Portale delle Reliquie, also by Antonuzzo, with bronze doors by Agostino Sarzana. In the chapel to the left of the sanctuary (behind glass doors) is a silver urn (illuminated on request), the masterpiece of Nibilio Gagini (signed 1604). In the sanctuary is a processional statue of *St Giacomo* by Vincenzo Archifel (1518) protected by a bronze canopy of 1964 (the original gilded throne is kept in the museum). This and the urn are carried through the streets of the town in a procession on 25 July.

From piazza del Municipio via Principe Amedeo returns to piazza Umberto I past (left) the **Chiesa del Collegio**, with a good façade decorated with statues, well seen below the road. It was built at the end of the 16C. It contains a painting of the *Annunciation* by Antonio Catalano, and a *Pietà* by Filippo Paladino.

Below piazza Umberto I is the **Museo Civico** (open 09.30–13.30; Tues, Fri, & Sat, also 16.00–19.00; closed Mon) housed in a massive building built as a prison in 1782 by Natale Bonaiuto. It is an interesting stone edifice with an interior court and double columns. The museum was founded in 1914. On the stairs are architectural fragments and, on the landing, four 19C terracotta vases by Bongiovanni Vaccaro. Beyond a room with modern local ceramics, another room contains the gilded throne of St Giacomo (16C, by Scipione di Guido; the statue is kept in the church of S. Giacomo), a bishop's 19C sedan chair, and a crib by Benedetto Papale (19C). There is a room dedicated to the works (paintings and ceramics) by the local artists Giuseppe, Francesco and Mario Vaccaro. There are also some 16C–17C paintings (including *Christ in the Garden* by Epifano Rossi), and two putti by Bongiovanni Vaccaro. On the top floor are modern works. The archaeological section is not yet open. Beside the museum is the fine façade, also by Bonaiuto, of **S. Agata** (closed).

Via Roma leads to **Ponte S. Francesco,** an 18C viaduct, which has pretty majolica decoration and a good view of Palazzo S. Elia below the bridge. The road continues past the piazza in front of the church of **S. Francesco d'Assisi,** founded in 1226 but rebuilt after 1693. It contains paintings by Francesco and Giuseppe Vaccaro and a Gothic sacristy. Behind the church (reached by via S. Antonio and via Mure Antiche) is **S. Pietro** with a 19C neo-Gothic majolica façade.

Via Roma continues past the **Tondo Vecchio** an exedra built by Francesco Battaglia in 1766. Beside the church of S. Francesco di Paola a road leads up past the **Teatro Politeama Ingrassia**, with interesting Art Nouveau details, to the entrance gate to the delightful **public gardens** laid out in 1846 by Giovanni Battista Basile. The exotic trees include palms, cedars of Lebanon and huge pines. There is a long balustrade on via Roma decorated with pretty ceramics from the workshop of Enrico Vella, and throughout the gardens are copies of terracotta vases and figures by Giuseppe Vaccaro and Giacomo Bongiovanni. There is also a fountain by Camillo Camilliani and a decorative bandstand. The palace of Benedetto Ventimiglia, also on via Roma, is preceded by a colourful ceramic terrace.

The **Museo Regionale della Ceramica** (open every day 09.00–18.30) is situated in the gardens, entered through the elaborate **Teatrino** (1792) by Natale Bonaiuto. From the top of the steps there is a view beyond a war memorial by Antonio Ugo, with four palm trees, to the pretty hills (with the town on the left). The museum contains a fine collection of Sicilian ceramics from the prehistoric era to the 19C. The rooms are not numbered and the exhibits poorly labelled. In the corridor to the right are 17C and 19C ceramics from Caltagirone. Beyond a room with 18C and 19C works, the archaeological material is displayed, including Hellenistic and Roman terracotta heads and figurines. Cases 19 and 20 contain fragments from Caltagirone (5C-4C BC). Nearby is a bas-relief in stone with sphynxes (6C BC). Prehistoric pottery from S. Mauro and Castelluccio is exhibited in cases 21 and 22. In case 26 is a krater depicting a potter at his wheel protected by Athene (5C BC). Case 27 contains the Russo Perez collection, including 5C BC red- and black-figure vases.

In the courtyard bases used in various potteries from the 11C to 13C are exhibited. In the large room on the left are Arab Norman stuccoes from S. Giuliano, 10C–12C Arab Norman pottery, and medieval works (Case 48 onwards). In the room by the entrance are 17C and 18C works from Caltagirone including tiles, and in a little room beyond part of a 17C tiled floor is exhibited, and elaborate 17C–18C ecclesiastical works.

On a lower level is a large hall with 17C–19C ceramics from Palermo, Trapani, Caltagirone and Sciacca, including blue enamelled vases and pharmacy jars. The fine collection of terracotta figures includes works by Giuseppe Bongiovanni (1809–89) and Giacomo Vaccaro (1847–1931). The hall is also used for exhibitions.

Via S. Maria di Gesù leads south from the public gardens to (10 minutes) the church of **S. Maria di Gesù** (1422), with a charming Madonna by Antonello Gagini.

Outside the town on the Grammichele road is the remarkable neo-Gothic **cemetery**, built in 1867 by Giovanni Battista Nicastro, with terracotta decorations by Enrico Vella.

## Environs of Caltagirone

**GRAMMICHELE**, 15km east of Caltagirone, was founded by Carlo Maria Carafa Branciforte, Principe di Butera, to house the people of Occhiolà, destroyed in 1693. Its remarkable concentric hexagonal plan is preserved around the hexagonal **piazza Carafa** with palm trees and a medley of houses between the six roads. Here the well-sited **Chiesa Madre** begun in 1723 by Andrea Amato stands next to the **Palazzo Comunale** (1896, by Carlo Sada). The **Museo Civico** (open 09.00–13.00 except Mon; Tues & Thurs also 16.00–18.00) was opened here in 1996. The small collection is very well arranged and contains finds from excavations in the district begun in 1891 by Paolo Orsi who identified a pre-Greek settlement at Terravecchia. Exhibits include prehistoric bronzes and Bronze Age ceramics, vases found in tombs (6C BC), terracotta votive statuettes and 15C–16C majolica from Occhiolà.

**Vizzini**, further east is a little town in a fine position on a spur (619m) surrounded by terraced hillsides. It occupies an ancient site, perhaps that of *Bidis* recorded by Cicero. In the central piazza is an 18C palace which used to be owned by Giovanni Verga's family: Vizzini claims to be the scene of Verga's *Mastro Don Gesualdo* and *Cavalleria Rusticana* (although the latter claim is contested by Francofonte).

**MILITELLO IN VAL DI CATANIA** is a pleasant town where the churches contain paintings by Vito d'Anna, Olivio Sozzi, Pietro Ruzzolone (attributed; *St Peter enthroned*) and others. Beside the Chiesa Madre is the interesting **Museo di S. Nicola** with 17C and 18C works, including vestments, church silver, sculpture and paintings. In the church of **S. Maria della Stella** there is an altarpiece in enamelled terracotta by Andrea Della Robbia (1487) with the *Nativity, Annunci-*

*ation to the Shepherds*, and (in the predella) a *Pietà* and *The twelve apostles*. The half-ruined **S. Maria la Vetere**, outside the town to the east, has a porch supported on lions and a good doorway of 1506. There is a prickly pear festival here in October.

**Mineo** is a little town on an ancient settlement founded by Ducetius, king of the Siculi in the 8C BC and later occupied by the Greeks and Romans. The Chiesa del Collegio and S. Agrippina have 18C stuccoes.

**Palagonia** is in a district well-known for its oranges. Outside the town is the 7C shrine of S. Febronia. The town is on the edge of the fertile **Plain of Catania**, known to the Greeks as the *Laestrygonian Fields*, the home of the cannibal Laestrygones. Its vast citrus fruit plantations are watered by the Simeto and its tributaries, the Dittaino and the Gornalunga.

The **Oasi del Simeto**, at the mouth of the Simeto, is an oasis for birds. Although numerous holiday villas were built here from the 1960s onwards, it was first protected in 1975 and became a nature reserve in 1984. In 1989 54 of the numerous houses erected within the area without building permission were demolished. The marshes and salt lakes offer protection to numerous nesting-birds as well as migratory birds, including moorhens, coots, grain weevils, herons, godwits, egrets, ibis, avocets and spoonbills. Amber can often be found on the shore here. The entrance to the reserve is on the left bank of the river near Ponte Primosole on the main road (SS 114). It can usually be visited from July to February at 09.00, 11.00, 14.00 and 16.00 (there are guides at the entrance, ☎ 095/388227 or 095/382112). On the left bank of the Simeto stood the ancient town of *Symaethus*, whose necropolis survives on the Turrazza estate.

# Messina

Messina, on the western shore of the Straits bearing its name, extends along the lowest slopes of the Monti Peloritani above the splendid harbour, one of the deepest and safest in the Mediterranean. The port, at the entrance to the island, is always busy with the movement of the ferries from the mainland. The city (population 270,000) remains the third largest town in Sicily despite the terrible earthquake that completely wrecked it in 1908, when 84,000 people died out of a population of 120,000. Rebuilt with exceptionally broad streets planted with trees and low buildings to minimise the danger of future earthquakes, the centre of Messina combines sea, sky and hills in a pleasant, open townscape. Unattractive higher buildings have been constructed on the outskirts in recent years.

## ■ Practical information

***Information offices***. APT Messina, via Calabria (corner of via Capra), ☎ 090/674236. Azienda Autonoma, 45 piazza Cairoli, ☎ 090/2935292.

**Getting there**
**Train-ferries, car-ferries and hydrofoils** from the Italian mainland. **Car ferries** from Villa S. Giovanni run by the State railways in connection with trains in 40min.; other car-ferries (*Caronte, Tourist Ferry Boat*) about every 20min. in 20min. Frequent **hydrofoil** services in 15min. from Reggio Calabria run by *SNAV*. The ferries run by the State railways arrive at the **stazione marittima**, going on to the **stazione centrale**, the station for Catania and Palermo. Other car-ferries and hydrofoils moor at the various jetties on the water-front parallel to via Vittorio Emanuele II and via della Libertà. There is a hydrofoil service once a day (in c 90min.) to the Aeolian Islands (see p.352).
**Buses.** No. 79 from the station via the Duomo, corso Cavour and via Garibaldi to the Museo Nazionale (going on to Ganzirri and Punta Faro). No. 29 from piazza Cairoli to the cemetery.
**Country bus** services run by *SAIS* (terminal in piazza della Repubblica) to Catania (direct via the motorway) in 90min. (going on to Catania airport); to Taormina (via N114) in 90min.; and to other towns in the province; to Rome in 9hr 30min. Coach service run by *Cavalieri* (from piazza Duomo) in connection with internal flights from Reggio Calabria airport (via piazza Duomo and piazza Stazione). From April–September services by *Giuntabus* from 8 via Terranova to Milazzo (for the Aeolian Islands; see p.352).
**Parking** is difficult in the centre of the town: space sometimes available in via La Farina and near the Fiera di Messina. There is a new car-park in piazza Cavallotti.

## Hotels

★★★★ *Royal Palace Hotel*, via T. Cannizzaro Is. 224, ☎ 090/6503, fax 090/2921075; *Jolly dello Stretto*, 126 via Giuseppe Garibaldi, ☎ 090/363860, fax 090/5902526.
★★★ *Villa Morgana*, 237 via C. Pompea, north of the town at Ganzirri, ☎ 090/325575, fax 090/2927233.
★★ *Monza*, 63 viale S. Martino, ☎ & fax 090/673755.

## Restaurants

**A** *Cotton Club*, 44 via del Vespro; *Nunnari*, 157 via Ugo Bassi.
**B** *La Trappola*, 15 via Verdi; *Osteria del Campanile*, 9 via Loggia dei Mercanti; *Da Mario*, 108 via Vittorio Emanuele.
**C** *Pizzeria Palastenese (JAD)*, piazza Francesco Lo Sardo; *Osteria Etnea*, piazza del Tribunale; *Al Padrino*, 54 via S. Cecilia.
   There are numerous restaurants and trattorie near the Lago Ganzirri, north of the town, including (**A**) *La Macina (Teo)*, 225 via Consolare Pompea and (**B**) *Salvatore*.
**Cafés and pasticcerie**. *Irrera*, piazza Cairoli; *Casaramona*, 242 viale S. Martino. Sandwich bar: *Procacciante*, 89 via T. Cannizzaro.
**Theatre**. Vittorio Emanuele, corso Garibaldi (for music and prose).

## Annual festivals

. The *Fiera di Messina*, a trade fair during the first 15 days of August coincides with the traditional processions of the *Giganti* on 13 and 14 August and the *Vara* (cart with tableau) on the Assumption (15 August). Other processions take place on 3 June (*Madonna della Lettera*, protectress of the city), on Good Friday (*Varette*) and on Corpus Domini (*Vascelluzzo*). Exhibitions are held (especially in winter) in various galleries.

### History

*Zancle*, as Messina was called by the Greeks in allusion to the sickle-shaped peninsula enclosing its harbour, was probably a settlement of the Siculi before its occupation by the Euboeans (from the island of Euboea east of Athens) and later by a colony from Chalcis. In 493 BC it was captured by Anaxilas, tyrant of Rhegium, and renamed *Messana*, in honour of his native country of Messenia in the Peloponnese. It took part in local wars against Siracusa and then against Athens, and was destroyed by the Punic general Himilco. Rebuilt by the Siracusans, it was occupied by the Campanian mercenaries of Agathocles, who called themselves Mamertini. These obtained the alliance of Rome against the Carthaginians and Messina prospered with the fortunes of Rome. Under the Normans it was renowned for monastic learning and was important as a Crusader port. Richard Palmer, an Englishman, who had arranged the marriage of William the Good to Joan Plantagenet in 1177, was Archbishop of Messina from c 1182 to his death in 1195. In 1190–91 Richard Coeur de Lion built the Castle of Mategriffon (in 1282 the stronghold of Herbert of Orleans, governor of Sicily) and wintered in the town, which he sacked as a warning to Tancred to surrender Joan and the Plantagenet share of William's inheritance. The Emperor Henry VI died of dysentery at Messina in 1197. After a heroic and successful resistance to Charles of Anjou in 1282, the city flourished until it lost its privileges by rebelling against Spanish misrule in 1674.

In 1492 Pietro Bembo came to Messina at the age of 22 in order to study Greek under Constantine Lascaris, and stayed two years. From Messina Cervantes sailed in the Marquesa to Lepanto (1571) and in Messina hospital recovered from the wound received in the battle. The action of Shakespeare's *Much Ado About Nothing* is set in Messina. The French geologist Dolomieu (1750–1801), returning from Napoleon's Egyptian expedition, was captured and imprisoned for two years (1799–1801) in Messina.

From then on its story is one disaster after another: the plague in 1743, an earthquake in 1783, naval bombardment in 1848, cholera in 1854, another earthquake in 1894, culminating in the catastrophe of 1908. The earthquake, which took place early in the morning of 28 December, not only ruined almost the entire city, but caused the shore to sink over half a metre. The subsidence caused a violent tidal wave which swept the coast of Calabria, rising to a height of 6m; its effects were felt in Malta 24 hours later. A series of lesser shocks continued almost daily for two months. Of the 100,000 victims, 84,000 lost their lives in Messina and its environs. Reconstruction, though assisted by liberal contributions from all over the world, was by no means complete when the city was again devastated in 1943 by aerial bombardment (when 5000 people lost their lives). In 1955 a preliminary agreement was signed by the 'six' in Messina to found the European Union (EU).

**Piazza del Duomo** was spaciously laid out in the 18C. Beside the cathedral the elaborate modern campanile overshadows the delicate **Orion Fountain**, a masterpiece by Montorsoli (1547; recently restored but sometimes dry). The **Duomo** (closed 12.00–15.30 or 16.00), despite successive reconstructions, retains much of the appearance of the original medieval structure.

Originally built by Roger II, and consecrated in 1197 in the presence of Henry VI, the cathedral was shattered in 1908, when the roof collapsed and the 26 monolithic granite columns, brought, it is believed, from the Temple of Neptune at the Punta del Faro, were smashed to pieces. The north corner of the façade and some of the mosaics and monuments survived, with the contents of the treasury, and the building was carefully restored following the Nórman lines, only to be even more thoroughly devastated by a fire, which, started on 13 June 1943 by incendiary bombs, raged for three days. Many of the treasures were completely destroyed including the mosaics and frescoes, the royal tombs and the stalls. But everything that could be salvaged was replaced in position in the rebuilt church; damaged works were painstakingly restored; and, where possible, lost works accurately reconstructed.

The lower part of the **façade** (covered for restoration) preserves much of the original sculptured decoration including panels in relief with delightful farming scenes, and three fine doorways, by 15C and 16C artists. The beautiful central doorway has a tympanum by Pietro da Bonitate (1468). On the south side is a doorway by Polidoro da Caravaggio and a pretty wall with fine Gothic Catalan windows.

The majestic basilican **interior**, in pink and grey tones, was remarkably well reconstructed after the fire. The side altars (copies of originals by Montorsoli), the columns, the marble pavement and the painted wooden roof were all restored. In the **south aisle** on the first altar is a statue of *St John the Baptist* by Antonello Gagini (1525). At the end of the aisle is the 14C Gothic arcaded tomb of five archbishops. On the nave pillar in the transept is the fragmented tomb slab of Archbishop Palmer (d. 1195; see above), with a Byzantine panel.

From the south aisle is the entrance to the **treasury**, recently re-opened (15.30 or 16.00–18.30 or 19.00 except Mon). Arranged in one room, it is particularly rich in 17C and 18C objects, including church silver made in Messina. Among the most important pieces are: a lamp in rock crystal dating from 969, altered in 1250; a 12C silver reliquary of an arm; a 15C silver reliquary of the arm of S. Nicola; an octagonal bronze reliquary of the *Madonna della Lettera* (14C); a 17C vase with silver and gilded bronze flowers; a 17C embroidered chasuble and two gilded silver chalices decorated with enamels (14C). The very fine reliquary of the arm of S. Marziano was commisioned by Richard Palmer (as the inscription states) when he was bishop of Siracusa, and brought here by him when he became Archbishop of Messina around 1182. It shows the influence of Islamic and Byzantine goldsmiths' art. Other works of particular interest include: a 13C processional Cross attributed to Perrone Malamorte (1194–1250); a large brightly coloured 17C silk embroidery; and a pair of silver candlesticks made in 1701 by Giuseppe d'Angelo and Filippo and Sebastiano Juvarra.

Outside the right apse chapel, elaborately decorated in marble, is the charming (but damaged) tomb of Archbishop De Tabiatis by Goro di Gregorio (1333). The sumptuous **high altar** bears a copy of the venerated Byzantine

*Madonna della Lettera* (destroyed in 1943). The baldacchino, the stalls (designed by Giorgio Veneziano in 1540), and the bishop's throne have all been reconstructed. The modern high altar encloses a silver altar frontal attributed to Francesco Juvarra (late 17C or early 18C). The mosaic in the apse has been recomposed. The monument to Bishop Angelo Paino (1870–1967), to the left of the apse, was sculpted by M. Lucerna. In the left apse chapel is the only original mosaic to have survived in the church from the 14C.

In the **north transept** the tomb effigy of Bishop Antonio La Lignamine is surrounded by 12 fine small panels of the *Passion* sculpted by the Gagini school. Nearby is a 17C bust of Archbishop Proto, and part of the tomb of Archbishop Bellorado by Giovanni Battista Mazzola (1513). In the **north aisle**, beside the doorway, is a 16C relief of *St Jerome* (the exterior of the 15C north doorway can be seen here). At the end of the aisle, the baptistery, with a reconstructed font, contains a striking wood Crucifix.

The **campanile** was designed by Francesco Valenti to house a remarkable astronomical clock, the largest of its kind in the world, built by a Strasbourg firm in 1933. At 12 noon a cannon-shot heralds an elaborate movement of mechanical figures.

A short way north of the cathedral is the circular **piazza Antonello**, laid out in 1914–29 with a group of monumental buildings: the post office, the Palazzo della Provincia, the Municipio (its façade faces corso Garibaldi), and an arcade with cafés and shops. In via Cavour is the circular domed church of **S. Maria Annunziata dei Teatini** (1930). To the south, reached by via Venezia, the **university** (1927), with a fine library dating from the foundation in 1548, faces **Palazzo di Giustizia**, a monumental neo-classical building in ochre stone by Marcello Piacentini (1928).

From piazza Duomo, via I Settembre (the stone on the corner records the outbreak of the Sicilian revolution in 1847) leads towards the station. It passes two Baroque corner fountains, which survived the earthquake, near (left) the church of **SS. Annunziata dei Catalani** (now the university chapel; open for services only), a 12C Norman church, shortened under the Swabians. It has been carefully restored. The **exterior** is remarkably fine. The apse, transepts and cupola, with beautiful arcading, date from the 12C, while the three doors at the west end were added in the 13C. The **interior** has a pretty brick apse and dome in yellow and white stone, and tall dark grey columns with Corinthian capitals. The windows and nave arches are decorated with red and white stone. The large stoup is made up of two capitals. In the piazza is a statue of Don John of Austria, by Andrea Calamech (1572).

Via I Settembre (which leads towards piazza Cavallotti with a statue of Carlo III of Bourbon and the station) crosses corso Garibaldi, a long broad thoroughfare, which continues south. Just off it, to the left, are the ruins of **S. Maria Alemanna** (c 1220), interesting as one of the few Gothic churches in Sicily. After years of neglect it is at last being restored. On the opposite side of the corso, the church of **S. Caterina di Valverde** contains a painting of the *Madonna dell' Itria between Sts Peter and Paul* by the local artist Antonello Riccio (restored in 1985). Corso Garibaldi ends in the huge **piazza Cairoli**, the centre of the town, which has a number of cafés. The fine evergreen ficus trees have remarkably thick foliage.

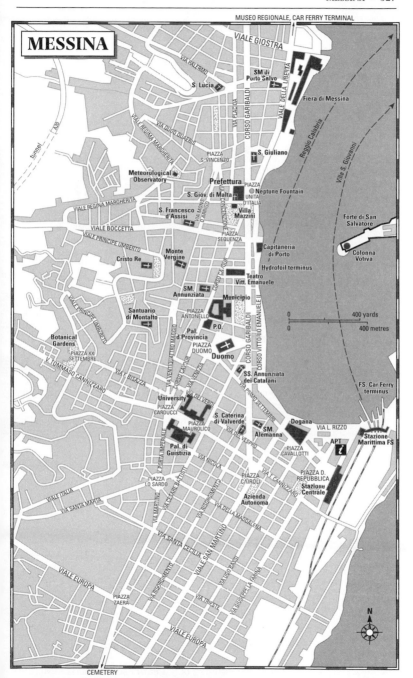

MESSINA

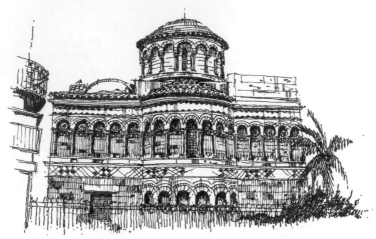

*SS. Annunziata dei Catalani in Messina*

Further south, viale S. Martino, one of the main shopping streets, traverses an area of well laid out streets, with homogeneous low buildings. It ends at the public gardens beside the monumental **cemetery**, designed in 1872 by Leone Savoia. The luxuriant garden, built in terraces on the slopes of the hill, has a lovely view of Calabria. The *Famedio*, or Pantheon, was damaged by the earthquake, but almost all the smaller family tombs were left intact; 80,000 victims of the disaster are buried here among the flowers. In 1940 the British cemetery, founded during the Napoleonic wars, was transferred here (reached by a path on the extreme left side of the cemetery) by the Italian authorities when its original site near the harbour was needed for defence works. It was the subject of a scandal in 1992 when legal proceedings were begun against those responsible for 're-ordering' the site, in an attempt to reduce it in size and use part of it for other purposes.

From piazza Cairoli (see above), corso Garibaldi runs north, parallel to corso Vittorio Emanuele and the waterfront, with a good view of the busy harbour, and the 'sickle', with the **Forte di S. Salvatore**, erected by the Spaniards in 1546. On its ancient wall rises a column (60m) surmounted by a *Madonna*. The east side of the harbour is a naval base. The **Teatro Vittorio Emanuele** (1842; by Pietro Valente), on corso Garibaldi, was re-opened in 1985 after its reconstruction.

The two parallel streets passing a statue of Ferdinando II, end in piazza Unità d'Italia, with the **Neptune Fountain** by Montorsoli (1557; the figures of Neptune and Scylla are 19C copies; the originals are kept in the Museo Regionale, see below). Behind it is the huge **Palazzo del Governo** (Prefettura), designed by Cesare Bazzani in 1920 (being restored). Nearby the little church of **S. Giovanni di Malta** (c 1590; by Camillo Camilliani and Giacomo del Duca) has also been reconstructed. Also facing the piazza is Palazzo Carrozza built in the 1930s in an eclectic style. There is a garden with pines and ficus trees facing the waterfront, and, behind, the public gardens of **Villa Mazzini**, where there is an aquarium.

Viale Boccetta leads inland to the church of **S. Francesco d'Assisi** (restored).

The exterior has an interesting apse; the deeply recessed arches retain some of the original masonry.

Viale della Libertà (bus, see above), which follows the shore in full view of the Calabrian coastline, passes the site of the Messina Fair, opposite which is the church of S. Maria di Porto Salvo with red domes in the Norman style, near the pretty Villino Tricomi-Sergio, built in the 1920s.

## Museo Regionale

The road runs alongside the beach to reach (c 3km from the Duomo) the important Museo Regionale (daily 09.00–13.30; Sun & PH 09.00–12.30; Tues, Thurs and Sat also usually 15.00–17.30 or 16.00–18.30 in summer) founded to house works of art saved from the earthquake. This remarkable collection of local art is particularly interesting for its fine examples of 15C and early 16C paintings (many of them recently restored). It was beautifully re-arranged in 1980–83. However, there are long-term plans to re-arrange the whole museum again and the exhibition space will be expanded when the new pavilion in the garden has been opened.

The **outer court** contains architectural fragments from the old city. The **inner court** has architectural fragments, including capitals from the Duomo, three church doorways (from S. Domenico, S. Maria della Scala and S. Maria di Basicò) and a 16C tomb. **Room 1** contains works of the **Byzantine and Norman** periods. It also contains 12C sculptural fragments; two fonts; the sarcophagus of the archimandrite Luke; an exquisite mosaic niche of the *Madonna and Child*, called *La Ciambretta* (13C); a painted *Madonna and Child* of the Byzantine type; fragments salvaged from the Duomo of the medieval painted wooden ceiling and a mosaic head of an apostle. The marble bas-relief of the *Virgin orans* was made in Constantinople in the mid or late 12C. Also here is a fine capital from the Duomo; a painting of *S. Placido*; and a damaged mosaic of the *Madonna and Child*. **Room 2**. **Gothic period**. This room contains a fragment of a 14C painting of the *Madonna and Child*, a triptych of the *Madonna and Child between Sts Agatha and Bartholomew* (very damaged) attributed to the Master of the Sterbini Diptych; a beautiful seated statue from the cathedral by Goro di Gregorio, known as the *Madonna 'degli Storpi'* (1333); and from the 14C–15C Veneto-Marchigiana school, a polyptych of the *Madonna and Child with four saints* (damaged).

**Room 3**. **Early 15C**. This room contains a very fine wooden Crucifix; architectural fragments from the duomo; a Della Robbian tondo of the *Madonna and Child*; bas-reliefs including *St George and the dragon* (attributed to Domenico Gagini) and the *Madonna and Child* (attributed to Desiderio da Settignano). **Room 4** contains works by **Antonello da Messina**, his school, and Flemish and Spanish works. Displayed on its own is the very beautiful polyptych of the *Madonna with Sts Gregory and Benedict* and the *Annunciation*, by Antonello da Messina (1473). It was much damaged in the earthquake but has since been restored. Also in room 4 are a *Madonna and Child* by the 15C Flemish school, attributed to Francesco Laurana; a very fine statue of the *Madonna and Child* (restored in 1983) attributed to the school of Antonello, *Madonna of the Rosary* (1489); Salvo d'Antonio (attributed), *Madonna and Child between Sts John the Evangelist and Peter*; Flemish Master of the St Lucy Legend (attributed), *Pietà and symbols of the Passion*; Henri Met de Bles (attributed), *St John the Baptist and*

## Antonello da Messina

Antonello da Messina, born around 1430 in Messina, was one of the masters of the Italian Renaissance and perhaps the greatest southern Italian painter. Antonello made a number of journeys from Sicily including several to Naples and Venice (in 1475, four years before his death). His work shows the influence of the Flemish school, particularly Jan Van Eyck, in its attention to detail and particular sense of light. He was one of the earliest Italian painters to perfect the art of painting in oil, and he had an important influence on Giovanni Bellini. His son, Jacobello, and his nephew Antonello de Saliba, were also painters. Some of his most beautiful works are still in Sicily (including the Virgin Annunciate in the Galleria Regionale in Palermo, and the portrait of a man in the Museo Mandralisca in Cefalù), while other masterpieces are now in the National Gallery of London, the Metropolitan Museum in New York, the Louvre in Paris, and in museums in Berlin and Dresden.

stories from his life; Giovannello da Itala, St Clare and stories from her life, St Thomas of Canterbury; Antonello de Saliba, Madonna and Child; 16C Spanish school, fragment of a triptych; school of Antonello, Madonna and Child; Antonello Freri, funerary monument of admiral Angelo Balsamo (restored in 1983–84); Jacob Cornelisz van Costzanen, triptych; Colijn de Coter, Deposition.

**Room 5**. **Girolamo Alibrandi and the early 16C**. This room contains a 16C statue of St Catherine of Alexandria (restored in 1983); Holy Family and St George, a particularly fine painting by Vincenzo Catena. Girolamo Alibrandi is well represented with paintings of the Last Judgement, St Peter, St Paul, St Catherine of Alexandria, the Circumcision and Presentation in the Temple (1519; restored in 1983–4); the last three are particularly interesting works. Also in room 5 is a statue of St Anthony of Padua (1534; restored in 1983) by Giovanni Battista Mazzolo, and the head of archbishop Pietro Bellorado (from his funerary monument, 1513); Antonello Gagini, ciborium, Madonna and Child.

**Rooms 6–9** contain **works of the 16C–17C**. **Room 6**. Stefano Giordano, St Benedict between Sts Mauro and Placido (1541); Polidoro da Caravaggio, Adoration of the Shepherds (1533); Montorsoli, Scylla (the original from the Neptune fountain; restored in 1983–84); Deodato Guinaccia, Resurrection, and works by Mariano Riccio and Stefano Giordano. **Room 7**. Deodato Guinaccia, Adoration of the Shepherds; 16C painting of Christ carrying the Cross; reliefs by Rinaldo Bonanno; Annunciation by Deodato Guinaccia.

**Room 8** contains a funerary monument of Francesca Lanza Cibo (1618); Alessandro Allori, Madonna of Istria (1590); Antonio Biondo, Marriage of St Catherine; and a case of majolica (from the Casteldurante and Venetian workshops). **Room 9**: Antonio Catalano il Vecchio, Madonna appearing to Sts Francis and Clare (1604); Giovan Simone Comandè, Miraculous draught of fish; Filippo Paladini, St Francis receiving the stigmata; Antonio Catalano il Giovane, Madonna 'della Lettera' (1629).

**Room 10** contains two **masterpieces** by **Caravaggio**, both very beautiful late works painted during his stay in Messina in 1608–09: Nativity (commissioned by the Senate of Messina) and Raising of Lazarus. Works by Sicilian artists of his school displayed here include: Alonzo Rodriquez (Meeting between Sts Peter *and Paul*, restored in 1984); Mario Minniti, *miracle performed by Christ for the widow of Nain*; and works by Matteo Stomer. **Room 11**. The **17C works** here include marble intarsia panels, and paintings by Domenico Maroli, Giovanni Battista Quagliata, Mattia Preti (tondo of the *Dead Christ*), Giovanni Fulcro, and Agostino Scilla. **Room 12** contains **18C works** including paintings by Giovanni Tuccari (*Marriage at Cana*, restored in 1985); Filippo Tancredi; Sebastiano Conca; and a state coach by Domenico Biondo.

From **room 12** stairs lead up to a mezzanine floor where the **Treasury** has recently been arranged. It includes vestments, altar frontals, church silver (16C–18C), a 17C ivory and ebony cabinet; an 18C silver altar frontal and ceramics.

The rest of the collection, which will be displayed when the new exhibition space is available, includes the archaeological section: Greek, Roman and Byzantine coins; the marble head of a *strategos* (1C AD, copy of a 5C original); fragment of an Egyptian statue (c 1413 BC); a Bronze Age pithos; a statue of *Igea* (3C–2C BC) found in piazza Duomo; a Roman sarcophagus showing *Leda and the swan*; Roman portrait busts; a sarcophagus with *Icarus* (mid-3C AD); Bronze Age pithos from the Aeolian Islands; and a bronze mirror showing *Eros in repose*. Also to be displayed here is Montorsoli's statue of *Neptune* (from his fountain; see above), church silver, tarsie and decorative arts.

On the slopes of the hillside above the town is **Cristo Re** (1939), a centrally planned church with a cupola standing on a prominence, and the conspicuous **Santuario di Montalto** (1930); nearby is the **Botanic Garden**. The long winding avenue here (viale Italia, Principe Umberto and Regina Margherita), marked by an almost continuous line of pine trees, used to provide a fine view of the Straits before new tower blocks were built.

**Punta Faro** (14km north; bus no. 79), at the extreme north-eastern tip of the island, can be reached by the old road lined with a modest row of houses facing the sea front, which, however, traverses the ambitiously named suburbs of Paradiso, Contemplazione, and Pace, where more high-rise building has taken place. The new fast road (*Panoramica dello Stretto*) which starts from viale Regina Elena and runs along the hillside above has a better view of the Calabrian coast; it is to be extended as far as Mortelle. Just short of the cape is the fishing village of **Ganzirri**, now a resort on two little lagoons (the **Pantano Grande** and the **Pantano Piccolo**) once famous for mussels, but now polluted. There are still mussel beds in the smaller lagoon, but no fishing takes place now in the prettier Pantano Grande, one side of which is lined with palm trees. Most of the mussels served at the numerous restaurants here are now imported from Taranto or Chioggia.

At Punta Faro is a lighthouse and a pylon bearing the Sicilian end of the cable that brings electricity from Calabrian power stations, over 229m high. The single span of 3653m of unsupported cable allows headroom for ships of 70m. Swordfishing has taken place off the coast here since ancient times; it was for many years considered one of the sights of Messina. The traditional method of harpooning the fish from characteristic small boats with tall look-out masts, has been carried out since the 1960s with modern equipment and motor boats. The catch usually takes place here in June and July and is still a tourist attraction.

Punta Faro is at the mouth of the **Straits of Messina**, the *Fretum Siculum* of the Romans. This is the site of the legendary whirlpool *Charybdis*, greatly feared by sailors in ancient times. The name of Cape Peloro recalls Pelorus, the pilot of Hannibal, who was unjustly condemned to be thrown into the sea for misleading the fleet. From here the Calabrian coast is sometimes, in hot weather, strangely magnified and distorted by the mirage called *Fata Morgana*.

Discussions have been going on for 25 years about the long-term project to connect Messina and Reggio di Calabria by land: the latest plan, proposed in 1986, and re-examined in 1997, involves a single-span suspension bridge for road and railway 3300m long, carried on two pylons 376m high. This would be the longest bridge in the world, but fears about its capacity to withstand earthquakes have been voiced, and there is some opposition to the project.

# Taormina and environs

Taormina is renowned for its magnificent position above the sea on a spur of Monte Tauro (206m), covered with luxuriant vegetation, commanding a celebrated view of Etna. With a delightful winter climate, it became a fashionable international resort at the end of the 19C, and during the 20C it has been the most famous holiday place on the island. The small town (population 11,000; with some 60 hotels), with one main street and many side lanes, is now virtually given over to tourism (extremely crowded in July and August), and it is a more expensive place to visit than the rest of Sicily. Many of the villas and hotels, built in mock-Gothic or eclectic styles at the beginning of the 20C, are surrounded with beautiful subtropical gardens. The appearance of the medieval town has deteriorated in recent years and since the 1960s new houses have been allowed to cover the hillside above, and new approach roads, on raised stilts, have spoilt some of the landscape below the town.

## ■ Practical information

***Information office***. Azienda Autonoma, Palazzo Corvaja (☎ 0942/23243).

### Getting there
**Railway station**. Taormina-Giardini, a pretty building on the sea front and on the coast road (N114). With two battlemented towers, it is built in an eclectic Romanesque-Gothic style. It is on the busy line along the coast from Siracusa via Catania to Messina. Blue buses (*SAIS*) and taxis up the hill to the town centre (via via Pirandello; 5km).

**Buses**. From the bus terminal in via Pirandello, services run by *ATM* via Porta Messina to the Lumbi car-park (going on to Castel Mola); other services to Mazzarò, Giardini Naxos and Forza d'Agro. *SAIS* buses to the railway station of Taormina-Giardini and Mazzarò, Giardini-Naxos, Castelmola, the Gola Alcantara and the towns in the foothills of Etna, as well as services to Catania (and Catania airport) and Messina. Coach excursions (it is preferable to book the day before) in summer run by *CIT*, *SAIS* and *SAT* from the bus terminal to Etna, Siracusa, Piazza Armerina and Enna, Agrigento, Palermo and Monreale, and the gorge of Alcantara. Taxis can be hired at fair prices for the excursion to Etna.

**Approaches by car**. The most pleasant approach is by the old road, via Pirandello (described below). Another approach road has been built to link up with the Catania–Messina motorway exit (*Taormina Nord*). This leaves the main coast road (N114) near Mazzarò and mounts on stilts past the huge Lumbi car-park to enter Taormina near the stadium and join via Pirandello. A third approach road (also on stilts), at the opposite end of the town, leads off from the N114 in the locality of Villagonia between Giardini–Naxos and the railway station. It terminates at Porta Catania, beside the Excelsior Hotel. A tunnel has been under construction for many years beneath the town which will link the two modern roads between the Lumbi car-park and the hillside below the Excelsior Hotel, but it is not clear how this will resolve the traffic problems.

**Car-parks**. The steep, narrow streets around the town, most of them one-way, are usually congested with traffic, and parking is difficult, especially in summer (only residents are allowed to park in the spaces marked 01, 02 and 03). The main street (corso Umberto I) is totally closed to traffic at all times; you are therefore strongly advised to park outside the gates. The car-park known as **Lumbi**, built in the late 1980s, on the northern approach road from the motorway is the only large car-park where space is almost always available. It charges an hourly tariff. A minibus service operates from the car-park to the centre of the town. There is also a convenient car-park at **Mazzarò**, on the coast at the foot of the hill, connected by cableway to Taormina (in 5 minutes; terminus outside Porta Messina). Access is allowed to hotels, and most of the large hotels have their own car-parks (signposted along the complicated one-way systems).

To leave the town from Porta Catania (or the Circonvallazione) the best route is to take the pretty via Roma (from piazza S. Domenico), one-way down, and rejoin via Pirandello via via Bagnoli Croce. The new road to Villagonia can also be used as an exit from the town.

**Cableway** from the foot of the hill at Mazzarò (car-park) to outside Porta Messina in 5 minutes.

## Hotels

The principal hotels provide transport from the station; they also have car-parks. Many hotels are in quiet positions with fine gardens and views. Many of them are only open from April–October and from Christmas to the New Year. Among the 60 or so hotels are:

★★★★★ *S. Domenico Palace*, 5 piazza S. Domenico, ☎ 0942/23701, fax 0942/625506.

★★★★ *Timeo*, 59 via Teatro Greco (closed for restoration for many years but due to re-open in 1998); *Miramare*, 27 via Guardiola Vecchia, ☎ 0942/23401, fax 0942/626223; *Excelsior Palace*, 8 via Toselli, ☎ 0942/23975, fax 0942/23978; *Villa Paradiso*, 2 via Roma, ☎ 0942/23922, fax 0942/625800; *Grande Albergo Monte Tauro*, 3 via Madonna delle Grazie, ☎ 0942/24402, fax 0942/24403.

★★★ *Isabella*, 58 corso Umberto, ☎ 0942/23153, fax 0942/23155; *Villa Fiorita*, 39 via Luigi Pirandello, ☎ 0942/24122, fax 0942/625967; *Villa S. Giorgio*, 46 via S. Pancrazio, ☎ 0942/23900; *Villa Sirina*, contrada Sirina, ☎ 0942/51776, fax 0942/51671; *Pensione Adromaco*, via Fontana Vecchia, ☎ 0942/23834, fax 0942/24985.

★★ *Elios*, 98 via Bagnoli Croce, ☎ & fax 0942/23431; *Villa Carlotta*, 81 via Luigi Pirandello, ☎ & fax 9942/23732; *Palazzo Vecchio*, 9 via Ciampoli,

☎ 0942/23033, fax 0942/625104.
★ *Soleado*, 41 via Dietro Cappuccini, ☎ 0942/24138, fax 0942/23617.

***Rooms and apartments to let*** all over the town, including the *Residence Circe*, on the corso Umberto (☎ 0942/23168): the others are shown in the hotel list provided by the Azienda Autonoma.

### Hotels in the environs of Taormina
The sea resort of **Taormina-Mazzarò** (described below) at the foot of the hill (cableway or road) also has numerous hotels including:

★★★★ *Mazzarò Sea Palace*, 147 via Nazionale, ☎ 0942/24004, fax 0942/626237; *Villa S. Andrea*, 137 via Nazionale, ☎ 0942/23125, fax 0942/24838; *Ipanema*, via Nazionale, ☎ 0942/24720, fax 0942/625821; *Park Hotel La Plage*, contrada Pagliara, località Isolabella, ☎ 0942/626095, fax 0942/625850.

★★★ *Villa Bianca*, piazzale Funivia, ☎ 0942/24488, fax 0942/24489.

Many large hotels in a much less attractive position at the undistinguished resort of **Giardini-Naxos** (see below), 4km west of Capo Taormina.

★★★★ *Hellenia Yachting Hotel*, 41 via Jannuzzo, località Recanati, ☎ 0942/51737, fax 0942/54310.

★★★ *Sabbie d'Oro*, 12 via lungomare, ☎ 0942/51227, fax 0942/56913; *Arethena Rocks*, 55 via Calcide Eubea, ☎ 0942/51348, fax 0942/51690; *Nike*, 27 via Calcide Eubea, ☎ 0942/651207, fax 0942/56315.

★★ *Alexander*, via Nixa, località Recanati, ☎ & fax 0942/54313; *Marika*, 2 via Vulcano, ☎ 0942/56583, fax 0942/56584; *Villa Mora*, 47 via Naxos, ☎ & fax 0942/51839.

At **Castel Mola**: ★★ *Villa Sonia*, 9 via Porta Mola, ☎ 0942/28082, fax 0942/28083.

**Campsites** on the sea to the north at Letojanni, see p.345. At S. Leo ★ *S. Leo*, ☎ 0942/24658.

### Restaurants
**A** *La Giara*, 1 via La Floresta; *La Griglia*, 54 corso Umberto; *Da Lorenzo*, 4 via Michele Amari.
**B** *A 'Zammara'*, 15 via Fratelli Bandiera; *La Piazzetta*, 5 via Paladini.
**C** *Trattoria Il Baccanale*, 13 piazzetta Filea; *La Botte*, 4 piazza S. Domenica (pizzeria).
In the environs at **Graniti** (above the Gola d'Alcantara): **C** *Paradise*, contrada Muscianò.

### Pasticcerie
*Giuseppe Chemi*, 112 corso Vittorio Emanuele; *Antonino Chemi*, 102 corso Vittorio Emanuele; *Roberto Chemi*, 9 via Calapitrulli (near the corner of via Bagnoli Croce and the public gardens).

Places to **picnic** in the public gardens. In the environs, at the archaeological site of Naxos.

**Anglo-American Church** (St George's), via Luigi Pirandello. A chaplain is shared with the Holy Cross in Palermo.

**Annual festivals**. Classical dance and music festival in the Greek Theatre, July–15 September. International film festival in July.

### History

*Tauromenium*, founded after the destruction of Naxos (see below) by Dionysius of Siracusa in 403 BC, was enlarged in 358 by a colony of Naxian exiles under Andromachus, father of the historian Timaeus.

Its harbour was the landing place of Timoleon in 334 BC, and of Pyrrhus in 278. It was favoured by Rome during the early days of occupation, and suffered in the Servile War (134–132), but forfeited its rights as an allied city by taking the part of Pompey against Caesar. In 902 it was destroyed by the Saracens, though rebuilt shortly afterwards, and it was taken by Count Roger in 1078. Here the Sicilian parliament assembled in 1410 to choose a king on the extinction of the line of Peter of Aragon.

The town was visited and described by numerous travellers in the 18C and 19C, when the famous view of Etna from the theatre was painted countless times. John Dryden was here in 1701, William Hamilton in 1769, Patrick Brydone in 1770, Henry Swinburne in 1778, and Goethe in 1787. John Henry Newman stayed in the town as a young man in 1833. In 1836 Viollet Le Duc recorded his distress at the poverty of the inhabitants of the town. In 1847 Edward Lear spent four or five days in 'Taormina the Magnificent'. In 1850 W.H. Bartlett complained that 'anywhere but in Sicily a place like Taormina would be a fortune to the innkeepers, but here is not a single place where a traveller can linger to explore the spot'. In 1863 the painter Count Otto Geleng settled in Taormina and stayed here until his death in 1939. He married a local girl and became deputy lord mayor, and founded a nursery school. Florence Trevelyan, daughter of Lord Edward Spencer Trevelyan (cousin of the historian) came to Taormina in 1881 and married the local doctor Salvatore Cacciola in 1890. She planted olives and cypresses and exotic trees on the hillside and created a lovely garden (now the public gardens) as well as dedicating herself to charitable works among the poor of the town.

Taormina was first connected to Messina by railway in 1866 and a year later the line to Catania was inaugurated. In 1874 the first hotel, the Timeo, was opened in the town, and it became internationally known as a winter resort soon after the first visit of the Kaiser (William II) in 1896 (when he stayed at the Timeo). The Kaiser returned in 1904 and 1905 with a large retinue, and set the fashion for royal visitors, many of whom came here in secret under false names. Augustus Hare complained that the town had become a 'fashionable loafing place' and that the Hotel Timeo was 'usually besieged by its patrons before Christmas and held against all comers, except royalties, who have done so much to spoil Taormina'. In 1906 Edward VII wintered at the S. Domenico Hotel and George V made a private visit in 1924. Before World War I the town had a considerable Anglo-American, German, and Scandanavian colony, including the impoverished Baron Wilhelm von Gloeden (1896–1931), who took up photography here and his famous studio became one of the sights of the town. The painter Robert Kitson built a villa for himself here where he lived from 1905 onwards, and C.R. Ashbee (see below) built a hotel here in 1908. Kitson was also concerned with the poverty of the local inhabitants and encouraged Mabel Hill, another English resident to set up a lacemaking school in the town. The writer Robert Hitchens arrived by car in Taormina in the winter of 1910, the first time a car had reached the town. The Anglican church was built in 1922. D.H. Lawrence and his wife Frieda lived here from 1920–23.

From the 1930s onwards Taormina became fashionable amongst the famous and wealthy as a place to visit. The town attracted the attention of allied aircraft in July 1943 when it temporarily became Kesselring's headquarters. In the 1950s it also became known as a bathing resort and for its film festival (famous visitors in this period included Truman Capote, Cecil Beaton, Jean Cocteau, Osbert Sitwell, Salvador Dalì, Orson Welles, John Steinbeck and Tennessee Williams). The hillside was disfigured with new buildings from the 1960s onwards when the motorway made it more accessible and since then the little town has been swamped by mass tourism.

The most pleasant **approach** is by the old road **via Pirandello** which branches off from the main road (N114) at Capo Taormina and winds up the hill past lovely gardens (beware of coaches at the hairpin bends). It passes the little 15C church of **SS. Pietro e Paolo** (open only for services), the ruins of the huge *Kursaal* and a series of Byzantine tomb-recesses in the wall below the former convent of S. Caterina. Shortly after the junction with via Bagnoli Croce (one-way down from the town) it passes the little **belvedere** where there is a fine view. Beyond the bus terminal, on the right (no. 24), surrounded by a garden of date palms, is the Anglo-American church of **St George's**, built by the British community in 1922, with lava decoration on the exterior. It contains British and American funerary monuments, and memorials to the two World Wars. Beyond the cableway station via Pirandello terminates outside Porta Messina, at the entrance to the town.

From piazza Vittorio Emanuele on the site of the ancient Agora, via Teatro Greco, lined with stalls selling wares for tourists, leads past a congress hall opened in 1990, and (on the right) the large Villa Papale (no. 41), once Palazzo Cacciolo and the residence of Florence Trevelyan (see above). It ends at a group of cypresses covered with bougainvillea beside the delightful **Hotel Timeo**, with its pergola, the first hotel to be opened in the town in 1874 by Francesco Floresta. It was moved here in 1883, but has been closed for renovation work for many years (due to re-open in 1998). Bernard Berenson first stayed here (when it was the only hotel in the town) in 1888: on another visit in 1953 he was appalled to find the town over-run by tourists. Other illustrious visitors to this hotel included the writers Andrè Gide, Thomas Mann and Somerset Maugham.

Here is the entrance to the magnificent **Theatre** (open every day, 09.00–dusk), famous for its remarkable scenic position. First erected in the Hellenistic period, it was almost entirely rebuilt under the Romans when it was considerably altered. This is the largest antique theatre in Sicily after that of Siracusa (109m in diameter; orchestra 35m across). The cavea, as was usual, was excavated in the hillside; above the nine wedges of seats, a portico (partially restored in 1955) ran

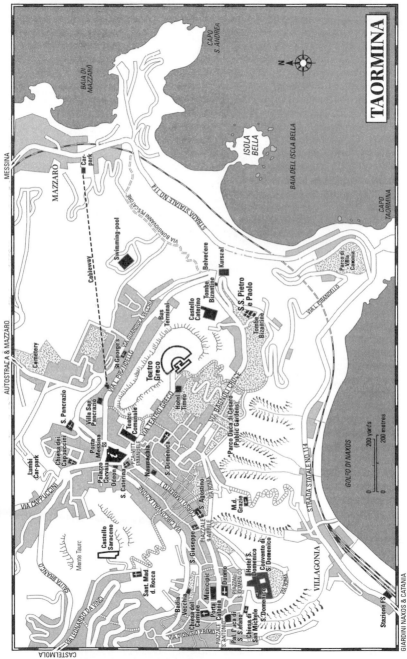

# TAORMINA

GIARDINI NAXOS & CATANIA

round the top (a few stumps of the 45 columns in front survive). The scena is in a remarkably fine state of preservation. The outer brick wall is pierced by three arched gates; the inner wall was once cased with marble. The foundations of the proscenium, or stage, remain, together with the parascenia, or wings, and traces of porticoes at the back (perhaps shelters from the weather). The theatre was famous for its acoustic properties, which can still be tested.

The celebrated view from the top of the cavea (reached from the steps to the left), one of the most breathtaking in Sicily, has been described by countless writers: Goethe in 1787 exclaimed 'Never did any audience, in any theatre, have before it such a spectacle.' On a clear day Etna is seen at its most majestic. In the other direction the Calabrian mountains extend to the northern horizon, and inland the hills stretch behind Monte Mola.

*The ancient theatre in Taormina*

The small **archaeological museum** has been closed indefinitely (and there are plans to move it to the Badia Vecchia, see below). It contains the torso of a youth (Hellenistic); the financial tablets of Tauromenium (150 BC to the Empire); list of strategoi on white marble (2C–1C BC); sculptural fragments including a leg, and a foot with sandal, etc.; and a female head attributed to the school of Scopas.

In piazza Vittorio Emanuele (see above) stands **Palazzo Corvaia** (late 14C), with good windows, a 14C side-portal, and a courtyard staircase decorated with reliefs of *Adam and Eve*. The limestone ornamentation with black and white lava inlay is characteristic of Taormina. The building houses the tourist information office. The great hall, meeting-place in 1410 of the Sicilian parliament and other rooms, are shown on request (09.00–13.00, 16.00–18.00). There are plans to open a local museum here. The church of **S. Caterina** has three large white stucco Baroque altars and a good painting on the high altar of the *Madonna and martyrs* by the Messina school (very damaged). In the floor of the nave, parts of the Odeon (see below) have been revealed. The macabre underground funerary chamber of 1662 is at present closed.

Behind the church are the scant remains of the **Odeon** or **Teatrino Romano**, incorporating part of an earlier Hellenistic temple. Recent excavations behind the barracks in the piazza have revealed public **baths** of the Imperial Roman period.

Outside Porta Messina, at the lower end of a large piazza busy with traffic, is **S. Pancrazio** (open on Sunday morning), built on the ruins of a Greek temple to Isis, whose cella is still traceable. The pretty little arcaded forecourt has a palm tree, and there is a view up to the Castello (see below), towering above the town. Below the church is Villa S. Giorgio, with its garden, built as a hotel in 1908 by C.R. Ashbee, the founder of the Guild of Handicraft at Chipping Camden, many features of which are incorporated in its decoration, using local motifs and materials.

Via Costantino Patricio (beware of cars) leads sharp left outside Porta Messina up to the remains of a public fountain. On the right, beyond Porta Cappuccini, via Fontana Vecchia continues past vestiges of an aqueduct and the Piscina Mirabile (left; under a school) to the church of the **Cappuccini**, with a doorway similar to the north door of the cathedral. The road passes under the arch to the left of the campanile and via Fontana Vecchia forks right, with (in front) a picturesque villa composed of ancient fragments. Just beyond the villa there is a view down to the huge Lumbi car-park and the mouth of the new road tunnel under the hill. The hillside beyond has been ruined by new buildings in the last two decades: the red villa where D.H. and Frieda Lawrence lived from 1920–23 survives in an abandoned state as the only old house on the hillside. It can be seen from here clearly, to the right, in a clump of cypress trees on the ridge of a hill. It is now recorded only by the name of the street which approaches it.

**Corso Umberto Primo** (totally closed to traffic) runs the length of the town. The shops here cater almost exclusively to tourists. To the right and left are glimpses of picturesque stepped alleyways, with colourful plants. At no. 42 is a pretty doorway and tiny rose window. Beyond no. 100 steps (via Naumachia) lead down to the so-called Naumachia, a long brick wall (122m) with niches (formerly decorated with statues) of late Roman date, now supporting a row of houses. Behind it is a huge cistern (no admission): it is thought to have been a monumental nymphaeum.

A series of narrow lanes (see the map) lead down to via Bagnoli Croce where the beautifully kept public gardens, **Parco Duca di Cesarò**, are situated. They were created in 1899 for Florence Trevelyan Cacciola (1852–1907), whose bust (a copy of her funerary monument) has been placed on the left of the main entrance on via Bagnoli Croce. They were presented to the town in 1922 by the Duca di Cesarò. They have exotic tropical plants, ficus, cactus, hibiscus, magnolia, bouganvillea, laurel and acacia plants as well as numerous fine trees (carob, olives, palms, cypress, cedars and pines). The most elaborate of the delightful Victorian follies here is the pagoda at the far end which resembles a beehive (but is inhabited by birds) with a maze of wooden terraces, antique fragments and lava decoration. In Florence Trevelyan's day the gardens were known, after this construction, as 'The Beehives'. There are now also aviaries, a children's playground and tennis courts, and in 1992 a reproduction of a human torpedo, used in 1941 to sink the British war ships *Queen Elizabeth* and *Valiant* in the port of Alexandria, was installed here as a memorial to local sailors who lost their lives in service. No dogs are allowed in the gardens which are therefore greatly favoured by cats (fed here by the local inhabitants). From the terrace there are superb views towards the sea and Etna. Although the lower part of the gardens further down the steep hillside is no longer accessible, there is a secluded little bar usually open here.

The corso (see above) opens into **piazza Nove Aprile**, where there is a superb south view across to the sea and Etna. Below, the railway station and the unspoilt hillside can be seen. Several cafés here have tables outside, including the *Mocambo*, one of the most famous cafés in the town still frequented both by residents and visitors. It now has a slightly decadent atmosphere: its fashionable past is charmingly depicted in a mural painted in 1978 by Christian Bernard. Another bar here has a better position with tables on the terrace overlooking the sea.

On the left is the former church of **S. Agostino** (1448), now the library, with a Gothic doorway, and to the right, approached by a pretty flight of steps, stands the 17C church of **S. Giuseppe**, which has a heavily decorated Rococo stucco interior. Beyond the **Torre dell'Orologio** (?12C; restored 1679), is the so-called **Borgo Medioevale**, usually less crowded with tourists. The corso is lined with many little medieval palaces, with doors and windows where supposedly Saracenic influences linger among the 15C details of the Gothic-Catalan doorways and windows. The first house on the left (no. 154) has two columns from the Roman theatre. At no. 185 is the former church of S. Giovanni (1533), which is now a club for war veterans and is full of trophies and photographs. Beyond no. 209 a wide flight of steps leads up to **Palazzo Ciampoli** built in 1412 and restored after war damage. In the garden the Hotel Palazzo Vecchio, built in 1926, is a miniature version of the Palazzo Vecchio in Florence.

Opposite the Municipio is the flank of the **Duomo** (S. Nicolò), founded in the 13C, with battlements, and two lovely side portals (15C and 16C). The façade has a late rose window and portal of 1636. In the **interior**, with six monolithic antique pink marble columns, are a painting of the *Visitation* by Antonino Giuffrè (1463) and a polyptych by Antonello De Saliba (1504; with a fine frame), from the former church of S. Giovanni, both in the south aisle, and particularly fine works. In the chapel at the end of the south aisle, there is a delicate tabernacle dated 1648, and an early 16C *Madonna and Child* in alabaster. In the north aisle, first altar, there is a *Madonna enthroned with saints* (in very poor condition) by Alfonso Franco; on the second altar, a 16C statue of *St Agatha*; and on the third altar, *Adoration of the Magi*. In the piazza is a charming fountain of 1635. The bizarre figure on the top recalls the symbol of Taormina with the bust of an angel on the body of a bull (adapted here as a female centaur with only two legs).

Steps on the right of the fountain ascend past a small black and white Roman mosaic (right; within an enclosure) and (left) the rebuilt church of the **Carmine** with a pretty campanile. More steps lead up to (left) the **Porta Cuseni** (or Saraceni), the name given to the village outside the walls. Outside the gate steps (the salita Castelmola) continue up to via Dionisio I which leads right to the **Badia Vecchia** (restored) with its large crenellated tower. There are long-term plans to arrange the archaeological museum here, formerly at the Teatro Greco (see above). Beyond it is a neo-Gothic hotel, typical of the hotels built in the town at the beginning of this century. In the other direction via Leonardo da Vinci leads past a wall in front of cypresses, bougainvillea and plumbago to **Casa Cuseni** (no. 5). It is preceded by terraced gardens and a fountain planted with papyrus. The villa was built by Robert Kitson in 1907. The painter lived in

Taormina from 1905 until the outbreak of World War II (but then returned here in 1946 and died in the villa in 1947). He was often visited here by Sir Frank Brangwyn who frescoed some of the rooms.

From piazza del Duomo a street descends to the convent of **S. Domenico** (first opened as a hotel in 1894), which has a late 16C cloister. Field-Marshal Kesselring set up his HQ here in July 1943, and many of his staff were killed by an allied air raid, which destroyed the church (the exterior was reconstructed in 1973; the interior is used as a conference hall).

The corso ends at **Porta Catania** or Porta del Tocco (1440). Across the walls here the Normans built one of their last refuges in Sicily at the end of the 12C, the **Palazzo del Duca di S. Stefano**. It was restored in 1973 and the upper floors and garden have a permanent display of works by the sculptor Giuseppe Mazzullo (d. 1988), while the lower floor is used for exhibitions (08.30–13.30, 16.00–19.00). Outside the gate are several busy roads. This area of the town suffered badly during the air raids of July 1943 (see above), when the little church of **S. Antonio** (good Gothic portal) was damaged and the Barbican gate all but destroyed. The church contains a crib made in 1953, which is modelled on the town. The neo-Saracenic Excelsior has been repainted in yellow and rose and now resembles a meringue cake. The view from the terrace (viale Toselli) in front of the hotel is spectacular, despite some ugly new buildings, and the new road, raised on stilts, which descends to the main coast road. Work is still in progress here on the tunnel which is to connect this road with the one on the other side of the hill by the Lumbi car-park.

### Walks in the vicinity of Taormina

There are a number of pretty walks (with signposted paths; see map p.337) from the town down to the coast at Mazzarò, Spisone and Villagonia. Above the town paths lead up to the Madonna della Rocca and the castle. They all have good views and lead through luxuriant vegetation.

Outside the Parco Duca di Cesarò (public gardens; see above) a narrow road with steps descends past a plaque (1908) which records the work of Mabel Hill (1866–1940), who came from the Royal School of Needlework in London to set up an embroidery school in the town to revive the traditional methods of making Taormina lace, and who, with the painter Robert Kitson (see above), took an interest in local social conditions between the wars. Beyond a modern hotel built on the steep hillside, a lane continues down to the coast at **Villagonia** near the railway station.

Steps lead down from the other end of the public gardens (beside the Jolly Hotel) to via Pirandello which can then be followed downhill to the coast by steps linking the loops in the road.

A path descends from the **Belvedere** on via Pirandello to **Mazzarò** opposite Capo S. Andrea. Another path, off the approach road from Mazzarò and the motorway, starts near the stadium and well-tended cemetery, part of which is reserved for non-Catholics and the town's foreign community (open 08.00–12.00, 14.00–16.00 except Friday; Sun & PH 09.00–12.00). The path descends to **Lido Spisone** beyond Mazzarò.

**Via Roma**, which runs from the public gardens to S. Domenico, although open to cars, provides magnificent views over luxuriant vegetation and precipitous ravines to the sea.

Above the town, from the Circonvallazione, a path (signposted) leads up through plantations of sub-tropical trees to the **Madonna della Rocca** and the **Castello** (see below), from which there are wonderful views. The return can be made by the 738 steps that link the serpentine loops of the Castel Mola road (described below). **Monte Ziretto** (579m) is also a fine viewpoint.

# Environs of Taormina

## Castel Mola

From the Circonvallazione above Taormina the Castel Mola road (with many hairpin bends) climbs up past numerous new houses. A turning (right) leads to the **Madonna della Rocca** and the **Castello** (398m), with a ruined keep (good view).

Castel Mola (550m) is a small village with hotels and restaurants on top of a rock with a ruined castle, high above Taormina. In the little piazza, with a view from the terrace of Etna and the bay of Naxos, the Caffè San Giorgio was founded in 1907 and has an interesting collection of autographs in its visitors' book. The village is well-known for its almond wine. The façade of the parish church opens onto a balcony with another wonderful view. The view is still better from **Monte Venere** or **Veneretta** (884m), reached by a long footpath from the cemetery of Castel Mola.

## Mazzarò

Mazzarò is a pretty bathing resort on **Capo S. Andrea** beneath the hill of Taormina, well supplied with hotels (see above). Three beaches of fine shale and pebbles are separated by rocky spurs. Offshore is the **Isola Bella**, of great natural beauty, finally acquired as a protected area by the Sicilian regional government in 1987. Off **Capo Taormina** 35 Roman columns lie submerged: they are unworked quarried stone, probably destined for a temple or the portico of a villa, which must have been lost in a shipwreck. Footpaths (signposted) and a cableway mount from Mazzarò to Taormina.

## Giardini-Naxos

Giardini, 4km south of Capo Taormina, once a quiet fishing village, with a long main street parallel to the sea, was developed in the 1960s into the large holiday resort (mostly catering for package holiday tours) of **Giardini-Naxos**. The wide bay is now lined with hotels, flats and restaurants from Capo Schisò as far as the railway station of Taormina-Giardini, and new buildings have been built wherever possible. There are no signposts to Giardini Naxos from Taormina: the older city seems to try to ignore its existence. From this bay, Garibaldi, with two steamboats and 4200 men, set out on his victorious campaign against the 30,000 Bourbon troops in Calabria (19 August 1860).

The point of the cape, **Capo Schisò**, was formed by an ancient lava-flow which can still be clearly seen at the water's edge here, by the little harbour. This was a natural landing-place for the navigators rounding the 'toe' of Italy from the East, and it was the site of the first Greek colony of **Naxos** which has been excavated here. From the sea front there is a view of Taormina, with Castel Mola above to the left.

By the modern harbour wall is the entrance to the **EXCAVATIONS OF NAXOS AND THE ARCHAEOLOGICAL MUSEUM** (the excavations are open every day, 09.00–dusk, the museum 09.00–19.00). The entrance is through a pretty, beautifully kept, little garden, through which the ancient lava-flow runs. An old Bourbon fort here has been restored to house the **Archaeological Museum** which has a good collection displayed chronologically on two floors and is well labelled.

**Ground floor**. Neolithic and Bronze Age finds from the Cape (Stentinello ware, etc.); Iron Age finds from the necropolis of Mola including geometric style pottery. **First floor**. Terracottas and architectural fragments from a sanctuary at S. Venera (6C BC); material found in the area of the ancient city including a fine antefix with polychrome decoration, and Attic pottery; a little altar dating from around 540 BC decorated with sphinxes in relief; a statuette of a goddess (end of 5C BC); a rare marble lamp from the Cyclades found in the sea (end of 7C BC); finds from a tomb near S. Venera of the 3C BC, including four pretty vases for perfume and a glass bowl; bronze objects (helmet of 4C BC, etc.). In the garden, beyond the lava-flow, a little museum of underwater finds has been arranged in a small fort. It contains anchors (7C–4C BC), amphorae, etc.

The very interesting **excavations** (well signposted) in the fields to the south are reached from the garden through a green gate. A path, lined with bougainvillea, leads through the peaceful site of the ancient city, beautifully planted and well labelled. The foundation date of the Greek settlement (Chalcidians from Euboea and Ionians from Naxos) is thought to be 734–3 BC. It was the first Greek colony on the island, closely followed by Siracusa and Megara Hyblaea. The town surrendered to Hippocrates of Gela (495) and to Hieron of Siracusa in 476. It was finally destroyed by Dionysius I in 405–4. Excavations were first carried out here in 1953, and digs continue in the area of the city. Exceptionally fine Greek coins, dating from 410–360 BC have been found here, many of them bearing the head of Dionysius.

On the right a path leads across a field planted with lemon trees to a stretch of Greek walls. The main area of excavation is about 15 minutes' walk from the museum in a beautiful orchard with lemon trees, palms, olives, orange trees, eucalyptus and medlar trees; between the trees flower bougainvillea, hibiscus and jasmine. Prickly pear, agave and oleander plants also flourish here.

There is an impressive stretch of **city walls** in black lava (c 500m) parallel to a line of eucalyptus trees. The **West Gate** is near a charming little olive tree raised on two circular terraces. A path leads to the original entrance to the **area sacra**, and remains of the 7C and 6C, including part of the walls, an altar and a **Temenos of Aphrodite**. A *sacello* or simple temple, constructed towards the end of the 7C was built over by a larger temple at the end of the 6C. Under cover two **kilns** are preserved, a circular one for pithoi, and a rectangular one for tiles; both were in use during the late 6C and 5C BC. Beyond is the **sea gate** with a fine polygonal lava wall. The pretty high wall, behind a row of cypresses, which blocks the view of the sea, was built during excavation work.

## The Alcantara Gorge

From Giardini-Naxos a road leads inland along the river valley of the Alcantara (*El Kantara*, meaning bridge in Arabic) which has numerous orange groves. Near Motta Camastra the *Gole Alcantara* are signposted. Beside the car-park is a lift (open daily) which descends into the **Alcantara Gorge**, an unexpectedly deep cleft of basalt prisms, now a protected area. This was originally formed by a lava-flow which was eroded by the river forming a narrow gorge in hard basalt. Waders can be hired to explore the gorge, which can also be reached by a path off the main road (signposted *Strada Comunale*).

# The Monti Peloritani

The Monti Peloritani, on the north-eastern tip of the island, were once thickly forested. The highest peak is the Montagna Grande (1374m). The southern slopes are barren and every drop of the scanty water supply is utilised by means of aqueducts from springs, and subterranean channels in the broad *fiumare*, conspicuous features of the countryside also on the northern slopes. These wide, flat-bottomed torrent-beds filled with gravel, similar to the *wadis* of the Syrian deserts, are usually waterless and stand out conspicuously in the surrounding landscape. In flood time the water descends these channels in spate, carrying a considerable quantity of alluvial matter. Although the mountains are for the most part inaccessible, there are a number of remote little upland villages reached by steep roads from the coast between Taormina and Messina, and between Messina and Tindari. The most interesting are Forza d'Agro on the southern coast, and S. Lucia del Mela and Castroreale on the northern coast. The church of SS. Pietro e Paolo near Casalvecchio Siculo is of great interest. Some of the most beautiful scenery on the island can be seen on the road which runs inland over the Peloritani from Castroreale Terme via Novara di Sicilia to Francavilla di Sicilia.

## ■ Practical information

*Information office*. APT Messina, ☎ 090/674236.

*Getting there.* A road and railway from Messina run along both the north and south coasts at the foot of the Peloritani. To visit the inland towns in the hills there are a few local buses.

### Hotels
**Letojanni**. ★★★★ *Park Hotel Lido Silemi*, 1 via Silemi, località Silemi, ☎ 0942/36228, fax 0942/652094. ★★★ *Antares*, Poggio Mastropietro, ☎ 0942/36477, fax 0942/36095. ★★ *Da Peppe*, 345 via Vittorio Emanuele, with restaurant, ☎ 0942/36159, fax 0942/36843. ★ *Da Nino*, 29 via L. Rizzo, ☎ 0942/36147, fax 0942/651060.
**Forza d'Agro**. ★★ *Souvenir*, via Belvedere, ☎ 0942/721078.
**Villafranca Tirrena**. ★★★ *Viola*, 90 via Antonello da Messina, località Ponte Gallo, ☎ 090/334042, fax 090/336607.
**Torregrotta**. ★★ *Redebora*, 7 via Siracusa, località Scala, with restaurant, ☎ 090/9981182, fax 090/9910900.
**Terme Vigliatore**. ★★★ *Grand Hotel Terme*, 85 via Stabilimento, ☎ 090/9781078, fax 090/ 978179.
**Francavilla di Sicilia**. ★★ *D'Orange Alcantara*, 15 via dei Mulini, ☎ 0942/981374, fax 0942/ 981704.

**Youth hostel** at **Castroreale** *Ostello della Gioventù delle Aquile*, via Federico II, ☎ 090/9746398 (open April–Oct).

### Campsites

**Letojanni.** ★★★ *Eurocamping Marmaruca*, località Marmaruca, ☎ 0942/36676. ★★ *Paradise International Camping*, località Melianò, ☎ 0942/36306.
**S. Alessio Siculo.** ★★ *La Focetta Sicula*, località Torrente d'Agrò, ☎ 0942/751657.
Near **Terme Vigliatore.** ★★★★ *Bazia Residenzial Camping*, at Bazia (Furnari), ☎ 0941/800130.

### Restaurants

**Letojanni.** A *Da Nino*, 29 via L. Rizzo. B *Il Ficodindia*, via Appiano, località Mazzeo, *Paradise Beach Club*, contrada Silemi.
Above Letojanni at **Gallodoro.** C *Noemi*, 8 via Manzoni.
**Forza d'Agro.** C *Il Giardinetto* and *l'Abbazia*.
**Itala.** C *Antica Pietrarossa*, 29 via Provinciale.
**S. Lucia del Mela.** B *Dal Pellegrino*.
**Castroreale.** C *Aquila*, 2 corso Umberto 1; *Trattoria Quattrocchi*, 18 contrada S. Croce.

## The southern slopes between Taormina and Messina

Above the resort of Letojanni just to the north of Taormina is **Mongiuffi Melia**, characteristic of the hill villages on the southern slopes of the Peloritani.

**Forza d'Agro** is a charming little medieval village, from which the views extend along the straight coastline towards Messina, across the straights to Calabria and south to Taormina. Above the piazza a lane leads up to circular steps which ascend through a pretty 15C Catalan Gothic archway which provides an entrance to the courtyard with six palm trees in front of the church of S. Trinità, with a pleasant 15C façade and campanile. It stands next to the former 15C convent of the Agostiniani with a cloister which is being restored. Behind the church a terrace, with a fine view of the coast, has recently been paved. Out of the other side of the piazza a narrow road leads through the village past the Chiesa Madre with a fine 16C façade (the crypt is being restored). Opposite is a charming abandoned old house with pretty balconies. The road continues past attractive old houses decorated with plants to the castle which was strengthened at the end of the 16C by a double circle of walls.

From S. Teresa Riva a byroad runs inland to **Savoca**, a village in a saddle between two hills which has spectacular views of the sea. In a private house at the entrance to the village is the Bar Vitelli, with a pretty garden, which has a collection of local artisans' tools, etc. Enquire here for the key to the churches. It is best to park here and walk up through the old gate past the 15C church of S. Michele with two pretty portals dating from the early 16C. Beyond the church of S. Lucia (with a 16C bust of St Lucy above the portal) the road continues up past the 17C church of the Immacolata (being restored). In via di Castello above are ruins of the castle. There are fine views of the coast and the little hill villages inland. The Chiesa

Madre contains a 16C stoup and a painting of *St Michael Archangel*. Outside the town in the church of the Cappuccini are catacombs which preserve naturally mummified bodies, fully dressed, of citizens who lived here in the 18C.

The pretty road continues over cultivated hills and valleys up to **Casalvecchio Siculo** charmingly situated on the slopes of a hill. Next to the Chiesa Madre a little diocesan museum has recently been opened. The narrow street continues through the village and 700m beyond, a very narrow road (in places single-track) leads left (signposted) and descends through lovely countryside to the old Basilian monastery of **SS. Pietro e Paolo d'Agro**. The imposing tall Norman church (unlocked by the custodian at the neighbouring farm; tip suggested) is in a beautiful peaceful spot near the Fiumara d'Agrò. Begun in 1116, it is extremely well preserved both inside and out. An inscription over the door relates how Gerardo il Franco dedicated it to Sts Peter and Paul for the Basilian monks in 1172; it was probably also restored at this time. Built of brick and black lava the exterior has splendid polychrome decoration. The Byzantine interior also shows Arab influence in the stalactite vaulting and the tiny domes in the apse and nave. The stucco was removed in this century from the walls to reveal the attractive brickwork. The columns made from Sardinian granite appear to be Roman in origin. It is possible to return to the coast road from here along a very rough road on the gravel bed of the wide torrent (*fiumara*).

At **Alì Terme**, with sulphur springs, the Calabrian coastline is in full view. A byroad leads inland to **Fiumedinisi** where the Chiesa Madre has a wooden statue of *St Lucy* by Rinaldo Bonanno (1589) and a painting of the *Madonna of the Rosary* by Agostino Ciampelli (both restored in 1985).

**Itala** is built on the side of a valley with lush vegetation. Above the village a road (very narrow in places) continues uphill and then left past ancient olive trees and lemon groves to the well-preserved church of **S. Pietro**. It is preceded by a delightful little courtyard with a garden and palm trees. The custodian who has the key lives in one of the houses here. The church was built in 1093 by Count Roger and has a handsome exterior with blind arcading and a little dome. Attached to the east end is a picturesque old palace in ruins.

**Scaletta Zanclea** has a long narrow main street (still the main coast road); fishing-boats are kept in the alleyways which lead down to the sea under the railway line. The street is particularly busy in the mornings when fresh fish is sold from stalls here. In the upper town the remains of a 13C castle lie beneath Monte Poverello (1279m), one of the highest of the Peloritani.

**Mili S. Pietro** is in a pretty wooded valley with terraced vineyards and orange groves. On the outskirts of the village (by the school) a primitive little Norman church (1082), founded by Count Roger, can be seen just below the road to the left. Steps descend to an abandoned farm, from which the church can be reached under the arch to the left. It is now in urgent need of restoration and the very interesting vaulted interior is closed (key at the parish church in the village).

## Messina to the Badiazza and Monti Peloritani

The road is well signposted from the centre of Messina (Colle S. Rizzo, Portella Castanea, S. Maria Dinnamare and Badiazza). Off N113 a very poor road (almost impassable in places) leads right (signposted) past S. Andrea, a little church built in 1929 and slums to the head of the valley. Here, in a group of pine trees, is **La Badiazza** (also called S. Maria della Scala or S. Maria della Valle). This fine 13C church (abandoned) belonged to a ruined Cistercian convent and has an interesting exterior with lava decoration.

The main road continues uphill to enter all that remains of the forest which once covered the slopes of the **Monti Peloritani**. Thick pinewoods survive here. The road sign indicating Palermo (250km) is a reminder that this was the main road to Palermo before the motorway was built. At **Colle S. Rizzo** (460m) is a crossroads. From here a spectacular road (signposted *Santuario di Maria S. di Dinnamare*) leads for 9km along the crest of the Peloritani range to a height of 1130m. The first stretch is extremely narrow and dangerous but further on the road improves. The views on either side are breathtaking: on the right Milazzo can be seen and on the left the toe of Italy. There are delightful picnic places and beautiful vegetation. Beyond a television mast is a car-park (signposted). The church of **Maria SS. di Dinnamare**, built in the 18C and restored in 1886, was rebuilt in 1899. The aerial view, one of the most remarkable in Sicily, takes in the whole of Calabria, the port of Messina and the tip of Punta Faro. On the other side the Aeolian Islands, including Stromboli (beyond Milazzo) and Mount Etna, can be seen.

From the Colle S. Rizzo crossroads (see above) the road signposted to Castanea leads through fine pinewoods (with views down of the port of Messina, and to the left of the Aeolian Islands, and the motorway in the hills). In May **Monte Ciccia** (609m) is on the migratory route from Africa to central Europe for hundreds of birds, especially falcons. On the approach to the village of **Castanea delle Furie** is a castellated villa. Castanea has two churches, one with a primitive dome. The road continues down to **Spartà** past olives and pines. As the road nears the sea there is a wonderful view of Stromboli.

## Northern slopes between Messina and Castroreale Terme

The coast road follows almost exactly that of the Roman via Valeria which joined Messina to Lilybaeum. At sea off Venetico, Agrippa defeated the fleet of Pompeius at the battle of Naulochos (36 BC). At the inland village of Rocca-valdina there is a remarkably well-preserved 16C pharmacy, complete with its jars, in piazza Umberto I.

S. LUCIA DEL MELA is in an open position beneath its prominent castle, but is now surrounded by new buildings. A narrow road leads up to the fine **Duomo** (if closed ring at no. 3 via Cappuccini), which has a lovely 15C portal and an interesting interior. In the south aisle, the first altarpiece of *The martyrdom of St Sebastian* (in poor condition) is attributed to Zoppo di Ganci; on the second altar is a painting of *St Mark the Evangelist* by Deodato Guinaccia (1581) and a statuette of the *Ecce Homo* attributed to Ignazio Marabitti. In the south transept, *St Blaise* by Pietro Novelli is situated. In the chapel to the right of the sanctuary there is a marble statue of *St Lucy* (1512). The high altarpiece of the *Assumption* is by Fra' Felice da Palermo (1771).

In the chapel to the left of the sanctuary is an unusual little sculpted *Last Supper* in the front of the altar attributed to Valerio Villareale. The altarpiece in the left transept is by Filippo Iannelli (1676), and on the third north altar is an 18C Crucifix. The font dates from 1485.

Also in the piazza is **Palazzo Vescovile**, with a little collection of works of art. Other churches of interest (open only for services) include: **SS. Annunziata** with a campanile of 1461 and a painting of the *Madonna and Child* of c 1400; **S. Maria di Gesù** (or S. Cuore) with a Crucifix by Fra Umile da Petralia; and the sanctuary of the **Madonna della Neve** (1673) with a *Madonna and Child* by Antonello Gagini. The **castle** of 1322, now a seminary, has a round tower.

A mountain road (surfaced as far as Calderado) leads into the Peloritani Mountains from S. Lucia del Mela as far as Pizzo Croce (1214m). The beautiful Bosco Scifo here, with chestnuts, oaks and ash has recently been preserved with the help of the local division of the Worldwide Fund for Nature.

**CASTROREALE** is an upland town (population 3560) which was the favourite residence of Frederick II of Aragon from whose castle (1324; now in ruins) it gets its name. Despite damage in the earthquake of 1978 the little town is unusually well preserved thanks to the efforts of its inhabitants. The numerous churches contain 16C–17C works of art.

The **Chiesa Matrice** contains a St Catherine by Antonello Gagini (1534). A Crucifix on a vara as high as the Chiesa Matrice is carried in procession through the little town on Good Friday. From piazza dell'Aquila there is a fine view of the fertile plain. The corso leads to the church of the **Candelora**, with a 17C carved wooden high altarpiece.

In via Guglielmo Siracusa is the church of **S. Maria degli Angeli** (open on Sunday and in the month of August) which contains a pinacoteca with interesting paintings and two sculptures (*St John the Baptist* by Andrea Calamech, 1568; and a *Madonna* by Antonello Freri, 1510). Further on is the fine **Museo Civico** (open 09.00–12.00, 15.00–18.00, except Wed afternoon) housed in the restored former Oratorio dei Filippini, with a charming balcony decorated with prancing horses and lions above the doorway. The collection of sculpture and paintings comes from local churches. In room 1 there are Crucifixes, including a painted one dating from the 14C–15C. Room 2 contains Antonello da Saliba's, *Madonna and Child enthroned, with angels*, and a sarcophagus with the effigy of Geronimo Rosso by Antonello Gagini (1507). Room 3 contains *St Lawrence and stories from his life* by Frate Simpliciano. In room 4 are 17C paintings. Upstairs vestments, precious books, ceramic tiles, 18C paintings, including works by Fra Felice da Sambuca (1733–1805) and an 18C–19C silver Cross from the Chiesa Matrice are displayed.

At the end of the street are the churches of S. Marina and **S. Agata**, with a charming *Annunciation* by Antonello Gagini, dated 1519. South of the town by the cemetery is the church of **S. Maria di Gesù** which dates from the 15C.

At the top of the town a circular tower survives of the **castle** founded by Frederick II of Aragon in 1324.

**Terme Vigliatore** became a comune in 1966. It is a thermal resort, with a tourist port. At S. Biagio, west of the town, are the remains of a large **Roman**

**villa** of the 1C AD (admission daily 09.00–dusk). The rooms, protected by a plastic roof, have black and white mosaics, mostly geometric, but one floor has a lively fishing scene, with dolphins, swordfish and other fish still found off the coast here. The main hall has a fine opus sectile pavement.

Inland near **Milici**, is the site of ancient *Longane*, a Sicel town of some importance, which was no longer inhabited by the 5C BC. Traces of the walls survive and the foundations of a sacred building.

From Castroreale Terme a road runs inland across the western side of the Peloritani (rising to a height of 1100m), connecting the Tyhrrenian coast with the Ionian Sea at Naxos. Fairly well engineered, and with very little traffic, it has some of the best scenery on the island. It follows the wide Mazzarrà and Novara valleys on the beds of which are extensive citrus fruit plantations and some 'pillbox' defences from World War II. **Mazzarrà S. Andrea** is surrounded with nurseries. Gravel is extracted from the grey waterless riverbed, beside which oranges are grown. A few lovely old abandoned farmhouses survive here.

**Novara di Sicilia** (675m), the ancient *Noae*, is now a quiet little town below the main road. From largo Bertolami, with a bronze statue of *David* by Giuseppe Buemi (1882), via Duomo leads up to the 16C Duomo. In the right aisle is a wooden statue of the *Assumption* by Filippo Colicci. Across the valley much new building has taken place at S. Basilio.

The fantastic bare horn-shaped **Rocca Novara** (1340m) stands at the end of the Peloritani range. The pass of **Sella Mandrazzi** (1125m) is surrounded by thick woods of pine and fir. The view extends to the coastline and the sanctuary of Tindari on its promontory, beyond the conspicuous Rocca Novara.

The scenery is particunrly fine in this area, and picnic places are provided. From here the fine mountain road descends through deserted country which provides pasture for sheep and goats. Almost all the farmhouses here are abandoned. On a clear day there is a spectacular view of Etna, and of the river torrents on the hillsides.

The road continues to descend and there are now some vineyards, persimmon trees and prickly pears. It crosses a bridge before reaching the junction with the road from Moio Alcantara (described on p.314), near an abandoned villa. The Francavilla road continues left along the side of the valley and then descends through orange groves to **Francavilla di Sicilia**. Above the cemetery on the outskirts is the well-signposted Convento dei Cappuccini (admission only for services), where the church has 17C and 18C works. A Greek sanctuary was excavated in the town in 1979–84 and the votive statues found here are now displayed in the archaeological museum in Siracusa. The Gola dell'Alcantara and Giardini Naxos on the coast are described on pp.342 and 344.

Another very winding minor road leads south-west from Terme Vigliatore to **Montalbano Elicona**, a little hill town (900m), in a fine position surrounded by woods, with a castle (1302–11) open for exhibitions and concerts.

# Milazzo and the Aeolian Islands

The interesting town of Milazzo is the port for the Aeolian Islands. These islands are the most beautiful islands off the Sicilian coast with wonderful scenery (including two volcanoes), important archaeological remains and good hotels.

## Milazzo

Milazzo is a port (population 32,100) with pretty buildings and an attractive sea front, standing on the isthmus of a narrow peninsula on the north-east coast of the island in the province of Messina. On the outskirts is a huge oil refinery and much new building has taken place.

## ■ Practical information

*Information office*. Azienda Autonoma, piazza Duilio (☎ 090/9222865).

*Railway station*. 3km from the centre. Services on the Messina–Palermo line. *Maritime services* to the Aeolian Islands, see below.

*Hotels*. ★★★ *Silvanetta Palace*, 1 via Mangiavacca, ☎ 090/9281633, fax 090/9222787; *Riviera Lido*, strada Panoramica (località Corrie), ☎ 090/ 9287834, fax 090/9283456; *Eolian Inn Park Hotel*, 25 via Cappuccini, ☎ 090/ 9286133, fax 090/9282855.

*Restaurants*. **A** *Villa Esperanza*, 191 via Baronia, località Capo Milazzo; *Salamone a Mare*, via Panoramica. **B** *Covo del Pirata*, lungomare Garibaldi; *La Vecchia Cucina*, 17 via Nino Ryolo. **C** *L'Ugghiularu*, 137 via Acquaviole; *Al Bagatto,*11 via Mario Regis; *Pignataro*, via L. Rizzo; *La Casalinga*, via D'Amico.

### History

Milazzo was the ancient *Mylai*, founded by Greeks from Zancle in 716 BC. Here Duilius defeated the Carthaginians in a sea battle (260 BC), and here in 1860 Garibaldi successfully assaulted the castle, garrisoned by Bourbon troops, promoting J.W. Peard, a Cornish volunteer, to the rank of colonel on the field.

The road for the centre passes the port, where the boats and hydrofoils for the Aeolian Islands dock. In via Crispi is the **Municipio** built at the end of the last century by Salvatore Richichi. On the other side of the building (reached through the courtyard) is piazza Duilio, with a copy made in 1990 of the *Fontana del Mela* (the original of 1762 by Giuseppe Buceti was destroyed in World War II). Here is the pleasant red façade of the former convent of the **Carmelitani** (16C; restored), with the Azienda Autonoma information office. Next to it is the Baroque façade of the **Carmine** (1574; rebuilt in 1726–52), and, on the other side, a handsome neo-classical palace. Opposite is Palazzo Proto which was Garibaldi's headquarters for a time in 1860 (see above). In via Pescheria fresh fish is sold in the mornings from stalls in the street.

The lungomare, planted with trees, is a continuation of via Crispi along the sea front. The 18C church of S. Giacomo is well sited at a fork in the road which leads inland to the **Duomo Nuovo** (1937–52) which contains paintings by Antonello de Saliba and Antonio Giuffrè. Further on, via Colombo leads away from the sea past two little Art Nouveau villas, now surrounded by unattractive buildings.

From piazza Roma via Impallomeni leads up towards the castle past the pretty 18C church of **S. Francesco di Paola**, which contains six paintings of miracles of the saint by Letterio Paladino (restored). The 17C church of the Immacolata can be seen above on the left, and on the right is the closed church of S. Salvatore. Pretty low houses surround the double walls of the **castle** (open 09.00–12.00, 14.30–15.30 (17.00–19.00 in summer; closed Mon) built by Frederick II in 1239, enlarged by Charles V and restored in the 17C. The walls date from the 16C and enclose a large area including an imposing keep with a Gothic doorway and great hall known as the *Sala del Parlamento*. The **Duomo Vecchio** (no admission), within the castle enclosure, is an interesting building of the early 17C, attributed to Camillo Camilliani or possibly Natale Masuccio. It was abandoned when the new cathedral was begun in 1937 (see above). The 16C walls survive here.

The unspoilt peninsula of Capo Milazzo is known as **Baronia**. Summer villas were built here in the 19C and early 20C. The road ends by a group of olive trees. There is a lighthouse, and paths descend to the rocky shore. The vegetation includes prickly pear, palms and olive trees. From the cape the view (on a clear day) encompasses the two active volcanoes of Etna and Stromboli.

## The Aeolian Islands

The Aeolian Islands form an archipelago of seven islands (Lipari, Salina, Stromboli, Panarea, Vulcano, Alicudi and Filicudi) and numerous rocks. Their name is derived from Aeolus, the Greek god of the winds, who was fabled to keep the winds imprisoned in his cave here. The islands are remarkable for their spectacular scenery and ever-changing views. They are extremely interesting from a geological point of view, with remarkable rock formations and volcanic phenomena on Stromboli (still active) and Vulcano.

Several prehistoric sites have been excavated on the islands, and the fine archaeological museum in Lipari is one of the most important collections of its kind in Europe. The local style of architecture adds charm to the picturesque villages on the smaller islands. They were developed for tourism in the 1960s and 1970s and are now crowded in the summer months. The islanders tend to have a tough and independent character. A lively fishing industry supplies the archipelago with a variety of fish.

## ■ Practical information

*Information office*. Azienda Autonoma del Turismo delle Isole Eolie, 202 corso Vittorio Emanuele, Lipari (☎ 090/9880095).

### Getting there

The most convenient starting-point in Sicily for the islands is **Milazzo.** Throughout the year **ferries** (run by *Siremar* and *Navigazione Generale Italiana*) leave about five times a day from Milazzo for the islands (to Lipari in c 2hr). A

**hydrofoil** and **catamaran** service (run by *Snav* and *Siremar*) operates about 12 times a day from Milazzo in 55min.

An overnight ferry from **Naples** (with sleeping accommodation and restaurant) operates about twice a week (more frequently in summer); it calls at Ginostra, Stromboli, Panarea, Salina, Lipari and Vulcano.

There is also a hydrofoil service from **Reggio Calabria** and **Messina** for Lipari. In summer, although the timetables are subject to change, there are usually hydrofoil services from **Palermo** and **Cefalù** for Alicudi, Filicudi, Salina, Vulcano and Lipari, and from Naples for Stromboli, Panarea, Salina, Lipari and Vulcano.

*Snav*: Agenzia Catalano, 17 via Rizzo, Milazzo, ☎ 090/9287821.

*Siremar*: Agenzia Alliatour, via dei Mille, Milazzo, ☎ 090/9283242.

*Navigazione Generale Italiana*, 26 via dei Mille, Milazzo, ☎ 090/9284091.

*Agenzia Ontano Tours*, piazza Municipio, Varco Angioino, Naples, ☎ 081/5800340.

**Sailing times**. Timetables vary annually and according to season, and all sailings are subject to sea conditions; the time of departure should always be checked locally since in rough weather services are suspended. Some ticket offices on the islands open only 30 minutes before sailing. Information from the Azienda Autonoma on Lipari (see above).

**Inter-island communications**. All the islands are connected by ferry and hydrofoil services; the services to Alicudi and Filicudi are less frequent. Extra hydrofoil services operate from Lipari to Vulcano (several times daily) and Salina, both of which can also be reached by local boat excursions. The ferries are slower and often less direct than the hydrofoil service, but are comfortable and provide an opportunity of seeing the coastal regions of the islands. The hydrofoils are relatively more expensive and less reliable, as they cannot sail in rough weather. Fishing-boats may be hired on all the islands, and the trip around the coast of most of the islands is strongly recommended.

**Cars** are allowed on Lipari, Vulcano, Filicudi and Salina; a car-ferry runs from Milazzo and Naples. However, visitors are not advised to take a car as distances are short and local transport good. Some car hire services operate on Lipari, Vulcano and Salina. On the other islands small motor vehicles are used to transport luggage. On Vulcano vespas and bicycles can also be hired at the port.

### Public transport on the islands

**Lipari**. Bus services from the corso Vittorio Emanuele to Canneto (every hour) and to the pumice quarries and Acquacalda (every 2hr); to Quattrocchi, Pianoconte, and Quattropani (every 2hr).

On **Vulcano** a few bus services a day from the port to Piano.

### Hotels

Good hotels are now to be found on most of the islands; the standard of accommodation is often higher than the official categories would suggest (especially in Panarea and Lipari). It is essential to book in advance in the summer months, and advisable to do so at all times of the year. All the islands also have numerous flats and rooms to let.

**Lipari**

★★★ *Giardino sul Mare*, 65 via Maddalena, ☎ 090/9811004, fax 090/9880150

★★ *Augustus*, 16 via Ausonia, ☎ 090/9811232, fax 090/9812233; *Poseidon*, 7 via Ausonia, ☎ 090/9812876, fax 090/9880252; *Oriente*, 35 via Marconi, ☎ 090/9811493, fax 090/9880198; *La Filadelfia*, via Madre Florenzia Profilio, ☎ 090/9812795, fax 090/9812486; *Villa Diana*, via Diana at Tufo, ☎ & fax 090/9811403.

**Apartments to rent** at *Residence La Giara*, via Barone, ☎ & fax 090/9880352.

**Youth hostel** on the Acropolis, ☎ 090/9811540, fax 090/9811715.

★★ **Campsite** *Baia Unci* at Canneto, ☎ 090/9811909.

**Vulcano**

★★★★ *Les Sables Noirs*, Porto Ponente, ☎ 090/9850, fax 090/9852454.

★★★ *Conti*, Porto Ponente, ☎ & fax 090/9852012; *Eolian Hotel*, Porto Ponente, ☎ 090/9852151, fax 090/9852153.

★★ *Orso Maggiore*, Porto Ponente, ☎ 090/9852018, fax 090/9852415.

On **Vulcanello**: ★★★ *Archipelago*, ☎ 090/9852002, fax 090/9852154.

**Salina**

★★★ *Signum*, 11 via Scalo, Malfa, ☎ 090/9844222, fax 090/9844102.

★★ *L'Ariana*, 11 via Rotabile, località Rinella, Leni, ☎ 090/9809075; fax 090/9809250.

★ *Punta Barone*, 8 via Lungomare Notar Giuffré, S. Marina, ☎ & fax 090/9843172.

**Furnished flats**. *Residence S. Isabel*, 12 via Scalo, località Malfa, ☎ & fax 090/9844018.

**Campsite** open in summer ★ *Tre Pini*, frazione Rinella, ☎ 090/9809155.

**Panarea**

★★★ *La Piazza*, via S. Pietro, ☎ 090/983154, fax 090/983003; *Cincotta*, via S. Pietro, ☎ 090/983014, fax 090/983211; *Lisca Bianca*, 1 via Lani, ☎ 090/983004, fax 090/983291.

★★ *Raya*, via S. Pietro, ☎ 090/983013, fax 090/983103.

**Stromboli**

★★★ *La Sciara*, via Soldato Cincotta, ☎ 090/986121, fax 090/986284; *La Sirenetta*, 33 via Marina, ☎ 090/986025, fax 090/986124.

★★ *Villaggio Stromboli*, via Regina Elena, ☎ 090/986018, fax 090/986258.

★ *Miramare*, 3 via Vito Nunziante, ☎ 090/986047, fax 090/986318; *Villa Petrusa*, 4 via Soldato Panettieri, ☎ 090/986045, fax 090/986126.

**Filicudi**

★★★ *Phenicusa*, via Porto, ☎ 090/9889946, fax 090/9889955.

★ *La Canna*, 43 via Rosa, ☎ 090/9889956, fax 090/9889966.

**Alicudi**

★ *Ericusa*, via Regina Elena, ☎ 090/9889902, fax 9889671, and numerous rooms to rent in private houses.

### Restaurants
**Lipari**. **A** *Filippino* and *Al Pirata; La Ginestra* at Pianoconte. **B** *Da Lauro*, at Acquacalda; *E Pulera* (only in summer); *Giardino sul Mare*. **C** *Pizzeria La Piazzetta (Nino Subba)*, piazzetta Monfalcone.
**Vulcano**. **A** *Da Gaetano*, at Gelso; *Da Maurizio*. **B** *Don Piricuddu; Il Diavolo dei Polli*, at Piano. **C** *A Zammara (*in the Hotel Conti), a pizzeria open in summer.
**Salina**. **B** *Il Gambero*, at Lingua.
**Panarea**. **B** *Da Pina; Da Antonio 'il macellaio'; Lisca Bianca* (which is also a good pasticceria).
**Stromboli**. **B** *Il Canneto* and *Barbablù*. **C** *Ai Geki*.
**Filicudi**. **B** *Villa La Rosa*.

### Pasticcerie
**Lipari**. *Laboratorio Ambra*, Marina Corta; *Pasticceria Subba*, piazzetta Monfalcone; and the three cafés at Marina Corta.
**Vulcano**. *Ritrovo Remigio*.

### History
The islands were important in ancient times because of the existence of obsidian, a hard volcanic glass used as a tool and exported in the Mediterranean. The earliest traces of settlement found belong to the Stentinello culture of the Neolithic age. In the Middle Bronze Age the islands were on the main trade routes between the Aegean Islands and the Western Mediterranean. The Greeks colonised Lipari in c 600 BC, and in the following centuries the islands were attacked by the Athenians and the Carthaginians. They fell to Rome in 252 BC. From then on their history has been closely related to that of Sicily.

**Vegetation**. The tropical plants which thrive on the rocky soil include prickly pear, carob trees and palms. Huge old olive trees survive on some of the islands. In spring, broom flourishes, and the wild flowers, particularly on Panarea, are exceptionally beautiful. Capers and excellent wine are exported from the islands. A strongly scented marjoram (*origano*) flourishes on the islands and is used a lot in the local cuisine.

# Lipari
Lipari (37 sq km), the chief island of the group and about 40km from Milazzo on the Sicilian mainland, has become a popular summer resort. About half its 8580 inhabitants are concentrated in the lively and attractive little port of **Lipari**. Here the castle commands the shore above the town, and separates the two harbours.

The town has low houses with balconies decorated with plants and charming narrow streets. Pleasant little shops sell local specialities and there are numberous *pasticcerie*, bars and restaurants. At **Marina Corta** the hydrofoils dock beside the picturesque church of the **Anime del Purgatorio** (in need of restoration). Another attractive church here is **S. Giuseppe** at the top of a ramp. Outside the church fishermen are often at work mending their nets, their colourful fishing boats pulled up on the quay beside a solitary palm tree. The three cafés here have tables outside.

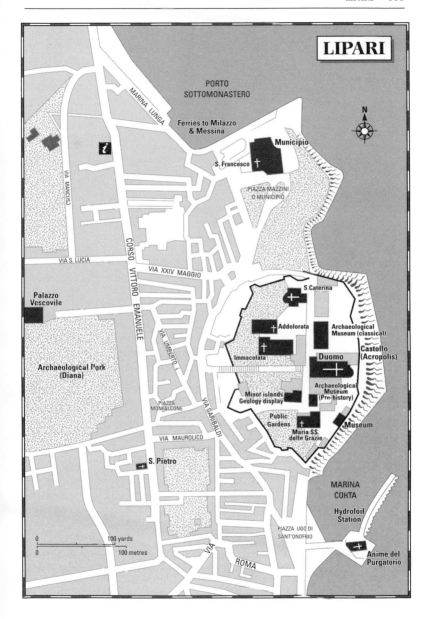

**Via Garibaldi** (closed to cars) winds uphill through the town. It passes a wide scenic flight of steps constructed at the beginning of the 20C up to the castle hill, framing the façade of the Duomo at the top (the second approach to the castle hill is described below). Via Garibaldi ends in **piazza Mazzini** with a garden and some pretty houses by the neo-Gothic town hall. The 18C church of **S. Francesco** has pretty marble altars. Steps lead down to the crypt which was the burial-place for the islanders before the cemetery (which can be seen nearby) was opened. From the terrace is a view of the sea and the port where the car-ferries dock, and the attractive sea front, with the boats pulled up on the quay in front of low houses.

From piazza Mazzini is the most interesting approach to the **Castle Hill** or **Acropolis** through the impressive 16C Spanish fortifications, with double gates and an entrance tunnel which incorporate classical fragments. The hill is a very peaceful spot since no cars are allowed here, and it is attractively planted with oleanders, prickly pear and ivy. On the summit there are archaeological remains as well as five churches, public gardens and an archaeological museum (see the map on p.355).

## Museo Archeologico

The Museo Archeologico is arranged in four separate buildings (open daily 09.00–14.00; 15.00–19.00; Sun & PH 09.00–13.00, 15.00–19.00; one of the buildings can sometimes be closed if there is a lack of custodians). The superb collection, beautifully displayed in chronological sequence (with labels also in English), contains finds from Lipari and other islands in the Aeolian group (as well as from Milazzo and southern Italy). Beyond the cathedral (described below) is the former Palazzo Vescovile (early 18C), with an attractive portal and balconies, which houses the first section dedicated to **prehistory**.

**Upstairs. Rooms 1–3** contain Neolithic finds from Lipari, including painted vases, *Serra d'Alto* style pottery (resembling southern Italian forms), and red pottery of the *Diana* style. **Room 4** has finds dating from c 3000 BC, from Piano Conte, and **room 5** contains early Bronze Age material from Capo Graziano on Filicudi. **Room 6** displays objects found here on the castle hill belonging to the Capo Graziano (1800–1400 BC) and Milazzese (c 1400–1250 BC) cultures, showing Greek influences. Notable are the vessels on tall pedestals, thought to have been used from a sitting position on the floor.

The display continues on the **ground floor**. The Ausonian culture (from southern Italy) is represented in **rooms 7–9**; the finds made on the castle hill show the influence of the Italian mainland, and the vessels have a great variety of strangely shaped handles. Here also are the remains of a small cooking device, and a large impasto pot, the repository of over 2cwt of bronze objects of the 9C BC. There are signs of a violent destruction of Lipari in the 9C BC, and the island appears to have remained uninhabited for the next three centuries.

The last **room 10** illustrates the Greek and Roman period on Lipari. The large restored Attic vase, used for mixing water and wine, has an exquisite delicate black-figure decoration on the rim showing the *Labours of Hercules* and (inside) a frieze of ships. It is attributed to the 'Painter of Antimenes' (540–30 BC). The couchant lion (c 575 BC) carved from volcanic rock, probably guarded a votive deposit. Also here are a Roman statue of a girl of the 2C AD, found in the bishop's palace, and a statuette of *Asklepios* (4C BC). A case displays Hellenistic and medieval ceramics. A door leads out to the garden which contains sarcophagi from contrada Diana (see below) and the **Epigraphic Pavilion** (not always open) which contains funerary inscriptions of 5C–1C BC.

On the other side of the cathedral is the pavilion, mostly dedicated to the **Clas-**

**sical** period. On the left are three rooms (**16–18**) with finds from Milazzo displayed in chronological sequence from the Middle Bronze Age to the 3C BC, with the reconstruction of a burial site, with the pithoi in situ. On the other side of the entrance **room 20** has a superb collection of terracotta and stone sarcophagi from Lipari, including the stone one in the centre (found in contrada Diana) which is perfectly preserved. It is thought to have been made by the sculptor in 2C–1C BC as his own tomb. In **room 19** beyond is a reconstruction of the piazza Monfalcone necropolis (1125–1050 BC) in Lipari.

**First floor. Room 21:** Attic red-figure kraters of the 5C BC and early Sicilian and Campanian red-figure vases (4C BC) including a splendid krater by the 'Painter of Adrasto' with columns (c 450 BC). In wall cases there are 5C BC grave goods, and Attic pottery on a white ground. **Room 22** contains more vases (350–30 BC). **Room 23** has a superb display of theatrical figurines in terracotta, statuettes (early 4C–mid-3C BC) found on Lipari (note: especially the statuettes of dancers, and *Andromica with her child*), and a fascinating and unique collection of **tragic masks** and **theatrical terracottas**. Also here is some very fine gold jewellery.

In **room 24** brightly-coloured vases are displayed by the 'Lipari Painter', a master who excelled in the representation of the female figure. The southern Italian vases include a krater with Dionysius watching a nude acrobat and two actors, and a bronze hydra with a female bust (early 5C BC). The Hellenistic gold jewellery includes a ring of the 4C BC with a female nude. **Room 25** consists of a reconstruction of part of the necropolis of Lipari at contrada Diana (6C–3C BC) with pithoi and situlae. Stairs lead up to **room 26** with the latest finds from the hill showing evidence of the destruction of Lipari in 252 BC, and then sporadic finds from the Roman and Norman periods, as well as medieval and Renaissance ceramics.

Downstairs in **room 27** is a section devoted to underwater archaeology, with finds dating from 2000 BC to the 5C BC, fished up off Capistello (Lipari), and near Filicudi and Panarea, including a magnificent display of amphorae. There are also finds from the wreck of a 17C Spanish warship.

Opposite the pavilion with the prehistoric section, a group of simple old houses displays prehistoric finds from the **minor islands:** Panarea (from the Calcara and Milazzese sites), Filicudi and Salina. In the entrance are three huge pithoi from Portella on Salina. Next door is a building which houses a **geological** display on three floors with diagrams, maps, reliefs and models which illustrate volcanic activity and the formation of the Aeolian Islands. In the courtyard is a small collection of epigraphs.

Outside, the extensive excavations begun in 1950 on the summit of the hill, have revealed a remarkable sequence of levels of occupation, uninterrupted from the Neolithic Age when the islands were first inhabited. The unique pottery strata (reaching a depth of 9m) make the acropolis the key dating site of the central Mediterranean. The different levels are well labelled and explained by diagrams.

The exterior of the church of **S. Caterina** (closed) has been restored. Beyond the excavations the small church of the **Addolorata** can be seen, which has a Baroque façade in need of restoration, and next to it the **Immacolata**, with another Baroque façade, and also in urgent need of restoration.

The **Duomo** (open 10.00–12.00) was first built on this site by King Roger (c 1084). The pretty interior, hung with chandeliers, has a vault frescoed in the 18C. On the side altars are 18C reliquary busts in gilded wood. In the north transept is a *Madonna of the Rosary*, attributed to Girolamo Alibrandi, and a statue in silver of *S. Bartolomeo* which dates from 1728. The statue, together with an elaborate silver reliquary of a boat, is carried in procession through the streets on 24 August, 16 November, 13 February and 5 March. The Benedictine cloister has been restored. Dating from 1131, with later additions, it has vaulted walks, and columns of different shapes and sizes (some of them Doric, and some re-used from Roman buildings), and primitive capitals with animals and birds.

The last church on the hill is **Maria SS. delle Grazie** (closed), with a fine restored façade, reached down a few steps in a little garden. On the other side of the road are **public gardens** (with fine views) which have a large number of Greek and Roman sarcophagi. These were found in the necropolis of contrada Diana (late 5C and 4C BC), at the foot of the acropolis (now covered by the modern town). There is also a little open-air theatre here, built in 1978.

The main road of the town is corso Vittorio Emanuele, which is congested with traffic. On the far (west) side is **Palazzo Vescovile**, eventually to be restored as the seat of a Diocesan Museum. Beside it is the archaeological zone of **contrada Diana** where two Roman hypogeum were found, and where excavations revealed part of the Greek walls (5C–4C BC) of the ancient city, and Roman houses. It is now very overgrown and is no longer open regularly to the public.

A road (26.5km) encircles the island. It leads north from Lipari via **Canneto** to traverse magnificent huge white cliffs of pumice, with deep gallery quarries. The loading jetties protrude into the sea, here washed clean by the pumice stone. Beyond **Porticello** the road crosses remarkable red and black veins of obsidian, some of which reach the sea. The beaches are covered with pumice and obsidian, and some of the paths in the villages are cut out of obsidian. A road connects Acquacalda with Quattropani. At **Piano Conte** lava battle-axes and Bronze Age weapons have been found. Near the coast (reached by a byroad) are the ancient hot springs of **S. Calogero** with remains of Roman baths. An ancient tholos has come to light here. The road returns to Lipari past the viewpoint of Quattrocchi.

**Monte S. Angelo** (594m; view), in the centre of the island, is an extinct stratified volcano of unusual form.

## Vulcano

Vulcano (21 sq km; population 717) is the most southerly of the isles (separated from the southern tip of Lipari by a channel less than 1km wide) and easily reached from the Sicilian mainland (see above) or by frequent hydrofoil services from Lipari (and by local boat excursions). It is of outstanding interest because of its geological structure, its spectacular volcanic landscape with black lava rocks on the sea and black lava beaches. The last volcanic eruption occurred in 1890. It has simple houses mostly built in the 20C in a disorderly way. It is deserted out of season but very crowded in summer when there are also discotheques etc. for the younger generation. The inhabitants are unusual in that many of them go barefoot.

The boats dock at **Porto di Levante** near the makeshift quay used by the hydrofoils. A road with simple shops and a few cafés leads to **Porto di Ponente** with mud pools on the beach fed by hot springs, where anyone can bathe. The 'castle' here was bought by a certain Stevenson from a Bourbon general in the last century and restored by him in neo-Gothic style. Stevenson left the island after his wife had been killed by an explosion of the volcano, and the building was bought by three islanders, the descendant of one of whom has recently restored the castle as a little spa centre, with facilities for Turkish baths, etc. The fine black lava beach nearby, with a number of hotels, is crowded in summer.

In the other direction from the port a straight road leads across the plain at the foot of the volcano. A narrow path (signposted; about 1km from the port) leads up across the fine volcanic soil and rocks to the top of the crater (375m) in about 1hr. The route can be damaged and almost impassible after heavy rain, but is normally quite easy (although sturdy shoes are necessary). There is a remarkable view of the inside of the **crater**, and the rim steams constantly with sulphur vapours. On a clear day most of the Aeolian Islands can be seen from here. You can follow the path right around the rim (in about 1hr).

Most of the islanders live in the upland plain of the island known as **Piano,** 7km from the port (reached by a few buses every day). Here there is one *pensione* and bar, a shop, a church and a school: most of the fields have now been abandoned, and some of the houses are now only used in summer. The Piano road passes close to the volcano and at the top of the hill by the first house on the corner a byroad leads left. Another turn left leads to the edge of a cliff with a number of caves and a view of the coast. The road continues gently uphill past a road on the left for **Gelso,** with some restaurants open in summer and good sea bathing. Another byroad leads to **Capo Grillo** which has the best panorama on the island. The Piano road ends in front of the parish church destroyed by an earthquake in 1978 and rebuilt in 1988.

On the northern tip of the island is **Vulcanello**, an excellent example of a volcanic cone which rose out of the sea in 183 BC. Near the **Faraglione della Fabbrica**, a high rock with alum quarries, are the hot springs of Acqua Bollente and Acqua del Bagno. Between Vulcano and Lipari are some striking basalt stacks, including the **Pietralunga**, an obelisk of rock, 72m high.

## Salina

Salina, 4km north-west of Lipari, is the highest of the islands (962m), and is formed by two twin volcanic cones and the saddle between them (27 sq km). The shape of Monte dei Porri is one of the most perfect mountain cones in the world. It has been identified with Homer's *Siren Island*, and was anciently called *Didyme*. Its population (2300) is divided into several picturesque villages: **S. Marina**, **Malfa** and **Leni**. The island is famous for its malvasia wine, but only two companies still bottle the grapes actually grown on the island (*Fenich* and *Caravaglio*). Capers are also grown here. The island is very green and lovely walks can be taken on the two mountains: the Fossa delle Felci has chestnut woods. The attractive old houses and the fine scenery are now protected thanks to an enlightened local administration. On the east coast, near the S. Marina lighthouse, a Middle Bronze Age village has been excavated (not open to the public), and traces of Roman houses have been found on the island (those at the north end of the lungomare can be seen). After the Arab conquest of the Aeolian

Islands in 838 the island remained virtually uninhabited until the 16C. The island was the setting for the film *Il Postino*.

## Panarea

Panarea lies to the north-east (15km from Lipari), towards Stromboli. It is perhaps the most charming of all the islands, and its natural beauty and the style of the local architecture has been carefully preserved by its 317 inhabitants. However, its hotels and restaurants, now frequented by famous and wealthy Italians, are a lot more expensive than those on the other islands. It is 3.5sq km in area. Electricity was brought to the island in 1982. Near the fishing harbour hot spring water mixes with the sea.

A walk (c 30 min.) leads to a naturally defended promontory on the southern tip of the island. On this superb site the Bronze Age village of **Milazzese** (probably inhabited in the 14C BC), with 23 huts, was excavated in 1948. Mycenaean ceramics and native vases showing Minoan influences were brought to light (now in Lipari Museum, see above).

At the opposite end of the island, near the last houses on the coast, a path descends to the shore at **Calcara** where the fumarole emit sulphureous gases. Nearby are traces of Neolithic pits made from boulders and volcanic clay, probably used for offerings. A Greek wreck was found offshore here in 1980, and from then until 1987 some 600 pieces of ceramics were recovered from its cargo of precious terracotta vases (5C–4C BC), some of which are now exhibited in the Lipari Museum.

In the sea near the island the beautifully coloured rocks of **Lisca Bianca** and **Basiluzzo** (with many traces of Roman occupation) provide a foreground to the ever-changing view of Stromboli. In hot weather, when the sea is very calm, the volcano takes on the appearance of a 'floating isle' (see *Odyssey*, x, 3).

## Stromboli

Stromboli (12.5sq km; c 28km from Lipari) is the most famous island of the archipelago on account of its continual volcanic activity. It consists of a single cone (926m); the present active crater is 200m below the summit. It has been abandoned several times after severe eruptions, but is now again increasing in population (407). It is visited by many tourists, especially from Germany.

The main village of **Stromboli** is on the north-east coast. The boats also call at **Ginostra**, an attractive small group of houses on a rocky headland on the south-west tip of the island. The construction of a port here in 1991 was blocked in an attempt to preserve the beauty of the coast. Eruptions occur on the north-west side of the volcano and are not visible from either of the villages. The cone may be ascended with a guide (c 3hr); but an easy footpath from Stromboli (S. Vincenzo) ascends as far as the Semaforo (c 1hr 30min.), from which point the explosions can usually be seen. Normally a small eruption occurs at frequent intervals; on days of unusual violence the spectacle (best seen at night from the sea) of the volcanic matter rushing down the **Sciara del Fuoco** into the sea is particularly impressive.

Off the north-east coast is the striking rock of **Strombolicchio**, a steep block of basalt (43m) ascended by a rock-hewn stair and commanding an unparalleled view of the islands and of Calabria. Around Strombolicchio are certain mysterious currents, sometimes violent enough to incline the vertically anchored fishing nets to an angle of 45 degrees. Shoals of flying fish can occasionally be seen offshore.

## Filicudi

The remote and picturesque island of Filicudi (9.5 sq km) lies 19km west of Salina. Anciently called *Phoenicoessa*, it has 301 inhabitants. It has recently become a fashionable place to visit. The landscape is pretty despite the construction of a road in the 1970s which destroyed the terraces. Two prehistoric villages have been excavated on Capo Graziano; on the point (Montagnola) 12 huts were uncovered showing evidence of rebuilding before their destruction in the Milazzese period, while just inland, three oval huts yielded Bronze Age vases. Off the cape in 1975 a hoard of Bronze Age ceramics was found on the site of a shipwreck.

## Alicudi

The most westerly isle is Alicudi. Its 5 sq km support a dwindling population of 102 inhabitants. It is a particularly beautiful island, with terraces and attractive local architecture. A number of foreigners have recently bought houses here. It has only had electricity since 1990.

# Tindari and the Parco dei Nebrodi

The ancient site of Tindari is in a very fine position on the sea. The Parco dei Nebrodi is a protected area with suberb mountain scenery. S. Marco d'Alunzio is an interesting little hill town here.

## ■ Practical information

### Information offices

APT Messina, ☎ 090/674236. Aziende Autonome local offices: Capo d'Orlando, 71 via Piave, ☎ 0941/912784; Patti, 11 piazza Marconi, ☎ 0941/241136; Tindari, 15 via Teatro Greco, ☎ 0941/369184.

For the Parco dei Nebrodi: main office at Caronia, 126 via Ruggero Orlando, ☎ 0921/333211; information offices at Alcara Li Fusi, 1 via Ugo Foscolo, ☎ 0941/ 793130, or 0941/793904, and at Cesarò (Strada Nazionale), ☎ 095/ 696008.

S. Marco d'Alunzio, local tourist office, ☎ 0941/797339 (or parish office, ☎ 0941/797045).

### Getting there

Tindari is just off the main coast road and motorway between Messina and Palermo. The Parco dei Nebrodi is approached by fine mountain roads from the north coast from Capo d'Orlando and S. Agata di Militello.

### Hotels

**Gioiosa Marea**. ★★★ *Capo Calavà*, contrada Calavà, ☎ 0941/301173, fax 0941/301188.

**Capo d'Orlando**. ★★★ *La Tartaruga*, Lido S. Gregorio, ☎ 0941/955012, fax 0941/955056, with restaurant.
**Rooms to rent** at Lido S. Gregorio (for information, ☎ 0941/914172 or 0941/955157).
**Parco dei Nebrodi**. Simple mountain refuge at the Passo del Miraglia: *Dun* (Villa Miraglia), on the road to Cesarò (SS 289), ☎ 095/7732133. *Agriturismo* accommodation near Caronia in contrada S. Mamma (Antonia Collura), ☎ 0941/701656.

### Restaurants
**Capo d'Orlando**. B *La Tartaruga*, Lido S. Gregorio. C *La Tettoia*, contrada Catutè.
**S. Marco d'Alunzio**. C *La Fornace*, 115 via Cappuccini. *Pasticceria* Basilio Castrovinci, 86 via Aluntina.

### Annual festivals
**S. Fratello** The ancient *Festa dei Giudei* is celebrated here on Maundy Thursday and Good Friday in traditional costume.
**Alcara Li Fusi** The summer solstice (24 June) is celebrated in the village with the pagan *Festa del Muzzuni*.

## Tindari
On the headland of **Capo Tindari** (230m) there is a conspicuous sanctuary and the excavations of the ancient city of *Tyndaris* founded in the 4C BC. The road leads to a car-park below the huge new church which was built onto the old in 1957–79 to house a seated statue of a black *Virgin* of Byzantine origin which has been greatly venerated since the 16C (pilgrimage on 8 September). The old sanctuary, with a portal of 1598, on the seaward side, is no longer visible.

From the car-park a path and steps lead up to a road in front of a small group of houses with a little bar and restaurant which leads to the entrance to the impressive ruins of **Tindari** (open daily 09.00–dusk). The ancient city of Tyndaris was founded by Dionysius the Elder in 396 after his victory over the Carthaginians. Tyndaris remained an ally of Siracusa until taken by the Romans in 254. It was later damaged by a landslide and then by an earthquake in AD 365. Excavations begun in the 19C, were resumed from 1949–64, and are still in progress.

A path leads down through a little garden to the excavations in a grove of olives and pines planted with bougainvillea and prickly pear. The beautiful peaceful site overlooks fields with olive trees on a cliff directly above the sea. There are splendid views out to sea of the Aeolian Islands. Unusual currents in the shallows at the foot of the cliffs produce pretty formations of sand and gravel and areas of temporary marshland of great interest to naturalists. The lagoon of Marinello has recently become a protected reserve (and there are plans to open a path down the cliff).

The small **museum** (open 09.00–dusk) has a plan of the excavations and finds from the site including two fragments of Hellenistic statues of winged victories, 4C–1C BC statuettes, a colossal head of the emperor Augustus (1C), female draped statues, vases, reliefs, a capital of 1C BC and a theatrical mask.

The paved **Decumanus Maximus** is flanked by remains of houses (those with mosaics are protected by a roof). To the right is a conspicuous building, once called the **Ginnasio**, but now thought to have been a monumental entrance to the public buildings. Its façade, which fell in Byzantine times, was excellently restored in 1956. It is an unusual building with barrel vaulting across the main road of the city: formerly dated in the 1C BC it is now thought to have been built in the 4C AD. The agora lies beneath the modern village.

To the left of the entrance is the large **theatre**, a Greek building adapted by the Romans for use by gladiators. To reach the top, from which there is a good view, there is a path on the right by a group of cypresses.

The Greek **walls** (3C BC), obscured by vegetation on the seaward side, survive in a good state of preservation to the south (beside the approach road below the sanctuary), extending, with interval towers, for several hundred metres on either side of the **main gate**, a dipylon with a barbican.

**Patti** (population 11,500), a short distance west of Tindari, stands on a hill, damaged by an earthquake in 1978. In the cathedral (damaged) is the Renaissance tomb of Adelaide (d. 1118), queen of Roger I. In a 19C villa in the sea resort of Marina di Patti there is a museum of local ceramics.

During the construction of the motorway from Messina part of a large **Roman villa** (4C AD) was uncovered here in 1973 (follow the signs for Marina di Patti and the motorway: the entrance to the site is beneath the motorway viaduct; open daily 09.00–dusk). The site is in an ugly position and is badly kept, and the museum which was built some years ago to house finds from the site has never been opened. The beautiful polychrome mosaic floors (protected by a roof, and seen from walkways), similar to those at Piazza Armerina, have geometric and floral designs as well as hunting scenes, but are rarely dusted.

**Gioiosa Marea** is a seaside resort. The island of Vulcano is only 19km offshore. The town was built in the 18C after an earthquake destroyed the medieval town of **Gioiosa Guardia**, the ruins of which survive high up (828m) on a hill beyond the motorway. A winding road leads up to the old town, from which there are wonderful views.

**Capo d'Orlando** is another seaside resort (population 12,000) which lies below its cape, off which Frederick II of Aragon was defeated in 1299 by Roger of Lauria, commanding the allied fleets of Catalonia and Anjou. The promontory, already occupied in the Greek era, is noted for its sudden storms. It is crowned by a 14C castle and a sanctuary. The town has been famous in Italy since 1991 for the courageous stand its shopkeepers, tradesmen and hoteliers have taken against the Mafia racket.

At **Lido di S. Gregorio** there is a delightful little museum in an old customs house which illustrates the life of the local fishermen, about 20 of whom still go out to fish from the bay here. To the east is another little port and (near the railway line) in the marshes just below the water level some circular carved discs of stone of unknown purpose, known as Le Cave del Mercadante can sometimes be seen. Nearby are the **Terme di Bagnoli** (open 09.00–dusk), surrounded by a little garden. These were Roman baths, part of a private villa built in the late 4C or 5C AD. Eight rooms have been unearthed, some of which were dislodged in an earthquake.

# The Parco dei Nebrodi

The Parco dei Nebrodi is a protected area of great natural beauty in the **Nebrodi Mountains**, which stretch from the Peloritani on the east to the Madonie on the west. They have an average height of 1200–1500m and are the largest forested area to survive on the island. The remarkable landscape changes constantly. The trees include oak, elm, ash, beech, holm oak, cork, maple and yew, and are especially fine in the Caronia forest. The area has abundant water, with many mountain torrents, small lakes and springs. The upland plains provide pastureland for numerous farm animals which roam free (with bells), including cows, horses, sheep, goats and black and white pigs. While grazing, they eat the low holly bushes into strange shapes. The S. Fratello breed of horses (identified by their characteristic noses) are now protected and allowed to run wild here. Delicious ricotta is made by the local farmers.

The park, created in 1993, is divided into four proteced areas, and the problem of its administration (with responsibility at present divided between the Comune, Regione, Ente Parco and Forestry Commission) still has to be resolved, as well as the opposition to the protection laws from the local hunters and some farmers.

Four mountain roads traverse the park from north to south, the most spectacular of which is that in the centre from S. Fratello to Cesarò. One of the best ways to explore the most beautiful and remote parts of the park is from **Alcara Li Fusi** by an organised tour in a jeep which takes a full day (with a picnic lunch). The visit must be booked in advance, ☎ 0338/8535301 or 0941/793213. There are no hotels inland but two simple mountain refuges, with restaurants at Floresta, and at the Passo del Miraglia (see above).

**Monte Soro** (1847m) is the highest peak of the Nebrodi. The Lago Biviere di Cesarò (1200m) is a lovely little natural lake with interesting birdlife (including herons), and a spectacular view of Etna. Nearby Lago Maulazzo is an artificial lake constructed in the 1980s for irrigation but never put into operation. In this area are numerous turkey oaks, maple trees and beech woods, and wild mushrooms (especially *porcini*) abound. In spring there are beautiful wild flowers and the hillsides are covered with broom, and the colours in autumn are spectacular.

A road leads inland from Capo d'Orlando across the eastern Nebrodi Mountains to Randazzo below Etna. It passes **Naso**, a small town of 5300 inhabitants, which has 15C–17C tombs in the church of the **Minori Osservanti**, including a monument to Artale Cardona (d. 1477). **Floresta** (1275m) is the highest village in Sicily, with winter sports facilities. The road reaches a summit level of 1280m before descending in full view of Etna to **Randazzo** (described on p.312).

At **S. Marco d'Alunzio** Robert Guiscard built the first Norman castle in Sicily in 1061 (it survives in ruins at the top of the hill). The interesting little hill town (population 2000) has numerous churches built of a distinctive local red marble (called *rosso di S. Marco*). At the entrance to the town on a spectacular site overlooking the sea, is the **Temple of Hercules,** dating from the Hellenistic era: on the red marble basement a Norman church (now roofless) was built. Later a Baroque portal and windows were added. Above the road on the right is the church of the **Aracoeli**, with a Baroque portal. The interior, including the columns, has local red marble decorations. On the south side a marble altar has a gilded wooden statue of *St Michael Archangel*, and another chapel has a fine red marble altarpiece.

Via Aluntina continues past (left) the deconsecrated 12C church of **S. Maria dei Poveri** (used for exhibitions) and then descends past the town hall and a fountain. On the left is the **Chiesa Matrice** (S. Nicolò) built in 1584. It has a very unusual triumphal arch with large marble sculptures and an 18C organ. On the north side, the fourth chapel has a 16C painting of the *Madonna of the Rosary* in a fine frame, and the fifth chapel a wooden 16C processional statue of the *Immacolata*.

A road leads uphill to the left past the tiny church of S. Giovanni and then down to the side of the hill where **S. Giuseppe** has another lovely portal. There is a fine view of the sea from here. On the left of the façade is the entrance to the **Museo Diocesano** (open 10.00–13.00, 16.00–20.00), inaugurated in 1996. In the vestibule are the original capitals from the portal of the church, as well as vestments and statues. The rest of the collection is arranged in the church which has a lovely red, grey and blue pavement and decorative stuccoes. The quaint collection of miscellaneous objects includes a sculpture of the *Madonna dell' Odigitria* by Giuseppe Li Volsi (1616), statues, reliquaries, and church furniture.

Higher up in the town is the tiny church of **Maria SS. delle Grazie** with a delightful carved high altar with a statue of the *Madonna and Child with the young St John*, and, on either side, two Filangeri tombs, one with an effigy (1481) and the other in red marble (1600). Opposite, built on to the rock, is the church of **S. Basilio**. Beneath **S. Teodoro** there is a Byzantine chapel with interesting remains of frescoes.

**S. Agata di Militello** is a seaside resort (population 12,600), from which climbing expeditions may be made in the Parco dei Nebrodi. A museum relating to the Nebrodi is open here on weekdays (09.00–13.30; for admission enquire at the town hall).

**Alcara li Fusi** is a pretty little mountain village beneath the Rocche del Crasto (1315m). The mountain, where golden eagles still nest, can be explored on foot to see the Grotta del Lauro (1060m), one of the most interesting caves in Sicily. Excursions by jeep into the Parco dei Nebrodi are organised from here (see above).

A picturesque road leads south from S. Agata di Militello through the Nebrodi mountains past **S. Fratello**, a Lombard colony founded by Adelaide, queen of Roger I, with a 12C Norman church.

**Caronia** is in the beautiful forest of Caronia. The town preserves a privately owned Norman castle. On the outskirts the site of the Greek and Roman colony of **Kalacte** has been identified. A mountain road leads across the Nebrodi to the hill town of **Capizzi**, one of the highest villages in Sicily. The road joins the beautiful A120 south of the Nebrodi from Nicosia (see pp.224-5) to Randazzo. It passes the village of **Cerami**: after his victory at the Battle of Cerami in 1063, Roger I presented four Saracen camels to Pope Alexander II in Rome. East of Troina (described on p.223) the road traverses rugged country with a superb view of Etna, passing below **Cesarò**, where the remains of its castle can be seen.

On the coast at the west end of the Nebrodi is **S. Stefano di Camastra** which has an interesting plan. It is noted for its fine ceramics, which are made and sold in potteries on the outskirts (most of which are east of the town on the road towards Messina). Local ware is also sold in numerous shops in the town.

A pretty road leads inland through the Nebrodi passing **Mistretta** (950m), an attractive old town (population 6600), with some good Baroque and Rococo buildings, on the site of the ancient *Amestratus*. The carved south portal of the church has been ascribed to Giorgio da Milano (1493). The Museo Civico is open 08.00–14.00, 16.00–19.00 except Mon, Sat 08.00–14.00. This magnificent mountain road continues south to Nicosia, described on p.224.

At the north-western corner of the province of Messina is **Castel di Tusa**. A road leads inland above the wide fiumara of the Tusa river to the pretty little hill town of **Tusa,** which has interesting sculptures in its church. The vast incongruous modern sculptures which were set up in the bed of the fiumara were ordered to be demolished by a court ruling in 1991, and again in 1993, but they are still here.

Off the road to Tusa is the site of *Halaesa* on a hill. A road leads up from the gate on the byroad to the car-park beside the restored convent and church and custodian's house. The attractive site (open daily 09.00–dusk), with ancient olives and almond trees, commands a fine view of the pretty Tusa valley, and the little towns of Tusa and (on the other side of the valley) Pettineo. On a clear day the Aeolian Islands can be seen.

Halaesa was a Greek city founded in the 5C BC by Archonides, tyrant of Herbita. The most conspicuous remains are those of the Agora (partly protected by a roof), which preserves part of its marble wall panelling and brick paving on the west side, and the walls of the city (a stretch further uphill is strengthened by buttresses). On the hillside below, looking towards the sea, was the theatre, and there was a temple at the top of the hill. Excavations begun in 1952–6 were interrupted in 1972 and have never been resumed.

Cefalù and the Madonie Mountains to the west, in the province of Palermo, are described on pp.120 and 124.

# Glossary

*For Greek architectural terms and vase types, see pp. 370–72.*

**Abacus**, flat stone in the upper part of a capital

**Acroterion**, an ornamental feature on the corner or highest point of a pediment

**Aedicule**, small opening framed by two columns and a pediment, originally used in classical architecture

**Agora**, public square or market-place

**Ambo**, (pl. ambones) pulpit in a Christian basilica; two pulpits on opposite sides of a church, from which the gospel and epistle were read

**Amphiprostyle**, temple with colonnades at both ends

**Amphora**, antique vase, usually of large dimensions, for oil and other liquids

**Antefix**, ornament placed at the lower corner of the tiled roof of a temple to conceal the space between the tiles and the cornice

**Antis**, *in antis* describes the portico of a temple when the side-walls are prolonged to end in a pilaster flush with the columns of the portico

**Architrave**, lowest part of the entablature, horizontal frame above a door

**Archivolt**, moulded architrave carried round an arch

**Atlantes**, (or *telamones*) male figures used as supporting columns

**Atrium**, forecourt, usually of a Byzantine church or a classical Roman house

**Badia**, (*abbazia*) abbey

**Baglio**, from the medieval word *Ballium* meaning a large fortified building. It is now usually used to describe the warehouse of a wine distillery

**Baldacchino**, canopy supported by columns, usually over an altar

**Basilica**, originally a Roman building used for public administration; in Christian architecture, an aisled church with a clerestory and apse, and no transepts

**Borgo**, a suburb; street leading away from the centre of a town

**Bottega**, the studio of an artist; the pupils who worked under his direction

**Bouleuterion**, council chamber

**Bozzetto**, sketch, often used to describe a small model for a piece of sculpture

**Bucchero**, Etruscan black terracotta ware

**Caldarium** or **calidarium**, room for hot or vapour baths in a Roman bath

**Campanile**, bell-tower, often detached from the building to which it belongs

**Camposanto**, cemetery

**Capital**, the top of a column

**Cardo**, the main street of a Roman town, at right-angles to the Decumanus

**Caryatid**, female figure used as a supporting column

**Cavea**, the part of a theatre or amphitheatre occupied by the row of seats

**Cella**, sanctuary of a temple, usually in the centre of the building

**Chiaroscuro**, distribution of light and shade, apart from colour, in a painting

**Chiesa Matrice**, (or *Chiesa Madre*) parish church

**Chthonic**, dwelling in or under the ground

**Ciborium**, casket or tabernacle containing the Host

**Cipollino**, onion-marble; a greyish marble with streaks of white or green

**Cippus**, sepulchral monument in the form of an altar

**Cista**, casket, usually of bronze and cylindrical in shape, to hold jewels, toilet articles, etc., and decorated with mythological subjects

**Console**, ornamental bracket

**Crenellations**, battlements

**Cuneus**, wedge-shaped block of seats in an antique theatre

**Cyclopean**, the term applied to walls of unmortared masonry, older than the Etruscan civilisation, and attributed by the ancients to the giant Cyclopes

**Decumanus**, the main street of a Roman town running parallel to its longer axis

**Diorite**, a type of greenish coloured rock

**Dipteral**, temple surrounded by a double peristyle

**Diptych**, painting or ivory tablet in two sections

**Duomo**, cathedral

**Entablature**, the part above the capital (consisting of architrave, frieze and cornice) of a classical building

**Ephebos**, Greek youth under training (military or university)

**Exedra**, semicircular recess

**Ex-voto**, tablet or small painting expressing gratitude to a saint

**Fiumare**, wide flat-bottomed torrent-bed filled with gravel, usually waterless

**Forum**, open space in a town serving as a market or meeting-place

**Fresco**, (*affresco*) painting executed on wet plaster. On the wall beneath the *sinopia* is sketched, and the *cartone* is transferred onto the fresh plaster (*intonaco*) before the fresco is begun, either by pricking the outline with small holes over which a powder is dusted, or by means of a stylus which leaves an incised line on the wet plaster. In recent years many frescoes have been detached from the walls on which they were executed

**Frigidarium**, room for cold baths in a Roman bath

**Fumarole**, volcanic spurt of vapour (usually sulphurous) emerging from the ground

**Gigantomachia**, contest of Giants

**Graffiti**. design on a wall made with an iron tool on a prepared surface, the design showing in white. Also used loosely to describe scratched designs or words on walls

**Greek cross**, cross with arms of equal length

**Hellenistic**, the period from Alexander the Great to Augustus (c 325–31 BC)

**Herm**, (pl. hermae) quadrangular pillar decreasing in girth towards the ground, surmounted by a bust

**Hexastyle**, temple with a portico of six columns at the end

**Hypogeum**, subterranean excavation for the interment of the dead (usually Etruscan)

**Intarsia**, inlay of wood, marble, or metal

**Kore**, maiden

**Kouros**, boy; Archaic male figure

**Krater**, antique mixing-bowl, conical in shape with rounded base

**Kylix**, wide shallow vase with two handles and short stem

**Latomiae**, the limestone quarries of Siracusa, later used as prisons, and now tropical gardens

**Loggia**, covered gallery or balcony, usually preceding a larger building

**Lunette**, semicircular space in a vault or ceiling, often decorated with a painting or a relief

**Marmi mischi**, inlay decoration of various polychrome marbles and pietre dure, used in church interiors in the 17C and 18C

**Medallion**, large medal, or a circular ornament

**Megalith**, a huge stone (often used as a monument)

**Megaron**, an oblong hall (usually in a Mycenean palace)

**Metope**, panel between two triglyphs on the frieze of a temple

**Monolith**, single stone (usually a column)

**Narthex**, vestibule of a Christian basilica

**Naumachia**, mock naval combat for which the arena of an amphitheatre was flooded

**Nymphaeum**, a sort of summer-house in the gardens of baths, palaces, etc., originally a temple of the Nymphs, and decorated with statues of those goddesses

**Octastyle**, a portico with eight columns

**Odeion**, a concert hall, usually in the shape of a Greek theatre, but roofed

**Ogee**, (arch) arch shaped in a double curve, convex above and concave below

**Oinochoe**, wine-jug usually of elongated shape for dipping wine out of a krater

**Opisthodomos**, the enclosed rear part of a temple

**Opus sectile**, mosaic or paving of thin slabs of coloured marble cut in geometrical shapes

**Ossuary**, deposit of or receptacle for the bones of the dead

**Palazzo**, any dignified and important building

**Pantokrator**, the Almighty

**Pax**, sacred object used by a priest for the blessing of peace, and offered for the kiss of the faithful, usually circular, engraved, enamelled or painted in a rich gold or silver frame

**Pediment**, gable above the portico of a classical building

**Pendentive**, concave spandrel beneath a dome

**Peripteral**, temple surrounded by a colonnade

**Peristyle**, court or garden surrounded by a columned portico

**Pietà**, group of the Virgin mourning the dead Christ

**Piscina**, Roman tank; a basin for an officiating priest to wash his hands before Mass

**Pithos**, large pottery vessel

**Podium**, a continuous base or plinth supporting columns, and the lowest row of seats in the cavea of a theatre or amphitheatre

**Polyptych**, painting or tablet in more than three sections

**Predella**, small painting attached below a large altarpiece

**Presepio**, literally, crib or manger. A group of statuary of which the central subject is the Infant Jesus in the manger

**Pronaos**, porch in front of the cella of a temple

**Propylon**, propylaea. Entrance gate to a temenos; in plural form when there is more than one door

**Prostyle**, edifice with columns on the front only

**Pulvin**, cushion stone between the capital and the impost block

**Putto**, figure of a child sculpted or painted, usually nude

**Quadriga**, four-horsed chariot

**Rhyton**, drinking-horn usually ending in an animal's head

**Situla**, water bucket

**Squinch**, arched space at the angle of a tower

**Stamnos**, big-bellied vase with two small handles at the sides, closed by a lid

**Stele**, upright stone bearing a monumental inscription

**Stereobate**, basement of a temple or other building

**Stilted arch**, round arch that rises vertically before it springs

**Stoa**, porch or portico not attached to a larger building

**Stoup**, vessel for Holy Water, usually near the west door of a church

**Stucco**, plasterwork

**Stylobate**, basement of a columned temple or other building

**Tablinum**, room in a Roman house with one side opening onto the central courtyard

**Telamones**, see *Atlantes*

**Temenos**, a sacred enclosure

**Tepidarium**, room for warm baths in a Roman bath

**Tessera**, a small cube of stone, terracotta, marble, glass, etc., used in mosaic work

**Tetrastyle**, having four columns at the end

**Thermae**, originally simply baths, later elaborate buildings fitted with libraries, assembly rooms, gymnasia, circuses, etc

**Tholos**, a circular building

**Tondo**, round painting or bas-relief

**Transenna**, open grille or screen, usually of marble, in an early Christian church

**Triclinium**, dining-room and reception room of a Roman house

**Triglyph**, blocks with vertical grooves on either side of a metope on the frieze of a temple

**Trinacria**, the ancient name for Sicily derived from its triangular shape

**Triptych**, painting or tablet in three sections

**Tympanum**, area above a doorway or the space enclosed by a pediment

**Villa**, country house with its garden

**Xystus**, an exercise court; in a Roman villa the open court preceding the triclinium

## Plan of Greek Temples

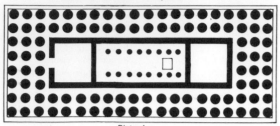

Dipteral
(Octastyle)

## Parts of Greek Temple

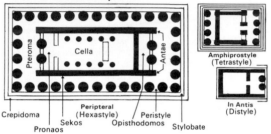

Pteroma · Cella · Antae

Amphiprostyle
(Tetrastyle)

In Antis
(Distyle)

Crepidoma · Sekos · Pronaos · Peripteral (Hexastyle) · Opisthodomos · Peristyle · Stylobate

## Walls

Uncoursed Polygonal
(rubble)

Archaic 'Lesbian'

Ashlar Isodomic
(Classical)

Coursed trapezoidal

Pseudo-Isodomic

'Lesbian' Polygonal
(Hellenistic)

## Greek Theatre

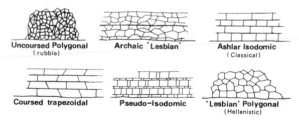

Diazoma · Kerkides (cunei) · Analemma · Cavea · Orchestra · Parodos · Paraskenia · Skene · Proskenion

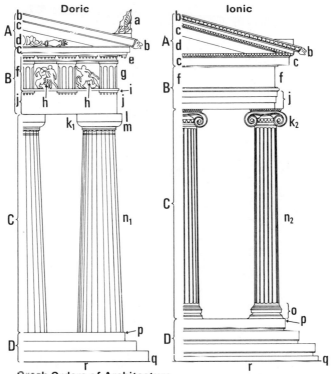

**Doric**

**Ionic**

# Greek Orders of Architecture

| | | | |
|---|---|---|---|
| A. | Pediment | f. | Frieze |
| B. | Entablature | g. | Triglyphs |
| C. | Column | h. | Metope's |
| D. | Crepidoma | i | Regulae & Guttae |
| a. | Acroterion | j. | Architrave or Epistyle |
| b. | Sima | $k_1$ | Capital (Doric) |
| c. | Geison or Cornice | $k_2$ | Capital (Ionic) with Volutes |
| d. | Tympanum | l. | Abacus |
| e. | Mutule & Guttae | m. | Echinus |

- $n_1$  Shaft with flutes separated by sharp arrises.
- $n_2$  Shaft with flutes separated by blunt fillets
- o.  Bases
- p.  Stylobate
- q.  Euthynteria
- r.  Stereobate

**Corinthian Capital**

**Pergamene Capital**

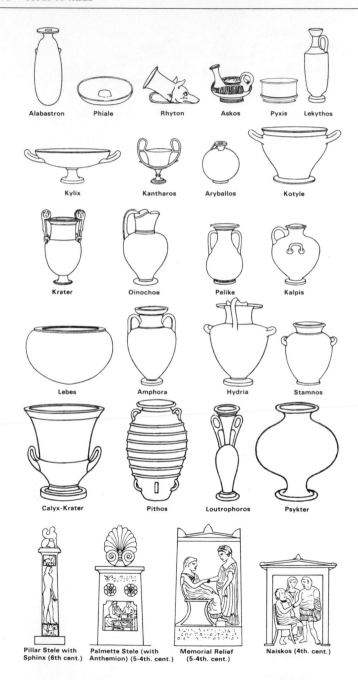

Alabastron   Phiale   Rhyton   Askos   Pyxis   Lekythos

Kylix   Kantharos   Aryballos   Kotyle

Krater   Oinochoe   Pelike   Kalpis

Lebes   Amphora   Hydria   Stamnos

Calyx-Krater   Pithos   Loutrophoros   Psykter

Pillar Stele with Sphinx (6th cent.)   Palmette Stele (with Anthemion) (5-4th. cent.)   Memorial Relief (5-4th. cent.)   Naiskos (4th. cent.)

# Index to artists

# Index